Psychological Testing

Psychological Testing

JOHN R. GRAHAM
Kent State University

ROY S. LILLY
Kent State University

PRENTICE HALL, Englewood Cliffs, New Jersey 07632

Library of Congress Cataloging in Publication Data

GRAHAM, JOHN R. (JOHN ROBERT), (0000)
   Psychological testing.

   Bibliography: p.
   Includes index.
   1. Psychological tests. 2. Personality tests.
3. Personality assessment. I. Lilly, Roy S., (0000)
II. Title.
BF176.G73 1984   150'.28'7   83-24560
ISBN 0-13-732652-1

Editorial/production supervision: *Edith Riker*
Interior design: *Edith Riker*
Manufacturing buyer: *Ron Chapman*
Cover design: *Lundgren Graphics, Ltd.*

**To Becky, John, Mary, and David
To Priscilla**

Printed in the United States of America

10 9 8 7

ISBN 0-13-732652-1

Prentice-Hall International (UK) Limited, *London*
Prentice-Hall of Australia Pty. Limited, *Sydney*
Prentice-Hall Canada Inc., *Toronto*
Prentice-Hall Hispanoamericana, S.A., *Mexico*
Prentice-Hall of India Private Limited, *New Delhi*
Prentice-Hall of Japan, Inc., *Tokyo*
Simon & Schuster Asia Pte. Ltd., *Singapore*
Editora Prentice-Hall do Brasil, Ltda., *Rio de Janeiro*

Contents

Preface

This book is intended primarily for courses at the undergraduate or graduate level in which consideration of psychological testing is a primary objective. Basic principles of tests and measurements are covered, and some of the most commonly utilized techniques are described and evaluated in detail. Although the book's orientation is primarily psychological, it also could be appropriate for students in education, business, and other disciplines in which testing is of interest.

Chapters 1 through 4 present some introductory material and discuss in detail characteristics of tests such as reliability and validity. Individual intelligence tests are covered in Chapters 5 through 7, and an entire chapter is devoted to assessing preschool children and special populations. Aptitude and achievement tests are discussed in Chapter 8. Chapters 9 and 10 deal with projective and objective approaches to personality assessment. Interviewing and behavioral assessment, topics often neglected in other books, are covered in Chap-

ter 11. Chapter 12 discusses interests, values, attitudes, and personal orientation, including detailed coverage of the Strong-Campbell Interest Inventory. Chapter 13 on the assessment process emphasizes that tests cannot be understood apart from those who use them and the purposes for which they are used. Finally, Chapter 14 includes a discussion of professional, ethical, and legal issues in testing.

We have tried to limit the number of tests discussed, choosing those that are most frequently used or representative of particular kinds of tests. Thus, although we describe many tests, we have tried to give enough detail about them so that the reader will understand their content, uses, and limitations. Although we may not have described all the tests an instructor believes are important or interesting, the ones we do describe should need relatively little elaboration. Thus, examples of tests that we do not describe can be introduced by the instructor.

We have also tried to simplify the technical discussion as much as possible without sacrificing accuracy. We have, therefore, stressed how tests are used rather than psychometric properties or measurement theories. In particular, we do not attempt to describe multivariate statistical techniques such as factor analysis or multiple regression even though such techniques are used in developing, evaluating, and applying tests. Latent trait theory or item response theory, an important new development in ability testing, is similarly not described because we believe it is too difficult for most undergraduate students to understand. These techniques are also just beginning to have an impact on applied problems in testing.

There are several other topics we chose to omit. First, construction techniques for classroom tests are not discussed. The actual writing of good items and item analysis, although obviously important topics, seem needlessly technical for a survey book on psychological testing. Unless they become teachers or test specialists, most students probably will never actually construct a test. We also did not attempt to describe computer-based testing, sometimes referred to as *adaptive testing* or *tailored testing*. We do describe computer-generated test interpretation. Tailored testing, which is often related to item response theory, may assume greater importance in the future. To us, its present applications seem more experimental than practical, although technological advances may soon increase its usefulenss. We have also not described specific aptitude tests, often useful in business and industry, but we have described the Differential Aptitude Tests. Test users often choose only one of the tests available in this battery, the one they believe is most suitable for their situation.

We are pleased to acknowledge the assist-

ance that we received in writing this book. First, Dan Waller, a former sales representative for Prentice-Hall, goaded us into writing the initial proposal. Without his persistent efforts, we probably would never have begun the project. We are especially grateful to the reviewers who made many constructive suggestions and added much to our finished product: Howard B. Lyman, University of Cincinnati; Richard M. Jaeger, The University of North Carolina at Greensboro; Fred H. Borgen, Iowa State University; John E. Stecklein, University of Minnesota; Kevin O'Grady, The University of Maryland; Lawrence E. Jones, University of Illinois–Urbana; Ellen Banks, Daemen College; Rick R. Jacobs, The Pennsylvania State University; B. Thomas Harwood, Forensic Mental Health Service, Buffalo, New York. Dr. Carolyn Williams and Dr. Michele Paludi read initial drafts on the nature of psychological testing and sex-role orientation, respectively, making many helpful suggestions. We, of course, are responsible for any errors or oversights that remain.

The editorial staff at Prentice-Hall, especially John Isley, psychology editor, has been most patient and encouraging even when we occasionally missed a deadline. In the final production of our book, we are most grateful for the professional assistance of Edie Riker, who patiently led us through the process of reading copy-edited manuscript, preparing artwork, and obtaining permissions for the use of copyrighted material. Also, the initial copy-editing by Barbara Conner improved our prose considerably—we will never use *while* for *although* again. Finally, clerical and secretarial assistance has been most ably, and usually cheerfully, provided by Kathleen Foltz, Joan Lash, and Diane Dinardo.

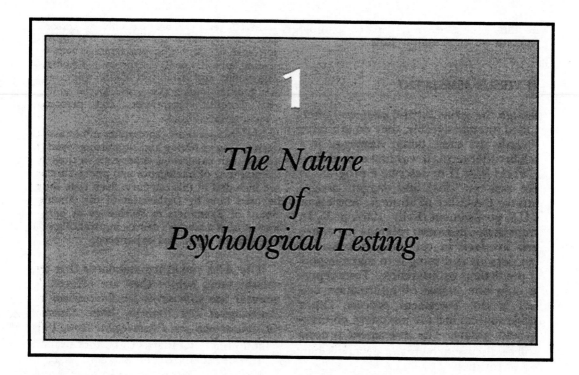

1

The Nature of Psychological Testing

Although the origins of testing can be traced to antiquity, modern psychological testing dates back only to the beginning of this century. Yet in its relatively short life span, testing has grown to the point where virtually every person in the United States will take at least one psychological test at some time in his or her lifetime. In this chapter we will discuss what is meant by the term *test*, who uses tests, for what purposes they are used, and where information about specific tests can be found. In addition, a brief account of the historical origins of testing is presented.

WHAT IS A TEST?

A test can be defined as a standardized sample of behavior from which other, more important, behaviors can be inferred or predicted. Note that a test involves a *sample* of behavior. Of all of the possible behaviors of an individual that we might observe, the responses obtained from testing represent only a small proportion. The nature of the sample usually is related directly to the predictions or inferences to be made. For example, the sample in a test to predict success as a typist might very well include actual typing. A test designed to predict success on an assembly line would probably include manual dexterity tasks.

It also should be noted that the behavior sample in a test is *standardized*. That is, the observations are made in a prescribed manner so that any differences can be attributed to differences in test subjects and not to variations in the manner in which the observations are made.

Our definition also makes clear that a test typically involves *prediction* or *inference* about behaviors more important than those observed during testing. Usually, the examiner has little interest in the actual test responses. What an individual sees in an inkblot test or the number of pegs placed into holes in a manual dexterity test are important only to the extent that they allow predictions or inferences about other behaviors, such as degree of psychopathology or success on an assembly line.

TEST VERSUS ASSESSMENT

Although the terms *test* and *assessment* often are used interchangeably, they do not refer to exactly the same thing. *Assessment* is a much broader term. It was first coined during World War II to describe a program to select men for "cloak and dagger" assignments for the Office of Strategic Services of the U.S. government (Kelly, 1967, p. 1). In current usage, *assessment* refers to the entire *process* involved in collecting information about persons and using it to make important predictions or inferences. Tests represent only one source of information collected in the assessment process. Other possible sources include interview, observation, and history. The assessment process will be discussed in greater detail in Chapter 13 of this book.

WHO USES TESTS?

Tests are used by psychologists and others who have the training and experience necessary for their administration and interpretation. In an attempt to assure that they are used only by qualified persons, the American Psychological Association (APA) specified the qualifications necessary for using tests of varying levels of complexity (*Ethical Standards of Psychologists*, 1953). Test distributers have assumed responsibility for verifying the qualifications of persons who want to purchase tests.

The APA standards divided tests into three levels of complexity:

Level A tests can be adequately administered, scored, and interpreted with the aid of a manual and a general orientation to the kind of organization in which one is working. Educational achievement and vocational proficiency tests are included in this category. Such tests may be used by responsible nonpsychologists such as school principals or business executives.

Level B tests can be used only by persons who have some technical knowledge of test construction and use and who are familiar with supporting subjects, such as statistics, psychology of adjustment, and so on. Included in this category are general intelligence tests, special aptitude tests, interest inventories, and personality screening inventories.

Level C tests are those that require substantial understanding of testing and supporting topics, together with supervised experience in their use. Clinical tests of intelligence and personality tests are included in this category. Such tests should be used only by Diplomates of the American Board of Examiners in Psychology or persons with at least a master's degree in psychology and one year of supervised experience.

The APA published standards that tests should meet before they are offered for general use (*Standards for Educational and Psychological Test Manuals*, 1966; *Standards for Educational and Psychological Tests*, 1974) and ethical standards to be met by persons who use them (*Ethical Standards of Psychologists*, 1977). Most states also have standards for test utilization that are enforced through state psychological associations or governmental bodies that control the practice of psychology.

SETTINGS AND PURPOSES OF TESTS

Most tests are used in educational institutions, businesses and industries, military services, and clinical settings (for example, hospitals and mental health centers). Educational institutions are by far the most frequent users of tests. Throughout a person's educational career important decisions about that person are based at least in part on test results. In some states a child may start school at an age younger than the one stated for admission if above-average scores are obtained on a standardized intelligence test. Decisions about placement levels, special classroom experiences, and many other educational matters are usually based primarily on test data. Most school systems regularly administer standardized achievement tests to all pupils. High school students who are seeking admission to college are expected to take appropriate aptitude tests (for example, Scholastic Aptitude Test and American College Testing Program Test Battery). College students seeking admission to graduate or professional programs are required to take especially designed aptitude tests (Graduate Record Examination, Law School Admission Test, Medical College Admission Test). At all educational levels tests are used to help identify the sources of academic or behavioral problems and to design appropriate remediation.

For many years businesses and industries have used tests as screening devices in personnel selection. State, federal, and local civil service commissions have relied heavily on testing procedures in selecting government employees. Tests also are used in business and industry to assist in decisions about placement and promotion of employees. The widespread use of tests in business and industry has been curtailed somewhat following the establishment of guidelines for selection procedures by the Equal Employment Opportunity Commission (1978). These guidelines require employers to maintain records of rejection and selection rates for minority and nonminority applicants. If the selection procedures utilized result in a greater proportion of minority than nonminority applicants being rejected for employment, tests and other parts of the selection procedures can be maintained only if the employer demonstrates to the satisfaction of the federal government that they have validity for the specific purposes for which they are being used. Although some large corporations have been able to present evidence of validity and nondiscrimination, many smaller businesses have discontinued using tests rather than assume the effort and expense involved in establishing such evidence.

The military services have been frequent users of tests since World War I. It was in response to their needs that the first group tests of intelligence and personality were developed. Tests are used to screen potential recruits, to place personnel into training programs and job assignments, and to identify potential officers.

Tests are often used by psychologists in clinical settings. Decisions about the need for treatment, selection of appropriate treatment programs, and evaluation of treatment outcomes often are based primarily on test data. Although tests often are used to try to answer some specific question, such as potential for acting-out or suicidal behavior, they also are used to help the professional staff gain a more complete understanding of clients' problems and personality functioning.

The importance of testing in contemporary life is by no means limited to the United States. For example, Cramer (1978) described the central role tests play in the lives of Egyptians. A test called *thanawia amma* (translated as "general secondary") is administered annually to all high school seniors. Not only does the test determine if students will graduate from high school, but also it is the exclusive determinant of which students will be admitted to the universities and what areas of specialization they will be allowed to pursue. Because of differences of a few points, some students who aspire to be physicians may have to enter the field of commerce or perhaps the postal service. The period of preparation for *thanawia amma* is important to the entire country. Virtually all social life and other nonacademic activities of students cease, and extraordinary consideration and support are given to those who will take the test. For example, the Cairo government set a fine of $7.50 for honking a car horn during *thanawia amma*.

SOURCES OF INFORMATION

Most tests in the United States are sold by one of several large distributors (for example, The Psychological Corporation, Consulting Psychologists Press, Science Research Associates). Their catalogs describe the tests, their costs, and qualifications required for persons using them, but little technical or evaluative information is given. A listing of all tests published in English-speaking countries is provided by *Tests in Print II* (Buros, 1974). Critical reviews of tests are published in *Mental Measurements Yearbooks* (Buros, 1941–1978). Appendices D and E of Anastasi's text (1982) list U.S. test publishers and representative tests classified according to type (intelligence tests, multiple aptitude batteries, educational tests, and personality tests).

By far the most useful information about a test can be found in its manual. An adequate manual should report construction procedures and directions for administering, scoring, and interpreting scores. In addition, information about norms, reliability, and validity should be included. Most publishers offer at nominal cost specimen sets of their tests. A specimen set typically includes samples of test booklets and answer sheets, scoring keys, and a test manual.

HISTORICAL PERSPECTIVE*

Early Civil Service Tests

DuBois (1970) credits the Chinese with inventing psychological tests. As early as 2200 B.C. the Chinese emperor examined public officials to determine their fitness to continue in office. By 1370 A.D. formal written examinations were an established part of the Chinese civil service system. Widespread use of tests continued in China until 1905, when it was discontinued so that those aspiring to public office would accept formal university training as a prerequisite. Both France (1791) and England (1833) introduced civil service tests patterned after the Chinese system. In 1883 the United States passed the Civil Service Act, which established the use of tests for selecting government employees.

Early Experimental Psychologists

Psychological tests as we know them today had their origins in the nineteenth century. Sir Francis Galton, an Englishman trained as a physician, became very interested in the genetic transmission of human characteristics and realized the importance of having some way of quantifying them. He developed a series of simple sensorimotor tasks and administered them to large numbers of people. In 1884 he established the Anthropometric Laboratory at the International Health Exhibition in London, where for a small fee a person could have a series of measurements taken. These measurements were the basis for many of Galton's scientific investigations.

James McKeen Cattell served as an assistant in Galton's laboratory and introduced the Galton methodology to the United States. Cattell established laboratories for studying individual differences first at the University of Pennsylvania (1885) and later at Columbia University (1891). Cattell first coined the term *mental test,* and he shared Galton's view that intelligence could be measured by sensorimotor tasks. Although many other early experimental psychologists shared Cattell's interest, the approach lost popularity as data accumulated indicating that an individual's performance varied considerably from one sensorimotor task to another and that the performance was virtually unrelated to teachers' ratings or school grades (Anastasi, 1982, p. 9).

Binet's Influence

While Cattell and other American psychologists were discovering that sensorimotor tasks were not good predictors of more complex mental functioning, another important development was taking place in France. Alfred Binet was a French psychologist who had an intense interest in the educational process. He was instrumental in having the French government assess school

*The reader who desires a more complete but concise history of psychological testing should consult DuBois (1970). Unless otherwise indicated, the material in this section is based on DuBois' interesting and informative account.

children to identify those who could benefit from special education. As part of the assessment process Binet and an associate, Theodore Simon, proposed a procedure that they called the *psychological method*. This method involved a series of thirty tests made up of such tasks as comparing the length of lines, copying a geometric design, identifying parts of the body, repeating sequences of digits, and finding similarities between two things.

In 1908 Binet and Simon published a revised and refined version of their earlier test, and just before his death in 1911, Binet published still more modifications of his test. As DuBois (1970, p.40) stated,

... Binet and his collaborators firmly established intelligence testing in a format which continues to this day: a well trained examiner testing a single child. In one place or another, Binet discussed many of the problems connected with individual testing: the need for the examiner to establish rapport with the child, the need to start the testing at a level at which the child is likely to succeed and to terminate it before the child is unduly fatigued, the need to maintain the child's interest, and the use of accurate records in evaluating results.

Intelligence Tests in America

Although a number of American psychologists translated and adapted the Binet-Simon scales, Lewis M. Terman at Stanford University deserves major credit for their widespread acceptance in the United States. In 1916 Terman published the Stanford-Binet Intelligence Scale, which was based to a large extent on the 1911 Binet-Simon scales. It was Terman who popularized the concept of intelligence quotient (IQ) as a ratio of mental age to chronological age. In collaboration with Maude Merrill, Terman revised the Stanford-Binet in 1936 and again in 1960. For many years after publication of the 1916 Stanford-Binet scale, the instrument was widely accepted as a standard measure of intelligence. Even today, the 1960 revision of the Stanford-Binet is used routinely to assess the intelligence of children who have been referred for individual study.

In 1939 David Wechsler, a clinical psychologist working at Bellevue Hospital in New York City, offered an alternative to the Stanford-Binet as an individual test of intelligence. In his work with adult psychiatric patients, Wechsler became dissatisfied with the Stanford-Binet because of its inadequate standardization with adults and because of its use of a single intelligence quotient. Wechsler noted that when persons developed serious emotional disorders, intellectual functioning often was selectively impaired. This selective impairment was difficult to assess with the Stanford-Binet scale, which yielded only a global IQ score. Wechsler's alternative, the Wechsler-Bellevue Intelligence Scale, was specifically designed for adults and yielded separate scores for various components of intellectual functioning as well as an overall IQ score. Subsequently, the Wechsler-Bellevue was revised in 1955 and 1981. In addition, tests patterned after it are now available for children ranging in age from four to fifteen years. In many cases, the appropriate Wechsler scale has replaced the Stanford-Binet as the intelligence test of choice.

Development of Group Tests

During World War I, the need for a group test of intelligence that could screen large numbers of military recruits became obvious. A team of psychologists, headed by Robert M. Yerkes, refined the work that Otis and others had started before the war began. The result was the Army Alpha, a paper and pencil test consisting of eight subtests covering such areas as practical judgment, arithmetical reasoning, and analogies. Before the war ended over a million men had completed the Army Alpha. To accommodate subjects with limited verbal ability, Yerkes and his group developed the Army Beta, a nonverbal version of the Alpha. Following the war Otis and a number of psychologists recognized the potential of group tests and developed versions for nonmilitary use in business and education. Group intelligence testing has mushroomed to the point that today almost every American will have taken one or more such tests during his or her lifetime.

Also during World War I the need for an efficient psychiatric screening device became evident. In 1918 Robert S. Woodworth, an experimental psychologist, developed a paper and pencil test which he called the Personal Data Sheet. The test asked subjects about one hundred different symptoms, and the subject received a point on a maladjustment scale when the response was in the direction expected for psychiatrically disabled individuals. The Personal Data Sheet and other early personality tests that used an intuitive construction strategy fell into disrepute when accumulating evidence indicated that some of the rationally selected responses indicative of pathology were not the ones actually chosen by maladjusted persons. In addition, it became obvious that subjects could easily fake or distort responses to make themselves appear better or worse off than they really were. In the late 1930s Starke Hathaway, a psychologist, and J. Charnley McKinley, a psychiatrist, utilized a new approach to the construction of a personality inventory, empirical keying. This approach involved selection of items and response direction for scales based on the performance of criterion groups known to differ on the variable being assessed. The resulting test was called the Minnesota Multiphasic Personality Inventory (MMPI). The MMPI was unique in that Hathaway and McKinley built into it several "validity" scales designed to identify persons who approached the test-taking task with the intention of creating an unrealistic picture of themselves. Although the manner in which the MMPI is used has changed considerably since its original publication in 1943, it is the most widely used personality inventory in the United States (Brown & McGuire, 1976).

Projective Personality Tests

The origin of projective tests of personality can be traced to 1921 when a Swiss psychiatrist, Herman Rorschach, developed a set of ten inkblots to elicit associations from patients. The Rorschach test was popularized in the United States in the 1930s by David M. Levy and Samuel J. Beck. In 1935 Henry Murray developed the Thematic Apperception Test (TAT) as a way of assessing constructs that were central to his personality theory. In the TAT, subjects tell stories about semiambiguous pictures. The resulting stories are analyzed to reveal needs, attitudes, and perceptions of the test subject. As the popularity of personality testing increased, many additional personality tests and scales were developed.

Tests in Education

Formal examinations and tests have not always been a part of education. The first formal examination in a university occurred at the University of Bologna in 1219. Oral exams were a part of the European university systems from the middle of the seventeenth century, and in 1803 formal written exams were introduced at Oxford University. The efforts of Joseph M. Rice in the late 1800s were instrumental in establishing standardized tests as part of the American educational system. Rice was trained as a physician, but he spent most of his professional life developing tests to assess educational achievement. Another significant figure in the history of educational tests is E. L. Thorndike. In the early 1900s Thorndike and his students at Columbia Teachers College contributed tests of arithmetic, handwriting, spelling, and other academic abilities. Today, routine achievement tests are a part of virtually every academic endeavor.

Interest Inventories

Thorndike also was instrumental in the development of interest tests. He and his students studied the interests of school students and related them to academic achievement. Vocational interests were first assessed systematically in the 1920s by men such as J. B. Miner and C. S. Yoakum. Probably the most significant development in interest testing was the publication of the Strong Vocational Interest Blank (SVIB) in 1927. The SVIB, the lifelong interest and work of Edward K. Strong, Jr., was a comprehensive inventory of interests with keys developed empirically by contrasting responses of persons in different occupations with a general reference group. The SVIB, has undergone numerous revisions, and in its present form, the Strong-Campbell Interest Inventory, the test is widely used for assessing vocational interests.

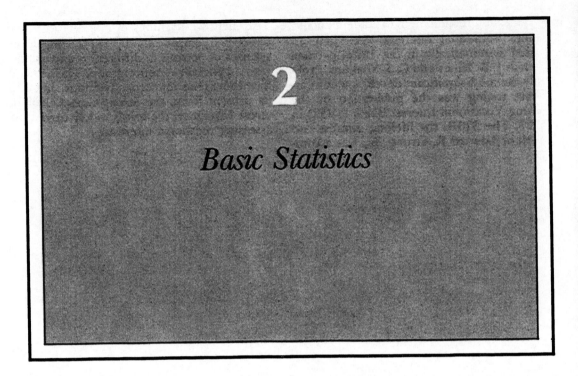

2

Basic Statistics

In this chapter we will discuss some elementary statistics that are often used in conjunction with tests. Our presentation is brief and is not designed to prepare students to perform statistical procedures. More information on all the topics covered is available in elementary statistics books (for example, McNemar, 1969; Runyon & Haber, 1980; Spence, et al., 1983).

ORGANIZING DATA

Using Numbers

The assignment of numbers to objects or events according to certain rules is important for any discipline. To the extent that characteristics of individuals can be accurately represented by numbers, it is easy to describe those characteristics and communicate more effectively with others about a given person or group of people. Physical or physiological measures are fairly direct and often very useful. For example, a person's

height (usually expressed in feet and inches) and weight (usually expressed in pounds) on a driver's license help identify that person. Physiological measures, such as blood pressure and heart rate, are important indicators of a person's physical condition. A physician may use these measures along with others to discover disease and determine a course of treatment. Having numbers available to represent any characteristic of interest about a person is usually very useful, as long as those interpreting the numbers are qualified to do so.

Suppose, however, we are interested in describing the characteristics of a large number of people. It is possible to list the names of all the people and describe the characteristics of each one. The first few names might look like this:

Doris Allen, height 5 feet, 2 inches; weight 120 lbs.
Robert Alsop, height 5 feet, 10 inches; weight 173 lbs.
Ray Best, height 6 feet, 2 inches; weight 211 lbs.

With relatively few people, such a list might be an effective way to describe a group. However, suppose there are 132 people in a group of interest. Listing all their names and characteristics is still possible, but such an exercise would not be very useful. There are simply too many names and too many numbers to be easily understood.

In Table 2-1 the weight in pounds for each of 132 people is listed. The names have been omitted, because we now intend to focus on characteristics of the group as a whole.

Frequency Distributions

TALLYING. The problem with the numbers in Table 2-1 is that they are not organized. The first number came from Doris Allen, the second from Robert Alsop, and the last from Myra Zele. Since we are no longer interested in individuals, there is no reason to organize the scores alphabetically or as they were collected. The main idea behind constructing a frequency distribution is to organize the scores in a more meaningful way.

TABLE 2-1 Weights (Measured in Pounds) of 132 People

120	154	159	115	204	170
173	119	175	145	184	164
211	168	150	89	141	135
112	150	170	153	122	216
130	207	175	140	183	200
153	137	188	142	220	155
157	195	134	197	161	134
154	195	158	165	145	185
124	100	188	209	153	179
173	160	162	142	100	162
105	143	150	108	192	157
137	182	108	155	125	151
187	95	182	165	128	166
94	168	124	156	164	186
170	167	176	119	179	135
187	143	115	144	151	150
158	152	160	140	139	134
129	162	110	146	165	174
128	191	169	155	140	145
103	136	131	147	164	174
153	118	200	119	175	151
144	130	185	113	125	115

TABLE 2-2 Ungrouped Frequency Distribution of the Weights of 132 People

X	f	X	f	X	f	X	f
220	1	175	3	152	1	125	2
216	1	174	2	151	3	124	2
211	1	173	2	150	4	122	1
209	1	170	3	147	1	120	1
207	1	169	1	146	1	119	3
204	1	168	2	145	3	118	1
200	2	167	1	144	2	115	2
197	1	166	1	143	2	113	1
195	2	165	3	142	2	112	1
192	1	164	3	141	1	110	1
191	1	162	3	140	3	108	2
188	2	161	1	139	1	105	1
187	2	160	2	137	2	103	1
186	1	159	1	136	1	100	2
185	2	158	2	135	2	95	1
184	1	157	2	134	3	94	1
183	1	156	1	131	1	89	1
182	2	155	4	130	2		
179	2	154	1	129	1		
176	1	153	5	128	2		

In Table 2-2, the scores have been better organized, being listed from highest (220) to lowest (89). In other words, the scores are now *ordered*. In addition, we have counted the number of times each score occurs. If you look carefully at Table 2-1, you will see there are two scores of 200, three of 175, and so on. The columns headed with f in Table 2-2 thus gives the *frequency of occurrence* for each weight in the group of 132 people. The process of counting how many times each score occurs is sometimes referred to as *tallying*.

Note that Table 2-2 has reduced the complexity of the scores from the way they initially appeared in Table 2-1. There are, in fact, 77 different scores. In addition, the fact that scores are now rank ordered makes it easy to see that the people in this group range between the weights of 220 pounds and 89 pounds, with most people weighing between 190 and 120.

GROUPING SCORES. Despite our progress in reducing the complexity of the 132 scores, the results in Table 2-2 are still not satisfactory. Seventy-seven different scores are still too many to understand very well. A common procedure is to group the scores into broader class intervals. A *class interval* is simply a group of scores considered as one for purposes of convenience. Considering the scores in Table 2–2, it seems reasonable to construct class intervals like those in Table 2–3. This means that all scores between 214 and 222 are grouped together. From Table 2–2, the reader can verify that there are two such scores (one at 220 and one at 216). Similarly, all scores between 205 and 213 have been grouped together. This grouping procedure is continued down to the lowest class interval, 88 to 96, in which there are three scores.

WIDTH OF A CLASS INTERVAL. Each class interval is the same width; that is, the distance between the highest and lowest scores in any interval is the same. For the example in Table 2–3, the width of the class interval is nine units. Potentially nine different scores could occur in each class interval and all be grouped together. Thus, for the highest class interval, weights of 214, 215, 216, 217, 218, 219, 220, 221, and 222 could occur within it. For whole numbers, the width of any class interval is given by subtracting the lowest number possible from the highest number possible and adding one. Thus, for the top interval we have

$$222 - 214 + 1 = 9$$

The same result occurs for all other intervals.

The numbers 222, 213, 204, and so on down to 96 are often referred to as the *upper score limits* of the class interval. The numbers 214, 203, 192, and so on down to 88 are often referred to as the *lower score limits* of the class intervals.

MIDPOINTS. It is useful to have a single number to represent all the scores in a given class interval. This number is called the class midpoint and, as the name suggests, is in the middle of the class interval. The midpoints for the class intervals given in Table 2–3 are 218, 209, 200, and so on down to 92, the midpoint of the last interval. It is very easy to determine the midpoint of a class interval. We simply add the upper and lower score limits together and divide by two. Thus, for the first interval we have

$$\frac{(214 + 222)}{2} = \frac{436}{2} = 218$$

GRAPHING FREQUENCY DISTRIBUTIONS. With many numbers to conceptualize, it is often desirable to display the frequency dis-

TABLE 2-3 Grouped Frequency Distribution of the Weights of 132 People

Class Interval	Midpoint	Frequency	Cumulative Frequency	Proportion	Cumulative Proportion
214–222	218	2	132	.015	1.000
205–213	209	3	130	.023	.985
196–204	200	4	127	.030	.962
187–195	191	8	123	.061	.932
178–186	182	9	115	.068	.871
169–177	173	12	106	.091	.803
160–168	164	16	94	.121	.712
151–159	155	20	78	.152	.591
142–150	146	15	58	.114	.439
133–141	137	13	43	.098	.326
124–132	128	10	30	.076	.227
115–123	119	8	20	.061	.152
106–114	110	5	12	.038	.091
97–105	101	4	7	.030	.053
88–96	92	3	3	.023	.023
		$N = \Sigma f = 132$			

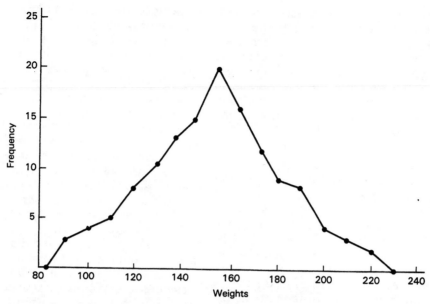

FIGURE 2–1 Frequency polygon of the weights of 132 people.

tribution in graphic form. In other words, we draw a systematic picture of the scores. One method for portraying a frequency distribution is called a *frequency polygon*. The frequency polygon for the scores in Table 2–3 is given in Figure 2–1. The vertical dimension or ordinate of a frequency polygon gives the frequency of occurrence for any given score. The horizontal axis or abscissa of a frequency polygon corresponds to the scores.

When scores have been grouped into class intervals, the question of what value to use on the horizontal axis naturally arises. The answer is to use the midpoint of each class interval. Thus, above the midpoint of the highest class interval the frequency of two has been plotted. At the lowest class interval the midpoint is ninety-two, and above this value is plotted the frequency of three. When the frequencies are all plotted as points, they are connected with straight lines.

In order to provide an accurate picture, the class intervals are extended one interval above the highest interval containing any scores (for example, 223–231) and one interval below the lowest interval containing

any scores (79–87). The frequency of occurrence in these intervals is of course zero, a point lying on the horizontal axis. By extending the class intervals in this way, the frequency polygon becomes a "closed" figure and is somewhat more pleasing to the eye. Of course, this "extension" is in fact what creates a polygon.

CUMULATIVE FREQUENCIES. Besides examining the frequency of occurrence within each interval, it is also useful to consider cumulative frequencies, which provide information about the relative position of scores. Cumulative frequencies tell us what number of scores are below or lower than a particular score of interest.

In obtaining cumulative frequencies, we begin at the lowest class interval and accumulate scores for each successive class interval. Thus, in Table 2–3, there are three scores in the interval 88 to 96. In the next interval, 97 to 105, there are four scores. The cumulative frequency through this second interval is seven; that is, there are seven scores 105 or lower in this frequency distribution. The next interval, 105 to 114, contains five scores. The cumulative frequency is, therefore, 12. We add successive frequencies within class intervals to the accumulated frequencies until the highest class interval is reached. At that point all the scores have been accounted for. In our example, when we reach the interval 214 to 222, all 132 scores have been accumulated. In Table 2–3, the fourth column gives the cumulative frequencies for each class interval.

PROPORTIONS AND CUMULATIVE PROPORTIONS. One problem with using frequencies and cumulative frequencies is that they are a function of the number of people in the group. In comparing frequency distributions from different groups we should be aware that differences in the number of scores occurring in any given class interval may be reflecting differences in the size of the groups rather than differences in the performance or characteristics of the two groups. In order to correct for differences in the size of the groups, we can simply divide the frequencies and cumulative frequencies by the total number of people in the group. Thus, we divide all the frequencies in Table 2–3 by 132 to change them to *proportions*. For example, the proportion of scores occurring in the class interval 142 to 150 is 15÷132, or .114.

Similarly, to change the cumulative frequencies to *cumulative* proportions we divide each entry in column four in Table 2–3 by 132. For example, the cumulative proportion of scores below the class interval 178 to 186 is .871. What this really means is that 87.1 percent of the scores are lower than 186 in this particular group of people. Note that when we reach the highest score in the group (222), all the scores are below this point—the proportion is 1.000 or 100 percent.

As we shall see in the next chapter, cumulative proportions (called percentile scores) are one common method of communicating the results of tests. They are meaningful in that they express very clearly the relative position of any score. Thus, each person knows where he or she stands in relation to others in the group or in similar groups.

CONCLUDING REMARKS. Frequency distributions are constructed and plotted to help us understand the scores produced by a group of people. In the construction of grouped frequency distributions, ten to fifteen class intervals are usually considered best. Fewer than ten intervals may obscure important characteristics of the data; more than fifteen intervals begin to make the data appear more complex. However, there is no immutable law that uniquely determines the number of class intervals to use. The persons constructing the frequency distribution must decide what will best serve their needs and convey information about the scores in the most useful manner.

As is the case with most tedious problems involving numbers and computations, there are now computer programs for constructing and plotting frequency distributions. It is, therefore, more critical to understand the purposes of frequency distributions than to spend a great deal of time learning how to construct and plot them.

Shapes of Frequency Distributions

In plotting or examining frequency distributions certain shapes occur rather often in practice. These variously shaped distributions have been given names to facilitate describing the frequency distributions, or groups of scores. The more common shapes are described in the next several paragraphs and are portrayed in Table 2–4. The figures represent ideal frequency distributions. Real groups of scores will, of course, only approximate these ideals. Again, as is true for all plotted frequency distributions, the height of the curve represents frequency, and the base line or horizontal axis represents scores.

SYMMETRIC DISTRIBUTIONS. Figure (a) in Table 2–4 shows the shape of one type of symmetric distribution. Such distributions are called symmetric because the scores are evenly divided around a central point; that is, the lower part of the curve is exactly like the upper part. Figure (a) is also referred to

TABLE 2–4 Shapes of Frequency Distribution

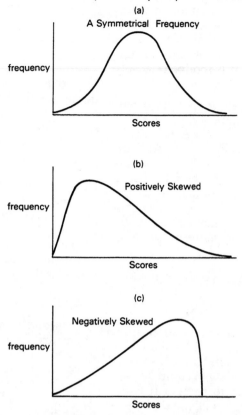

(a)
A Symmetrical Frequency

frequency

Scores

(b)
Positively Skewed

frequency

Scores

(c)
Negatively Skewed

frequency

Scores

as a *normal distribution* or a *normally distributed* set of scores. This curve is of great theoretical importance in statistics and has a specific mathematical formula to describe it very precisely. However, for our purposes, note that in a normal distribution there are more scores toward the center of the distribution than at the upper or lower ends. Extreme scores, either very high or very low, occur with low frequency in a normal distribution. Test scores such as IQ scores are often almost normally distributed. However, it is well to keep in mind that the normal distribution or normal curve is a theoretical distribution. Real data typically will only approximate the theoretical curve. It should also be noted that not all symmetric distributions follow the normal distribution.

POSITIVELY SKEWED DISTRIBUTIONS. Figure (b) in Table 2–4 shows a positively skewed distribution. Positively skewed means that the low scores tend to occur with greater frequency than the high scores. If a class of students is given a test that is too hard, for example, the resulting distribution of scores will tend to be positively skewed. Most students will receive rather low scores, but a few students will do very well and receive high scores. Reaction time scores can also be positively skewed because most people respond very quickly to a stimulus but occasionally turn their head, stop paying attention, or for some other reason do not respond for a long period of time.

NEGATIVELY SKEWED DISTRIBUTIONS. Figure (c) in Table 2–4 shows a negatively skewed distribution. This distribution, of course, is the opposite of a positively skewed one. Most scores tend to be rather high, and there are relatively few low scores. If a class of students is given a test that is too easy, for example, the resulting distribution of scores will tend to be negatively skewed. Most students will receive rather high scores, but a few (perhaps those who never come to class or read the text) will still receive relatively low scores.

OTHER SHAPES. Other shapes have also been named. For example, a *rectangular distribution* is one in which all scores occur with about the same frequency. *Leptokurtic distributions* are symmetric but with more scores in the center and fewer in the tails than a normal curve. *Platykurtic distributions* are the opposite of leptokurtic, having a flatter appearance than a normal curve, with fewer scores in the center and more in the tails.

MEASURES OF CENTRAL TENDENCY

Mean

By far the most commonly used measure of central tendency is the arithmetic mean. It has many desirable mathematical and statistical properties, it is easy to compute, and it is generally familiar to people. It is defined simply as the sum of all the scores in a given group divided by the total number of people in the group. In symbols* it is written as

$$\bar{X} = \Sigma X/N \qquad (2\text{-}1)$$

where $\bar{X}$ represents the mean, Σ is the Greek letter sigma and is the symbol for summation, ΣX means add up all the X scores, and N is the number of scores or the number of people in the group.

If there are five scores in a group (7, 4, 5, 8, 6), the mean of this set of scores is

$$\bar{X} = \frac{(7 + 4 + 5 + 8 + 6)}{5}$$

$$\bar{X} = \frac{(30)}{5} = 6$$

Note that in this example $\Sigma X = 30$. That is, the sum of the X's or the sum of the scores is 30. The mean of the X's or the mean of the scores is 6.

The arithmetic mean, $\bar{X}$, is one way of summarizing the average score of a group. It does not imply that everyone in a particular group has received this score. In fact, no one may have. It also does not imply that persons receiving scores close to the mean are "average" in an absolute sense. For example, if the test scores of the group as a whole tend to be high, the mean of the group will tend to be high.

Median

A second measure of central tendency is the median. Just as the median strip divides interstate highways into two equal roadways, the median of a group of scores divides the distribution into two equal halves. The median is that score in a group above which 50 percent of the scores lie and below which 50 percent of the scores lie. In other words, the median is always exactly in the middle (fiftieth percentile) of any group of scores.

Unless the scores appear in a grouped frequency distribution, there is no explicit formula for computing the median. For small sets of data it can be found by inspection. Consider the five scores for which we computed the mean—7, 4, 5, 8, 6. The first step in computing the median is to *rank order* the scores. These five scores are rank ordered as follows:

4, 5, 6, 7, 8

The score that divides the distribution into two equal halves is the third score, 6. The median for these five scores is 6. Note that this value is exactly the same as the mean, which does not always occur.

*We are using the conventional symbols for descriptive statistics in our discussion of basic statistics. We do this to simplify the presentation, recognizing that formulas for inferential statistics would often be used in practice. Sampling problems and statistical inference are not discussed in detail in this or subsequent chapters.

Suppose a sixth score were added to the group. And suppose this score were 54. The six scores would be rank ordered as follows:

4, 5, 6, 7, 8, 54

Which score now divides the distribution into two equal halves? In this case, there should be three scores in each half. Therefore, the dividing point is between the third score (6) and the fourth score (7). By convention we define the median as being halfway between these two scores, or at the location 6.5. The median for these six scores is, therefore, 6.5.

What would the mean ($\overline{X}$) of these six scores be? Note that we have added a very large score, 54, relative to the others. The sum of the six scores ($\sum X$) equals 84. Therefore,

$$\overline{X} = \frac{84}{6} = 14$$

Note that in computing the mean we have obtained a value, 14, that is larger than all but one of the six scores. The median, however, is still exactly in the center of the distribution. What this implies in general is that the mean is not a very good measure of central tendency when the scores have a skewed distribution. When the distribution is positively or negatively skewed, the median is a better measure of central tendency.

Mode

The third measure of central tendency is the mode, which is the most frequently occurring score in the group. It is found by inspection. Referring back to Table 2–2, the most frequently occurring score is 153. Thus, the mode for this group would equal 153. The mode is most useful when there are rather large numbers of scores. For small groups of people, the mode is not particularly meaningful. For instance, in the small example we used in computing the mean and median (4, 5, 6, 7, 8), no score occurs more than once.

Unlike the mean and the median, for which there is always only a single value for a particular group, a distribution of scores may have two or more modes. When there are two scores occurring with equal frequency, the distribution is said to be *bimodal*. This type of distribution can occur, for example, when half the group taking a test does very well and the other half does very poorly.

Summary Remarks

Of the three measures of central tendency, the mean is the one most often used. Computer programs exist to compute the mean when large numbers of scores are available. Hand calculators can also be used to compute the mean for smaller sets of data. The median requires rank ordering the scores and then finding the median by inspection. Explicit formulas are available in elementary statistics books for computing the mean and the median from a grouped frequency distribution. The mode implicitly requires that a frequency distribution be available in order to determine its value. The mode is perhaps the easiest to obtain but is the crudest measure of the three.

If the scores follow a normal distribution, the three measures of central tendency are all equal. If the scores follow a skewed distribution, the median is the preferred measure. (The three measures will all typically be different in skewed distributions.) If the scores follow a symmetric distribution, the mean and median will be equal.

MEASURES OF VARIABILITY

In our discussion of measures of central tendency, we were looking for a single number to characterize the average performance of a group. However, the average score in a group is not the one everybody in the group receives. Rather, many different scores are usually obtained—some above the mean, some below the mean, and some close to the mean. Measures of variability are very important in testing, because *variability reflects individual differences.* One of the primary goals in giving tests is to measure individual differences. If people were all the same, there would be no variability in the scores and no need to give tests.

Range

The simplest measure of variability is the range, which is defined as the difference between the highest and lowest score in a group. For example, in the five scores we used in defining the mean and median—4, 5, 6, 7, 8—the range is equal to 4. (Range = 8 − 4 = 4.) That is, there are four units between the highest and lowest score. When we created a second example with six scores, we had the numbers 4, 5, 6, 7, 8, 54. The range for this set of scores is 50 units (54 − 4 = 50). Clearly there is a wider range of scores in the second example. The group is more diverse; the people are more heterogeneous in whatever characteristic is being measured.

Although the range is easy to compute and conveys some useful information, it has a major drawback as a measure of variability. Because it is a function of only two scores, the highest and the lowest, it is not a very stable index of variability.

Variance

In statistical applications, the variance is an important measure of variability. The standard deviation, which is also a commonly used measure of variability, is derived directly from the variance. Therefore, the variance will be discussed first, although the standard deviation is in some ways more useful in testing. The symbol used for variance is S^2.

In order to define precisely what variance is, a new type of score must be introduced. This score is called a *deviation score* (x) and is defined as the difference between a raw score (X) and the mean ($\overline{X}$) for a particular group. In other words, a deviation score measures how far each raw score is from the mean. Thus, for any individual, the equation is

$$\text{deviation score} = \text{raw score} - \text{mean}$$

or

$$x = X - \overline{X} \qquad (2\text{-}2)$$

In the left panel of Table 2–5 the five scores used earlier in defining the mean and median are given as Data Set 1. The mean

TABLE 2-5 Calculation of Deviation Scores, Means, Variances, and Standard Deviations for Three Sets of Data

Data Set 1			Data Set 2			Data Set 3		
X	x	x^2	X	x	x^2	X	x	x^2
8	2	4	11	5	25	6	0	0
7	1	1	7	1	1	6	0	0
6	0	0	6	0	0	6	0	0
5	−1	1	5	−1	1	6	0	0
4	−2	4	1	−5	25	6	0	0
$\Sigma X = 30$	$\Sigma x = 0$	$\Sigma x^2 = 10$	$\Sigma X = 30$	$\Sigma x = 0$	$\Sigma x^2 = 52$	$\Sigma X = 30$	$\Sigma x = 0$	$\Sigma x^2 = 0$
$\overline{X} = \dfrac{\Sigma X}{N}$		$S^2 = \dfrac{\Sigma x^2}{N}$	$\overline{X} = \dfrac{\Sigma X}{N}$		$S^2 = \dfrac{\Sigma x^2}{N}$	$\overline{X} = \dfrac{\Sigma X}{N}$		$S^2 = \dfrac{\Sigma x^2}{N}$
$\overline{X} = \dfrac{30}{5}$		$S^2 = \dfrac{10}{5}$	$\overline{X} = \dfrac{30}{5}$		$S^2 = \dfrac{52}{5}$	$\overline{X} = \dfrac{30}{5}$		$S^2 = \dfrac{0}{5}$
$\overline{X} = 6$		$S^2 = 2$	$\overline{X} = 6$		$S^2 = 10.4$	$\overline{X} = 6$		$S^2 = 0$
	$S = \sqrt{2} = 1.41$			$S = \sqrt{10.4} = 3.22$			$S = \sqrt{0} = 0$	

$(\bar{X})$ for this set of data is 6. The raw scores appear in rank order under the column headed by X. The second column gives the corresponding deviation score (x). The five deviation scores were obtained as follows:

$$8 - 6 = 2$$
$$7 - 6 = 1$$
$$6 - 6 = 0$$
$$5 - 6 = -1$$
$$4 - 6 = -2$$

Note that if we add the five deviation scores they total zero. This is always true because the positive and negative deviation scores are perfectly balanced around the mean. Positive deviation scores are, of course, above the mean; negative deviation scores are below the mean.

Now that we have defined deviation scores, it is possible to define the variance of a group of scores. *The variance is the average of a set of squared deviation scores.* That is, we square each deviation score in our group, add the squared scores, and then divide by the number of scores in the group. The corresponding formula is

$$S^2 = \frac{\Sigma x^2}{N} \qquad (2\text{-}3)$$

In the left panel of Table 2–5 the five squared deviation scores are listed under the column headed by x^2. Thus, the five deviation scores we have just computed

$$2, 1, 0, -1, -2$$

are squared

$$2^2, 1^2, 0^2, (-1)^2, (-2)^2$$

which gives

$$4, 1, 0, 1, 4$$

and added

$$4 + 1 + 0 + 1 + 4 = 10$$

to give

$$\Sigma x^2 = 10$$

The variance, S^2, for this group of scores is

$$S^2 = \frac{\Sigma x^2}{N} = \frac{10}{5} = 2$$

The deviation scores are squared to overcome the minus numbers. Any number squared will be positive. The variance of a set of scores is always a positive number. We have also used a definition formula. There are computational formulas using only raw scores in all elementary statistics books. However, for our purposes it is more important to understand the basic ideas about variance than to learn computational methods. Besides, computers can easily compute variances for almost any number of scores that may be obtained.

Two other examples of variance are presented in Table 2–5. For Data Set 2, there are again five scores and the mean is again 6. However, the scores are more spread out, ranging from a high of 11 to a low of 1. The variance, correspondingly increased, equals 10.4. For Data Set 3, all the scores equal 6. Accordingly the mean is still 6, but the variance of these scores is 0. That is, there are no differences at all among the scores. These two examples illustrate that the variance of a set of scores reflects how different the scores are from each other.

Another important point to notice about the three sets of data is that the mean is exactly the same. In other words, the mean and variance of most sets of scores are independent of each other. Knowing one tells us nothing about the other.

Standard Deviation

The variance is mathematically a useful statistic. However, it does involve the squares of scores rather than the scores themselves. The standard deviation is a measure of variability designed to remove the squaring effects from the variance. It is symbolized by the letter S and is simply the square root of the variance. Implicitly a variance is computed whenever the standard deviation is. Knowing either of these two statistics implies we know the other. The formula for the standard deviation can be written as

$$S = \sqrt{\Sigma x^2/N} \qquad (2\text{-}4)$$

In Data Set 1 in Table 2–5, the variance is 2. Therefore, the standard deviation would equal the square root of 2:

$$S = \sqrt{2} = 1.41$$

For Data Set 2, the variance is 10.4, so that

$$S = \sqrt{10.4} = 3.22$$

And for Data Set 3, the variance is 0 so that

$$S = \sqrt{0} = 0$$

For the moment the important thing to notice is that the standard deviation, as did the variance, reflects individual differences. The more spread out the scores are, the larger will be the variance and the standard deviation. Also, these two statistics, unlike the range, are a function of all the scores in the group. They are, therefore, more stable indicators of variability than is the range.

Before we can make these two statistics more meaningful, it will be necessary to make some assumptions about how the raw scores, the Xs, are distributed. In the next chapter, we shall see how the standard deviation can be used if the raw scores follow a normal distribution. For now it will be sufficient to understand how the variance and standard deviation are defined and that they both reflect how different the scores are from each other.

CORRELATION

The statistics we have discussed up to this point have all required only a single score per person. However, for measures of relationship or association there must be at least two scores or measurements per person. In this section we shall consider a relatively simple way of describing the relationship between two variables. We shall also consider an elementary method of predicting scores on one variable from the knowledge of scores on another variable.

The example we shall use is very common in terms of the two variables involved. We shall assume that we have ACT composite scores (a measure of scholastic aptitude) for a number of college students as well as their grade point averages (GPA). We are interested in determining if there is a relationship between ACT scores and GPA and, ultimately, in predicting a student's GPA when we know his or her ACT score. In order to keep our example reasonable, we shall limit our group to only eight students. In any application of this method there would typically be large numbers of students involved. Practical work with correlation might involve data from several hundred students. Even with our small example, however, we shall be able to illustrate the important principles.

z-Scores

Before we identify the measure of relationship we intend to use, it is helpful to define a new kind of score. We have previously discussed and used raw scores, symbolized by X, and deviation scores, symbolized by x and defined as the raw score minus the mean. The new score is called a *standard score* or a *z-score*. It is defined as follows:

$$z\text{-score} = \frac{\text{deviation score}}{\text{standard deviation}}$$

or in symbols

$$z_x = \frac{x}{S_x} = \frac{(X - \bar{X})}{S_x} \qquad (2\text{-}5)$$

These z-scores have two useful and convenient properties: the mean of a set of z-scores is always zero, and the variance and standard deviation are equal to one. In other words, z-scores are corrected for both differences in the means and variances of variables.

Note that z-scores represent an important use for the standard deviation, S. *The z-scores are expressed in standard deviation units of measurement.* A z-score of one is one standard deviation above the mean; a z-score of − .5 is one-half a standard deviation below the mean. As was true for deviation scores, positive z-scores are above the mean and negative z-scores are below the mean. Using the standard deviation as the unit of measurement gives a precise way to assess how far away from the mean any given score is.

In Table 2–6 are the z-scores for the students for whom we have ACT composite scores and GPAs. Student A has a z-score of +1.5 on the ACT and a z-score of +1.0 on the GPA variable. Student B has a z-score of − 1.5 on the ACT and − 1.5 on the GPA variable. Student A is 1.5 standard deviations *above* the mean on the ACT and 1.0 standard deviation *above* the mean on the GPA variable. Student B is *below* the mean by the same amounts, − 1.5 on the ACT and − 1.5 on the GPA variable.

Correlation Coefficient

The correlation coefficient, symbolized by r, is probably the most commonly used measure of relationship. It is defined as the average of a set of cross products of z-scores; that is, each student's z-score on the ACT and the student's z-score on the GPA variable are multiplied. These products are then added together and the sum divided by the number of students for whom we have scores. Let z_x, read as "z sub x," stand for the z-score on the ACT; and let z_y, read as "z sub y," stand for the z-score on the GPA variable. In symbols, the correlation coefficient is defined as

$$r = \frac{\Sigma z_x z_y}{N} \qquad (2\text{-}6)$$

In Table 2–6 the cross products, $z_x z_y$, have been computed in the fourth column. The sum of these cross products is 7.5, and therefore, the correlation coefficient for these eight students is

$$r = \frac{\Sigma z_x z_y}{N} = \frac{7.5}{8} = .9375$$

Correlation coefficients are usually reported with only two significant figures. In our case, r would be reported as .94. How-

TABLE 2-6 Calculation of Correlation Between ACT Scores and GPA's by Using z-Scores

Student	ACT z-score (z_x)	GPA z-score (z_y)	Cross Product $z_x z_y$
A	+1.5	+1.0	1.50
B	−1.5	−1.5	2.25
C	+1.0	+1.5	1.50
D	+1.0	+1.0	1.00
E	−1.0	−1.0	1.00
F	+ .0	− .5	.00
G	− .5	+ .0	.00
H	− .5	− .5	.25
	$\Sigma z_x = 0$	$\Sigma z_y = 0$	$\Sigma z_x z_y = 7.50$
	$\Sigma z_x^2 = 8$	$\Sigma z_y^2 = 8$	$\dfrac{\Sigma z_x z_y}{N} = \dfrac{7.5}{8} = .9375$
	$\dfrac{\Sigma z_x^2}{N} = \dfrac{8}{8} = 1$	$\dfrac{\Sigma z_y^2}{N} = \dfrac{8}{8} = 1$	

ever, in order to illustrate some properties of correlations, we are maintaining four places to the right of the decimal.

The first thing we can say about the r we have just computed is that it is positive. This means that persons who have scores above the mean on one variable will tend to have scores above the mean on the other variable. The converse is also true. Persons who score below the mean on one variable will tend to score below the mean on the second variable. On the other hand, of course, a negative r suggests that persons scoring above the mean on one variable tend to score below the mean on the other. Many tests of academic achievement and aptitude correlate positively with grade point averages in both high school and college. However, correlations are rarely as high as our example. The variables of height and weight are two other variables that are also positively correlated. The heavier a person is the taller the person is likely to be; similarly, shorter people tend to weigh less. The relationship between height and weight is also not perfect. As an example of two variables that would tend to be negatively correlated, consider the weight of an automobile and the miles per gallon of gasoline it uses. Here, heavier automobiles tend to get fewer miles per gallon of gasoline whereas lighter automobiles tend to have higher mileage.

Basically, a correlation coefficient measures the extent to which the scores are arranged in the same rank order for the two variables. For positive correlations, high scores tend to go with high scores, average scores with average scores, and low scores with low scores. Negative correlations are the reverse.

In our example we have used a definition formula to obtain r. Elementary statistics books give formulas in raw scores so that they do not need to be transformed into z-scores first. However, whether we correlate raw scores, deviation scores, or z-scores, the r obtained is the same.

INTERPRETING r. In Figure 2–2 the pairs of z-scores presented in Table 2–6 are plotted. The points are labeled A, B, C, and so on for the various students. The horizontal axis is z_x, the ACT z-score; the vertical axis is z_y, the GPA z-score. In our example

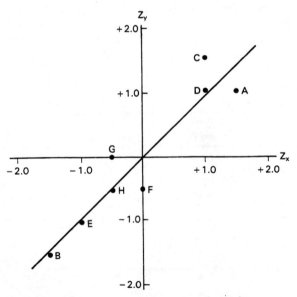

FIGURE 2–2 Plot of z_y versus z_x scores for eight students with a best-fitting regression line ($\hat{z}_y = .9375z_x$).

we shall use the z_x scores to predict the z_y scores. In other words, we are using test scores to predict grades, a very common practice.

How could we describe the relationship between the z_x and z_y scores? There are many possible functional relationships and mathematical formulas that could be used. However, we shall consider the simplest mathematical function of all, a *straight line* relationship (a *linear* relationship).

In Figure 2–2 we have drawn a straight line. This line does not go through any of the points, yet it is maximally close to all of them. It is a best-fitting straight line, and its slope is r. In our example its numerical value is .9375.

This line is best-fitting in a *least squares sense;* that is, by choosing the straight line with a slope of .9375 we have minimized the *squared* differences between the line and the observed points. Mathematically, our linear equation is

$$\hat{z}_y = rz_x \qquad (2\text{-}7)$$

or in our case,

$$\hat{z}_y = .9375z_x$$

where $\hat{z}_y$ is the z_y score predicted from a person's z_x score. The differences that are made as small as possible are

$$(z_y - \hat{z}_y)^2$$

That is, we are making the squared differences between the observed z_y scores and the predicted $\hat{z}_y$ scores as small as possible. Choosing to define r as we did accomplishes this goal.

One way of interpreting or thinking about r, then, is as *the slope of the best-fitting straight line relating two sets of z-scores.*

A second way of thinking about correlation coefficients is as an index of how well we can predict one variable from another. The total variance that can be explained or accounted for in a set of z-scores is 1.0. If we compute $\hat{z}_y$ for every z_x score in our group,

and then compute the variance of these predicted scores, we will find that this variance equals r^2. This result gives us our second way of interpreting correlation coefficients. In our example $r^2 = (.9375)^2 = .8789;$ that is, about 88 percent of the variance can be explained. *The square of a correlation coefficient (r^2) gives the proportion of variance accounted for by a linear relationship between the two variables.*

If the correlation between two variables is perfect, $+1.00$ or -1.00, we can explain all the variation in scores for one of the variables from knowledge of the scores for the other variable. If the correlation is zero or close to zero, we can say the two variables are not linearly related. We cannot account for any of the variance in one of the variables from knowledge of the other.

CAUSATION VERSUS CORRELATION. Strictly speaking, a significant correlation between two variables establishes a relationship. Correlation does not necessarily imply that one variable causes or produces variation in the other. There may well be, for example, a high positive correlation between the number of personal fouls that basketball players commit and the number of points they score. We might argue that players who commit more fouls tend to be aggressive and get more points because of this aggressiveness. However, it is more likely that both variables, personal fouls and points scored, are a function of a third variable—the total amount of playing time. This third variable probably reflects the coach's assessment of how skilled the player is. Although it is often tempting to argue for causal relationships when significant correlations are discovered, it is a very tricky argument to make in most instances. Fortunately, in the use of correlation coefficients to describe the relationships between test scores and behaviors of interest, causation is of little importance. The user is typically satisfied with the significant relationship because it enables predictions to be made. The correlational results can sometimes be extended through more rigorous experimental techniques to establish causative models.

CORRELATION AND LINEAR RELATION-SHIPS. It is well to keep in mind that a correlation of zero between two variables does not necessarily imply they are unrelated. It may well mean they are *linearly* unrelated, but they could still be related in a nonlinear manner. "Test anxiety" is one example of a variable that might be related in a nonlinear manner to performance in classroom examinations. Students with no test anxiety may receive low scores on examinations because they have no motivation to succeed. Students with high test anxiety would also tend to receive low scores on examinations, but in this case, because they are traumatized by fear and "freeze" on examinations. Students with a medium amount of "test anxiety" might tend to perform best because they are motivated but do not "freeze up." If the test anxiety scores and classroom examination scores were correlated, they could yield a correlation approaching zero. Yet the two variables would be systematically related through a nonlinear function.

STATISTICAL SIGNIFICANCE VERSUS IMPORTANCE. Before any correlation coefficient is interpreted, it should be *statistically significant.* By this we mean the correlation should not have occurred by chance. Even more precisely, we mean the correlation is significantly different from zero. Testing hypotheses and probability are not the subjects of this book, but there are formulas to determine whether or not a correlation coefficient is statistically significant. In general, the further it is from zero, the more likely it is to be statistically significant. Negative and positive correlations are equally useful. However, statistical significance is partially a function of sample size. When the sample size is very large, a very small correlation coefficient may be statistically significant. For example, if the sample size is 502, a correlation of .088 would be statistically significant at the 5 percent level. That is, it would occur by chance only 5 times in 100 if the true or population correlation were zero. However, if the sample size is 6, then a correlation of .811 would be needed to be statistically significant at the 5 percent level.

Obviously no one should use or interpret correlation coefficients that are not statistically significant. However, even if the correlation is statistically significant, it may not be important in terms of the amount of variance accounted for. In our example from the preceding paragraph, the correlation of .088 was statistically significant when it was based on 502 observations. But squaring this correlation gives an indication of the proportion of variance accounted for:

$$r^2 = (.088)^2 = .0077$$

This means that less than 1 percent of the variance can be accounted for even though the correlation is statistically significant. In conclusion it seems fair to say that a statistically significant correlation may still not be important or useful.

FACTORS THAT INFLUENCE CORRELATION. There are many factors that can influence the correlation between two variables. We note two of the most important.

1. *Homogeneous groups.* When all people receive about the same score on a test, we call the group *homogeneous.* They do not differ very much on whatever the test was measuring. When there is little variability on either or both of the variables being correlated, *r* is likely to be small. When groups are *heterogeneous,* the scores differ widely and the *r* has a better chance of being high.
2. *Unreliable scores.* If the scores obtained on either or both variables are not consistent or are subject to many random sources of error, they will usually not correlate highly with other variables.

CORRELATION AND TESTING. As we shall see in the following chapters, correlation coefficients are used in many ways to determine how good a test is. The basic characteristics of any test, reliability and validity, can be expressed by particular kinds of correlation coefficients. In using test scores we are typically assuming that they relate with other important variables of interest. The use of correlation coefficients is pervasive among test developers, test users, and researchers.

SPECIAL TYPES OF CORRELATION COEFFICIENTS. Depending on the kind of variables being correlated, correlations have been given special names. Without providing formulas for these special cases, we will give their names and defining features. The first two involve a *dichotomous* or *binomial variable*. A dichotomous variable is one having only two possible values, and it is usually coded 0 or 1. For scoring test items, for example, correct answers are coded 1 and incorrect answers are coded 0. Gender, male or female, is another variable that can be coded dichotomously, although the numbers assigned to male and female are arbitrary. All males could be scored 1 and females 0 or vice versa. A *point biserial correlation* is one between a dichotomous variable and a continuous variable, for example, correlations between the total test score on a classroom examination and the score on an individual item (correct or incorrect). A *phi coefficient* is the correlation obtained when two dichotomous variables are correlated. For example, when scores (correct or incorrect) on items are correlated, we have a phi coefficient.

When a dichotomous variable is presumed to have been artificially created and to have a continuous distribution underlying it, different correlation coefficients are obtained. These are called *biserial correlation* (one dichotomous variable, one continuous variable) and *tetrachoric correlation* (two dichotomous variables). These two correlations are largely of theoretical interest and require special computational formulas.

SUMMARY STATEMENTS ABOUT *r*.

1. Correlation coefficients vary between +1.0 and −1.0.
2. A positive correlation means that persons scoring above the mean on one variable tend to score above the mean on the second variable. A negative correlation implies the opposite—persons above the mean on one variable tend to be below the mean on the other.
3. The farther the correlation coefficient is from zero in either direction the stronger the relationship is between the two variables.
4. A zero correlation means that the two variables are not linearly related. They still may be related in a curvilinear fashion.
5. The square of the correlation coefficient tells us what proportion of variance is explained or accounted for by a linear relationship, that is, how much variance can be predicted from one variable given knowledge of the other.
6. Correlation does not necessarily imply causation.
7. A correlation coefficient can be computed for any pair of variables, even if neither of them is normally distributed.
8. If the scores on one or both variables are homogeneous, the correlation coefficient will tend to be lower than if the scores are relatively heterogeneous.
9. If the scores on one or both variables contain large errors, the correlation coefficient will be lower than if there is relatively little error.

REGRESSION EQUATIONS

In order to simplify our presentation of correlation we have used z-scores to define various concepts of interest. However, in using correlation coefficients for prediction purposes in various settings (educational, industrial, clinical), the user is not usually interested in predicting z-scores. Rather, the user is interested in predicting the actual raw scores—the student's GPA, the worker's production capacity, the client's potential for successful psychotherapy. Regression equations are equations for predicting one variable from another. Again, to illustrate some principles, we will use a very small example. Applied work with regression equations would usually involve large samples of people.

With z-Scores

In defining and interpreting the correlation coefficient, r, we have already used the z-score regression equation. It is written as

$$\hat{z}_y = rz_x \qquad (2\text{-}7)$$

where $\hat{z}_y$ is the z-score on the Y variable predicted from a given person's z-score (z_x) on the X variable. Once r has been determined for a group of people, the prediction of z_y is straightforward since we multiply r times each z_x to obtain the predicted value.

The term *regression* arises from the fact that r is typically less than 1.00; that is, the correlation between two variables is rarely perfect. Whenever z_x is multiplied by r to obtain $\hat{z}_y$, the predicted $\hat{z}_y$ is typically smaller than the z_x from which it was predicted. If $z_x = 1.0$ and $r = .9375$, $\hat{z}_y = (.9375) (1.0) = .9375$, which is smaller than 1.0. The predicted $\hat{z}_y$'s thus *regress* toward the mean or get closer to the mean of the z_y scores. Remember that the mean of any set of z-scores is zero. In prediction, then, it is statistically safer to predict that scores will be close to the mean than to predict that they will be far away.

In the left panel of Table 2–7 the z-score example used in computing r is repeated, but we have now included a third column of predicted z-scores ($\hat{z}_y$'s) for the Y variable, the GPAs. Note that in no case does the $\hat{z}_y$ exactly equal the observed z_y. The regression equation was determined so that the squared differences between $\hat{z}_y$ and z_y across all eight students are as small as possible.

Remember that if the $\hat{z}_y$'s are squared, summed, and divided by N, we have the variance of the $\hat{z}_y$ scores. This result is equal to r^2. The square of the correlation gives the proportion of variance that is predictable by using a linear relationship.

With Raw Scores

As we indicated previously, the main interest of any user of correlations for prediction purposes is to predict raw scores. Conventionally, Y is the symbol used for the variable to be predicted. This variable is often called the *dependent variable*, since its values are assumed to depend on the values of another variable, the *independent variable*. The independent variable is conventionally symbolized by X. It is the predictor variable, or the one from which we predict Y. The predicted Y scores are symbolized by $\hat{Y}$.

In order to make predictions about raw scores, five statistics are needed. They are the following:

1. $\bar{X}$, the mean of the X's.
2. $\bar{Y}$, the mean of the Y's.
3. S_x, the standard deviation of the X's.
4. S_y, the standard deviation of the Y's.
5. r, the correlation between the X and Y variables.

The regression equation for predicting the raw scores of Y from the raw score of X is

$$\hat{Y} = r\frac{S_y}{S_x} X + (\bar{Y} - r\frac{S_y}{S_x} \bar{X}) \qquad (2\text{-}8)$$

This is an equation for a straight line having a slope equal to $r\frac{S_y}{S_x}$ and a Y-intercept equal to $(\bar{Y} - r\frac{S_y}{S_x}\bar{X})$. The Y-intercept is where the straight line crosses the Y axis, which occurs when $X = 0$.

TABLE 2-7   Observed and Predicted Scores for Eight Students: z-scores and Raw Scores

	z-scores				Raw Scores		
Student	z_x	z_y	$\hat{z}_y$	Student	X	Y	$\hat{Y}$
A	+1.5	+1.0	+1.40625	A	24	2.90	3.0625
B	−1.5	−1.5	−1.40625	B	12	1.90	1.9375
C	+1.0	+1.5	+ .93750	C	22	3.10	2.8750
D	+1.0	+1.0	+ .93750	D	22	2.90	2.8750
E	−1.0	−1.0	− .93750	E	14	2.10	2.1250
F	+ .0	− .5	+ .00000	F	18	2.30	2.5000
G	− .5	+ .0	− .46875	G	16	2.50	2.3125
H	− .5	− .5	− .46875	H	16	2.30	2.3125

In the right panel of Table 2–7 are listed the raw score equivalents of the z-scores given in the left panel. The five statistics are

$$\overline{X} = 18$$
$$\overline{Y} = 2.5$$
$$S_x = 4$$
$$S_y = .4$$
$$r = .9375$$

The resulting raw score regression equation is

$$\hat{Y} = .9375 \frac{.4}{4} X + \left[2.5 - .9375 \left(\frac{.4}{4} \right) 18 \right]$$

$$= .09375\, X + .8125$$

In our example, to predict the GPA for any student, we multiply the student's ACT score, X, by .09375 and add .8125. Student D has an ACT score of 22; the predicted GPA, $\hat{Y}$, is 2.88. Note that for every student the predicted GPA is not equal to the GPA actually obtained. As was true for relating two sets of z-scores, the raw score regression equation makes the squared differences between the observed and predicted Y scores as small as possible. For the entire group of eight students the predicted scores are as good as we can make them, although for any particular student we may well be considerably in error. This is a common problem in statistics and in testing. Predictions that are very good on the average, for many people, can be rather poor for particular individuals in the group.

Errors in Prediction

STANDARD ERROR OF ESTIMATE. In the right panel of Table 2–7 we have computed all the predicted grades for the eight students. A GPA of 3.0625 is predicted for Student A; the lowest GPA, 1.9375, is predicted for Student B. The predicted grades all differ somewhat from grades the students actually earned. Some of the predicted grades are higher than the students earned, as is the case with Students B, E, F, and H, and

some predicted grades are lower, as is the case with Students A, C, D, and G. How could we measure the accuracy with which these predictions are made? One way is to compute the standard deviation of the differences between the observed and predicted scores. For the GPAs in Table 2–7, these differences would be $-.1625$ for Student A, $-.0375$ for Student B, .225 for Student C, down to a difference of $-.0125$ for Student H. Squaring these differences for all eight students and adding them gives a sum of .155. In symbols we have

$$\Sigma (Y - \hat{Y})^2 = .155$$

To change this sum to a variance we divide by N to obtain

$$S_{y|x}^2 = \frac{\Sigma (Y - \hat{Y})^2}{N} = \frac{.155}{8} = .019375$$

$S_{y|x}^2$ is defined as the variance of the errors we make in predicting Y from X.

Because computing $S_{y|x}^2$ in this manner would be a great deal of work, there is a mathematically equivalent formula that uses some statistics we already know.

$$S_{y|x}^2 = S_y^2 (1 - r^2) \qquad (2\text{-}9)$$
$$= (.16)\, (1 - .93752)$$
$$= (.16)\, (1 - .87890625)$$
$$= (.16)\, (.12109375)$$
$$= .019375$$

Remember that S_y^2, the variance of the Y scores, is the square of the standard deviation of the Y scores ($.4^2 = .16$).

The standard deviation of the errors we make in predicting Y from X is called the *standard error of estimate* and is symbolized by $S_{y|x}$. It is, of course, equal to the square root of the variance we have just computed,

$$S_{y|x} = \sqrt{.019375} = .13919411$$

The standard error of estimate can also be computed from the following formula:

$$S_y|_x = S_y \sqrt{1 - r^2} \qquad (2\text{-}10)$$

In our example, $S_y = .4$ and $r = .9375$, giving the following results:

$$
\begin{aligned}
S_y|_x &= .4 \sqrt{1 - .9375^2} \\
&= .4 \sqrt{1 - .87890625} \\
&= .4 \sqrt{.12109375} \\
&= (.4)(.34798527) \\
&= .13919411
\end{aligned}
$$

which is the same value that we previously obtained.

Note that the standard error of estimate depends on two quantities: (1)how spread out the Y scores are as measured by S_y and (2)how strongly the two variables are correlated. If $r = +1$ or -1, there is no error in our predictions, and the standard error of estimate will equal zero. The closer r gets to zero, the less accurate our predictions become and the larger the standard error of estimate.

CONFIDENCE INTERVALS. The standard error of estimate can also be used to set confidence limits around a predicted score. To do so, considerable statistical knowledge is required, and we must assume that the errors we make in prediction follow a normal distribution. In a normal distribution 95 percent of the scores are within 1.96 standard deviations of the mean. In our case we can write the following equation for setting the 95 percent confidence limits around a predicted score:

$$\text{Upper limit} = \hat{Y} + 1.96 S_y|_x \qquad (2\text{-}11)$$
$$\text{Lower limit} = \hat{Y} - 1.96 S_y|_x \qquad (2\text{-}12)$$

In our example, in predicting the GPA of a student having an ACT score of 22, we obtained a $\hat{Y}$ of 2.875. Using $S_y|_x = .139$ we would obtain the following limits around 2.875:

$$
\begin{aligned}
\text{Upper limit} &= \hat{Y} + 1.96 S_y|_x \\
&= 2.875 + 1.96(.139) \\
&= 2.875 + .272 \\
&= 3.147
\end{aligned}
$$

$$
\begin{aligned}
\text{Lower limit} &= \hat{Y} - 1.96 S_y|_x \\
&= 2.875 - 1.96(.139) \\
&= 2.875 - .272 \\
&= 2.603
\end{aligned}
$$

We can, therefore, say that 95 percent of the time a student having an ACT score of 22 will have a GPA between 2.603 and 3.147.

Confidence intervals serve one very useful purpose. They make clear that for any degree of correlation, unless it is perfect, there is a range of Y scores that is reasonable to obtain for a given X score. The lower the correlation, the wider the confidence interval. In our example, the ACT score of 22 yields a predicted GPA of 2.875. However, any GPA between 2.603 and 3.147 would be a reasonable one to obtain. Test scores in particular rarely allow the user to make fine predictions; the confidence intervals are usually rather wide.

Summary Remarks

In this section we have tried to give the essentials of using simple linear equations to make predictions. We have not tried to be rigorous in our presentation because this is not a statistics book. Nevertheless, the basic concepts used in regression equations have been presented so that their use in evaluating and using tests will be meaningful. We have also presented a rather simple picture of prediction. It would be more common in practice to use several predictor or independent variables, combining them in an optimum fashion to predict a dependent variable of interest. Such techniques are called *multiple regression analyses* and are described in advanced statistics books (for example, Kleinbaum & Kupper, 1978; Pedhazur, 1982).

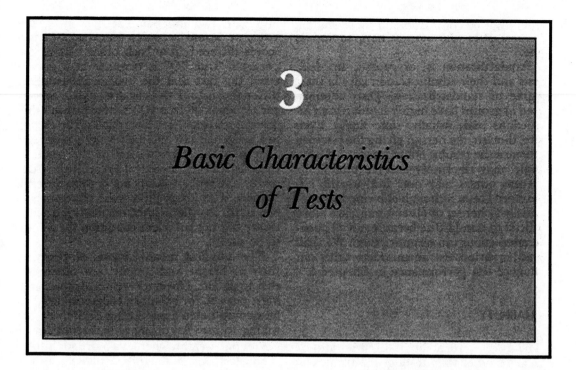

3

Basic Characteristics of Tests

In this chapter three broad characteristics are discussed: standardization, reliability, and validity. *Standardization* refers to the conditions under which the test is administered. *Reliability* refers to the consistency of the test scores. *Validity* refers to what the test measures. These latter two topics have a voluminous technical literature associated with them. Because they are important, they will be considered at some length, but we shall attempt to minimize and simplify the statistical aspects as much as possible. By determining the basic characteristics of a test, it is possible to evaluate and compare tests and decide which one or ones, if any, might be useful in a particular situation.

STANDARDIZATION

Standardization sometimes refers to the procedure of establishing norms for a test; that is, a test is said to be standardized if it uses a particular group of people to establish its statistical properties. We are not using the term in this way. Rather, by *standardization*, we mean that the conditions under which the test is administered are as clearly and completely specified as possible. The instructions are standardized; the time allowed to complete the test is specified; the method of scoring the test is standardized. Standardization really means that everyone taking a particular test is treated exactly the same. The only reason, then, that two people receive different scores is because they really differ on the trait or characteristic being measured.

When the Scholastic Aptitude Test, for example, is administered on a Saturday morning in Boise, Idaho, and in Chicago, Illinois, the students receive the same tests, the same instructions, and the same time to complete the various sections of the test. If such matters were not standardized, numerically equal test scores obtained at different times and different locations would not in fact be equivalent. For example, if the students in Boise were allowed an additional half hour to complete the test, their scores would not be comparable to those students in other cities who did not have additional time.

Standardization is, of course, an ideal. Tests and their administration vary in their degree of standardization. Tests administered in groups have highly standardized instructions and, usually, time limits. Even here, though, the person giving the test may influence the results. Some teachers, for example, may rigorously enforce time limits whereas others may not. Individually administered tests, although allowing for a potentially richer set of observations, are more difficult to standardize because not all possible interactions can be anticipated. We shall consider various extraneous factors that can influence test performance in Chapter 4.

RELIABILITY

The study of reliability is an important one in areas other than testing. Electronic components are checked for reliability before being installed in computers, television sets, and other devices. Manned space flight in complex rockets has necessitated the determination of the reliability of the numerous components and systems within the rocket. *Reliability* in this context refers to the confidence we have that parts will function as they are supposed to. Even the most sophisticated electronic system is subject to flaws of various kinds. To make the total rocket as reliable as possible, a certain amount of redundancy is required. Thus, several components may be installed to accomplish a certain task so that if one or even two fail, the remaining components can still accomplish the task. If the physical parts and construction were perfect (that is, there were no error), the redundancy would be unnecessary and a single component would be sufficient, since it would always function reliably (that is, perfectly).

In testing, the study of reliability explicitly recognizes that any particular measurement is not perfect. If we were able to make simultaneous measurements of a person's IQ with two independent measuring devices, we would probably find that the two scores differed from each other. Since the person's "true IQ" is constant at a given time, the fact that the two measurements differ means our devices are subject to error. A person's "true IQ" is, of course, a theoretical abstraction. How much error exists in a particular test and the resulting scores is an important characteristic of the test. If there is a large amount of error in the test scores, they will probably not be very useful. If there is relatively little error, the test *may* be useful. In other words, reliability is a necessary but not sufficient condition for a test to be useful.

The physical measurements of people, such as height and weight, are relatively easy to obtain. The error we make in weighing a person, for example, is determined by how complicated a measuring device we are willing to use. An ordinary bathroom scale gives one weight, whereas a more sophisticated electronic scale with a digital readout would give another. Also, if we weighed a person twice in a very short period of time, say fifteen minutes, we would expect the person's weight to be the same, particularly if we used a good scale. However, weighing a person twice on a poor scale might well give two different weights, even though we know that the person's "true weight" remained constant. Weight is an example of a reliable variable that might not be useful in predicting other variables of interest. For example, it is probably not related to a student's college GPA.

Psychologists, educators, and other behavioral scientists are often interested in much more complicated characteristics of people than simple physical ones. Intelligence; anxiety; achievement in reading, science, and mathematics; or potential for alcoholism are examples of complex variables that might be of interest. Unfortunately, they are difficult to define very precisely and are correspondingly often difficult to measure. Such variables may also not remain constant for individuals but may vary across time or situations. For these reasons and more, tests measuring some psychological variables may be rather unreliable. On the other hand, many tests, particularly those measuring aptitude for school work, are quite reliable.

Two Approaches to Reliability

Historically, reliability has been assessed by using the correlation coefficient (refer to the appropriate section of Chapter 2 for a discussion of this statistic). In this approach, a group of people is given the same or a similar test on two separate occasions over a relatively short period of time (say, within one week). If the test is reliable, we would expect a person's score to be approximately the same on the two separate occasions. By correlating the two sets of scores, we are determining to what extent the scores are related. If the test were perfectly reliable, we would expect the correlation between the two sets of scores to be 1.00. If the test scores were totally unreliable, we would expect the correlation to approach zero. The correlational approach to reliability requires two scores for each person, although the two scores may be obtained at one time. The two scores may, of course, come from observers who are rating each person's behavior. The pairs of scores need not come from tests.

The second approach to reliability has been to recognize more explicitly the sources of error in obtaining a test score and systematically vary those sources of error. This approach has its origin in the analysis of variance methodology that is very predominant in experimental psychology. Cronbach and his associates (1972) have been the main proponents of this approach, which has several desirable features. For one, it allows the size of the various sources of error to be estimated. These terms can be computed rather easily from the results in an analysis of a variance summary table. Second, the investigator is not restricted to pairs of scores but may have three or more scores. Third, the extensive statistical literature on the analysis of variance may be applied in determining the reliability of test scores.

Conceptual Model

As we have previously indicated, any observation or measurement is subject to error. The measurement is imprecise because of limitations of the measuring device, a poor definition of what is to be measured, inconsistencies in the person being measured, and other possible reasons. As far as testing is concerned, there are several possible approaches to expressing in a mathematical way the ideas we have been discussing. Spearman (1904, 1907, 1910) first introduced the technical results in the psychological literature. Gulliksen (1950, Ch. 2) in *The Theory of Mental Tests* systematically presented this traditional approach, often referred to as the "strong true-score theory." This approach, in simplified form, begins with the expression

$$X = T + E \qquad (3\text{-}1)$$

where

> X represents an observed score;
> T represents a "true score;"
> E represents an "error score."

Every observed score is conceptualized as arising from two sources. One source, the true score (T), is systematic and reflects true differences among persons. The second source, the error score (E), is nonsystematic and reflects the random influences in the measurement process. When test scores are highly reliable, the true score is large relative to the error score. On the other hand, if the test scores are unreliable, the error score is dominant. One important goal in developing tests and procedures for administering them is to eliminate as many sources of error as possible. We wish, in other words, to maximize the opportunity for true individual differences to emerge and minimize the extent to which test scores reflect chance differences among people.

Although the model we have presented is intuitively appealing, it has an obvious problem. The observed score, X, is the only term that we have immediately available: X is simply the total score on a test. The true score, T, and error score, E, are unknown. Since we have only one equation but two unknowns, we cannot compute T and E directly. These two scores will have meaning only if we assume certain characteristics about either of them. Perhaps the simplest approach is to make some assumptions about E. Traditionally, the three assumptions (Gulliksen, 1950, Ch. 2) most often used are these:

1. The mean of the error scores is zero.
2. The true scores and error scores are independent of each other.
3. Error scores on different tests are independent of each other.

The first assumption is intuitively reasonable. It implies that the error scores for all the people tend to balance out. Some people receive higher scores than they deserve, whereas other people receive lower scores than they deserve. The second assumption also appears reasonable. If error scores are due to chance, then they should not be related to a systematic source of individual differences. In other words, if the error scores were related to another score, it would suggest that the error scores were systematic rather than chance—which would be contradictory to our intuitive ideas about what error is. The third assumption is a natural extension of the second. If error scores are unrelated to true scores, they should certainly be independent of other error scores. Two chance outcomes would not be related. The second two assumptions imply that the correlation between T and E is zero, and the correlation between E_1 and E_2 (error scores on two different tests) is zero.

Using these assumptions, it is possible to derive several useful results. For example, it can be shown (Gulliksen, 1950, p. 9) that the variance of the observed scores is equal to the variance of the true scores plus the variance of the error scores. In symbols,* we have

$$S_x^2 = S_t^2 + S_e^2 \qquad (3\text{-}2)$$

This formula says simply that variability in the observed scores is a function of the variability in the true scores and error scores.

Of course, the model and assumptions we have presented may not be exactly true for a given set of test scores. However, in most cases the model probably is a good approximation. Other more mathematically sophisticated approaches (Allen & Yen, 1979; Lord & Novick, 1968) are possible, but they give very similar results to the one we have presented. Also, even though it is not possible to determine T and E exactly for an individual, by using the assumptions made it is possible to determine statistics characterizing the entire group. The conceptual model we have used and its more sophisticated versions are not without critics. Lumsden (1976), for example, suggests that the study of reliability is largely irrelevant to how tests are used and that the principle results of reliability theory are based on untenable assumptions.

Sources of Error

Lyman (1978) identifies five sources of error in test scores. One is the *person taking the test*. Individuals will differ in their motivation for taking the test, in their physical health, and in a large numnber of other ways that potentially could influence their scores. These extraneous individual differences can never be totally eliminated.

A second potential source of error is the *examiner-scorer*, who is relatively unimportant when tests are administered to

*We are presenting these and future results in the symbols for sample statistics because these symbols are probably more familiar to students. However, technically speaking, the results in Equation 3-2 are true for population values and are not necessarily true for sample data.

groups of people by a single person. However, if the test is administered individually, the person giving it may inadvertently influence the examinee. Thus, the same examinee might receive different scores from two different examiners on the same test. Scoring the test, as a second part of the examiner's task, is usually not a serious source of error. Objective tests can be scored by machine. On tests involving subjective evaluations, such as individually administered intelligence tests, the test manual is usually precise as to how particular responses are to be scored. However, this latter case represents a potential source of error in any subjectively scored test.

A third source of error is *test content*. All tests are composed of a finite number of items. If a different set of items had been used, the individuals would have probably received somewhat different scores because they would know the answers to some items but not others. Most methods of measuring reliability have been developed to assess how well a particular test has sampled items from a given domain.

A fourth source of error is *time*. This source reflects the amount of temporal consistency or lack of consistency in test scores. Are scores stable over time or do they change markedly? Some variables, such as intelligence, remain fairly constant over rather long periods of time. Other variables, such as mood, almost by definition change greatly from one time to the next.

The final source of error identified by Lyman is *situation-induced*. This last category is used for all aspects of the testing situation that are not clearly attributable to any of the other sources. The physical conditions of the place in which the testing occurs could be important. Cheating is another possible example, although it may also be more a function of the person than the situation. Even though these five sources may not be independent and may interact in complex ways, it is useful to identify them as major potential sources for error.

Parallel Tests

Two tests are said to be parallel if they have similar item content, if persons have the same true score on the two tests, and if the error variance on the two tests is the same. From these assumptions, it can be demonstrated that for tests (Gulliksen, 1950, pp. 12–13) to be truly parallel, the means of the observed scores for the two tests must be equal, as must the variances. Note that the observed score each person obtains on each parallel test will usually not be the same. "Classical" test theory also leads to two additional criteria for parallel tests: (1) the scores on all parallel tests correlate with one another equally, and (2) the scores on parallel tests correlate equally with the scores on any other variable (Ghiselli et al., 1981, p. 205).

Parallel tests could be constructed by randomly sampling items from a given domain of interest. For example, in testing the mathematical ability of people to add two three-digit numbers together, almost a limitless number of items could be constructed. For other variables of interest, such as anxiety, it may not be easy to construct many good items. Parallel tests are perhaps of more theoretical than practical interest, because most tests are used only once with a particular group of people. However, in some instances, having parallel tests available would be very useful. For example, in assessing the impact of a particular educational program on reading or mathematics it would be necessary to have two equivalent tests measuring achievement in order to determine if people improved, stayed the same, or did worse after participating in the program. However, the main reason we have introduced the definition of a parallel test is so that we can more precisely define reliability.

In practice it is unlikely that tests are constructed by randomly sampling items from a domain of interest. It is much more likely that two tests are constructed to be similar in content but that they will not satisfy all the criteria of strictly parallel tests. Such tests, designed to approximate parallel tests, are usually referred to as *alternate forms* of the test (Allen & Yen, 1979, p. 77; Nunnally, 1978, p. 228).

Reliability Defined

The reliability of a test can be defined as the correlation between two parallel tests. It is usually symbolized as r_{xx}. The x subscripts imply we are correlating a test with a parallel form and not with another variable. If a test were perfectly reliable, this correlation would be 1.00. If the test were totally unreliable, the correlation would be zero. Note that in assessing reliability in this way we are assuming that the true scores remain constant. The only reason people would differ on the two tests is because of error. Even with our restrictive definition of reliability, it should be apparent that a test could have many reliability coefficients, depending on the time between the administration of the two parallel forms.

There are several interesting results to be mentioned in connection with reliability coefficients. The first is that r_{xx} gives *the proportion of total variance because of true score differences among the persons taking the test*. In symbols,

$$r_{xx} = \frac{S_t^2}{S_x^2} \qquad (3-3)$$

where S_t^2 equals the true score variance and S_x^2 equals the observed score variance. Therefore, if the observed score variance is 100 and the true score variance is 90,

$$r_{xx} = \frac{90}{100} = .90$$

Thus, 90 percent of the observed score variance would be caused by true score differences among the people. To what is the other 10 percent attributable? The answer, of course, is error. Therefore, $1 - r_{xx}$ gives *the proportion of error in the observed score vari-*

ance. In our example, 10 percent of the variability is due to error.

A second result that should be mentioned is that r_{xx} provides an index of how well we could estimate a person's true score from the observed score. That is, what is the correlation between observed scores, X, and true scores, T? The result is $r_{xt}^2 = r_{xx}$. *The reliability coefficient of a test gives the proportion of true score variance that can be predicted from the observed score.* It is a general index of how close the observed scores are to the true scores. The square root of the equation is written as

$$r_{xt} = \sqrt{r_{xx}} \qquad (3-4)$$

The square root of the reliability coefficient is called the *index of reliability*. It has the interesting property of setting the upper limit to the validity of a test. If $r_{xx} = .81$, then $\sqrt{r_{xx}} = .9$. This means $r_{xt} = .9$, which is the highest correlation the test could theoretically have with any other variable. Paradoxically, then, it is possible for a test to have a larger correlation with another variable than its own reliability coefficient. In practice, however, such results are uncommon.

EMPIRICAL METHODS OF ESTIMATING RELIABILITY

Test-Retest

Test-retest methods, as the term suggests, involve testing the same group of people on two separate occasions. In testing each person twice, we are implicitly assuming that the only reason a person's score differs is because of error. Test-retest methods are designed mainly to assess the stability of scores over time.

SAME TEST. To assess how stable scores are over time, exactly the same test can be given on two separate occasions. The scores of each of the two separate administrations of the test are then correlated. This correlation represents a measure of temporal reliability. Because there may be many time periods between the two administrations, a test can have many different reliability coefficients. In general, the longer the period between the first and second administration of the test, the lower the reliability will be. The test-retest method, using the same test, has a serious weakness if examinees remember specific items. Memory will prejudice examinees to answer the questions in the same way the second time. Thus, the two measures are not independent assessments of the variable of interest and will tend to correlate more highly. This higher correlation, of course, in this context means that the reliability coefficient is higher than it should be. Test-retest methods using the same set of items are acceptable when items are not easily distinguishable. Tests involving sensory discrimination are a possible example, as in tests of musical aptitude.

PARALLEL FORMS. A second method of assessing reliability is to test the same examinees on two different occasions but with parallel or alternate forms of the test. Thus, in addition to changes arising over time, the items in the two tests are completely different. The scores on the two parallel forms are correlated, which gives a classic definition of the reliability of the test. Once again, depending on the time interval, the test can have many different reliability coefficients. Reliabilities based on parallel forms for a particular time interval would be generally lower than those based on the same test for the same time interval. Such results would occur because the parallel form allows error arising from content to influence the reliability coefficient.

A special problem with test-retest methods of estimating reliability is that the examinees may really change over long periods of time. The method assumes that any difference in a person's score from one time until another occurs because of error. In fact, if the time interval is long enough, a person may well have truly changed. A formerly anxious person, for example, may upon retesting two years later not be anxious at all, the change in score reflecting a true change in the person being tested and not a defect in the test.

Internal Consistency

Internal consistency estimates of reliability are based on the average intercorrelations among the items on a test. A test is internally consistent if the items tend to intercorrelate.

Unlike test-retest methods, internal consistency permits estimating the reliability of a test from a single administration. This approach has an obvious advantage since the person administering the test does not depend on the examinees being available for a second testing session. A limitation of these methods, of course, is that they do not assess any temporal stability of scores. The examinee's characteristics on the day of the test will not be taken into account. A second limitation is that these methods cannot be used with tests that are quickly paced. They will overestimate the reliability of such tests. On very easy tests, for example, a person's score is largely determined by the number of items attempted. Internal consistency methods of estimating reliability do not work with such tests.

SPLIT-HALF. This method essentially involves creating two parallel forms from a single test. Half the items are scored as one test and the other half are scored as a second test. The scores on the two halves are correlated, and the resulting correlation is the split-half reliability of the test. A very convenient way of dividing the test into two halves is to score the odd-numbered items as one test and the even-numbered items as another. Note that the split-half method determines the reliability of a test *half as long* as the one that is actually used. Therefore, a formula has been developed to estimate the reliability of the score on the total test from knowledge of the correlation between the two halves:

$$r_{xx} = \frac{2r_{12}}{1 + r_{12}} \qquad (3\text{-}5)$$

where r_{12} is the correlation between the scores on the two halves of the test, and r_{xx}

is the reliability of the total test. For example, if the two halves of the test correlate .75, the reliability of the total test would be computed as follows:

$$r_{xx} = \frac{2(.75)}{1 + .75} = \frac{1.50}{1.75} = .857$$

Although the split-half technique is relatively straightforward, it has fallen into disuse because of a more general approach to determining internal consistency.

CRONBACH'S COEFFICIENT α. Cronbach (1951) introduced the term coefficient α ("alpha") to represent the internal consistency of a test. This coefficient measures how well the items are measuring a single variable. Coefficient α is a function of all the items in the test and the total score on the test. The formula is

$$\alpha = \left(\frac{k}{k - 1} \right) \left(1 - \frac{\sum\limits_{g=1}^{k} S_g^2}{S_x^2} \right) \quad (3\text{-}6)$$

where k equals the number of items in the test, S_g^2 equals the variance of the scores on the gth item, and S_x^2 equals the variance of the scores on the total test.

Essentially, in this approach to reliability each item is conceptualized as a test. In a way we are trying to estimate the reliability of the score on the total test, the entire k items, from knowing the reliability of each individual item. Instead of creating two parallel tests from the k items, as we did in the split-half method, we are conceptualizing the k items as k parallel tests, each consisting of a single item. After considerable mathematical manipulation, Equation 3-6 results.

To understand Equation 3-6 consider a three-item test ($k = 3$). Note what happens if the sum of the item variances, $\sum\limits_{g=1}^{k} S_g^2$, equals the variance of the total test scores. For example, let $S_1^2 = 6$, $S_2^2 = 8$, and

$S_3^2 = 10$. Then suppose that $S_x^2 = 24$. Coefficient α would equal

$$\alpha = \left(\frac{3}{3 - 1} \right) \left(1 - \frac{24}{24} \right)$$

$$\alpha = \frac{3}{2} (1 - 1) = \frac{3}{2} (0) = 0$$

That is, the internal consistency or reliability of this test is zero because the variance of the total test scores is a sum of the individual item variances, $S_x^2 = S_1^2 + S_2^2 + S_3^2$.

Suppose, however, that the items were not independent of each other but were intercorrelated. Then, the variance of the total test scores is a function of the individual item variances and the *intercorrelations* among the items. (See Nunnally, 1978, for a more detailed discussion of the variance of a sum.) If each item is designed to measure some aspect of a variable of interest, we expect the items to intercorrelate; we expect them to be internally consistent with each other. When the items intercorrelate, the variance of the total test scores will be considerably higher than the sum of the individual item variances. Suppose, for example, our item variances remain the same as before but the variance of the total test score, S_x^2, is now 48. Coefficient α is now

$$\alpha = \left(\frac{3}{3 - 1} \right) \left(1 - \frac{24}{48} \right)$$

$$\alpha = \left(\frac{3}{2} \right) (1 - .5)$$

$$\alpha = (1.5)(.5) = .75$$

Note that the reliability of this three-item test is now fairly high because the items are intercorrelated; they are measuring the same variable.

Coefficient α has several interesting and important properties. For one, it is the average of all possible split-half reliabilities. Second, it permits an efficient estimate of the reliability from a single administration of a test.

Earlier developments of coefficient α were made by Kuder and Richardson (1937) using somewhat more restrictive assumptions. For this reason coefficient α is also often referred to as $K-R_{(20)}$, coming from the twentieth formula in Kuder and Richardson's article.

Analysis of Variance

An important recent development is the use of analysis of variance (ANOVA) procedures for estimating reliability. This work flows mainly from Cronbach and his associates (Cronbach et al., 1972). Because this development assumes a rather sophisticated knowledge of statistics, we shall give only a brief indication of the principles involved. Those readers who are unfamiliar with analysis of variance terminology should refer to a statistics textbook (Myers, 1979) for the necessary fundamentals.

We shall only consider the simplest example in estimating reliability by ANOVA methods. In Table 3-1 are some hypothetical data from five people on four parallel forms of the same test. These four tests could also be considered as different judges who rated each person on some characteristic of interest. ANOVA methods analyze the sources of variance in tables such as Table 3-1. In our example, the total variability among all twenty scores, ignoring the person and test, can be divided into three *components of variance*, or sources of variance. These are assumed to be additive, independent sources of variance and are identified as follows:

Total variability = Variability due to persons
+ Variability due to tests
+ Residual

In ANOVA terminology, the variability due to persons would be estimated from the MS_{rows} (mean square for rows); the variability due to tests would be estimated from the $MS_{columns}$ (mean square for columns); the residual would be estimated from

TABLE 3-1 Analysis of Variance Approach to Estimating Reliability for Five People on Four Tests

Person	Test Forms 1	2	3	4	Means
A	10	9	11	13	10.75
B	12	13	14	16	13.75
C	13	12	15	10	12.75
D	15	14	18	18	16.25
E	10	10	7	8	8.50
Means	12.0	11.6	13.0	13.0	

ANOVA Summary Table

Source	SS	df	MS
Rows (people)	130.8	4	32.70
Columns (tests)	7.6	3	2.53
Error (residual)	42.4	12	3.53
Total	180.8	19	

MS_{error} (the mean square for error). These mean squares would be computed with standard ANOVA procedures.

To estimate the reliability of the average or total score on the four tests, which should be a better estimate of a person's "true score" than any single score, we must estimate the components of variance. These components* may be estimated as follows:

1. $S_t^2 = \dfrac{1}{k}(MS_{rows} - MS_{error})$ (3-7)

2. $S_o^2 = \dfrac{1}{n}(MS_{columns} - MS_{error})$ (3-8)

3. $S_e^2 = MS_{error}$ (3-9)

where S_t^2 represents our estimate of true score variance among the people; S_o^2 represents our estimate of true variance among test means or judge's mean ratings; S_e^2 is the error variance implicit any time we measure a variable; k is the number of tests or judges; n is the number of people.

As part of our previous discussion, we in-

---

*These components represent unbiased estimates of population parameters. We will continue to use the same symbol (S^2) to simplify our presentation, although to be technically correct, different symbols should be used.

dicated that the observed score variance, S_x^2, was a sum of the true score variance and the error variance. This result is still used in the present ANOVA context. That is,

$$S_x^2 = S_t^2 + S_e^2 \qquad (3\text{-}2)$$

where S_x^2 is the estimate of the observed score variance. However, the important result is that the reliability of the average scores can still be computed from the ratio of S_t^2 to S_x^2, both of which can be estimated from the ANOVA results. That is,

$$r_{xx} = \frac{S_t^2}{S_x^2} \qquad (3\text{-}3)$$

In the lower half of Table 3-1 is the ANOVA summary table. The sums of squares (SS), degrees of freedom (df), and mean squares (MS) have all been computed by standard ANOVA methods. Using these results, we can compute the estimates of the three components of variance.

$$S_t^2 = \frac{1}{k}(MS_{\text{rows}} - MS_{\text{error}})$$

$$S_t^2 = \frac{1}{4}(32.70 - 3.53)$$

$$S_t^2 = \frac{1}{4}(29.17)$$

$$S_t^2 = 7.29$$

$$S_o^2 = \frac{1}{n}(MS_{\text{columns}} - MS_{\text{error}})$$

$$S_o^2 = \frac{1}{5}(7.6 - 3.53)$$

$$S_o^2 = \frac{1}{5}(4.07)$$

$$S_o^2 = .81$$

$$S_e^2 = MS_{\text{error}}$$

$$S_e^2 = 3.53$$

Therefore, S_x^2 would be given by

$$S_x^2 = S_t^2 + S_e^2$$

$$S_x^2 = 7.29 + 3.53$$

$$S_x^2 = 10.82$$

The reliability is then computed from the ratio of true variance relative to observed score variance:

$$r_{xx} = \frac{S_t^2}{S_x^2}$$

$$r_{xx} = \frac{7.29}{10.82} = .67$$

Cronbach and his associates use the term *generalizability coefficients* to refer to reliability coefficients. The statistic computed indicates how generalizable the observed test scores are to the universe scores that would be obtained from using all possible tests or all possible test items. The *universe score* is another way of referring to a person's *true score*, the term we have been using. Saying a test has a high coefficient of generalizability means that the observed test scores would correlate highly with the true scores.

Ratings and Percent Agreement

In some situations, it may be impossible or difficult to compute reliability coefficients. Such situations often occur in making behavioral ratings. For example, two raters might be observing the play of nursery school children on the playground and deciding whether or not a child exhibited aggressive behavior in a given period of time. If the ratings are made on a quantitative scale, the usual correlational methods could probably be applied. But often during a small time interval, say thirty seconds, the only rating made is whether or not the behavior occurred. In such situations, investigators often use percent agreement during the total observation period as an index of consistency of judgment. Such measures are descriptive of the rating process but have none of the properties associated with reliability coefficients.

Factors Influencing Reliability

TEST LENGTH. In general, the longer a test is, the more reliable it will be. By adding items to a test we are sampling more and more of the domain of interest. Persons taking a longer test can be more finely differentiated. A test having twenty-five items will potentially have scores ranging from zero to twenty-five, whereas a test having fifty items will potentially have scores ranging from zero to fifty. The fifty-item test has the potential for a finer gradation among the people taking it.

A well-known formula has been developed to estimate the relationship between test length and reliability. It is called the *Spearman-Brown formula* and takes the following form:

$$r_{kk} = \frac{kr_{11}}{1 + (k - 1)r_{11}} \quad (3\text{-}10)$$

where r_{11} is the reliability of the original test (unlengthened or unshortened); k is the factor by which the test will be lengthened or shortened; r_{kk} is the estimated reliability of the lengthened or shortened test. The formula for split-half reliability (Equation 3-5), which we have already discussed, is a special case of the Spearman-Brown formula. In that special case, $k = 2$.

For example, suppose a test contains twenty items and has a reliability of .60. If the test is made three times as long, lengthened to sixty items, what will its reliability be? The Spearman-Brown formula answers questions such as this one. Where $r_{11} = .60$ and $k = 3$, the resulting estimate of reliability is

$$r_{kk} = \frac{kr_{11}}{1 + (k - 1)r_{11}}$$

$$= \frac{3(.60)}{1 + 2(.60)}$$

$$= \frac{1.80}{2.20} = .82$$

This result suggests that by adding forty items to the existing twenty we could increase the reliability from .60 to .82.

The assumption involved in deriving the Spearman-Brown formula is that we can add items that are similar to those we already have. If the items are equivalent, the formula will give exact results. Usually, however, it provides a reasonable estimate, even though the items added are not all equivalent. Of course, we are also assuming that making the test longer will not unduly fatigue the persons taking it.

Interestingly enough, the Spearman-Brown formula works in the opposite direction as well. That is, if our twenty-item test is reduced by one-half, what would the resulting reliability be? In this case, $k = \frac{1}{2}$ and $r_{11} = .60$. The computation would be

$$r_{kk} = \frac{kr_{11}}{1 + (k - 1)r_{11}}$$

$$= \frac{1/2 \, (.60)}{1 + (-1/2) \, .60}$$

$$= \frac{.30}{1 - .30}$$

$$= \frac{.30}{.70} = .43$$

In this example, reducing the number of items from twenty to ten will reduce the reliability from .60 to .43.

HOMOGENEITY OF PEOPLE. Since the reliability of a test reflects true individual differences, a homogeneous group of people will tend to reduce reliability. Having a homogeneous sample is also referred to as *restriction of range* by many authors. In the most extreme case, if all people were identical (had the same true scores), the only differences among them would be due to error. On the other hand, people who are widely different from each other will permit higher reliability coefficients to appear. Homogeneous groups are often created by implicit or explicit selection. The same intelligence test would have different reliabilities when given to students at a highly selective private university as contrasted to students from a large public university with open admission. We would expect the students at the private university to be more similar than those at a public university. Such a selection process would mean that the intelligence test would have a lower reliability coefficient when used at the private university and a higher reliability coefficient when used at the public university.

Standard Error of Measurment

Although the reliability coefficient provides one useful index of how consistent the scores on a test are, it does not give the total picture. It provides no direct indication of how much error is present in an individual score. The standard error of measurement, however, does provide such information.

As we indicated previously, the variance of the observed test scores, the X's, may be conceptualized as arising from two independent sources, the true scores and the error scores. The variance of the observed scores thus may be written as

$$S_x^2 = S_t^2 + S_e^2$$

Assuming the reliability of the test is known, it is then possible to solve this equation for the error variance S_e^2, as follows:

$$S_e^2 = S_x^2 (1 - r_{xx}) \qquad (3\text{-}11)$$

This formula merely states that the error variance, S_e^2, is the portion of observed score variance that is not reliable. Recall that $1 - r_{xx}$ gives the proportion of error in the

scores. Multiplying this proportion by the observed score variance, S_x^2, gives an estimate of the error variance. Note that in Equation 3-11, if r_{xx} equals 1.00, the test is perfectly reliable; then S_e^2 equals zero. Conversely, if r_{xx} equals 0, the test is totally unreliable, and S_e^2 equals S_x^2. That is, all the observed score variance is due to error.

The *standard error of measurement* is the square root of Equation 3-11. We are now talking about the standard deviation of the error scores. The formula is

$$S_{meas} = S_x \sqrt{1 - r_{xx}} \qquad (3\text{-}12)$$

Of what use is this formula? It permits the interpreter of test scores to set confidence intervals or limits around a given score. That is, the standard error of measurement makes explicit the fact that test scores contain error. The score received by an examinee is only one value of a rather wide range of possible scores the examinee could have obtained.

As an example, suppose S_x equals 100 and the r_{xx} equals .91. The standard error of measurement would be

$$
\begin{aligned}
S_{meas} &= 100 \sqrt{1 - .91} \\
&= 100 \sqrt{.09} \\
&= 100(.3) \\
&= 30
\end{aligned}
$$

Note that the standard error of measurement is a function of the variability of the observed scores, S_x, and the reliability of the test, r_{xx}.

In using observed scores to set confidence intervals for a person's true score, several assumptions are made. First, the assumptions of classical theory (given previously in this chapter) are used. Second, the error scores are assumed to follow a normal distribution. Third, it is assumed that the standard error of measurement is the same for all people, regardless of their true score.* Confidence intervals can then be set by using the following formulas:

$$\text{Upper limit} = X + 1.96S_{\text{meas}} \quad (3\text{-}12)$$

$$\text{Lower limit} = X - 1.96S_{\text{meas}} \quad (3\text{-}13)$$

These limits are for the 95 percent confidence interval, which means if we set the limits in this way for any value of X, we would include the true score 95 percent of the time. The number 1.96 comes from the normal curve and encompasses 95 percent of the area in a normal distribution.

Using our present example, suppose we have an observed score of 550 and wish to set a confidence interval around this value. The values would be

$$
\begin{aligned}
\text{Upper limit} &= 550 + 1.96(30) \\
&= 550 + 58.8 \\
&= 608.8 \\
\text{Lower limit} &= 550 - 1.96(30) \\
&= 550 - 58.8 \\
&= 491.2
\end{aligned}
$$

These results suggest that 550 is not an immutable score. Rather, any score between 608.8 and 491.2 would be quite reasonable for the examinee to receive. Thus, if a parallel form of the test were administered, we would expect the examinee to receive a score lower than 609 but higher than 491. It would be rather unlikely that the examinee would receive a score of exactly 550 again because of the error in the test.

Conceptually, the standard error of measurement indicates the variability we expect to appear in the test scores of a single

person. The only reason we would expect the test scores from one person to vary over a short time span is because of error. The more reliable the test, the less variability we expect. Alternatively, we may also conceptualize the standard error of measurement as indicating the variability among observed scores for those individuals who all have exactly the same true score. Again, the only reason the observed scores would differ for persons having the same true score is because of errors of measurement.

The standard error of measurement has one feature that distinguishes it from the reliability coefficient. The former remains constant regardless of the homogeneity of the group. This property makes it very useful in selecting tests for various groups.

In using the standard error of measurement to set confidence intervals, we have assumed that the test is equally accurate for high and low scores. In fact, the standard error of measurement is an average. A test may be more or less accurate for a given range of scores than for another range of scores. A test, for example, may be very good at differentiating among various levels of mental retardation but rather inaccurate in differentiating among persons of normal or above-average intelligence.

VALIDITY

Although reliability is an important attribute, the most critical property of any test is its validity. *Validity* refers to what the test measures and how useful the test is. There are several kinds of test validity and several ways of assessing it. Most often, however, the validity of a test is determined by correlating the test scores with another variable of interest. This other variable is called the *criterion*. Because validity coefficients are typically correlation coefficients, the reader may wish to review the sections in Chapter 2 that discuss correlation and regression.

Common criteria that tests are validated

*The second two assumptions made here can be shown to be unreasonable, particularly for persons having true scores far from the group mean (Allen & Yen, 1979; Lord, 1953; Nunnally, 1978). It is also technically necessary to estimate true scores from the observed scores and substitute these estimated values for X in Equations 3-12 and 3-13. In order to keep our discussion at an appropriate level, we have ignored these technical points.

against or correlated with include grades in college, high school, and elementary school; teachers' ratings; job success; completion of a training program; length of hospitalization in a mental hospital; success in psychotherapy; marital adjustment; and other test scores. The criterion often represents a variable of importance to an institution. For example, grades are important to a college because they determine which students will graduate. At selective colleges, admission counselors will not admit students who have a low probability of successfully completing the college program.Similarly, being able to predict who will be successful in a given job, whether as a police officer or airline pilot, saves the person involved from an embarrassing failure and the institution from possible economic loss.

It should also be clear that many criteria are themselves far from perfect. Grades in college, for example, are undoubtedly a function of many factors besides academic aptitude. Criteria are often subject to the same error of measurement as test scores. More important, many criteria represent a measure of convenience rather than the ultimate variable of interest. For example, in admitting students to medical school the ultimate criterion might be which students are most likely to make good physicians. However, defining what characteristics a good physician should have is a very difficult task. In selecting a criterion to validate a test used to help determine admission into medical school, therefore, grades in medical school are substituted for the more important criterion of excellence as a physician. Grades are a more convenient criterion, but more important, if a medical student does not earn satisfactory grades, the student will never become a physician at all. The point to keep in mind is that any criterion may be a compromise between a variable that is readily available and one that would be ideal.

Just as a test may have many different reliability coefficients, a test may have many different validity coefficients. Indeed, most tests are valid for predicting some variables but not valid at all for predicting other variables. Obtaining validity data is often an expensive, time-consuming, and difficult task. It is, however, essential if test scores are to be accurately used and interpreted.

Face Validity

Face validity refers to the apparent appropriateness of the test items for measuring the trait of interest. In other words, does the person taking the test believe the items are appropriate? It is important to note that this type of validity does not involve a statistical assessment of the utility of the test scores. A test could appear to be valid on the surface yet not be related to any behavior of interest. Conversely, the test items may appear invalid or irrelevant to a trait of interest yet be highly related to a behavior of interest. To the professional using a test, face validity is important only when it interferes with an examinee's cooperation. Most ability and achievement tests have reasonable face validity if they involve verbal items. However, some tests of mental ability that involve manipulation of geometric forms and similar activities may not appear relevant to the layperson. Personality tests may be more likely to lack face validity for the layperson, for example, the Rorschach projective test, which uses inkblots for stimuli.

Content Validity

Content validity refers to how adequately the items in a test sample a domain of interest. As was true of face validity, there is no quantitative index of this type of validity. However, content validity can be approached by systematically sampling the different areas a test is to cover. Content validity is critical in evaluating achievement tests and other tests designed to measure how much a person has learned in a given training program. Classroom examinations are another example of tests that should have high content validity. In the construction of such tests, the items and responses required can be systematically sampled. In measuring students' knowledge of American history, for example, one would ask questions about various periods of time and not limit questions to those dealing with the Revolutionary War. In constructing a classroom examination to assess knowledge of statistics, an instructor would probably include items to measure computational skills and the use of various tables as well as items to measure more abstract concepts.

Although content validity is important and reasonable for tests of educational achievement, it is not particularly relevant for aptitude tests or personality tests. Such tests do not cover a limited domain of interest but, rather, reflect a multitude of past experiences.

Criterion-related Validity

Perhaps the most important practical use of test scores is in predicting performance on nontest behaviors of interest. Such use requires that a criterion be defined and test scores be related to that criterion. As we indicated previously, selecting and measuring a criterion measure is often a difficult task. However, if a test is to be validated, a criterion must be available. There are two types of criterion-related validities: concurrent validity and predictive validity. The two differ with respect to the availability of the criterion scores. In concurrent validity, the test scores and criterion measure are both immediately available. In predictive validity, the test scores are available before the criterion measure. The two are similar in that they both usually involve correlating test scores with scores on another variable, the criterion. They both involve an explicit, statistical index of the relation between scores on a test and the criterion measure.

CONCURRENT VALIDITY. In the establishment of the concurrent validity of a test, the criterion scores are immediately available. Therefore, choosing a test to administer to a group of people already available is the major task. For example, if the employment records of a group of industrial workers are available, the criterion measure available might be the number of units of a product each worker produced. The more units produced, the better the worker. The more production a company has, the higher its profits and the more successful it will be in the marketplace. The company's success is ideally translated into better wages and fringe benefits for its employees. In any event, it is clearly in the company's interest to select workers who are productive. If the company can identify skills that are related to productivity, perhaps tests are available or can be constructed to measure those skills. The tests selected are administered to those workers already employed, and the resulting test scores are correlated with the criterion measure. Tests having a statistically significant correlation with the criterion would possess concurrent validity. That is, the test scores are related to an empirical criterion. In this case the criterion is a variable of importance to the company and is not simply a score on another test. The test scores themselves are of no interest in and of themselves. They are of interest only because they are related to an important variable—productivity.

In establishing the concurrent validity of a test, one's goal is usually to use such evidence to predict the behavior of people for whom the criterion is not available. That is, given a test has concurrent validity, it may then ideally be used to predict the criterion scores of people for whom only the test scores are available. It may also be used for selection. Although concurrent validity is often used to infer predictive validity, such a use is not always appropriate. The inferences regarding predictive validity may be inappropriate when the test scores change as a function of the criterion. For example, in studying the outcome of psychotherapy, a clinical psychologist may wish to correlate scores on a personality test with the person's personal adjustment (the criterion) after six months. However, the process of psychotherapy may well have changed the person's scores on the personality test (that is, the person is no longer highly anxious). In some instances, then, a test could have concurrent validity but might have little or no predictive validity.

PREDICTIVE VALIDITY. In establishing the predictive validity of a test, one administers the test first. At a later time the criterion scores become available. The correlation between the test scores and the criterion represents the statistical index of the predictive validity of the test. As was the case with concurrent validity, the criterion used will often be an important nontest variable. For example, at many large state-assisted universities, entering students are required to take a nationally administered test designed to predict academic achievement. One such test is the ACT. Assuming a university has an essentially open admissions policy, students are admitted to the university regardless of their test scores. Thus, at the beginning of the first year, every entering student has a test score. One measure of success in college is a student's GPA. If this variable is chosen as a criterion, it is not available immediately, along with the test score, but will be available after each successive term. If the ACT scores correlate significantly with grades, the test would have predictive validity.

In establishing the predictive validity of a test it is critical that the scores not be used to select persons to enter a program, college, or company. If not all people can be accepted by an institution, those admitted should be randomly selected in the absence of any validity information. Only if the test scores are not used in the selection process can an accurate determination of the predictive validity of a test be made.

In terms of practical applications, predictive validity is probably the most important characteristic a test can have. If psychologists, for example, could administer a personality test to children that would accurately predict which ones were likely to develop severe emotional or adjustment problems, they could possibly intervene with appropriate therapeutic techniques. Unfortunately, no such test exists. One reason it does not is that the criterion would be very difficult to define—what is deviant behav-

ior? A second reason is that the same children would have to be followed for long periods of time. Longitudinal studies are notoriously difficult to conduct. A third reason is that psychologists' understanding of personality and personality development is too imprecise to permit the development of very good tests.

Construct Validity

The term *construct validity* was introduced by Cronbach and Meehl (1955) to provide a means of evaluating tests designed to measure hypothetical psychological traits. Cronbach and Meehl (p. 283) define a construct as "some postulated attribute of people, assumed to be reflected in test performance." In contrast with criterion-related validity, construct validity involves the theoretical meaning of the test scores and is not directly concerned with predicting a particular criterion. However, the correlation of the test scores with various criteria is one source of information used to determine the construct validity of the test. In other words, construct validity refers to the accumulated body of research in which the test has been used and through which the psychological meaning of the trait being measured is refined and sharpened. Such research may also lead to changes in the test itself in order to make it reflect more closely a particular psychological characteristic. Construct validity is, at least to some extent, a restatement of the general method of scientific inquiry in which hypotheses are generated, tested empirically, and confirmed or disconfirmed.

Cronbach and Meehl list several procedures that could be used to examine construct validity. Examining *group differences* is one possible way. If our interpretation of a construct leads us to believe that two groups would differ in their average test scores, we can test for these differences statistically. *Correlation matrices and factor analysis* are a second way to assess construct validity. If two tests measure the same construct, they should be positively correlated. In factor analysis, one examines the intercorrelations among a large number of tests to determine an underlying structure. If all the tests are measuring a single construct, one factor or one underlying dimension can explain all the intercorrelations. The technique can help researchers understand the relationships among many tests and thus help them understand the construct(s) being measured by the various tests.

Studies of internal structure are also relevant in judging construct validity. Cronbach's coefficient α provides one way to index the internal consistency of the items in a test. In general we can say that if the items are all measuring the same construct, they should be positively intercorrelated with each other and positively correlated with the total test score. *Studies of change over occasions* may provide evidence of construct validity, if an experimental intervention is expected to affect the construct under study. *Studies of process* give additional insight into what kind of behavior produces a particular type of test score. By *process* is meant the methodology a person uses to perform a particular task. For example, to understand what a test of mathematical aptitude measures, we might ask people to describe verbally how they are solving the problems. Insight into this process could provide information about what construct the test is measuring.

In a very real sense, then, construct validity subsumes all other types of validity studies of a test. Each of the other types of validity information (content, concurrent, and predictive) can be used as evidence about the construct validity of a test. However, in terms of making decisions about people, predictive validity remains the most important property for a test to possess.

The three categories of content, criterion, and construct validity are somewhat artificial and represent convenient labels for particular procedures for evaluating a test. Messick (1980a) wrote a sophisticated article stressing the centrality of construct validity in providing a rational foundation for predictions from and relevance of test scores. Messick also suggests that the consequences

of test use, even a valid test, pose ethical questions that need to be considered. Cronbach (1980) also noted that the tripartite division of validity is incorrect and all evidence on tests is construct validation. Cronbach, too, noted that value judgments will always be part of how tests are used. Society, the courts, and the political process may determine that highly valid tests are still inappropriate for use. Several authors (Fitzpatrick, 1983; Guion, 1978; Tenopyr, 1977) have argued forcefully, in particular, that content validity is not a viable concept.

Convergent and Discriminant Validity

Campbell and Fiske (1959) presented an intriguing and important analysis of test validation. They pointed out that validation is typically convergent. That is, tests are expected to correlate with other tests or with a particular criterion. However, particularly for the establishment of construct validity, tests should not correlate with other tests from which they are supposed to differ. This predicted noncorrelation with some tests is referred to as *discriminant validation*. Even more important is the use of a multitrait-multimethod matrix in the validation process. A *multitrait-multimethod matrix* is a table in which the intercorrelations among several traits measured by several methods are presented.

As an example, we will use the multitrait-multimethod matrix constructed by Campbell and Fiske (1959, p. 82). Their example, Table 3-2, presents three traits, labeled A, B, and C, and three methods. Thus, A_1 refers to trait A measured by method 1, A_2 refers to trait A measured by method 2, and C_3 refers to trait C measured by method 3. The various regions in Table 3-2 are defined as follows:

1. *Reliability diagonals.* These are the entries in parentheses running from upper left to lower right. They indicate the reliability of each trait measured by each method.
2. *Heterotrait-monomethod triangle.* These are the entries enclosed with a solid-line triangle and adjacent to each reliability diagonal. They

TABLE 3-2 A Synthetic Multitrait-Multimethod Matrix

	Traits	Method 1 A₁	B₁	C₁	Method 2 A₂	B₂	C₂	Method 3 A₃	B₃	C₃
		A_1	B_1	C_1	A_2	B_2	C_2	A_3	B_3	C_3
Method 1	A_1	(.89)								
	B_1	.51	(.89)							
	C_1	.38	.37	(.76)						
Method 2	A_2	.57	.22	.09	(.93)					
	B_2	.22	.57	.10	.68	(.94)				
	C_2	.11	.11	.46	.59	.58	(.84)			
Method 3	A_3	.56	.22	.11	.67	.42	.33	(.94)		
	B_3	.23	.58	.12	.43	.66	.34	.67	(.92)	
	C_3	.11	.11	.45	.34	.32	.58	.58	.60	(.85)

Note: The validity diagonals are the three sets of italicized values. The reliability diagonals are the three sets of values in parentheses. Each heterotrait-monomethod triangle is enclosed by a solid line. Each heterotrait-heteromethod triangle is enclosed by a broken line.
Campbell, D. T., & Fiske, D. W. (1959), Convergent and discriminant validation by the multitrait-multimethod matrix. *Psychological Bulletin, 56,* 81–105. Copyright 1959 by the American Psychological Association. Reprinted by permission of the authors.

give the correlations among different traits measured by a single method.

3. *Monomethod block.* These blocks consist of the reliability diagonal and the adjacent heterotrait-monomethod triangle. They contain all the correlations among different traits that use a single method along with the reliabilities of the various traits.

4. *Validity diagonal.* These are the entries in italics. They are the correlations among the same trait as measured by different methods.

5. *Heterotrait-heteromethod triangle.* These entries are enclosed by a dashed-line triangle. They represent correlations among different traits as measured by different methods.

6. *Heteromethod block.* This block consists of the validity diagonal and the two heterotrait-heteromethod triangles lying on each side of it. Unlike the monomethod block, these two triangles contain different sets of correlations.

What aspects of Table 3-2 are important for the validation process? First, we would expect the correlations in the validity diagonal to be statistically significant and reasonably high, and therefore, evidence for convergent validity. Second, the validity diagonal should be higher than the correlations occurring in the same row and column of the heterotrait-heteromethod triangles. All this requirement means is that different ways or methods of assessing the *same* trait should correlate more highly with each other than with other traits measured by another method. Third, we expect that the trait correlates more highly with independent methods of measuring it than with different traits measured by the same method. Fourth, the same pattern of correlations among the traits should appear in all methods.

In Table 3-2 it can be seen that all the measures have acceptable reliabilities. The lowest, .76, is trait C measured by method 1. All the entries in the validity diagonals are higher than those in the same row and column of the heterotrait-heteromethod triangles. For example, the correlation between A_1 and A_3, trait A measured by method 1 and method 3 respectively, is .56, which exceeds the entries of .22 and .11 in the row of one triangle and the entries of .23 and .11 in the column of the other triangle. With respect to the correlations among traits measured by different methods as compared with the correlation among traits measured by the same method, Table 3-2 shows that only tests A_1, B_1, and C_1 have this property. Thus, there is little evidence that traits A, B, and C are generalizable across different measuring techniques. With respect to the last requirement, the pattern of intercorrelations, the traits have this property to a high degree. Thus, traits A and B correlate more highly than do A and C or B and C, these latter two correlations tending to be approximately equal in all the triangles.

Campbell and Fiske (1959) present many examples of multitrait-multimethod matrices. The general conclusion is that method or apparatus factors contribute a great deal to the positive correlations among many variables. It is possible, therefore, that the correlation between two personality traits measured by a self-report test is due more to the fact that the two traits were measured by the same method rather than the fact of any psychological relationship. The evidence in the literature suggests that discriminant validity is sadly lacking in many psychological tests.

Factors Influencing Validity

HOMOGENEOUS GROUPS. In Chapter 2, we mentioned several factors that influence the correlation between two variables. Those factors, of course, influence the validity of a test (if validity is assessed by using a correlation coefficient). One important factor that could limit the validity of a test is group homogeneity. To the extent that members of a particular group are similar in the test (predictor variable), criterion variable, or both variables, it will be difficult to find high correlations. Thus, the validity of the test is limited when the people to whom the test is administered are very similar. Consider an extreme example, a case in which people all receive exactly the same score. There is, therefore, no opportunity to differentiate among them on the basis of the test scores. We are able, correspondingly, to make no differential predictions, since whatever prediction equation or procedure we use, we would predict the same criterion score for each individual. Homogeneity means, essentially, that the scores have little variability—the variance and standard deviation are small.

The group taking a test may be homogeneous because of explicit or implicit selection. In explicit selection, an institution selects people above or below a particular test score. Thus, only those students having very high test scores are admitted to medical school. Selecting students for admission to medical school on the basis of test scores also produces selection on other variables that are correlated with the test scores. For example, in explicitly selecting students on the basis of test scores, we also would probably implicitly select students who had high grades. The practical consequences of such selection procedures are to produce rather homogeneous groups of people and limit how highly their scores will correlate with other variables.

Besides selection effects, scores may be limited in range by the nature of the variable. For example, it is common to use ratings of various kinds as a criterion measure. Ratings often are made on five-point scales (strongly agree to strongly disagree). It would not be likely that ratings would involve more than nine categories. People making the ratings also tend not to use the extreme categories (say, 1 or 9). Such rating scales limit differences among people and, therefore, limit the test's validity in predicting those ratings. When we consider that the ratings themselves are probably rather crude indicators of the criterion of interest, it is not surprising that tests often do not correlate very highly with behaviors of interest.

The homogeneity problem again illustrates the importance of validating test scores by using unselected groups. That is, to determine the validity of a test, that test should initially not be used for selection purposes. If a limited number of persons must be selected, they should be randomly selected. If the test demonstrates predictive validity, then it can be subsequently used for selection.

RELIABILITY. A second factor influencing validity has already been mentioned in this chapter. However, it is well to remember that reliability places an upper limit on the validity of a test. Unreliable measures, whether they are predictor or criterion variables, will allow tests to show little if any validity. If scores on a test or on the criterion are random or largely due to chance, correlations with such scores will typically approach zero. Reliability is a necessary, but not a sufficient, condition for the test to have validity.

Evaluating Validity

In this section we will consider some of the more important ways of evaluating the validity of a test. Most of the methods that we consider involve correlating test scores with a criterion of interest.

STATISTICAL SIGNIFICANCE. The first condition a validity coefficient must satisfy to make a test useful is that it must be statistically significant. *Statistical significance* simply means that the relationship discovered is unlikely to have occurred by chance. In most applications of statistical methods, to be accepted as statistically significant, the result must occur with a probability .05 or less. That is, events that could occur by chance more than five times in a hundred are not interpreted as significant. Therefore, if a test did not correlate significantly with a criterion, it would not be interpreted as possessing validity for that particular purpose. A correlation of zero ($r = 0$) would mean that the test scores are unrelated to the criterion of interest. In testing the statistical significance of a correlation coefficient, we are deciding whether or not the observed correlation is different from zero. As far as statistical significance is concerned, it does not matter whether the correlation is positive or negative. All that matters is that the correlation coefficient departs significantly from zero.

Statistical significance is, however, partially a function of the sample size. With larger samples, smaller correlation coefficients are statistically significant. Conversely, if a sample is small, a rather large correlation coefficient is needed to reach statistical significance. Tests being validated with small samples may thus not have much chance of demonstrating any validity. The following correlation coefficients are those needed for various sample sizes to be significant at the .05 level (nondirectional):

n	Correlation
7	.754
12	.532
22	.423
42	.304
102	.195
402	.098

As we indicated in Chapter 2, the square of the correlation coefficient indicates the proportion of variance predictable with a linear relationship. In the preceding example, then, using a sample size of 42, a correlation of .304 is necessary for statistical significance. However, the square of .304 equals approximately .09. Thus, even when the correlation is statistically significant, it only accounts for 9 percent of the total variance. In other words, statistical significance may not guarantee that a test will be useful in making decisions. Schmidt and Hunter (1980), however, have persuasively argued that the usefulness of tests in criterion-related validity studies may have been seriously underestimated because many such studies are based on very small sample sizes. As noted, with small samples large correlations are needed to be statistically significant. When adequate samples are used, systematic results often demonstrate that the tests have modest but consistent correlations.

STANDARD ERROR OF ESTIMATE. This concept, introduced in Chapter 2, provides an index of the error made in predicting a dependent variable (the criterion) from an independent variable (often a test). The formula, for the standard error of estimate, for large samples is

$$S_y \mid_x = S_y \sqrt{1 - r_{xy}^2} \qquad (3\text{-}14)$$

where S_y equals the standard deviation of the criterion variable and r_{xy}^2 is the square of the correlation between the predictor variable (X) and the criterion variable (Y). To be used, of course, this formula assumes that the validity coefficient is statistically significant. The standard error of estimate is a measure of the variability around a predicted score generated by a regression (prediction) equation such as

$$\hat{Y} = r_{xy} \frac{S_y}{S_x} (X - \bar{X}) + \bar{Y} \qquad (3\text{-}15)$$

where $\hat{Y}$ equals the predicted score on the criterion; S_x equals the standard deviation of the predictor variable; S_y equals the standard deviation of the criterion variable; r_{xy} equals the correlation between the predictor and criterion variable; X equals the score on the predictor variable; $\bar{X}$ equals the mean of the predictor variable; $\bar{Y}$ equals the mean of the criterion variable. The standard error of estimate measures, for all values of X (the test scores), the amount of variability in the differences between the observed scores, the Y's, and the predicted scores, the $\hat{Y}$'s. For more details, refer to the appropriate section in Chapter 2.

The standard error of estimate gives a conservative picture of the usefulness of a test in predicting a criterion. The test user is typically not interested in predicting the performance of all people but only in assessing how well the test distinguishes between those who are "successful" and those who are "failures." The standard error of estimate is largely irrelevant for placing persons into categories of those who do well and those who fail. On the other hand, it

can set confidence intervals around the predicted score. If we assume the errors in prediction are normally distributed, the confidence interval around the predicted score can be determined by the following formula:

$$\hat{Y}_{\text{Upper}} = \hat{Y} + 1.96 S_y \mid_x \qquad (3\text{-}16)$$

$$\hat{Y}_{\text{Lower}} = \hat{Y} - 1.96 S_y \mid_x \qquad (3\text{-}17)$$

The value of 1.96 represents the point in a normal distribution beyond which 5 percent of the total area occurs. Thus, the confidence interval will contain the obtained score 95 percent of the time if this method is used to determine the upper and lower limits of the interval.

As an example of how the standard error of estimate might be used, consider the problem of admitting applicants for graduate study in psychology. Suppose it has been found that the scores on the verbal section of the Graduate Record Examination (GRE-V) correlate .40 with grades (GPA) in graduate school. Grades represent the criterion of interest, and the GRE-V is the test score to be used as a predictor. Suppose the other statistics are as follows:

The mean GPA in graduate school = $\bar{Y} = 3.45$;
The mean GRE-V = $\bar{X} = 560$;
The standard deviation of GPA = $S_y = .15$;
The standard deviation of GRE-V = $S_x = 80$.

We are, of course, assuming that .40 is a statistically significant correlation. Then, the standard error of estimate would be

$$
\begin{aligned}
S_y \mid_x &= S_y \sqrt{1 - r_{xy}^2} \\
&= .15 \sqrt{1 - .40^2} \\
&= .15 \sqrt{1 - .16} \\
&= .15 \sqrt{.84} \\
&= .15(.92) \\
&= .14
\end{aligned}
$$

Graduate school grades would be predicted by using the regression equation of

$$\hat{Y} = r_{xy} \frac{S_y}{S_x} (X - \bar{X}) + \bar{Y}$$

$$\hat{Y} = (.40) \frac{.15}{80}(X - 560) + 3.45$$

$$\hat{Y} = .00075(X - 560) + 3.45$$

or $\hat{Y} = .00075X + 3.03$

Using this equation, we would predict the following grades for various GRE-V scores:

X(GRE-V)	$\hat{Y}$ (Predicted GPA)	$\hat{Y}_{Upper}$	$\hat{Y}_{Lower}$
450	3.368	3.642	3.094
500	3.405	3.679	3.131
550	3.443	3.717	3.169
600	3.480	3.754	3.206
650	3.518	3.792	3.244

Using the equation for establishing the confidence interval around a predicted score, we have for our example

$$\hat{Y}_{Upper} = \hat{Y} + (1.96)S_y \,|\, x$$
$$\hat{Y} + (1.96)(.14)$$
$$\hat{Y} + .2744$$

$$\hat{Y}_{Lower} = \hat{Y} - (1.96)S_y \,|\, x$$
$$\hat{Y} - (1.96)(.14)$$
$$\hat{Y} - .2744$$

Note that as the test score increases so does the predicted GPA. However, in selecting students for admission to graduate study, we might decide that students will not be admitted unless the lowest GPA they are likely to obtain is above 3.20. In our example, then, only students having GRE-V scores 600 or higher would be admitted for graduate study, because the lowest GPA we expect from students having a GRE-V score of 600 is 3.206 ($\hat{Y}_{Lower}$). Without taking into account the error in our predictions, it should be noted that the predicted GPA for all students is above 3.20.

The example we have presented is oversimplified. Other sources of information besides test scores would determine whether or not a student is admitted for graduate study. In principle, however, the information from whatever sources could be combined statistically to develop a prediction equation. The resulting predicted GPA could be evaluated in the same manner. Using GPA as a criterion is only one of many possible variables of interest. We could develop equations to predict grades in particular courses or particular groups of courses or the time until the degree is earned. Finally, the ultimate criterion might be the professional competence of the graduates.

EXPECTANCY TABLES. Another way of expressing the validity of a test is with expectancy tables. Test scores are one dimension of an expectancy table, and the probability or proportion of successes associated with each test score or interval of scores is given in the body of the table. Expectancy tables are empirically determined in much the same way that life insurance companies determine life expectancies for people of various ages. Thus, in expectancy tables there is the proportion of people with a particular test score who have been a "success" on a specific criterion. For example, if we consider scores on the verbal section of the GRE, we might determine the proportion of students who graduate at each possible GRE-V score or score interval. Table 3-3 gives a possible set of results for these two variables.

Note that again as test scores increase the proportion of students graduating also increases. We are still assuming that there is a relationship between test score and graduation. The information conveyed in an expectancy table has the advantage of being fairly easy to understand. In our example 95 percent of the students having test scores between 750 and 799 have received degrees, whereas only about 5 percent of the students having test scores between 350 and 399 have graduated. Expectancy tables are also useful aids in counseling students because the counselor can describe the relative likelihood of the student's success. A stu-

TABLE 3-3 Example of an expectancy table.

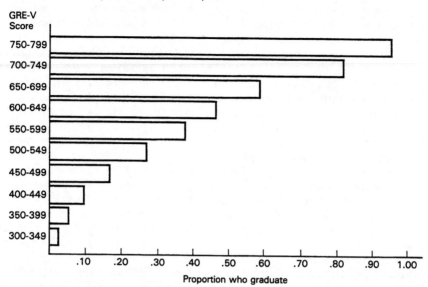

GRE-V Score / Proportion who graduate

dent whose chances of graduating are only 10 percent, for example, might well be advised to consider other career options.

BASE RATES. The base rate of a particular characteristic is defined as the proportion of people possessing that characteristic in the population. Base rates are determined by empirical methods, counting the number of times a particular trait occurs. For example, in measuring the base rate of success in graduate school, we might count the number of students who receive their Ph.D. The base rate of success would then be defined as the proportion of admitted students who graduated. Other examples of base rates are the proportion of patients who are diagnosed as schizophrenics, the proportion of heart attacks suffered by men of a particular age, and the proportion of college students receiving average grades of B or higher.

Base rates are important because they greatly influence how useful test scores are likely to be in making predictions. If the base rates are either very low or very high, tests may not be useful. For example, if every student who enters graduate school receives a Ph.D., no test score could differenti-

ate between those students who will be successful (graduate) and those who will not be successful (not graduate). The predictions will be perfectly accurate if we say everyone who is admitted will graduate. Similarly, if the base rate for a particular type of brain damage is very low, a screening test will have to be extremely sensitive to detect people who have that affliction. Our best prediction is to guess that a patient does not have brain damage, and we will be correct almost all the time.

Test scores are more likely to be useful when the base rate is close to .5. Then, we would expect our predictions to be correct only half the time. Test scores could thus potentially increase our accuracy of prediction above chance, assuming that the test correlated with the criterion of interest. However, some phenomena occur infrequently but are extremely important to predict. A prime example is suicide. For such events it is still worthwhile to search for tests that would improve our ability to predict these rare but important occurrences. It may be possible, for example, to identify subgroups of people among whom suicide occurs more frequently and for whom tests might significantly improve prediction. Rosen (1954) used the detection of suicidal patients as an excellent, although tragic, example of the difficulty in predicting infrequent events.

SELECTION RATIOS. Another factor that will influence how useful a test will be is the selection ratio, the proportion of people selected from the total number who are available. In admitting students to medical school there are typically many more applicants than there are available openings. The selection ratio in this situation would be very low, perhaps only one in ten. On the other hand, admission to many large state universities is essentially open to almost everyone who applies. In this case, the selection ratio is very high. If a test is valid (that is, related to the criterion of interest), it will be most useful when the selection ratio is low. Then the persons with the highest scores could be selected. For example, if ten students are to be admitted into a Ph.D. program and one

hundred apply, the students with the ten highest scores would be admitted.

The relationships among the proportion of successes, base rate, selection ratio, and test validity have been reported in a series of tables by Taylor and Russell (1939). Different tables were prepared for different base rates. For example, Table 3-4 is for a base rate of .50. Across the top of the table are various selection ratios; the rows represent various possible validity coefficients, the correlation of the test with the criterion. In the body of the table are the expected proportion of successes for the particular validity coefficient and selection ratio.

The first two indicate what happens if the test validity is zero. The expected proportion of successes is .50, the base rate, regardless of the selection ratio. On the other hand, Table 3-4 illustrates numerically that as validity increases and the selection ratio decreases the expected proportion of successes becomes larger. For example, if the selection ratio is .05 and the validity coeffi-

TABLE 3-4 Proportion of Employees Considered Satisfactory = .50

					Selection Ratio						
r	.05	.10	.20	.30	.40	.50	.60	.70	.80	.90	.95
.00	.50	.50	.50	.50	.50	.50	.50	.50	.50	.50	.50
.05	.54	.54	.53	.52	.52	.52	.51	.51	.51	.50	.50
.10	.58	.57	.56	.55	.54	.53	.53	.52	.51	.51	.50
.15	.63	.61	.58	.57	.56	.55	.54	.53	.52	.51	.51
.20	.67	.64	.61	.59	.58	.56	.55	.54	.53	.51	.51
.25	.70	.67	.64	.62	.60	.58	.56	.55	.54	.50	.51
.30	.74	.71	.67	.64	.62	.60	.58	.56	.54	.52	.51
.35	.78	.74	.70	.66	.64	.61	.59	.57	.55	.53	.51
.40	.82	.78	.73	.69	.66	.63	.61	.58	.56	.53	.52
.45	.85	.81	.75	.71	.68	.65	.62	.59	.56	.53	.52
.50	.88	.84	.78	.74	.70	.67	.63	.60	.57	.54	.52
.55	.91	.87	.81	.76	.72	.69	.65	.61	.58	.54	.52
.60	.94	.90	.84	.79	.75	.70	.66	.62	.59	.54	.52
.65	.96	.92	.87	.82	.77	.73	.68	.64	.59	.55	.52
.70	.98	.95	.90	.85	.80	.75	.70	.65	.60	.55	.53
.75	.99	.97	.92	.87	.82	.77	.72	.66	.61	.55	.53
.80	1.00	.99	.95	.90	.85	.80	.73	.67	.61	.55	.53
.85	1.00	.99	.97	.94	.88	.82	.76	.69	.62	.55	.53
.90	1.00	1.00	.99	.97	.92	.86	.78	.70	.62	.56	.53
.95	1.00	1.00	1.00	.99	.96	.90	.81	.71	.63	.56	.53
1.00	1.00	1.00	1.00	1.00	1.00	1.00	.83	.71	.63	.56	.53

(Taylor & Russell, 1939, p. 575.)

cient is a very modest .20, the expected proportion of successes is .67. This represents a sizeable improvement in performance over the base rate of .50. The important point is that with low selection ratios, even tests with relatively low validity coefficients can be useful. On the other hand, if the selection ratio is high, even tests with high validity coefficients may not be useful. For example, if the selection ratio is .95 and the validity coefficient is .90, the expected proportion of successes is .53. This increase over the base rate of .50 is not very great.

Other tables from the Taylor and Russell (1939) article provide information about what happens when the base rates change. Consider the results when the test validity is .35, a reasonably modest but not uncommon finding in research. Table 3-5, constructed from the relevant tables developed by Taylor and Russell, illustrates what happens to the expected proportion of successes as the base rate and selection ratios change. Table 3-5 clearly demonstrates the dramatic effect base rate and selection ratio have on the proportion of successes expected. When base rates are very low or very high and the selection ratio is high, little improvement is possible using a test with a validity of only .35. For example, when the base rate is .10 and the selection ratio is .90, the expected proportion of successes is .11. However, if the base rate is less extreme, say, .40, and the selection ratio is low, say .10, then the expected proportion of successes is .69,

which is a marked improvement over the base rate.

DECISION THEORY. The Taylor and Russell (1939) approach to evaluating the utility of a test was later expressed in terms of decision theory (Cronbach & Gleser, 1965; Wald, 1950), in which mathematical analysis is used to help reach decisions under specified conditions. Strategies can thus be developed to reach optimum decisions about people. Decision theory has obvious implications for testing when test scores are used, for example, to select people for available positions in industry, training programs, or education. It is, of course, still fundamental that test scores be significantly correlated with the criterion before a decision theory approach can be used.

For example, consider predicting success in graduate school in clinical psychology from scores on the GRE-V. Suppose that data are available for several classes so that sixty students have both GRE-V scores and GPAs for their first year of graduate study. A plot of these hypothetical data is presented in Figure 3-1, which shows that there is a correlation between the GRE-V and GPA. The correlation is about .85, which is statistically significant. This correlation is, of course, considerably higher than we would obtain with actual data. In general, we see that the higher the test score is the higher the GPA is likely to be. We also can identify a "success" as any student who has a GPA

TABLE 3-5 Proportion of Successes Expected When the Validity Coefficient (r) is .35 for Various Selection Ratios and Base Rates

		Selection Ratio								
		.10	.20	.30	.40	.50	.60	.70	80	.90
	.10	.24	.20	.18	.16	.15	.14	.13	.12	.11
	.20	.41	.36	.32	.30	.28	.26	.24	.23	.22
	.30	.54	.49	.45	.42	.40	.38	.36	.34	.32
	.40	.69	.65	.60	.56	.53	.50	.48	.45	.43
Base	.50	.74	.70	.66	.64	.61	.59	.57	.55	.53
Rate	.60	.82	.78	.75	.73	.71	.69	.67	.65	.63
	.70	.89	.86	.83	.82	.80	.78	.76	.75	.73
	.80	.94	.92	.90	.89	.89	.87	.85	.84	.82
	.90	.98	.97	.96	.95	.95	.94	.93	.93	.92

(Adapted from Taylor & Russell, 1939, pp. 573-575.)

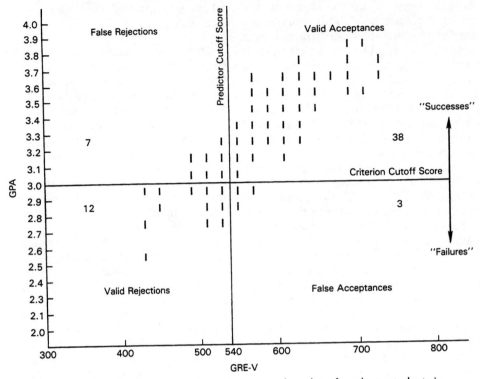

FIGURE 3–1 The relation between GRE-V scores and grades of graduate students in clinical psychology.

above 3.00 in graduate school. The university has determined that all graduate students must maintain a GPA of 3.00 or higher to remain in graduate school. A "failure" is any student who has a GPA below 3.00. A GPA of 3.00, then, defines a cutoff score for the criterion. Students above the cutoff score are making adequate academic progress, whereas students below the cutoff score are not.

The question to be answered by the decision-maker is what cutoff score to use on the predictor variable. That is, which GRE-V cutoff score shall be used so that those scoring above the cutoff will be admitted to graduate study and those below will be denied admission? There is no generally accepted method of determining such a cutoff score, and the decision-maker must consider a variety of factors. Suppose, however, that 540 was initially and arbitrarily established as the cutoff score. In Figure 3-1 the

vertical line corresponds to a GRE-V score of 540 and the horizontal line corresponds to the GPA of 3.0. We can now determine what the effects of setting the cutoff score at 540 would be.

There are two groups of students about whom we would have made correct decisions: those scoring above 540 and having a GPA above 3.00. This group is what we might call *valid acceptances* and numbers thirty-eight students in our example. The second group about whom we would have made a correct decision are those scoring below 540 and having a GPA below 3.00. This group is called *valid rejections* and numbers twelve students in our example. Of the sixty students, then, we would be correct in fifty of sixty instances or 83.3 percent of the time. The proportion of students about whom we would make a correct decision is called the *hit rate*.

It should also be noted that by using a

cutoff score of 540 we would increase the proportion of admitted students who succeed over the base rate. In our example, forty-five of sixty students were "successes." This corresponds to a base rate of 45/60 = .75. However, if the cutoff score of 540 were used, forty-one students would have been admitted and thirty eight of them would have been "successes." The proportion of successes would rise to 38/41 = .927.

However, there are also two groups of students about whom we would have been in error. One group is those students who had scores below 540 but who had GPAs above 3.00. This group is referred to as *false rejections* and numbers seven students in our example. By using 540 as a cutoff score, we would have denied admission to seven students who actually could have succeeded. On the other hand, we also would have been in error about three students who scored above 540 on the GRE but had GPAs lower than 3.00. This group is referred to as *false acceptances.*

Now that we have defined some terms, we can discuss the options for setting a cutoff score more precisely. Note that there is an obvious reciprocal relationship between the number of false rejections and the number of false acceptances. From an institution's point of view or perhaps from the viewpoint of the graduate faculty in clinical psychology, minimizing the number of false acceptances is the important goal. To accomplish it, we simply raise the cutoff score until no more false acceptances are admitted for graduate study in clinical psychology. In our example if a cutoff score of 600 were used, there would be no false acceptances. That is, no student admitted would have had a GPA below 3.00. However, by raising the cutoff score to 600, many more false rejections would be produced. In our example, twenty-one students would have been denied admission, although they could have achieved GPAs above 3.00. From the prospective student's point of view false rejections are more serious than false acceptances. From the clinical faculty's point of view, the situation is reversed. The main difficulty in determining a cutoff score is in balancing these two different perspectives.

Meehl and Rosen (1955) have presented a detailed and compelling discussion of the problems in setting cutoff scores. They noted that under some conditions (base rates on the criterion markedly different from .50 and a moderately valid test), there can be more erroneous decisions made when a test is used than when one is not used. They also point out that no single cutoff score is maximally efficient when the base rates of the criterion groups are different. For example, we can attempt to maximize the number of correct predictions for all cases, the number of valid acceptances, or the number of valid rejections. Different cutoff scores would be needed for each of these goals. Which approach is chosen would depend on the cost (human, social, economic, and so on) associated with the various outcomes. Such costs are almost impossible to quantify, and as a result, the use of decision theory in its mathematical form has not been widespread.

As a final note, it is also rather unlikely that a single test score would be used to make decisions about people. Information from other tests as well as other nontest variables would be combined in some fashion, either statistically or judgmentally, to reach a decision about a person. The use of multiple cutoff scores is a possible approach to decision making. Also, tests can be used as rough, screening devices in order to determine those people who warrant further, more intensive testing.

SUMMARY

In this chapter we have presented some characteristics that all good tests should possess. A test should be highly standardized, reliable, and most of all, valid. In discussing various tests we shall continually emphasize and use the concepts introduced in this chapter. The various types of reliability and validity coefficients should become more meaningful as they are discussed in connection with particular tests.

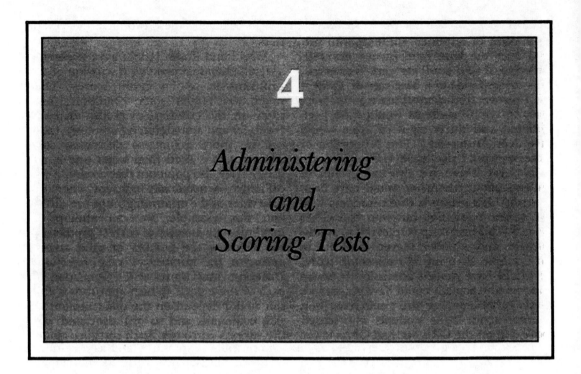

4

Administering and Scoring Tests

In this chapter we will present the basics of administering and scoring tests. All commercially available tests give explicit and detailed instructions in the test manual, which also contains other important information about the test. We begin by presenting some ways in which tests traditionally have been classified. The various categories may not be mutually exclusive, but they are useful descriptive terms to have available.

CATEGORIZING TESTS

Group versus Individual Tests

Tests can be classified as those administered to a single individual or those administered to a group of people. Individual tests typically require a trained examiner, whereas group tests may be administered by a person less formally trained in assessment techniques. As was suggested in Chapter 1, the first tests that were developed were individually administered. World War I pro-

vided the impetus for the development of group tests in the United States, because although the large numbers of draftees could not be tested individually, personnel decisions had to be made. For many individual tests, only a selected number of items may be used. That is, depending on a person's performance on one or more items, the person may not be asked certain other questions. In most group tests, all persons are given all the items, and it is implicitly assumed that the test is appropriate for the particular people being tested. It should be obvious that group tests also could be individually administered. The main advantage of group tests is that information can be obtained from large numbers of people quickly and inexpensively. The time of a trained examiner, who is needed to administer an individual test, is what makes such tests expensive. However, individual tests may be the only tests that can be used with some populations, for example, preschool children, mentally retarded, and some types of handicapped people. Another possible advantage of individual tests is that they permit qualitative observational data to be obtained. The examiner can note particular characteristics of the subject that interfered with performance. Such observations are not available in group testing.

Examples of individual tests include the Stanford-Binet Intelligence Scale, Wechsler intelligence scales, Rorschach, and Bayley Scales of Infant Development. Examples of group tests include standard achievement tests administered in elementary and secondary schools, California Personality Inventory, Strong-Campbell Interest Inventory, Minnesota Multiphasic Personality Inventory (MMPI), Scholastic Aptitude Test (SAT), and American College Testing (ACT) program.

Typical versus Maximum Performance Tests

The distinction between typical and maximum performance tests was suggested by Cronbach (1970). Typical performance tests are those tests that contain items to which there are no necessarily correct or good responses. These are most often personality tests of various kinds, interest inventories, or attitude scales. What is of interest is how the person typically responds to such items. For example, the statement "I like to go to parties" might appear in a personality inventory designed to measure extroversion-introversion. People are to respond to this statement by saying that it is generally true or it is generally false about them. There is nothing intrinsically right or wrong about answering the item either way.

Maximum performance tests, on the other hand, typically involve a correct answer, and the subject's task is usually to answer as many questions as possible correctly. Intelligence tests are examples of maximum performance tests. In most situations it is to the person's advantage to score as high as possible on such tests.

Objective versus Projective Tests

These terms are typically applied to personality tests, although they might be ap-

plied to some types of ability tests. With ability tests, however, the word *subjective* is usually used instead of *projective*. Objective and projective tests actually lie on a continuum. The critical dimension is the degree to which the test is structured. Structure or ambiguity may exist in both the stimulus and in the response. Objective tests are those that have both structured stimulus materials and structured responses. Projective tests are those that have either unstructured stimulus materials, unstructured responses, or both. Objective personality tests typically involve a series of written items and require the subject to answer true or false, yes or no, agree or disagree, or to use other similar specific replies. The scoring of such tests is completely objective, since the answers are unambiguous. Examples of objective personality tests are the California Personality Inventory, MMPI, and Guilford-Zimmerman Temperament Survey.

In projective tests, the subject often must construct the answer from very limited information. Scoring the subject's response is more subjective, because it involves interpretation and inference rather than simply counting the number of questions answered in a particular way. Projective tests were developed under the assumption that in ambiguous situations a person will impose structure dictated by his or her own unique personality. Projective tests were in fact developed before objective tests of personality. Projective tests require a highly trained professional to administer, score, and interpret. Examples of projective tests include the Rorschach and the Thematic Apperception Test. (The distinction between projective and objective tests is discussed in more detail in Chapter 9.)

Speed versus Power Tests

Many tests, particularly ability or aptitude tests administered to groups, have time limits. A pure speed test is one containing relatively easy questions so that a person's score is essentially the number of questions attempted. That is, how quickly a person can answer questions determines the score. Tests of clerical aptitude or fine motor coordination are examples of speeded tests. Speed and accuracy of response are necessary to obtain high scores. Power tests contain questions of varying difficulty so that answering a question does not necessarily imply a correct answer. Problems can arise when power tests are partially speeded. Examinees may respond, for example, by guessing at test items toward the end of the test. Partially speeded tests can thus be partially measuring the examinee's willingness to guess. Most power tests are speeded to some degree, since examinees are unable to reach all the items. Most college students periodically complain about classroom examinations being too speeded, even though the professor believes that the tests are always pure power tests. Most ability and achievement tests are, however, largely power tests.

Limited-Response versus Free-Response Tests

In multiple-choice tests the examinee must choose one of several available alternatives. Most aptitude or achievement tests administered in groups are multiple-choice tests, giving examinees four or five alternatives from which to choose. Only one of the alternatives, of course, is correct. Personality inventories may also use a multiple-choice format in which the examinee's task is to answer true-false or agree-disagree to various statements. The obvious advantage of multiple-choice tests is that they are easily scored. In fact, the large testing programs such as the ACT and SAT would probably not exist if multiple-choice questions were not used. Computer scoring means that thousands of tests can be accurately and quickly scored.

Free-response tests require the examinee to produce the answer. A common classroom example of a free-response test is the essay examination in which students are required to write an expository statement in response to one or more questions. Most individually administered intelligence tests require the examinee to produce the response

rather than recognize the correct answer among several alternatives. Similarly, projective tests of personality are free-response tests in that examinees construct stories or otherwise generate a response to the projective stimulus.

Although multiple-choice tests have an obvious advantage in terms of the ease with which they are scored, they also permit examinees to answer correctly by guessing. Free-response tests are much less likely to be influenced by guessing. The major problem with free-response tests is that the scoring can be difficult and is almost always time-consuming.

There are undoubtedly other ways of categorizing tests, although we have listed several major ones. The terms we have introduced are not necessarily mutually exclusive. The type of test being used has implications for its administration and scoring. Therefore, we have defined various characteristics of tests so that we can refer to them in connection with administration and scoring procedures.

ADMINISTERING TESTS

Tests permit standardized observation of a specified kind of behavior. To obtain results that are useful and interpretable it is necessary for tests to be administered exactly as specified in the manual. The standardization of instructions is what makes scores comparable from person to person and group to group. The examiner or person who administers the test must be familiar with the instructions and other mechanical details of administration. Thus, for example, time limits must be strictly enforced and questions from examinees must be answered in the prescribed manner. Clemans (1971) wrote a good summary of the many details involved in administering group tests, and Sattler (1982) provided a similar overview for administering individual tests of intelligence to children. Almost all test manuals provide extensive discussion of and suggestions for administering the particular test.

Environmental Conditions

Obviously, the location in which the test is given should be quiet and free from distraction. Individually administered tests should usually be given in a private office with only the examiner and examinee present. Group tests should be given in rooms that will comfortably seat the number of examinees being tested. The amount of light, noise, and temperature should be controlled as much as possible to permit optimum performance. The furniture used should also be conducive to optimum performance. For example, students being tested in a relatively cold room with many burnt-out lights and broken armrests will probably do more poorly than those tested under better conditions. Extraneous factors such as these contribute to the error variance in the test scores and should be minimized. The factors mentioned refer mainly to standardization of conditions.

In most testing, then, it is likely that the extraneous factors are largely eliminated. If the group taking the test is fairly well motivated and is experienced in taking tests, it is unlikely that distractions will seriously disrupt performance. Research studies with undergraduate and graduate students have demonstrated that average test performance is not greatly influenced by disturbances of various kinds (Ingle & de Amico, 1969; Super et al., 1947). Younger children are probably more easily distracted than adults. Thus, preschool children are given individual tests so that the examiner has more influence and control over the testing situation. At least one study reported that children as old as sixth-graders are influenced by outside distractions and earn lower average scores than a comparable group without the distractions (Trentham, 1975). However, Bateman (1968) tested a group of mentally retarded children under very poor conditions such as high heat and high noise levels. The resulting average IQs were only slightly lower than those obtained under optimum conditions. Bateman's study did use an individually administered test, which suggests that such tests may be less influenced by environmental factors than are group tests. Bateman's study might also be interpreted as reflecting a "floor effect." That is, retarded children are likely to obtain low IQs under any set of conditions.

Rapport

To insure that test results will be useful to the examinee and examiner, the cooperation of the former must be elicited and maintained by a process called *rapport*.

On maximum performance tests, the examiner encourages the subjects to do their best. It is assumed that subjects are motivated to do well and are generally familiar with the material to be covered. For typical performance tests, the subject is encouraged to answer the questions as truthfully and honestly as possible. For both kinds of tests, the subject is encouraged to pay close attention to the instructions. In addition, the examiner should convince the examinees that the test data are important and that they are not wasting their time on a trivial task. If rapport between the examiner and subjects is established, the subjects' performance on the test is apt to represent their true capabilities. Mutual trust and respect represent the ideal situation between examiner and subject.

Rapport is undoubtedly easier to establish with individual tests than with group tests. With many group tests, however, the subject's motivation to do well, as on the GRE for example, will usually insure close cooperation and attention to instructions. On the other hand, individual tests are often administered because outside authorities such as courts or school administrators require the assessment. The purpose for and conditions under which the test is given greatly influence the degree to which rapport is established. The same subject may be much more cooperative if he or she has voluntarily sought counseling than if testing has been ordered by a court. Despite a psychologist's best attempt to establish rapport, it may be all but impossible if the subject is being tested in a jail or prison.

Establishing rapport with preschool children represents a special problem. These children may be shy, inattentive, and restless. They also have limited verbal ability and usually are unfamiliar with testing. Examiners must have patience and empathy to secure the needed cooperation.

Many testing situations involve some threat to a subject's self-esteem. To do poorly on an ability test or a classroom examination makes most people unhappy. The knowledge that one is being evaluated and compared with others is not a necessarily pleasant state of affairs. Personality tests sometimes ask embarrassing questions dealing with sexual matters and require high levels of concentration from the examinee. Given the generally unpleasant characteristics of testing, the examiner must often overcome a good deal of antipathy and resentment. It is not surprising that intensive training is needed to develop competent experts in test administration and interpretation.

Although there is no exhaustive list of ways to insure establishing rapport between the examiner and examinee, several factors appear important.

1. *Personality of the examiner.* It is obvious that a person with sensitivity to other people's needs, with warmth, and with a generally friendly attitude toward others will be more successful in dealing with individuals than a person not having these characteristics, which are especially important in testing children. On the other hand, a businesslike attitude is probably more effective for group testing.
2. *Sensitivity to the testing situation.* A clear understanding of why the person is being tested will help alleviate suspicion, hostility, or fears. Persons being tested during a time crisis are the most difficult cases, and the examiner must take the situation into account when interpreting the scores.
3. *Training in interview techniques.* Specific training, usually at the graduate level, in interview techniques is very desirable. It enables an examiner to anticipate and avoid many potential problems. Interviewing is often taught as part of a graduate assessment course, but books on the topic are also available (Benjamin, 1981).

4. *Familiarity with the test being administered.* It is essential that the person administering the test be familiar with the materials, instructions, and methods of administration. If a subject doubts an examiner's competence, there is little hope of any mutual respect.
5. *Professionalism.* The examiner should appear to be an authority figure in the best sense of the word. The examiner should exhibit self-confidence and conviction that the testing process is important. If the examiner attempts to demean the test in any way, rapport will suffer.
6. *Legitimate interests of the examinee.* If the examinee is convinced that cooperation is in his or her best interests, rapport will be more easily established. Part of an examiner's professionalism is to convince the person being tested, regardless of the situation, that maximum performance or answering questions as honestly as possible is in his or her best interest.

SCORING TESTS

Summative Scoring

Most tests, regardless of how they are categorized, consist of a series of questions or statements to which the examinee must respond. The individual questions or statements are referred to as items. These items are usually numbered sequentially in group tests so that examinees can respond on an answer sheet rather than on the test booklet itself. The items may be organized into several different sections according to their type, age for which they are intended, or some other principle. In aptitude tests it is common to have easier items at the beginning of the test and more difficult items at the end. Permitting examinees to answer successfully the first few questions helps increase their motivation so that they can maximize their performance. In personality inventories, the concept of difficulty has no meaning because there is no necessarily correct answer to an item. For all group tests, all items are administered to all examinees in the same order. For individual tests, only the items appropriate to the particular examinee may be administered. The order of administration of the items is, however, fixed for individual tests once the particular set of items has been selected.

If psychologists, educators, and other social scientists were measuring variables such as length or weight, it would be reasonably simple to devise a test. A single item or measurement would do the job, since the trait being measured is not complex. However, if we are interested in assessing a complex trait like scholastic aptitude, there is no simple and obvious single measure. Therefore, many items believed to be related to this trait are constructed. Although any single item may not be a good indicator, many such items should sample more adequately the domain of interest. Test scores, therefore, represent the sum of performance on many different items. *Summative scoring* simply means combining in a systematic way the examinee's performance on many items rather than using a single item.

The items on a test may be grouped in several different ways. For example, the MMPI contains 566 items, from which a large number of different scales can be scores. Similarly, the Graduate Record Examination (GRE) has three scores, the SAT has two, and the ACT has five. Of course, many test have only one score—most achievement tests and classroom examinations, for example.

It is interesting to note that whenever human judgments are involved, it is common for several "items" or independent measurements to be made. In athletic events of many kinds several judges are used, particularly when timing is involved. In swimming and track there are usually several different people timing each participant. In rating the performance of divers, ice skaters, and gymnasts, several judges are used, and an average rating is assigned as the final score. In our criminal justice system, juries typically consist of twelve people who must agree on a verdict. Graduate students have several faculty members on the dissertation committee for their final oral examination. In all these cases we have recognized that a single individual may make wrong decisions

or judgments and that by adding more judges we increase the opportunity for a more accurate assessment of the true performance. It is the same with tests. By adding more items, there is a better opportunity to make an accurate assessment of a complex bit of behavior. Although we may find that the examinee's response to a single item is not very useful, we may be much more confident in interpreting a score based on many items.

Expression of Performance

RAW SCORES. The first step in interpreting a person's performance on a test is to obtain that person's raw score. On an aptitude test, the raw score is simply the number of items answered correctly. On a personality inventory, the raw score is the number of items answered in a particular, predefined manner (say, the number of questions answered that reflect anxiety). Items are usually combined in an unweighted manner. That is, all correctly answered items on an aptitude test are scored as one point and incorrectly answered items are scored as zero. The total score simply reflects the number of correct items. More complex weighting schemes are theoretically possible and quite feasible given the availability of computers. However, the simple weighting scheme seems to work well and is almost universally used for commercially available tests.

Raw test scores may vary from zero up to the number of items on the test. Note that the more items there are, the greater the potential range of scores. Since individual differences in performance are more likely to occur when there are more items, long tests, other factors being equal, are preferred. As we noted in Chapter 3, longer tests will tend to be more reliable than shorter tests.

Unless a raw score is compared to some absolute standard—for example, in passing an examination for a driver's license—the raw score a person obtains is not very meaningful. Consider a girl in an elementary school who reports to her parents that she received a score of 85 on a spelling test and a score of 52 on an arithmetic test. On the surface, the student's parents should be pleased with her spelling but unhappy with her arithmetic. However, these two raw scores are in and of themselves meaningless. In the first place, we have no way of knowing if the number of items on the two tests were the same. If the spelling test had 120 items and the arithmetic test had 60 items, our interpretation of the two scores would be quite different. Even if both tests had 100 items, we could easily be misled into believing the student was a good speller and poor at arithmetic. What is lacking for us to interpret the scores adequately is the student's relative standing in the class. That is, how do her scores compare with those of other students in her class? More broadly, we might be interested in how her scores compare with all students of a similar age in the United States. The number of different groups of which this student is a member could be virtually limitless. However, to interpret the test scores adequately, several different comparison groups will usually be sufficient. In fact, in many cases a single group will be enough. The comparison groups to which the test has been given are called *normative groups* and establish the "norms" for the test. We will discuss norms later in this chapter; let us now turn to some other ways of expressing performance.

PERCENTILE SCORES. Perhaps the most direct way of expressing performance is in terms of percentiles. A percentile score gives the proportion of people in a group scoring below a particular score. Implicitly, percentile scores require that a frequency distribution (see Chapter 2) of all the raw scores be constructed for a group. Any particular raw score can then be placed in its relative position, and we can see what percentage of scores are above or below that score. Percentile scores convey essentially rank order information; that is, they give the relative standing of an individual. They are often referred to as percentile ranks. In our previous example, if the score on the

spelling test were exceeded by 25 percent of the students in the class, the student would have a percentile score of 75. Similarly, the score on the arithmetic test might be at the ninety-fifth percentile, which would be a very high score. Note that there is a direct relationship between the size of the test score and the percentile score *within* a test. That is, within the same test high scores are associated with high percentile scores. However, the same raw score on two different tests could have different percentile scores.

Percentile scores have several advantages. They convey an immediate and clear picture of an examinee's relative standing. They are easily communicated to parents, patients, and other test consumers. They are not influenced by the shape of the distribution of raw scores—the fiftieth percentile remains exactly in the middle of a set of scores regardless of the shape of the distribution. They are expressed on a familiar scale—percentage or proportion—and will always be between zero and one hundred for all tests. Percentile scores may be directly compared from test to test as long as the normative groups are the same, although such comparisons are necessarily approximate without appropriate statistical tests.

The major difficulty with percentile scores is that the differences between percentiles have a different meaning depending on the location of the score in the distribution of scores. Thus, small differences among test scores in the middle of the distribution of raw scores are reflected in rather large differences between percentiles. On the other hand, rather large differences in high or low raw scores have small differences between the corresponding percentile scores. Stated more simply, percentile scores tend to overemphasize differences in the middle of the distribution and underemphasize differences in the extremes of the distribution.

In the interpretation of a percentile score, it is always critical to know what group is being used as a reference. Consider, for example, how an examinee's interpretation of the same raw score on a mathematical aptitude test might change as a function of the group with which it is compared. In the following example, we see how the person would seem to have a reasonably high score compared to first-year high school students and even high school seniors. However, compared with those students who majored in mathematics, our student is only average. And if the person were compared to people with a doctorate in mathematics, the score would be rather low. Which group is best to use? It depends on the aspirations and goals of the person being tested.

Group	Percentile Score for a Raw Score of 62
First-year high school students	90
High school seniors	75
First-year college students	66
BA graduates in mathematics	50
Ph.D's in mathematics	25

All things considered, percentile scores are probably the best and most generally used method of presenting test results to persons not familiar with statistical methods.

STANDARD SCORES. A major problem in interpreting raw scores is that no information about the relative standing of the score is conveyed. As we indicated in Chapter 2, two essential characteristics of any distribution of scores are a measure of central tendency, or average, and a measure of variability. Standard scores take these two characteristics into account. In fact standard scores are "standard" because they refer to a standard average (mean) and standard measure of variability (standard deviation). Standard scores are linear transformations of the raw scores. All standard scores are *derived from* z-scores, to which we now turn.

A *z-score* is defined by the following formula:

$$z_x = \frac{X - \bar{X}}{S_x} \qquad (4\text{-}1)$$

where $\bar{X}$ is the mean of the raw scores and S_x is the standard deviation of the raw scores.* To convert raw scores to standard scores, the mean and standard deviation of the raw scores must be available. Suppose, for example, we know that the mean, $\bar{X}$, is 36 and the standard deviation, S, is 4 for a particular set of test scores. Any raw score in this distribution could then be converted to an equivalent z-score by the following formula:

$$z_x = \frac{X - 36}{4}$$

If the raw score was 42, z_x would be

$$z_x = \frac{42 - 36}{4} = \frac{6}{4} = 1.50$$

If the raw score was 29, the corresponding z_x would be

$$z_x = \frac{29 - 36}{4} = \frac{-7}{4} = -1.75$$

Note that raw scores above the mean have positive z-scores whereas raw scores below the mean have negative z-scores. The z-scores are expressed in standard deviation units. Thus, a person who has a z-score of 1.50 has a score one and one-half standard deviations above the mean. A person with a z-score of -1.75 has a score one and three-fourths standard deviations below the mean. Standard scores do, therefore, convey rather precisely where a person is in a distribution of scores.

Another useful characteristic of z-scores and other standard scores is that they make

*Recall that in Chapter 2, $\bar{X}$ was defined as the sum of the raw scores divided by the total number of observations (that is $\bar{X} = \Sigma X/N$) and S_x was defined as the square root of the average of the sum of the squared deviation scores $(S_x = \sqrt{\dfrac{\Sigma(X - \bar{X})^2}{N}})$.

it possible to compare performances on different tests. This is possible because standard scores have a predefined mean and standard deviation. For z-scores, the mean is zero and the standard deviation is one. In addition, z-scores can be manipulated mathematically and are thus convenient to use in theoretical derivations.

Equation 4-1 assumes nothing about the shape of the distribution of raw scores. If the distribution follows the standard normal curve, we can say even more about the meaning of particular z-scores. The normal distribution has two parameters that completely determine its shape: the mean and the standard deviation. These are, of course, the same two parameters needed to convert raw scores into z-scores by using Equation 4-1. If the X's, the raw scores, in Equation 4-1 are normally distributed, the z-scores associated with each raw score will also be normally distributed. The important difference is that the normally distributed z-scores (like all sets of z-scores) will have a mean of zero and a standard deviation of one. This distribution is called the *standard normal distribution* and has been extensively tabled. By referring to it we are able to determine the proportion of scores above, below, or between any z-scores of interest. In other words, the z-score, when it follows a normal distribution, allows us to determine percentile scores by referring to the tables for the standard normal distribution.

Figure 4-1 presents the standard normal curve, which is symmetric around the mean. Theoretically the curve extends without limit in the positive and negative directions. It is also a continuous distribution, that is, decimal values of the z-score are permitted. In the standard normal curve, 68 percent of the scores occur between the z-scores of +1.00 and −1.00; 95.4 percent, between +2.00 and −2.00; and 99.7 percent, between +3.00 and −3.00. Most scores occur around the mean, and only about 5 percent of the z-scores will be above +2.00 or below −2.00.

Another way of evaluating z-scores in the standard normal distribution is to note that 97.7 percent of the scores are lower than a z-score of +2.00. In other words, the percentile score for a person obtaining a z-score of +2.00 is about 98. Similar percentile scores could be obtained for any z-score from a table of the standard normal distribution. The converse is also true. By knowing the percentile score, the z-score can be obtained from the tables for the standard normal distribution. For example, a z-score of 1.65 has a percentile score of 95.

The z-scores computed from Equation 4-1 are often called *normal deviates* when the raw scores are assumed or known to be normally distributed. However, the transformation of a raw score to a z-score by Equation 4-1 does not change the shape of the distribution. In other words, converting raw scores that are not normally distributed to z-scores will *not* result in a standard normal distribution.

As a final warning, we should note that the normal distribution is a mathematical abstraction. It is probably fair to say that no trait or characteristic that psychologists measure follows the normal distribution exactly. If the normal distribution is critical to a researcher, there are statistical tests to determine if a given set of data departs significantly from a normal distribution. It appears that scores from many tests tend to be distributed approximately as the normal distribution requires. However, the general shape of the distribution depends greatly on the group to whom the test is administered and the items it contains. Intelligence test scores, for example, will certainly not be normally distributed if the test is administered to graduating seniors at a highly selective university. Often the process used in developing tests and selecting items and persons to be tested was designed to insure that the scores follow approximately a normal distribution. Such a construction process is justified if we assume that most people are "average" and that there will be relatively few extreme "deviations" in either direction from the mean.

One problem with z-scores is that the average score is zero. In the United States to

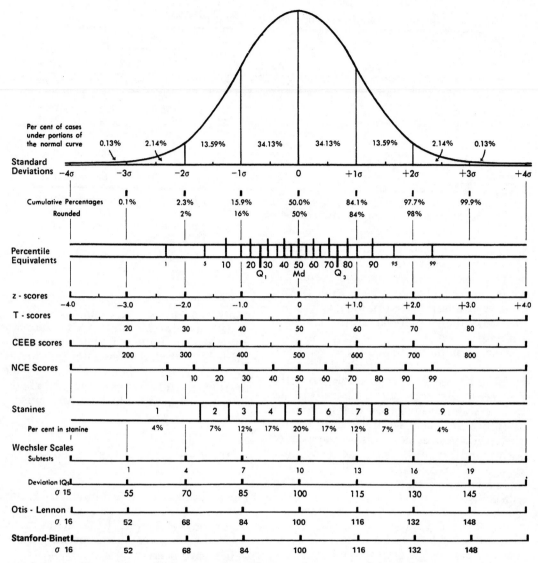

FIGURE 4–1 Types of standard score scales and percentile scores and their relation to the normal distribution. (Adapted from Test Service Bulletin No. 48. A publication of The Psychological Corporation. All rights reserved.)

have zero of anything is usually considered bad. Even worse, z-scores permit persons to have negative scores. Again, negative scores tend to have a negative connotation in U.S. society and would undoubtedly create problems in communicating their meaning to nonprofessionals. For this reason, and for matters of convenience and tradition, other derived scores were developed. All are standard scores and are derived from z-scores. To convert a z-score to any other standard score, we could use the following formula:

$$X_{NEW} = S.D._{New}(z_x) + Mean_{New} \quad (4\text{--}2)$$

TABLE 4-1 Illustrative Raw Scores and Associated Standard Scores

Person	Raw Score (X)	z-score	T-score	Deviation IQ		SAT-V
				S-B	Wechsler	
A	42	+1.50	65	124	123	650
B	36	.00	50	100	100	500
C	45	2.25	73	135	134	725
D	29	−1.75	32	72	74	325
E	27	−2.25	27	64	66	275
Mean*	36	.00	50	100	100	500
Standard Deviation*	4	1.00	10	16	15	100

*The mean and standard deviation refer to the characteristics of the entire group of scores and not to the five we have selected for illustrative purposes.

S.D.$_{New}$ is the desired standard deviation of the new standard scores; Mean$_{New}$ is the desired mean of the new standard scores; z_x is the z-score to be converted; and X_{New} is the new standard score for any given z_x. We will now define several other common standard scores.

A very common one is the *T-score*, which has a mean of 50 and a standard deviation of 10. The MMPI, for example, uses the T-score to express performance on the various scales available on this personality inventory. In Table 4-1 we present several selected raw scores along with the associated z-score and T-scores. As can be seen, a raw score of 42 has a z-score of 1.50. To convert this z-score to a T-score, we use Equation 4-2 as follows:

$$T = S.D._{New} (z_x) + Mean_{New}$$
$$T = 10(1.50) + 50$$
$$T = 65$$

The other T-scores in Table 4-1 can be obtained in the same fashion. It should be noted that they are all perfectly correlated with one another. That is, the subjects remain in exactly the same relative position. The only things that change are the means and standard deviations of the various types of scores.

IQ scores represent another type of standard score. When intelligence tests were first developed, *IQ* referred to *intelligence quotient*. It was obtained by division from the formula

$$IQ = \frac{MA}{CA} \times 100 \qquad (4-3)$$

where MA is the examinee's mental age in months and CA is the examinee's chronological age in months. This ratio was multiplied by 100 to eliminate the need for decimals. Note that when a person's mental age equaled his or her chronological age, the IQ was 100. For example, if a child 7 years old (84 months) had a mental age of 7 years, the IQ would be

$$IQ = \frac{84}{84} \times 100 = 1.00 \times 100 = 100$$

The child was of average intelligence, since the mental age matched that of other 7-year-olds. However, if the child's mental age had been 9 years (108 months), the IQ would have been

$$IQ = \frac{108}{84} \times 100 = 1.29 \times 100 = 129$$

Such an IQ is above average, since the mental age is higher than the chronological age.

However, the IQ as a ratio has been replaced for a variety of technical reasons by the *deviation IQ*, a standard score having a mean of 100. Again, as was historically true, a deviation IQ of 100 represents average performance on the test. However, the meaning of other IQ scores depends on the standard deviation that was chosen for this standard score. The Stanford-Binet Intelligence Scale specifies a standard deviation of 16 whereas the Wechsler tests specify a standard deviation of 15. Thus, on purely statistical grounds, IQ scores from the Stanford-Binet and the Wechsler tests are not really equivalent, except perhaps at the mean. Table 4-1 gives examples of the deviation IQs from these two tests if the same raw scores were simply converted directly to standard scores.

Another set of standard scores is used by the Educational Testing Service for many of its large testing programs. Test scores on the SAT and GRE are expressed as standard scores having a mean of 500 and a standard deviation of 100. Table 4-1 contains illustrative scores on the SAT–Verbal, again assuming the raw scores were converted directly to the standard scores.

NORMALIZED STANDARD SCORES. It would theoretically be possible to convert raw scores into a set of standard scores that follow the normal distribution exactly. As indicated, by first determining percentile scores, the associated z-score in the normal distribution could be found. These normal deviates could then be converted to any standard score scale that was of interest. An example of such a normalized standard score is the *stanine*. The stanine scale has nine categories (one through nine) with a mean of five and a standard deviation of approximately two. This scale has the virtue of having a single number for a score, which could be punched in a single column on a computer card. Normalized scores have also been used in several tests for large and representative groups. Lyman (1978, Ch. 6) describes several such examples and gives more details about *stanines*.

Normalizing test scores is a process that should not be routine. Lord (1953) gave a detailed theoretical account of how the characteristics of the items in a test determine the shape of the distribution of test scores. Careful consideration of the purpose for which a test is to be used is often more important than a normally distributed set of test scores. For example, if the purpose is to discover those individuals in need of special education, an easy test creating a negatively skewed (see Chapter 2) distribution of scores would be most useful. That is, most students would score high on the test, but the few who scored low would be the ones most in need of assistance. However, if we assume that the scores in a population are normally distributed, but the scores in our sample are not normally distributed because of certain deficits in the test, we might choose to convert the sample raw scores into normalized standard scores.

Norms

Implicit in the use of derived scores, percentile scores, and standard scores is the concept of a normative group. The word *norms* has been used to refer to the groups of people to whom a test has been administered and for whom descriptive statistics are available. Percentile scores and standard scores must be interpreted with reference to the characteristics of the groups to whom the test has been administered, because an individual score is interpreted by comparing it with scores made by other individuals. Most tests in use today are norm-referenced. That is, a test score is given meaning by its relative standing among those from a particular group.

Suppose we are developing a personality inventory to measure aggressive behavior in ten-year-old children. Once the potential items have been pretested and the good ones selected for use, we must now obtain our normative sample. We assume the test is to be used only in the United States, and thus all ten-year-old children in the United States become the population of interest. Since we cannot test every ten-year-old child, we must be content with a *representative* sample. *Representative* means that the characteristics of the sample must match closely the characteristics of the population. In our case, it means that demographic characteristics, such as sex, socioeconomic status, ethnic group, geographic location, and other potentially important variables, should exist in our sample to the same degree that they exist in the population. Such a normative sample would represent an ideal and one which is never obtained in practice. In the first place, children and their parents would have to agree to participate in such a study. The sample, almost immediately, is somewhat unrepresentative because it excludes those children whose parents will not give their consent. It is often difficult to have minority groups adequately represented in a normative sample. Rural children are less likely to be included, and any children not attending school are likely to be overlooked. For these reasons and others, samples truly representative of large populations are difficult to obtain.

However, norms are often based on well-planned sampling procedures designed to insure appropriate representation of minority groups, ages, sexes, and other demographic characteristics thought to be important. The description of the norm group in the test manual should explicitly state the manner in which people were selected to participate in the testing program, the method of sampling, any source of bias in the sampling procedure, and the number of cases in various demographic categories. The test user must be certain that a person being tested can reasonably be regarded as a member of the normative group. If the person tested is not, that score is not interpretable with reference to those particular norms.

What characteristics should a normative group have? We will identify several of the most important.

1. *Representative of the population.* The people tested should match the more important demographic variables in the population of interest. These might include sex, age, ethnic status, socioeconomic level, locale, and educational status. Another way of defining *representative* is to say that the sampling should be unbiased. The norms should not be biased against any significant number of people having a particular characteristic if the test is likely to be used with people having that characteristic.
2. *Large number of cases.* The number of persons tested should be as large as possible. With large samples, any statistics computed are less subject to error. This requirement presumes that we have a representative sample, of course.
3. *Current.* It is desirable for the test to have been recently administered. Tests that have not been revised in, say, ten or fifteen years probably cannot be safely interpreted unless research indicates that the population has remained largely unchanged with respect to test performance. For example, if the normative group were given a test in 1970, it may well be that educational and cultural changes since that date would make current scores uncomparable to those obtained in 1970.

It may be possible and desirable to develop *local norms.* As the name suggests, local norms can be developed by maintaining records of the scores obtained by persons taking the test at a given location, a school or industry, for example. Such norms could be used in conjunction with national norms to provide a more accurate description of a person's test performance. Local norms can be particularly useful in making predictions about job success or academic progress. Whether local norms or national norms are used, it is important to choose the normative group that most closely approximates the group with whom the person will compete.

Profiles

In making inferences about a person, it is usually desirable to consider several sources of information. Some testing procedures involve a battery of tests, several different tests measuring somewhat different characteristics. Some tests with a large number of items permit multiple scores to be obtained from a single test. Multiple scores from one or several tests are often presented graphically to illustrate the examinee's *profile* of performance, which is usually expressed as percentile or standard scores. By inspecting the profile, a trained professional can see the relative strengths and weaknesses of a particular individual.

As an example of a profile of test scores generated by a computer, we have reproduced a report from the Metropolitan Achievement Tests in Figure 4-2. This test

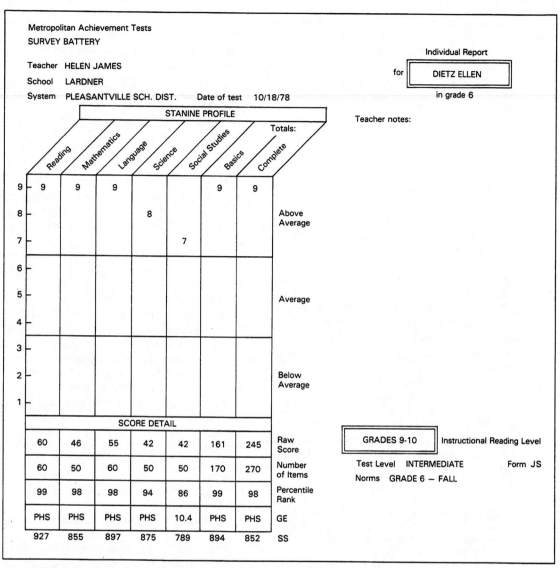

Metropolitan Achievement Tests
SURVEY BATTERY

Teacher HELEN JAMES
School LARDNER
System PLEASANTVILLE SCH. DIST.   Date of test   10/18/78

Individual Report

for   DIETZ ELLEN

in grade 6

Teacher notes:

STANINE PROFILE

Reading   Mathematics   Language   Science   Social Studies   Basics   Complete   Totals:

9	9	9	9			9	9	
8				8				Above Average
7					7			
6								
5								Average
4								
3								
2								Below Average
1								

SCORE DETAIL

60	46	55	42	42	161	245	Raw Score
60	50	60	50	50	170	270	Number of Items
99	98	98	94	86	99	98	Percentile Rank
PHS	PHS	PHS	PHS	10.4	PHS	PHS	GE
927	855	897	875	789	894	852	SS

GRADES 9-10   Instructional Reading Level

Test Level   INTERMEDIATE   Form JS
Norms   GRADE 6 — FALL

FIGURE 4–2 Example profile of a student's performance on the Metropolitan Achievement Tests. (Reproduced by permission of the publisher. Copyright © 1978 by Harcourt Brace Jovanovich, Inc. All rights reserved.)

has sections on reading, mathematics, language, science, and social studies as well as totals based on the basic battery (the first three sections) and all five sections. Thus, a student's profile consists of his or her relative standing on six scores. This test uses stanines as the standard scores in plotting the profile. However, the computer printout gives other types of scores as well—percentiles, grade equivalents (GE), and standard scores (SS). As can be seen in Figure 4-2, this particular student had very high test scores in reading, mathematics, and language and was only slightly lower in science and social studies. Other students could demonstrate different patterns of performance. Some could be high in one or two subjects and average in others, for example. Such differences may have diagnostic importance and suggest a student's need for a particular kind of remedial work.

Criterion-referenced Testing

The psychometric tradition in testing focuses on individual differences, and test scores are interpreted on a relative basis. Thus, norm-referenced testing is designed to measure a particular characteristic of an individual relative to a normative group. Criterion-referenced testing interprets scores on a more absolute basis. Glaser (1963) first introduced the term in connection with measuring the outcomes of learning. Popham and Husek (1969) were also early advocates of criterion-referenced testing.

Various definitions are available. Glaser and Nitko (1971), for example, define criterion-referenced tests as those designed to yield scores directly interpretable in terms of specified performance standards. Lindvall and Nitko (1975, p. 76) list four defining characteristics of a criterion-referenced test:

1. The classes of behaviors that define different achievement levels are specified as clearly as possible before the test is constructed.
2. Each behavior class is defined by a set of test situations (that is, test items or tasks) in which the behaviors and all their important nuances can be displayed.
3. Given that the classes of behavior have been specified and that the test situations have been defined, a representative sampling plan is designed and used to select the tasks that will appear on any form of the test.
4. The obtained score must be capable of being referenced objectively and meaningfully to the individual's performance in these classes of behavior.

Popham (1975) defines a criterion-referenced test as one used to determine an individual's status with respect to a well-defined behavior. Criterion-referenced testing does not yet have a completely satisfactory, single definition, which has led to considerable confusion about what such testing can accomplish (Glass, 1978; Hambleton et al., 1978).

Carver (1974) distinguishes between two dimensions of tests—psychometric (norm-referenced) and edumetric (criterion-referenced). The first dimension (psychometric) comes from the long tradition of focusing on between-individual differences, whereas the second dimension (edumetric) reflects the within-individual growth that has been of primary interest in educational testing. A test that is very good for psychometric purposes may be very bad for edumetric purposes and vice versa.

Table 4-2 summarizes the differences between psychometric (norm-referenced) and edumetric (criterion-referenced) tests with respect to purpose, item selection, validity, reliability, and score interpretation (Carver, 1974). Although the mathematical-statistical theory of psychometric or norm-referenced tests is well developed and extensive (for example, Gulliksen, 1950; Lord & Novick, 1968), the corresponding theory for criterion-referenced tests is largely nonexistent (Hambleton et al., 1978). Berk (1980), however, has provided guidance on obtaining reliability estimates for criterion-referenced tests.

Criterion-referenced test scores are used in two important ways (Hambleton et al., 1978). One is the estimation of an examinee's domain score, that is, basically, the proportion of items a person answers correctly in a given domain of interest. Although this is undoubtedly useful information, it is unclear what to do with it (Glass, 1978). The second use is the allocation of examinees to mastery states. That is, criterion-referenced tests are used to determine which students have reached a minimally acceptable level of performance on the test and presumably on the construct of interest. The terms *mastery*, *competence*, and *proficiency* all appear to be used interchangeably in this context and appeal to the

TABLE 4-2 Type of Test

Test Characteristic	Psychometric	Edumetric
Purpose	Measures individual differences	Measures gain or growth of individuals
Item selection	Has items that approximately half the subjects pass and that have high item and test correlations	Has items that are maximally sensitive to growth or gain; items that show the most increase in proportion passing from pre- to posttreatment
Validity	Relates individual differences on test to those on another variable of interest	Shows the test's sensitivity to gain or growth
Reliability	Discriminates consistently between individuals from one occasion to the next, which directly depends on variability in test scores	Is concerned with consistency of gain or growth within individuals
Score interpretation	Compares to an average score, a deviation from a mean, or the percentile of a normative group; raw scores not interpreted	Has meaning in relationship to a criterion, objective, or scale independent of individual differences; raw scores interpreted

Carver, R. P. (1974). Two dimensions of tests: Psychometric and edumetric. *American Psychologist, 29,* 512-518. Copyright © 1974 by the American Psychological Association. Adapted by permission of the author.

vague concept of "standards." According to Glass (1978), the essential problem is establishing a criterion score on a criterion-referenced test. That is, what score should an examinee obtain to be classified as a "master" rather than a "nonmaster"?

Glass identifies six methods of determining cutoff scores but finds none of the procedures acceptable. For example, one technique is labeled "Counting backwards from 100 percent." Mastery status is declared if an examinee is correct on 95 percent or 90 percent or 85 percent of the items. Clearly the number of examinees reaching mastery status will vary depending on the percentage deemed appropriate, and that percentage appears to be largely arbitrary. A second approach is called "judging minimal competence." Experts, however defined, examine the test and decide what a minimally competent person should score. Such an approach is used to establish competency-based graduation requirements in some school districts and states. For example, a task force for the National Association of Secondary School Principals (*Competency Tests and Graduation Requirements*, 1976) suggested that potential high school graduates be certified for graduation by passing competency measures of (1) functional literacy in reading, writing, and speaking; (2) the ability to compute, including decimals

and percentages; and (3) knowledge of the history and culture of the United States, to include the concepts and processes of democratic governance. Glass argued that it has not been demonstrated that the experts (judges) can make determinations of such cutoff scores consistently and reliably and the concept of minimal competence has virtually no foundation in psychology. Thus, we can imagine a continuum for most skills and performances running from complete absence of the skill to clear excellence. Recognizing complete absence of a skill is very different from recognizing the minimum needed for success. The educational concept of minimum competence is analogous to the notion of cure in psychotherapy. Both are imprecise. Glass' conclusion is that every attempt to derive a criterion score is either blatantly arbitrary or derives from a set of arbitrary premises.

The technical literature on criterion-referenced testing has, however, been growing rapidly. An issue of *Applied Psychological Measurement* (1980, volume 4, number 4) was entirely devoted to criterion-referenced testing technology. Shaycoft (1979) published a useful book describing in a direct manner the characteristics, uses, and evaluation of criterion-referenced tests. We recommend her book as an excellent starting point for those needing more detailed and practical information on criterion-referenced tests as well as their relationship to norm-referenced tests.

FACTORS INFLUENCING PERFORMANCE

The administration and scoring of a test ideally is a neutral process, like that of weighing a truckload of corn or measuring the length of a board. Factors extraneous to performance are minimized by careful attention to instructions and establishing rapport with the subject. However, the testing situation is dynamic and involves many factors beyond the examiner's control. In this section we identify some of the potential factors that could influence performance—by which we mean factors that could contribute to a person receiving a higher or lower score than the person would receive if the factors were eliminated or under better control.

Characteristics of Examinee

An obvious factor is the characteristics of the examinee. Young children, for example, are incapable of taking some types of tests. People who do not read or understand English cannot be expected to take tests requiring that fundamental skill. Older people may not be able to respond quickly enough to some types of items. The physically handicapped present special problems in assessment. However, these characteristics and others are generally taken into account by the testing process. Special tests are available for children. We do not expect young children to be given intelligence tests designed for adults. A blind person would not take the SAT in the usual group setting. The characteristics with which we are concerned are those that may not be immediately obvious impediments but which may, nevertheless, have an important affect on how well a person performs.

COACHING, PRACTICE, "TEST-WISENESS." Often examinees view their test scores as extremely critical to their future. This perception may or may not be true, but examinees behave as if it were. For example, as part of the admission process for medical school, applicants must take the Medical College Admission Test (MCAT). Since admission to medical school is in fact a highly competitive situation, applicants want to score as high as possible. Thus, it is not surprising that commercial courses are developed to teach people how to do well on the MCAT and other aptitude tests used for selection. *Coaching* is the general term used to refer to explicit instruction on how to improve performance on a particular test. If the coaching has the ancillary effect of actually improving the skills that the test was designed to measure (in this instance, aptitude for medical school), it will not reduce the validity of the test score. However, if the main consequence of coaching is to enable the examinee to answer the types of questions on a given test, the score obtained is misleading and not valid. Another way of stating the problem (Anastasi, 1982, p. 41) is to say that coaching invalidates the test if it improves performance on the test without producing a corresponding improvement in the behavior the test was designed to predict.

As is true of most other human endeavors, test performance can be improved with practice. Maximum performance tests are constructed under the assumption that the test will be administered only once. However, many people take similar tests throughout their years in school. In the United States, it seems likely that most people are familiar with the general format of multiple-choice tests designed to measure scholastic ability or achievement. The large testing programs such as the SAT and ACT provide sample questions and instructions to registering students. Such information is designed to overcome disparate previous experience with tests and testing procedures. The distinction between coaching and practice is not clear since coaching must involve practice with items on a particular test. In addition, coaching usually involves instruction on particular test-taking strategies (that is, when to guess at questions of which the examinee is unsure, using time efficiently, and eliminating incorrect alternatives). Practice involves the notion of repeated test-taking, which may or may not involve instruction on test-taking strategies beyond those suggested by the test instructions.

The result of coaching, practice, or experience in taking tests is called *test-wiseness*. This term refers to the person's capacity to utilize the characteristics and formats of the test and/or the test-taking situation to receive a high score and is logically independent of the person's knowledge of the subject matter (Millman et al., 1965). Test-wiseness involves both the purpose of the testing and the nature of the test. In analyzing test-wiseness, Millman et al. suggest that some factors are independent of test construction and purposes whereas other factors are not. Regardless of the test, examinees can avoid losing points by employing efficient time-using strategies and avoiding errors; they can gain points by using an appropriate guessing and deductive reasoning strategy (that is, eliminating alternatives in multiple-choice questions).

The evidence concerning the effects of coaching and practice on performance is rather mixed (Fueyo, 1977). In summarizing the results of several British studies, Vernon (1954) noted agreement among investigators on several points. Among them was the finding that previous practice and/or coaching did affect intelligence test performance enough to change the decision about a proportion of children near the cut-off point for selection into an academic curriculum. However, the effects were found to be limited, and a few hours of practice or coaching seemed to produce the maximum achievable average gain. Vernon also concluded that some types of items were much more susceptible to practice or coaching than others. For example, straightforward multiple-choice items on an information test were affected least, whereas nonverbal items were more affected. Practice on a particular test (Teich, 1976) and training in test-taking skills (Eakins et al., 1976–77)

have also been shown to improve the test performance of children. It thus appears that practice and/or coaching can influence the test performance of children on a variety of different tests, although the improvement may be small and is likely to occur with only a limited amount of practice or coaching.

Earlier results of studies with young adults appeared to demonstrate that coaching had little or no effect on test performance. The College Entrance Examination Board, the executive body responsible for the Scholastic Aptitude Test (SAT) program, was concerned about the ways special coaching may affect students' scores. The SAT is used to help in the selection of students for admission into many colleges and universities. Even in times of declining enrollment, admission into more prestigious universities is highly competitive. Students are thus motivated to score as high as possible on the SAT in order to improve, at least potentially, their prospects for admission into a college or university of their choice. In summarizing the results of seven studies on coaching and the SAT, the College Entrance Examination Board (*Effects of Coaching on Scholastic Aptitude Test Scores,* 1965) concluded that score gains directly attributable to coaching were of such small magnitude that it was unlikely decisions on college admissions would be affected. Although a student's scores on the SAT will change over time, the report concluded that the changes that do occur are approximately of the same degree and the same frequency whether or not a student is coached.

However, more recent results questioned these earlier conclusions. The Federal Trade Commission (FTC) investigated the advertising claims of three commercial firms that offered instruction in taking the SAT and other aptitude tests used in selection decisions. The first FTC report (*Staff Memorandum . . . ,* 1978), prepared by the Boston regional office, concluded that coaching did significantly improve performance on the SAT. The second FTC report (*Effects of Coaching . . . ,* 1979), however, recognized several methodological flaws in the data analyses used in the first report and was more cautious in its conclusions. This report concluded that coaching improved performance by twenty to thirty points on both the verbal and mathematical sections of the SAT at one of the schools, but that the effects were negligible at the other. The 1979 FTC report concluded that coaching can be effective for those who do not score well on standardized tests.

Messick (1980b) reviewed the effect of coaching on the SAT and provided an excellent summary of the methodological problems. The main point is that students who choose to utilize a coaching school do so for a wide variety of reasons. There is not a random assignment of students to "coached" and "uncoached" conditions. That is, the students who have been coached are also those who were self-selected. They may be more highly motivated to obtain high scores, may have parents who want them to do well in school, and may differ in many other ways from those students who do not attend a coaching school. Thus, the improvement in SAT performance is due to the combined effects of coaching and self-selection. Messick (1980b) correctly notes that without an appropriate control group it is impossible to conclude that coaching is effective or not.

Messick and Jungeblut (1981) provided an additional insight into the effects of coaching on SAT scores. They examined improvement in SAT scores as a function of time and effort expended and concluded that each additional score increase requires increasing amounts of time and effort. The time needed to increase SAT performance by more than twenty to thirty points rapidly approaches that of full-time schooling. This conclusion appears especially true for the verbal section of the SAT. Pike (1978) has, however, suggested that short-term instruction may have some benefits for the mathematical section. Such instruction might be quite useful, for example, for students not currently enrolled in mathematics classes or

for those who had not taken any mathematics for a period of time.

As might be expected, however, taking the identical test twice does result in improved performance. In one study (Nevo, 1976) first-year college students were given two batteries of aptitude tests ten months apart. The study was designed to permit comparison of performance on two identical tests, two parallel forms, and two completely different tests. General test sophistication was not a significant factor in this study, but there was improvement in performance because of specific practice and item familiarization. Other investigators (Droege, 1966; Hutton, 1969; Longstaff, 1954) found that repeated administration of the same test or of a parallel form results in improved performance. Wing (1980) reported data from 66,303 test-takers in a nationwide federal employment program. Her results demonstrated small but consistent increases in performance in the second administration of alternate forms. The effects of practice appeared to be larger for items that can be solved by a systematic approach (arithmetic reasoning, geometric classifications) than for items requiring more general knowledge that has been previously acquired (vocabulary, comprehension). Since most tests are given only once to each person, practice is unlikely to influence scores for most commercially available aptitude and achievement tests. If the same test or even a parallel form is given to the same person, this fact should be considered in interpreting the score on the second administration.

Test-wiseness can have an important influence on scores obtained from maximum performance tests. However, the concept may not be directly relevant to tests of typical performance, such as personality inventories. Stricker (1969) concluded that test-wiseness is not an important source of distortion on the personality scales that he studied, but at least one investigation disagrees with his conclusion (Hess & Neville, 1977). However, since test-wiseness has been more commonly restricted to those cases in which people earn a higher or lower score than deserved by their ability, the concept does not seem as critical for typical performance tests—although personality inventories are subject to faking. This issue and other related ones will be examined in Chapters 9 and 10 in the discussion of projective and objective personality tests.

TEST ANXIETY. It would be a rare college professor who has not heard a student say something like "I don't know why I did so poorly on the exam. I knew the material, but I panicked and missed even the easy questions." The pervasive research finding is that persons who are anxious about taking tests score significantly lower than those who are not.

The term *test anxiety* was first introduced in the early 1950s by Mandler and Sarason (1952, 1953; S. B. Sarason & Mandler, 1952), and I. G. Sarason (1957, 1972), among many others, continued to explore its nature. I. G. Sarason (1972) developed a thirty-seven-item scale to measure test anxiety among college students. Representative items, all answered true by test-anxious students, are the following:

While taking an important exam I find myself thinking of how much brighter the other students are than I am.

If I were to take an intelligence test, I would worry a great deal before taking it.

While taking an important examination I perspire a great deal.

It is somewhat ironic that a test has been developed to assess how much anxiety a person has about taking tests. Other similar scales are available and are reviewed by Spielberger et al. (1976).

When confronted with an evaluation situation, the inherent threat in such an evaluative situation produces self-centered interfering responses (I. G. Sarason, 1975), which contribute to the poorer performance exhibited by persons who have high test anxiety. Investigators (Liebert & Morris, 1967; I. G. Sarason, 1975; S. B. Sarason and Mandler, 1952; Wine, 1971) tended to identify two components of the test anxiety response: an emotional reaction (for example, sweating) and a cognitive one (for example, worrying about not doing well). Spielberger et al. (1976, p. 323) continued this theoretical analysis:

Trait test anxiety may be conceptualized as reflecting individual differences in the tendency to perceive evaluative situations as threatening: high test-anxious persons respond to evaluative situations with elevations in state anxiety (A-state) and task-irrelevant, self-centered interfering worry. Elevations in A-state and worry responses both seem to contribute to the performance decrements that have been observed for high test-anxious persons. In test situations, the high levels of A-state that are evoked in trait test-anxious persons activate: (1) task-related error tendencies which compete with correct responses, and (2) task-irrelevant worry responses that distract the test-anxious individual from effective task performance.

The elimination of test anxiety among secondary and college students would undoubtedly make the educational process more enjoyable and effective. Behavioral approaches, such as desensitization, to modify or eliminate the emotional reaction have been attempted. Spielberger et al. (1976) state that twenty-nine of thirty-three studies reported success in reducing test anxiety. Although these approaches have been successful in reducing test anxiety, they have not been correspondingly successful in improving academic achievement and performance on cognitive tasks. Desensitization in combination with some form of counseling on study skills seems to be the most helpful and better than either alone (Mitchell & Ng, 1972).

GUESSING. Another troublesome problem with multiple-choice tests is what to do when examinees guess the answers to questions about which they are unsure. Even if responses were entirely random, examinees would be correct a certain proportion of the time just by chance. Thus, if a test has four alternatives per question and a subject does not even read the item, the subject would choose the correct alternative on one-fourth of the questions. If all examinees had the same willingness to guess or were instructed to guess when they did not know or were unsure of the answer, the problem would not be especially serious. Also, if tests were not highly speeded and had few omitted items, again guessing would present no great problem.

To compensate for guessing, formula scoring has been used. That is, a certain proportion of correct answers are deducted from an examinee's score because it is assumed that some of those correct answers were obtained by guessing. The basic assumption in developing this formula is that all alternatives are equally attractive or plausible if the examinee does not know the correct answer. If there are k alternatives per item, the probability of choosing the correct one by chance (guessing) is $1/k$. The probability of an incorrect guess is, therefore, $(k - 1)/k$. On the average, then, we expect examinees to be correct once for every $k - 1$ times they are wrong when they guess. The assumption of equally attractive alternatives leads to the following formula:

Estimated number correct =

$$\text{Right} - \frac{\text{Wrong}}{k - 1} \qquad (4\text{--}4)$$

Suppose, for example, an examinee answers fifty questions and has thirty-eight right and twelve wrong. If there were four alternatives per item, the estimated number correct would be

$$\text{Estimated number correct} = 38 - \frac{12}{4 - 1}$$
$$= 38 - \frac{12}{3}$$
$$= 38 - 4$$
$$= 34$$

Unfortunately, the basic assumptions on which the correction formula is based are undoubtedly largely incorrect. That is, each alternative is not an equally plausible choice for those who guess, and items cannot be divided into those that an examinee knows perfectly and those that the examinee does not know. Rowley and Traub (1977) conclude that the choice between formula scoring and number-right scoring will be decided by value judgment. Those persons who value number-right scoring will do so because the resulting score is unbiased by irrelevant personality factors that determine an examinee's willingness to guess. These investigators note that the empirical evidence for the effectiveness of formula scoring on validity and reliability is not strong, at least for unspeeded tests. Formula scoring will be selected by those who favor the reduction of error variance, since guessing introduces error into the test score. Diamond and Evans (1973) provided a good review on the correction-for-guessing formula, and Lord (1975) provided a different and elegant rationale for using the usual guessing formula.

Effects of Examiner

There is no doubt that the examiner can have a significant effect on test performance. Individually administered tests appear more subject to such effects than group tests. It also seems clear that children are more influenced by the examiner than adults, but this may be because less research has been done with adults. Tests of both maximum performance (for example, intelligence tests) and typical performance (personality tests) can be influenced by characteristics of the examiner. Following are several characteristics that could influence or have influenced test performance.

RACE. The possibility that examiners of one race testing people of another race could adversely affect performance is a reasonable hypothesis. Most research has focused on studies in which black children have been tested by white and black examiners. If race is an important variable, we would expect black children to score lower on intelligence tests, for example, when the examiner is white than when the examiner is black. As far as individually administered intelligence tests are concerned, Sattler (1970) concluded that there was no convincing evidence that racial differences between the examinee and examiner were important. Shuey (1966) in her review of the literature also concluded that white examiners did not lead to poorer performance of black examinees. Sattler (1974) also noted that relatively few studies have been done to assess the importance of racial differences between examinee and examiner.

Jensen (1980) reviewed and summarized the results of thirty studies published between 1936 and 1977. To address the question adequately, a study should have examinees of each race tested by examiners of each race. If race is a critical variable, we would expect examinees to do better when tested by an examiner of the same race than when tested by an examiner of a different race. Of the thirty studies reviewed by Jensen, only seventeen were adequately designed. Jensen's (p. 602) conclusion is that the results of all these studies indicate that the race of the examiner is not an important variable in determining performance on tests of mental ability. Other authors have reached the same conclusion based on thorough reviews of the literature (Graziano et al., 1982; Sattler & Gwynne, 1982).

SEX. As was hypothesized with race, one might expect that examinees tested by examiners of the same sex would do better than those tested by examiners of the opposite sex. There appear to be no systematic trends because of the sex of the examiner in intelligence tests of children (Sattler, 1974). One study (Black & Dana, 1977), for example, found that female examiners elicited higher scores on the Wechsler Intelligence Scale for Children, whereas another study (Cieutat & Flick, 1967), using the Stanford-Binet Intelligence Scale, found no differences attributable to the examiner's sex. Even when studies are well designed and find statistically significant effects because of the sex of the examiner, the effects appear to be small in size (Samuels, 1977).

Rumenik et al. (1977) reviewed experimenter sex effects in the psychological literature. Their conclusion is that the results from personality and intelligence testing are mixed. There is some hint that an examinee's response to test items of a sexual nature may be affected by the sex of the examiner. Milner and Moses (1972) found, for example, that sexual associations were repressed with opposite-sex test administrators. Rumenik et al. (p. 874) concluded that no clear trends have emerged with respect to sexual effects in personality or intelligence testing. As was probably true for examiners of the same race, examiners of the same sex probably differ considerably concerning their skill in administering tests. This large within-group variability probably contributes to the lack of systematic trends in the effects of the examiner's sex on test performance.

EXPECTANCY. Previous information given to examiners can influence their perceptions of or judgments about an individual. That is, certain expectancies are produced in the examiner and these expectancies, rather than the actual performance of the examinee, determine or greatly influence the test scores that are assigned. Rosenthal (1966) demonstrated that expectancy can influence experimental results in a variety of areas of psychological research. It is less clear, however, that expectancy is an important influence in test scoring and administration.

Rosenthal and Jacobson (1968) in their book *Pygmalion in the Classroom* claimed to have demonstrated that expectancies did influence the IQ scores received by elementary school children. In this study, elementary school teachers were given the names of several children who were expected to show a marked increase in cognitive ability during the year because of their scores on a special pretest. Actually, the names were determined randomly. Thus, any significantly greater cognitive growth demonstrated by the children named over that of the other children in the class could be attributed to the teacher's positive expectancies. Those children were expected to do well and they did. Although Rosenthal's results apparently supported the self-fulfilling prophecy, the study has since been severely criticized on methodological grounds (for example, Elashoff & Snow, 1971; Snow, 1969; Thorndike, 1968). Cronbach (1975) summarizes the study and resulting controversy by stating that it merits no consideration as research. Expectancy, at least in teachers and others, has apparently not been demonstrated to affect IQ scores (Jensen, 1980).

However, studies more specific to the testing situation have demonstrated expectancy effects. Sattler (1974) summarizes several studies that show that ambiguous responses on the Wechsler Intelligence Scale for Children are given more credit when they supposedly come from bright examinees than from dull ones. Such studies present groups of "examiners" with the same record so that the examiners do not actually conduct the testing. When examiners actually test subjects, halo effects appear to occur less often, although several studies have found such effects (Jensen, 1980; Sattler, 1974).

OTHER VARIABLES. One can easily imagine many other characteristics of examiners that could influence test performance: experience, personality traits, style (for example, warm versus cold), and familiarity with the examinee. The evidence regarding these characteristics suggests they can be important, but it is extremely difficult to specify exactly when they will influence test results. By careful attention to details of administration and after suitable training, these variables should not significantly influence results.

Although this discussion has focused mainly on tests of ability, personality tests can also be influenced by situational and interpersonal variables, as Masling (1960) noted, in reviewing research on projective tests. Of course, given a projective test like the Rorschach, its unstructured nature almost guarantees that subjects will be more sensitive to any other cues available in the testing situation. Typical performance tests are perhaps more easily distorted as a function of the total testing situation simply because there is no "correct" response to most items. These problems in personality assessment are considered in Chapters 9 and 10.

SUMMARY

Test administration and scoring represent the first steps in obtaining data for making judgments and decisions about people. In the following chapters we will consider a variety of specific tests and will describe the methods for administering and scoring most of them. The information in Chapters 3 and 4 should provide a basis for understanding and evaluating all the tests that we discuss.

5

Intelligence and the Stanford-Binet Scale

The concept of intelligence has undoubtedly been used implicitly by human beings for a long time. Surprisingly, however, explicit measures of intelligence were not developed until relatively recently. The first practical intelligence test was developed in France by Alfred Binet and Theodore Simon between 1905 and 1911. A modern form of this test is still being used, the Stanford-Binet Intelligence Scale. In this chapter we will first consider various definitions of and approaches to intelligence and then will focus our discussion on the Stanford-Binet Intelligence Scale. In Chapter 6 we will cover the various Wechsler scales of intelligence. Additional individually administered tests of mental ability will be discussed in Chapter 7. Chapter 8 will be devoted to group tests of mental ability and academic achievement.

Before we consider possible definitions of intelligence, we should indicate that there are several terms virtually synonymous with *intelligence: Mental ability, cognitive ability, and scholastic aptitude.* Also, tests that measure intelligence are maximum performance tests. Thus, items on intelligence tests have correct answers, and subjects are encouraged to score as high as possible. Generally speaking, the more ability one has, the better one is regarded in the United States. In particular, a deficit in intelligence or mental ability limits how well a person can function in our technological society.

INTELLIGENCE

Intelligence is one of the most highly studied areas in psychology. The *Psychological Abstracts* in the years 1967 through August 1980 referred to 7,045 publications dealing with some aspect of intelligence. Despite this voluminous literature, the concept of human intelligence remains, in many ways, as mysterious now as it has ever been. In fact, psychologists are better at measuring intelligence than at understanding it. This lack of understanding is reflected in the many definitions that have been proposed.

Definitions of Intelligence

The *American Heritage Dictionary of the English Language* (1976, p. 682) defines *intelligence* as (1) the capacity to acquire and apply knowledge, (2) the faculty of thought and reason, and (3) superior powers of mind. Psychologists have not progressed very far in sharpening this definition. To illustrate the diversity of opinions on what constitutes intelligence, we will cite a sizeable number of examples.

Binet defined intelligence as "the tendency to take and maintain a definite direction; the capacity to make adaptations for the purpose of attaining a desired end; and the power of auto-criticism" (Terman, 1916, p. 45). Thus, an intelligent person, according to Binet, is one whose activity is purposeful and goal-directed but also one who is flexible and adaptable.

In 1921, in a symposium on intelligence and its measurement, fourteen leading researchers were asked to summarize current definitions of *intelligence* and suggest where research might be headed. We provide some of these definitions from more than half a century ago.

Thorndike (1921) suggested that the intellect in general is the power of making good responses from the point of view of truth or fact. The power of making good responses to abstract qualities and relations rather than gross total facts, and to ideas rather than direct experiences, may be called the more intellectual variety of intellect.

For Terman (1921), an individual is intelligent in proportion as he or she is able to carry on abstract thinking.

Colvin (1921) stated that an individual possesses intelligence insofar as one has learned or can learn to adjust oneself to one's environment.

Pintner (1921) defined intelligence as the ability of the individual to adapt adequately to relatively new situations in life, which fundamentally leads us back to the general modifiability of the nervous system.

One can contrast the opinions in the 1921 symposium with those from a more recent symposium held in 1974 at the University of Pittsburgh. Resnick (1976) edited a surprising mixture of papers from this symposium in which both experimental psychologists and psychometricians address the nature of human intelligence.

Some papers suggest that intelligence can be understood in terms of underlying, more basic cognitive processes (Hunt, 1976).

Simon (1976) emphasizes computer simulation of complex tasks as one method for potentially understanding components of human intelligence.

In viewing human intelligence from an ethological perspective, Charlesworth (1976, p. 149) sees intelligent behavior "as having two major characteristics: (1) it is behavior that generally aids individuals in their attempts to adapt to problematic situations resulting from imbalance in their interactions with the environment; and (2) it is behavior having certain characteristics which compel us to conclude that cognitive processes are organizing and controlling it."

Resnick and Glaser (1976) argue that a major aspect of intelligence is the ability to solve problems. They further indicate that intelligence "can be viewed as the ability to acquire new behavior in the absence of direct or complete instruction, and that this ability involves processes that can facilitate the transition from simple to more complex cognitive performance."

Clearly, the evidence suggests that psychologists have never agreed on a single definition of *intelligence*. As might be expected, there are even more possible definitions available. We wish to note three more definitions from researchers who have strongly influenced the contemporary measurement and study of intelligence:

Wechsler (1944, p. 3), a psychologist who developed a series of widely used intelligence scales, defined *intelligence* as the "aggregate or global capacity of the individual to act purposefully, to think rationally, and to deal effectively with his environment."

Jensen (1969, p. 19) defined *intelligence* as a "capacity for abstract reasoning and problem solving."

Elkind (1969), in representing the ideas of Jean Piaget, the famous Swiss developmental psychologist, says that "for Piaget the essence of intelligence lies in the individual's reasoning capacities."

At about the same time as the 1921 symposium, a famous operational definition of *intelligence* appeared. Boring (1923), a psychologist especially noted for his book on the *History of Experimental Psychology*, stated simply that intelligence is what IQ tests measure. Interestingly enough, in the 1974 symposium, in summarizing the points of view on human intelligence, Voss (1976, p. 309) concluded, only somewhat facetiously, that *"intelligence may be defined as what the participants report they measure."* To understand the meaning of intelligence, then, is to understand how it is measured. The score on an intelligence test has meaning to the extent it is related to other variables of interest or to the extent it is useful. If an intelligence test has predictive validity, a user need not necessarily be interested in its construct validity. The construct of intelligence is a theoretical explanation of the test score, perhaps, for example, by referring to more basic cognitive processes that are essential for answering particular items. For our purposes, then, we wish to focus on the more commonly used tests of general mental ability. We shall concentrate on the manner in which these tests measure human intelligence and how the resulting scores are used.

Conceptual Approaches to Intelligence

The multitude of definitions of *intelligence* that we have cited illustrate the diversity of viewpoints regarding its nature. It is a construct rather than a directly observable characteristic of individuals. It is possible, however, to note different approaches to the study of intelligence, which we will now briefly discuss.

HEREDITY (GENETIC) VERSUS ENVIRONMENT (CULTURAL). A fundamental question for any characteristic of human beings is whether that characteristic is genetically or environmentally determined. For many characteristics, both influences are probably important, although one component may be more important than the other. In other words, the biology of human beings is an important determinant of our behavior; but our behavior is also influenced by learning and culture. The color of our eyes is genetically determined, and we cannot modify this characteristic. However, the particular language that we speak depends entirely on the culture in which we are reared, although the capacity for language may be biologically based. Is intelligence, then, largely fixed at birth or is it largely modifiable by interaction with the environment? The social, political, and human consequences of this debate have been controversial, bitter, and important. For example, *if* intelligence were entirely determined by heredity, remedial or early intervention programs would be worthless. Block and Dworkin (1976) edited a book, *The IQ Controversy*, that reprints a large number of articles bearing on the heritability of intelligence and the social and political aspects of the controversy. Their book is a good place to begin for anyone especially interested in this subject. For those interested in a recent debate between two persons holding very divergent opinions see Eysenck versus Kamin (1981). We will examine these issues in Chapter 14.

When intelligence tests were first developed, it was assumed that intelligence was innate. That is, a child's intelligence was determined by the genes inherited from the child's parents. This view gradually changed to reflect a stronger environmental position. The "nature-nurture" problem remains with us today, although the debate seems to be over the relative rather than exclusive importance of each component (see Vernon, 1979, for a lucid account of these issues).

Hebb (1949) attempted to resolve some of the controversy by conceptualizing two different kinds of intelligence: Intelligence A and Intelligence B. Intelligence A is the basic potentiality of the organism to learn and adapt to the environment. It is genetically determined and is a product of the central nervous system. Such potential is subject to environmental influences—biological, physical, and social—but the limits of its development are biologically fixed. Intelligence B, on the other hand, is a product of genetic potential and environmental interaction. It is what we can estimate, perhaps by using many different tests of intelligence. Intelligence B is still perhaps best thought of as a theoretical term or construct, since it represents *general intelligence,* which is not specific to the manner in which it is assessed. Intelligence A cannot be measured by any techniques currently available. Even newborn infants, for example, will be influenced by prenatal environmental conditions. Hebb's Intelligence A and Intelligence B are similar to a biologist's distinction between genotype and phenotype.

Vernon (1969) suggested the addition of Intelligence C to Hebb's two types. Intelligence C is the actual sample of "intelligent" behavior obtained from a particular test. For example, Intelligence C could be the IQ score obtained on the Stanford-Binet Intelligence Scale. Any test can measure only a limited number of cognitive skills. Thus, Intelligence C scores will differ from test to test. They also can be thought of as one instance or sample from Intelligence B.

R. B. Cattell (1963, 1971), whose work could also be considered under psychometric approaches to intelligence, identified two aspects of intelligence that appear to be similar to Hebb's Intelligence A and Intelligence B: *fluid intelligence* and *crystallized intelligence.* Fluid intelligence has the following characteristics: (1) requires adaptation to new situations, (2) depends more on speed of responding, (3) reaches a maximum at 14 to 15 years of age, (4) appears to be more constant and biologically determined, (5) is more directly physiologically (genetically) determined, (6) changes less over short periods of time because of its physiological basis, (7) will be more adversely effected by brain damage, (8) is best measured by culture-fair tests, and (9) is more important in influencing the rate of learning in completely new areas (Cattell, 1963). Crystallized intelligence, on the other

hand, tends to have the opposite characteristics. That is, crystallized intelligence is a result of the interaction between fluid intelligence and the environment, and it is greatly influenced by culture, education, and past experiences. Cattell also believes that most intelligence tests measure both fluid and crystallized intelligence. He advocated the use of culture-fair tests, those using novel materials and emphasizing perceptual relations, as the best measure of fluid intelligence. To oversimplify, fluid intelligence is natural ability that does not depend on acquired knowledge; crystallized intelligence does depend on acquired knowledge and on fluid intelligence.

PIAGET. Another conceptual approach to intelligence is that of Jean Piaget, a Swiss developmental psychologist. Piaget's approach is biologically based but is also developmental in nature. His position has had considerable influence on the study of cognitive development. Piaget believed that children proceed through stages of cognitive growth as a function of age. Children of different ages display qualitatively different ways of thinking. Piaget wrote voluminously on his theory of cognitive development. His writing has a philosophical character quite different from the approach of most psychologists in the United States. Flavell (1963) wrote a comprehensive and comprehensible book on Piaget's developmental psychology and also a text (1977) on cognitive development that refers extensively to Piaget's theory of intelligence. Books written by Piaget are also available but more difficult to read (Piaget, 1950, 1954; Piaget & Inhelder, 1969, 1973). Although there has been some interest in constructing tests to assess a child's Piagetian developmental status (Uzgiris & Hunt, 1975), his theories have not yet widely influenced the development of intelligence tests.

PSYCHOMETRIC AND FACTOR ANALYTIC. The psychometric approach to the study of intelligence rests on the analysis of correlations among mental tests. Despite rather diverse content, most measures of mental ability tend to be positively correlated. We often observe among our friends and acquaintances that those who have high levels of ability in one area tend to have correspondingly high levels in other areas. Spearman (1927) was perhaps the first to note this observation in a systematic fashion. He called the single factor that produced the intercorrelations among mental tests g, standing for *general factor*. It also represents in a statistical way the concept of general intelligence. Spearman was a student of Karl Pearson, the English statistician who developed the correlation coefficient. These early psychometricians and those who followed have all been interested in studying individual differences. The correlation coefficient (r), a measure of linear relationship between two variables, has been their most commonly used statistic. The statistical technique by which the intercorrelations among many mental tests are analyzed is called *factor analysis*. Several excellent texts are available on this statistical technique, but they all require a rather sophisticated mathematical background (Gorsuch, 1974; Harman, 1976; Mulaik, 1972). The basis of factor analysis is to discover the underlying structure in a table of intercorrelations. Is there a single influence or factor that can explain the intercorrelations or are there many such influences or factors? In the case of intelligence, is there one general factor that adequately explains or accounts for the intercorrelations, or are many "ability" factors needed to explain the intercorrelations among mental tests? Psychometricians are still studying this fundamental question. Another way of stating the problem is to ask if a single IQ score tells us almost everything we need to know about a person's level of cognitive functioning, or do we need many scores to describe completely a person's cognitive abilities?

Spearman (1927) originally hypothesized a two-factor theory of intelligence. As already noted, he called the general factor g. The second factor, s, was specific to each test. Thus, each mental test measures some-

thing in common with all other mental tests (g) and something unique to that test.

The next step was taken by Thompson (1939), another English psychologist. Although keeping the general factor, he thought that *group* factors also existed. Thus, instead of a mental test containing variance due only to g and s, it also shared variance with several other tests. Through the admission of group factors, the importance of g is deemphasized. That is, group factors suggest that there are important aspects of intelligence not adequately represented in a single score.

It was left for psychologists in the United States to eliminate the general factor from the model. Thurstone (1938) was one of the first to do this. He found seven group factors in his analysis, which he called *primary mental abilities*, and no general factor. The factors included number, word fluency, verbal meaning, memory, reasoning, space, and perceptual speed. The interpretation of the factors was made on the basis of the tests that correlated with each one. Scores on each of these primary mental abilities could be obtained by combining the scores from the tests contributing to that factor.

Guilford (1967) perhaps pushed the factor analytic approach the farthest from g, or general intelligence. His model of human ability, called the *structure of intellect*, identified three major ways in which tests of cognitive ability can be classified. These are summarized as follows:

1. Contents: figural, symbolic, semantic, behavioral.
2. Operations: cognitive, memory, divergent production, convergent production, evaluation.
3. Products: units, classes, relations, systems, transformations, implications.

A vocabulary test, in which a subject is given a word to define, would be classified as follows: semantic in content, cognition as the mental operation needed, and units (words) as the product used. Guilford's model thus implies that "intelligence" can be divided into $4 \times 5 \times 6 = 120$ abilities. Guilford and Hoepfner (1971) claim to have evidence for ninety-eight of these hypothesized ability factors, although others are less convinced (Eysenck, 1973; Horn & Knapp, 1973).

The psychometric approach has thus left the unanswered question of whether or not intelligence is a uni- or multidimensional trait. As a statistical technique, factor analysis permits many abilities to emerge, but it cannot demonstrate that such abilities are necessarily more useful than a single score. McNemar (1964), among others, strongly argues that a single score is most useful. Jensen (1980) also suggests that the evidence supports g, since methods exist for reducing multiple factor solutions to a single, underlying factor.

It is possible that heterogeneous groups may tend to produce a single factor of general intelligence whereas more homogeneous groups produce several ability factors (Maloney & Ward, 1976, p. 190). Thus, for example, Guilford's structure of intellect model with its large number of dimensions was developed mainly through Air Force recruits and college students. Such homogeneous groups may largely eliminate the possibility of observing a large general factor. Using children of several chronological ages, however, may make a factor of general intelligence more likely to appear. It is possible that general intelligence is a concept more meaningful with young children than with adults. For example, it appears that for adults it is possible to separate verbal ability from mathematical ability. Such a distinction could be useful in predicting success in various training programs. Such abilities are, however, due to previous experience and education. They are not innate.

In the remainder of this chapter we will describe the development of the Stanford-Binet Intelligence Scale in considerable detail. We do this because this test and its resulting IQ scores were almost synonymous with intelligence for many years. Other tests of intelligence, as they were developed, were often validated against the Stanford-Binet. The test is still widely used, and we discuss the content and characteristics of the current version.

STANFORD-BINET INTELLIGENCE SCALE

Alfred Binet was born in Nice, France, on July 8, 1857, and died on October 18, 1911. He was a prodigious scholar, publishing some 336 books and articles during his career. (Wolf, 1973, has written a comprehensive and interesting biography of Binet.) The original impetus for Binet's intelligence scale came from the requirements of universal education. The problem was one that we still face today—how do we provide appropriate education for retarded children? Thus, Binet's first step was to identify in an objective fashion those children who were

FIGURE 5-1 Alfred Binet (1857–1911) was a French psychologist who originated the first practical test of intelligence. (Archives of the History of American Psychology, University of Akron.)

retarded and assign them to special classes. To do this, he and his colleague, Theodore Simon, recognized that the simple, sensory tasks that other experimental psychologists were using were not adequate. What was needed were tasks more complex in nature to permit wide individual differences in mental functioning to appear.

Historical Development

ORIGINAL VERSIONS FROM BINET AND SIMON. The first scale appeared in 1905. As suggested, it was developed to classify retarded children and to distinguish between normal and retarded children. The scale consisted of thirty tests arranged in order of difficulty. In this original scale and in all its subsequent modifications and revisions, the term *test* refers to an item or group of items of a particular kind (for example, naming objects or tracing mazes). The simplest test was visual coordination, in which the subject responded to a lighted match moved slowly before his or her eyes. The ninth test was naming objects in a picture (this test being the upper limit of a normal child of age three). Test fourteen was giving definitions of familiar objects (for example, *house, horse*) and was the *limiting* test for a normal child of age five. The last test was giving distinctions between abstract terms such as *liking* and *respecting*. The entire 1905 scale is given in Sattler (1982, pp. 100-101) and Edwards (1971, pp. 25-26). This early scale was successful in distinguishing between the academically successful child and one doing poorly in school, using school marks as the indicator of academic performance. Only fifty children were used in the standardization sample.

In 1908, a revision of the 1905 scale was published. The 1908 version was the first age scale. The tests were graded by years— the youngest age level being three and the oldest thirteen. The tests at any age level should be passed by intellectually average children of that age. As Wolf (1973, p. 190) notes, the shift in emphasis from the 1905 scale to the 1908 scale is clear in the change

of titles. The 1905 scale was called "New methods for the diagnosis of the intellectual level of the abnormal," whereas the 1908 scale was called "The development of intelligence in children." The revision was indeed extensive, and many items were added. The items were placed at various age levels based on empirical results and not because of theoretical conceptions. The 1908 scale also introduced the idea of *mental age,*[*] which was used to identify various categories of mental retardation. Thus, an eight-year-old who has a mental age of six is more severely retarded than an eight-year-old who has a mental age of seven. The labels for these categories are no longer in use (for example, idiots were mental age levels zero to two, imbeciles two to seven, and morons seven and above). The 1908 scale also had a much larger "standardization" sample—203 children were tested.

In 1911, Binet, without the help of Simon, published the final version of his scale. He did some additional testing, although the number tested was not clear. Certain tests were moved to different age levels, and fifteen-year and adult levels were added. There were fifty-four tests in all. The 1911 scale also established the *basal year,* the highest age at which all tests were passed, and granted fractional credit for all tests passed at older age levels. Terman (1916) listed the tests for various ages in Binet's 1911 scale. There were generally five tests per age level. The following are tests for several ages to illustrate the kinds of performance required:

AGE THREE:

1. Points to nose, eyes, and mouth.
2. Repeats two digits.
3. Enumerates objects in a picture.
4. Gives family name.
5. Repeats a sentence of six syllables.

---

[*]According to Wolf (1973, p. 203), Binet in fact used the term *mental level* rather than *mental age.* The latter term was introduced by the German psychologist Wilhelm Stern in 1911.

AGE SIX:

1. Distinguishes between morning and afternoon.
2. Defines familiar words in terms of use.
3. Copies a diamond.
4. Counts thirteen pennies.
5. Distinguishes pictures of ugly and pretty faces.

AGE TWELVE:

1. Resists suggestion.
2. Composes one sentence containing three given words.
3. Names sixty words in three minutes.
4. Defines certain abstract words.
5. Discovers the sense of a disarranged sentence.

These tests or revisions of them have remained in the scale until the present time.

Binet's 1905 and 1908 scales were translated into English and made available to American psychologists by Whipple (1910). The 1911 scale was similarly translated by Town (1914). Interestingly enough, although Binet's tests were not widely accepted in France, they soon found a ready audience in the United States. Goddard (1908, 1911) used the tests in institutions for the retarded, and Terman (1906) based an early study on "genius and stupidity" on Binet's work. Terman and Childs (1912) administered a translation of Binet and Simon's 1908 scale to 396 children in and around Stanford University. This later study led to the development of the Stanford-Binet Intelligence Scale, to which we now turn.

1916 STANFORD-BINET SCALE (FIRST REVISION). Lewis M. Terman published the first version of the Stanford-Binet Scale in 1916. Terman noted that Binet was the first to use age standards or norms in the measurement of intelligence. Terman (1916, p. 41) believed that Binet's ingenious idea of an age-grade scale for measuring intelligence ranked, from the practical point of view, as the most important in all the history of psychology. A second contribution was that the Binet scales were designed to test

FIGURE 5–2 Lewis M. Terman (1877–1956) was an American psychologist who revised Binet's test of intelligence for use in the United States in 1916 and participated in later revisions of this test, the Stanford-Binet Intelligence Scale, as well. (Courtesy News Service, Stanford University.)

the higher, more complex mental processes rather than the simpler sensory processes. The Binet scale undertook to measure the general level of intelligence rather than its many specific aspects.

The Stanford-Binet Scale (S-B) was an extensive revision and restandardization of Binet's original work. The 1916 revision consisted of ninety tests: six at each age level from age three to ten, eight at age twelve, six at "average adult," and six at "superior adult," along with sixteen alternate tests to be used as substitutes if a regular test could not be used for some reason. Terman also tested 2,300 subjects—1,700 normal children, 200 defective and superior children, and more than 400 adults. The actual test norms were based on a sample of approximately 1,000 children and 400 adults. By contemporary standards, the sampling procedure was not adequate, but at the time it was an enormous improvement over previous work. The 1916 revision used the intelligence quotient (IQ) as the ratio of mental age to chronological age multiplied by 100. One of the goals in choosing tests was to have the median IQ of children at each age equal 100. That is, on the average, the mental age should equal the chronological age.

The 1916 scale included, for the first time, a detailed guide for administering and scoring each test. Examiners were cautioned that unless they followed a standardized procedure the "tests lose their significance." The instructions also emphasized the importance of establishing rapport, and the examiner was cautioned not to show displeasure at a response, "however absurd it may be." It is clear that Terman expected the 1916 S-B to be administered and scored by trained examiners.

This earliest version of the S-B also attempted to address the reliability and validity of IQs. For example, Terman (1916, p. 75) reported a correlation of .48 between IQ and teachers' rankings of intelligence. He also presented many individual cases of various IQs along with what we would now call their behavioral correlates. He thus concluded that no child with an IQ between 70 and 80 was able to do satisfactory school work in the age-appropriate grade (p. 104).

1937 REVISION. The 1916 S-B had several major faults. For one thing, abilities at the extremes (below four or above average adult) were inadequately sampled. Above age ten, the scale yielded scores that were progressively too low. After many years of research, a number of the tests were found to be unsatisfactory for a variety of reasons. The lack of precision in the instructions for administration and scoring was also a weakness. Finally, the cultural changes in the twenty-one years between 1916 and 1937 were undoubtedly great and needed to be reflected in a revised S-B.

Maud Merrill collaborated with Terman in revising the S-B. The 1937 S-B consisted of two parallel forms, Form L and Form M,

FIGURE 5–3 Maud M. Merrill (1888–1978) was an American psychologist who collaborated with Lewis Terman in revising the Stanford-Binet Intelligence Scale in 1937 and 1960. (Courtesy News Service, Stanford University.)

each having 129 subtests. This revision remained an age scale, using age standards of performance and assuming that general intelligence is a trait that develops with age. The primary goal was to select subtests in such a way that the mean mental age of a representative group of children closely approximated their chronological age. Thus, at each age, the mean IQ should be 100. In the development of the revised scale two problems were apparent. First, a representative sample of persons had to be selected at each age, and second, the subtests had to be assigned to the proper age level. Terman and Merrill were thus faced with sampling both tasks (age-appropriate intelligent behaviors) and people (Terman & Merrill, 1937).

Items were initially selected for three reasons: (1) they correlated with acceptable criteria of intelligence; (2) they allowed an increased percentage of children to pass them as a function of mental or chronological age; (3) they differentiated, essentially, between the mean mental age of those passing and those failing the item. Of course, practical considerations, such as ease of administration, objectivity in scoring, and variety of content, were also important. In the final statistical analysis, the items included had to show an increase in percent passing for each successive age level and had to correlate sufficiently high with the total score to indicate that the item was measuring what the total scale was measuring (Terman & Merrill, 1973).

The final standardization sample consisted of 3,814 native-born white subjects. Approximately 100 subjects were tested at each half-year interval from 1½ to 5½ years, 200 at each age from 6 to 14, and 100 at each age from 15 to 18. At each age, the group was evenly divided between the two sexes. Subjects had to be within one month of a birthday to be included in the age group, a procedure that gave very homogeneous groups for each age level. The 1937 S-B made extensive efforts to secure a sample representative of U.S. society, including such factors as geographical location, socioeconomic status, urban versus rural residence, and types of elementary or high schools attended. The standardization sample, however, did contain somewhat more subjects from the higher socioeconomic levels and urban areas than would be appropriate, based on the 1930 census figures. It also contained no blacks.

The 1937 S-B proved to be a valuable test and was used extensively by psychologists. The construction procedures were largely successful in that at each age level the average IQ was 100 with a standard deviation of about 16. This meant that IQs had approximately the same meaning at each age. Administration and scoring instructions were improved. The test was quite reliable, although it was more reliable for older than

TABLE 5-1 Distribution of Stanford-Binet IQs for the 1937 Standardization Group

IQ	Percent	Classification
160–169	0.03	
150–159	0.2	Very superior
140–149	1.1	
130–139	3.1	Superior
120–129	8.2	
110–119	18.1	High average
100–109	23.5	Normal or average
90–99	23.0	
80–89	14.5	Low average
70–79	5.6	Borderline defective
60–69	2.0	
50–59	0.4	Mentally defective
40–49	0.2	
30–39	0.03	

From Terman & Merrill, 1973, p. 18. Reproduced by permission of Houghton Mifflin Company

for younger children and for lower than higher IQs.

The 1937 S-B provided a means of empirically classifying IQs. Table 5-1 gives the distribution of IQs in the 1937 standardization sample (Terman & Merrill, 1973, p. 18). The distribution is surprisingly normal in shape.

1960 STANFORD-BINET. The 1960 S-B incorporated the best items from the L and M Forms of the 1937 scale. The scale was not restandardized, and the 1937 standardization group was retained. The 4,498 subjects tested from 1950 to 1954 were used to determine changes in the difficulty of the subtests which were eliminated or relocated if they changed significantly in difficulty. Other subtests were eliminated or replaced if they were no longer suitable because of cultural changes. The 1960 scale remained an age scale, and the subtests retained had to correlate highly with total score and demonstrate an increased percentage passing at successive mental age levels. The result was 142 tests (Terman & Merrill, 1960).

Besides the changes in content, statistical innovations were introduced. First, the IQs were adjusted for the slight differences in variability at the various age levels. The revised IQs are deviation IQs, standard scores with a mean of 100 and a standard deviation of 16. The MA/CA ratio is no longer used. Second, the tables were extended to include chronological ages seventeen and eighteen, a recognition that mental growth as measured by the S-B extends beyond age sixteen.

1972 STANFORD-BINET RESTANDARD-IZATION. As indicated, the 1960 S-B did not develop new norms, but in the school year 1971-1972, a new standardization group was tested. The S-B content remained unchanged with two minor exceptions. Thus, any changes in performance could be attributed to differences in the characteristics of the subjects tested. Approximately 100 subjects at each of twenty-one age levels were tested, a total of approximately 2,100 subjects. Finding and individually testing this many subjects was a massive undertaking. The normative testing was accomplished in conjunction with a large-scale norming of a group test, the Cognitive Abilities Test. Stratified sampling was used to obtain students representative of the country as a whole, and about 20,000 students per age group were tested. Seven communities provided test records so that the S-B could be administered. The group test was given in grades three through twelve. Younger siblings were identified from among those tested and chosen in a stratified manner based on verbal scores on the Cognitive Abilities Test. In this way, a range of S-B scores was reasonably assured. Although a description of the final standardization sample is not presented, it was intended to be representative of the U.S. population. Minority subjects were included in the 1972 standardization sample, whereas they were not included in the 1937 group.

The 1972 norms represent the most appropriate ones to evaluate persons tested with the S-B. Again presented as deviation scores, IQs have a mean of 100 and standard deviation of 16.

As can be seen in Table 5-2, the performance of the 1972 group was better than the 1937 group at every age. Assuming the 1937 IQs averaged about 100, it is evident that the 1972 standardization sample had improved performance most markedly at preschool ages. The average preschool child in 1972 received an IQ ten points higher than the 1937 counterpart. What cultural changes could have produced these differences? One thinks immediately of television and better health (nutrition, prenatal care, preventive medicine). On the other hand, maybe children of the 1970s were simply more familiar with games or tests.

The roots of the current scale go back to the earliest versions developed by Binet and

TABLE 5-2 Smoothed Estimates of Means and Standard Deviations of Stanford-Binet IQs for the 1972 Standardization Sample

Age	Mean	SD
2–0	110.4	15.7
2–6	110.6	15.9
3–0	110.7	16.0
3–6	110.8	16.1
4–0	110.7	16.2
4–6	110.4	16.3
5–0	109.7	16.4
5–6	108.4	16.6
6–0	107.1	16.7
7–0	105.0	17.0
8–0	103.3	17.2
9–0	102.1	17.2
10–0	101.9	16.9
11–0	102.2	16.6
12–0	102.5	16.4
13–0	102.9	16.5
14–0	103.3	16.8
15–0	103.9	17.2
16–0	104.7	17.6
17–0	105.7	17.9
18–0	106.9	18.0

From Terman & Merrill, 1973, p. 359. Reproduced by permission of Houghton Mifflin Company

Simon. We have gone into considerable detail on the development of the S-B for several reasons: (1) it illustrates the type of procedures used with an age scale; (2) it illustrates the difficulties in standardizing a test; and (3) the S-B has been so closely identified with the concept of IQ.

Characteristics

CONTENT. In content, the version of the S-B currently in use is virtually identical to the 1960 scale. The scale is organized by age level. The twenty age levels available include the years two through fourteen; "average adult"; three levels of "superior adult"; and half-year levels at ages two, three, and four. There are six tests per age level except for "average adult," which has eight. One alternate test is provided at each age level to be used if one of the regular tests is spoiled. There are 142 tests available, although some are used at several age levels with different standards for scoring.

Examples of the tasks used at three different age levels are given in Table 5-3. The Vocabulary Test is an example of a test that

TABLE 5-3 Subtests at three age levels of the Stanford-Binet Intelligence Scale

Year Three	*Year Six*	*Year Twelve*
1. *Stringing Beads.* Beads of three different shapes are to be strung on a shoelace. Subject must string at least four beads within two minutes to pass.	1. *Vocabulary.* Subject is asked to define a series of words of increasing difficulty. Six or more must be identified to pass. Testing stops when six consecutive words are failed.	1. *Vocabulary.* Same subtest as year six except fifteen or more words must be identified to pass.
2. *Picture Vocabulary.* Eighteen cards with pictures of common objects are presented, and subjects are asked what they are called. Ten or more must be identified to pass.	2. *Differences.* The subject is asked to state a difference between two animals, two types of footwear, and two common substances. Two or more must be correct in order to pass.	2. *Verbal Absurdities II.* Five statements, each of which contains an inconsistency, are read to the subject. The subject must identify what is foolish about the statement. Four or more must be correctly identified to pass.
3. *Block Building: Bridge.* The examiner builds a "bridge" from three blocks. The subject must build one exactly like it.	3. *Mutilated Pictures.* The subject is shown five pictures of things that have parts missing and is asked to identify what is missing. Four or more must be answered correctly to pass.	3. *Picture Absurdities II.* A picture, which contains an inconsistency, is shown to the subject, who must identify what is foolish about the picture.
4. *Picture Memories.* Four cards with animal pictures are used. The subject is shown the picture of an animal. The picture is then removed and the subject must find the same animal among four others from memory. One or more must be correctly identified to pass.	4. *Number Concepts.* The subject is asked to select various numbers (three, ten, six, nine, seven) of blocks from among the twelve available. Four or more correct responses are required to pass.	4. *Repeating Five Digits Reversed.* Three series of five digits each are presented and the subject must recall them correctly in reversed order. At least one series must be correctly repeated backwards to pass.
5. *Copying a Circle.* The subject must copy a circle, using a pencil.	5. *Opposite Analogies II.* The subject is asked to complete four analogies of the type "A ball is round; a block is. . . ." Three or more must be answered correctly to pass.	5. *Abstract Words I.* The subject is asked to define four abstract words, such as *jealousy*. Three or more must be correctly identified to pass.
6. *Drawing a Vertical Line.* The examiner draws a vertical line and asks the subject to make one like it.	6. *Maze Tracing.* The subject is presented three mazes and asked to trace the shortest path from a starting point to an end point. Two or more must be traced correctly to pass.	6. *Minkus Completion I.* Subjects are given four sentences with a word missing and must write in the missing word. Three or more must be answered correctly to pass.
Alternate. Repeating Three Digits. Three series of three digits are spoken. The subject must repeat at least one in the correct order to pass.	*Alternate. Response to Pictures Level II.* The subject is presented three pictures and asked to tell about each.	*Alternate. Memory for Designs II.* The subject is shown a geometric design for ten seconds and then must draw it from memory.

FIGURE 5–4 Test materials of the Stanford-Binet Intelligence Scale. (Courtesy of The Riverside Publishing Company.)

appears at several age levels with different criteria for passing. Thus, at year six, six words must be correctly defined whereas at year 12, fifteen or more words must be defined. As can be seen from Table 5-3, many of the tests at younger age levels require the use of blocks, toys, and other objects. Particularly for preschool children, performance tests (for example, Stringing Beads) are used, although verbal skills (for example, Picture Vocabulary) are assessed at all age levels. A picture of the S-B test materials is given in Figure 5-4.

ADMINISTRATION AND SCORING. The administration, scoring, and interpretation of the S-B all require a trained examiner. This person is usually a psychologist, school psychologist, or counseling psychologist who has a graduate degree and at least one graduate level course in intellectual assessment. Detailed instructions for administering and scoring the S-B must be followed. These instructions occupy 204 pages in the test manual (Terman & Merrill, 1973). The order in

which the tests are given must follow that given in the manual. The test usually takes from thirty to forty minutes to administer to a young child but may take ninety minutes for an older child. An experienced examiner requires much less time to administer the S-B than does a less experienced one. As suggested in Chapter 4, the examiner should establish good rapport with the subject so that high motivation and optimal performance are obtained.

An important question is the age level at which to begin testing. For children of average ability, it is recommended that the testing begin with the age level just below the child's chronological age. The examiner, however, must be ready to shift to a different age level if the initial starting point is obviously too difficult or too easy.

Scoring rules are quite precise. Examples of correct responses (pluses) and incorrect responses (minuses) are given as well as general guidelines for scoring a particular test. Examiners are explicitly cautioned against the "halo effect" and instructed to judge each response on its merits, ignoring successes or failures on other tests or responses. Ambiguous responses call for further questioning in order to determine whether or not the subject should be given credit for them.

In computing test scores, the *basal age* refers to the highest age level (1) at which all tests are passed and (2) which just precedes the first age level at which the first failure occurs. It is assumed that all tests below the basal age would be passed. The *ceiling age* is the lowest age level at which all tests are failed. Testing is terminated at this point, and it is assumed that all tests above the ceiling age would be failed. Subjects often show a scatter of success across a wide range of age levels. Thus, a five-year-old child might pass all tests at age IV-6, five tests at age V, and then pass one or two tests at each of the next four or five age levels. Such scattering of successes is more likely to occur at older age levels than younger ones and appears to have no justifiable diagnostic significance.

It should be noted that subjects are not given any credit for tests on which they give some correct responses but do not reach the criterion for passing that test. For example, at age VI subjects are required to identify six vocabulary words to receive credit for that test at that level. A subject who correctly identifies five or fewer items receives no credit whatsoever. A major psychometric weakness of the S-B is that much informa-

tion on performance is lost because no partial credits are given.

In computing the mental age (used much as a raw score), the subject is credited with the basal age plus all additional credits beyond the basal age. At the lower age levels (II through IV-6) each test that is passed earns one month credit. From age levels V through XIV and for average adult, each test passed earns two month's credit. At superior adult levels I, II and III, each test passed earns four, five, and six month's credit, respectively. The tests above year XIV are thus given more weight in order to make the IQs at those "ages" comparable to those at the younger age levels.

An example of mental age (MA) computation for a boy who is three years and zero months of age is given in Table 5-4. Note that this child has "scattered" his successes across seven different age levels. He passed all tests at age II and missed one at age II-6. His basal age is thus age II. He failed all tests at age VI, which is his ceiling age. Appropriate credit has been assigned to the tests passed and the total has been computed. His MA is 3-5 (three years, five months).

Once the MA has been computed, the subject's IQ can be determined from tables provided by Terman and Merrill (1973). Tables are provided for both the 1972 standardization sample and the 1960 revision. These are deviation IQs (standard

TABLE 5-4 Computation of mental age score for a boy three years and zero months of age

Year Level	Number of Tests Passed	Months Credit per Test	Total Credits	
			Years	Months
II	6 (basal age)	—	2	—
II-6	5	1	—	5
III	4	1	—	4
III-6	3	1	—	3
IV	2	1	—	2
IV-6	1	1	—	1
V	1	2	—	2
VI	0 (ceiling age)		2	17

Mental Age Score: 3-5
Deviation IQ: 98

scores), not ratio IQs. The IQ is obtained by entering the appropriate part of the tables, Chronological Age (CA) being the row heading and Mental Age being the column heading. The tables provide IQs for CAs between two and eighteen and for MAs from two years to twenty-two years, ten months. For adults over eighteen years of age, the CA of eighteen is used. In our example in Table 5-4, the IQ equivalent to the obtained MA score of 3-5 is 98.

RELIABILITY. As we indicated in Chapter 3, reliability is an important characteristic of any test. How consistent are IQ scores obtained on the S-B? Surprisingly enough, there is no evidence presented on the current version of the S-B in the test manual. Waddell (1980) commented that she was unable to find any published reliability studies on the S-B since the 1972 restandardization. Thus, the reliability of the current S-B must be judged entirely on the basis of research done on earlier versions of the scale. Terman and Merrill (1973), in fact, reported reliability data obtained from the 1937 scale as evidence for the 1960 scale's reliability.

The 1937 S-B scale had two forms, L and M. In order to assess reliability, scores on Forms L and M given less than a week apart were correlated. McNemar's (1942) extensive statistical analysis found that the 1937 S-B was more reliable for lower IQs than higher IQs and for older subjects than for younger subjects. The median reliabilities (across IQ levels) for subjects aged 2½ to 5½, 6 to 13, and 14 to 18 were .899, .926, and .944, respectively. After grouping subjects into ten IQ categories, reliabilities ranged from a high of .979 for those having IQs between 60 and 69 at ages 14 to 18 to a low of .823 for those having IQs between 140 and 149 at ages 2½ to 5½. With respect to the 1960 scale, Brittain (1968) reported an internal consistency reliability of .94 for a group of normal eight-year-olds, and one of .88 has been reported for a group of retarded children (Share et al., 1964).

Since only the best items have been kept

in the 1960 scale, it seems likely that the short-term reliability of S-B IQs is still acceptable. The evidence available suggests, then, that the 1972 S-B has a reliability of around .90. This would be the correlation expected between IQ scores obtained with a short interval between testing or a measure of the internal consistency of the scale.

A second aspect of the reliability of a test is the question of *stability* of scores over longer periods of time. Longitudinal studies, which are required to determine the stability of test scores, are ones in which the same subjects are tested at several different times after the initial testing. Such studies are difficult and expensive to conduct, since records of and access to subjects must be maintained for long periods of time. Again, the 1972 version of the S-B has no data available on the stability of IQ scores.

As was true of other estimates of reliability for the S-B, information on the stability of IQ scores is available from earlier versions of the test. The Berkley Guidance Study began testing children at age twenty-one months and continued testing these same children through age eighteen (Honzik et al., 1948). Much of this testing involved the 1916 and 1937 forms of the S-B. The study began in the late 1920s and continued until the late 1940s. The 1916 scale was administered when the children were six and seven years old, and Form L or Form M at ages eight through ten and twelve through fifteen. The correlations reported indicate high stability of scores when the interval between tests is short. Also, for older children the IQ remains fairly constant. For example, the correlation of 1937 Form L IQs at age eight with those at ages nine, ten, eleven, twelve or thirteen, and fourteen yielded stability coefficients of .91, .88, .85, .85, and .85, respectively. On the other hand, the correlation of IQs at age six on the 1916 scale with Form L IQs at age fourteen was only .67 (Honzik et al., 1948, Table III, p. 323).

Other data, summarized by Bloom (1964), suggest that S-B IQs obtained from preschool children do not correlate particularly high (r's of about .60) with IQs obtained nine or ten years later. Jensen (1980, p. 279) summarizes S-B intercorrelations from a longitudinal study conducted by Robert McCall at the Fels Research Institute for children from age 2½ to 17. These data clearly show that as the interval between testing increases, particularly for younger ages, the correlation between S-B IQs decreases. For example, consider the following correlations of IQ at age 17 with those of earlier ages: 2½, .36; 4, .49; 6, .62; 8, .65; 10, .69; 12, .74; 14, .71; 15, .89. Thus, the correlation between IQs obtained at ages 2½ and 17 was only .36, whereas at ages 15 and 17 the correlation was .89. On the other hand, the median of twenty-eight intercorrelations from age 8 to age 17 is about .86.

The results suggest, then, that S-B IQs are fairly stable for relatively short periods of time (one to two years) at all ages. However, S-B IQs obtained from preschool children are not accurate predictors of those obtained at progressively later ages. The results also suggest that beginning about age ten, the S-B IQs are relatively stable. However, all the results cited were obtained on earlier versions of the S-B scale. Since the 1960 scale uses the best items from earlier versions, it seems reasonable to assume that the stability of S-B IQs obtained from the current scale is no worse than that obtained from earlier versions. It is also possible that one of the reasons correlations over short intervals are high is that subjects are simply repeating the same test items. Thus, on a vocabulary test, a person who knows the definition of a word at age ten is likely to know that definition at age eleven as well.

Besides the reliability of a test at a given time and its stability over time, scores can be examined in terms of the *standard error of measurement*. Recall that in Chapter 3 the standard error of measurement was defined as

$$S_{meas} = S_x \sqrt{1 - r_{xx}}$$

where

S_{meas} is the standard error of measurement;
S_x is the standard deviation of the test scores; and r_{xx} is the reliability of the test.

Terman and Merrill (1973) present no information on the standard error of measurement of the S-B. However, assuming that the reliability of the S-B (r_{xx}) is about .90 and that the standard deviation is 16, a reasonable estimate of the standard error of measurement would be

$$S_{meas} = 16 \sqrt{1 - .90}$$
$$S_{meas} = 16 \sqrt{.10} = 16 (.32) = 5.12$$

Assuming the errors are normally distributed, and rounding S_{meas} to the nearest whole number (5.00), we can expect the following proportions of changes in IQ because of error or unreliability in the test:

Change in IQ Points	Expected Proportion
16 or more	.0013
6 to 15	.1474
−5 to 5	.6826
−6 to −15	.1474
−16 or more	.0013

For example, consider persons whose true IQs were 110. We would expect such persons to obtain IQs between 105 and 115 about 68 percent of the time. Only about 15 percent of such persons would change by 6 to 15 IQ points, and only about one in a thousand would change by 16 or more IQ points. These results indicate that large changes in IQ can occur but typically would not over short periods of time. The IQ scores on the S-B do not change much in a statistical sense. However, for any given person, the change could be dramatic. The statistics simply tell us that for the group as a whole, it is unlikely that a person's IQ will shift dramatically in either direction. The results we have computed are, of course, illustrative of what we would expect from "normal" subjects. As McNemar (1942) demonstrated, the 1937 scale was in fact more accurate for lower IQs than for higher ones. Although we suspect this is true for the current version of the test, almost no published results are available to refute or support the earlier finding.

VALIDITY. As was true for reliability studies, there is relatively little validity information available on the 1972 S-B norms (Waddell, 1980), and no new validity data were presented with the 1960 scale (Sattler, 1982). Thus, to a large extent, the validity of the current S-B scale is based on results accumulated over many years with earlier versions of the scale.

In judging the *content validity* of the S-B, we can examine the kinds of tests used at various age levels. The S-B contains a wide variety of content, ranging from simple discrimination tasks at younger age levels to complex verbal tasks at older age levels. The wide variety of content and the care with which the tests were chosen insures good content validity of the scale. In examining the correlation between each test and the IQ score, it is again apparent that items having a strong relationship to the total score have been selected. For the 1960 scale, the average correlation for nineteen age levels range from .80 to .53. These correlations also indicate that the S-B's vocabulary test correlates very highly with the IQ score at the four adult age levels, the values being .86, .96, .91, and .90 (Terman & Merrill, 1973). Other similar results suggest that the S-B becomes more and more a measure of verbal ability as the age level increases, although other, more complicated analyses of item content have also been proposed (Sattler, 1982, Ch. 8). As a measure of general mental ability, then, the tests in the 1972 scale seem to be largely appropriate.

With respect to *criterion-related validity*, there is relatively little evidence. Waddell

(1980), in fact, found no published predictive studies using the 1972 S-B. However, Thiel and Reynolds (1980) reported evidence on the predictive validity of the S-B for a small ($n = 40$) group of trainable retarded students. The S-B IQ was correlated with scores on achievement tests. The resulting correlations were .54 for Reading, .63 for Arithmetic, and .54 for Spelling. Himelstein (1966) reviewed the available research on the 1960 revision and found mainly studies of the concurrent validity of the scale. That is, scores on the S-B were correlated with a criterion measure available at very nearly the same time as the S-B scores were obtained.

Concurrent validity has been demonstrated mainly in terms of the correlation between the S-B and other tests of intelligence or cognitive development. Waddell (1980) found a similar situation in her review of research on the 1972 scale, citing eleven published studies. Davis (1975), for example, reports a correlation of .91 between the General Cognitive Index on the McCarthy Scales of Children's Abilities (McCarthy, 1972) and the S-B for kindergarten children of low ability. Using the same two tests with preschool children of average ability, Harrison and Wiebe (1977), however, found a correlation of only .45. Himelstein (1966) and Waddell (1980) both report numerous studies correlating S-B IQs with those obtained from tests developed by David Wechsler—the Wechsler Preschool and Primary Scale of Intelligence, the Wechsler Intelligence Scale for Children–Revised, and the Wechsler Adult Intelligence Scale. The Wechsler scales and the S-B do correlate fairly well, ranging from .52 to .81 for various tests. It also appears that the correlation between the S-B and other intelligence tests is higher for retarded groups than for subjects of normal or superior intelligence. There also appears to be an almost total lack of recent studies using adult subjects.

With respect to the relationship of the S-B to academic achievement, there is little recent information. Most studies also establish concurrent rather than predictive validity. One recent study, employing the 1972 norms, correlated IQ with achievement test scores (Bossard et al., 1980). These investigators tested 120 children who had been referred for evaluation because of learning or behavior problems. The sample was evenly divided by sex and race (black or white) and averaged 8.4 years of age. For black children the IQ-achievement test (reading, spelling, and arithmetic) correlations were .74, .78, and .70, whereas for white children they were .81, .81, and .82.

Kennedy et al. (1963) reported the following correlations between the S-B and California Achievement Test for a large ($n = 1800$) sample of black elementary school children: Reading, .68; Arithmetic, .64; Language, .70. They also reported correlations between the S-B and teacher ratings as follows: Reading, .30; Spelling, .31; Writing, .25; and Discipline, .15.

Using a sample of eleven-year-old students in Britain, Phillips and Bannon (1968) reported correlations of .85 (concurrent validity) between S-B scores and scores on both a mathematics and an English achievement test. Freeman (1962, p. 215) reports that the 1937 S-B scale had often been correlated with grades at the elementary school level with the following results: Reading, mostly between .60 and .69; Arithmetic, mostly between .50 and .59; Spelling, mostly between .45 and .55. He similarly reports approximate median correlations between 1937 S-B IQs and high school grades as follows: Reading Comprehension, .70; Knowledge of Literature, .60; English Usage, .60; History, .60; Algebra, .60; Biology, .55; Geometry, .50; Spelling, .45; Reading Rate, .45. Freeman's summary reflects a mixture of concurrent and predictive studies.

Although the current evidence is less convincing than it could be, it does appear that the S-B still correlates with other tests of intelligence and scholastic achievement. This is not surprising because most tests of intelligence contain a large amount of verbal material and because the S-B was originally designed to assess functions important to succeed in school. Much of the concurrent and predictive validity of the S-B rests on results obtained with the 1937 scale. Again, since only the best items from the 1937 scale were retained in the 1960 scale, and since these items are still in use, it is assumed that the current version of the S-B continues to be a valid predictor of scholastic achievement and other similar variables.

Since the S-B was not designed for use with adults, it is not surprising that little or no validity data have been reported for adults. The S-B should be used mainly with children or retarded adults and should probably be used with adults only for research purposes.

The *construct validity* of the 1972 S-B again rests largely on studies of earlier versions of the scale. Construct validity, understanding the psychological qualities being measured by a test, is based on accumulated research using the scale. A fundamental construct or hypothesis of the S-B is that intelligence is a developing function. Thus, the number of examinees passing an item should increase with age. Garfinkel and Thorndike (1976) have demonstrated that this important characteristic is satisfied for the 1972 S-B. A second indication of its construct validity comes from the criterion-related studies previously cited. The S-B does tend to correlate, although not perfectly, with other intelligence tests and with measures of academic performance.

Finally, the S-B provides a single measure of mental ability, the IQ. Thus, the tests should all correlate highly with the total score, and the IQ should mean the same thing at different age levels. As indicated previously, the tests do have high correlations with the total score. The second question has been approached through the statistical technique of factor analysis. McNemar (1942) presented results from the 1937 scale at fourteen different age levels suggesting that one "factor" could account for the intercorrelations among the tests. That is, the S-B at each age level measured largely one major construct. The results of the factor analyses and other data do suggest that the IQ obtained became increasingly related to performance on the vocabulary tests in the S-B. Other studies, however, using fewer age levels, have found that more than one factor was needed to account for the correlations among the tests (for example, Jones, 1949, 1954; Ramsey & Vane, 1970). Further such analyses on the current version of the S-B would help to clarify its underlying structure.

S-B IQs are related to other characteristics of the individuals, although again there appears to be relatively few recently published studies. Thus, several studies report that S-B IQs vary as a function of socioeconomic status, with subjects whose parents are in higher status occupations tending to obtain higher mean IQs (Kennedy et al., 1963; Phillips & Bannon, 1968; Terman & Merrill, 1937). As is true of many ability tests, black children usually obtain much lower mean S-B IQs than do white children of the same age. Kennedy et al., for example, report a twenty-point difference between their sample of black children and the 1960 normative group. Such differences raise challenging questions about using the S-B and other ability tests with minority groups. We deal with this question in Chapter 14.

Evaluation

Following are several summary points regarding the Stanford-Binet Intelligence Scale:

1. The scale is well constructed and has been carefully developed. The content is generally current.
2. The scale provides a single measure of mental functioning and does not provide diagnostic scores for components of mental functioning.
3. Reliability and validity information on the 1960 S-B and the 1972 norm data are not presented in the test manual. The majority of studies on which the interpretation of the S-B is based occurred in connection with the 1937 version of the test.
4. Although the 1972 normative sample is probably more representative of the general population than earlier samples, the demographic characteristics of the normative sample are not adequately specified.
5. The S-B measures a subject's current mental functioning and is consequently a function of both environmental influences and heredity.
6. The S-B is useful mainly in assessing the IQ of children and the mentally retarded of all ages. It does not appear to be as useful for adults, particularly those of superior intelligence.
7. The S-B is designed to predict academic achievement and does correlate with various measures of academic achievement.
8. The S-B becomes progressively more dependent on verbal skills (for example, vocabulary) as it is used with older subjects. Thus, it cannot be properly or accurately used with subjects who have a language deficit.

6

Wechsler Intelligence Scales

David Wechsler was one of the best known psychologists connected with intelligence testing. Three intelligence scales that he developed—Wechsler Adult Intelligence Scale–Revised, Wechsler Intelligence Scale for Children–Revised, Wechsler Preschool and Primary Scale of Intelligence—are very widely used. The Wechsler scales are all individually administered, as is the Stanford-Binet (S-B), but they differ in several ways from the S-B. First, none of the Wechsler scales is organized by age level. Rather, the items in each subtest are grouped by the nature of the task and ordered in terms of difficulty. Second, the Wechsler scales provide separate scores on ten or more subtests as well as a Verbal IQ, Performance IQ, and a Full Scale IQ. The Full Scale IQ is similar to the IQ obtained from the S-B, although a person taking both tests would probably not receive exactly the same IQ.

The first form of the Wechsler scales appeared in 1939, the Wechsler-Bellevue Scale (W-B). Wechsler observed that other tests that existed at that time had largely been developed for use with children. That is, the existing tests had not been standardized on adults. The type of material used in the tests appealed to children but was unlikely to appeal to adults. The tests also emphasized speed as opposed to accuracy. The concept of mental age, which was very widely used at the time, had limited utility in assessing adult intelligence. As a clinical psychologist working with hospitalized patients, Wechsler also found that a single IQ score was often not helpful in treating psychiatric patients. Thus, Wechsler believed that IQ was not globally affected by psychiatric problems but was affected in different areas (Wechsler, 1944, Ch. 2).

Edwards (1971) provided a good summary of Wechsler's contribution to the theory and measurement of intelligence. Matarazzo (1972) presented a comprehensive review of material on assessing adult intelligence with the Wechsler scale. We will now consider the three Wechsler scales cur-

FIGURE 6–1 David Wechsler (1896–1981) was an American clinical psychologist responsible for developing three widely used intelligence scales —Wechsler Adult Intelligence Scale–Revised, Wechsler Intelligence Scale for Children–Revised, and Wechsler Preschool and Primary Intelligence Scale. (Courtesy of the Psychological Corporation.)

rently available, beginning with the Wechsler Adult Intelligence Scale–Revised (WAIS–R).

WECHSLER ADULT INTELLIGENCE SCALE–REVISED (WAIS–R)

The WAIS–R was published in 1981 (Wechsler, 1981) and is a revision of the Wechsler Adult Intelligence Scale (WAIS) that appeared in 1955 (Wechsler, 1955). These more recent tests are, of course, based on the original W-B that appeared in 1939 (Wechsler, 1939). The objectives in constructing the WAIS–R were to update

the content and provide new norms based on contemporary samples of people. Since the WAIS was published in 1955, a new version of the test was needed to ensure its continued effectiveness. The WAIS–R content is similar to that in the WAIS, about 80 percent of the items being identical or slightly modified. Item changes included (1) dropping or substantially modifying those items whose content appeared dated, (2) changing the order in which items were administered to reflect any changes in difficulty, and (3) modifying the scoring of some items. With respect to test administration, a major change in procedure was made. In the WAIS, the verbal tests were all administered first, followed by the performance tests. In the WAIS–R, verbal and performance tests are administered alternately. This is the same procedure followed in the other two Wechsler scales. This change is justified by the claim that varying the tasks often helps maintain the subject's interest. Other changes in administering the various subtests appear relatively minor (simplifying and rewording directions, giving assistance to the subject under slightly different conditions, and so on).

Content

The WAIS–R consists of eleven tests grouped according to the ability assessed. Six are combined to form the Verbal Scale, and the remaining five form the Performance Scale. All eleven tests are combined to give a Full Scale score. Within each test, the items are ordered in terms of difficulty. That is, the first items are easy, whereas those toward the end of each test are more difficult. The six verbal tests are Information, Digit Span, Vocabulary, Arithmetic, Comprehension, and Similarities. The five performance tests are Picture Completion, Picture Arrangement, Block Design, Object Assembly, and Digit Symbol. All the tests in the Performance Scale have time limits. Only the Arithmetic test is timed among those tests in the Verbal Scale. Each of the tests is described briefly as follows, and the questions presented are analogous to those actually used.

VERBAL SCALE

1. *Information.* The twenty-nine questions in this test cover the range of knowledge a person has. One point is given for each correct answer. Testing is stopped after five consecutive failures. A sample question would be "How many seconds are in a minute?" Knowledge about geography, U.S. society, and literature is assessed.

2. *Digit Span.* In this test, series of digits are presented orally and the examinee must repeat them in the same order as presented (Digits Forward) or in reverse order (Digits Backward). The Digits Forward portion is administered first. The number of digits begins with three and increases by one until nine is reached (that is, seven items). For Digits Backward, there are also seven items, but the number of digits begins with two and increases by one digit until eight is reached. Two trials are presented for each number of digits, and a point is awarded for each trial correctly recalled. Testing is discontinued when both trials are missed for a given number of digits.

3. *Vocabulary.* Thirty-five words are presented for the examinee to define. Each item is scored 2, 1, or 0 and testing is discontinued after five consecutive failures.

4. *Arithmetic.* This test assesses the person's ability to solve arithmetical problems. There are fourteen items, and one point is given for each correct response. Testing is stopped after four consecutive failures. A sample question would be "How many feet are there in four and two-thirds yards?" All the problems involve common situations or practical calculations. The questions are presented orally and the examinee must provide answers without using paper and pencil. Varying time limits are set, and bonus points are added for especially fast solutions to the more difficult items.

5. *Comprehension.* The sixteen questions in this test assess a person's understanding of abstractions. Each item is scored 2, 1, or 0. Testing is stopped after four consecutive failures. A sample question would be "Why should the state make people have a license to drive a car?" Proverbs are also included for interpretation.

6. *Similarities.* Examinees are given fourteen pairs of words and must indicate in what way they are alike. Items are scored 2, 1, or 0. Testing is discontinued after four consecutive failures. A sample question would be "In what way are a ring and a necklace alike?" This test requires the examinee to see or discover the common elements of the terms being compared.

PERFORMANCE SCALE

1. *Picture Completion.* In this test twenty cards having pictures of common objects or scenes are presented. The pictures are incomplete, some important part being missing. The examinee must identify the part that is missing. For example, a picture of an automobile might be presented without one of the wheels. There is a time limit of twenty seconds per item. One point is given for each correct response, and testing is discontinued after five consecutive failures.

2. *Picture Arrangement.* In this test, pictures can be arranged to show a logical series of events. These are much like a series of panels in a newspaper cartoon strip. Ten sets of pictures are presented, varying in the number of components from three to six. The time limit for the first four is 60 seconds; for five through eight, 90 seconds; and for the last two, 120 seconds. Testing is discontinued after four consecutive failures.

3. *Block Design.* In this test blocks are used to make designs. The blocks are all alike: two sides are white, two sides are red, and two sides are half red and half white (triangular in shape). Using varying numbers of blocks (four or nine), the examinee must match the designs pictured on cards. The first five designs use only four blocks and have a time limit of 60 seconds. Designs six through nine use nine blocks and have a time limit of 120 seconds. For the first two designs, two points are awarded if the design is completed within 60 seconds on the first trial; one point if completed on the second trial. Successful completion of the latter designs within the time limit earns four points. Bonus points are awarded for especially fast completion of designs three through ten.

4. *Object Assembly.* This test requires the examinee to put the pieces of a puzzle together to form a familiar configuration. Each of four cut-up objects is presented in a disarranged

pattern to the examinee, who must arrange the pieces to form the whole objects. The first two objects have time limits of 120 seconds, and the latter two, 180 seconds. Nine to five points are awarded for perfect performances, depending on the complexity of the object. Again, bonus points are added for especially rapid responses.

5. *Digit Symbol.* This test is essentially a coding task. Digits are associated with a particular symbol. Ninety-three symbols are presented, and the examinee's task is to complete as many digits as possible in ninety seconds. Responses are made on the record form provided with the test.

Administration and Scoring

As is true of the Stanford-Binet, a trained examiner is required for the administration and scoring of the WAIS–R. Detailed directions for administering and scoring occupy thirty-nine pages of the test manual (Wechsler, 1981). The eleven subtests are ordinarily administered in the following order: Information, Picture Completion, Digit Span, Picture Arrangement, Vocabulary, Block Design, Arithmetic, Object Assembly, Comprehension, Digit Symbol, and Similarities. As we mentioned earlier, the alternation of verbal and performance tests is a major change from the 1955 WAIS, in which the six verbal tests were presented first, followed by the five performance tests. It is, of course, essential that the directions be followed exactly in testing subjects. In most cases, according to the test manual, the WAIS–R requires from sixty to ninety minutes to administer.

The rules for scoring are quite precise, although all possible responses cannot be anticipated. Items from the various subtests of the Verbal Scale are scored 2, 1, or 0, with bonus points awarded in Arithmetic for especially rapid correct answers on some of the items. The scoring for several of the subtests thus recognizes that some answers may be better than others. Thus, in Vocabulary two points are awarded for a good synonym, whereas only one point is awarded for a vague or inexact synonym. Several exam-

ples of responses deserving a two or a one are given for each item. A zero is given to a response on any item that is obviously wrong. For each subtest from the Verbal Scale, testing is stopped when a specified number of consecutive failures occur. For example, Information is halted after five consecutive failures; Digit Span is halted after the subject misses both trials for a particular series of digits. The subtests of the Performance Scale are all timed, and two (Object Assembly and Block Design) award points for especially rapid correct responses.

After all the subtests have been administered, the raw scores for each subtest must be converted to scaled (standard) scores, which for each subtest have a mean of 10 and a standard deviation of 3. The scaled scores are obtained from a single table, regardless of the age of the subject tested. They were derived from five hundred subjects in the standardization sample between the ages of twenty and thirty-four. Table 6–1 gives an example of scaled scores for a particular subject. In this case, for example, a raw score of 25 in Information converts to a scaled score of 13. To obtain the verbal IQ, we add the *scaled scores* on the six verbal tests and then convert them to an IQ score by referring to the table appropriate to the subject's age. Nine such tables are available for the following ages: 16 and 17, 18 and 19, 20 to 24, 25 to 34, 35 to 44, 45 to 54, 55 to 64, 65 to 69, and 70 to 74. For the subject in Table 6-1, the verbal IQ equivalent to the Verbal Scale score of 80 is 125. Performance and Full Scale IQs are obtained in the same manner. That is, for the Performance Scale IQ, the scaled scores on the five performance subtests are added and then converted to an IQ score. For the Full Scale IQ, the scaled scores for all eleven subtests are added and this sum is converted to an IQ score (see Table 6-1).

For each age group, the Verbal, Performance, and Full Scale IQ distributions were constructed to have a mean of 100 and a standard deviation of 15. The IQs are thus

TABLE 6-1 WAIS–R Raw Scores, Scaled Scores, and IQs for a 20-Year-Old Adult

	Subtest/Scale	Raw Score	Scaled Score[a]
Verbal Scale	Information	25	13
	Digit Span	17	11
	Vocabulary	61	13
	Arithmetic	18	15
	Comprehension	30	16
	Similarities	23	12
Performance Scale	Picture Completion	17	11
	Picture Arrangement	18	13
	Block Design	49	16
	Object Assembly	36	12
	Digit Symbol	54	9
	Verbal Scale	80[b] IQ = 125[e]	
	Performance Scale	61[c] IQ = 115[e]	
	Full Scale	141[d] IQ = 125[e]	

[a]Regardless of the subject's age, scaled scores are obtained by reference to the 20 to 34 age group in the standardization sample.
[b]The verbal scaled score is obtained by adding the scaled scores on the six verbal tests.
[c]The performance scaled score is obtained by adding the scaled scores on the five performance tets.
[d]The full scale scaled score is obtained by adding the scaled scores on all eleven subtests.
[e]The IQ is obtained by using the appropriate sum of scaled scores and referring this sum to the age group appropriate to the subject. In this example, age group 20 to 24 is used.

expressed as standard scores or deviation IQs. Each subject tested is compared with the performance of other persons of his or her age. The same sum of scaled scores could have a different IQ, depending on the subject's age. For example, the sum of scaled scores equal to 123 would have a Full Scale IQ of 119 at ages 16 and 17, of 115 at ages 18 and 19, of 108 at ages 20 to 24, of 106 at ages 25 to 34, of 111 at ages 35 to 44, of 114 at ages 45 to 54, of 120 at ages 55 to 64, of 122 at ages 65 to 69, and of 127 at ages 70 to 74.

With respect to diagnostic categories, Table 6-2 gives the suggested method of classifying IQ scores. Those subjects receiving IQs 69 and below, for example, are considered to be mentally retarded. The full scale IQ of 125 obtained by the person in Table 6-1 would be considered superior.

Reliability

As reported in the WAIS–R manual, for all subtests except the Digit Span and Digit Symbol, reliability coefficients were obtained by the split-half method (scores on the odd items were correlated with scores on the even items). The Spearman-Brown formula (see Chapter 3) was then used to estimate the reliability of full-length (using all items) subtests, except for the Digit Span and Digit Symbol. Because Digit Symbol is a speeded test, the split-half method could not be used. It is known that the reliability of a speeded test is overestimated when the split-half method is used.* The nature of

*The split-half method is inappropriate for speeded tests because any items not answered by the examinee at the end of the test are all scored zero, and almost all

TABLE 6-2 Intelligence Classifications for WAIS–R IQs

		Percent Included	
IQ	Classification	Theoretical Normal Curve	Actual Sample[a]
130 and above	Very Superior	2.2	2.6
120–129	Superior	6.7	6.9
110–119	High Average[b]	16.1	16.6
90–109	Average	50.0	49.1
80–89	Low Average[b]	16.1	16.1
70–79	Borderline	6.7	6.4
69 and below	Mentally Retarded[b]	2.2	2.3

[a]The percents shown are for Full Scale IQ, and are based on the total standardization sample ($N = 1,880$). The percents obtained for Verbal IQ and Performance IQ are essentially the same.
[b]The terms *High Average, Low Average,* and *Mentally Retarded* correspond to the terms *Bright Normal, Dull Normal,* and *Mental Defective,* respectively, used in the 1955 *WAIS Manual.*

From Wechsler, 1981, p. 28. Reproduced by permission of the Psychological Corporation.

the Digit Span does not permit splitting the test into two halves. Reliabilities for the Digit Span and Digit Symbol were estimated by the test-retest method for subjects from four age groups. For the Verbal, Performance, and Full Scale IQs, the reliability coefficients were estimated statistically from the reliabilities of the various subtests (Guilford 1954, p. 393). A detailed summary of these results appears in Table 6-3.

The reliability (an average of .97) of the Full Scale IQ is quite high for all age groups. The reliability of the Verbal IQ is essentially equivalent (an average of .97) to the Full Scale IQ for all age groups. The reliability of the Performance IQ is quite consistent in all age groups and only slightly lower (an average of .93) than the other two IQ scales. The reliability of individual subtests is, in some cases, markedly less than the IQ scores—for example, Object Assembly has a reliability of only .52 for ages 16 to 17—partially because of the restricted range

items answered will be answered correctly. Thus, any person's score on each "split half" of a speeded test will be about half the number of items answered. The correlation between the split-half totals for all examinees will therefore usually approach 1.00.

of scores possible on some of the subtests. Also, Vocabulary alone is about as reliable as the IQ scores, suggesting that verbal ability is an important component of the test as a whole. It should be noted that these reliabilities are measures of internal consistency and do not reflect stability of the test scores across time. The Verbal, Performance, and Full Scale IQs do, however, appear to have high reliability for the standardization groups.

With respect to stability of the WAIS–R scores over time, the 1981 manual presents information based on small samples ($n = 71$, $n = 48$) for two age groups (25 to 34, 45 to 54). These subjects were retested within two to seven weeks. The stability coefficients, in general, parallel the results of the split-half coefficients presented in Table 6–3, although the values tend to be slightly lower. Stability coefficients for the Full Scale IQ are, for example, .95 and .96 for the 25 to 34, and 45 to 54 age groups, respectively, as contrasted with split-half coefficients of .98 and .97 for the same two age groups. The test-retest results also demonstrated an increase in the mean IQ at the second testing. The gains suggest that there is a practice effect when the WAIS–R is admin-

TABLE 6-3 WAIS–R Reliability Coefficients (r_{11}) of the Tests and IQ Scales, by Age

Test	Age Group									Average r_{11}[a]	Average SE_m
	16-17	18-19	20-24	25-34	35-44	45-54	55-64	65-69	70-74		
Information	.90	.89	.90	.90	.90	.87	.91	.90	.88	.89	.93
Digit Span	.70	—[b]	—[b]	.89	.85	.82	—[b]	—[b]	—[b]	.83	1.23
Vocabulary	.96	.96	.94	.96	.96	.95	.96	.96	.95	.96	.61
Arithmetic	.73	.81	.83	.86	.87	.84	.87	.87	.86	.84	1.14
Comprehension	.78	.80	.77	.84	.85	.87	.84	.90	.84	.84	1.20
Similarities	.80	.83	.78	.82	.85	.85	.86	.87	.86	.84	1.24
Picture Completion	.71	.74	.76	.85	.84	.82	.82	.89	.83	.81	1.25
Picture Arrangement	.66	.70	.68	.76	.78	.82	.77	.71	.73	.74	1.41
Block Design	.87	.87	.88	.89	.89	.84	.83	.87	.84	.87	.98
Object Assembly	.52	.71	.71	.68	.73	.71	.71	.67	.62	.68	1.54
Digit Symbol	.73	—[b]	—[b]	.86	.84	.82	—[b]	—[b]	—[b]	.82	1.27
Verbal IQ	.95	.96	.96	.97	.97	.97	.97	.97	.97	.97	2.74
Performance IQ	.88	.90	.92	.94	.94	.94	.93	.94	.92	.93	4.14
Full Scale IQ	.96	.96	.97	.98	.98	.97	.97	.98	.97	.97	2.53

Note—The reliability coefficients for all tests except Digit Span and Digit Symbol are split-half correlations corrected by the Spearman Brown formula. For Digit Span and Digit Symbol, test-retest correlations are presented for four age groups; these coefficients are based on samples of between 48 and 80 individuals tested twice (1- to 7-week interval). (See manual for further discussion of retest groups.) The coefficients for the IQ Scales were obtained from the formula for the reliability of a composite group of tests (Guilford, 1954, p. 393).

[a]The average r was computed using Fischer's z transformation.

[b]The best estimate of the reliability coefficient of Digit Span or Digit Symbol at an age level where retesting was not done is the value obtained at the nearest age group that was retested; e.g., the .82 obtained for Digit Span at age 45-54 is the best estimate for age 65-69. These "best estimates" were used when computing the reliability of the three IQs at ages 18-19, 20-24, 55-64, 65-69, and 70-74.

From Wechsler, 1981, p. 30. Reproduced by permission of the Psychological Corporation.

istered to the same subject after a relatively short period of time.

Because the WAIS–R is a relatively new test, there are no longitudinal data yet available for it. However, there are several such studies available for the 1955 WAIS. These studies tested the same subjects after varying lengths of time, from thirteen years to one day. Among the groups used were geriatric patients, college students, police applicants, adult retardates, and psychiatric patients. Kangas and Bradway (1971) tested twenty-four men and twenty-four women in 1956 when they averaged about thirty years of age and then again in 1969, thirteen years later. Their results showed correlations of .70, .57, and .73 for Verbal, Performance, and Full Scale IQs, respectively. These results suggest that from young adulthood to middle age there can be fairly substantial changes in a person's IQ as measured by the WAIS, particuarly for the Performance Scale, which exhibits a test-retest correlation of only .57. For shorter time intervals, the WAIS test-retest correlations are considerably higher.

Catron and Thompson (1979), using college students as examinees, reported correlations of .83, .85, and .90 for Verbal, Performance, and Full Scale IQs, respectively, over a four-month period. Matarazzo et al. (1973), using applicants for police training, reported corresponding correlations of .87, .84, and .91 over a test-retest interval averaging about five months. After a one-day interval, and using patients sixty or older as subjects, Meer and Baker (1965) reported test-retest correlations ranging from a high of .97 to a low of .81 for four of the subtests in the Verbal Scale. Brown and May (1979), in a sample of fifty psychiatric patients having an average age of forty-four, and after an average retest interval of two years, reported test-retest correlations of .91, .90, and .92 for the Verbal, Performance, and Full Scale IQs, respectively. Similarly, Kendrick and Post (1967) administered the WAIS at six-week intervals to elderly and brain-damaged subjects (average age 70.5) and reported test-retest corre-

lations ranging from .95 to .66. Another study, using mentally retarded subjects whose average age was 26.2, and retesting after 2½ years, found correlations of .87, .92, and .88 for the Verbal, Performance, and Full Scale IQs, respectively (Rosen, et al., 1968). A similar sample of retarded subjects (mean age thirty-four) retested after thirty-two months yielded a correlation between Full Scale IQs of .90 (Dinning, et al., 1977).

It thus appears that adult IQs as measured by the WAIS remain reasonably stable over periods of two years or less. The results of Kangas and Bradway (1971) also suggest that over longer periods of time (thirteen years), WAIS IQs may change a considerable amount. Since the WAIS–R was designed to be similar to the 1955 WAIS, it is likely that IQs obtained from it will parallel those of the earlier test.

In addition to considering the correlation between WAIS–R scores, it is also possible to examine the *standard error of measurement* (S_{meas}) associated with each subtest and each IQ score. The average (computed for the nine age groups) S_{meas} for each subtest and IQ are given in Table 6–3. For the subtests, the S_{meas} are reported in terms of the scaled scores (mean of 10, standard deviation of 3), and those of the IQ scores are reported in terms of a mean of 100 and standard deviation of 15. The S_{meas} for the subtests thus appears smaller because the standard deviation of the scaled scores from the subtests is smaller.

For the Full Scale IQ, as can be seen in Table 6-3, the average S_{meas} is 2.53. Thus, assuming the errors of measurement are normally distributed, we would expect the obtained IQ to be within approximately ± 5.06 IQ points of the true score 95 percent of the time. Rounding the 5.06 to 5.0 and using a person who obtained an IQ of 110 as an example, we would expect such a person to obtain IQs between 105 and 115 about 95 percent of the time. These errors, of course, are what might be expected over relatively short periods of time.

Reliability of Difference Scores

Unlike the Stanford-Binet, the WAIS–R provides eleven separate subtest scores and two IQ scores in addition to the Full Scale IQ. It is thus possible to examine differences between scores on the various subtests and between the Verbal and Performance IQs. These differences may have diagnostic significance. For example, a person who obtains a very high Performance IQ and a very low Verbal IQ may come from a family where English is rarely or never spoken. A large difference between the Verbal and Performance IQs would at least suggest a special problem of some kind.

Difference scores, however, are relatively unreliable, largely because the errors of measurement associated with the two scores are additive or cumulative; the errors in the two scores do not balance each other out when difference scores are computed. Thus, the error of measurement associated with a difference score will be larger than the error of measurement of either score alone. McNemar (1969, p. 173) provides a good discussion of the technical reasons for the unreliability of difference scores.

The reliability of difference scores is a function of the reliabilities of the two tests involved and of the intercorrelation between them. If the variance of the two tests is equal, the following formula gives the reliability of the difference scores:

$$r_{dd} = \frac{\frac{1}{2}(r_{xx} + r_{yy}) - r_{xy}}{1 - r_{xy}} \qquad (6\text{-}1)$$

where

r_{xx} = the reliability of test X,
r_{yy} = the reliability of test Y,
r_{xy} = the intercorrelation between test X and test Y.

Thus, for the reliability of the difference between Verbal and Performance IQs on the WAIS–R for the age group twenty-five to thirty-four, we have the following:

r_{xx} = reliability of the verbal scale = .97;
r_{yy} = reliability of the performance scale = .94;
r_{xy} = correlation between the verbal scale and performance scale = .76; and

$$r_{dd} = \frac{\frac{1}{2}(.97 + .94) - .76}{1 - .76} = \frac{.195}{.24} = .81$$

As can be seen from this result, the reliability of the difference scores is much lower than the reliability of either component. What this means is that we must be very cautious in interpreting difference scores. Unless they are very large, they can easily be due to chance or error rather than to true or important differences in ability.

Although data on the WAIS–R are not available, McNemar (1957) has computed reliabilities for difference scores for all eleven WAIS subtests for the same age group. Since the reliabilities of the subtests tend to be lower than the IQ scales, these reliabilities of difference scores are even lower than Verbal-Performance IQ differences, ranging from a low of .25 (Picture Arrangement-Object Assembly) to a high of .84 (Vocabulary-Digit Symbol). The median reliability of the fifty-five possible differences between the eleven subtests is .60. Similar results would be expected with the WAIS–R. Thus, one must be even more cautious in attributing meaning to differences between subtest scores than between Verbal and Performance IQ scores.

The error component in the Verbal-Performance IQ difference score has, on the average, a standard error of about five. Verbal-Performance IQs should thus differ by at least ten points before we attempt to attach any diagnostic significance to the difference obtained. The WAIS–R manual (Wechsler, 1981, p. 36) suggests that a Verbal-Performance IQ difference of fifteen or more points merits further investigation.

Field (1960) and Fisher (1960) both provide additional data on interpreting differences between the Verbal and Performance

IQs for the 1955 WAIS. These investigators computed the proportion of people in the "normal" standardization sample who obtained differences of varying amounts between Verbal and Performance IQs. Their tables indicate that about five percent of the "normal" standardization sample had a twenty or more point difference and about twenty-five percent had a ten or more point difference. The size of these differences clearly suggests that it would be relatively easy to overinterpret Verbal-Performance IQ differences. McNemar (1957) makes a similar point about differences between scores on the 1955 WAIS subtests. These conclusions are probably valid for the WAIS–R, although similar data have not been published.

Validity

The test manual for the WAIS–R presents almost no validity information. The manual argues that the evidence available on the 1955 WAIS and the 1939 W-B is relevant, because the WAIS–R measures the same abilities and there is considerable overlap in content with the two earlier scales.

One study reported in the test manual (Wechsler, 1981, p. 47) correlated WAIS–R and WAIS scores. Seventy-two subjects in the age group 35 to 44 were tested with both scales in a counterbalanced order. The time interval between testing was three to six weeks. The correlations among the subtest scaled scores ranged from a low of .50 (Object Assembly) to a high of .91 (Vocabulary). The correlations among Verbal, Performance, and Full Scale IQs were .91, .79, and .88, respectively. It was also found that WAIS Verbal, Performance, and Full Scale IQs were approximately seven, eight, and eight points higher than the respective WAIS–R IQs. Although these results suggest that the WAIS–R will provide similar scores to those obtained from the WAIS (high correlations), they also suggest that the IQs are probably not completely equivalent on the two scales. Of course, the study reported is based on a relatively small

sample for a particular age group. Additional data will undoubtedly be obtained as the WAIS–R is used in other studies.

The Wechsler Intelligence Scale for Children–Revised (WISC–R) and WAIS–R can both be administered to subjects at age sixteen. The WAIS–R manual (Wechsler, 1981, p. 48) reported a study in which subjects, age sixteen, were given both tests in a counterbalanced order. The time between testings was one to six weeks. Correlations between the subtest scaled scores ranged from a low of .39 (Picture Arrangement) to a high of .86 (Vocabulary). The Verbal, Performance, and Full Scale IQs were correlated .89, .76, and .88, respectively. The mean IQs were very similar for both scales, differing by at most two points. Again, although more research would be useful, these results suggest that the WAIS–R and WISC–R are measuring similar mental functioning and seem to provide, on the average, equivalent IQs.

As suggested, a truly voluminous literature exists on the earlier versions of the WAIS–R. Buros' *Eighth Mental Measurements Yearbook* (1978) contains almost 1,300 publications or other reports that cite one of the Wechsler adult scales. Guertin and his colleagues provided evaluative summaries of research using the WAIS (Guertin et al., 1966, 1971; Guertin et al., 1962). Matarazzo (1972) provided an extensive discussion on the clinical use of the WAIS in addition to updating Wechsler's *Measurement and Appraisal of Adult Intelligence* (1958). Zimmerman and Woo-Sam (1973) wrote a book entitled *Clinical Interpretation of the WAIS*, which should be quite useful to clinical psychologists and other professionals who use the WAIS for diagnostic purposes. From this voluminous literature on the WAIS we are only able to include what we believe are the significant generalities of the results and give some specific examples on validity. Validity studies in which the WAIS–R is used should rapidly supplant the 1955 WAIS results.

With respect to *content validity*, tests were

originally selected for inclusion "based on their correlation with other established tests of intelligence and empirical judgments of intelligence, on ratings by experienced clinicians, and on other empirical studies of several groups of known intellectual functioning" (Wechsler, 1981, p. 49). The tests were designed to appeal to adults rather than children and the items were chosen on this basis. The content of the WAIS–R is in keeping with Wechsler's goal of measuring overall competency, or global capacity.

Criterion-related validity of a test is established by comparing its scores with scores from other tests and with nontest measures of performance. *Concurrent valdity* of the WAIS–R has been demonstrated in two previously mentioned studies that reported correlations of WAIS–R scores with scores on the 1955 WAIS and the WISC–R. Both these studies provided preliminary evidence that the WAIS–R is related systematically to test scores from these other two Wechsler scales. Since the 1955 WAIS and the WAIS–R are similar in content and design, such results are not surprising, but they are necessary if validity evidence on the WAIS is to be generalized to the WAIS–R.

Most concurrent validity studies in the literature used the 1955 WAIS. For years the Stanford-Binet (S-B) was accepted as the standard measure of intelligence. The scores from the WAIS were correlated with those from the S-B in a variety of studies (see Zimmerman and Woo-Sam, 1973, for an extensive compilation). Wechsler (1955) reported a study using fifty-two reformatory inmates between the ages of 16 and 26. The correlation between the WAIS Full Scale and the 1937 S-B IQs was .85. Although the mean S-B IQ for this group was 100, the WAIS Full Scale IQ was 95, five points less than "average." The main point here is that even though the S-B and WAIS IQs were highly correlated, the IQs obtained were not equivalent. This study also demonstrated that the Verbal Scale IQ correlated much more highly with the S-B than did the Performance Scale IQ (.86 versus

.69). This result is not surprising because the upper levels of the S-B are largely verbal in nature. It is interesting to note that this study is the only validity study cited in the test manual for the 1955 WAIS.

Fisher et al. (1961) used a sample of 180 retardates ranging in age from eighteen to seventy-three to compare WAIS and S-B IQs. They reported correlations between WAIS and S-B IQs ranging from .74 to .78. Higher correlations, .90 to .79, were found by Cochran and Pedrini (1969) in another sample of adult male retardates ranging in age from 16 to 35. It also appears the 1955 WAIS IQs are typically higher than S-B IQs among adult retardates, even though the IQs obtained from the two tests are usually highly correlated. Part of the reason for this difference is undoubtedly due to the age norms provided for the WAIS. The S-B uses age 18 norms for all adults regardless of their age. As noted by Guertin et al. (1971), studies comparing the S-B and WAIS have largely disappeared, probably because of the greater popularity and appropriateness of the WAIS over the S-B for assessing adult intelligence.

Matarazzo (1972, pp. 246–247) and Zimmerman and Woo-Sam (1973, Ch. 2) presented summaries of the correlations between the WAIS and other intelligence scales. For example, Pool and Brown (1970) found a correlation of .81 between the Peabody Picture Vocabulary Test (PPVT) and the WAIS IQ for 150 psychiatric outpatients. The PPVT is an individually administered test evaluating word recognition and does not require the subject to verbalize any responses. Using thirty adolescents suspected of being mentally retarded, Covin and Covin (1976) found a correlation of .92 between the WAIS IQ and the PPVT.

The WAIS also has been correlated with intelligence tests that can be administered to groups. For example, Cowden et al. (1971) correlated WAIS scores with a group test of general mental ability, using 209 male prisoners. They found that the two tests correlated .78. The correlations between the WAIS Full Scale IQ and other intelligence scales, as presented in Zimmerman and Woo-Sam (1973, Ch. 2), range from a low of .32 to a high of .93. The majority of correlations were in the .70s. Later studies also support Zimmerman and Woo-Sam's conclusions (Duvall & Maloney, 1978; Hubble, 1978; Maloney et al., 1978; Martin & Rudolph, 1972; Watson & Klett, 1973). The large number of studies using many different tests and many different subjects provide good evidence for the concurrent validity of the WAIS. It is assumed that additional studies on the WAIS–R will demonstrate a similar pattern of results.

The WAIS IQs have been used to predict academic success. Conry and Plant (1965), for example, reported a correlation of .62 between WAIS Full Scale IQ and high school rank ($n = 98$) and of .44 between WAIS Full Scale IQ and college GPA ($n = 335$). The criterion variable was obtained twenty months after testing for the high school students and about six months for the college students. The mean IQ of the high school seniors was 107; for the college students it was 115. As might be expected the Verbal IQ correlated more highly with the measures of academic success than did the Performance IQ (.63 versus .43 for the high school students, and .47 versus .44 for the college students). Plant and Lynd (1959) reported similar results for first-year college students. In their sample of 161 students, the WAIS Full Scale IQ correlated .53 with the GPA at the end of the first year. The Verbal IQ also correlated more highly with the criterion than did Performance IQ (.58 versus .31). The mean Full Scale IQ for a large sample of college freshmen was 115. In nonacademic areas, the WAIS is, however, less successful in predicting criteria of interest. Lowe (1967), for example, reported that the WAIS IQs were unrelated to the work adjustment for released psychiatric patients. Another study reported that the performance of managerial personnel is largely unrelated to WAIS IQs, the highest correlation being .32 between Verbal IQ and the criterion variable (Balinsky & Shaw, 1956).

As was mentioned earlier, the fact that the WAIS–R has eleven subtests and two IQs in addition to the Full Scale IQ permits many possible differences among test scores to be constructed. There are, for example, fifty-five possible pairs of differences among the eleven subtests. However, it is well known that difference scores tend to be unreliable, and only large differences should be interpreted. Since the standard error of difference for subtests is approximately three, a difference of six scaled score points between two subtests should be statistically significant, although it does not establish any clinical or diagnostic significance.

We will focus on the difference between Verbal and Performance IQ scores and not consider differences among the subtests. The concurrent validity of difference scores is evaluated by examining their relationship to various other measures. In summarizing the available literature on the 1955 WAIS, Zimmerman and Woo-Sam (1973, p. 8) suggested that having a Verbal IQ significantly greater than a Performance IQ is characteristic of right-hemisphere or diffuse brain damage. Matarazzo (1972, p. 390) also summarized data that largely demonstrate this difference. On the other hand, having a Performance IQ significantly greater than a Verbal IQ has generally been found in persons with lesions in the left-hemisphere of the brain (Guertin et al., 1971; Matarazzo, 1972, p. 390; Zimmerman & Woo-Sam, 1973, p. 8). Thus, Verbal-Performance IQ differences on the WAIS–R may be a useful indicator of various kinds of brain damage.

In addition to the possible indication of brain damage, having a Verbal IQ below Performance IQ has often been characteristic of juvenile delinquents (and perhaps other diagnostic groups exhibiting antisocial behavior). Guertin et al. (1971, p. 318) concluded, however, "that test score patterns are a function of psychiatric diagnoses, cultural background, race, age, educational level, and sex. Although IQs tend to be low and PIQ > VIQ, there are exceptions." For example, Henning and Levy (1967), using a large sample ($n = 2,361$) of black and white male delinquents of various ages, found virtually no evidence on the WAIS that Verbal IQ was less than Performance IQ. However, Kendall and Little (1977) found such a difference for both black and white juvenile delinquents. The latter investigators had both males and females in their sample.

Differences between Verbal and Performance IQs would, of course, not be the only information used in diagnosing a patient as brain damaged or a potential delinquent. The results cited are also group tendencies and do not translate immediately into use with an individual. Such differences, if they are reliable, also do not explain why they appear. Henning and Levy (1967), for example, hypothesized that a Verbal IQ lower than a Performance IQ for delinquents reflected a pattern of reading disability rather than a sociopathic pattern of behavior.

The *construct validity* of the WAIS–R depends to a large extent on the published research dealing with earlier versions of the scale. The results previously cited tend to support the construct validity of the 1955 WAIS. By implication the WAIS–R should also possess a high degree of contruct validity. When intelligence is viewed as a global capacity, the subtests are expected to be highly interrelated. From the tables of intercorrelations, it appears that all the subtests are intercorrelated and also correlate with the Full Scale IQ. Silverstein (1982) factor analyzed standardization data for both the WAIS and the WAIS–R. The results indicated almost identical factor structures for the two instruments. Two factors, Verbal Comprehension and Perceptual Organization, were identifed for each instrument. However, Silverstein also pointed out that 60 percent of the total variance in the WAIS and 55 percent of the total variance in the WAIS–R were accounted for by a single, general factor. From these results one could argue that both Wechsler scales measure nothing but a general factor and that interpretations should be limited to Full Scale IQ.

The studies on the 1955 WAIS concerning academic achievement also support the construct of intelligence. Gibson and Light (1967) reported an interesting study on 148 scientists at Cambridge University. The scientists were in such areas as biology, chemistry, physics, and social science and had IQs above the seventieth percentile. That is, they all had IQs higher than 70 percent of the adult U.S. population. We would expect a scientist at a prestigious research university like Cambridge to have a high level of mental ability. Gibson and Light suggested that there may be a threshold IQ necessary before one can function as or is likely to become a scientist. Within this select group of scientists, however, IQ was largely unrelated to measures of academic achievement. Wechsler (1958, p. 258) also reported that the correlation between years of education and WAIS Full Scale IQs was about .70 for three different age groups. We also noted several studies in which college students had average IQ scores of 115 to 120. As we would expect, these are considerably above average. The 1955 WAIS has been used successfully for years to identify retarded individuals. Although far from conclusive, the fact that Verbal IQ is less than Performance IQ for those subjects having brain damage in the dominant hemisphere is consistent with our understanding of brain function (that is, language behavior is controlled by the dominant hemisphere).

Despite the years of work with the 1955 WAIS, we are not convinced that the WAIS–R will ever prove useful in diagnosing psychiatric disorders or in correlating with personality variables of various kinds (Loro & Woodward, 1976; Matarazzo, 1972, Ch. 14). The possible exception is the suggestive finding that delinquents, on the average, often have lower Performance IQs than Verbal IQs. The explanation for this finding remains unclear.

WECHSLER INTELLIGENCE SCALE FOR CHILDREN–REVISED (WISC–R)

Ten years after publishing the W-B for adults, Wechsler (1949) published a corresponding scale for children, the Wechsler

Intelligence Scale for Children (WISC). This test was well received and widely used. In 1974, Wechsler published a revised scale for children, the WISC–R, designed for children between the ages of six and sixteen; the WISC was appropriate for children aged five through fifteen. The WISC–R contains many items from the 1949 WISC but also many new items or ones that were substantially changed. It seems to be the most frequently used individually administered test of intelligence for school-age children. It is widely used with both normal children and those with special problems, such as mental retardation or learning disabilities.

As is true of all the Wechsler scales, the WISC–R consists of subtests scored separately and then combined to yield Verbal, Performance, and Full Scale IQs. The IQs are expressed as deviation IQs, having a mean of 100 and a standard deviation of 15. The scores on the subtests are scaled to have means of 10 and standard deviations of 3. As would be expected, the WISC–R and WAIS–R are similar in design, the content and scoring of the former reflecting the age groups with which each is used. There are some differences between the two scales, however, and we will note these in our discussion of the WISC–R.

FIGURE 6–2 Test materials for the Wechsler Intelligence Scale for Children–Revised. (Courtesy of the Psychological Corporation.)

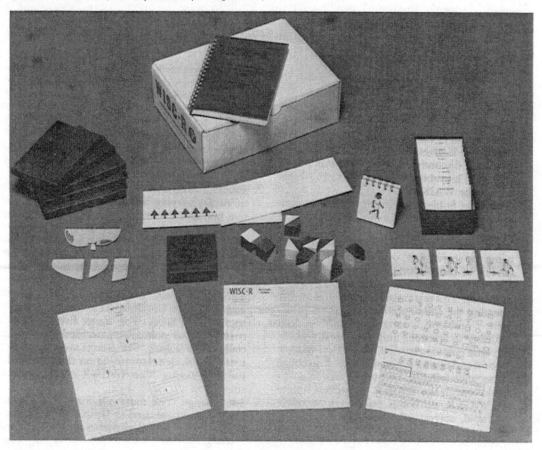

Content

The WISC–R consists of twelve subtests, ten of which are used to compute the IQ scores. Two are called supplementary tests and are suggested for administration. The WAIS–R has no supplementary tests. All items within a subtest are ordered in terms of difficulty, easier items appearing first. For seven of the subtests, the examiner begins testing at different places in the sequence of items, depending on a child's age. Thus, an older child is not asked the easiest items on some tests. However, if a child does not answer the first two items correctly, then the easier items (the ones omitted) are administered. Items are scored zero if the answer is incorrect, but some items are given more than one point depending on the quality of the correct response. Bonus points are awarded for especially rapid completion of some of the timed tests. As is true of the WAIS-R, all the performance tests and one verbal test (Arithmetic) have time limits. The subtests are described as follows.

VERBAL SCALE

1. *Information.* This test has thirty questions dealing with a child's range of information. One point is given for each correct answer. Testing is discontinued after five consecutive failures. This subtest is analogous to Information in the WAIS-R.
2. *Similarities.* Subjects are given seventeen pairs of words and asked to indicate in what way they are alike or the same. The first four items are scored 1 and 0 and the remaining items are scored 2, 1, or 0 depending on the quality of the response. Testing is stopped after three consecutive failures.
3. *Arithmetic.* This test consists of eighteen items assessing the child's ability to perform arithmetic problems, ranging from simple counting to fractions and numerical reasoning. One point is awarded for each correct response, and testing is discontinued after three consecutive failures. This test is analogous to Arithmetic in the WAIS-R. However, unlike the WAIS-R, no bonus points are awarded for rapid, correct solutions. The time limits per item vary from thirty to seventy-five seconds.

4. *Vocabulary.* This test consists of thirty-two words to be defined. Each item is scored 2, 1, or 0 depending on the quality of the response. Testing is stopped after five consecutive failures. This test is analogous to Vocabulary in the WAIS-R.
5. *Comprehension.* The seventeen questions in this test assess the child's understanding of a variety of situations, including the body, societal activities, and dealings with other people. Each item is scored 2, 1, or 0 and testing is discontinued after four consecutive failures. This test is similar to Comprehension in the WAIS-R.
6. *Digit Span (Supplementary Verbal Test).* This subtest is exactly like Digit Span in the WAIS-R. Varying numbers of digits are to be recalled in order (Digits Forward) or backwards (Digits Backward). Two trials for each set of digits are allowed. Two points are awarded if both trials are passed; one point if one trial is passed. Testing is stopped if both trials are missed.

PERFORMANCE SCALE

1. *Picture Completion.* In this test twenty-six cards having pictures of common objects or scenes are presented. The pictures are incomplete, having some important part missing. There is a time limit of twenty seconds per picture. One point is awarded for each correct response, and testing is discontinued after four consecutive failures. This test is similar to Picture Completion in the WAIS-R.
2. *Picture Arrangement.* This test has thirteen sets of cards, varying in number from three to five per set. The subject's task is to arrange the pictures in the correct order so that they make sense or tell a story. The task is like arranging the panels of a cartoon strip in the correct order. A sample item is included so that twelve sets are actually scored. The first eight items have a forty-five second time limit, and the last four items have a sixty-second time limit. For items five through twelve, bonus points are awarded for especially fast solutions. The points awarded vary from one to five depending on the item and the time bonus. The WAIS-R has a similar subtest.
3. *Block Design.* The materials for this test are exactly like those used in Block Design in the WAIS-R. Eleven designs are constructed, using four or nine blocks. Bonus points are

given for especially rapid correct solutions for designs four through eleven. The child is given a second trial for designs one through three if the first attempt is incorrect. Testing is stopped after two consecutive failures (design is incorrect or design is not completed within the time limit).

4. *Object Assembly*. This test requires the subject to put the pieces of a puzzle together to form a familiar object. Five items are presented. The first is a sample item; the remaining four are scored. The puzzles vary in number of pieces (six to eight), time limit (120 to 180 seconds), maximum score without time bonus (five or six), and bonus points possible (one to three). Time bonus points are awarded only for perfect assemblies. All four items are administered to all children. The WAIS-R has a similar subtest.

5. *Coding*. This test has two forms. Coding A is used with children under eight; Coding B with those over eight. Coding A consists of five geometric figures (for example, a circle) repeated in random order. Each figure has a "code." The child must put the appropriate "code" in each geometric figure. Forty-five figures are presented in Coding A. One point is awarded for each item correctly filled in. For those children correctly completing all forty-five items, up to five bonus points can be awarded for especially rapid completion. The time limit is 120 seconds. The WAIS-R does not have a coding test like this. For Coding B, symbols are associated with the numbers one through nine. Ninety-three numbers are then printed on the form, and the child must write the symbol associated with each number in the box below. The time limit is 120 seconds. One point is awarded for each correct coding. There are no time bonus points for Coding B. Coding B is like Digit Symbol in the WAIS–R.

6. *Mazes (Supplementary Performance Test)*. A booklet of mazes of varying difficulty is used in this test. A boy or girl is pictured in the center of a maze, and the subject must find his or her way out without going through any "walls." Nine mazes, varying in complexity, are used. Time limits vary from 30 to 150 seconds. An error is defined as entrance into a blind alley. No errors earn the maximum number of points. Less than perfect performance earns fewer points. Failures (0 points) occur when the time limit is exceeded, the number of errors exceeds the maximum, the tracing begins beyond the starting point, the goal is not reached, or the tracing cuts through a wall of the maze. The WAIS-R has no test comparable to Mazes.

Administration and Scoring

A trained examiner is required for the administration and scoring of the WISC–R. Since it is designed to be used with children as young as six, the examiner must often exercise special skills to establish and maintain rapport. The test manual (Wechsler, 1974, p. 55) makes the following remarks on this matter:

Making the testing experience satisfying to both child and examiner places great demands on the examiner's clinical skills. He must put the child at ease, keep him interested in the tasks at hand, and encourage him to do his best. There is no magic formula for "reaching" a child; approaches that succeed with some children may antagonize others. With experience, the examiner will develop a perceptiveness enabling him to establish sympathetic relationships with children and to adapt to the specific needs of each one.

As is true of all testing procedures, the instructions in the test manual for administering and scoring the test must be closely followed. Unless the standardized procedures are followed, the test scores will not be valid.

The subtests are usually administered in the following order: Information, Picture Completion, Similarities, Picture Arrangement, Arithmetic, Block Design, Vocabulary, Object Assembly, Comprehension, Coding, Digit Span (Supplementary Verbal Test), and Mazes (Supplementary Performance Test). As is true for the WAIS-R, the WISC-R alternates administration of the verbal and performance tests. The analogous performance tests appear in the same position for both the WISC-R and WAIS-R, whereas the analogous verbal tests vary slightly in position. The two supplementary tests of the WISC-R are usually administered last when they are used.

Unlike the WAIS-R, the starting point for some WISC-R tests varies as a function of the child's age. For example, on three verbal tests (Information, Arithmetic, and Vocabulary), children aged 8 to 10 years, 11 to 13 years, and 14 to 16 years begin at different points in the sequence of items. Thus, the easiest items are not administered to older children unless they do not exhibit perfect performance on the first two items. If the child fails, the items appropriate for the next youngest age group are administered until perfect performance is exhibited. Several WAIS-R tests also start with an advanced item and follow the same administration procedures as the WISC-R if either the first or second "advanced" item is missed. Four of the WISC-R performance tests have different starting points, depending on the child's age.

For the WISC-R, when a child fails the first item of a test, the examiner provides the correct answer to insure that the child understands the task. Coding is the only test that does not permit such corrections. This correction procedure is followed for most WAIS-R tests but not all of them. According to the WISC-R manual, approximately fifty to seventy-five minutes are required to administer the regular set of ten subtests.

The rules for scoring a subject's responses are reasonably complete. At least one reviewer, however (Freides, 1978), notes that the scoring instructions are too often logically inconsistent. That is, the rationale for giving some responses 2 points and others only 1 point is not clear. The scoring appears to be a problem mainly on the Similarities, Vocabulary, and Comprehension tests. For these tests, the manual provides fairly extensive examples of responses deserving 2, 1, or 0 points. Some studies of interrater reliabilities of the scoring on these tests would perhaps have been helpful. The bonus points awarded for especially rapid correct responses require that the examiner be very accurate in timing items.

As is true of all the Wechsler scales, the raw scores for each subtest must be converted to scaled (standard) scores. These scaled scores have a mean of 10 and standard deviation of 3. The conversion of raw scores to scaled scores on the WISC-R differs from that on the WAIS-R. For the former, the *raw scores* are referred to an age-appropriate table. Tables for thirty-three age groups are provided, beginning at ages 6-0 to 6-3 (six years-zero months to six years-three months) and progressing in four-month intervals to ages 16-8 to 16-11. The WAIS-R, it will be recalled, converts raw scores to scaled scores by reference to a single age group.

Once scaled scores on the ten subtests have been obtained, the three IQs can be determined. The sum of the five scaled scores on the Verbal Scale is converted to a Verbal IQ by reference to a single table; the sum of the five scaled scores on the Performance Scale is converted to a Performance IQ; and the sum of all ten scaled scores is converted to a Full Scale IQ. Unlike the WAIS-R, the sums of scaled scores are converted to IQs by reference to a single table, regardless of the child's age. The resulting IQs are deviation IQs, having a mean of 100 and standard deviation of 15. One conversion table is used for all ages, because age differences are taken into account when subtest raw scores are converted to scaled scores. Children are thus still compared with other children of their own age, because the IQs are based on scaled scores derived separately for each age group.

The WISC-R IQs are classified in the same manner as WAIS-R IQs. (This classification scheme appears in Table 6-2.) The IQs can also be treated in a descriptive way by noting the percentile score associated with each IQ. Thus, an IQ of 130 is at the ninety-fifth percentile (95 percent of the sample have IQs below 130), and an IQ of 80 is at the ninth percentile (only 9 percent of the sample have IQs below 80). Verbal and Performance IQs range from a low of 45 to a high of 155. Full Scale IQs can range from 40 to 160. Ogdon (1975) suggested a statistical technique for extending the range slightly.

Reliability

The reliabilities reported in the WISC-R manual were, in general, computed in the same fashion as those reported for the WAIS-R. They are split-half reliabilities, except for the Digit Span and Coding tests. Split-half reliabilities, corrected for test length, reflect the *internal consistency* of test scores. The reliabilities for the twelve subtests and three IQs were computed separately for each of eleven age groups (6½ to 16½). The reliabilities of the IQ scores show remarkably little change across ages and are all high. The average reliabilities in the eleven age groups are .94, .90, and .96 for the Verbal, Performance and Full Scale IQs, respectively. The subtests demonstrate somewhat lower reliabilities but do not appear to vary in any systematic way as a function of age. Again, looking only at the average reliabilities across ages, Object Assembly has the lowest average reliability (.70) and Vocabulary has the highest (.86).

To assess the *stability* of the WISC-R subtest scores and IQs, three groups were retested after an interval of about one month. About 100 children in each of three age ranges (6½ to 7½, 10½ to 11½, 14½ to 15½) were used. The resulting reliabilities were similar to those obtained by the split-half method. Within a one-month period the subjects remained in essentially the same rank order with respect to test scores. However, on the second testing, the average scores increased for all subtests as did the three IQ scores for all age groups. These results suggest that there is some practice effect in retaking the WISC-R. For example, for the age group 14½ to 15½, the Full Scale IQ increased from 96.1 to 103.0 even though the correlation between the two sets of scores was .95 (Wechsler, 1974, p. 33).

Extensive longitudinal studies of the WISC-R are not yet available. That is, the stability of WISC-R scores over long intervals of time remains to be demonstrated. However, one study reported the stability of WISC-R scores for a sample of seventy-five "exceptional" children over a two-year interval (Vance et al. 1981). The IQs from the two administrations correlated .80, .91, and .88 for the Verbal, Performance, and Full Scale, respectively. The differences between the means of the IQs were also small. This study strongly suggests that WISC-R IQs are relatively stable over a two-year interval. A second study, using forty-five normal children, retested children after about six months (Tuma & Appelbaum, 1980). The IQs were quite highly correlated, .95, .89, and .95 for the Verbal, Performance, and Full Scale, respectively, but some practice effect was demonstrated. The Performance and Full Scale IQs were, on the average, significantly higher on the second testing. Finally, Covin (1977b) retested thirty children classified as learning disabled after a one-day interval and found stability coefficients of about .84 for all three IQ scales with little difference in the mean IQs.

Stability studies of the 1949 WISC, as summarized by Zimmerman and Woo-Sam (1972), also did not cover particularly long intervals of time. The limited data available on the WISC suggest that IQ reliabilities may be in the .70s over three- to four-year intervals and that subtest reliabilities are too low for profile analysis. Based on what happens with other tests as well as with the WISC, it is probably fair to infer that WISC-R scores will be stable over relatively short periods of time but could show considerable change over longer periods of time.

As we have mentioned earlier, scoring individually administered tests that permit relatively free or unstructured responses is a difficult task. The studies on the reliability of the WISC-R just reported implicitly assume that scoring is accurate and that error arises mainly because of random processes originating in the subject. Thus, if the same WISC-R protocol (responses to all items on the test) were given to trained examiners, we would expect the same scores to be earned by all examinees. The only reason scores would differ is because of differences among the examiners in how they scored the responses. Bradley et al. (1980) constructed two experimental protocols—one easy to score, the other difficult. A sample of sixty-three school psychologists scored the two protocols. The results demonstrated that the score an examinee receives for a given set of responses on the WISC-R can easily vary from six to eight IQ points. Unreliable scoring is potentially a serious problem for the WISC-R and other tests that permit unstructured responses.

Responses on the Similarities, Comprehension, and Vocabulary subtests are difficult to score and undoubtedly contributed to the results reported by Bradley et al. When only unusual, atypical, or ambiguous responses on these three subtests were submitted to examiners for scoring, it was found that 80 percent agreement among raters occurred for less than half the 726 responses (Sattler et al., 1978).

The *standard error of measurement* provides another index of the consistency of test scores on the WISC-R. Wechsler (1974, p. 30) presents the standard errors of measurement for all twelve subtests and three IQs at each of the eleven age levels. There is somewhat more error for younger than older children on all tests and IQ scales, but the differences are not very large. As might be expected, there is somewhat more error in Performance than in Verbal IQs. The standard error of measurement for the Full Scale IQ varies from a high of 3.49 for age 6½ to a low of 2.96 for age 12½. The average S_{meas} is 3.19. Using 3.00 as an approximation to S_{meas}, we would expect a child's Full Scale IQ to be within ± 6 IQ points of the "true" IQ about 95 percent of the time.

As with the WAIS-R, it is possible to examine differences between scores on the various WISC-R subtests and between the Verbal and Performance IQs. Again, difference scores are unreliable and must be interpreted with caution. Wechsler (1974, p. 35) provides tables that give the differences between scaled scores on the subtests and between Verbal and Performance IQs that are required for statistical significance. In all age groups, the average difference between Verbal and Performance IQs required to be statistically significant at the .05

level is 11.55. Thus, differences smaller than eleven or twelve points could occur by chance more than 5 percent of the time. Wechsler (p. 34) suggests that a difference of fifteen or more points is important and deserves further investigation.

Other investigators have approached the differences between Verbal and Performance IQs in an empirical fashion or examined the abnormality of subtest score differences with a different statistical procedure. Kaufman (1976b), for example, examined Verbal-Performance IQ discrepancies on the WISC-R in the 2,200 subjects in the standardization sample. He found that 24 percent of the standardization sample differed by fourteen or more points and four percent differed by twenty to twenty-four points. These figures provide base rates useful in interpreting obtained differences in Verbal and Performance IQ. Thus, a child could have a statistically significant discrepancy yet still not have an abnormally deviant score. Silverstein (1981a, b) and Piotrowski (1978, 1981) provide additional discussion and formulas on this topic.

Validity

The validity information presented in the WISC-R manual is very limited. It consists of three studies in which the WISC-R was correlated with three other tests of intelligence, two of them being other Wechsler scales—the Wechsler Preschool and Primary Scale of Intelligence (WPPSI) and the 1955 WAIS. These studies all demonstrated the concurrent validity of the WISC-R.

In the WISC-R and WPPSI comparison, fifty children six years of age were administered both tests (one to three weeks between testings). The three IQs correlated about .80, and the average IQs were similar for both tests.

In the 1955 WAIS study, forty children of age sixteen years, eleven months were given the WISC-R and 1955 WAIS (one to three weeks between testings). The correlations between IQs were .96, .83, and .95 for the Verbal, Performance, and Full Scale

IQs, respectively. These correlations clearly indicate that the two Wechsler scales were measuring similar mental functions and that subjects were in similar rank orders on the two scales. However, it was also found that the 1955 WAIS IQs were, on the average, six points higher than the WISC-R IQs. The WISC-R and WAIS-R results reported earlier in connection with the WAIS-R produced somewhat lower correlations but smaller differences between mean IQs.

Finally, the WISC-R and Stanford-Binet Intelligence Scale (S-B) were given to about thirty children at four different age levels (6, 9½, 12½, 16½). Wechsler (1974, p. 52) presents the results for each age level, but we will consider only the average correlations for the four age groups. The S-B correlated, on the average, .71, .60, and .73 with the WISC-R Verbal, Performance, and Full Scale IQs. In addition, the mean IQs on both scales were quite similar. The relationship between the S-B and the WISC-R is thus reasonable but not as high as between the 1955 WAIS and WISC-R. Because the S-B and WISC-R did not correlate more highly, it is certainly the case that the IQs from the two tests are not interchangeable or equivalent.

Although the 1974 test manual did not include a detailed examination of the validity of the WISC-R, much validity information exists in the literature. Research on the 1949 WISC, which was used in numerous studies, has been reviewed by Littell (1960) and Zimmerman and Woo-Sam (1972). To the extent that the 1949 WISC and WISC-R are similar, research on the earlier edition of the scale provides at least suggestive validity data for the WISC-R.

As might be expected, there are many studies relating WISC and WISC-R scores. Swerdlik (1977), for example, who reviewed twelve studies, demonstrated that WISC IQs are always higher on the average. Of course, one would expect this finding since the 1949 WISC norms were undoubtedly outdated by 1974. Schwarting (1976), using a random sample of fifty-eight children between the ages of six and fifteen, administered the WISC and WISC-R in counterbalanced order. The time between tests was about two months. He found that the WISC IQs were significantly higher—109 versus 105 for the Verbal, 115 versus 106 for the Performance, and 113 versus 106 for the Full Scale. Although Schwarting did not report correlations, they can be computed from his results and are .88, .74, and .86 for the Verbal, Performance, and Full Scale IQs, respectively.

Many studies comparing the WISC and WISC-R used special subject groups such as retarded persons and special education classes. For example, Berry and Sherrets (1975) found correlations between WISC and WISC-R IQs of .74, .85, and .86 for the Verbal, Performance, and Full Scale IQs. The subjects in this study were twenty-eight special education students ranging in age from 8.7 to 15.6 years. The order of test administration was counterbalanced, with about two weeks between tests. Similar results were obtained by Brooks (1977) with thirty students referred for psychological evaluation. The WISC and WISC-R Full Scale IQs correlated .91, for example, and mean WISC IQs were all higher, on the average, than the corresponding WISC-R IQs. Fairly low correlations (.21, .65, .54) between WISC and WISC-R IQs have been reported, however, for twenty retarded students tested over an interval of time averaging three years. The WISC had always been administered first when subjects averaged eleven years of age (Gironda, 1977). In a fairly large study, Thomas (1980) used students who were "mildly mentally handicapped." One hundred eighty-three students were tested twice with the WISC. Ninety-three students were tested first with the WISC and then with the WISC-R. There were approximately three years between administrations, and the children had a median age of 9½ at initial testing. The WISC IQs showed, on the average, a slight increase over time, whereas the means for the WISC-R IQs were slightly lower than the WISC IQs obtained three years earlier. The correlations (not reported in the study but computed from the results published) between WISC-R and WISC IQs were .87, .90, and .92, for the Verbal, Performance, and Full Scale, respectively. Other investigators have also found WISC IQs tended to be higher than WISC-R IQs (Stokes et al., 1978). Others have examined the effects of different socioeconomic backgrounds in comparing the 1949 WISC with the WISC-R (Tuma et al., 1978).

Based on these results it does appear that the WISC and WISC-R measure similar mental functioning. This is not surprising since the content of the two scales is highly similar. Perhaps because of the renorming, it also appears that WISC IQs, on the average, are higher than WISC-R IQs. Thus, although the two scales would tend to rank order children in the same manner, diagnostic categories would not necessarily be the same because of the differences in mean IQs. Kaufman (1979b) reviewed the available studies and concluded that the WISC-R, being the most recently developed test, should always be used. On balance, however, it appears reasonable to assume that validity information about the WISC is relevant in evaluating the WISC-R.

The *content validity* of the WISC-R is judged on the adequacy of the items and subtests selected for inclusion. As Littell (1960) noted in his review of research on the WISC, the content validity of the WISC-R is difficult to determine because Wechsler's definition of intelligence is so broad. However, the test was constructed with care and the items seem appropriate for various age levels. Also, the subtests differ in content to reflect Wechsler's more global conception of intelligence. Since it is well known that mental capacity increases with age, information on the percentage of children of various ages passing items on the subtests would be useful and would help establish the content validity of the items in a statistical sense. The scoring criteria reflect an increase in ability as a function of age. Thus, for example, a scaled score of 10 on the Information test is received for raw scores of 5, 10, 13, 17, 19, and 22 at ages 6, 8, 10, 12, 14, and 16, respectively. Older children must, there-

fore, exhibit higher levels of performance than younger children to receive the same scaled score.

The *concurrent validity* of the WISC-R was examined mainly by correlating its scores with other measures of intelligence. We have already noted the studies reported in the WISC-R manual. The S-B has appeared in several studies with the WISC-R (Brooks, 1977; Kaufman & Van Hagan, 1977; Raskin et al., 1978). In these studies, which involved retarded children or others referred for evaluation, the S-B IQ and WISC-R Full Scale IQ correlated between .82 and .95. The mean IQs were generally similar, although one study (Kaufman & Van Hagan, 1977) found the S-B IQ to be seven points higher than the WISC-R full scale IQ. These results parallel those reported in the WISC-R manual (Wechsler, 1974). The WISC-R Verbal IQ correlated more highly with the S-B than did the Performance IQ. The 1949 WISC also correlated with the S-B in much the same manner (Littell, 1960; Sattler, 1974, Ch. 11; Zimmerman & Woo-Sam, 1972). Previous research on the WISC also indicated that the WISC IQ for superior children was always lower than the mean S-B IQ. This also appeared to be true for children of above average intelligence. The two scales appeared to provide comparable IQs for subjects of below average intelligence (Sattler, 1974, p. 155). The comparability of mean IQs for the WISC-R and S-B largely remains to be established.

In addition to the S-B, the WISC-R has been correlated with other tests of intelligence, academic achievement, or cognitive functioning. The Wide Range Achievement Test (Jastak et al., 1976) seems particularly popular. In many of these studies the Verbal IQ correlates with the other test scores as well as or better than the Full Scale IQ. Recent studies suggest that the WISC-R Full Scale and Verbal IQs correlated fairly well (r's = .60 to .80, in general) with scores on other tests of mental ability, whereas the Performance IQ typically correlates less well. The studies, however, often were based on rather small samples, were for different age groups, and were often composed of "special" children (for example, learning disabled or retarded). Examples of studies correlating the WISC-R with other test scores[11] include the following: Brooks (1977); Covin (1976); Covin (1977a); Crofoot and Bennett (1980); Hale (1978); Hartlage and Steele (1977); Hodapp and Hodapp (1980); Ivimey and Taylor (1980); Lowrance and Anderson (1979); Mize et al. (1979); Nicholson (1977); Raskin et al. (1978); Reeve et al. (1979); Reynolds and Gutkin (1980a); Reynolds and Hartlage (1979); Reynolds et al. (1979); Wikoff (1979).

Based on the S-B results and the studies just cited, it appears that the concurrent validity of the WISC-R is comparable to that of the 1949 WISC. In this case, we limit our definition of concurrent validity to correlations between WISC-R IQs and scores on other tests of mental ability and achievement. Although the correlations are generally satisfactory, there are often differences between the mean IQs on the WISC-R and the other tests. The test scores are, thus, usually not equivalent or interchangeable even though they may be correlated.

There are surprisingly few studies of the WISC-R that provide information on its *predictive validity*. As would be expected, the WISC-R has been used to predict scholastic achievement. Hartlage and Steele (1977) tested thirty-six predominantly black children with a mean age of seven years and nine months. Grades in several subjects at the end of the first and second grade were used as the criteria. The WISC-R Full Scale IQ correlated significantly with grades in several areas, the highest *r* being .72 for reading and spelling in grade two, but it did not correlate significantly with grades in social studies for either grade one or grade two. The Verbal IQ was a better predictor of grades than was the Full Scale IQ. The Performance IQ correlated less well or not at all with grades except for writing, where it was about as good as or better than the other two IQ scales.

In a well-designed study, Dean (1979) tested forty-nine Mexican-American children between the ages of 8 and 10½. Approximately a year and a half later achievement test scores in vocabulary, reading, and arithmetic skill were obtained. The predictive validity coefficients were all statistically significant and ranged from a low of .35 for the Performance IQ, predicting performance on the reading test, to a high of .61 for the Verbal IQ, predicting scores on the vocabulary achievement test. Considering the homogeneous sample, the WISC-R does possess satisfactory validity in predicting academic achievement as measured in Dean's study.

Reschly and Reschly (1979) reported data on the predictive utility of the WISC-R for a large group (n = 787) of children from four ethnic groups (anglo, black, chicano, and native American Papago). Although there were some differences among groups, the Full Scale IQ correlated modestly (.41 to .62) with achievement test scores in reading and mathematics. Full Scale IQ also correlated with teachers' ratings of academic performance, although these correlations were generally lower than the ones with achievement tests.

Given the paucity of predictive validity studies on the WISC-R, it seems important to examine such evidence from the 1949 WISC. Unfortunately, again relatively little information is available. Littell (1960, p. 135) noted that restricting the term *predictive validity* to refer to correlations between the WISC and a criterion behavior obtained some time after the test scores were obtained resulted in finding no relevant studies in the ten years immediately following the publication of the 1949 WISC. A later review of WISC research (Zimmerman & Woo-Sam, 1972) cited no studies specifically dealing with the predictive validity of the WISC. Sattler (1974), however, contends that the WISC did have predictive validity based on studies cited in his section on diagnostic applications of intelligence tests. Sattler uses predictive validity more in the sense of establishing behavioral correlates of WISC scores or determining their clinical utility. It thus appears to us that the WISC-R cannot rely to any great degree on studies done with the WISC to establish its predictive validity. More evidence on the WISC-R's predictive validity is clearly needed.

The evidence on the *construct validity* of the WISC-R continues to accumulate. Obviously, the many studies cited demonstrate that the WISC-R correlates with other tests of mental ability and academic achievement. The WISC-R, along with the S-B, has been accepted as a criterion measure of intelligence, and other tests are considered valid if they correlate with the WISC-R.

The WISC-R demonstrated expected differences between mean IQs when criterion groups were created on the basis of other information. For example, Ivimey and Taylor (1980) found that a learning disabled group had a mean WISC-R Full Scale IQ of 102, whereas a nonlearning disabled group had a mean of 113, a highly significant difference. Thompson (1980) reported significant mean differences between all three of his diagnostic groups and the standardization sample of the WISC-R. For all three IQs, Thompson found that the mentally retarded group had the lowest, a learning disability group next lowest, and a psychological or behavioral disorder group the highest mean IQ. However, all groups had means significantly below 100, the mean of the standardization group. Other investigators found much higher Verbal, Performance, and Full Scale IQs among children from higher socioeconomic groups (Appelbaum & Tuma, 1977; Tuma et al. 1978; Zingale & Smith, 1978).

The rational dichotomy of the subtests, verbal versus performance, was suggested by Wechsler for all three of his scales. Other researchers used factor analysis to determine empirically how the subtests were organized. Kaufman (1975a) factor analyzed the intercorrelations among the twelve WISC-R subtests at the eleven age levels in the standardization sample. His results suggested that there were three factors under-

lying performance on the WISC-R subtests: (1) *Verbal Comprehension*—Information, Similarities, Vocabulary, and Comprehension; (2) *Perceptual Organization*—Picture Completion, Picture Arrangement, Block Design, Object Assembly, and Mazes; (3) *Freedom from Distractibility*—Arithmetic, Digit Span, and Coding. These same factors have generally appeared in other studies of a variety of different groups (for example, Cummins & Das, 1980; Gutkin & Reynolds, 1980; Karnes & Brown, 1980; Lawlis et al. 1980; Reschly, 1978; Reynolds & Gutkin, 1980b; Shiek & Miller, 1978; Swerdlik & Schweitzer, 1978; Van Hagan & Kaufman, 1975). It thus appears that the first factor, Verbal Comprehension, corresponds fairly closely to Wechsler's Verbal Scale and that the second factor, Perceptual Organization, is similar to Wechsler's Performance Scale. The third factor, Freedom from Distractibility, may be in the behavioral or affective domain rather than in the cognitive domain (see Kaufman, 1979a, for an extensive discussion of this factor and its interpretation). The results of the several factor analyses seem to support Wechsler's rationale for constructing the two IQ scales, although a third factor is also present.

Given that the verbal-performance dichtomy is a meaningful one, it is possible to examine differences between Verbal and Performance IQs for possible diagnostic significance, assuming, of course, that such differences are reliable. Usually a difference of at least 12 to 15 points is required before the difference is significant, and larger differences would be worthy of consideration. Kaufman (1979a) does an excellent job in discussing the contradictory results on verbal and performance differences. He suggests that they can arise for a variety of reasons, including differences in verbal versus nonverbal intelligence, psycholinguistic deficiency, bilingualism, problems in coordination, time pressure, and socioeconomic influences. It appears to us that such discrepancies remain a rich source of clinical hypotheses but that empirically based correlates are, as yet, lacking in consistency. Kaufman (1979a, p. 25), for example, notes that the discrepancies should not be used to infer brain damage without data from other sources. He also notes that virtually the entire literature on verbal-performance differences is replete with contradictory studies and a lack of success in identifying characteristic patterns associated with various diagnostic groups.

As is true of all the Wechsler scales, profile analysis can be used with the WISC-R. That is, patterns of scores on the subtests can be used for diagnostic purposes. *Scatter* refers to large differences among the scores on subtests within the Verbal or Performance Scales. For example, a child having high scores on two of the verbal tests and relatively low scores on the other three tests would be exhibiting scatter. A more "normal" pattern would be for a child to receive either consistently high, average, or low scores on all the verbal subtests, for example. The clinical or diagnostic significance of scatter remains more of an art than a science. As Kaufman (1979a, p. 196) reports, rather large differences between subtest scores occur routinely. He found, for example, that the average difference between each child's highest and lowest subtest scaled score was seven points (over two standard deviations). The point is that it is easy to overinterpret scatter on the WISC-R subtests. Other investigators have questioned the utility of scatter in differentiating among groups (Gutkin, 1979; Ollendick, 1979; Thompson, 1980).

More complex methods of statistical analysis have been employed to examine the utility of profile analysis of the WISC-R subtest scores. Hale and Landino (1981), for example, had four carefully defined criterion groups of boys in their study: a conduct problem group, a withdrawn group, a mixed group (not clearly a conduct problem or withdrawn), and a nonproblem group. Their investigation demonstrated that behaviorally disturbed and normal children could not be meaningfully separated by WISC-R subtest differences. Hamm and Evans (1978) reported a similar lack of success in differentiating severely emotionally disturbed children from other groups. Three more recent studies (Bloom & Raskin, 1980; Vance et al., 1980; Zingale & Smith, 1978) suggested a lack of diagnostic utility of patterns of subtests scores for learning disabled children. Hale (1979) reported a similar failure in discriminating between adequate and underachieving children. Other investigators have found that subtest scores did not differentiate among a large group ($n = 238$) of retarded children (Vance et al., 1978). Hirshoren and Kavale (1976) refer to the profile analysis of the WISC-R as a continuing malpractice because of the unreliability of the subtest scores.*

Kaufman's (1979a) book, *Intelligent Testing with the WISC-R,* provides an excellent description of and prescription for clinical use of the WISC-R. This book will undoubtedly be of great use to professionals who use the WISC-R in their work. His chapters on profile analysis are rich in clincal insight and are balanced against the empirical work that we have already mentioned. Profile analysis, however, remains an indefinite science.

In summary, the accumulated evidence on the construct validity of the WISC-R is encouraging. There is already a vast literature on this test and it grows yearly. Additional studies on the predictive validity of the WISC-R would be helpful, as would longitudinal studies on the stability of WISC-R IQs. Wechsler's hope that a profile analysis of the subtests would be useful and clinically relevant as yet appears to have been only marginally fulfilled.

*Other investigators have been able to differentiate among groups (for example, Dean 1978, using learning disabled and emotionally disturbed children), but the available evidence suggests that such findings are certainly not universal.

WECHSLER PRESCHOOL AND PRIMARY SCALE OF INTELLIGENCE (WPPSI)

The WPPSI is the baby of the Wechsler scales (Wechsler, 1967). It was published in 1967 well after the WAIS and WISC were developed; in fact, the WAIS had already been revised once. The WPPSI was designed for children ranging in age between three years, ten months, and sixteen days to six years, seven months, and fifteen days. Children older than the upper age limit must be tested with the WISC-R. Children younger than the lower limit cannot be tested with any Wechsler scale, and another test (for example, Stanford-Binet) must be used.

The WPPSI was developed to extend the age range of children that could be tested by the WISC-R. The lowest age appropriate for testing with the WISC-R is six. There is thus some overlap between the two scales, but the WPPSI is intended for preschool children. Its age range covers an important developmental period. The early identification of mental dysfunction, for example, is necessary so that remedial educational programming can begin. At this period, children are also beginning to exhibit fairly sophisticated verbal skills.

The WPPSI is organized like the other two Wechsler scales. There are eleven subtests divided into two types—verbal and performance. Ten subtests (five verbal and five performance) are combined to yield Verbal, Performance, and Full Scale IQs expressed as standard scores with a mean of 100 and standard deviation of 15. The subtests are scaled to have a mean of 10 and standard deviation of 3. Eight of the subtests provide the same measures as the WISC-R. Two subtests on the Performance Scale, Animal House and Geometric Design, are unique to the WPPSI. A Supplementary Verbal test, Sentences, is unique to the WPPSI, but it is not used in computing the Verbal or Full Scale IQs. The eight subtests of the WPPSI in common with the 1949 WISC contain some identical items and some new items. The modifications of the WISC subtests for the WPPSI include the addition of easier items and the deletion of more difficult items. In other words, the WISC tests are modified to be appropriate for younger children, a modification that includes some adjustments in both content and the mode of administration. The WPPSI was the first Wechsler scale to alternate the administration of verbal and performance tests, a practice now followed in the WISC-R and WAIS-R.

Content

The WPPSI consists of eleven subtests, ten of which are used to compute the IQ scores. The subtests are organized according to content, and all items within a subtest are ordered in terms of difficulty, easier items appearing first. For each subtest, all children begin with the first item and are presented items until they fail a critical number consecutively. Items are scored zero if answered incorrectly. Correct answers are usually given one point, but some subtests allow higher scores for higher quality correct answers. Bonus points are awarded for especially rapid correct responses on some of the timed tests. There are fewer timed tests and items on the WPPSI than on the other Wechsler scales. Three of the performance tests have time limits, and the Arithmetic test has eleven of twenty items that are timed. The Verbal Scale tests are the following: Information, Vocabulary, Arithmetic, Similarities, Comprehension, and Sentences (Supplementary Test). The Performance Scale tests are these: Animal House, Picture Completion, Mazes, Geometric Design, and Block Design. Because eight of these subtests are similar in design and content to those in the WISC-R, we will not discuss them again. Sattler (1982, Ch. 13) and Wechsler (1967) provide descriptions of all WPPSI subtests. We will describe the three tests unique to the WPPSI.

1. *Sentences (Supplementary Test).* This Verbal Scale test was developed to replace the WISC Digit Span test. Ten sentences, varying in complexity, are read to the child, who must repeat them verbatim. If the first sentence, containing five words, is failed, three easier sentences, containing two, three, and four words, are administered. An error in repeating the sentence is defined as an omission, transposition, addition, or substitution. Subjects are awarded 1 to 4 points per sentence depending on the number of errors made. For example, four or more errors on sentences seven to ten earn 0 points, and no errors on these same sentences earn 4 points. Testing is discontinued after three consecutive failures.
2. *Animal House.* This Performance Scale test is like the coding test on the WISC–R and requires the child to associate an object with a symbol. The test consists of a form board and twenty-eight colored cylinders. In each square of the form board is a hole and a picture of one of four animals (dog, chicken, fish, or cat). A different colored cylinder is associated with each animal's picture. The child's task is to place a cylinder of the appropriate color in each hole in the form board. The examiner demonstrates what is expected by doing the first five or six pictures. The demonstration cylinders are then removed, and the child is told to continue the task. Twenty squares are to be completed in five minutes. Scores are based on the time needed to complete the test and the number of errors and omissions. For example, a child making five errors but completing the task in two minutes would be awarded 34 points, whereas a child making the same number of errors but taking four minutes would receive 16 points. Thus, to do well on the test, children must perform both quickly and accurately. The maximum score possible is 70.
3. *Geometric Design.* In this Performance Scale test, geometric designs are presented, and the child must draw the figure. The designs vary in complexity (the first and easiest, for example, is a circle). Testing is discontinued after two consecutive failures. No fixed time limit is imposed, but about 30 seconds are allowed for the child to make an attempt. The points awarded for correct designs vary from 1 to 4 depending on the accuracy of the drawing. The maximum score possible is 28.

Administration and Scoring

A trained examiner is required for the administration of the WPPSI. Since it is used with children between the ages of 4 and 6½, it is important for the examiner to establish rapport. The examiner's approach should be objective yet sympathetic. As Wechsler (1967) suggests, the general aim is to establish rapport in order to maintain the child's interest and encourage maximum performance. There are special problems in testing young children. The WPPSI manual notes the following: "Some of the test materials are quite small, and some children may try to put them into their mouths. The examiner must guard against this to prevent accidents" (Wechsler, 1967, p. 38). Young children thus pose a special challenge. At least, when testing adults, examiners need not worry about the subject swallowing the test materials.

Instructions for administering and scoring the WPPSI must be followed precisely in order for the resulting test scores to be valid. Scoring procedures for some of the subtests differ rather markedly from those used on the WISC-R. Further inquiry for ambiguous responses is permitted. Because younger children may pronounce words less accurately than adults or older children, this can be one source of ambiguity that needs further inquiry by the examiner.

The subtests are usually administered in the following order: Information, Animal House, Vocabulary, Picture Completion, Arithmetic, Mazes, Geometric Designs, Similarities, Block Design, Comprehension, Sentences (Supplementary Test), and Animal House Retest. The WPPSI manual notes that Animal House occasionally may be administered again at the end of the session if the examiner is interested in the qualitative evaluation of the child's ability to learn a simple task. However, only the first test score is used in determining IQs, not the retest score.

According to the WPPSI manual, the test can be administered in fifty to seventy-five minutes. However, the manual notes that this may be too long for some children. With younger children or those having handicaps, two sessions may be needed. The manual strongly recommends, however, that all ten subtests be administered in a single session.

The instructions for scoring the subtests seem reasonably detailed. However, three verbal tests—Similarities, Vocabulary, and Comprehension—are somewhat subjective in that items are given two, one, or zero points depending on the quality of the response. Geometric Design, a test unique to the WPPSI, is also difficult to score, since children's drawings can reflect a lack of hand-eye coordination in addition to perceptual and organizational deficits. The manual does provide fairly extensive examples of drawings for each design that merit two, one, or zero points. Again, information on interrater agreement on these more subjective subtests would be useful. Accurate timing is required for several subtests since bonus points are awarded for especially rapid correct responses.

As is true of all Wechsler scales, the raw scores received on each subtest must be converted to scaled (standard) scores. The scaled scores, as noted, have a mean of 10 and standard deviation of 3. The scaled score equivalents of raw scores on each of the subtests are obtained from tables in the test manual for the age-appropriate group. Eleven age groups are available, essentially varying in three-month intervals from 4 to 6½ years of age. The scaled scores are then converted to IQs by reference to a single table. The WPPSI scaled scores and IQs are obtained in the same way as those on the WISC-R.

As is true for the WISC-R, the sums of scaled scores for the five verbal tests and five performance tests are virtually identical for all age groups. Thus, a single table for converting the scaled scores to the corresponding IQ is provided. Children are still being compared with others of their own age, since scaled score equivalents of raw scores do vary as a function of age. That is,

older children must earn higher raw scores than younger children to obtain the same scaled score. The resulting WPPSI IQs have means of 100 and standard deviations of 15. The percent included in the various categories of IQ are similar to those of the WAIS-R that are presented in Table 6-2. The IQs from the WPPSI follow approximately a normal distribution.

Reliability

The WPPSI manual reports split-half reliabilities for all subtests except Animal House, which has test-retest reliabilities. The reliability of the Verbal, Performance, and Full Scale IQs are determined statistically from the results of the subtests. Thus, the reliabilities for the WPPSI were determined in the same way as those of the other Wechsler scales. They were computed separately for each of six age groups—4, 4½, 5, 5½, 6, and 6½. The reliabilities did not change across ages and were generally quite high. The IQ scores had average reliabilities of .94, .93, and .96 for the Verbal, Performance, and Full Scale, respectively. Among the subtests, Animal House had the lowest average reliability (.77) and Mazes had the highest (.87). The reliability of the IQs is particularly impressive, especially considering that the scores were obtained from relatively young children. Similar reliabilities were reported for a group of gifted preschool children (Ruschival & Way, 1971), for disadvantaged Mexican-American children (Henderson & Rankin, 1973) and for a group of mentally retarded subjects (Richards, 1970).

The manual also reports one study on the *stability* of WPPSI test scores. Fifty kindergarten children were retested with the WPPSI after an average interval of about eleven weeks. The test-retest reliabilities generally were lower than those obtained by the split-half method. The Verbal, Performance, and Full Scale IQs had test-retest reliabilities of .86, .88, and .91, respectively. These are also lower than the corresponding split-half reliabilities previously noted.

The mean Verbal, Performance, and Full Scale IQs also exhibited some increase (3, 6, and 4 points, respectively) because of practice effects. No other stability studies on the WPPSI are currently available. Such information would be useful in evaluating the scale for preschool screening, since it is possible scores could change dramatically in children between ages four and six.

The reliability of the WPPSI could be affected by errors in scoring. Sattler (1976) reported that the Geometric Design test is difficult to score for both experienced and inexperienced raters. He used five protocols (responses from five subjects) that were scored by all the raters. The agreement on scoring was as low as 48 percent for one of the designs. Similar poor interscorer reliability of the Geometric Design test was reported in one other study (Morsbach et al., 1978). Kaufman (1978) also presented an interesting analysis of the use of basic concepts (for example, same, different, next) in the directions of several intelligence tests, including the WPPSI. If a child cannot understand the directions, it will be impossible for the child to perform adequately. That is, if understanding the task is not part of the test, a child's low IQ could reflect a complete or partial lack in understanding the instructions.

The *standard error of measurement* provides another index of the consistency of scores on the WPPSI. As was true of reliability, the standard errors of the subtests and of the IQ scores appear to remain comparable in the six age groups in the standardization sample. Among the subtests, Mazes has the lowest standard error (1.04) and Information the highest (1.50). The standard errors of the three IQ scores are 3.69, 3.99, and 2.98 for Verbal, Performance, and Full Scale IQs, respectively. We would thus expect children to obtain Full Scale IQs within ± 6 points of their "true" IQ about 95 percent of the time. Again, these figures are similar to results with the other Wechsler scales.

The WPPSI manual also provides tables for interpreting differences between pairs of subtest scores and between the Verbal and Performance IQs. Milliren and Newland (1968–69) provided additional information on subtest differences needed for statistical significance. For the Verbal-Performance IQs, a difference of about ten points is needed for statistical significance.

Validity

As was true of the other Wechsler scales, the WPPSI manual presents limited validity information based on ninety-eight children between the ages of 5 and 6 who were concurrently given three other intelligence tests—Stanford-Binet (S-B), Peabody Picture Vocabulary Test (PPVT), and Pictorial Test of Intelligence (PTI). The WPPSI IQs correlated as follows (Wechsler, 1967, p. 34):

		S-B	PPVT	PTI
	Verbal IQ	.76	.57	.53
WPPSI	Performance IQ	.56	.44	.60
	Full Scale IQ	.75	.58	.64

The WPPSI thus demonstrates positive correlations with these other tests but the correlations are not strikingly high. Mean IQs are roughly comparable on the three tests, all being about ninety. However, the correlations are low enough to suggest that the scores are not interchangeable.

With respect to *content validity*, it appears that the WPPSI is a well-designed test. The items should appeal to children and are appropriate for the targeted age groups. Cooley (1977) demonstrated that the items in the subtests are generally correctly ordered in terms of difficulty based on results from a sample of 151 black children. Similarly, the raw scores needed to obtain the same scaled score show an expected increase with age. Thus, for a child of four, a raw score of 12 on the Comprehension test earns a scaled score of 14; a child of six with the same raw score, however, would earn a scaled score of 8.

The *concurrent validity* of the WPPSI has

been demonstrated mainly by correlating it with other tests of intelligence. We have already noted the correlations cited in the WPPSI manual. In addition, the correlation between the WPPSI and the WISC-R was reported in the WISC-R manual (Wechsler, 1974). These correlations between WPPSI and WISC-R IQs were in the .80s, and the means were similar. Since the WPPSI is an extended version of the WISC, these correlations perhaps provide evidence on the content validity of the WPPSI as well as indicating that the two scales measure similar mental functions.

As might be expected, the WPPSI has been correlated with the S-B in several studies. Sattler (1974) summarized the results of thirteen such studies by noting that the median correlations between the S-B IQ and the WPPSI Verbal, Performance, and Full Scale IQs were .81, .67, and .82, respectively. Two additional studies, not cited by Sattler, generally support the relationship between the S-B and WPPSI. Anthony (1973) reported a correlation of .90 between WPPSI Full Scale IQ and S-B IQ. Sewell (1977) reported a parallel correlation of .71. This latter study involved the newest available norms of the S-B, and both studies used black, disadvantaged children as subjects. Although the S-B and WPPSI study in the WPPSI manual suggested that the mean IQs on both tests were similar, Sattler (1974) noted that the S-B IQs were generally higher. However, the most recent study by Sewell (1977), in which newer S-B norms were used, found that the mean WPPSI IQs were higher. Thus, differences between means on the two tests may be a function of which has the more contemporary norms. In the earlier studies cited by Sattler, the S-B norms were based on the 1960 version of that test, whereas the WPPSI norms were dated from 1967. The newest S-B norms, however, date from 1972. The safest interpretation is probably to conclude that WPPSI and S-B IQs are not interchangeable.

The WPPSI also has been correlated with a variety of other tests. For simplicity, we will focus only on correlations between the WPPSI Full Scale IQ and scores on other tests. The Full Scale IQ score on the WPPSI correlated .61 with the Slosson Intelligence Test (Baum & Kelly, 1979), .58 with the Metropolitan Reading Readiness Test (Pasewark et al., 1974), .74 with the General Cognitive Index of the McCarthy Scales of Children's Abilities (Phillips et al., 1978), and .70 with the Vane Kindergarten Test (Scherr et al., 1973). These modest correlations follow the results summarized by Sattler (1974) in which eleven studies published between 1968 and 1971 were examined. Sattler (p. 210) reported that the median correlation between the WPPSI and a variety of other tests was .64. Given the size of these correlations, although positive, it is clear that the average scores or IQs on the WPPSI and other tests will usually not be equivalent. Gerken (1978), for example, tested a group of Mexican-American children with the WPPSI and the Leiter International Performance Scale and found the WPPSI Verbal and Full Scale IQs significantly lower.

Based on the results with S-B and with other tests, the evidence on the concurrent validity of the WPPSI is good. Many of the studies involved learning disabled, gifted, or culturally disadvantaged subjects, which limited the range of scores and the correlations. However, the generally modest correlations reported clearly indicate that WPPSI IQs and those of other tests will not usually be equivalent. This is important if cutoff scores are being used to identify children who are mentally retarded, for example.

The *predictive validity* of the WPPSI has been examined in a number of studies. Since the WPPSI is appropriate for preschool or kindergarten children, scores can be related to later achievement in first grade. The scores can also be used to predict IQs obtained on other tests given when the child is older. In one study (Crockett et al., 1975), the WPPSI was administered to forty-two children age 6½ in a Head Start program, and the 1949 WISC was administered about four years later. Correlations between WPPSI and WISC IQs were .41, .61, and .54 for the Verbal, Performance, and Full Scale, respectively. The S-B was, in fact, a better predictor of WISC scores than the WPPSI.

A second study involved the prediction of WISC-R scores for ninety children after a one-year interval (Rasbury et al., 1977). Correlations between WPPSI and WISC-R IQs were .69, .68, and .75 for the Verbal, Performance, and Full Scale. Both these studies had a restricted range of scores, Crockett et al. (1976) reporting mean IQs significantly below average, and Rasbury et al. (1977) reporting mean IQs significantly above average. The latter study, using the WISC-R, replicated the relation between the WPPSI and WISC-R mean IQs reported in the WISC-R manual—the WPPSI IQs being consistently higher.

Finally, the WPPSI was used to predict WISC-R scores in a sample of 139 British children (Bishop & Butterworth, 1979). These children were initially tested with the WPPSI at an average age of 4½ and then tested with the WISC-R after an interval of about four years. The children differed rather widely in ability but had average IQs of about 100 on both tests. The correlations between Verbal, Performance, and Full Scale IQs on the two tests were .66, .70, and .75, respectively. Thus, the preschool WPPSI IQs were predictive of WISC-R IQs obtained four years later, although the standard error of estimate was reported as 9.2 for the Full Scale IQ.

The WPPSI has also been used to predict reading achievement in first grade. White and Jacobs (1979) cited the results of six such studies, including their own, that found significant, positive correlations between the WPPSI Full Scale IQ and several tests of reading achievement. The median correlations were .54, .51, and .41 for the Verbal, Performance, and Full Scale, respectively. White and Jacobs noted, however, that two studies using disadvantaged, and probably bilingual, subjects did not find any relationship between WPPSI IQs and first-grade reading achievement (Crockett

et al., 1976; Henderson & Rankin, 1973). One additional study (Serwer et al., 1972), using forty-one "high risk" children, found no significant correlation between WPPSI IQs and reading achievement or other types of achievement in first grade. It is important to note that several of these studies undoubtedly had a restricted range of IQ scores and possibly of reading achievement scores. This restriction would decrease the size of the correlation coefficient. Second, the studies were truly predictive in that scores on the reading achievement tests were usually obtained at least one year after the WPPSI was administered and sometimes as long as three years. At least with respect to middle-class children, WPPSI scores obtained in nursery school or kindergarten provide modest prediction of reading achievement in first grade.

The results on the predictive validity of the WPPSI are encouraging but limited. It would be useful to have more predictive studies relating WPPSI IQs obtained in the preschool years to scholastic achievement as measured by tests and other indices. Such data would provide evidence on the diagnostic utility of the WPPSI when used with preschool children. In our opinion, much of the data in the literature arises from samples of convenience rather than from more carefully designed research. It appears that the WPPSI, perhaps because of the extensive familiarity of professionals with the other Wechsler scales, has gained fairly wide acceptance as a criterion measure of intelligence with preschool children.

The *construct validity* of the WPPSI depends mainly on the evidence previously cited. Thus, the fact that WISC-R and WPPSI IQ scores are correlated is evidence that the two tests measure similar mental functions. The correlations between WPPSI IQ scores and other tests of intelligence also support the supposition that the WPPSI is measuring intelligence. The limited number of studies on the WPPSI's utility in predicting achievement in first grade is also confirmatory evidence of the construct validity of the WPPSI.

One interesting study employed the WPPSI to determine the pattern of cognitive development in 142 pairs of preschool twins (Wilson, 1975). Twins were classified as monozygotic (genetically identical) or dizygotic (genetically different or fraternal). Subjects were tested at ages four, five, and six, and some subjects were tested more than once. For the monozygotic pairs, correlations between Full Scale IQs were significantly higher than for dizygotic pairs. The same results were indicated on subtests. That is, the profiles of monozygotic twins tended to be more similar than those of dizygotic twins. Thus, to the extent that one believes intelligence is strongly influenced by genetic factors, Wilson's study provides evidence that the WPPSI is an indicator of this expected finding.

The means of WPPSI IQ scores have been shown to vary as a function of the criterion group in many studies. That is, when a group is defined as being disadvantaged or at risk, the mean IQs are typically less than 100 and often substantially less (Anthony, 1973; Baum & Kelly, 1979; Crockett et al., 1975; Dlugokinski et al., 1976; Henderson & Rankin, 1973). Gerken (1978), in her study of Mexican-American children, reported sizeable differences on the WPPSI Verbal IQ as a function of the language spoken in the child's home. Thus, the mean Verbal IQs were 62, 84, and 104 for groups from Spanish-, bilingual-, or English-speaking homes. The studies demonstrating expected differences in mean IQs support the construct validity of the WPPSI. Other studies indicated that WPPSI IQs vary as a function of socioeconomic status (Dlugokinski et al., 1976; Kaufman, 1973). Children from families in higher socioeconomic groups have higher mean IQs than those from lower occupational groups. These differences between mean IQs for various criterion groups support the construct validity of the WPPSI as a measure of intelligence.

Factor analyses of the standardization data have tended to support the use of two IQs—Verbal and Performance (Coates & Bromberg, 1973; Hollenbeck & Kaufman, 1973; Ramanaiah & Adams, 1979; Wallbrown et al., 1973). That is, when the intercorrelations among the eleven WPPSI subtests are analyzed, it has been found that the verbal tests are related to one factor or dimension and the performance tests are related to the second factor or dimension. Results similar to those from the standardization sample have been obtained for educationally deprived and normal children (Heil et al., 1978). The empirical results provide some justification for reporting and using WPPSI Verbal and Performance IQs. However, the studies typically report that the first factor is very large in relation to the other, suggesting that one general factor could be used to explain the intercorrelations among the tests. On balance, however, the factor analytic results support the construct validity of the WPPSI.

EVALUATION OF THE WECHSLER SCALES

Following are several points regarding the Wechsler scales of intelligence.

1. Each scale has been carefully developed. The content is current and appropriate for ages for which it is to be used.
2. The standardization samples for all three scales are representative of contemporary U.S. society and are completely described.
3. The WAIS-R, published in 1981, and the WISC-R, published in 1974, are both quite recent additions. The WPPSI, published in 1967, may need new normative data or more evidence that children tested in the 1980s are performing similarly to the 1967 normative sample.
4. Unlike the Stanford-Binet, which provides a single IQ, each Wechsler scale provides ten to eleven subtest scores as well as Verbal, Performance, and Full Scale IQs. Although differences among the subtest scores and between the Verbal and Performance IQ may be of clinical use, they may also be over-interpreted.

5. The Verbal, Performance, and Full Scale IQs appear to be highly reliable (internally consistent) but the subtest scores are much less so. More data on the stability of IQs over longer periods of time would be desirable, although the available evidence is encouraging.

6. The manuals for all three scales report little validity information. Much of the voluminous literature on the three scales deals with their concurrent validity, mainly the correlation between the Wechsler scales and other intelligence tests. More studies of the predictive validity of the three scales are clearly needed.

7. All the Wechsler scales measure a subject's current mental functioning and thus measure the effects of both heredity and environment.

8. Speed of responding is a factor of importance for some subtests on all the scales.

9. Taken as a package, the three Wechsler scales provide the best available means for the individual assessment of intelligence from age four through old age.

7

Individual Tests
of Mental Ability

Tests Used with Preschool Children
and Special Populations

In this chapter, we will consider individually administered tests that are used with preschool children and special populations such as infants and the handicapped.

The Wechsler scales and Standford-Binet (S-B) are undoubtedly the most widely used individually administered tests of intelligence. The WISC-R, in particular, is extremely popular and is generating much research. The WAIS-R will surely follow shortly with a wealth of new studies. However, at the preschool level, although the S-B and WPPSI are widely used and good instruments, it appears to us that the McCarthy Scales of Children's Abilities (MSCA) is becoming an increasingly important assessment tool. This test was published in 1972 and was the creation of Dorthea McCarthy (now deceased), a developmental/clinical psychologist on the faculty of Fordham University. The scales were developed in recognition that the early years of a child's life are very important. Thus, psychologists have become increasingly interested in testing younger and younger children.

McCARTHY SCALES OF CHILDREN'S ABILITIES (MSCA)

The items or tasks on the MSCA were designed to appeal to children and to be nonthreatening. Children do largely enjoy the MSCA, since it is much less "testlike" than the S-B or WPPSI. The MSCA can be administered to children between 2½ to 8½ years of age. There are eighteen separate tests (or types of tasks) grouped into six scales, which are based on both statistical and clinical grounds. The scores on the six scales are often referred to as *indexes*. Unlike the S-B and Wechsler scales, the MSCA does not use the term *intelligence* or *IQ*. However, one of the indexes is the General Cognitive Index, which for all practical purposes can be regarded as a deviation IQ. The McCarthy also permits some observations

128

FIGURE 7–1 Dorthea McCarthy (1905–1974) was a clinical psychologist who spent most of her professional career in the Psychology Department at Fordham University. She developed the McCarthy Scales of Children's Abilities. (Courtesy of Archives, Fordham University.)

on laterality (left- or right-handedness), because, unlike the Wechsler scales or S-B, it assesses a child's coordination.

Recent reviews of research on MSCA (Kaufman & Kaufman, 1977b; Nagle, 1979) attest to its growing popularity. A book (Kaufman & Kaufman, 1977a) on the clinical use of the McCarthy should help increase its acceptance by clinical and school psychologists who deal with young children.

Content

The MSCA's organization is similar to that of the Wechsler scales in that it consists of subtests. It is not organized by age level as in the S-B. Unlike the Wechsler scales, however, the subtest scores are not typically used for diagnosis or prediction. Instead, the subtests are combined to form six scales, which are not all independent of each other. That is, some of the same subtests contribute to more than one of the scales. The six scales are Verbal, Perceptual-Performance,

Quantitative, General Cognitive, Memory, and Motor. The first three do not overlap in content and are combined to yield the General Cognitive Index. Items within each subtest are ordered in terms of difficulty. Most tests begin with the first item, but some allow older children to begin with more difficult items. In such cases, credit is given for the easier items if the more difficult item is passed. If it is failed, the easier items are administered. The six scales or indexes will be described in the following section on administration and scoring, but first we will describe the eighteen subtests.

1. *Block Building.* In this test, the child copies four structures (towers) built by the examiner out of blocks (one-inch wooden cubes). The examiner's model remains standing during the entire trial. A second trial on each of the four items is permitted if a perfect score is not obtained on the first trial. The points awarded vary from 0 to 3 depending on how well the child constructs the model. Children five and older begin with item three. Testing is discontinued after two consecutive failures.

2. *Puzzle Solving.* Six puzzles are presented for the child to put together appropriately. They are all pictures of common objects or animals (a cat) and vary in the number of pieces from two to six. Children five or older begin with item three. For items four through six, bonus points are awarded for rapid, correct performance. These latter items have time limits of 60, 90, and 120 seconds. Partial credit is possible, and the points awarded can vary from 0 to 9. Testing stops after three consecutive failures.

3. *Pictorial memory.* A card with six pictures of common objects is shown to the child while the examiner names the six objects. After ten seconds of exposure the card is removed and the child is asked to tell the examiner what the objects were. Ninety seconds are allowed for recall.

4. *Word Knowledge.* Part I: Picture Vocabulary for children below age five begins with a card of six pictures of common objects. The child is asked to identify five of the six objects by pointing to the one the examiner

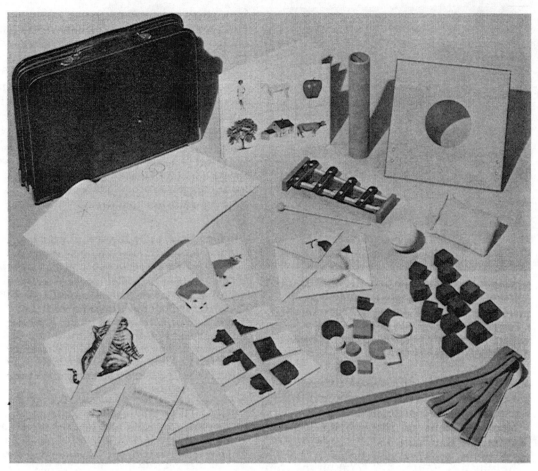

FIGURE 7–2 Test materials for the McCarthy Scales of Children's Abilities.(Courtesy of the Psychological Corporation.)

names. Cards two through five have a picture of a single object, and the child is asked to identify it. Part II: Oral Vocabulary consists of ten words that the child is asked to define. Testing is discontinued if the child receives five or fewer points on Part I or after four consecutive failures on Part II.

5. *Number Questions.* This test consists of twelve items assessing number information or quantitative skills. The harder items require simple arithmetical operations (for example, dividing). The questions are read to the child, and testing is discontinued after four consecutive failures.

6. *Tapping Sequence.* This test uses a toy xylophone to assess the child's immediate mem-ory for nonverbal material. The xylophone has four "keys." The examiner "plays" sequences of "notes,"varying in number from three to six. After the examiner plays the "tune," the examiner hands the mallet to the child and asks the child to play it. Eight trials or sequences are presented. On the first trial, the child is given three chances to play the tune correctly. If the child is unsuccessful after three chances on item one, testing is discontinued. If the child plays item one correctly, items two through eight are administered. Testing is discontinued after two consecutive failures.

7. *Verbal Memory.* Part I: Words and Sentences consists of words or sentences read to the

child, whose task is to repeat them. The first two items have three words, the second two items have four words, and items five and six are complete sentences with seven and nine key words. Sequence is important in recalling the words but not in recalling the sentences. Part II: Story is administered only if the child earns eight or more points (out of thirty) on Part I. Part II: Story is a short paragraph, consisting of eight sentences. The child's task is to recall the story. For ease in scoring, eleven elements of the story are noted. The child receives one point for each element correctly recalled.

8. *Right-Left Orientation.* This test is not administered to children below age five. It consists of nine items. The first five involve directions for the child to follow or questions that would indicate knowledge of the right versus left side of the body (Which is your left ear?). For items six through nine, a picture of a boy (Roger) is used for the child to indicate right-left orientation (Show me Roger's right elbow). Testing is discontinued after five consecutive failures.

9. *Leg Coordination.* This test has six items requiring movements or balancing or both. The child is asked to walk backwards, walk on tiptoe, walk a straight line (along a nine-foot tape measure), stand on one foot and then on the other, and skip. To earn 2 points for standing on one foot, the child must do so for ten seconds or more.

10. *Arm Coordination.* This test consists of three parts. In Part I: Ball Bouncing, the child bounces a small rubber ball without catching it. The points awarded depend on the number of bounces; the maximum being seven points for fifteen bounces. If the child bounces the ball fewer than fifteen times on the first trial, a second trial is permitted. The better of the two scores is used. Part II: Beanbag Catch Game involves three tasks—catching a beanbag with both hands, with one hand, and then with the other hand. There are three trials or tosses per task, and one point is awarded for each catch. Part III: Beanbag Target Game involves a small board with a hole. The child stands six feet from the board and throws the beanbag through the hole. The child uses one hand and then the other, with three trials per hand. Two points are awarded if the beanbag goes through the hole, one point if the beanbag hits the board.

11. *Imitative Action.* This test consists of four actions (for example, folding hands) that the examiner performs and that the child is asked to imitate.

12. *Draw-A-Design.* This test is similar to Geometric Design on the WPPSI. It consists of nine figures, varying in complexity, that the child is asked to draw. The first three figures are the simplest and are drawn by the examiner. The child is asked to imitate the drawing. Designs four through nine are copied without the examiner's drawing them first. The first three designs are awarded 1 or 0 points (correct or incorrect) depending on the quality of the drawing; designs four and five are awarded 2, 1, or 0 points; and designs six through nine are awarded 3 to 0 points. Testing is discontinued after three consecutive failures.

13. *Draw-A-Child.* This test is administered only if the child earned one or more points on Draw-A-Design (Test 12). In this test, the child is asked to draw a same-sex child. No model is given. Points are based on ten elements (hair, mouth, and so on); and about five minutes are allowed for the child to complete the drawing.

14. *Numerical Memory.* This test is exactly like Digit Span in the Wechsler scales. A series of numbers is read and the child is asked to repeat them in either the same or reverse order. There are two trials per item. Two points are awarded for correct repetition on the first trial, one point for correct repetition on the second. Testing is discontinued after failure of any item on both trials. The backward series is administered only if the child earns three or more points on the forward series.

15. *Verbal Fluency.* The child is asked to think of words falling into each of four categories (for example, things to eat). Twenty seconds per item is allowed. One point is awarded for each acceptable response up to a maximum of nine.

16. *Counting and Sorting.* If the child passes nine or more items on Number Questions (Test 5), this test is not administered and the child is given full credit (nine points) for it. The test consists of nine items and ten blocks. The items require the child to count, ("take two of the blocks") using the blocks as concrete objects. One point is awarded for each correct response.

17. *Opposite Analogies.* This test consists of nine

items in which the child is asked to give the antonym for adjectives used in a simple analogy (for example, An elephant is *big,* and a mouse is _____.). If the child fails item one or two, the examiner supplies the correct response. If the child fails both item one and two, testing is discontinued. For children proceeding to items three through nine, testing is discontinued after three consecutive failures.

18. *Conceptual Grouping.* This test consists of nine problems orally presented to the child, who must select, group, or eliminate the blocks used as stimuli. There are twelve blocks varying in three dimensions—shape, size, and color. The first three items test the child's ability to determine size, color, and shape, respectively. On the first three items, one point is awarded for correct answers. On items four through nine, more complex grouping or selection of objects is required. Scoring involves a correction for the number of wrong choices. Depending on the child's accuracy of choice, 2, 1, or 0 points are awarded for items four through nine. Testing is halted after four consecutive failures.

Administration and Scoring

As is true for the S-B and Wechsler scales, the McCarthy requires a highly trained examiner to administer and score the test. Establishing rapport with the child is emphasized as a crucial aspect of testing. The manual (McCarthy, 1972, p. 45) makes the following comments on how to introduce the test to the child:

With children of all ages, the examiner should be satisfied that the child is at ease in his surroundings before beginning the examination. A good, positive introduction to the test is to tell the child that the examiner is going to show him some new puzzles and blocks, ask him some questions, and play some games with him. A supplementary toy (not part of the test kit), placed at the edge of the table, may attract the child's attention while the examiner fills in identifying data. A smile by the examiner, along with his reassurance that the child will see the games in a minute, may calm the child and engage his curiosity.

The examiner may also provide verbal encouragement if a child stops after beginning a task.

The eighteen tests are administered in the order indicated. The first two tests, Block Building and Puzzle Solving, should serve as icebreakers, since they do not require a verbal response from the child. The tests vary in content so that no strain, fatigue, or boredom should develop as from a consecutive series of cognitive tests. Tests 9 through 13, which test motor coordination, occur together near the middle of the eighteen tests and provide a natural break from the cognitive tests.

As noted, some of the tests may be omitted depending on the child's age and performance on other tests. Thus, Test 8, Right-Left Orientation, is administered only to children aged five or older. Test 13, Draw-A-Child, is administered only if the child scores one or more points on Test 12, Draw-A-Design. And finally, Test 16, Counting and Sorting, is not administered if the child passes nine or more items on Test 5, Number Questions. If Test 16 is not administered, however, the child is given full credit for it. We have noted those tests (1, 2, and 4) that permit older children to begin with more difficult items. The examiner must be highly familiar and comfortable with the testing procedures to prevent awkward pauses in the session. The estimated time for testing is forty-five to fifty minutes for children younger than five and sixty minutes for older children.

Detailed scoring instructions with examples are provided for tests that involve subjective scoring. In particular, example drawings are given for Draw-A-Design and Draw-A-Child. The Word Knowledge test also has many examples of responses earning 2, 1, or 0 points. No information is given in the manual on the reliability of scoring (that is, interrater agreement) for any of the subtests.

The scores on the eighteen subtests are used to compute six scale indexes. These and the subtests composing them are as follows:

Verbal Scale (V)	Perceptual-Performance Scale (P)
3. Pictorial Memory	1. Block Building
4. Word Knowledge	2. Puzzle Solving
7. Verbal Memory	6. Tapping Sequence
15. Verbal Fluency	8. Right-Left Orientation
17. Opposite Analogies	12. Draw-A-Design
	13. Draw-A-Child
	18. Conceptual Grouping

Quantitative Scale (Q)	General Cognitive Index (GCI)
5. Number Questions	All fifteen tests on the V, P, and Q Scales.
14. Numerical Memory	
16. Counting and Sorting	

Motor Tests (Mot)	Memory Scale (Mem)
9. Leg Coordination	3. Pictorial Memory
10. Arm Coordination	6. Tapping Sequence
11. Imitative Action	7. Verbal Memory
12. Draw-A-Design	14. Numerical Memory
13. Draw-A-Child	

The raw scores on each subtest are not necessarily used in combination with other subtests to obtain a scale index. Weights were determined by two factors: (1) the test author's judgment of the relative importance of each test and (2) the size of the standard deviations of the raw scores in the standardization sample. The first criterion reflects the clinical judgment of the test author, whereas the second is a statistical consideration. That is, weights were assigned to yield scores that would be approximately equal in variability, but high weights were also assigned to tests measuring especially important abilities. Actually, most tests were assigned a weight of one. That is, the raw scores were used for most subtests. The exceptions were Test 5, Number Questions; Test 14, Numerical Memory (Part II); and Test 17, Opposite Analogies, which were assigned weights of two; and Test 2, Puzzle Solving and Test 7, Verbal Memory (Part I), which were assigned weights of one-half. To determine a child's weighted raw score, which would be used in computing the raw score on a scale index, the child's raw score is multiplied by the test's assigned weight. It is important to note that unlike the Wechsler scales, the subtest scores on the McCarthy are not routinely used for diagnostic or interpretative purposes; many of the subtests are short and hence likely to be relatively unreliable.

The composite raw score for a scale index is computed by adding the weighted raw scores of each subtest on that scale index. Thus, the composite raw score on the Verbal Scale Index (V) is obtained by adding the weighted raw scores on Tests 3, 4, 7, 15, and 17. The General Cognitive Index (GCI) is obtained by adding the V, P, and Q composite raw scores. Table 7-1 illustrates how scores are obtained.

All scale indexes except for GCI are expressed as standard scores with a mean of 50 and a standard deviation of 10. The GCI is a standard score having a mean of 100 and a standard deviation of 16. Note that the GCI is expressed in exactly the same fashion as the deviation IQ on the Stanford-Binet. (The Wechsler IQs, it will be recalled, have a mean of 100 but a standard deviation of 15.)

The scale index equivalents of the composite raw scores are given in tables in the manual. Twenty-five tables are provided in three-month increments for ages 2½ (2 years, 4 months, 16 days through 2 years, 7 months, 15 days) through 8½ (8 years, 4 months, 16 days through 8 years, 7 months, 15 days). For example, a composite raw score of 128 on the GCI for a child of four years and nine months has a scale index of 109. A child of seven years and nine months with the same raw score would have a GCI

TABLE 7-1 Example of scoring on the McCarthy Scales of Children's Abilities[a]

Test	Raw Score	Weight	Weighted Raw Score	Verbal	Perceptual-Performance	Quantitative	Memory	Motor
1. Block Building	6	1	6		6			
2. Puzzle Solving	18	½	9		9			
3. Pictorial Memory	3	1	3	3			3	
4. Word Knowledge: Part I	5	1	5	5				
Word Knowledge: Part II	0	1	0	0				
5. Number Questions	4	2	8			8		
6. Tapping Sequence	5	1	5		5		5	
7. Verbal Memory: Part I	14	½	7	7			7	
Verbal Memory: Part II	4	1	4	4			4	
8. Right-Left Orientation	NA[b]	1	NA		NA			
9. Leg Coordination	8	1	8					8
10. Arm Coordination: Part I	4	1	4					4
Arm Coordination: Part II	5	1	5					5
Arm Coordination: Part III	5	1	5					5
11. Imitative Action	2	1	2					2
12. Draw-A-Design	10	1	10		10			10
13. Draw-A-Child	9	1	9		9			9
14. Numerical Memory: Part I	5	1	5			5	5	
Numerical Memory: Part II	3	2	6			6	6	
15. Verbal Fluency	18	1	18	18				
16. Counting and Sorting	5	1	5			5		
17. Opposite Analogies	4	2	8	8				
18. Conceptual Grouping	5	1	5		5			
Composite Raw Scores				45	44	24	30	43
				V	P	Q	Mem	Mot

General Cognitive Index (GCI) = V + P + Q

GCI = 45 + 44 + 24 = 113

Scale Index Scores[c]: GCI = 117; V = 50; P = 68; Q = 67; Mem = 58; Mot = 69

[a] Scoring is based on that for a four-year-old child.

[b] NA stands for not administered; Test 8 is not administered to children below the age of five.

[c] The scale index scores are standard scores. The GCI has a mean of 100 and a standard deviation of 16; the other indexes have a mean of 50 and a standard deviation of 10.

TABLE 7-2 Classification of ability levels for the general cognitive index (GCI) in the McCarthy Scales of Children's Abilities

GCI	Descriptive Classification	Theoretical Percent	Actual Percent (MSCA Normative Sample)
130 and above	Very Superior	3.0	3.1
120–129	Superior	7.5	8.5
110–119	Bright Normal	16.0	15.9
90–109	Average	46.8	46.7
80–89	Dull Normal	16.0	15.7
70–79	Borderline	7.5	7.3
69 and below	Mentally Retarded	3.0	2.8

From McCarthy, 1972, p. 25. Reproduced by permission of the Psychological Corporation.

of only 60. Table 7-2 lists ability classifications suggested for use with GCI scores.

For example, children having GCI scores 69 and below are classified as mentally retarded. The GCI scores follow a normal distribution fairly closely. The similarity between ability classification in Table 7-2, based on the McCarthy, and those in Table 6-2, based on the WAIS-R, should be noted. The McCarthy has an upper limit of 150 on the GCI for all age levels and a lower limit of 50. Harrison and Naglieri (1978) suggested a statistical procedure for obtaining extrapolated values beyond the limits of the test, although Levenson and Zino (1979b) suggest it may not work well with retarded children.

Reliability

Reliability coefficients are reported for each of the six scales. They are based on the split-half reliabilities of the component tests unless that method was inappropriate. The reliabilities of several tests (Memory tests, Right-Left Orientation, and Draw-A-Child) were thus based on the test-retest method. The reliabilities were determined separately for ten different age groups in the standardization sample. There were about 100 children per group. These results are given in Table 7-3.

The scales are quite reliable, especially considering the ages of the children who were tested. There appears to be no striking change in reliability as a function of age for any of the scales except the Motor Scale Index, which tends to be less reliable for older children (see Table 7-3). The GCI, in particular, is quite reliable, having an average reliability of .93 and ranging from a low of .90 for age 6½ to a high of .96 for age 3½. The reliability coefficients for the GCI are only slightly lower than those obtained for the Full Scale IQ of the WPPSI, for example.

With respect to stability of McCarthy scores over time, the manual reports the results of one study. Three age groups (3 to 3½, 5 to 5½, and 7½ to 8½) of forty to forty-five children were retested after three to five weeks. The GCI stability coefficient was about .90 for all three groups, whereas that of the other cognitive scores ranged from a low of .75 to a high of .89. The Motor Scale Index had the lowest test-retest correlation (.69) at ages 7½ to 8½. For a short time interval, the scale indexes appear stable and the stability coefficients are similar to the split-half reliabilities previously reported. Bryant and Roffe (1978) retested thirty-eight children with a median age of six after an interval of three to six weeks. Their results were similar to McCarthy's, the GCI having a test-retest correlation of .84, despite the use of a rather select group (the mean GCI was 114). The other cognitive scales showed acceptable stability coefficients (.71 to .75) given the restricted range of scores.

TABLE 7-3 Reliability coefficients and standard errors of measurement of the six MSCA scales, by age, for the standardization sample

Age in Years	N	Verbal		Perceptual-Performance		Quantitative		General Cognitive		Memory		Motor	
		r	SE_M	r	SE_M	r	SE_M	r	SE_M	r	SE_M	r	SE_M
2½	102	.90	3.2	.76	4.8	.77	4.9	.93	4.2	.78	4.6	.84	4.0
3	104	.89	3.2	.87	3.6	.82	4.2	.94	3.8	.73	5.0	.82	4.2
3½	100	.92	2.8	.90	3.2	.83	4.2	.96	3.4	.83	4.1	.84	4.1
4	102	.90	3.2	.86	3.6	.70	5.3	.91	4.7	.83	4.0	.78	4.6
4½	104	.88	3.5	.89	3.3	.79	4.6	.94	3.8	.74	5.0	.84	4.1
5	102	.87	3.6	.87	3.7	.86	3.7	.94	3.9	.78	4.9	.82	4.3
5½	104	.87	3.5	.84	3.9	.86	3.7	.93	4.2	.72	5.3	.80	4.5
6½	104	.84	3.9	.77	4.7	.80	4.3	.90	5.0	.84	4.0	.69	5.5
7½	104	.90	3.3	.84	4.1	.82	4.1	.94	3.9	.83	4.0	.75	5.1
8½	106	.86	3.7	.75	5.0	.83	4.2	.92	4.5	.82	4.3	.60	6.2
Average r and SE_M for the 10 Age Groups[a]		.88	3.4	.84	4.0	.81	4.3	.93	4.1	.79	4.5	.79	4.7

Note—The reliability coefficients presented here are based on split-half correlations corrected by the Spearman-Brown formula for the component tests, except for the Memory tests, Right-Left Orientation, and Draw-A-Child, for which that method was inappropriate. For these, test-retest correlations, based on smaller groups and corrected for restriction of range, were used in the computation of Scale reliability coefficients (Guilford, 1954, pp. 392–393).

The standard errors of measurement are in GCI units for the General Cognitive Scale, and in Scale Index units for the other 5 Scales.

[a]The average coefficients were obtained by using Fisher's z transformation (Walker and Lev, 1953, p. 254).

From McCarthy, 1972, p. 31. Reproduced by permission of the Psychological Corporation.

There is also some evidence on stability of McCarthy scores over longer periods of time. Davis and Slettedahl (1976) tested forty-three children in kindergarten and then about one year later when they were in first grade. The test-retest correlation for the GCI was .85, indicating good stability of the scores on this index. The cognitive scales ranged in test-retest correlations from .62 to .76, whereas the Motor Scale lacked stability, having a test-retest correlation of .33. Ernhart et al. (1980) retested sixty-eight black children after an interval of five years. The retesting occurred after the majority of children were older than 8½, which exceeds the upper age limit of the McCarthy. However, the scores were estimated by extrapolation. The GCI demonstrated a test-retest correlation of .61. The other cognitive indexes ranged from a low of .24 (Perceptual-Performance) to a high of .51 (Verbal). The Motor Scale again lacked stability, the test-retest correlation equaling .31.

It thus appears that the GCI is fairly stable over time. The Motor Scale is not. The other cognitive scales demonstrate fairly good stability over a one-year interval but may not be stable over longer periods. More systematic longitudinal studies are clearly needed. However, as we discuss later in this chapter, mental ability is not particularly stable in younger children, regardless of the test used. The stability of the GCI thus reflects the typical finding that younger children may change rather dramatically in mental ability over longer time periods.

As is true of other individually administered tests of intelligence, part of the unreliability in the McCarthy scales could be due to inaccurate scoring. Reynolds (1979b) has provided some initial evidence that the Draw-A-Design and Draw-A-Child subtests can be reliably scored by trained examiners. Reynolds had the drawings of fifty children independently scored by two school psychologists. The interscorer reliabilities were

.93 for Draw-A-Design and .96 for Draw-A-Child. The average scores assigned were also in close agreement. These results suggest that the scoring instructions for these two tests are quite good and that scoring inaccuracies are probably not a great source of error. Similar information on other more subjectively scored subtests would be useful.

The standard error of measurement provides another way of evaluating the consistency of the McCarthy Scales. Table 7-3 gives the standard errors of measurement for the six scale indexes. The GCI is based on a standard deviation of 15, whereas the other scale indexes are based on a standard deviation of 10. As can be seen in Table 7-3, the standard errors do not vary systematically by age, except for the Motor Scale, in which older children have more inconsistency. For the GCI, the average standard error of measurement is about 4. Thus, we would expect a child's "true" GCI to be between ± 8 points of the one obtained about 95 percent of the time. There is, relatively speaking, much less consistency in the other scale indexes.

The test manual (McCarthy, 1972, p. 35) also gives the differences needed for statistical significance between some pairs of the scale indexes. These vary from about ten (Verbal versus Perceptual-Performance) to thirteen (Memory versus Motor). There has been some empirical work on the reliability of profiles on the McCarthy but not as much as with the Wechsler scales. Kaufman (1976) notes that the children in the standardiza-

tion sample exhibited considerable scatter—the difference between a child's highest and lowest index, or the number of indexes differing significantly from a child's mean. Thus, even normal children apparently have considerable scatter in their profiles. For further results and discussion, other publications are available (Kaufman, 1975c; Reynolds, 1979a; Roffe & Bryant, 1979).

Validity

The manual of the MSCA presents limited validity information (McCarthy, 1972, pp. 40–43). The concurrent validity was evaluated by correlating the scores on the McCarthy with the WPPSI and the S-B (see Table 7-3a).

It should be noted that these correlations are based on thirty-five white, parochial school children from New York City who were between 6 and 6½ years of age. The GCI correlates fairly well with both the WPPSI Full Scale and S-B IQs. The Motor Scale is unrelated to IQ scores on the other two tests. On the whole, the scores on the McCarthy appear somewhat more related to the S-B than to the WPPSI. McCarthy attributes this to a possible ceiling effect on the WPPSI. That is, children in this age range are approaching the upper limit of the WPPSI.

A second study, based on thirty-one of the children in the correlational study just mentioned, examined the predictive validity of the McCarthy. Scores on the Metropoli-

TABLE 7-3a

| | WPPSI | | | |
MSCA Scales	Verbal IQ	Performance IQ	Full Scale IQ	S-B (1960) IQ
Verbal	.51	.43	.54	.66
Perceptual-Performance	.47	.59	.61	.70
Quantitative	.41	.27	.38	.41
General Cognitive	.63	.62	.71	.81
Memory	.42	.39	.46	.67
Motor	.02	.10	.07	.06

tan Achievement Test were obtained four months after the McCarthy was administered. Two of the cognitive scales (Perceptual-Performance and Quantitative) and the GCI correlated significantly with the achievement tests. The Verbal Scale, however, did not correlate significantly with the achievement test scores. The significant correlations ranged from a low of .38 to a high of .57. The GCI correlated .49 with a total score on the achievement test. The McCarthy thus demonstrated modest predictive validity in this small sample of children.

In addition to the studies reported in the test manual, the *concurrent validity* of the McCarthy has been evaluated by correlating its scores with those of other intelligence tests. Although McCarthy did not use the term *IQ*, her test has been compared with the S-B in at least seven published studies. These studies indicate that the GCI generally does correlate with the S-B IQ, with correlations ranging from a high of .91 to a low of .45. As might be expected, the relationship is stronger among normal children than among retarded ones. Although the McCarthy and the S-B are correlated and designed to have the same average score (100) and standard deviation (16), the IQs are not interchangeable. The GCI and IQ discrepancies that may exist have not yet been related in a systematic fashion to group characteristics, although Kaufman and Kaufman (1977b) hypothesized that such discrepancies might indicate a learning disability. The available literature at least suggests that the MSCA and S-B are measuring similar abilities (Davis, 1975; Davis & Rowland, 1974; Davis & Walker, 1976; Gerken et al., 1978; Harrison & Wiebe, 1977; Levenson & Zino, 1979a; Naglieri & Harrison, 1979), although the S-B may be a better test to use with retarded children. Some of the studies suffer by having very small samples.

In addition to the S-B, the concurrent validity of the McCarthy has been assessed by correlating it with other intelligence and cognitive tests. One study administered the WPPSI and the McCarthy to sixty kindergarten children (Phillips et al., 1978). The GCI correlated .75, .59, and .74 with the WPPSI Verbal, Performance, and Full Scale IQs. Other McCarthy scales, including the Motor Scale, were significantly correlated with the WPPSI IQs. In general, the results were similar to those reported by McCarthy (1972), except that the Motor Scale correlated significantly with the WPPSI IQs and the mean GCI score was significantly smaller than the mean WPPSI IQs.

Davis and Walker (1977) reported correlations between the GCI and WISC-R IQs of .65, .62, and .75 for the Verbal, Performance, and Full Scale, respectively. This study, which involved fifty-one second-graders, twenty-eight of whom were Hispanic, also found that the mean WISC-R IQs and the mean GCI scores were not significantly different.

Goh and Youngquist (1979) reported GCI and WISC-R correlations of .71, .45, and .69 for the Verbal, Performance, and Full Scale, respectively. The other scales generally correlated significantly with the WISC-R IQs, although the Motor Scale tended to have lower correlations than the others. The mean GCI was also found to be significantly lower than the WISC-R IQs. The forty children tested in this study were learning disabled, having a mean age of about seven.

Ivimey and Taylor (1980) found a correlation of .40 between the WISC-R full scale IQ and the GCI for a group of thirty learning disabled children and a correlation of .87 for a comparable group of thirty normal second-graders. The learning disabled group also had a lower mean GCI than WISC-R Full Scale IQ. It thus appears that the McCarthy is measuring abilities similar to those of the WPPSI and WISC-R, although the scores on the instruments are not interchangeable.

Although work with the Weschler scales and S-B constitute the bulk of concurrent validity studies, other researchers have examined other tests. These include the Columbia Mental Maturity Scale (Phillips et al., 1978), Detroit Tests of Learning Aptitude (Wiebe & Harrison, 1978), Illinois Test of Psycholinguistic Abilities (Davis & Walker, 1976), Peabody Picture Vocabulary Test (Taylor, 1979), Test for Auditory Comprehension of Language (Davis & Walker, 1976), and Wide Range Achievement Test (Ivimey & Taylor, 1980). In general, the results of these studies provide support for the concurrent validity of the McCarthy.

The evidence on the *predictive validity* of the McCarthy remains meager. The study in the manual has already been noted. Published by Kaufman (1973), it compares the McCarthy's predictive validity with that of the WPPSI and S-B. Kaufman concludes that the McCarthy is as good as the WPPSI or the S-B in predicting achievement test scores in first grade. Harrison (1981) administered the McCarthy to sixty-two first-graders at the beginning of the school year and correlated the scores with the Metropolitan Achievement Test given nine months later. The GCI correlated .75 with the achievement test score, and the Motor Scale correlated .53. The children (blacks and whites) in this study were from rural Georgia and from relatively poor families.

One additional study (Ernhart et al., 1980) used the McCarthy to predict reading achievement test scores in the first grade. This study was already cited in the section on the stability of McCarthy scores. The sixty-eight urban, black children were administered the McCarthy five years before the reading achievement test as well as concurrently with that test. The preschool GCI correlated significantly ($r = .52$) with scores on the reading achievement test. Thus, after an interval of five years, the GCI demonstrated a reasonable, though modest, amount of predictive validity. The other cognitive scales were also related to achievement test scores, although less strongly than the GCI. For achievement test scores in first grade, then, the McCarthy does appear to have predictive validity; but although these results are encouraging, they are not definitive. Further longitudinal studies are needed, and criteria in addition to achievement test scores should be used.

The *construct validity* of the McCarthy, of course, rests on the empirical research in which the test has been used. Its concurrent and predictive validity contribute to our understanding of what it measures. It appears, in particular, that the GCI functions very much like the IQ from the S-B or the Full Scale IQ from the Wechsler scales. That is, the GCI correlates with other measures of intelligence and also with achievement test scores. The Motor Scale, on the other hand, does not appear to be as highly related or to correlate significantly as often with these same criteria as the cognitive scales. The GCI also detects expected mean differences for groups diagnosed as "special" on other grounds (Goh & Youngquist, 1979; Harrison, et al., 1980; Ivimey & Taylor, 1980; Kaufman & Kaufman, 1974; Levenson & Zino, 1979a; Naglieri & Harrison, 1979; Ramey & Campbell, 1979). Such groups have mean GCIs considerably below the standardization group's mean of 100. Kaufman and Kaufman (1975) also reported that children from higher socioeconomic classes have higher mean scores on the GCI and other scale indexes. However, the cognitive scales showed a greater mean difference than did the Motor Scale.

The construction of the six scales apparently followed a curious blend of clinical intuition and statistical analyses. In attempting to verify the construct validity of the six scales, Watkins and Wiebe (1980) used multiple regression techniques to predict the six scale indexes. The eighteen subtests were the predictor variables. The GCI, Verbal Scale, and Perceptual-Performance Scale were predictable in the study, thus supporting McCarthy's scoring methods. However, the Quantitative Scale was marginally supported, and neither the Memory nor Motor Scale was predictable. Although there were some technical problems with the Watkins and Wiebe study, the constructs or theoretical conception of the scales were not completely justified. McCarthy's relatively intuitive grouping of the subtests may not be the best way to organize them.

Kaufman and Hollenbeck (1973) reported the results of a factor analysis of the McCarthy subtests for three different age groups from part (60 percent) of the standardization sample. These results were apparently used to some extent in McCarthy's decision on how many scales to include in the final version of her test.

Kaufman (1975b) subsequently examined the factor structure of McCarthy subtests for the entire standardization sample in five age groups (2½ to 7½). He found that four of six factors appeared at age 2½ and tended to appear at all other ages. These were a general cognitive factor, a verbal factor, a memory factor and a motor factor. These factors, empirically determined, clearly correspond to scales used by McCarthy. Also, Kaufman found that a perceptual-performance factor emerged at age 3 to 3½ and a quantitative factor at age 5 to 5½. He interprets the results as being largely consistent with the final scale structure chosen by McCarthy, even though an alternative placement of some of the subtests could be justified.

The factor analytic results and others (Mishra, 1981; Naglieri et al., 1981) do, therefore, support the construct validity of the McCarthy. The GCI appears to have construct validity based on regression and factor analytic techniques. The other scales may be less secure, and criterion-related validity studies will be needed to determine their utility and theoretical implications.

Although the McCarthy has six scale index scores and eighteen subtest scores, relatively little attempt has been made to use subtest patterns to differentiate within or between groups. One study demonstrated differences among subtest patterns and other regroupings of the McCarthy scales for a group of educable mentally retarded (EMR) children (Harrison et al., 1980).

These investigators, for example, found that the EMR children had higher scores on tests assessing memory for common objects and lower scores on tests of acquired knowledge (that is, numerical reasoning and conceptual thinking). The GCI-IQ discrepancy, as another possible diagnostic aid, remains to be demonstrated (Bracken, 1981; Nagle, 1979).

As noted earlier, the McCarthy permits the determination of hand dominance by observation of the preferred hand used during the subtests composing the Motor Scale. Although hand dominance could be determined by observation or interview, the McCarthy includes it as part of the testing procedure. Other commonly administered tests of intelligence have no such determination. It is commonly assumed that hand dominance is directly related to cerebral dominance (a dominant half of the brain). The importance of left- or right-handedness, then, is related to language development. Such studies are concerned with *laterality*. Kaufman et al. (1978) studied differences between the dominance-established groups and dominance-not-established groups in the standardization sample. They found no significant differences between the groups on demographic variables (for example, sex or race). The comparisons involving the 2½ to 4½ age group found statistically higher scores on the GCI and Motor Index for the children with established hand dominance. These differences were not significant for children at ages 5 to 8½. For the older children, there was a significant relationship between dominance being established and right versus left awareness as measured by the Right-Left Orientation subtest. These findings suggest that the emergence of hand dominance may be a useful indicator of developmental progress for young children, although the investigators are appropriately cautious in interpreting their results. They suggest using dominance as only one of many signs in assessing a child's developmental and intellectual status.

Evaluation

The reliability and validity evidence on the McCarthy is quite encouraging. It is a well-designed test and appears to be gaining acceptance. We should note in passing that it has also been used as a dependent variable in an interesting variety of studies assessing cognitive functions in young children. Such studies include the early development of twins (Wilson, 1978), children with sickle-cell trait (Kramer et al., 1978), children with elevated lead absorption (Baloh et al., 1975), children of low birth weight (Eisert et al., 1980), and effects of chronic undernutrition (Ashem & Janes, 1978).

TESTS FOR SPECIAL POPULATIONS

The Stanford-Binet, Wechsler scales, and McCarthy were all designed for children or adults who are largely free of physical handicaps. They also were not designed to be used with infants or children younger than two years of age. However, the assessment of infant behaviors, for example, is becoming increasingly important and widespread (Osofsky, 1980). Special tests are clearly needed to assess the sensory-motor and possibly cognitive capacities of infants. Also, children and adults with severe motor or sensory impairments need special tests if their cognitive strengths and weaknesses are to be identified and remedial programs developed. Persons who are blind, deaf, suffering from cerebral palsy, multiply handicapped, or severely retarded are examples of special populations that need special tests. Persons from other cultures or those whose native language is not English also require special tests, since the tests discussed to this point all assume some familiarity with English and have been standardized on persons from contemporary U.S. society. In the following section, we will briefly discuss some tests that can be used with special populations. Some of them are not intelligence tests, but we include them here since they do assess the developmental or cognitive status of individuals.

Infants

A recent survey of tests available for infants listed sixty-one such assessment devices (Katoff & Reuter, 1979). Yang (1980) summarized the early attempts to assess the behavior of infants, identifying Arnold Gesell as the primary source of the initial efforts in this field. Two women, Nancy Bayley and Psyche Cattell, were other early participants in infant assessment. All three developed tests to be used with infants and young children.

Early Developments. Gesell (1925) published developmental schedules in which 144 items were designed to cover four general areas—motor behavior, language behavior, adaptive behavior, and personal and social behavior. There have been essentially no revisions in the scale since 1925. The Gesell Developmental Schedules is not an intelligence test but rather establishes the norms for behaviors that infants are capable of exhibiting. Knobloch and Pasamanick (1974) published the latest version of the Gesell schedules and supplied more adequate norms for the scales.

Psyche Cattell (1940), on the other hand, attempted to design a scale that would be a downward extension of the Stanford-Binet Intelligence Scale. For the ages of 22 to 30 months, she in fact intermingled Stanford-Binet items. She relied on Gesell's work but attempted to eliminate items that measured only motor performance. She also wanted the items to appeal to the infants and young children being tested and to be an improved psychometric product (to have, for example, objective scoring and standardization). Like the Stanford-Binet, the Cattell Test of Infant Intelligence is an age scale, organized in one-month intervals from two months to 12 months, in two-month intervals from 14 to 24 months, and in three-month intervals from 27 through 30 months. The organization and scoring of the Cattell test parallels that of the S-B. A mental age is obtained and is converted to a ratio IQ. Although the Cattell test suffers from an inadequate standardization sample and a lack of validity information and does not use deviation score IQs, it does represent a major attempt to assess important mental functioning in infants.

BAYLEY SCALES OF INFANT DEVELOPMENT. Bayley published the most extensively used and cited set of scales for infants. The Bayley Scales of Infant Development were published in 1969 but had their origins in the California First Year Mental Scale (Bayley, 1933). As Bayley (1969) notes,

testing infants represents a special challenge. For one thing, infants and young children do not consistently follow directions. Thus, the testing method must capture the child's attention and interest. Second, tests for infants involve abilities that differ from those assessed with tests designed for older individuals. Simple functions develop first and these are then gradually differentiated with growth.

The current edition of the Bayley has 163 items composing the Mental Scale and 81 items composing the Motor Scale. The Bayley was standardized on a representative sample of 1,262 children at fourteen different age groups (two through thirty months).

FIGURE 7–3 Test materials for the Bayley Scales of Infant Development. (Courtesy of the Psychological Corporation.)

The test is designed for children in the first two and one-half years of life.

Bayley (1969, p. 3) describes the two scales obtained as follows:

1. The Mental Scale is designed to assess sensory-perceptual acuities, discriminations, and the ability to respond to these; the early acquisition of "object constancy" and memory, learning, and problem-solving ability; vocalizations and the beginnings of verbal communication; and early evidence of the ability to form generalizations and classifications, which is the basis of abstract thinking. Results of the administration of the Mental Scale are expressed as a standard score, the MDI, or Mental Development Index.

2. The Motor Scale is designed to provide a measure of the degree of control of the body, coordination of the large muscles and finer manipulatory skills of the hands and fingers. As the Motor Scale is specifically directed toward behaviors reflecting motor coordination and skills, it is not concerned with functions that are commonly thought of as "mental" or "intelligent" in nature. Results of the administration of the Motor Scale are expressed as a standard score, the PDI, or Psychomotor Development Index.

The standard scores have a mean of 100 and a standard deviation of 16. The Bayley also provides a score on a third scale—the Infant Behavior Record—which is completed after the Mental and Motor Scales have been administered. It helps the clinician assess the child's social and objective orientation toward the world.

The items on the two scales are arranged in order of "difficulty." That is, an item is placed at an age level by noting the age at which approximately 50 percent of the children passed the item. Table 7-4 lists the behaviors assessed at several age levels for the Mental and Motor Scales. As can be seen from the examples, the content of the Bayley is quite different from intelligence tests given to adults or older children.

The administration of the Bayley requires a highly trained examiner. Unlike most other tests, the order of administering the items is flexible and behavior may be scored at any time (not just when the item is administered). This flexibility is necessary to measure maximal performance. Also, some items are administered while the infant is in its crib or lying flat on a table. The Mental Scale is given first, followed by the Motor Scale. Many of the early items of the Motor Scale may be observed at any time. The examiner must establish a *basal* and *ceiling level* of responding, similar to the Stanford-Binet. The manual suggests ten successive items passed or failed to assign a basal level or ceiling on the Mental Scale and six successive items for the Motor Scale. The raw score on each scale is simply the number of items passed plus all those items below the basal level.

Raw scores on the Mental and Motor

TABLE 7-4 Representative items from the mental and motor scales of the Bayley Scales of Infant Development

Age Placement in Months	Mental Scale Items	Motor Scale Items
.4	Prolonged regard of red ring	Crawling movements
2.3	Vocalizes 2 different sounds	Sits with support
6.0	Looks for fallen spoon	Sits alone 30 seconds or more
14.6	Closes round box	Walks backward
20.6	Sentence of 2 words	Walks with one foot on walking board
30+	Understands 3 prepositions	Jumps over string 8 inches high

Scales are converted to standard scores by reference to the age-appropriate table. Thirty-two different age groups are listed, ranging from two through 30 months. The younger ages (up to 5½ months) go up by one-half a month, the older ages by one month. The standard scores obtained are called the Mental Development Index (MDI) and Psychomotor Development Index (PDI) in order to reflect the nature of the variables used. As noted, the MDI and PDI have been standardized to means of 100 and standard deviations of 16.

The reliability of the Mental Scale, as estimated by the split-half method, appears quite good. The coefficients range from a low of .81 at ages 8 and 10 months to a high of .93 at age 3 months. The Motor Scale shows relatively low reliability (.68) at age 2 months but is acceptably reliable after that, although somewhat lower than the mental scale. The manual also provides information on the standard error of measurement for the two scales and on the reliability of differences between the MDI and PDI scores. These scores do correlate, but the correlations vary widely across ages (from .18 to .75). They also tend to correlate less as age increases.

In validating the Bayley scales, children of twenty-four, twenty-seven, and thirty months were administered the Bayley and Stanford-Binet (S-B). The MDI and S-B IQs correlated .53, .64, and .47 for the ages of 24, 27, and 30 months, respectively. The children tested had means above 100 on both tests at all ages and exhibited some restriction of range (standard deviations smaller than 16). Thus, the modest correlations are probably due to the measurement of different constructs and to the restricted range of scores.

Another study (Ramey et al., 1973) found that the Bayley scores from previous testings were not related to S-B IQs at 24 months, but paradoxically, some were related at 36 months. The PDI obtained at 6 to 8, 9 to 12, and 13 to 16 months correlated .77, .56, and .43 with the S-B IQ obtained at 36 months. The MDI obtained at 6 to 8 months did not correlate significantly with S-B IQs obtained at 36 months but did for MDIs obtained at 9 to 12 months ($r = .71$) and at 13 to 16 months ($r = .90$). Such confusing results may be caused by several factors. First, the stability coefficients of both the MDI and PDI are not high in this study. The highest was only .52. Second, the number of subjects at 36 months was also small, and selection effects may have occurred.

Another study illustrates the intrinsic difficulties of obtaining consistent scores from infants. Horner (1980) tested 9- and 15-month-old infants in the home and in a clinic after an average interval of one week. Although the setting did not influence scores on the Bayley, three of four test-retest correlations were below .75. (The sample had been divided into four groups on the basis of sex and age with a sample size of only twelve in each group.) Nevertheless, these results suggest that infant behavior can be highly variable, making predictive studies difficult or impossible to accomplish. Berk (1979) also examined the utility of the Bayley for classifying infants as neurologically suspicious and neurologically normal. The Bayley was administered to 194 black infants at eight months of age. The criterion variable was the physician's classification of these infants. Children diagnosed normal at both one and seven months were classified as normal. Those labeled normal at one and neurologically suspicious at seven months were classified as neurologically suspicious. The Bayley was found to have only modest discriminating power, with the Motor Scale being a better predictor of which infants were classified as neurologically suspicious.

It appears to us that the Bayley scales are useful in establishing developmental norms and may be helpful in identifying infants and young children who may develop some disability. The scales do not appear to be highly predictive of future behavior on either the Bayley scales or other measures of intelligence. There are, of course, reasons why such predictions are poor. We will discuss some of these problems under infant assessment in a subsequent section of this chapter.

CAREGIVER ASSESSMENT. All the tests previously discussed assume that trained professionals administer, score, and interpret the results. The administration of individual tests to infants is very time-consuming. Also, the infant may not perform at maximum capacity for an examiner, who is usually a stranger. Thus, a different method of assessment that does not use a professional examiner could provide both more accurate data and much less expensive results. There are several scales that use a caregiver's assessment of infant behaviors (Katoff & Reuter, 1979, 1980). A caregiver is often a parent or guardian, the person with whom the infant lives, but caregivers can also be teachers, nurses' aides, or anyone who provides care to the infant on a regular daily basis. By using caregiver ratings, developmental status can be determined without explicitly testing the infant or involving a highly trained professional. If the scores from caregiver assessment are valid and reliable, they can be substituted for those obtained from tests administered by highly trained professionals. Accurate information could thus be obtained in a relatively inexpensive fashion, although test scoring and interpretation would still require an appropriately trained person.

The Kent Infant Development Scale (KID Scale) is one example of a caregiver assessment instrument (Katoff, 1978; Katoff et al., 1979). The KID Scale is an inventory of 252 items describing behaviors that could be observed in the first year of life. These descriptions are rated by the caregiver of the infant. The following items are examples:

1. Nurses from breast or bottle.
2. Pulls off hat.
3. Sucks food off a spoon.
4. Plays peek-a-boo.

Each item is answered with one of the following four alteratives: (1) yes, (2) used to

do it but outgrew it, (3) is no longer able to do it, (4) no, cannot do it yet.

The KID Scale is a developmental scale based on the normative sample of 357 infants. The item norm represents the age at which 65 percent of the infants passed an item. Thus, item 4 (plays peek-a-boo) has an age norm of eight months. That is, this behavior does not appear routinely until infants are about eight months of age. In addition to a full scale score the KID Scale provides scores in five domains: (1) cognitive (watches TV), (2) motor (sits on your lap), (3) social (laughs aloud), (4) language (has one clear word), and (5) self-help (swallows soft foods).

Although the KID Scale was recently developed, it appears to have excellent prospects for assessing the developmental status of infants and possibly profoundly handicapped children as well. The domain scores are highly intercorrelated ($r = .90$) and highly related to the full scale score (r's = .95 to .98). Internal consistency is high (approaching 1.00) for the full scale and domain scores. Also, as reported in the manual, test-retest reliabilities over an average interval of sixty-nine days are about .90. In addition, for twenty infants whose father and mother both completed the KID Scale, the correlation between ratings was quite high (.88 to .95). Thus, the KID Scale appears to provide reliable ratings of the developmental status of normal infants (Katoff et al., 1979).

In the one concurrent validity study reported in the manual (Katoff et al., 1979) the KID Scale full scale score correlated .88 and .90 with the mental and motor indexes, respectively, of the Bayley scale, an individually administered test of infant development. Although more validity evidence is needed, the KID Scale appears to have great promise as a caregiver assessment instrument. It might be particularly useful, for example, as a screening instrument to identify infants with developmental deficits. These infants could then be examined by more highly trained specialists to determine both the accuracy of the screening test and cause of the problem. The early detection of developmental delay is an important task for pediatricians, clinical psychologists, and other professionals working with young children. The KID Scale represents one attempt to meet this problem in an economical, realistic fashion for infants younger than twelve months (Katoff & Reuter, 1980).

THE GENERAL PROBLEM IN INFANT ASSESSMENT. The problems of discovering the skills possessed by infants have been nicely summarized by Yang (1980, p. 165).

Assessment techniques for infants are as unique as the organism itself. To wit: the infant, although not uncommunicative, is linguistically incompetent. Therefore, control of the testing situation by instructions is not possible; the guile of the examiner and the inherent interest of the test items are critical to successful testing. While the infant cannot be relied upon to be cooperative, he can effectively control the behavior of others (especially adults) with the most compelling communications: cries and smiles. In addition to being guileful, therefore, the examiner must be wary of overresponding to a particularly skillful infant. These considerations, prior to any theoretical perspective, make infant assessment a distinctive part of the testing field. At no other time is development so rapid and the available forms of measurement so restricted.

The fact is that scores on infant tests of intelligence or development status are not predictive of later IQ and do not even predict very well the scores on the same infant test obtained within a reasonably short period of time. McCall (1980), for example, notes that the correlation between scores on various tests administered during infancy is about .50. On the other hand, the correlation between IQ scores obtained during childhood (ages 9 to 12) is about .90. Thus, individual differences in intelligence remain reasonably consistent in later childhood but are not particularly stable as measures during the first two years of life. These are similar to the results obtained with the GCI score on the McCarthy scales. McCall also provided information on the prediction of later IQ from scores on tests administered in the first 2½ years of life. McCall's summary suggests that scores obtained in the first six months of life are essentially unrelated to later measures of IQ. Scores obtained at 7 to 12 months are marginally related (correlating at about .26), and those obtained from 13 to 18 and 19 to 30 months correlate moderately (r's of about .40 and .50, respectively) with later measures of IQ. For normal infants, then, test scores are not very predictive of later status on measures of intelligence. This conclusion is particularly justified, based on the evidence presented by McCall, for scores obtained in the first 18 months of life.

Given that infant tests are not predictive of later cognitive functioning, are such instruments invalid and of no utility? The answer to this question is no. McCall argued that developmental psychology is concerned with both the stability of individual differences over time and the developmental function. Developmental function refers to the qualitative and quantitative changes that occur over time and the fact that certain behaviors may replace or grow out of other behaviors. The rapidity with which behavior changes or evolves during infancy, along with the differences with which infants exhibit such behavior, undoubtedly contributes to the failure of prediction. Certainly having norms available makes the identification of atypical infants more possible, and at the extremes, such atypical infants do remain relatively stable over time. That is, a brain-damaged infant is likely to score poorly at every age tested. A normal infant, on the other hand, will score in the normal range at later ages but could still vary rather widely in this "normality."

Finally, infant tests and later measures of intelligence are strikingly different in content. To be intelligent is, almost by definition, to be able to use language. Until language skills develop, it seems unlikely that a person's test scores will be predictive of later performance on IQ tests or any other criterion where such skills are important.

Motor and Speech Handicaps

A person who is unable to speak or speaks with difficulty could not be given the standardized tests discussed previously. Similarly, if a person has a disability that prevents him or her from writing or marking answers on an answer sheet, ordinary tests are inappropriate. *The Peabody Picture Vocabulary Test–Revised* (PPVT-R) (Dunn & Dunn, 1981) is an example of a test that can be used with many people who have difficulty speaking or writing, as well as with people who have no handicaps.

The PPVT-R consists of 175 items or plates. Each item has four pictures. The examiner gives the name of one of the four objects, and the subject's task is to choose the 'one alternative that best represents the word spoken by the examiner. The drawings are free of fine detail and appear readily identifiable. The test may be given to persons between the ages of 2½ and 40 years of age who are able to hear, see the drawings, and communicate a choice in some fashion. The items are ordered in terms of difficulty, easier items appearing first. It is important to note that the person taking the test does not need to know how to read. The most recent edition (Dunn & Dunn, 1981) of the PPVT-R consists of two separate forms (L and M). The test may be administered by anyone familiar with the administration and scoring procedures. It does not require a highly trained examiner, although scores would typically be interpreted only by a trained professional.

The testing starts with different items, depending on the subject's age. Like the S-B, a basal and ceiling point are established. The basal item is established as the lowest item number after which eight consecutive items are answered correctly. Testing is continued until the subject makes six errors in any eight consecutive presentations. The last item presented is the ceiling. Thus, each subject is presented with a limited set of items and the PPVT-R may be rapidly administered (ten to fifteen minutes).

Scoring the test is very easy. The raw score is the number of correct responses plus credit for all items below the basal. The raw score is converted to a deviation IQ by reference to tables provided for each of the over 100 chronological ages. The resulting IQs have been standardized to have a mean of 100 and a standard deviation of 15.

The PPVT-R IQ is reasonably reliable. The coefficients range from a low of .61 at age group 7-6 to 7-11 to a high of .88 at age group 18-0 to 18-11. The manual contains an extensive list of studies in which the previous PPVT (Dunn, 1965) has been used. The PPVT IQs have been correlated with many other tests of intelligence. We have cited several such studies in connection with other tests (for example the S-B and WISC-R). Scores on the PPVT also correlate with measures of academic achievement. Thus, the PPVT-R is a valid indicator of verbal ability as measured by a vocabulary test. Since it is quickly and easily administered, the PPVT-R is a potentially valuable screening test. However, tests assessing more diverse aspects of intellectual functioning should be used in reaching diagnostic or treatment decisions about subjects.

The manual of the PPVT-R is exceptionally fine—concise and informative. The technical methods followed, including constructing the test and obtaining the normative sample, are meritorious. For the type of test and its intended use, the PPVT-R is an excellent assessment instrument. Moreover, it appears to be much improved over its earlier edition (Dunn, 1965).

Learning Disabilities

The S-B, WISC-R, and other intelligence tests are used to identify children who are learning disabled. A child suffering from a learning disability is one who has normal intelligence but is having learning difficulties in one or more areas (for example, reading). We will discuss one test, the Illinois Test of Psycholinguistic Abilities (ITPA), that was designed primarily for children encountering learning difficulties. The ITPA attempts to provide information on specific psycholinguistic functions (strengths and weaknesses) that can be used for remediation. The test focuses on intraindividual (within a single person) differences, and its main purpose is to diagnose a child's psycholinguistic abilities and disabilities so that remediation can follow (Paraskevopoulos & Kirk, 1969).

The ITPA is based on the communication model of Osgood (1957a, 1957b), although the theoretical model has been adapted for clinical use. The model consists of three dimensions: (1) the channel of communication (auditory or visual memory input); (2) psycholinguistic processes (recognizing, organizing, or expressing ideas); and (3) levels of organization (a representational level requiring the use of symbols or an automatic level requiring less voluntary but highly organized and integrated patterns of behavior).

The following twelve tests were constructed to reflect various aspects of Osgood's model. They are described within an outline of the processes being assessed.

I. Functions Tested at the Representational Level
   A. The Receptive Process (Decoding)
      1. *Auditory Reception.* This test assesses the child's ability to understand verbally presented material. Short sentences requiring a yes or no answer are used.
      2. *Visual Reception.* This test assesses the same ability as Test 1 except a different sense modality is used. The child is shown a picture and is then asked to find the one of four alternatives that is conceptually similar.
   B. The Organizing Process (Association)
      3. *Auditory Association.* The child's task is to relate concepts presented orally. This is a verbal analogies test.
      4. *Visual Association.* This is a picture association test. A picture is presented with four pictures surrounding it. The child must choose the one picture that is most closely related to the stimulus picture.

C. The Expressive Process (Encoding)
      5. *Verbal Expression.* This test assesses the child's ability to express concepts vocally. The child is shown four familiar objects and asked to tell the examiner about each one.
      6. *Manual Expression.* The child is shown fifteen pictures of common objects and asked to pantomime the appropriate action.
II. Functions Tested at the Automatic Level
   A. Closure
      7. *Grammatical Closure.* This test assesses the child's ability to complete sentences with the appropriate grammatical or syntactical form (for example, plurals).
      8. *Auditory Closure (Supplementary Test 1).* In this test, words are orally presented in an incomplete form, much as one might hear on a bad telephone connection. The child's task is to provide the complete word from the parts provided.
      9. *Sound Blending (Supplementary Test 2).* In this test the component sounds in a word are spoken at half-second intervals. The child must integrate the sounds and identify the entire word.
      10. *Visual Closure.* This test measures a child's ability to find a specified object in a picture. The object appears many times but in various degrees of concealment.
   B. Sequential Memory
      11. *Auditory Sequential Memory.* This is a digit-span test analogous to those on the WISC-R except the numbers are read more slowly.
      12. *Visual Sequential Memory.* In this test the child is shown a sequence of nonmeaningful figures which must then be recalled. The test measures ability to remember visually presented material.

Paraskevopoulos and Kirk (1969, p. 23) summarize the general design of the ITPA as follows:

These twelve subtests are designed to isolate abilities in (a) three processes of communication; (b) two levels of language organization; and/or (c) two channels of language input and output. Performance on specific subtests of this battery should aid in pinpointing specific psycholinguistic abilities and disabilities. The identification of specific deficiencies in psycholinguistic functions lead to the crucial task of remediation directed to the specific areas of defective functioning. This is the sine qua non of diagnosis.

In addition to generating discrete tests, it should be pointed out that the model also assists in designing a curriculum for young children, and its theoretical base allows for developing remedial procedures for specific deficits. It is, therefore, a diagnostic-remedial model.

In addition to the twelve subtests, a composite score is computed by adding all subtest scores except for the two supplementary tests.

The ITPA was standardized with a total of 962 midwestern children from eight age groups. The normative group was selected to be "normal" with respect to intellectual, academic, and physical functioning. Minorities were not adequately represented in the normative group, and the ITPA may not be appropriate for such groups.

The subtests appear reasonably reliable. Chase (1972) notes that of the 104 reliability coefficients reported in the manual, fifty-one are below .80, twenty-three are below .70, and fifteen are above .90. Visual Closure and Auditory Closure are the least reliable subtests. The stability coefficients for a five- to six-month test-retest interval presented in the manual are not particularly impressive, ranging from a low of .12 to a high of .86 with a median of .50. Given the intended purpose of the ITPA, the reliability of differences between subtest scores is important. Median reliabilities are reported for each possible pair of subtests. These coefficients range from a high of .88 to a low of .57. The manual also provides appropriate information on the size of differences between pairs of subtest scores that are needed to be statistically significant.

The ITPA was designed (1) to be used as a diagnostic test of functioning in language and other forms of communication; (2) to measure areas in which a child succeeds or fails, and not to measure general intelligence; (3) to be used principally with young children, especially those between four and eight; and (4) to identify deficits that require remediation (Kirk & Kirk, 1978). If the ITPA is to be used for designing remedial programs, it must at least demonstrate that the functions it measures are trainable. That is, the psycholinguistic functions measured must be responsive to training. Although there is disagreement in the literature, a recent, sophisticated review of studies in which the ITPA was used as the criterion variable in measuring the effectiveness of psycholinguistic training demonstrates that such training is effective (Kavale, 1981). In addition, it appears that although some ITPA subtests and constructs respond more to training, all areas of psycholinguistic functioning can be enhanced by various kinds of training programs (Kavale, 1981).

Kirk and Kirk (1971) provide an extensive discussion on the ITPA for the diagnosis and remediation of psycholinguistic learning disabilities. For example, consider a child who receives a low score on the Auditory Reception subtest. Such a child has difficulty understanding spoken language. Kirk and Kirk (p. 137) suggest that this deficit arises from one or more of the following four sources:

1. The child may not recognize and identify sounds in his or her environment.
2. The child may not have developed a listening attitude.
3. The child may have difficulty attaching meaning to words.
4. The child may not understand consecutive speech.

After the deficits are identified, Kirk and Kirk (pp. 138-185) suggest guidelines for remedial training. For example, for source 3, a teacher could associate auditory input with pictures, actions, and motor activity. For instruction in groups, Vance (1975-76) suggests asking short questions and using short, one-concept phrases.

Silverstein (1978), however, has questioned the construct validity of the ITPA. He notes that the correlation between the ITPA and S-B IQ is .78. He suggests, then, that the ITPA is nothing more than another individual test of general intelligence. The ITPA has also been severely criticized for its inability to predict academic achievement. Newcomer (1974-75), for example, suggests that the test is of no practical importance in designing remedial programs. Kirk and Kirk (1978) answer many criticisms of the ITPA and provide a balanced view of its utility in diagnosing certain kinds of developmental disabilities.

The ITPA has proved to be a popular test. However, Carroll (1972) notes that it is perhaps misnamed and could more accurately be called the "Illinois Diagnostic Test of Cognitive Functioning." That is, the ITPA does not deal specifically with language skills such as reading, writing, or spelling. Carroll, in fact, concludes that it assesses a limited number of intellectual abilities, including verbal comprehension and general information, immediate memory span, and perhaps special capacities in the areas of visual and auditory perception. At least one reviewer suggests that the test has enough technical defects so that it should not have been published at all and certainly not used (Lumsden, 1978).

Visual and Hearing Impairments

Persons who are visually or hearing impaired cannot typically be given most tests. In particular, of course, persons who are blind cannot be expected to take tests that require reading printed words or that have performance tasks that require sight (block designs, picture completion, and so on). Although modifications of some standardized tests have been attempted for persons having sensory deficiencies, special tests have been designed for these populations.

Langley (1978-79) summarized the tests available for assessing the capacities of multiply handicapped children. She briefly describes forty-two instruments of potential utility in assessing blind children, ranging from tests of visual acuity to standard measures of cognitive or developmental status that we have already discussed (for example, Bayley, McCarthy, and ITPA). Other summaries of tests that can and have been used with the visually impaired are also available (Coveny, 1976; Scholl & Schnur, 1976; Swallow, 1981). It should be noted that PL 94-142, the Education of the Handicapped Act, mandates that all exceptional persons between the ages of 3 and 21 must be provided with both an appropriate educational program in the least restrictive environment and an individualized educational program (IEP) that has been approved by the child's parents. Thus, the evaluation of learning potential and outcome for handicapped persons is receiving increasing attention.

One specially developed test is the *Haptic Intelligence Scale for Adult Blind (HIS)* (Shurrager & Shurrager, 1964). This is a nonverbal scale designed to be similar to the performance tests of the WAIS. The test's authors suggest that the verbal scale of the WAIS be used in conjunction with their test to provide a more complete picture of a subject's mental functioning. Four of the HIS tests are modifications of the WAIS performance tests: Block Design, Digit Symbol, Object Assembly, and Object Completion. Two performance tests, Bead Arithmetic and Pattern Board, were especially developed. The HIS performance tests require tactile discrimination and manipulation of parts. The standardization and scoring procedures parallel those used in the WAIS. The HIS subtests and performance IQ have respectable reliability and stability coefficients. Streitfeld and Avery (1968) correlated IQs obtained on the WAIS Verbal Scale and HIS with a measure of academic achievement for a group of thirty-one blind students. The WAIS Verbal IQ was a better predictor ($r = .79$) than the HIS ($r = .57$). The Verbal and Performance Scales correlated .65. It appears to us that little is known about the predictive or concurrent validity of the HIS.

With minor modifications, the Verbal Scale of the Wechsler can be administered to persons who are visually impaired or blind. Other tests can also be modified for the visually impaired by using braille or larger print. In reviewing the available research, Vander Kolk (1977) concluded that the blind, as a group, obtain average scores on tests of intelligence. That is, in terms of group averages, the blind do not differ significantly from sighted persons on verbal measures of intelligence or on other tests that have been appropriately modified for the blind. There is also some evidence that the totally blind and partially sighted do not differ substantially in average IQ (Jordan & Felty, 1968).

Assessing the mental ability of persons suffering a partial or total hearing loss provides problems almost the opposite of those encountered with the blind. Persons who are deaf cannot be directly administered the verbal test of the Wechsler scales since the items are presented orally. However, the performance tests, with appropriate modification of instructions, can be given to the deaf. A survey of professionals involved in testing the deaf found that the Wechsler Performance Scales were the most highly used tests (Levine, 1974). The Performance Scale of the WISC-R, for example, has been standardized with a sample of 1,728 deaf children (Anderson & Sisco, 1977). Deaf children have a mean WISC-R Performance IQ of 96, which is slightly lower than that of hearing children (Sisco & Anderson, 1978). Unfortunately, there appear to be almost no WISC-R validity studies available in which deaf children were tested.

The Levine (1974) survey also identified one test, the Hiskey-Nebraska Test of Learning Aptitude, that was developed for and standardized on a sample of deaf children as well as a sample of hearing children (Hiskey, 1966). It is one of the few tests that provides norms for deaf children. The test consists of twelve subtests (such as Bead Patterns, Memory for Color, Picture Identification), which are essentially performance tests. The test is an age scale like the Stanford-Binet and provides parallel instructions for deaf and hearing children. For the deaf children the instructions are pantomimed, whereas for hearing children they are presented orally. The test yields a "learning age" score for deaf children and a "mental age" score for hearing children. Norms are also provided to compute a deviation IQ score for hearing children and a "learning quotient" for deaf children. Split-half reliabilities appear quite acceptable for both hearing and deaf children (in the .90s). For deaf children, the Hiskey-Nebraska correlated with teacher ratings and scores on achievement tests. Newland (1972) suggested that the Hiskey-Nebraska provides a good means of assessing the abilities necessary for school in deaf children.

Relatively few published studies are available in which the Hiskey-Nebraska has been used. Buros (1978) lists thirty-eight such studies. However, most of these refer to earlier versions of the test. Currently, then, the validity information available is not especially encouraging or extensive. One relatively recent study (Petrie, 1975), for example, is based on a sample of only eleven children, and another study (Shutt & Hannon, 1974) used bilingual (not deaf) children. A study (Giangreco, 1966) using an earlier version of the Hiskey-Nebraska found modest correlations between measures of academic achievement and the Hiskey-Nebraska for lower elementary students (grade two) and advanced high school students (grades eleven and twelve). The test did not, however, predict achievement very well, if at all, for children between these extreme ages.

Different Cultures

The tests that we have discussed so far have been designed for use in the United States. That is, a common background of experiences is assumed, and the language in which the test is given is typically English. A limited time is usually provided for accomplishing a given test or subtest; in many instances strict time limits are imposed. And, finally, content is largely based on people, objects, and information characteristic of contemporary U.S. society. All these characteristics might, of course, be inappropriate for persons from other cultures (for example, Australian aborigines, African bush people, or even American Eskimos). Thus, if we wish to assess cognitive functioning independent of culture, rather special assessment devices must be used. Whether such *culture-fair* tests are of practical utility or not, establishing the cross-cultural similarity (and differences) of human intellectual functioning is of considerable theoretical and scientific interest. It is, however, probably impossible to develop tests that are totally culture-fair and certainly impossible to develop ones that are *culture-free*. What can be done is to minimize the more obvious cultural effects, especially by eliminating language and cultural content.

We will briefly discuss two tests that have been used in cross-cultural testing programs. Such tests can also be used, of course, with persons in the United States. Often such use is intended to obtain a "truer" or "less biased" estimate of intelligence for persons from minority groups. Members of minority groups can be conceptualized as coming from a cultural milieu at least somewhat different from that of U.S. society as a whole. Thus, it is often argued that tests such as the Wechsler scales are appropriate for white, middle-class children and adults but not for black children from the inner city. Black inner-city children live in a different culture from that on which the tests were developed. We will examine the possible problem of test bias in Chapter 14.

CATTELL'S CULTURE FAIR INTELLIGENCE TEST. One example of a culture-fair test is that developed by Raymond B. Cattell. His Culture Fair Intelligence Tests (CFIT) were designed to reduce as much as possible the effects of verbal fluency, cultural climate, and educational level on test performance. The tests have no verbal content and require examinees to perceive relationships in shapes and figures. Three tests are available. Scale 1 is for children between 4 and 8 years of age and for adult retardates. Scale 2

is for children between 8 and 14 years of age and for adults in the average range of intelligence. Scale 3 is designed to discriminate among people of higher levels of intelligence. Scales 2 and 3 are similar in form except that the latter is more difficult. Scale 1 is not wholly figural in content, must in part be individually administered, and requires some simple apparatus. We will describe Scales 2 and 3 to illustrate the test.

Scales 2 and 3 both consist of four rather short subtests called Series, Classification, Matrices, and Conditions. Table 7-5 gives an example item for each of the subtests in Scale 2. Note that all items are presented in a multiple-choice format with five alternatives per item. For Series items, the subject must determine which choice would complete the series. For Classification items the subject must determine which alternative is different from the others. For Matrices, the subject must determine the pattern of change occurring in the figures and choose the one that completes the matrix; this subtest is a more complicated version of Series. For Conditions, the subject must select the alternative that duplicates the conditions given in the target stimulus. Both Scale 2 and Scale 3 have two forms (A and B). The subtests are timed, having limits of 2½ to 4 minutes, and are quite short (ten to fourteen items). Using an appropriate age group, we can convert raw scores (the sum of the number correct on the four subtests) to a normalized IQ having a mean of 100 and standard deviation of 16.

In the manual for Scales 2 and 3, *Measuring Intelligence with the Culture Fair Tests* (1973a), and an associated *Technical Supplement for the Culture Fair Intelligence Tests: Scales 2 and 3* (1973b), a number of studies on the CFIT are summarized. The full test scores (Forms A and B) for both Scale 2 and Scale 3 have reliabilities in the .80s. Using only Form A, the reliabilities range from .76 to .69. Although the sample characteristics from which these statistics were obtained are not completely specified, they are typically based on large numbers of students. Validity information also indicates that the CFIT correlates with other tests of

TABLE 7–5 Example items from the Cattell Culture Fair Intelligence Test
(Copyright © 1949, 1957 by the Institute for Personality and Ability Testing, Inc. Reproduced by permission.)

NOTE: The present notice is intended only as a brief first exposure to IPAT Culture Fair Intelligence Tests, from which, it is hoped, the reader will go on to study much more complete evidence and information in the Manuals and Technical Handbooks for the scales. They cannot effectively be evaluated or used without this fuller study.

Do the following sample problems:

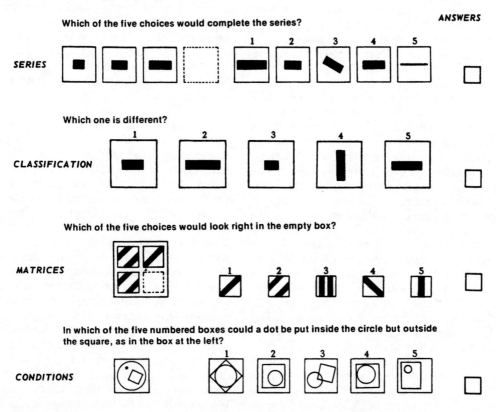

INTRODUCTION: You have just been introduced to an IPAT Culture Fair Intelligence Test, much as an examinee would be; that is, you have started taking the test. The examinee, however, has several examples of each type to work through, in the process of discovering what is required in the test proper. Also, such supplementary explanation as is necessary, oral or written, is given him in his primary language, whatever that is: English, Spanish, German, Italian, French, Japanese, Hindi, etc. This includes telling him the answers to examples, after he has worked them for himself (in this case, alternatives 1, 4, 1, and 3, respectively).

intelligence (an average correlation of .77 for Scale 2 and .69 for Scale 3). Chissom and Hoenes (1976), using eighth- and ninth-graders also reported excellent split-half reliabilities (about .90) and significant prediction of achievement test scores for both grades. The latter results are evidence of predictive validity because the CFIT scores were obtained in the fall whereas the achievement tests were obtained in the spring.

In examining cultural differences, the manuals for the CFIT report studies from Germany, Pakistan, Canada, Finland, Mexico, Britain, and Taiwan. A recent study (Weiss, 1980) used rural Peruvian Indians, and the CFIT was also used in Costa Rica (Fletcher et al., 1975). The CFIT has been used to predict academic achievement in other cultures and seems to be a promising assessment tool for measuring intelligence while minimizing cultural influences. However, a systematic presentation of the results of such studies is badly needed. For example, the Weiss study with Peruvian Indians found that they scored much lower on the average than the normative American group, although they scored in the average range on a second measure of intelligence. Similarly, Fletcher et al. found that the average score of the Costa Rican subjects was below normal on the CFIT but somewhat above normal on a Spanish version of the WAIS. The two measures of intelligence were, however, highly correlated ($r = .86$).

As previously indicated, culture-fair tests have also been proposed for minority groups in contemporary U.S. society. The CFIT manuals summarize some evidence that suggests that the test yields higher average scores for blacks than do several other tests of intelligence. Zoref and Williams (1980) analyzed the content of several intelligence tests (WAIS, WISC-R, S-B, Slosson, PPVT, and CFIT), and their results demonstrate that the CFIT does not contain biased content. That is, it does not reflect white, male dominance. However, Chissom and Hoenes (1976) found that the CFIT did correlate with race, blacks having lower scores for both eighth- and ninth-graders. One other study using white and nonwhite juvenile delinquents found that the CFIT yielded higher scores for nonwhites than did the WISC-R, although nonwhites had lower mean scores on both tests (Smith et al., 1977). The CFIT and WISC-R IQs also correlated at .76 in this study. The authors suggest that the CFIT may be a useful measure of intelligence because it eliminates at least some of the cultural bias in the WISC-R.

Jensen (1980, p. 652), however, suggested that it should not be used with low-IQ, culturally disadvantaged children in elementary school because many such children obtain the lowest possible score on the CFIT. Whether such a "basement effect" is due to the test's instructions and motivational factors is unknown. As previously noted, the subtests also have short time limits, which could contribute to the low scores.

RAVEN'S PROGRESSIVE MATRICES. A British psychologist, J. C. Raven, developed the most widely used culture-fair test, Raven's Progressive Matrices (Raven, 1938). Buros' *Eighth Mental Measurement Yearbook* (1978) lists 699 references to the various forms and revisions of the test, which was first published in 1938 and has been revised and improved since then (Raven, 1960). The tests do not use language but rather depend on perceptual forms that change in a systematic way that must be discovered by the subject. The key is to find the progressive change or changes that occur in the vertical dimension, horizontal dimension, or both dimensions of a matrix. Typically eight sections of a matrix are provided and the lower right corner is blank. Subjects must then choose from among the six alternatives available. We provide two ficticious examples in Table 7-6. Note that what the subject must do is select the alternative that most logically completes the pattern in the matrix. Thus, for the first example, answer 1 is correct because it continued the pattern of plus (+) signs found in the remainder of the matrix. For the second example, the rows change from circles to squares to triangles and also change in shading. In the columns the figures increase in size. Thus, answer 5 is correct because the next figure should be the largest, completely blackened, triangle to complete the progression of figures in the matrix. There are three versions of the pro-

TABLE 7-6 Example items similar to those used in Raven's Progressive Matrices

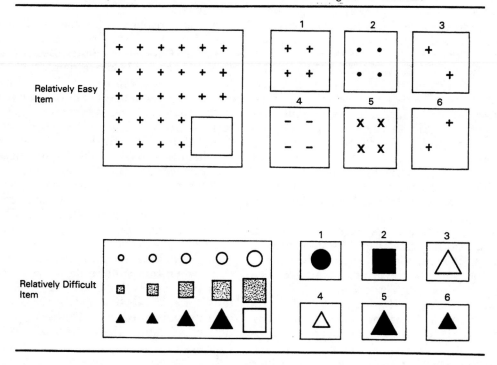

gressive matrices, differing in difficulty and in the age for which they are appropriate.

The most recent Standard Progressive Matrices (SPM) (Raven, 1960) is virtually identical to the 1938 edition of the test. It consists of five sets of matrices (A through E) with twelve matrices per set. Subjects thus answer sixty items. Each set of matrices involves a different principle in solving the problem. Also, within each set of matrices, the items increase in difficulty. After twelve items the subject begins a new type of problem with an easy item. Such an arrangement should encourage subjects to do well and maintain their interest. The test can be administered to subjects six years of age and older, individually or in groups. The instructions and content are obvious enough to most subjects so that they can be pantomimed if necessary (with deaf subjects or those who do not speak English). Instructions and content for the other forms of the test are also quite obvious. The test is scored in terms of the total number of correct answers. Scores on the five sets of matrices are not reported separately. The raw scores are not converted to standard scores, although norms are provided for conversion into five percentile ranks (Group I is the top 5 percent; Group V is the lowest 5 percent). The test has a time limit of sixty minutes.

The second version of the test, Colored Progressive Matrices (CPM) (Raven, 1965b), consists of three sets of matrices, two of which (A and B) are identical to those in Standard Progressive Matrices except for the addition of color. The subject thus solves thirty-six matrices in this test, which is designed for children between the ages of 5 and 11, mental patients, and the elderly. For younger children (ages 5 and 6), the test is individually administered; for older children it can be administered in groups. The scoring is the same as that of Standard Progressive Matrices. Elementary school children can complete the whole test in thirty to forty minutes. The addition of color to the matrices apparently makes the test somewhat more appealing to children. This version is less difficult than the standard version of the test.

The third version, Advanced Progressive Matrices (Raven, 1965a), consists of thirty-six matrix items that are more difficult than those in the standard test. It is designed for subjects 11 years of age and older who are above average in intelligence. The test is more appropriate for college students, for example, than is the standard test.

The most recent compilation of references to Raven's Progressive Matrices demonstrates its extensive cross-cultural use (Buros, 1978). Studies have been done in Iran, Iraq, Israel, Canada (Eskimos and Indians), Poland, Nigeria, Japan, and Britain, to note some of the groups that have been tested. Also, within the United States, the test has been used with blacks, Mexican-Americans, the hearing impaired, Indians, the elderly, the mentally retarded, and patients of various kinds. Jensen (1980) and Valencia (1979), along with others, conclude that Raven's Progressive Matrices is the best available culture-fair test, although both describe the test as culture-reduced rather than culture-fair.

Unfortunately, there is no recent comprehensive review of research in which Raven's Progressive Matrices have been used. Over twenty years ago, Burke (1958) published a very thorough review of the research available at that time, the bulk of which had used Standard Progressive Matrices (SPM). Burke concluded, among other things, that SPM had fairly good concurrent and predictive validity, correlated reasonably well with other tests of intelligence, differentiated among groups known by other criteria to vary in intelligence, and although demonstrating reasonable reliability, had insufficient reliability at various age levels to be useful in making decisions about individuals. Burke also questioned the adequacy of SPM as a measure of Spearman's g, general intelligence. The test has been accepted as the purest available measure of g, and

Jensen (1980) contends that this is still largely true.

A major problem with Raven's Progressive Matrices is the lack of adequate normative data in the United States. Burke (1972) provided some normative data on 567 VA patients, all of whom were males. Additional results with adults suggest that SPM has rather high split-half reliabilities and has correlations with other measures of intelligence in the .70s (Burke, 1972; Burke & Bingham, 1969). Other investigators (McLaurin & Farrar, 1973; McLaurin et al., 1973) reported lower correlations (in the .50s) with other measures of intelligence. Kyle (1977) suggested that the British norms are now outdated and a restandardization is needed.

The available manuals are also inadequate when compared to those available for tests such as the Wechsler scales. Raven's tests, for example, have time limits that may or may not be used. Also, the use of percentile scores rather than standard scores is contrary to most other tests of intelligence. Additional psychometric work on the items, perhaps increasing the number of items and revising some so that the difficulty levels are more evenly distributed, is needed. Such improvements would make the test more sensitive to differences in intelligence.

Cross-cultural studies suggest a rather mixed set of findings. Subjects from other cultures sometimes obtain average scores similar to that found in the English normative groups or other groups from Western cultures. For example, MacDonald and Netherton (1969) found no differences between the mean of a group of Canadian Eskimos and Indians when compared with the mean of a group of white Canadian children. Comparing Filipino and Canadian children, Flores and Evans (1972) found no differences in average performance for sixth-graders but some difference for eighth-graders. Using a large sample ($n = 3692$) of Tanzanian secondary students, Klingelhofer (1967) found no striking differences in average performance among various tribes. On the other hand,

Baraheni (1974), using a large sample ($n = 4561$) of Iranian school children, found very large differences between their performance on the Raven's test and the performance of the British normative group. The Iranian children were far below the British norms. Wiltshire and Gray (1969) reported a similarly large difference in favor of the British normative group for a sample of Canadian Indians. It should be noted that cross-cultural studies demonstrated the satisfactory reliability of Raven's test. Baraheni (1974), for example, reported split-half reliabilities for his Iranian sample ranging from .89 to .95. The predictive validity in cross-cultural studies of the Raven's test has been modest, and one fairly large study ($n = 534$) of Nigerian children (Ogunlade, 1978) found no correlation with school marks at all.

Irvine (1969), in reviewing the use of the SPM in Africa, noted that its scores do reflect environmental differences in African cultures. He also presented evidence that item difficulties varied in African cultures and between African culture and normative data from Britain. He concluded that for tests like the SPM, cultural biases still exist but in ways that are different from verbal tests and perhaps more difficult to define. Irvine's analysis also suggests that even if cultural groups do not differ in average performance, they may differ in the items that are correctly answered. Thus, the same test score could be obtained for very different reasons, which would reflect different cognitive functioning between people in two different cultures.

As we mentioned earlier, culture-fair tests are also used for minority groups in contemporary U.S. society. Since such tests have no verbal content, they may be better indicators of intellectual potential than other tests of intelligence. Raven's test has been used in several studies with black and Mexican-American children. According to Fitz-Gibbon (1974), the SPM could be used to select mentally gifted children from populations of "disadvantaged" children, who were predominantly black and Mexican-

American in her study. Although average performance was lower than the normative data for the SPM, it was better than other measures of intelligence based on verbal items. Sewell and Severson (1974) suggested that CPM scores may be useful in predicting learning potential for first-grade black children. In comparing Mexican-American and white third-grade boys, Valencia (1979) found that CPM average scores did not differ in a practical sense, although the difference was statistically significant in favor of the white children. McManman and Cohn (1978) also found that for third- and fifth-graders there was no difference in average SPM scores for English- and Spanish-speaking children. These investigators all concluded that Raven's Progressive Matrices was a good nonverbal measure of intelligence and could be used with these two minority groups to obtain less biased estimates of cognitive functioning.

However, other investigators demonstrated that the RPM does not yield higher scores for minority groups than other standard tests of intelligence. One study, for example, demonstrated that the WISC was a better predictor of achievement test scores than was the CPM and that the CPM correlated .75 with the WISC IQ (Hartlage et al., 1976). Another study reported that black applicants for a vocational rehabilitation program had average scores much below that of white applicants, the difference being of the same order as that obtained on the WAIS (Vincent & Cox, 1974). Black fifth- and sixth-graders in lower socioeconomic groups have also been found to have average SPM scores lower than white children from the same social class (Tulkin & Newbrough, 1968). In one of the best studies we have seen on cognitive development, Hall and Kaye (1977) report results on a number of measures for 600 boys at six, seven, and eight years of age. With respect to CPM, they found (1) that white children received higher scores than black children, (2) that middle-class children do better than lower-class children, and (3) that older children do better than younger children. Also, although all groups improved in performance across age, middle-class white boys showed a greater gain in performance between 6 and 7 years than did any of the other groups. Thus, CPM scores showed patterns that would be expected in more "culture-loaded" tests. Hall and Kaye did find, however, that the CPM and the PPVT were equally good predictors of academic achievement for all groups. This finding is one piece of evidence against these tests being culturally biased.

In summary, it appears to us that RPM shows promise as a culture-reduced measure of intelligence. The available literature continues to demonstrate that a completely culture-free measure of intelligence is still beyond our reach. It is also clear that RPM would be a more valuable test if its manual, norms, and items were revised. Jensen's (1980, p. 648) summary of RPM largely represents our opinion as well:

Because the RPM is an excellent culture-reduced measure of fluid g, one of its chief values is for screening illiterate, semiliterate, bilingual, and otherwise educationally disadvantaged or socially depressed populations for potential academic talent that might easily remain undetected by parents and teachers or by the more conventional culture-loaded tests of scholastic aptitude. It is probably the surest instrument we now possess for discovering intellectually gifted children from disadvantaged backgrounds, so that they can be given the special attention needed for the full realization of their ability in school and in the world of work.

The practical usefulness of culture-fair tests is largely still to be demonstrated. As Jensen and others suggested, the tests may be useful in identifying persons of high ability whom other tests miss. They also provide one interesting method of measuring mental ability in widely different cultures. However, it appears to us that in predicting most criteria of interest, culture-fair tests do less well than standard tests of intelligence. This, of course, is not surprising since criterion measures reflect culturally important behaviors. For example, to predict achievement in school, it should not be surprising that the WISC–R is a better predictor than Raven's Progressive Matrices. The WISC-R was specifically designed to be culturally relevant and to be able to predict such things as academic achievement.

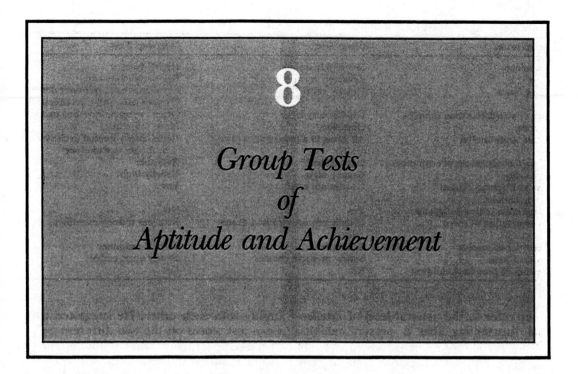

8

Group Tests
of
Aptitude and Achievement

In the previous three chapters, we discussed tests of mental ability that are usually individually administered. Such tests cannot be efficiently used with large numbers of people. In this chapter we will discuss tests of mental ability that can be administered to groups. Standardized achievement tests, given to millions of students each year, measure academic progress in such areas as mathematics, reading, and social science. Other tests are administered to students entering college in order to assess their aptitude for college work. These tests can be used to select students for admission and to provide information on their academic strengths and weaknesses. Other group tests can also be used by professional schools (medicine, law, business) to help select students for admission.

Group tests can be administered and scored by relatively untrained people and usually have strict time limits. They often contain multiple-choice items for which answers are recorded on separate answer sheets. The answer sheets are often on op-

tical scanner forms and are eventually scored by a computer. The items have a single correct or best answer. Although individually administered intelligence tests are usually used in a clinical setting, group tests are widely used in education, industry, civil service, and the armed forces, where it is necessary to test large numbers of people as efficiently and effectively as possible. Group tests are the only practical way to accomplish this task. In Table 8-1, we summarize some characteristics of tests and indicate how group and individual tests of mental ability compare.

APTITUDE-ACHIEVEMENT DISTINCTION

As noted in Chapter 5, a person's test score is a product of past experiences, genetic endowment, and probably some complex interaction between these two components. We use the terms *intelligence, mental ability,* and *aptitude* more or less interchangeably.

TABLE 8-1 Contrast between group and individual tests

Characteristic	Group Tests	Individual Tests
Examiner	Not highly trained	Highly trained
Cost	Relatively inexpensive	Relatively expensive
Time limits	Usually restrictions	For many tests, examiner determines pace and time necessary
Size of standardization samples	Usually very large	Often representative but small
Scoring	Objective	More subjective
Items administered	All items to all examinees (usually)	Items largely limited to those appropriate to examinee
Clinical observations of examinee	Unavailable	Available
Reliability	Usually high	Usually high
Use with special clinical populations	Usually not used	Yes
Large-scale testing programs	Yes	No
Interpretation of score	Usually requires trained examiner	Requires trained examiner
Recorder of answer	Examinee	Usually examiner
Type of item	Mostly multiple choice	Mostly open-ended
Testing of preschool children	No	Yes

They refer to the general level of intellectual functioning that a person exhibits. They do not refer to innate capacity but rather are a joint function of environmental and genetic influences. It is obvious that formal education should have a large influence on cognitive growth. In fact, modern societies depend on the educational system (largely the public schools) to teach the fundamentally important skills, such as reading, writing, and mathematics, needed to survive in our modern world. Thus, an intelligence test administered after a child begins school will reflect to some degree how much that child has benefited from the educational system. Intelligence tests or aptitude tests, however, are not necessarily designed to determine how much a child has learned in specific subjects. The amount of academic achievement is usually measured by tests designed specifically for that purpose. That is, achievement tests are designed to measure the outcomes of relatively specific learning experiences (instruction in various subjects) in a particular setting (the public schools).

Is it meaningful and important to distinguish between aptitude and achievement? Kelley (1927), for example, noted that intelligence and achievement tests correlate highly with each other. He suggested that since test scores on the two different types of tests essentially ranked students in the same manner, the tests did not differ in the trait being measured. He referred to this false distinction as the "jangle" fallacy—achievement and intelligence sound as though they are different but in truth are not. Other investigators supported Kelley's position (Coleman & Cureton, 1954; Coleman & Ward, 1956). Humphreys (1974) also called the distinction between aptitude and achievement misleading. He stressed that although there are different kinds of tests, they are more accurately described by different terms. For example, Humphreys suggested that the items on aptitude and achievement tests could differ in three ways: (1) breadth of items, aptitude tests having more different kinds of items than achievement tests; (2) variety of experience, aptitude tests measuring a wider variety of experiences; (3) age of learning sampled, aptitude tests typically depending on older learning. These differences, of course, are ones of degree. In examining any single item it might be difficult to determine if it came from an aptitude test or from an achievement test. Humphreys does not believe the distinction is worthwhile.

To us it appears that it may be important to consider how tests are used rather than the labels that are attached to them. Thus, aptitude tests are used to predict future behavior whereas achievement tests are used to assess the results of previous training (usually education). This is a distinction used by Becker (1974) and many others. Carroll (1974) also presented a sophisticated analysis of the difference between aptitude and achievement, using the example of an aptitude for studying a foreign language (Mandarin Chinese). Carroll noted that aptitude tests can predict who will learn foreign languages most rapidly but that scores on these tests are largely unchanged as a result of foreign language instruction. Achievement occurs because people who could not speak or understand Chinese before instruction are able to use the language after instruction. Their achievement in learning Chinese can be measured after the instruction has occurred.

Anastasi (1980) suggested that we use the term *developed abilities* rather than distinguishing between aptitude and achievement. The continuum that differentiates tests is the precision with which antecedent experience is specified. Thus, tests used to measure outcomes in the classroom assume relatively specific previous experiences. The Stanford-Binet tests a more general set of previous experiences, growing up in U.S. society, but possibly including formal education. A culture-fair test, like Raven's Progressive Matrices, provides the most extreme example of testing for a general, unspecified set of previous experiences. Cronbach (1970, p. 282) suggested a similar continuum for conceptualizing tests of ability. On one end of his continuum are those tests reflecting maximum direct training (subject matter proficiency); on the other extreme are tests reflecting maximum adaptation or transfer (analytic or fluid ability).

It is most important to recognize that the aptitude-achievement distinction is somewhat arbitrary. There is not necessarily a clear division between tests that are obviously measuring aptitude and those measuring achievement. We shall use the term *achievement test* to refer to those tests generally designed to measure educational progress in various subjects. For us, *aptitude tests* will be those tests used most typically to predict future behavior. We recognize, however, that scores on some tests may be used for both purposes.

APTITUDE TESTS

Aptitude and *cognitive* or *mental ability* are terms that we use interchangeably, and different tests may have either of these terms in their titles. Group aptitude tests have been designed for children as young as age five (kindergarten) through adulthood. There are many such tests available, and we shall discuss only a representative sample of them, focusing mainly on those often taken by college students. Ability or aptitude tests usually provide several scores for each person, each score reflecting a different area of mental functioning.

Multilevel Tests—Cognitive Abilities Test (CAT)

The Cognitive Abilities Test (Form 3), developed by Robert L. Thorndike and Elizabeth Hagen (1978a, b, c), is an excellent example of a well-constructed multilevel aptitude test. The CAT consists of two components—the Primary Battery (Levels 1 and 2) and the Multilevel Edition (Levels A through H). Primary Level 1 is used with children in kindergarten and grade one; Level 2 is used mainly with children in grade two. The eight levels (A through H) of the Multilevel Edition are used in the ten grade levels from three through twelve. The current edition of the CAT evolved from the earlier Lorge-Thorndike Intelligence Tests, which are also still in use (Lorge et al., 1964). The CAT is designed to measure scholastic aptitude and abstract reasoning. Thus, it could be helpful in determining students' strengths and weaknesses. It also could help assess students' developed abilities in relation to their academic achievement.

PRIMARY BATTERY. Because the Primary Battery is administered orally, reading is not a required skill. The Primary Battery consists of four short subtests: Relational Concepts, Object Classification, Quantitative Concepts, and Oral Vocabulary. The number of items in each subtest ranges from eighteen to twenty-eight. Figure 8-1 gives sample items from the Primary Battery (Level 1).

Items are referred to by a common figure associated with each row (for example, moon, flower, star) rather than by a number. For the first example, the children are instructed to identify the shortest tree. In the second example, they are instructed to find the dog behind the house. All items in the Primary Battery have three to five pictures (alternatives) from which children choose the correct answers based on the examiner's oral instructions.

The Primary Battery does not have strict time limits. The examiner, typically a classroom teacher, is encouraged to adjust the pace of testing to suit the characteristics of the children being tested. The test's authors (Thorndike & Hagen, 1978b) also recommend that the four subtests for Primary Level 1 be administered on separate days. For Level 2, the authors recommend administering two subtests per day (Thorndike & Hagen, 1978c). The manual suggests that each subtest can be administered in about fifteen minutes. Only a single score is provided for the Primary Battery.

The technical characteristics of the Primary Battery have been obtained from the manual provided by the publisher (*Technical Manual . . : , 1982*). Items were chosen from studies with children in kindergarten through grade three. A high correlation between the total subtest score and answering an item correctly was the main statistical criterion for including an item in the subtest. These correlations between items and total score are quite high (*r*'s ranging from .54 to .71). Other indices and procedures indicate that the content is appropriate and that the tests are well constructed.

The standardization sample tested in the spring of 1978, for example, consisted of students from four grade levels (kindergarten through three). The standardization

FIGURE 8–1 Example Items from the Cognitive Abilities Test Primary Battery, Level 1, Form 3. (Copyright © 1978 by Houghton Mifflin Company. Reproduced by permission of the Publisher, The Riverside Publishing Company.)

Oral instructions. For "moon" item: "Find the shortest tree." For "flower" item: "Find the dog behind the house."

sample is large enough to produce statistically stable results and appears to be reasonably representative of the U.S. population.

The reliability of the Primary Battery, as measured by internal consistency formulas, appears quite high. For Level 1, grades kindergarten and one, the internal consistency coefficients are .92 and .89. For Level 2, grades two and three, the values are both .89. The standard error of measurement, another index of error in test scores, suggests that the Primary Battery has somewhat less error for children of lower ability than for those of higher ability. The technical manual notes that the Primary Battery contains a large number of relatively easy items. It may not, therefore, be a good test to use with groups that are predominantly average or above average in ability.

The four subtests of the Primary Battery are intercorrelated, r's ranging from .42 to .60. These results are based on a sample of 429 third-grade students who also took the appropriate level of the Multilevel Edition of the CAT. For these students, it was found that the score on the Primary Battery was correlated with the three scores on the Multilevel Edition. No other validity information is presented in the manual regarding the interpretation of the score on the Primary Battery. More research on the Primary Battery would be desirable before it is routinely used in the schools or other settings.

MULTILEVEL EDITION. The CAT for older children (grades three through twelve) is organized into three batteries—verbal, quantitative, and nonverbal. Each subtest within a battery is divided into eight different but overlapping levels (A through H). The items are ordered in terms of difficulty so that older children start at a higher level. Each series of items begins with those easy enough for a slow third-grader and ends with those difficult enough for superior high school students. By varying the point where examinees begin and end, age-appropriate items are available for any group. Thus, a single test booklet can be used with children of any age.

The Verbal Battery consists of four subtests: Vocabulary, Sentence Completion, Verbal Classification, and Verbal Analogies. The Quantitative Battery consists of three subtests: Quantitative Relations, Number Series, and Equation Building. The Nonverbal Battery consists of three subtests: Figure Classification, Figure Analysis, and Figure Synthesis. Examples of these items appear in Table 8-2.

All subtests are separately timed, each having limits of seven to twelve minutes. Each of the three batteries can be administered in less than an hour. The manual recommends three successive testing days for younger children. For older children, two testing periods in a single day and a single testing period on the following day are recommended.

With two exceptions, all subtests have five-choice responses. The Quantitative Relations items have three choices, and Figure Synthesis items have yes or no responses to each of five alternatives. The formats can be seen in Table 8-2.

Three total scores are reported—verbal, quantitative, and nonverbal—using six types of scores: raw scores (number right); standard scores, percentile ranks, and stanines for age groups; and percentile ranks and stanines for grades. The standardization sample is quite large, about 200,000 students tested in 1977 and 1978 and selected to be representative of the U.S. population with respect to geographic region, school district size, and socioeconomic level. Information provided in the manual suggests that ethnic groups are also reasonably represented (*Technical Manual . . .*, 1982).

The internal consistency of the three tests is uniformly high. For the verbal test, it varies from .92 to .95 for the eight levels A through H; for the quantitative test, the corresponding range is .88 to .92; and for the nonverbal test the range is .91 to .93 (*Technical Manual . . .*, 1982). These values have been corrected to eliminate any possible effects caused by speeding (inadequate time limits). In addition to internal consistency, some information is available on the stability

TABLE 8-2 Example from Cognitive Abilities Test, Form 3

Example Items from Verbal Battery Subtests

Vocabulary: Which word means most nearly the same thing as wish?

  Wish   A agree   B bone   C over   D want   E waste

Sentence Completion:

  The fire is _____.

    A wet   B green   C hot   D running   E round

Verbal Classification:

  Think in what way the words in dark type go together. Then find the word on the line below that belongs with them.

                 mouse   **wolf**   **bear**

    A rose   B lion   C run   D hungry   E brown

Verbal Analogies:

                      big—large : little—

    A girl   B small   C late   D lively   E more

Example Items from Quantitative Battery Subtests

Quantitative Relations:

  Mark A if the amount in Column A is *greater* than that in Column B.

  Mark B if the amount in Column B is *greater* than that in Column A.

  Mark C if the amount in Column A is exactly *equal to* that in Column B.

               Column A   Column B

                  3 + 2   2 + 3

Number Series:

  1 2 3 4 5 — A 4 B 5 C 6 D 7 E 8

Equation Building: In this test, you will try to discover how to put numbers together to make true equations or number sentences. You are to discover how to put together *all* of the numbers and signs given in a problem in a way that gives you *one of the answer choices supplied in that problem.*

    2 3 1 + +   A 4 B 5 C 6 D 7 E 8

Example Items from Nonverbal Battery Subtests

Figure Classification: Each question starts with a set of figures or drawings that are alike in some way. You are to figure out how they are alike, and then find among the answer choices on the right the figure that belongs with them.

                                 A   B   C   D   E

TABLE 8-2   (Continued)

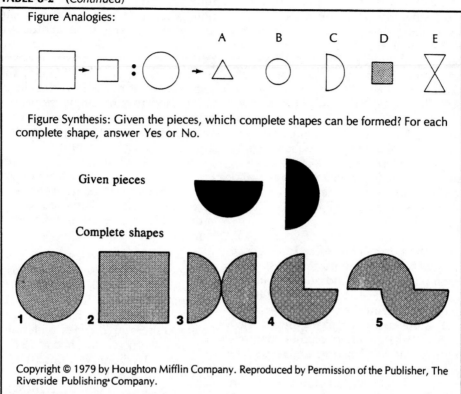

Figure Analogies:

Figure Synthesis: Given the pieces, which complete shapes can be formed? For each complete shape, answer Yes or No.

Given pieces

Complete shapes

of scores over time. Test-retest correlations over a six-month interval yield representative values of .91 for the verbal, .86 for the quantitative, and .85 for the nonverbal. Thus, the available evidence suggests that the Multilevel Edition of the CAT is reliable, although information on the long-term stability of scores would be of interest.

Items in the Multilevel Edition were selected to have high correlations with the subtest's total score. These correlations are generally high for all subtests and all grades, ranging from .85 to .53. Further, item difficulties were appropriately chosen so that maximum differentiation among students would be possible. The content was designed to help measure a person's educational and work potential. Thus, the content validity of the test appears to be good.

The three scores are not, however, independent of each other. The median correlations (in ten age groups) between verbal and quantitative, verbal and nonverbal, and nonverbal and quantitative are .78, .72, and .78, respectively. Given the reliabilities of the tests, rather sizeable differences (ten or fifteen points at least) between standard scores must occur before such differences could possibly reflect differential abilities. The manual explicitly recommends against averaging the three separate scores. However, given the high intercorrelation, the usefulness of the three separate scores will need continued scrutiny and research. The manual does note that based on further statistical analyses (factor analysis), each of the verbal and nonverbal subtests measures unique aspects of mental functioning. This result is the justification for reporting three scores rather than a single index of mental ability (*Technical Manual . . .*, 1982, p. 33).

The Multilevel Edition of the CAT does

possess criterion-related validity. It correlates with other tests and with school grades. For example, typical correlations with the Iowa Tests of Basic Skills achievement test composite is in the high .80s for the Verbal Battery, about .80 for the Quantitative Battery, and in the low .70s for the Nonverbal Battery. These correlations support the concurrent validity of the CAT. An earlier edition of the CAT, Form 1, was also shown to have predictive validity. The GPA in grade nine was correlated with CAT scores obtained in grades five and seven, four and two years earlier. Thus, there is every reason to suppose the CAT, Form 3, will have similar predictive validity.

The previous editions of the CAT, including the Lorge-Thorndike Intelligence Tests, have been used in numerous studies. For example, the CAT and an achievement test were administered to over 250,000 students in grades four, eight, and twelve as part of a statewide program in Georgia (Osborne, 1975). Other studies demonstrated that the CAT scores are related to achievement test scores in social studies (Lewis & Todd, 1978), mathematics (Good & Beckerman, 1978), and first-grade reading (Busch, 1980). The CAT was also found to correlate positively with tests of musical aptitude and social status (Phillips, 1976). We anticipate that the CAT, Form 3, will continue in this tradition. It is an excellent example of a group test of general mental ability that is recently normed and carefully constructed. Further research should continue to clarify its validity.

Aptitude Batteries

To be successful in a job requires that a person have the skills and aptitudes necessary to perform that job. Aptitude batteries typically consist of many tests whose scores are then differentially related to success in different jobs. They are used in educational and vocational counseling of high school and college students and with special programs, such as those in the military services and state employment bureaus.

The principle underlying the use of aptitude batteries is that of differential prediction. That is, it is assumed that success in any job is related to some aptitudes or abilities but not to others. Thus, depending on a person's strengths and weaknesses as measured by the tests in the battery, success in some careers is more likely than in others. It is assumed that no single measure, like an IQ, is universally useful in predicting job success. Rather, different aptitude profiles are needed, it is assumed, for different types of jobs. Most aptitude tests providing only one or a limited number of scores are used to predict academic achievement. Differential aptitude batteries are perhaps more likely to be used in vocational prediction or counseling.

DIFFERENTIAL APTITUDE TESTS (DAT). One of the most widely used aptitude batteries is the DAT. Sell and Torres-Henry (1979), for example, reported that it was the most widely used aptitude battery in 284 counseling centers at colleges and universities. The test was first published in 1947, but the most recent edition was published in 1982 and has two alternate forms (V and W). The DAT yields the following eight test scores:

1. Verbal Reasoning: a verbal comprehension test using analogies.
2. Numerical Ability: a computational test requiring knowledge of arithmetic operation.
3. Abstract Reasoning: a nonverbal test requiring the examinee to determine the rule used in constructing a series of figures.
4. Clerical Speed and Accuracy: a speed test requiring the examinee to find the pair of symbols that match a target pair.
5. Mechanical Reasoning: a test of basic physical and mechanical principles.
6. Space Relations: a test requiring the examinee to determine the shape of an unfolded figure.
7. Spelling: a test requiring examinees to recognize whether or not a word is correctly spelled.
8. Language Usage: a test requiring examinees to recognize grammatical and other errors in sentences.

Examples from these tests are given in Figure 8-2.

Verbal Reasoning

Each of the fifty sentences in this test has the first word and the last word left out. You are to pick out words that will fill the blanks so that the sentence will be true and sensible.

For each sentence you are to choose from among five pairs of words to fill the blanks. The first word of the pair you choose goes in the blank space at the beginning of the sentence; the second word of the pair goes in the blank at the end of the sentence. When you have picked the pair to fill in the blanks, mark the letter of that pair on the Answer Sheet, after the number of the sentence you are working on.

Example X. . . . . . . is to water as eat is to . . . . . .

    A   continue — drive
    B   foot — enemy
    C   drink — food
    D   girl — industry
    E   drink — enemy

Numerical Ability

This test consists of forty numerical problems. Next to each problem there are five answers. You are to pick out the correct answer and mark its letter on the Answer Sheet. If you do not find a correct answer among the first four choices, blacken the circle for N as your answer. Choice N for every problem is **none of these**, which means that a correct answer is **not** among the first four choices. Only one answer should be marked for each problem. Do your figuring on the scratch paper you have been given, and reduce fractions to lowest terms.

Example X.   Add

            A   14
    13   B   16
    12   C   25
            D   59
            N   none of these

Abstract Reasoning

In this test you will see rows of designs or figures like those below. Each row across the page is **one** problem. You are to mark your answers on the Answer Sheet.

Each row consists of four figures called Problem Figures and five called Answer Figures. The four Problem Figures make a series. You are to find out which one of the Answer Figures would be the next (or the fifth one) in the series of Problem Figures.

PROBLEM FIGURES   ANSWER FIGURES

Example X.

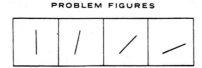
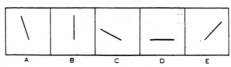

FIGURE 8-2 (Continued)

Clerical Speed and Accuracy
This is a test to see how quickly and accurately you can compare letter and number combinations. On the following pages are groups of these combinations; each test item contains five. These same combinations appear after the number for each test item on the Answer Sheet, but they are in a different order. You will notice that in each test item one of the five is **underlined**. You are to look at the **one** combination that is underlined, find the **same** one after that item number on the Answer Sheet, and fill in the circle under it.

Examples

V. <u>AB</u> AC AD AE AF

W. aA aB BA Ba <u>Bb</u>

X. A7 7A B7 <u>7B</u> AB

EXAMPLES

AC AE AF AB AD
V ○○○●○

BA Ba Bb aA aB
W ○○●○○

7B B7 AB 7A A7
X ●○○○○

Mechanical Reasoning
This test consists of a number of pictures and questions about those pictures.

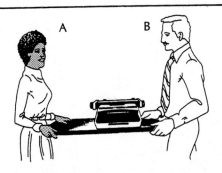

Example X.

Which person has the heavier load?
(If equal, mark C.)

Space Relations
This test consists of 60 patterns which can be folded into figures. To the right of each pattern there are four figures. You are to decide which **one** of these figures can be made from the pattern shown. The pattern always shows the **outside** of the figure.

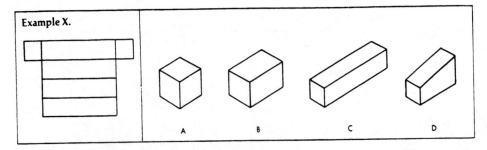

Example X.

A   B   C   D

FIGURE 8-2 (Continued)

Spelling

This test is composed of a series of words. Some of them are correctly spelled; some are incorrectly spelled. You are to indicate whether each word is spelled right or wrong by blackening the proper circle on the Answer Sheet. If the spelling of the word is **right**, fill in the circle that has the R, for RIGHT. If it is spelled **wrong**, blacken the circle that has the W, for WRONG.

Examples

W. man

X. gurl

Language Usage

This test consists of fifty sentences, each divided into four parts, lettered A, B, C, and D. You are to consider each sentence as an example of formal, written English. In many of the sentences, one part has an error in punctuation, grammar, or capitalization. Decide which part, if any, is wrong. Then, on the Answer Sheet, fill in the circle that has the letter that matches the part of the sentence that has an error. Be sure the item number on the Answer Sheet is the same as that of the sentence on which you are working.

Some sentences have no error in any part. If there is no error in a sentence, fill in the circle for the letter N.

Example X. I just / left / my friends / house.
           A   B   C   D

Example Y. Ain't we / going to / the office / next week?
            A   B   C   D

Example Z. I went / to a ball / game with / Jane.
            A   B   C   D

All the tests have multiple-choice items, most with five alternatives. However, Space Relations has four alternatives, and Mechanical Reasoning and Spelling have two. The time limit for all tests except Space Relations, which takes thirty-five minutes, is forty minutes. The entire battery takes about four hours to administer. The manual suggests several testing periods that can be used to finish testing in one day (Bennett et al., 1982b).

Although most of the tests are reasonably called *aptitude tests*, the Spelling and Language Usage tests are more reflective of the effects of education and are probably better classified as *achievement variables* (Bouchard, 1978).

The DAT emphasizes the importance of measuring separate abilities, but it also provides a composite score: VR + NA (verbal reasoning plus numerical ability). This composite score is similar to that provided by IQ tests yielding a single score. All test scores are based on the number of correct answers.

The raw scores may be converted to either percentile scores or to stanine scores by reference to the appropriate tables.

As the manual states, the DAT battery was constructed mainly to be used for counseling with students in junior and senior high school (Bennett et al., 1982a). The DAT has also been used for educational and vocational counseling with adults not in school and for selecting employees. However, the norms for the DAT are based on the students tested at five grade levels (eight through twelve) in November and December 1980. Separate norms are available for fall and spring semesters for grades eight through eleven. The spring norms were obtained by interpolation. The same norms are used for both Forms V and W, because the separate forms were judged to be essentially equivalent. Separate norms are available for males and females. These separate norms are provided because the two sexes score somewhat differently on the tests in the DAT battery. For example, males tend to score higher than females on Mechanical Reasoning, whereas the converse is true for Language Usage.

The DAT standardization sample, 61,722 students in grades eight through twelve, came from sixty-four school districts in thirty-two states. The sample appears to be reasonably representative of school districts across the United States with respect to enrollment and socioeconomic status. Ethnic minorities and nonpublic schools are also represented. Some school systems refused to participate, which undoubtedly contributed to some bias in the norms. However, the current version of the DAT appears to have followed a carefully conceived process to assure a reasonably representative normative sample.

The reliability of the DAT was determined by the split-half method for all tests except Clerical Speed and Accuracy. Reliability for this test, because it is highly speeded, was estimated by correlating scores on the alternate forms (V and W) for relatively small samples in grades eight and ten. Essentially the internal consistency of the DAT is reported in the manual for all tests (except as noted) at all grade levels for males and females (Bennett et al., 1982a, pp. 43-45). The split-half reliabilities for all tests are uniformly high for all groups and both forms, the lowest being .83 and the highest .96. Although these initial results on reliability are encouraging, no stability or alternate form coefficients have yet been reported. Such results would provide useful information. They are, of course, available for earlier forms of the DAT.

Surprisingly enough, the manual of the most recent DAT (Forms V and W) presents no information on the test's validities (Bennett et al., 1982a). The recent publication date is undoubtedly the reason for this obvious omission. However, because the manual also fails to report the intercorrelations among the eight tests for the normative sample, it is difficult to determine whether or not the DAT actually measures different aptitudes. The validity of the current DAT must thus be inferred from the evidence available on the 1974 edition (Forms S and T).

Extensive research on earlier editions of the DAT exists, Buros (1978) citing 388 studies. The manual for the previous edition of the DAT (Forms S and T) provides an extensive summary of validity information available at that time (Bennett et al., 1974). This 1974 manual explicitly devotes forty-six pages to the validity of the DAT and presents twenty-two tables reporting correlations with grades in various specific courses (for example, English, science, mathematics). Bennett et al. (1974) noted, for example, that VR + NA, Verbal Reasoning, Numerical Ability, and Language Usage, are the best predictors of grades in the more common high school courses, that Clerical Speed and Accuracy is a good predictor of grades in business and office practice, and that Mechanical Reasoning can be expected to have its greatest validity with respect to occupational criteria rather than course grades.

Bennett et al. (1974, p. 125) also reported some longitudinal data on students' post-high school accomplishments. The data appeared to support several general conclusions:

1. College students tended to have special aptitudes in verbal and language skills.
2. Those students who had special strengths were found in curricula which call for those strengths.
3. The level of endeavor at which students were found was clearly related to their level of aptitudes. The students seeking college degrees obtained higher average test scores than the nondegree-seeking students, who in turn scored higher than the already-employed groups.
4. Job level within an occupational area was related to scores on the most relevant tests. For example, in Numerical Ability, Mechanical Reasoning, and Shape Relations, engineering students were clearly best and were followed by nondegree technical students; skilled mechanical, electrical, and building trades employees; and unskilled workers in that logical order.

The 1974 manual thus presents voluminous information on the predictive validity of the DAT, although it was limited to the prediction of course grades. In addition, the 1974 manual cites numerous studies in which the DAT was correlated with other aptitude and achievement tests. These correlations tend to be substantial and largely support the concurrent validity of the DAT (Forms S and T). For example, when the DAT composite score (VR + NA) was correlated with other aptitude tests, the correlations were between .48 and .89 for males and between .53 and .86 for females.

How useful is the DAT in making differential predictions? Reviewers of the previous editions have concluded that the DAT achieves very little differential validity and measures mainly general intelligence (Bouchard, 1978; Linn, 1978; McNemar, 1964). Although the intercorrelations among the tests in the DAT (Forms V and W) are not reported, it is likely that they are high. Thus, differential prediction is unlikely to be demonstrated by the current version of the DAT. This problem is, of course, not unique to the DAT and certainly also reflects a lack of differentiation among criterion measures as well (Hanna, 1974; Linn, 1978). However, when used with the DAT Career Planning Program (Super, 1982), the DAT provides the counselor and student with a data-based starting point for exploring career options. Thus, it will continue to be useful in counseling students in vocational and educational options.

OTHER APTITUDE BATTERIES. Although the DAT has been used with adults, it is largely designed for high school students. Other aptitude batteries have been developed for adults to aid in occupational placement. The U.S. Employment Service (USES), for example, developed several batteries. One, the General Aptitude Test Battery (GATB), available in state employment offices, has twelve tests that are condensed to yield nine factor scores: Intelligence, Verbal Aptitude, Numerical Aptitude, Spatial Aptitude, Form Perception, Clerical Perception, Motor Coordination, Finger Dexterity, and Manual Dexterity. The entire battery can be administered in 2½ hours. The tests are rather highly speeded and some require simple apparatus. Performance on the GATB has been related to performance in several thousand occupations (U.S. Department of Labor, 1979). Thus, on the basis of test scores, an employment counselor could suggest possible occupations for a particular client. A nonreading version of the GATB has also been developed.

The U.S. Employment Service also provides the Basic Occupational Literary Test (BOLT), which is made up of five separate tests. The first test is a Wide Range Scale used to determine which level of the other four tests to administer. Scores are provided in Reading Vocabulary, Reading Comprehension, Arithmetic Computation, and Arithmetic Reasoning. This test was developed specifically for educationally disadvantaged adults. Counselors can compare the skills on the four tests with those needed in various occupations. Reviewers have noted that relatively little is known about the predictive validity of the BOLT (Cronbach, 1978; Tuckman, 1978).

The military services of the United States use a common aptitude test battery—the Armed Services Vocational Aptitude Battery (ASVAB). As might be expected, this is a very large testing program. Friedman and Williams (1982) report that the ASVAB was administered to 601,782 applicants for military service in 1978 and to another 965,409 high school students during the 1978-1979 school year. Because the ASVAB is provided free to high schools, there is evidence that it is being widely used (Engen et al., 1982). It provides tests on Paragraph Comprehension, Numerical Operations, Coding Speed, Word Knowledge, Arithmetic Reasoning, Mathematical Knowledge, Electronics Information, Mechanical Comprehension, General Science, Automotive, and Shop Information.

The Armed Forces Qualification Test (AFQT) is a composite of four subtests (Word Knowledge, Paragraph Comprehension, Arithmetic Reasoning, and Numerical Operations) from the ASVAB. It is used for screening purposes by placing individuals in five categories. Recruits in the lowest category, commonly called CAT V, usually are not accepted for military service. Once accepted into military service, a recruit's scores on the ASVAB are used for assignment to duties. Typically, pass or fail cutoff scores on two or more ASVAB composites are used to select personnel for enlisted men's training programs in all branches of the armed services (Friedman & Williams, 1982).

College Level Aptitude Tests

The use of aptitude test scores for college admission and placement is probably one of the most familiar and accepted current uses of tests. Most colleges and universities in the United States require students to submit aptitude test scores before enrolling. Although more selective colleges and universities often use these scores, along with other information, to assist in decisions on admission, less selective colleges and universities usu-

ally use them to place students in courses, particularly in English and mathematics, and to help identify students with either high or low academic potential.

Rather than develop their own tests, most colleges and universities rely on one of two national testing programs. The College Entrance Examination Board (CEEB), which is responsible for the Scholastic Aptitude Test (SAT), is one such program. The test is popularly referred to as the "College Boards" or the "SAT." The SAT is developed and maintained by the Educational Testing Service at Princeton, New Jersey, under contract from the CEEB. The second nationally administered program is the American College Testing Program, located in Iowa City, Iowa. The test from this organization is commonly referred to as the ACT. Because these two testing programs are widely used and because almost all students admitted to an institution of higher education in the United States will have taken one or both of them, we will describe their characteristics in some detail in the next two sections of this chapter.

Scholastic Aptitude Test (SAT)

The SAT has been administered to college-bound high school students since 1926. Since 1948, the Educational Testing Service has designed and administered the SAT under contract from the College Entrance Examination Board. In 1981-1982, the SAT was taken by 1,478,100 students (*ETS 1982 Annual Report*, 1983). Based on statistics from previous years, the SAT may be taken by as many as 70 percent of those students intending to enroll in college. Because it is used at many universities as part of the admission process, it is an important source of information. Moreover, as is true of testing in general, its usefulness has been questioned—by consumer advocate Ralph Nader, for example, (Nairn, 1980)—and some public controversy surrounds its use. A very large research literature on the SAT also exists. Buros (1978), for example, lists over 784 references to it.

The SAT is a multiple-choice test designed to measure general verbal and mathematical abilities. As its name suggests, the SAT is designed to predict academic success (usually measured by GPA) in college, and it is typically taken by college-bound juniors and seniors. The SAT is not an achievement test in that it does not measure specific outcomes of a high school's curriculum. As is true of any ability test, it reflects both in-school and out-of-school experiences. It purports to measure developed abilities and makes no claim to measure innate intelligence. Two separate scores are provided—verbal (SAT-V) and mathematical (SAT-M).

CONTENT AND ADMINISTRATION. This information on content and administration pertains largely to the SAT given in March 1980 (*An SAT,* 1980). The SAT is administered as a series of tests. Each test booklet has six separately timed thirty-minute sections:

Two SAT-V sections (eighty-five questions).
Two SAT-M sections (sixty questions).
One Test of Standard Written English (TSWE) (fifty questions).
One experimental section which does not count toward a student's score.

The SAT-V and SAT-M thus require two hours of testing, and the total testing time required is three hours. The TSWE is administered along with the SAT in order to help colleges place students in first-year English courses. The experimental section is used to pretest items for possible inclusion in future versions of the SAT or for equating purposes.

Developing a new edition of the SAT is a time-consuming process. Questions are written by high school and college teachers, by test specialists at the Educational Testing Service, and by others with appropriate backgrounds. The review process is excrutiatingly detailed. The psychometric art of test construction has undoubtedly reached its peak with the SAT (DuBois, 1972). The selection of items follows a consistent logical and statistical progression.

Those that are included have been rigorously screened.

In the SAT-V, there are four types of five-alternative items. (1) *Antonyms* test the breadth and depth of a student's vocabulary. (2) *Analogies* test a student's ability to establish relationships between pairs of words and to recognize similar or parallel relationships in other pairs. (3) *Sentence Completions* test a student's ability to recognize logical relationships among parts of a sentence. (4) *Reading Comprehension* requires the student to read a passage and .answer questions on its content. The passages have been adapted from published materials and vary in length between 200 and 450 words. The passages, which vary in content, may consist of a single paragraph but usually are of three to six paragraphs. The questions ask the student to recognize a restatement of specific information in the passage, to recognize main ideas, to make inferences based on the passage, to analyze the arguments presented, to recognize tone or attitude, and to make generalizations from the information in the passage. Examples from the first three types of items are presented in Figure 8–3.

The SAT-M items are of two types: (1) the usual five-alternative item and (2) four-alternative quantitative comparisons emphasizing the concepts of inequalities and estimation. The SAT-M seems to be more dependent on curriculum-based learning than is the SAT-V, but the items are designed to test a student's ability to apply mathematical knowledge in new situations. Content is divided almost equally among arithmetic reasoning, algebra, and geometry. There are a few miscellaneous questions that do not fit these categories. The items assume that students have studied at least a year of algebra and some geometry. For example, special triangles, properties associated with parallel lines, and measurement-related concepts such as area and the Pythagorean Theorem are assumed to be familiar to the students. Clearly, the more mathematics a student has taken in high school, the better prepared the student will be for the SAT-M. Basic geometric formulas

ANTONYMS

Directions: Each question below consists of a word in capital letters, followed by five lettered words or phrases. Choose the word or phrase that is most nearly *opposite* in meaning to the word in capital letters. Since some of the questions require you to distinguish fine shades of meaning, consider all the choices before deciding which is best.

> **EXAMPLE:**
>
> GOOD: (A) sour (B) bad (C) red
>   (D) hot (E) ugly
>
> Ⓐ ● Ⓒ Ⓓ Ⓔ

ANALOGIES

Directions: Each question below consists of a related pair of words or phrases, followed by five lettered pairs of words or phrases. Select the lettered pair that *best* expresses a relationship similar to that expressed in the original pair.

> **EXAMPLE:**
>
> YAWN : BOREDOM : : (A) dream : sleep
>   (B) anger : madness (C) smile : amusement
>   (D) face : expression
>   (E) impatience : rebellion
>
> Ⓐ Ⓑ ● Ⓓ Ⓔ

SENTENCE COMPLETIONS

Directions: Each sentence below has one or two blanks, each blank indicating that something has been omitted. Beneath the sentence are five lettered words or sets of words. Choose the word or set of words that *best* fits the meaning of the sentence as a whole.

> **EXAMPLE:**
>
> Although its publicity has been ----, the film itself is intelligent, well-acted, handsomely produced, and altogether ----.
>
> (A) tasteless .. respectable (B) extensive .. moderate
> (C) sophisticated .. amateur (D) risqué .. crude
> (E) perfect .. spectacular
>
> ● Ⓑ Ⓒ Ⓓ Ⓔ

FIGURE 8–3 Examples from Verbal Sections of the Scholastic Aptitude Test. (Adapted from *Taking the SAT: A Guide to the Scholastic Aptitude Test and the Test of Standard Written English*. College Entrance Examination Board 1981. Reproduced by permission of Educational Testing Service, the Copyright owner of the sample questions.)

needed to answer certain questions are provided in the test booklet.

In addition to varying in mathematical content, the SAT-M items also vary across six levels of thought processes necessary to answer the question. Thus, a lower-level item requires the student to perform mathematical manipulation. A higher-level item requires the student to solve nonroutine problems requiring insight or ingenuity. Examples from the SAT-M are given in Figure 8–4.

For both the SAT-V and SAT-M, there is a wide range of difficulty. Within any section, the items tend to be ordered in terms of difficulty—earlier items being easier than later ones. For example, for a representative sample of 2,245 candidates who took the SAT in March 1980, the SAT-V items ranged in difficulty (measured as percentage of the sample answering an item correctly) from 93 percent to 10 percent correct. For the SAT-M, item difficulty ranged from 92 percent to 5 percent correct. For the same SAT, the mean percents correct for the eighty-five SAT-V items and sixty SAT-M items were 48 percent and 47 percent, respectively. Thus, the SAT, for most students, is a challenging test.

The SAT is typically administered to groups of students at a specified time at about 5,000 locations throughout the United States and the world. The sections of the test are separately timed, thirty minutes being allowed for each. Students respond on separate answer sheets that are optically scanned and then scored by computer. The instructions and informational materials available are models of completeness and utility. Administration of the test begins at 9:00 A.M. and is completed by noon.

SCORING. Raw scores are determined by the number of correct answers, and there is a correction for guessing. For questions with five alternatives, one-fourth of a point is subtracted for each wrong answer; for questions with four alternatives, one-third of a point is subtracted for each wrong answer. The principle scores reported are the SAT-V and SAT-M. No total score for the two content areas is provided. The SAT-V raw scores can range between −21 and 85. For the SAT-M, the range is −17 to 60. For the SAT-V, a vocabulary subscore, based on the forty-five antonym and analogy questions, and a reading subscore, based on the forty sentence completion and reading comprehension questions, are reported. The subscores are T-scores, varying from 20 to 80, with a mean of 50 and standard deviation of 10. No subscores are reported for the SAT-M. Both the SAT-V and SAT-M scores are reported on a 200 to 800 scale, having a mean of 500 and standard deviation of 100. Thus, for the March 1980 SAT, a verbal raw score of 65 was converted to a scaled score of 640; a math raw score of 20 was converted to a scaled score of 440. For both sections of the test, raw scores of -9 or lower were converted to scaled scores of 200.

Because about twenty different editions of the SAT are administered each year, students obviously cannot be directly compared unless scaled scores are used. The scaled scores are linked to a standardization sample of 10,654 students who took the test in April 1941, for whom the mean of 500 and standard deviation of 100 were arbitrarily chosen. Through a complicated statistical procedure all later editions of the SAT have been linked to this standardization sample. New editions are thus equated by including a limited number of items used in older versions of the test. More details on this unique equating procedure are available (Angoff, 1971). The point to keep in mind is that for any particular group taking the SAT there is no reason to expect the mean score to be 500 or the standard deviation to be 100.

RELIABILITY. The SAT is quite reliable. For example, the internal consistency measures of reliability were .92 and .91 for the March 1980 SAT-V and SAT-M, respectively (*An SAT*, 1980). These coefficients clearly support the construction procedures used, since they indicate a high degree of

FIGURE 8–4 Examples from mathematical sections of the Scholastic Aptitude Test. (Adapted from *Taking the SAT: A Guide to the Scholastic Aptitude Test and the Test of Standard Written English.* College Entrance Examination Board 1981. Reproduced by permission of Educational Testing Service, the Copyright owner of the sample questions.)

STANDARD MULTIPLE-CHOICE

Directions: In this section solve each problem, using any available space on the page for scratchwork. Then decide which is the best of the choices given and blacken the corresponding space on the answer sheet. The following information is for your reference in solving some of the problems.

1. If $2a + b = 5$, then $4a + 2b =$
   (A) $\frac{5}{4}$ (B) $\frac{5}{2}$ (C) 10 (D) 20 (E) 25

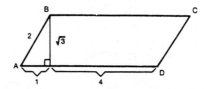

8. The figure above shows a piece of paper in the shape of a parallelogram with measurements as indicated. If the paper is tacked at its center to a flat surface and then rotated about its center, the points covered by the paper will be a circular region of diameter.

   (A) $\sqrt{3}$ (B) 2 (C) 5 (D) $\sqrt{28}$ (E) $\sqrt{39}$

QUANTITATIVE COMPARISONS

Directions: Each of the following questions consists of two quantities, one in Column A and one in Column B. You are to compare the two quantities and on the answer sheet blacken space

   A if the quantity in Column A is greater;
   B if the quantity in Column B is greater;
   C if the two quantities are equal;
   D if the relationship cannot be determined from the information given.

Notes: 1. In certain questions, information concerning one or both of the quantities to be compared is centered above the two columns.
   2. In a given question, a symbol that appears in both columns represents the same thing in Column A as it does in Column B.
   3. Letters such as x, n, and k stand for real numbers.

EXAMPLES Column A	Column B	Answers	
E1. 2 × 6	2 + 6	●ⒷⒸⒹⒺ	(The answer is A because 12 is greater than 8.)
E2. 180 − x x° / y°	y	ⒶⒷ●ⒹⒺ	(The answer is C because x + y = 180, thereby making 180 − x equal to y.)
E3. p − q	q − p	ⒶⒷⒸ●	(The answer is D because nothing is known about either p or q.)

homogeneity among the questions. Estimates of internal consistency for twelve SATs administered in 1966 through 1969 range from .898 to .917 for the SAT-V and from .888 to .913 for the SAT-M (Donlon & Angoff, 1971). Given the care and methods with which the SAT is constructed, it is not surprising that its internal consistency is quite high. It appears to us that .90 is a convenient representative value to use as a measure of the SAT's internal consistency.

Information is also available on the stability of SAT scores over time. It is not uncommon for high school students to take the SAT twice—often as juniors and again as seniors—which provides parallel-form reliability estimates. The reliabilities are based on juniors who retook the SAT as seniors after time intervals of seven to ten months. The resulting correlations ranged from .88 to .91 for the SAT-V and from .85 to .89 for the SAT-M (Donlon & Angoff, 1971). Again, these data are based on SATs administered between 1962 and 1970. However, they are undoubtedly representative of the results expected from current editions.

The standard error of measurement is another indicator of the precision of any test. For the SAT administered in March 1980, the standard errors of measurement were 31 for the SAT-V and 33 for the SAT-M. Thus, if a student's true SAT-V ability score is 570, for example, the chances are about two out of three (68 percent) that the student would obtain a score between 539 and 601. That is, the observed score would be within one standard error about two-thirds of the time. Ninety-five percent of the time the score would be between 508 and 632 (two standard errors). Donlon and Angoff (1971) report data on the standard error of measurement for twelve SATs administered in 1966 through 1969. For the SAT-V, standard errors of measurement ranged from 30.9 to 33.3. For the SAT-M, the corresponding values were 32.8 to 36.3. The SAT has a long history of excellent psychometric characteristics, which continue in the present versions of the test.

VALIDITY. Because the main purpose of the SAT is to predict academic achievement in college, its predictive validity is of primary importance. However, the *content validity* of the SAT can also be considered. First, the items are very carefully developed, pretested, and reviewed. Content is thus highly appropriate for the goal of the SAT. We know of no other test that has been constructed in a more psychometrically excellent manner. In addition to their content, items must satisfy certain statistical requirements. Items are selected at various levels of difficulty to assure that the SAT will be appropriate for a wide range of ability. The second major statistical criterion used to select items is the correlation of each item with the total score. That is, items that correlate positively with the total test score suggest that students answering the item correctly tend to have higher total test scores than those students who answer the item incorrectly.

The SAT is also designed to be largely a power test rather than a speeded test. The time limits are such that most students will be able to attempt almost all items. For the SAT administered in March 1980, for example, virtually all students completed at least three-fourths of each section. The number of students completing all but the last question in a secton varied from 58 percent to 90 percent (*An SAT*, 1980). These results are similar to those reported for earlier editions of the SAT (Donlon & Angoff, 1971). Thus, the SAT appears to be largely unspeeded, although it is undoubtedly true that some students must work at a rate faster than their accustomed one if they are to attempt all items.

A final matter of concern on the content validity of the SAT is the extent to which the SAT-V and SAT-M measure different abilities. For the SAT administered in March 1980, the correlation between SAT-V and SAT-M scores was .66 (*An SAT*, 1980). Similarly, Donlon & Angoff (1971) reported that the average correlation for twelve SAT forms administered was .67. It is thus obvious that the SAT-V and SAT-M are not in-dependent scores and share about 44 per-cent of their variance. A reviewer noted that "the value of separate scores needs con-certed scrutiny in the light of this phenome-non." (Wallace, 1972b, p. 334).

The *predictive validity* of the SAT has been examined in thousands of published and unpublished studies. In the vast majority the criterion variable of interest is the first-term or first-year college GPA. Scores from the SAT-V and SAT-M are usually used, along with some indicator of a student's aca-demic success in high school (high school GPA or rank in class). Schrader (1971) sum-marized a large number of studies on the predictive validity of the SAT. For example, considering men and women separately (be-cause not all colleges are coeducational), Schrader reported median validity coeffi-cients for 310 different colleges for students in liberal arts and general progams. These data appear in Table 8-3. Each of these 310 studies involved at least 85 students and few were less than 100.

Note that for all groups, the high school record is the best single predictor of college GPA. The SAT-V and SAT-M median cor-relations are in the .30 to .39 range. Note also that the inclusion of the SAT scores along with the high school record improves the prediction. The improvement is not large but is typically statistically significant. That is, the multiple correlation, using all these predictors, is higher than any single predictor. Schrader also reported results for more specialized student groups, such as en-gineering, science, and business. For these groups, the high school record was still the best predictor (median *r*'s from .39 to .42), but the SAT did correlate with the GPA. Schrader also found that the SAT-M had a higher median correlation with GPA than did the SAT-V (.33 versus .23) for engineer-ing students. Other investigators found that the SAT-M is a better predictor of grades in college mathematics courses than is the SAT-V (Gusset, 1974; Troutman, 1978).

Other large-scale studies of the SAT's ef-

TABLE 8-3 Validity coefficients of SAT and high school record: Selected percentiles of validity coefficients based on students in liberal arts and general programs classified by sex

Percentile	SAT-V	SAT-M	High School Record	Three Predictors Combined
Men				
90	.48	.47	.62	.68
75	.42	.40	.56	.62
50	.33	.30	.47	.55
25	.24	.24	.39	.48
10	.17	.16	.31	.40
Number of groups	116	116	116	116
Women				
90	.55	.52	.68	.74
75	.48	.45	.61	.68
50	.41	.36	.54	.62
25	.32	.27	.44	.52
10	.23	.21	.35	.43
Number of groups	143	143	143	143
Men and Women				
90	.54	.48	.67	.73
75	.48	.41	.62	.68
50	.39	.33	.55	.62
25	.35	.24	.44	.54
10	.26	.20	.33	.46
Number of groups	51	51	51	51

From Schrader, W. B. (1971), The predictive validity of college board admissions tests. In W. G. Angoff (Ed.), *The College Board Admissions Testing Program: A technical report on research and development activities relating to the Scholastic Aptitude Test and Achievement Tests.* New York: College Entrance Examination Board. Copyright 1971 by College Entrance Examination Board. Reproduced by permission of the Educational Testing Service.

fectiveness in predicting college grades are available. For example, Fincher (1974) re-ported summary results on the predictive validity of the SAT in admission procedures in Georgia's state university system. These summary values were based on thousands of students that entered the state's universities in the years 1958 through 1966 and in 1970. Table 8-4 presents average validity coeffi-cients for the SAT and high school GPA as

TABLE 8-4 Summary of mean correlation coefficients between predictor variables and college grades in the university system of Georgia, 1958-66 and 1970

College Means	SAT-Verbal	SAT-Math	HSA	SAT V + M	V + M + HSA
Less than 300	.363	.354	.470	.450	.570
(N = 3)	.460	.414	.590	.537	.680
300—399	.363	.388	.490	.422	.592
(N = 6)	.500	.478	.610	.572	.731
400—449	.371	.345	.501	.420	.594
(N = 7)	.530	.488	.611	.582	.714
450 and above	.345	.360	.478	.362	.572
(N = 3)	.447	.440	.610	.500	.650
All Groups	.363	.362	.491	.416	.586
Combined	.500	.468	.598	.562	.706

Note—Means are based on simple arithmetic averages of equivalent Fisher z-coefficients across N-institutions for a variable number of years (i.e., data have not been weighted by institutional enrollment). Superior coefficients are for male students; inferior coefficients for females.

Fincher, C. (1974), "Is the SAT worth its salt? An Evaluation of the Scholastic Aptitude Test in the University System of Georgia over a thirteen-year period." *Review of Educational Research, 44*, pp. 293–305. Copyright 1974, American Educational Research Association, Washington, D.C.

well as for combinations of the predictors. These results demonstrate that the high school GPA is the best predictor of college GPA but that both SAT-V and SAT-M scores contribute incrementally to predicting college GPA. Fincher's results also indicate that the predictive validity does not vary much as a function of the ability level of the college. That is, the SAT is as useful at colleges enrolling students with low SAT-V scores as at those enrolling high scores. Another striking result in the Georgia system is that the college GPAs of female students are more predictable than male students. Thus, based on the analysis of data over the thirteen-year period, Fincher concluded that the SAT's incremental effectiveness as a predictor of the first-year GPA had been demonstrated.

Aleamoni and Oboler (1978), using 1,750 entering students at the University of Illinois-Urbana, found limited evidence on the validity of the SAT in predicting the first-semester GPA. The SAT-V and

SAT-M correlations with the GPA were .268 and .228, respectively. However, the high school rank was again the best single predictor of college GPA ($r = .429$). Dalton (1976) provided additional results from Indiana University suggesting that the SAT in combination with high school GPA has validity for predicting the first-semester college GPAs. This study demonstrated no sex differences.

It thus seems reasonable to conclude that the SAT does, in general, possess predictive validity. In most instances, it will increase the predictability of the first-year GPA over that of high school GPA alone. This incremental validity is typically not large but is usually statistically significant. In summary, based on 827 studies from various colleges and universities, the following median validity coefficients are fair, although perhaps somewhat conservative, estimates of the relationship between the SAT and high school GPA with college GPA (*Test Use and Validity*, 1980):

PREDICTOR(S)	MEDIAN VALIDITY COEFFICIENT
SAT-V	.37
SAT-M	.32
SAT-V + SAT-M	.41
High School GPA	.52
SAT-V, SAT-M, HS GPA	.58

Is the SAT's validity related to other criteria of interest? Larson and Scontrino (1976) presented evidence on the SAT's utility in predicting college GPA across eight years (1966-1973). Their results demonstrated that the correlations between graduating seniors' GPA and SAT scores were usually statistically significant. However, high school GPA was the single best predictor of the four-year cumulative college GPA. Adding the SAT scores to high school GPA for males increased predictability slightly but proved largely ineffective for females.

In another study, Mauger and Kolmodin (1975) also demonstrated that the SAT scores predict the GPAs of graduating seniors, although their reported correlations were quite small (SAT-V: $r = .26$; SAT-M: $r = .14$). They reported that the SAT scores are much more predictive of performance of achievement test results in a student's major (SAT-V: $r = .47$; SAT-M: $r = .43$). Nevertheless, considering the restriction of range that occurs in the GPAs of graduating seniors and the fact that the SAT was administered four and one-half years before graduation, the results suggest that the SAT has some validity for predicting the final college GPA.

Although the SAT and other aptitude tests can predict college GPA, they are not good predictors of later, nonschool accomplishments. Wallach (1976), for example, summarized results demonstrating that SAT scores were unrelated to accomplishments in literature, science, art, music, dramatics, political leadership, or social service. Heath (1977), using a sample of sixty-eight Haverford College men, found a similar lack of prediction of adult maturity and competence when SAT scores, as well as other measures of academic achievement, were used as predictors. These results suggest, then, that the SAT does not differentiate among people once a certain threshold of competence is reached. Although this fact should be known because of the SAT's standard error of measurement, it is apparently often ignored by many test consumers. Of course, college GPA is itself an imperfect criterion and does not predict future accomplishments either.

The *construct validity* of the SAT is supported by the numerous studies on its predictive validity. As a measure of aptitude for college work, it should and does correlate with academic achievement in college. Given the restricted range of scores in many studies, it is in fact surprising that it correlates as well as it does with college GPA.

Because the SAT is supposed to measure abilities that develop over long periods of time, performance should not be markedly affected by short-term coaching. We have already referred in Chapter 4 to the effect of coaching on test scores. Although early studies suggested that the SAT was relatively unaffected by coaching (*Effects of Coaching on Scholastic Aptitude Test Scores*, 1965), a more recent study by the Federal Trade Commission showed that coaching did improve performance on the SAT (*Effects of Coaching on Standardized Admission Examinations*, 1979). Messick (1980b) provided a summary of studies in which some type of control group was used, and Messick and Jungeblut (1981) noted that the amount of coaching time needed to increase SAT scores markedly rapidly approaches that of full-time schooling. It thus appears that the effect of coaching on SAT scores is relatively small and difficult to disentangle from the self-selection of highly motivated students choosing to participate in commercial coaching programs. A review of mathematical concepts, particularly for students not enrolled in mathematics courses, would probably be beneficial (Messick, 1980b). It thus appears to us that the SAT does largely measure verbal and mathematical abilities that develop over relatively long periods of time.

The SAT should reflect any changes in the average ability of students who take the test. The fact that the average SAT score, both verbal and mathematical, has declined since about 1963 has been a source of considerable interest and public concern (Jones, 1981). This eighteen-year decline appears to have halted in 1981 (Biemiller, 1981). The average SAT-V declined from 478 in 1963 to about 424 in 1980 and 1981. The average SAT-M declined from 502 in 1963 to about 465 in 1980 and 1981. In 1982, both averages increased slightly—the SAT-V to 426 and the SAT-M to 466. The average SAT-V declined somewhat more than SAT-M, but the average score for both sections fell a significant amount. The reasons for this decline are, of course, of considerable interest. Are students less well-educated than in previous years? Are they less interested or motivated to do well on standardized tests? It has even been suggested that the decline in scores is due to the atmospheric testing of nuclear weapons (Barnes, 1978) or to radiation effects from television sets (Kubey, 1979). Wharton (1977) counted seventy-nine hypotheses that have been suggested to explain the decline in average SAT scores. With the importance of the phenomena, it is not surprising that such a large number of explanations have been proposed.

It is possible, of course, that content or the scale on which the SAT is scored has changed, but this explanation is not viable. If anything, the slight problems in equating new forms of the SAT to older forms, if eliminated, would produce a larger decline in the average score (Jones, 1981). An advisory panel created by the College Entrance Examination Board suggested several reasons for the decline (On Further Examination, 1977). In the first place, the SAT-taking population has been enlarged to include more students who formerly would not have considered enrolling in college—students from lower socioeconomic status, members of minority ethnic groups, and women. The change in the composition of the group taking the SAT accounts for most of the decline until 1970. After 1970, the composition of the group has been relatively stable, and six additional factors have been proposed (On Further Examination, 1977).

1. The high school curriculum reflects the use of more elective courses and a reduction in required courses in English and mathematics.
2. There is less emphasis on the mastery of skills and knowledge in the learning process in the schools, in the home, and in society in general. This is popularly referred to as a "lowering of standards."
3. Television clearly has an enormous impact on children and may be the dominant mechanism for their learning about the world. There appears to be a corresponding lessening of interest in reading and more traditional modes of learning.
4. The nature and role of the family has undoubtedly affected the educational process. The single-parent family, for example, has become increasingly common.
5. The decline of scores in the early 1970s is due partly to the disruption in society because of protests against the war in Vietnam. Young people were active in such protests, and many students preparing to take the SAT were undoubtedly affected.
6. Students appear less motivated to learn than they perhaps once were.

Beaton et al., (1977) suggested that the decline in average SAT-V scores between 1960 and 1972 is related to a corresponding decline in reading comprehension. The number of college students taking remedial English is stark testimony to their results. Jones (1981) also noted that the number of eighteen-year-olds increased by nearly four million (a 50 percent increase) between 1960 and 1972. This large number of students leaving high school at the same time conceivably saw limited opportunities for assimilation into society and thus contributed to lower motivation and achievement. An intriguing hypothesis, offered by Zajonc (1976), that the decline in SAT scores is due to birth order effects, earlier-born children having higher scores than later-born children, appears not to be supported by the data (Zajonc & Bargh, 1980).

Despite the general decline in average SAT scores, the SAT-M is used to identify children who are gifted in mathematics. Stanley (1976) reported that the SAT-M is very useful in differentiating among students in the upper 1 or 2 percent of mathematical ability. It is a much better predictor of achievement in mathematics than is the judgment of a child's mathematics teacher.

On the whole, the SAT appears to have construct validity, and its scores vary in ways largely consistent with the theory and purpose underlying its construction.

American College Testing Program (ACT)

The second widely used college aptitude testing program is the ACT. In the 1978-1979 academic year, for example, about 900,000 junior and senior high school students took this test, and Buros (1978) lists 584 references to it. This testing program was first initiated in 1959 and is administered by the American College Testing Program located in Iowa City, Iowa. The ACT tends to be used by many colleges in the midwestern United States and by relatively fewer colleges on the East and West Coasts.

The ACT Assessment Program consists of three separate parts:

1. The Academic Tests, a set of four cognitive tests providing four separate scores and a composite.
2. The ACT Interest Inventory, ninety items measuring a student's interests in six different academic and vocational areas.
3. The ACT Student Profile Section, 192 items providing information about a student's background and plans, including out-of-class accomplishments and demographic characteristics.

The last two sections are completed when the student registers for the Academic Tests. The four Academic Tests are administered five times per year at about 15,000 locations throughout the United States. We will focus our discussion on the four Academic Tests, which measure academic abilities in English, mathematics, social studies,

and natural sciences. The tests are designed as measures of academic development. They depend partly on students' reasoning abilities and partly on students' knowledge of subject matter. The ACT, then, is perhaps somewhat closer to an achievement test than is the SAT. The ACT is, of course, designed to predict scholastic achievement in college and it attempts to measure as directly as possible the skills students will need to succeed.

CONTENT. The ACT is made up of four separate Academic Tests. Each test is separately timed and consists of four- or five-alternative items. The following descriptions of the tests are taken from material provided by ACT (*Contents of the Tests in the ACT Assessment*, 1980b).

The English Usage Test is a 75-item, 40-minute test that measures the student's understanding of the conventions of standard written English and the use of the basic elements of effective expository writing: punctuation, grammar, sentence structure, diction, style, logic, and organization. The test does not measure the rote recall of rules of grammar, but stresses the analysis of the kind of effective expression which will be encountered in many postsecondary curricula. The test consists of several prose passages with certain portions underlined and numbered. For each underlined portion, four alternative responses are given. The student must decide which alternative is most appropriate in the context of the passage. [Examples are given in Figure 8-5.]

The Mathematics Usage Test is a 40-item, 50-minute test that measures the student's mathematical reasoning ability. It emphasizes the solution of practical quantitative problems that are encountered in many postsecondary curricula and includes a sampling of mathematical techniques covered in high school courses. The test emphasizes quantitative reasoning, rather than memorization of formulas, knowledge of techniques, or computational skill. Each item in the test poses a question with five alternative answers, the last of which may be "none of the above." In general, the mathematical skills required for the test involve proficiencies emphasized in high school plane geometry and first- and second-year algebra. Six types of content are included in the test. These include arithmetic

Directions: Questions on the English Usage Test are based on passages containing expressions that are inappropriate in standard written English; you are to decide how these expressions can be made appropriate and effective. The passages are presented in a spread-out format in which various words, phrases, and punctuation marks have been underlined and numbered. In the right-hand column, opposite each underlined portion, you will find a set of responses numbered to correspond to that underlined portion. Each set of responses contains a "NO CHANGE" option and three alternatives to the underlined version. Since your judgment about the appropriateness and effectiveness of a response will depend on your perception of the passage

as a whole, the author's purpose, and the type of audience, first read through the entire passage quickly. Then reread the passage slowly and carefully. As you come to each underlined portion during your second reading, look at the alternatives in the right-hand column and decide which of the four words or phrases is best for the given context. Since your response will often depend on your reading several of the sentences surrounding the underlined portion, make sure you have read ahead far enough to make the best choice. If you think that the original version (the one in the passage) is best, choose the response marked A or F. If you think that an alternative version is best, choose the letter that corresponds to that alternative. In every case, consider only the underlined words, phrases, and punctuation marks; you can assume that the rest of the passage is correct as written.

Thor Heyerdahl became famous for a unique sailing expedition, which he later described in *Kon-Tiki*. Having developed a theory that the original Polynesians had sailed or drifted to the South Sea Islands from South America, it then had to be tested. After careful study he
1

built a raft that was as authentic as possible. Using only primitive equipment, he and five other men sailed into the South Seas from Peru, which he judged to be in the same
2

general area as the land of the original Polynesians. As a result, his group and him will
3

long be remembered not only as thorough scientists but also as courageous men.

Heyerdahl's courage was first tested in Ecuador. His search for trees that was large enough for the expeditionary
4

raft sent him to Quito, a city high in the Andes. There, he and his companions were warned about headhunters and bandits on the trail. Feeling undaunted, they hired a driver
5

and jeep from the U.S. Embassy, going on with their dangerous task.
6

1. A. NO CHANGE
   B. he set out to test it.
   C. it was decided that it must be tested.
   D. the theory was then to be tested.

2. F. NO CHANGE
   G. Peru, being judged as
   H. Peru, which had been
   J. Peru judged as being

3. A. NO CHANGE
   B. him and his group
   C. his group and himself
   D. he and his group

4. F. NO CHANGE
   G. which would be of sufficient size
   H. of adequate size
   J. of certainly sufficient size

5. A. NO CHANGE
   B. trail. Undaunted, they
   C. trail, but they were undaunted, and
   D. trail; undaunted they

6. F. NO CHANGE
   G. Embassy; and went on with
   H. Embassy and proceeded with
   J. Embassy, and kept on

After the raft was done, Heyerdahl made
7

final preparations for the expedition. Even before his crew came aboard, the courage which Heyerdahl possessed was
8

tested again. As the raft was being towed out of the harbor, it drifted under the stern of a tug. Heyerdahl had to struggle to save it.

Dangers at sea were present, but Heyerdahl
9

and his men did not show fear. Instead they developed games that were actually tests of courage. Although man-eating fish were nearby, the men swam to relieve their tension, maintaining that the fish were not
10

dangerous unless a man had already been cut or scratched. One game consisted of luring sharks within reach, catching them, and then they would yank it onto the raft.
11

Being on the raft, the sharks thrashed about
12

7. A. NO CHANGE
   B. When the raft was ready,
   C. The raft was speedily completed and
   D. The raft having been constructed,

8. F. NO CHANGE
   G. Heyerdahls' manly courage
   H. Heyerdahl's courage
   J. the courage of this man

9. A. NO CHANGE
   B. (Do not begin new paragraph) At sea, dangers
   C. (Begin new paragraph) Dangers, at sea
   D. (Begin new paragraph) At sea, dangers

10. F. NO CHANGE
    G. tension. Maintaining
    H. tension. He maintained
    J. tension, because it was maintained

11. A. NO CHANGE
    B. then to yank it
    C. and then to yank them up
    D. and yanking them

12. F. NO CHANGE
    G. At that point,
    H. Once there,
    J. At that time,

FIGURE 8–5 Examples from the English Usage Test of ACT. (Copyright © 1981 by the American College Testing Program. Reproduced by permission.)

---

and algebraic operations, arithmetic and algebraic reasoning, geometry, intermediate algebra, number and numeration concepts, and advanced topics. [Examples are given in Figure 8–6.]

The Social Studies Reading Test is a 52-item, 35-minute test that measures the comprehen-

sion, analytical and evaluative reasoning, and problem-solving skills required in the social studies. There are two types of items: the first is based on reading passages, the second on general background or information obtained primarily in high school social studies courses. All

1. Two wells pump oil continuously. One produces 4000 barrels of oil per day, which is 33 1/3 percent more than the other well produces. How many barrels of oil are produced daily by the 2 wells?

   A. 5333 1/3
   B. 6666 2/3
   C. 7000
   D. 8333 1/3
   E. 9000

2. If a car travels a miles in b minutes, how many minutes will it take to travel c miles?

   F. c/a
   G. c/b
   H. c/ab
   J. ab/c
   K. cb/a

3. In the figure below, what is the sum of the measures of the angles labeled x and y?

   A. 90°
   B. 100°
   C. 130°
   D. 140°
   E. None of the above

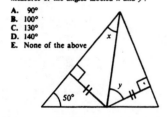

FIGURE 8–6 Examples from the Mathematics Usage Test of ACT. (Copyright © 1981 by The American College Testing Program. Reproduced by permission.)

items are multiple choice with four alternatives. The items based on the reading passages require not only reading comprehension skills, but the ability to draw inferences and conclusions, to examine the interrelationships and import of ideas in a passage, to extend the thoughts of a passage to new situations, to make deductions from experimental or graphic data, and to recognize a writer's bias, style, and mode of reasoning. The discrete information items ask the students to apply what they have learned in high school social studies courses to familiar, new, and analogous problems. The test is based on the content taught in basic high school social studies courses. The items require inferential reasoning and the application of general information rather than the rote recall of specific facts. The five content areas include history, government, economics, sociology/anthropology, and psychology. [Examples are given in Figure 8–7.]

The Natural Sciences Reading Test is a 52-item, 35-minute test that measures the interpretation, analysis, evaluation, critical reasoning, and problem-solving skills required in the natural sciences. There are two types of items: the first is based on reading passages, the second on information about science. All items are multiple choice with four alternatives. The passages concern a variety of scientific topics and problems. Descriptions of scientific experiments and discussions of current scientific theories are the most common formats. The items require the students to understand and distinguish among the purposes of experiments, to examine the logical relationships between experimental hypotheses and the generalizations which can be drawn from experiments, to predict the effects of ideas in a passage on new situations, to propose alternate ways to conduct experiments, and to judge the practical value of the ideas and theories presented in a passage. The discrete information items ask the students to apply what they have learned in high school science courses to familiar, new, and analogous problems. They require the understanding only of significant facts and minimal algebraic and arithmetic computations. The test is based on content taught in basic high school natural science courses. The items require inferential reasoning and the application of general information rather than the rote recall of specific facts. The four content areas include biology, chemistry, physics, and physical sciences. [Examples are given in Figure 8–8.]

ADMINISTRATION AND SCORING. The ACT is given to groups of students five times per year at about 15,000 testing centers, mainly located at high schools and colleges. Each of the four Academic Tests is separately timed, and the total testing time required is about 3½ hours. Students respond on optical scanner forms which are computer scored.

Raw scores are obtained on each of the four tests. Unlike the SAT, there is no correction for guessing. Raw scores are thus the

Directions: The Social Studies Reading Test measures your ability to comprehend, analyze, and evaluate reading materials in such social studies fields as history, political science, economics, sociology, anthropology, and psychology. To answer these questions, you will have to draw on your background in social studies as well as on your ability to understand new material. Read the material through once. Then return to it as often as necessary to answer the questions. In addition to the questions based on reading passages, there are some questions that test your general background knowledge in social studies. For each question in the test, choose the letter that corresponds to the alternative that you think is best.

Over the past several decades the growth of the United States economy has been marked by expansion of metropolitan areas and by "regionalization" of production—that is, a more even geographical distribution of industries over the United States. Such rapid growth causes drastic changes in the geographical structure of metropolitan areas. Manufacturing industries, which were initially attracted to the core of the city by the proximity of the railroads, a steady labor supply, and the economic advantages of mass production, are now moving toward peripheral locations.

No single explanation can be given for this trend toward suburbanization, but as cities have grown, the supply of undeveloped land has decreased. The advantages of the central metropolis continue to attract economic activity, but congestion in the central city and the development of production techniques which demand more space have tended to push industry into the suburbs. The net result has been a pattern of geographical specialization within metropolitan regions. The central city increasingly becomes geared to white-collar and service activities, and the periphery attracts manufacturing, transportation, and other blue-collar job activities.

The development of residential areas has followed industrial movement to some extent, but suburban living (undoubtedly desired for its amenities) is still largely reserved for those who can afford it. Consequently, the central city has been losing middle- and upper-income families to the suburbs. Now people can live in dispersed residential locations; rising incomes and the pro-liferation of automobiles have made this both economically and technically feasible. However, this "urban sprawl" creates serious financial problems. Since tax-paying industry has fled to the suburbs, the central city has had to bear the cost of public assistance payments and other welfare service for low-income groups.

When housing developers began building on a large scale, many suburbs rapidly doubled and tripled in size. This new population required more schools and teachers, more fire and police protection, and sizable expenditures for water and sewer lines and roads. Frequently, these towns were entirely dependent on property taxes for their revenues.

To meet ever increasing expenses and broaden their tax base, some communities have tried to attract new industry. However, when town officials found themselves competing intensely for these industries, they often conceded partial exemption from property taxes to new industry in order to bargain more favorably. As a result, an area often found its tax base weakened rather than strengthened by winning new industry. As a consequence of all these changes, both the suburbs and the central city are entangled in thorny financial problems.

1. According to the author, a rise in wages earned by employees of service industries will principally tend to:

   A. increase the physical separation between zones of residence and zones of work.
   B. decrease the tax revenues of the suburbs.
   C. decrease the tax revenues of the metropolitan areas.
   D. increase the work force in the periphery.

2. The most efficient way to solve the financial problems of a metropolitan area would be to:

   F. cut personal taxes in central cities.
   G. cut personal taxes in the suburbs.
   H. decrease public expenditures in central cities.
   J. place the entire area under one fiscal authority.

3. Which of the following problems should be given first consideration on the basis of the changing urban structure outlined in the passage?

   A. Commuter traffic between areas of residence and areas of work
   B. Highway passenger traffic between two metropolitan areas
   C. Congestion due to heavy truck traffic in downtown areas
   D. The centralization of railroad freight stations in downtown areas

4. The author would consider the giant modern city essentially a by-product of the:

   F. invention of the internal-combustion engine.
   G. development of monopolistic industries.
   H. Industrial Revolution.
   J. capitalist system.

5. If the trend outlined in paragraph two continues, the centers of large American cities are more likely than the suburbs to have a high percentage of:

   A. small-scale manufacturing firms.
   B. large-scale factories.
   C. railroad stations.
   D. banks and insurance companies.

FIGURE 8–7 Examples from the Social Studies Reading Test of ACT. (Copyright © 1981 by The American College Testing Program. Reproduced by permission.)

---

number of questions correctly answered on each test. These can vary from zero to the number of items in the test. The raw scores on each test are converted to standard scores by a scale varying from one to thirty-six. This scale was designed to have a mean of about twenty and a standard deviation of about five. As is true of the SAT, students currently taking the ACT produce scores somewhat different from these values.

Based on college-bound students, the ACT also reports percentile scores for students from a particular high school, the state, and the nation. For example, an ACT composite score of twenty-five would be placed at about the 85 percentile, based on

Test 4: NATURAL SCIENCES READING

Directions: The Natural Sciences Reading Test measures your ability to understand, analyze, and evaluate reading passages about scientific topics and descriptions of experiments in such fields as biology, chemistry, physics, and physical science. To answer these questions you will have to draw on your scientific background as well as on your ability to understand new material. Read the material through once. Then return to it as often as necessary to answer the questions. In addition to the questions based on reading passages, there are some questions that test your general background knowledge in the sciences. For each question in the test, choose the letter that corresponds to the alternative that you think is best.

As the cells that make up different tissues and organs differ in structure and function, so also do they differ in their response to radiation. The law of Bergonie and Tribondeau states that the radiosensitivity of a tissue is directly proportional to its reproductive capacity and inversely proportional to its degree of specialization. In other words, immature, rapidly dividing cells will be most harmed by radiation. In addition, three other factors are important: undernourished cells are less sensitive than normal ones; the higher the metabolic rate in a cell, the lower its resistance to radiation; and cells are more sensitive to radiation at specific stages of division.

Radiation alters the electrical charges of the atoms in the irradiated material, breaking the valence bonds holding the molecules together. For example, radiation passing through a cell is most likely to strike water molecules. The breakdown products from these molecules may combine with oxygen to form bleaches, which in turn can break down protein molecules in the cell. One class of these proteins comprises the enzymes that not only play a role in nearly all biochemical reactions but also control cell division. Such inhibition of cell division may permit cells to grow to an abnormal size; when such a cell dies there is no replacement to fill the void in the tissue. If the cell has been altered so that its daughter cells are genetically different from the parent cell, the daughter cells may die before they reproduce themselves; they may continue to grow without dividing; or they may divide at a higher or lower rate than the parent cell.

Because of these possible effects, doctors and scientists have been concerned about the exposure of humans to radiation. A study of the effects of radiation on the human body indicates that the following organ and tissue groups are most affected by radioactivity: (1) blood and bone marrow, (2) lymphatic system, (3) skin and hair follicles, (4) alimentary canal, (5) adrenal glands, (6) thyroid gland, (7) lungs, (8) urinary tract, (9) liver and gallbladder, (10) bone, (11)

eyes, and (12) reproductive organs. Although very small amounts of radiation may not cause any observable reaction in humans, large amounts can be permanently damaging, even lethal.

1. In the first paragraph, the "metabolic rate" of a cell refers to the cell's:
   A. chemical activities.
   B. degree of specialization.
   C. stage of division.
   D. maturity.

2. Why is muscle tissue relatively unaffected by radiation?
   F. Its cells contain no water.
   G. It is highly specialized.
   H. It is protected by the bony skeleton.
   J. Its cells have a unique method of reproduction.

3. If radiation can *cause* cancer, as implied in the second paragraph, then which of the following best justifies the use of radiation in treating cancer?
   A. Cancer tissue is highly specialized, hence very sensitive to radiation.
   B. Only the cancer cells receive the radiation.
   C. Cancer cells divide relatively rapidly.
   D. The patient may die anyway, and desperate measures are appropriate in such instances.

4. Which of the following would the author probably consider the most serious long-range effect of exposure to radiation on human populations?
   F. Possible destruction of natural resources essential to survival
   G. Hereditary changes that might occur in the population
   H. The world's population increasing at a higher rate than the world's food supply
   J. The daughters of people exposed to radiation dying before they can have children

5. Why would a man in outer space be in greater danger from radiation than a man on earth?
   A. He would not be shielded from cosmic rays by the earth's atmosphere.
   B. The reduced pressure in a space vehicle inhibits cell division.
   C. Biochemical reactions essential to life cannot occur in outer space.
   D. In a weightless condition, cells are more vulnerable to radiation.

FIGURE 8–8 Examples from the Natural Sciences Reading Test of ACT. (Copyright © 1981 by the American College Testing Program. Reproduced by permission.)

the national norms obtained from over 2,600,000 college-bound students who took the ACT from 1976 to 1979. The ACT (*College Student Profiles*, 1980a) also provides norms for various subgroups (geographical region, sex, type of college, and so on) based on a sample of 45,516 and representative of those college students who took the ACT assessment but not of all college students.

RELIABILITY. The ACT (*Highlights of the ACT Technical Report*, 1973b) summarized the results of studies on the internal consistency and stability of scores on the four Academic Tests and the composite score. Median internal consistency reliabilities are given in Table 8–5. The internal consistency of the ACT suggests a range of values from .80 to .85 for the four tests and about .90 for the composite.

The stability of test scores over periods of less than six months and for two years is also quite good. For short periods of time, the median reliabilities range from .73 to .80 for the four tests, and for the composite score the median value is .90. These values decrease only slightly when a longer period of time (two years) separates the testing dates. These results, given in Table 8–6, also suggest that there is a very small increase in average scores over a two-year period, which is probably due to educational growth during that time. The smaller increase for the shorter time interval probably represents a practice effect.

The ACT is scaled in such a manner that its *standard error of measurement* is about one point on the one to thirty-six scale. In other words, two-thirds of an individual's repeated scores are expected to fall within one point of that person's true score.

Although the composite score is the most reliable, it appears to us that the ACT demonstrates fairly high reliabilities for all four tests. In reviewing the ACT, Hills (1978) noted that the reliabilities for the four tests were somewhat lower than might be expected from a carefully constructed test. However, Hills also considered the reliabilities acceptable.

VALIDITY. As is true for the SAT, the main purpose of the ACT is to measure ap-

TABLE 8-5 Summary of median reliability estimates for the ACT Assessment

	Estimates of Reliability and Standard Error of Measurement					
	Split-half[a]		K-R 20[b]		Coefficient Alpha[b,c]	
	Rel.	*S.E.M.[d]*	*Rel.*	*S.E.M.[d]*	*Rel.*	*S.E.M.[d]*
English Usage	.90	1.49	.89	1.74	.77	2.37
Mathematics Usage	.88	2.21	.89	2.14	—	—
Social Studies Reading	.87	2.34	.85	2.56	.77	3.17
Natural Sciences Reading	.85	2.41	.84	2.37	.73	3.16
Composite	.96	1.04	.91	1.44	.85	1.91

[a]Based on 10 forms of the ACT Assessment in use from 1967 to 1971. Each reliability given is the median of 10 reliability estimates based on random samples of approximately 1,000 students each. Data are from Table 5.1 of The American College Testing Program (1973a).

[b]Based on 12 forms of the ACT Assessment in use from 1968 to 1972. Each reliability given is the median of 12 reliability estimates based on random samples of from approximately 1,000 to 3,000 each. Data are from Tables 5.2 and 5.3 of The American College Testing Program (1973a).

[c]The coefficient alphas were computed by treating the questions associated with each passage on the test as a unit and the information items as a single additional unit. Each test had approximately five units while alpha for the Composite was based on the four tests as units.

[d]The standard errors of measurement (S.E.M.) were based on scaled test scores which range from 1 through 36 with a national mean of approximately 20. Like reliability figures, the S.E.M. is a type of quantification of the amount of error in measurement. If the same individual took a test many times, the scores would not be identical because of error. Instead, the scores would form a distribution around a central score and the standard deviation of that distribution would be the S.E.M. A standard error of measurement of *one* (such as the split-half S.E.M. for the Composite) can be interpreted as follows: two-thirds of an individual's repeated scores would be expected to fall within *one* standard score of his average or central score.

From the American College Testing Program, 1973b, p. 16. Reproduced by permission of the author.

TABLE 8-6 Summary of parallel-form reliability estimates for the ACT Assessment

	Less than 6 Months Apart[a]		Two Years Apart[b]	
	Median R[c]	Mean Increase[d]	Median R[c]	Mean Increase[d]
English Usage	.80	.97	.75	.93
Mathematics Usage	.80	.62	.81	.71
Social Studies Reading	.78	.39	.74	2.69
Natural Sciences Reading	.73	.35	.72	1.61
Composite	.90	.58	.87	1.46

[a]Based on five studies in which two parallel forms of the ACT Assessment were administered from 2 weeks to 5 months apart to samples ranging from 433 to 3,089 students. Data from Tables 5.5 and 5.6 of The American College Testing Program (1973a).
[b]Based on two studies in which parallel forms of the ACT Assessment were administered before entry to college and at the end of 2 years of college to samples of 63 and 972 students. Data from Table 5.7 of The American College Testing Program (1973a).
[c]The correlations are adjusted for the standard deviations of the samples to provide comparable estimates across studies.
[d]The mean increase is the average difference between the second test score and the first for scores on the ACT standard score scale ranging from 1 through 36.
From the American College Testing Program, 1973b, p. 15. Reproduced by permission of the author.

titude for college. The ACT's predictive validity is, therefore, of primary importance in evaluating its utility. With respect to *content validity*, the ACT certainly uses the usual psychometric criteria in selecting items and does extensive pretesting. Wallace (1972a) suggested that many of the ACT items are of poor quality, but a more recent reviewer (Hills, 1978) judged content validity to be adequate. Hills also noted, however, that the four Academic Tests do intercorrelate rather substantially (.55 to .75), the mathematics test being the least related to the other three. Given the structure of the items, it seems to us that the ACT measures mainly verbal comprehension, although different subject areas are included.

The *predictive validity* of the ACT is typically assessed by correlating ACT scores with first-term or first-year college GPA. In addition, studies often determine if the ACT contributes more to predicting college GPA than does high school rank alone. As is true of the SAT, thousands of published and unpublished studies examined the predictive validity of the ACT. Summary data (*Highlights of the ACT Technical Report*, 1973b) demonstrate that the ACT does predict college GPA. Based on data from 419 colleges and 297,980 students, the study showed that high school grades had a me-

dian correlation of .512 with first-term college grades; ACT scores had a corresponding median correlation of .465. The combination of high school grades and ACT scores yielded a median multiple correlation of .576. Thus, high school grades are the best predictor of college GPA, but the ACT does help improve prediction over high school grades alone. Munday (1967) presents similar results based on a study of 211,324 students from 398 colleges.

The two previously cited studies used combinations of the four ACT tests to predict college GPA. Aleamoni and Oboler (1978), using 4,100 freshman at the University of Illinois-Urbana, combined high school rank and the ACT composite to predict first-term GPA. They found high school rank to be by far the best single predictor ($r = .429$), whereas the ACT composite correlated at .267. These two predictors combined yielded a multiple correlation of .443. The ACT did contribute a small amount of incremental validity to the prediction of first-term college GPA. Other studies also confirm that the ACT can predict college GPA. Such studies include large public universities (Halpin et al., 1981), a liberal arts college enrolling predominantly black students (Thomas, 1979), a college of business students (Price & Kim, 1976), nursing students (Halpin et al., 1976), and the prediction of course grades in basic skills courses (Snowman et al., 1980). The ACT mostly can perform the function for which it was developed.

The *construct validity* of the ACT rests mainly on the fact that it does predict academic success in college. In addition, the extensive norms provided by ACT (*College Student Profiles*, 1980a) demonstrate that test scores vary in expected ways as a function of other variables. For example, average ACT scores steadily increase as family incomes increase. Also, students' average ACT scores vary in an expected manner according to the type of college they attend. Students in two-year colleges have the lowest average scores, and students in colleges that grant doctorates have the highest average scores. The ACT average scores have declined similarly to those of the SAT, and this fact has been noted by several researchers (Ferguson, 1976; Jones, 1981; Munday, 1976). Although the reasons for the decline are complex, two factors, a more diverse pool of test-takers and weaker academic preparation, appear to be major sources. Thus, the ACT scores do reflect a rather widely recognized or inferred change in U.S. society from the late 1960s through much of the 1970s. Although the ACT can predict college grades reasonably well, the limited information available (Richards et al., 1967) suggests that it cannot predict other college achievement criteria (artistic achievement, scientific achievement, writing achievement). Although there is no particularly compelling reason for the ACT to predict musical achievement in college, it might be expected to predict scientific or writing accomplishments, which would seem to require academic potential for students to be highly successful.

Given the similar purposes for which the ACT and SAT were developed, it would be expected that scores on the two tests would be correlated. This seems to be the case. Gordon (1974) reports a correlation between SAT-V and ACT's English Usage Test of .65; the corresponding correlation between SAT-M and ACT's Mathematics Usage Test is .80. Aleamoni and Oboler (1978) report correlations of .61 and .79 for verbal and mathematics tests, respectively. Thus, the ACT and SAT do seem to be related, although the mathematics tests are apparently more similar than the verbal tests. Based on their sample of over 4,000 first-year college students, Aleamoni and Oboler also report that the ACT composite score and the total score on the SAT (V + M) correlate at .81. These results suggest, then, that both the ACT and SAT would yield approximately the same rank ordering of students. A correlation of .52 between SAT total and ACT composite was reported for a much smaller sample of college first-year students (Halpin et al., 1981).

On balance, then, the ACT does appear to possess construct validity. It predicts college GPA, in particular, and is a measure of academic potential. The studies we have noted demonstrate that, in general, ACT scores are related to other variables in expected ways.

Comparison of the SAT and ACT

Both the SAT and ACT are designed to measure academic potential. Both accomplish this goal equally well. Both are typically combined with a measure of academic achievement in high school optimally to predict college GPA. The available evidence suggests that both tests have about the same validity for predicting college GPA (Aleamoni & Oboler, 1978; Halpin et al., 1981; Lenning & Maxey, 1973).

The differences are perhaps more stylistic than substantive. The SAT provides a verbal score and a mathematics score but no total. The ACT provides scores from four different areas (English, mathematics, social studies, and natural sciences) plus a composite score. The SAT scores vary on a standard scale of 200 to 800; the ACT standard scores range from 1 to 36. The SAT uses formula scoring to correct for guessing whereas the ACT does not. The ACT has no provisions for reporting scores for students taking the test a second time; the instructions specifically recommend against this practice. The SAT does have provisions for reporting scores when the test is retaken. Although the ACT has adequate psychometric properties and is carefully constructed, the SAT is commonly judged to have attained the highest standards of construction and design for an aptitude test. The SAT provides a Test of Standard Written English that is designed to place students appropriately in first-year English classes. The utility of the ACT for placement purposes has not yet been convincingly demonstrated (Hills, 1978). The ACT assessment package also provides information on student's interests and background; the SAT does not. At extra cost, the SAT program does offer achievement testing in several areas.

Although the bulk of the evidence demonstrates that both the SAT and ACT predict college GPA, the importance of obtaining high scores is probably greatly exaggerated by many parents and their children. The fact is that high test scores are of importance only if a student is applying to highly selective and prestigious universities. Skager (1982) noted that most students are admitted to a college or university of their choice and that cutoff scores, if used at all, are surprisingly low. Others also noted that it is relatively easy to gain admission to some college in the United States regardless of academic talent or motivation (Astin et al., 1978; Hargadon, 1981; Hartnett & Feldmesser, 1980). Undoubtedly, a good deal of self-selection occurs when students apply to colleges. A student with very high grades from a good high school and high academic aspirations (motivation) will probably obtain relatively high scores on the SAT or ACT. This student may also be interested in applying to prestigious, selective universities, if it is economically and personally feasible. If the student applies, he or she is very likely to be admitted. Certainly such a student will be admitted to a less selective college of his or her choice. Students who have low grades and little or no academic as-

piration will probably obtain low test scores. Their choices for college, if they have any interest in attending, will be more limited. But in times of declining enrollment, they will find many colleges willing to admit them, perhaps on probation.

The more interesting cases, of course, are those students who have high grades and low test scores or those who have low grades and high test scores. For the former group, since high school GPA is the single best predictor of college GPA, having low test scores will eliminate them from only the most highly selective colleges. For the latter group, the combination of high test scores and low grades suggests unrealized or underrealized academic potential. The high test scores may thus provide these students with a "second chance" for academic success at a college of their choice. Again, only the most highly selective institutions might eliminate such students.

Thus, although both the ACT and SAT can predict college GPA, they do so less well than high school GPA. The prediction is also far from perfect. The criterion measure, college GPA, has many problems—among which are unreliability; differing grading practices among faculty, colleges, and departments; and restriction of range. In short, the problem may be more with the criterion than with the tests (Goldman & Slaughter, 1976). It is also unfortunately true that academic success in college appears to be largely unrelated to later accomplishments in business, teaching, engineering, medicine, and scientific research (Hoyt, 1966). Aptitude tests are similarly unable to predict such accomplishments. Test scores do provide a common basis for comparing students. That is, they are standardized. High school grades, of course, are relatively unstandardized, depending on the quality of the high school or its grading practices.

Postcollege Aptitude Tests for Graduate and Professional Schools

In our increasingly technological world, advanced training is becoming more necessary and common. Professions such as medicine and law have always required several years of intensive study after an undergraduate degree has been obtained, and doctorates are typically required for those wishing to pursue careers in college teaching. Most research scientists also have considerable training in graduate school. Graduate training in business, particularly a Master of Business Administration (MBA), is now often regarded as essential for advancement in business and industry.

Many graduate programs and professional schools are very selective, and only the most talented and highly motivated tend to apply for advanced training. Because the training is both intellectually demanding and costly, great care is used in selecting students for such programs; aptitude tests are part of the selection process. We will first discuss the Graduate Record Examinations, probably the most widely used testing program at the postcollege level, and we will then briefly describe several tests used by professional schools in their admission procedures.

GRADUATE RECORD EXAMINATIONS (GRE). The GRE was first administered in 1937 and is now produced by the Educational Testing Service in Princeton, New Jersey. Two types of tests are available—an Aptitude Test and advanced tests in twenty disciplines. The Aptitude Test measures developed abilities in three areas—verbal, quantitative, and analytic. These abilities are ones students are presumed to need for success in graduate school, although different disciplines might emphasize the importance of one of the abilities more than another. For example, verbal ability might be important for success in a graduate program in English whereas quantitative ability might be less important. The advanced tests can perhaps best be thought of as achievement tests because they deal with material taught in most undergraduate curricula as part of a specific major. Advanced tests for most undergraduate majors are available. Among the twenty disciplines represented are, for example, the following: biology, chemistry, economics, French, mathematics, philoso-

phy, and psychology. The Aptitude Test and the relevant advanced test are often both required for students seeking admission to a particular graduate program (for example, chemistry). Our discussion will focus mainly on the Aptitude Test.

The GRE is administered on five dates at several hundred locations in the United States and in many foreign countries. The GRE was taken by 831,650 students between October 1, 1977, and June 30, 1980 (*Guide to the Use of the GRE*, 1981). In 1981-1982, about 279,000 examinees took the GRE (*ETS 1982 Annual Report*, 1983).

The GRE Aptitude Test consists of seven thirty-minute sections. Each advanced test is two hours and fifty minutes long. Thus, examinees will typically spend a Saturday morning of three and one-half hours of testing time in taking the Aptitude Test and most of the afternoon taking an advanced test.

The verbal measure (GRE-V) is similar to the SAT-V but does require a higher level of performance. It is designed to test a student's ability to reason with words in solving problems. Four types of questions are used—antonyms, analogies, sentence completion, and reading comprehension. The following descriptions of the various types of verbal questions and those in the other sections of the test were taken from materials provided by the Educational Testing Service (*GRE 1982-83 Information Bulletin*, 1982).

Analogy questions test the ability to recognize relationships among words and the concepts they represent and to recognize when these relationships are parallel. The process of eliminating four wrong answer choices requires one to formulate and then analyze the relationships linking pairs of words (the given pair and the five answer choices) and to recognize which answer pair is most nearly analogous to the given pair. Some examples of relationships that might be found in analogy questions are kind, size, contiguity, or degree [1982, p. 9].

Although *antonym questions* test knowledge of vocabulary more directly than do any of the other verbal question types, the purpose of the antonym questions is to measure not merely the strength of one's vocabulary but also the ability to reason from a given concept to its opposite. Antonyms may require only rather general knowledge of a word or they may require one to make fine distinctions among answer choices. Antonyms are generally confined to nouns, verbs, and adjectives; answer choices may be single words or phrases [1982, p. 10].

The purpose of the *sentence completion questions* is to measure the ability to recognize words or phrases that both logically and stylistically complete the meaning of a sentence. In deciding which of five words or sets of words can best be substituted for blank spaces in a sentence, one must analyze the relationships among the component parts of the incomplete sentence. One must consider each answer choice and decide which completes the sentence in such a way that the sentence has a logically satisfying meaning and can be read as a stylistically integrated whole. Sentence completion questions provide a context within which to analyze the function of words as they relate to and combine with one another to form a meaningful unit of discourse [1982, p. 11].

The purpose of the *reading comprehension questions* is to measure the ability to read with understanding, insight, and discrimination. This type of question explores the examinee's ability to analyze a written passage from several perspectives, including the ability to recognize both explicitly stated elements in the passage and assumptions underlying statements or arguments in the passage as well as the implications of those statements or arguments. Because the written passage upon which reading comprehension questions are based presents a sustained discussion of a particular topic, there is ample context for analyzing a variety of relationships; for example, the function of a word in relation to a larger segment of the passage, the relationships among the various ideas in the passage, or the relation of the author to his or her topic or to the audience.

There are six types of reading comprehension questions. These types focus on (1) the main idea or primary purpose of the passage; (2) information explicitly stated in the passage; (3) information or ideas implied or suggested by the author; (4) possible application of the author's ideas to other situations; (5) the author's logic, reasoning, or persuasive techniques; and (6) the tone of the passage or the author's attitude as it is revealed in the language used.

In each edition of the Aptitude Test, there are two relatively long reading comprehension passages, each providing the basis for answering seven or eight questions, and two relatively short passages, each providing the basis for answering three or four questions. The four passages are drawn from four different subject matter areas; the humanities, the social sciences, the biological sciences, and the physical sciences [1982, p. 12].

Quantitative ability (GRE-Q) is similar in design to the SAT-M and measures basic mathematical skills, the understanding of mathematical concepts, and the ability to reason within a quantitative content. Advanced training in mathematics is not required, although general knowledge of arithmetic, algebra, and geometry is assumed. The three types of questions used are described as follows.

The *quantitative comparison questions* test the ability to reason quickly and accurately about the relative sizes of two quantities or to perceive that not enough information is provided to make such a decision. To solve a quantitative comparison problem, you compare the quantities given in two columns, Column A and Column B, and decide whether one quantity is greater than the other, whether the two quantities are equal, or whether the relationship cannot be determined from the information given. Some questions only require some manipulation to determine which of the quantities is greater; other questions require you to reason more or to think of special cases in which the relative sizes of the quantities reverse [1982, p. 15].

Each *discrete question* contains all the information needed for answering the question except for the basic mathematical knowledge assumed to be common to the backgrounds of all examinees. Many of these questions require little more than manipulation and very basic knowledge; others require the examinee to read, understand, and solve a problem that involves either an actual or an abstract situation [1982, p. 16].

The *data interpretation questions*, like the reading comprehension questions in the verbal measure, usually appear in sets. These questions are based on data presented in tables or graphs and test one's ability to synthesize information, to select appropriate data for answering a question, or to determine that sufficient information for answering a question is not provided [1982, p. 18].

The measure of analytical ability (GRE-A) is a relatively recent addition to the GRE, first appearing in October 1977, and in October 1981, the types of questions were changed. Thus, relatively little is known about the utility of the GRE-A scores, and current GRE-A scores are not comparable to those obtained before October 1981. The two kinds of questions—analytical reasoning and logical reasoning—are designed to measure a person's ability to think analytically.

Analytical reasoning questions test the ability to understand a given structure of arbitrary relationships among fictitious persons, places, things, or events; to deduce new information from the relationships given; and to assess the conditions used to establish the structure of relationships. Each analytical reasoning group consists of (1) a set of about three to seven related statements or conditions (and sometimes other explanatory material) describing a structure of relationships, and (2) three or more questions that test understanding of that structure and its implications. Although each question in a group is based on the same set of conditions, the questions are independent of one another; answering one question in a group does not depend on answering any other question.

No knowledge of formal logic or mathematics is required for solving analytical reasoning problems. Although some of the same processes of reasoning are involved in solving both analytical reasoning problems and problems in those specialized fields, analytical reasoning problems can be solved using knowledge, skills, vocabulary, and computational ability (simple addition and subtraction) common to college students [1982, p. 19].

Logical reasoning questions test the ability to understand, analyze, and evaluate arguments. Some of the abilities tested by specific questions include recognizing the point of an argument, recognizing assumptions on which an argument is based, drawing conclusions from given passages, applying principles governing one argument to another, identifying methods of argument, evaluating arguments and counterarguments, and analyzing evidence.

Each question or group of questions is based on a short argument, generally an excerpt from the kind of material graduate students are likely to encounter in their academic and personal reasoning. Although arguments may be drawn from specific fields of study such as philosophy, literary criticism, social studies, and the physical sciences, materials from more familiar sources such as political speeches, advertisements, and informal discussions or dialogues also form the basis for some questions. No specialized knowledge of any particular field is required for answering the questions, however, and no knowledge of the terminology of formal logic is presupposed.

Specific questions asked about the arguments draw on information obtained by the process of critical and analytical reading described above [1982, p. 22].

Because the GRE-A has yet to be validated, we will not discuss this score any further. Research will undoubtedly establish whether or not it is a useful addition to the GRE-V and GRE-Q scores.

Most questions on the GRE are five-alternative items. Unlike the SAT, there is no correction for guessing on the GRE Aptitude Test. Raw scores are simply the number of questions for which the best answer was chosen. The raw scores are then converted to standard scores. As is true for the SAT, GRE standard scores are reported on a scale of 200 to 800, with a mean of 500 and standard deviation of 100. For the GRE, the reference group consisted of 2,095 seniors at eleven undergraduate institutions who took the test in 1952. For this reference group, the mean and standard deviation were set at 500 and 100, respectively. Later additions of the GRE were statistically equated to this reference group so that the scale of measurement, like that of a thermometer, stays constant. However, for current students there is no reason to expect the mean and standard deviation to be the same as they were for the reference group. Thus, the mean GRE-V and GRE-Q scores for over 800,000 students who took the GRE in 1977-1980 were 479 and 518, respectively; the corresponding standard deviations were 129 and 135. A GRE-V score of 580, for example, is at the 76th percentile; one of 400 is at the 27th percentile.

The internal reliability for the GRE-V

and GRE-Q scores was reported to be .93 and .90, respectively (*GRE 1982-83 Information Bulletin,* 1982). The corresponding standard errors of measurement reported were thirty-four and forty-four. The GRE is thus quite reliable, comparing favorably with other group aptitude tests, although the GRE-Q is slightly less reliable than the GRE-V.

With respect to validity, the selection of items follows very high standards of test construction. Thus, the content validity of the GRE-V and GRE-Q is commendably high.

Since the GRE is used to help select students for admission into graduate school, evidence on its predictive validity is of primary importance. Predicting success in graduate school is even more difficult than predicting success in college. In the first place, specifying the appropriate criterion measure is not easy. Graduate school GPA is typically highly restricted in range because grades of A and B are used almost exclusively in graduate courses. The students have typically been highly selected, which means their undergraduate GPAs, test scores, and other predictors are highly similar. Thus, statistically, the size of the correlation between graduate school GPA and predictors, including the GRE, will be limited.

Other criteria of success are, of course, available. These could include, for example, faculty ratings, performance on departmentally administered examinations, attainment of a doctorate or other advanced degree, the time taken to obtain a doctorate, and research accomplishments while in graduate school. Of course, these and other criteria of success in graduate school are intermediate indicators of interest. Ultimately, what is of interest is a person's success in a career. Willingham (1974) summarized information on the predictive validity of the GRE and other predictors for five different criterion measures of success in graduate school. These results are presented in Table 8-7.

Willingham based his results on forty-three studies for the period 1952 to 1972. As can be seen from Table 8-7, the median validity coefficient for the combination of GRE scores and undergraduate GPA was .45 in the prediction of graduate GPA. The GRE does possess modest predictive validity and contributes to the prediction of various criteria of success in graduate school. Willingham (p. 275) concluded that (1) at the graduate level, validity coefficients for all predictors were somewhat lower than at the undergraduate level; (2) the GRE composite is as good or better at predicting

TABLE 8-7 Median validity coefficients for various predictors and criteria of success in graduate school. (The number of coefficients upon which each median is based is given in parentheses. Coefficients involving dichotomized criteria were sometimes reported as biserials and sometimes as point-biserials.)

	Criteria of Success				
Predictors	Graduate GPA	Overall faculty rating	Departmental examination	Attain Ph.D.	Time to Ph.D.
GRE-verbal	.24 (46)	.31 (27)	.42 (5)	.18 (47)	.16 (18)
GRE-quantitative	.23 (43)	.27 (25)	.27 (5)	.26 (47)	.25 (18)
GRE-advanced	.30 (25)	.30 (8)	.48 (2)	.35 (40)	.34 (18)
GRE-composite	.33 (30)	.41 (8)	*	.31 (33)	.35 (18)
Undergraduate GPA	.31 (26)	.37 (15)	*	.14 (30)	.23 (9)
Recommendations	*	*	*	.18 (15)	.23 (9)
GRE-GPA composite	.45 (24)	*	*	.40 (16)	.40 (9)

*No data available.
Willingham, W. W. (1974), Predicting success in graduate education. *Science, 183,* 273–278.
Copyright 1974 © by the American Association for Advancement of Science.

graduate criteria than the undergraduate GPA; (3) the GRE-V and GRE-Q scores are differentially related to the field of study in the expected way; (4) the GRE advanced test is generally the most valid single predictor; (5) recommendations are fairly poor predictors of the criteria studied; (6) the departmentally administered examination appears somewhat more predictable than the other measures available; and (7) the weighted composite of GRE and undergraduate GPA appears to have modest validity coefficients (.40 to .45) across various criteria and academic fields. More recent data involving 130 graduate departments and more than 400 validity coefficients (Wilson, 1979) tend to support the general trend of the earlier findings.

The GRE thus appears to function largely as intended, although its predictive validity is modest. The problem of defining appropriate measures of success in graduate school remains largely unsolved. GRE scores should, of course, not be the only information used in selecting students for admission to graduate school.

There are several other aptitude tests used for selecting students for professional schools. We will describe each very briefly in the following sections. Students intending to attend professional schools such as in medicine or law would be well advised to obtain information on these aptitude tests. It appears that they are almost universally required for admission. Given that admission to such schools, particularly medical school, is highly competitive, students should maximize their chances by being familiar with the test that is used.

MEDICAL COLLEGE ADMISSION TEST (MCAT). Skager (1982) reports that all but two of the 126 medical schools in the United States require applicants to submit MCAT scores. He also notes that approximately 48,000 new students take the MCAT yearly, along with about 6,000 repeaters. His estimate is that these approximately 54,000 students are competing for about 15,000 openings.

The earlier version of the MCAT, admin-istered since 1962, was largely a measure of general ability. The current version, first administered in 1977, is produced by the American Institute for Research in Washington, D.C., under contract with the Association of American Medical Colleges. Administration and scoring are provided by the American College Testing Program in Iowa City, Iowa.

The MCAT requires a full day of testing. Science Knowledge and Science Problems are given in the morning; Skills Analysis: Reading and Skills Analysis: Quantitative are given in the afternoon. The MCAT provides six separate scores measuring knowledge in three natural sciences, problem solving in the three science fields, reading skills, and quantitative skills. The six scores are biology, chemistry, physics, science problems, reading, and quantitative. MCAT scores are reported on a standard score scale ranging from one to fifteen, eight being a median value.

Because the MCAT has recently been revised, little information on its validity is yet available. The preliminary results do suggest that MCAT scores are positively correlated with specific course grades in medical school (*New Medical College Admission Test*, 1977). Skager (1982) reports data that suggest high MCAT scores do give a student a higher probability of receiving at least one offer of admission into medical school. He also notes that the undergraduate GPA is the most heavily weighted factor in medical school admissions.

LAW SCHOOL ADMISSION TEST (LSAT). The LSAT is produced and administered by the Educational Testing Service at Princeton, New Jersey, under contract to the Law School Admission Council. In 1980-1981, the LSAT was taken by over 100,000 students. All the law schools approved by the American Bar Association require applicants to take the LSAT (Skager, 1982).

The LSAT yields a general aptitude score that reflects a student's verbal comprehension and reasoning ability. There is a separate section measuring writing ability, but this score is not widely used for admission purposes (Skager, 1982). Scores on the LSAT range from 200 to 800, with a mean of 500. Many law schools rely on an index based on the combination of LSAT and undergraduate GPA to predict first-year grades in law school. This index is undoubtedly used as an initial screen at highly selective law schools where the number of applicants far surpasses the number of openings. Skager (1982) presents data strongly suggesting that students with high LSATs have a high probability of receiving at least one offer of admission. Thus, doing well on the LSAT appears to be an important factor in gaining admission into a highly selective law school.

Linn (1982) notes that the LSAT does predict first-year grades in law school. He attributes its success at least partially to the fact that law school grades in the first year are more varied than in other advanced schools, that entering classes are often large enough to justify adequate validity studies, and that first-year curriculums have much in common so that comparisons across schools are reasonable. The LSAT is in fact a better predictor of law school GPA than is undergraduate GPA. The Educational Testing Service (*Test Use and Validity*, 1980) reports that the median correlations for predicting first-year law school GPA, based on 116 studies, are .36. for the LSAT, .25 for previous GPA, and .45 for the two predictors combined.

GRADUATE MANAGEMENT ADMISSION TEST (GMAT). The GMAT is developed and administered by the Educational Testing Service under contract to the Graduate Management Council. The test is required by most graduate schools of business and by all of the largest and most highly regarded schools (Skager, 1982). Approximately 204,000 students took the GMAT in 1981-1982 (*ETS 1982 Annual Report, 1983*). This testing program is unlikely to diminish given the increasing interest among undergraduate students and those already in the business world for advanced training.

Three scores are reported for the GMAT—verbal, quantitative, and total.

Based on sixty-seven studies with graduate schools of management, the Educational Testing Service (*Test Use and Validity,* 1980) reports median validity coefficients for predicting first-year grades of .29 for GMAT, .21 for previous GPA, and .38 for both predictors combined. The GMAT thus has some predictive validity, particularly when combined with undergraduate GPA. Business schools often prefer entering students to have previous business or practical experience, which implies that test scores may be of secondary importance in the admissions process. The selection process used by graduate schools, at least those using the GMAT, has not yet been extensively researched and is not well understood. At selective schools, the GMAT is probably used in a manner similar to the GRE, LSAT, and MCAT.

MILLER ANALOGIES TEST. Another test designed to screen applicants for graduate study and for high-level positions in business and government is the Miller Analogies Test (MAT). Six parallel forms are available, each consisting of 100 analogy items and taking fifty minutes to administer. The items are based on various areas of knowledge (literature, biology, general information, and so on) but require recognition of relationships. The analogies are formed on a variety of principles (sound, for example), not only those based on word meanings. The items vary in difficulty so that even persons of the highest ability will be challenged. The items are of the common analogy form A : B : : C : D (Night is to day as dark is to _____.), and any one of the elements may be blank. Examinees select the one option, among the four available, that completes the analogy.

The 1981 edition of the *Miller Analogies Test Manual* (1981) provides educational and industrial norms. The educational norms are of two types—applicants and enrolled students. Educational norms are available for thirteen different areas of study (clinical psychology, social work, elementary education, and so on). Based on data presented in the manual, the MAT is mainly used in screening graduate applicants in psychology and education. The industrial norms are based on cases tested before 1970 and include mostly persons already employed, but some applicants for positions are included as well. Although the norms provide useful information, a user of the MAT would be well-advised to develop local norms for any selection procedure.

The reliability of the MAT appears to be quite good. The 1981 manual reports split-half reliabilities ranging from .92 to .95 for thirteen studies of various forms of the test. Also, alternate form reliabilities range from .85 to .91. The manual also reports that the stability coefficient of the MAT over an interval averaging five months is .75. This figure was obtained by correlating two alternate forms of the test.

The 1981 manual summarizes validity studies of the MAT that were completed after 1970, including primarily ones in which the MAT was correlated with graduate GPA or with other ability tests. Many of these studies had very small samples. Nevertheless, the MAT does correlate modestly (r's in the .30s) with graduate GPA. The correlations with the GRE are substantially higher, ranging from .48 to .83. The MAT does, therefore, exhibit positive correlations with relevant criteria. The disparate nature of the various samples reported makes it impossible to conclude how generally valid the MAT is. Therefore, we would recommend, as is true for any test, that local validity studies be conducted if the MAT is being considered for use as a screening test.

ACHIEVEMENT TESTS

The aptitude tests we have discussed are taken by large numbers of students each year. However, it appears to us that even larger numbers of students take standardized achievement tests each year. It has been estimated, for example, that in the United States six to twelve full batteries of achievement tests will be given to a student between kindergarten and twelfth grade (Houts, 1975). Anderson (1982) suggests that the number of achievement tests administered to elementary and secondary school students is in the hundreds of millions.

As we indicated in the initial section of this chapter, the differences between aptitude and achievement tests rest largely on the purpose for which the test is used. Achievement tests are designed to measure the results of a relatively specific set of experiences. In elementary and secondary education, achievement tests measure how students compare with others in areas such as reading, mathematics, language arts, and science. Commercial publishers have developed tests in many subjects. Commercially available tests are almost universally used by schools in reading and mathematics. Of course, this is understandable since schools must teach students how to read and to use mathematics if the students are to function in modern society. Thus, scores on achievement tests provide one index of how successful schools have been in teaching critically important skills.

Anderson (1982) suggests that among other uses, tests in the elementary and secondary schools can be used in instructional management. For one thing, tests are often used for diagnostic purposes to identify the strengths but more often the weaknesses of particular students. Achievement tests are of little assistance in this area, however, because they are too broad in content. Diagnostic tests measure fairly specific skills, particularly in reading and mathematics. A second use for tests is to place students in the best available instructional environment. Achievement tests can be useful for such placements. A student having a low reading score on a reading achievement test, for example, might need additional instruction or might need a special class in this area. Finally, test scores can be used as part of the information in guidance and counseling given to students regarding their general program of study.

Anderson further notes that tests can be used in making programmatic decisions. First, in survey assessment, data are collected on groups of students to determine general educational development. Such surveys are often made on a regular basis so that trends in accomplishment can be determined. The results of such testing can identify general areas that may need more instructional resources. They also demonstrate how well the schools are meeting the goals set by public representatives (school boards) and government (state boards of education). Anderson also suggests that tests are often part of formative and summative evaluation. *Formative evaluation* assesses the outcome of an ongoing program that may be relatively new. The program can be modified depending on the results of testing. *Summative evaluation* determines if a program should be continued, terminated, or revised. Federally funded programs, for example, strongly recommend that a nationally normed test be used to evaluate the educational outcome of such programs.

Achievement tests are thus used in almost all school districts to assess change in performance over time within a district and to compare a district's performance to national norms. Commercial test publishers have a large market for achievement tests. It was reported (Floden, et al., 1980) that four tests dominate the market in elementary reading and mathematics: The Stanford Achievement Test (Psychological Corporation), Iowa Test of Basic Skills (Riverside Publishing Company), Metropolitan Achievement Tests (Psychological Corporation), and California Test Bureau/McGraw-Hill Comprehensive Tests of Basic Skills (CTB/ McGraw-Hill). Commercially available achievement tests are typically provided for each grade level (kindergarten through twelve). These tests provide scores with the same or similar names and do tend to be correlated. However, Floden et al. show that commercially available fourth-grade achievement tests in mathematics do differ in content.

According to a survey supplied by the Association of American Publishers, schools purchased 90 percent or more of standardized tests sold in the years 1972 through 1978. In 1977, educational sales totaled $44.9 million, or about .1 of 1 percent of the total school instructional budget (Wigdor & Garner, 1982, p. 153). There is no doubt that educational testing is a sizeable industry and significant money is involved. Wigdor and Garner (p. 153) further suggest that six commercial publishers furnish the majority of tests used in schools: Addison-Wesley Publishing Company; California Test Bureau/McGraw-Hill; Houghton Mifflin Company (through its subsidiary, Riverside Publishing Company); Scholastic Testing Service, Inc.; Science Research Associates; and the Psychological Corporation/Harcourt Brace Jovanovich, Inc. All these publishers, as well as others, provide high-quality tests and testing services. We will discuss one achievement battery in some detail in order to understand their characteristics.

Achievement tests are evaluated chiefly on the basis of their content validity. That is, they must adequately sample the domain of interest. The tests should measure the important skills being taught in a school's curriculum. Hopkins and Stanley (1981, Ch. 14) discuss in detail the general principles that educators should use in evaluating and selecting achievement tests. Iwanicki (1980) reviewed recent editions of five achievement batteries and has found all to be excellent tests. A summary of these five and of the Stanford Achievement Test (7th edition) is in Table 8-8. As Iwanicki and others (Ebel, 1978) noted, any of these achievement batteries could be used in a school system with the assurance that they are of high quality and that a variety of scoring and reporting services is available.

Stanford Achievement Test (SACHT)

The SACHT was first published in 1923 and has had a long history of use. Buros (1978) lists 268 references to the various editions of this test. As Ebel noted in his review, "the 1973 edition of the Stanford Achievement Test embodies most of the best that is currently known about the mea-

TABLE 8-8 Summary description of six standardized achievement test batteries

Battery Name	California Achievement Tests	Iowa Tests of Basic Skills	Metropolitan Achievement Tests	SRA Achievement Series	Sequential Tests of Educational Progress	Stanford Achievement Tests
Areas Measured — Basic Skills	Reading Vocab. Reading Comp. Math Computation Math Concepts & Appl. Spelling Language Mech. Language Expr.	Reading Vocabulary Math Computation Math Concepts Math Problems Language Spelling Lang. Capitalization Lang. Punctuation Language Usage	Reading Mathematics Language	Reading Vocab. Reading Comp. Math Computation Math Concepts Math Problem Soln. Language Spelling Language Mechanics Language Usage	Reading Vocabulary Math Computation Math Basic Concepts Writing Skills	Vocabulary Reading Comprehension Math Concepts Math Computation Math Applications Spelling Language/English Word Study Skills
Areas Measured — Other	Reference Skills	Work Study-Reference Materials Work Study-Visual Materials	Science Social Sci.	Reference Materials Science Social Sci.	Study Skills Listening Science Social Sci.	Social Science Science Listening Comprehension
Basic Skills Test Time	143 min.	179 min.	120 min.	190 min.	180 min.	215[a] min.
Grade Span	K-12	K-8	K-12	K-12	3-12	1-9
No. of Levels/Forms	10/2	10/2	8/2	8/2	6/2	6/2
Publisher and Publication Date	CTB/McGraw-Hill 1977, 1978	Houghton Mifflin 1978	Psychological Corporation 1978	Science Research Associates 1978	Addison-Wesley 1979	Psychological Corporation/ Harcourt Brace & Jovanovich 1982

[a]Based on Primary Level 3 Battery

Based on Iwanicki, E. F. (1980), "A New Generation of Standardized Achievement Batteries: A Profile of Their Major Features." *Journal of Educational Measurement, 17,* 155–162. Copyright © 1980, National Council on Measurement in Education, Washington, D.C.

urement of educational achievement" (1978, p. 98). Lehman (1975) praised the quality of the test. The seventh edition of the SACHT was published in 1982, building on the strengths of the previous editions. As indicated in Table 8-8, the SACHT has forms appropriate for administration to students in grades one through nine. In addition, the Stanford Early School Achievement Test is available for use in kindergarten and first grade. The Stanford Test of Academic Skills is available for use in grades eight through thirteen. The Stanford Measurement Series thus provides for assessing the achievement status in important skill areas across all grades (kindergarten through grade twelve and entry into community colleges). In the following sections we will describe the 1982 edition of the SACHT.

MATERIALS, ADMINISTRATION, SCORING. The SACHT is available at six different levels with two forms (E, F). The six levels and corresponding grades are as follows: Primary 1 (Grades 1.5–2.9), Primary 2 (Grades 2.5–3.9), Primary 3 (Grades 3.5–4.9), Intermediate 1 (Grades 4.5–5.9), Intermediate 2 (Grades 5.5–7.9), and Advanced (Grades 7.0–9.9). The number and types of tests vary somewhat across levels as does the total amount of time required. Thus, there are nine tests at the Primary 1 level, which would require three hours and thirty-five minutes of testing time. At all other levels, there are ten or eleven tests, requiring from three hours and forty-five minutes to five hours and fifteen minutes of testing time to complete an entire battery. As is true of most achievement batteries, the SACHT requires a considerable amount of testing time. A school system could easily devote at least one full day to achievement testing. It is suggested, however, that the Primary 2 Battery be administered over a three-day period. A teacher would typically use several days to administer an achievement test battery. The SACHT was designed to be used toward the beginning (October) or toward the end (May) of the school year.

Because achievement testing is probably most important in the primary grades, we use the Primary 2 Battery to illustrate the SACHT content. We believe that it is most important, for example, to identify children who are not learning basic skills in reading and mathematics as soon as possible. Such children could then be targeted for special instruction, assuming adequate resources are available. The SACHT provides practice items to be administered prior to the test battery. We illustrate the content of the SACHT, Primary 2 Battery, by using items from the practice test. Ten tests may be administered at this level. These include: Word Study Skills, Word Reading, Reading Comprehension, Vocabulary, Listening Comprehension, Spelling, Concepts of Number, Mathematics Computation, Mathematics Applications, and Environment. In Figure 8-9, we present descriptions of the content of the ten tests in the Primary 2 Battery. These descriptions are taken from the teacher's manual on administering the SACHT (Gardner, Rudman, Karlsen, & Merwin, 1983).

For the Primary 2 Battery, the teacher reads many of the questions. The students must then choose the appropriate answer. Example instructions used by the teacher along with example items from the ten tests are given in Figure 8-10. Students may respond on the test sheets if hand scoring is used or on answer sheets if computer scoring is used.

Raw scores on each test are obtained. Because the tests are designed to be power tests with sufficient time limits for almost all students to attempt all items, no correction for guessing is used. In addition to the ten single test scores, total scores are also obtained. These totals including Reading, Listening, Language, Mathematics, Basic Battery, and Complete Battery. In addition to the scores on the ten subtests, a score labeled *Using Information* is obtained from items in the Mathematics and Language subtests. These items are designed to measure a student's ability to use reference sources and to read graphs and charts. The

Description of the Stanford Primary 2 Battery

The Primary 2 battery includes measures of reading, listening, spelling, mathematics, and understanding of the environment. The concepts and skills that are assessed in each content area are those ordinarily taught during the second half of Grade 2 and in Grade 3.

THE SUBTESTS AND WHAT THEY MEASURE

The content of the subtests in the Primary 2 battery is described briefly below; detailed lists of objectives are presented in the Primary 2 *Guide for Classroom Planning*.

Word Study Skills

The Word Study Skills subtest has two major emphases: *structural analysis* and *phonetic analysis*. Structural analysis has to do with the decoding of words by analyzing word parts, and phonetic analysis is concerned with the relationships between sounds and letters.

At this level, the structural analysis portion of the Word Study Skills subtest assesses pupils' ability to recognize compound words and to identify the appropriate use of contractions and inflectional endings in context. In the phonetic analysis portion, pupils are asked to determine particular sounds in words and relate each sound to a common spelling of that sound. Half the sounds are represented by single consonant letters, consonant blends, and consonant digraphs; the remaining sounds include long and short vowel sounds, as well as some vowel-sound variants. All words included in this subtest are expected to be in the listening vocabulary of most pupils in the second and third grades, and pupils should be able to decode them if they have learned the sound-letter relationships being measured.

Word Reading

This subtest measures pupils' ability to recognize words and attach meaning to them. As such, it provides an assessment of pupils' ability to function at a very basic level in reading, going from the printed word to the spoken word.

The test-taking task involves the identification of words that describe, or are associated with, a particular illustration. The test words represent words that are typically taught in grades 1, 2, and 3, such that the correct word can be identified through the use of phonics or memory. Each word is also conceptually simple and included in pupils' speaking and listening vocabularies.

Reading Comprehension

Given the wide range of reading ability that exists in the second and third grades, this subtest has been designed to provide adequate measurement of pupils who are having difficulty reading connected discourse, as well as those who are capable of interpreting brief reading selections. Thus, two different formats are used to assess reading comprehension.

The subtest begins with three short passages presented in a multiple-choice, modified cloze format. This rather simple format enables pupils to respond in a way that approximates the reading process and should provide all children with the motivation to continue. The rest of the subtest consists of complete passages with accompanying questions. The reading vocabulary of the passages has been limited to words found in reading materials designed for the primary grades, with the content of the passages selected to be interesting and varied in content.

Vocabulary

The Vocabulary subtest is dictated in order to provide a measure of pupils' language competence without requiring them to read. The words were selected to represent the various parts of speech, as well as the vocabulary encountered in school and in ordinary conversation. Though vocabulary, as such, is generally not a part of the school curriculum, the information that can be derived from the assessment of language development in this way has considerable diagnostic utility.

Listening Comprehension

Listening and reading are the modes through which most learning takes place. Thus, the primary purpose of the Listening Comprehension subtest is to evaluate pupils' ability to process information that has been heard, both in terms of the retention of specific details and the organization, or understanding, of the material as a whole. The stimulus material for this subtest has been selected to represent listening tasks that are related to school learning and to obtaining information outside of school.

FIGURE 8-9

Description of the Stanford Primary 2 Battery

Spelling

The format of this subtest requires pupils to identify the misspelled word from a group of four words. Each incorrectly spelled word contains the error that is most commonly made by children at this level, as presented by Gates in *A List of Spelling Difficulties in 3876 Words* (New York: Teachers College Press, Columbia University, 1937). The misspellings to be detected have been selected to represent errors frequently found in the spelling of sight words, which are so "irregular" as to require memorization; errors resulting from the improper use of letter-sound relationships (phonetic principles); and errors resulting from the incorrect spelling of inflectional endings and affixes when they are added to basic word forms (structural principles).

Concepts of Number

The purpose of this subtest is the assessment of pupils' understanding of basic number concepts. Since an understanding of these concepts is requisite to facility with computation and problem solving, it is important that basic number concepts be developed as instruction in mathematics proceeds. At this level, the whole number concepts measured include naming numbers, counting, reading numerals, place value, and ordering. Concepts of part-whole relationships expressed as fractional numbers and of the operations and their properties are also assessed.

Mathematics Computation

This subtest includes the addition, subtraction, and multiplication facts and the addition and subtraction of whole numbers, with and without renaming.

Mathematics Applications

The Mathematics Applications subtest provides information about pupils' ability to apply the number concepts and computation skills they have learned by assessing understanding of the language of mathematical problems and the ability to solve problems by the choice of the appropriate mathematical operation. Reading and interpreting graphs and principles of geometry and measurement, including the use of various units of measure, are also assessed.

Environment

The Environment subtest is designed to assess pupils' understanding of the basic concepts reflecting the social and natural environments of their world. While formal instruction in the sciences and social sciences often does not begin until the third or fourth grade, the acquisition of an understanding of these concepts in the early school years is important to future learning in these areas.

FIGURE 8-9   *(Continued)*

raw scores and totals are converted to various other scores including percentile ranks, stanines, grade equivalents, normal curve equivalents, and scale scores. For the Primary Level 2, empirically based norms are available for the fall (beginning of grade three) and for the spring (end of grade two). The test user is faced with a large array of scores for each student.

Grade Equivalent Scores are commonly reported for achievement tests. A grade equivalent is a score that represents the average performance of students tested in a given month of the school year. Even though such scores have many technical problems associated with them, they have

obvious relevance to teachers in that they indicate whether or not a particular student is performing below, at, or above grade level. Grade equivalents are often used as a measure of growth. However, grade equivalents are not comparable from test to test or at the various grade levels. Gardner et al. (1983, p. 14) have specifically noted that grade equivalents can be misinterpreted. If, for example, a fourth grader obtains a grade equivalent of 6.2 on a mathematics test constructed for fourth graders, it does *not* mean the student has mastered all the mathematics taught in grade five. The student's attainment in mathematics is not necessarily similar to that of an average sixth grader.

FIGURE 8-10 Stanford Achievement Test, Primary 2 Battery: Example Instructions and Items. For brevity, transitional instructions have been omitted as have some items. (Reproduced by permission of the publisher. Copyright © 1982 by Harcourt Brace Jovanovich, Inc. All rights reserved.)

Instructions	Test Items

WORD READING

First, we are going to look at a picture and find the words that tell about the picture. Look at the box with questions 1, 2, and 3 in it. You see a picture of a clown. Now look at the three rows of words below the picture. In each row there is one word that goes with the picture. Pick out the word in each row that goes with the picture. Look at row 1. Read the words to yourself as I read them aloud: "many . . . clown . . . came." Which word goes with the picture? Yes, the word "clown" goes with the picture. That's why the space under "clown" has been filled in in your booklet. Now look at row 2 in your booklet. Read the words in row 2 to yourself. Mark the space under the word that goes with the picture of the clown. When you are finished with row 2, go on to row 3.

1   many   clown   came
       ○   ●   ○

2   father   make   funny
       ○   ○   ○

3   jolly   just   join
       ○   ○   ○

READING COMPREHENSION

Now move down to the box with question 4. Look at the picture and read the sentences to yourself. The last two words of the second sentence are missing. Which group of words completes the sentence correctly? Mark in front of the two words that complete the sentence.

The door handle came off.
Jim got a tool so he could

4   ○ close it   ○ bend it
    ○ fix it   ○ cut it.

WORD STUDY SKILLS

Look at row 8. You see the words "until," "candy," and "doorway." One of these words has two words in it. Find the word and mark under it. Which word did you mark? Yes, you should have marked under the third word, "doorway," because "doorway" is made up of two words, "door" and "way." Does everyone understand? Now look at row 9.

8   until   candy   doorway
       ○   ○   ○

9   who's   who'll   who'd
       ○   ○   ○

You see the words "who's," "who'll," and "who'd." Each of these is a shortened form of two words. The shortened form has the same meaning as the two words from which it comes. I will say two words and use them in a sentence. Then you will find the one word in row 9 that has the same meaning, and mark under it. Listen to the two words: WHO IS. WHO IS bringing the food? WHO IS.

CONCEPTS OF NUMBERS

Now we are going to do some work with numbers. Find the box with 13 in it. All but one of these are names for six. Mark the space under the answer that is *not* a name for six.

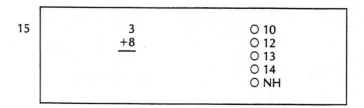

13

7−1	2+4	six	1+6
O	O	O	O

MATHEMATICS COMPUTATION

Now move down to box 15. Here you see an additional example, "three plus eight." Next to the sample, you see four numerals, "ten," "twelve," "thirteen," "fourteen," and the letters "NH." "NH" stands for "Not Here." Three plus eight equals . . . what? Is it ten, twelve, thirteen, fourteen, or is the answer not here? If the answer is not here, mark next to "NH" for "Not Here."

15

$$\begin{array}{r} 3 \\ +8 \\ \hline \end{array}$$

O 10
O 12
O 13
O 14
O NH

MATHEMATICS APPLICATIONS

Now move down to the box with 18 in it. Here you see four numerals, "one," "three," "four," "seven," and the letters "NH." Listen carefully to this problem: "Bob has four books, and Dick has three. How many books do they have altogether?" Do they have "one," "three," "four," "seven," or is the answer not here? Mark the space under your answer.

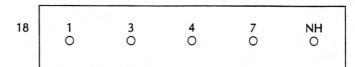

18

1	3	4	7	NH
O	O	O	O	O

SPELLING

We are now going to work on spelling. You will look at a group of words and choose the one word that is *not* spelled correctly. Look

20

O bathed
O naughty
O shuv
O troubles

FIGURE 8-10 *(Continued)*

Instructions	*Test Items*

at the number 20. Here you see four words, "bathed," "naughty," "shove," and "troubles." Which word is spelled incorrectly? Mark the space next to the word that is *not* spelled correctly.

ENVIRONMENT

Move down to box 23. Here you see three pictures. Which picture shows a family? Mark the space under the picture you have chosen.

23

Move down to box 24. Here you see three pictures of a cucumber plant. Which picture shows the arrow pointing to the stem? Mark the space under the picture you have chosen.

24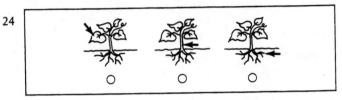

VOCABULARY

Look at question 25. You see the words, "beat him," "rescue him," and "chase him." I will read part of a sentence and then the three groups of words. You will decide which one of these groups of words completes the sentence correctly. Here is the sentence: "When you run after someone you . . . beat him . . . rescue him . . . chase him." Mark next to the words that best complete the sentence.

25
○ beat him
○ rescue him
○ chase him

LISTENING COMPREHENSION

Now I am going to read some stories to you. Listen very carefully so that you will be able to answer questions about them. I will read everything only once, so listen carefully and try to remember what I say. Look at number 27. Listen to this story: "Tracy wanted a pet that she could keep in her apartment. Dogs weren't allowed, and her mother didn't like cats." Mark the space under the picture of the animal that Tracy might get.

27

Gardner et al. suggest that grade equivalents are best used in interpreting the performance of groups of students.

RELIABILITY. As estimated by internal consistency and alternate-form methods, the reliability of the SACHT is quite good. For the Primary 2 Battery (Forms E and F) subtests, for example, Gardner et al. reported KR-20 coefficients between .64 and .93. The lowest KR-20 coefficient is .64 for Environment. As would be expected, KR-20s are higher (.89 to .97) for the total scores such as Total Reading and Mathematics. Gardner et al. reported no direct evidence on the stability of the SACHT. However, they did report alternate-form (E and F) reliabilities obtained within a four-week period. These alternate-form reliabilities were between .68 and .86 for the subtests and .85 and .92 for the total scores. Because Primary 2 is designed for the youngest age group and because younger children yield less reliable scores, it has the lowest reliabilities. The reliabilities increase somewhat when the batteries used with older children are examined.

For the previous edition of the SACHT, Suddick and Bowen (1981) reported strong and stable test-retest reliability coefficients for total mathematics scores on three of the batteries. The study was conducted over a three-year period with 139 third, fourth, and fifth grade children. Since two forms of the SACHT are available, stability information can be obtained over periods of time. However, since student growth in educational competence undoubtedly occurs at differential rates, the stability of SACHT scores over long periods of time is perhaps not a critical issue.

VALIDITY. As we indicated earlier, achievement tests must have content validity to be useful. Thus, to measure educational achievement, the test development process of the SACHT identified what was being taught in schools throughout the nation. The sources of curricular information included textbook series in the various subjects, course syllabuses, state guidelines, and research pertaining to children's concepts, experience, and vocabulary at successive ages and grades (Gardner et al., 1983, p. 7).

Before the final forms were constructed, an extensive field testing program was used to obtain data on each item. A sample of approximately 100,000 students from fifty school systems across the country participated in the field testing (Gardner et al., 1983, p. 7). This field testing provided the data on which the final selection of test items was based. Items included in the final forms also had to cover all instructional objectives for each subject area and to vary in difficulty. As Gardner et al. (1983, p. 7) noted:

The final tests were created to conform to the test blueprints, which specified the objectives to be measured and their relative emphases, appropriateness of difficulty, comparability in content and difficulty between test forms, and continuity across levels. The skill clusters were also built to be parallel in coverage and average item difficulty across forms. No item in the mid-range of difficulty was chosen unless the correlation between the item and the subtest (biserial correlation coefficient) was positive and significant, (at least .35).

All items selected for the final forms were reviewed again for clarity, style, and bias. Proper names, pronouns, pictures, activities, and implied status were checked for balance between male and female references and across racial and ethnic groups. The final forms were reviewed by the bias panel that had served for the Item Analysis forms. The total composition of each form was checked again to eliminate clues from item to item, similarity of pictures, and repetition or overlap of content.

In summary, the methods of test construction followed by the SACHT authors were excellent. The review of item content and the statistical analysis were thorough and complete.

To be useful, however, the SACHT scores must be related to appropriate norms. Thus, the standardization sample must be representative of the population of interest. Gardner et al. (1983) give details on the standardization samples. In the fall of

1981, a total of 300 school districts partici- pated, and approximately 250,000 students were tested. In the spring of 1982, approxi- mately 200,000 students were tested. The standardization sample for the SACHT ap- pears largely to match the national popula- tion based on the 1980 census. In particular, the standardization sample was similar to the U.S. population on the following charac- teristics: school system enrollment, geo- graphic region, socioeconomic status, public or nonpublic schools, and student ethnicity. However, only schools that chose to cooperate participated in the testing pro- gram. Undoubtedly, some bias is produced by the voluntary nature of a school system's participation. That is, schools that refused to participate could do so for a variety of reasons. But we remain ignorant of the ef- fect their students would have on the SACHT norms. This problem is, of course, not unique to the SACHT. In general, the standardization sample for the SACHT is as representative as can be expected.

In addition to measuring individual pupil growth, and the general accountability of schools in meeting educational goals, an- other major use of achievement tests is as a dependent variable in studies of variables influencing educational growth. Previous editions of the SACHT have been used in numerous such studies. For example, it was used in studies of self-esteem and educa- tional achievement (Maruyama, Rubin, and Kingsburg, 1981; Rubin, 1978), school per-

formance of offspring of young adolescent mothers (Morrow, 1979), teaching learning strategies to learning-disabled children (Snart, 1979), the neuropsychological corre- lates of academic success (Townes, Trupin, Martin, and Goldstein, 1980), and the use of senior citizens as psycho-educational agents in improving the performance of learning- disabled and emotionally handicapped chil- dren (Matefy, 1978). The use of the SACHT in these studies as well as others illustrates its wide acceptance as a measure of educational achievement.

It is, however, apparent that the tests are intercorrelated. For example, for the Pri- mary 2 Battery (Form E, administered at the beginning of Grade 3), the lowest correla- tion between two tests is .42 (Spelling with Environment); the highest correlation is .82 (Word Reading with Reading Comprehen- sion). There is thus evidence that there is re- dundancy in SACHT scores; students who do well on one test tend to do well on other tests. For previous editions of the SACHT, this result has also been noted by other in- vestigators (Klein, 1979; Merrifield and Hummel-Rossi, 1976), who suggested the need for discriminant validity studies of the SACHT.

On balance, however, we find the SACHT to be among the best available measures of educational achievement. The other batteries noted in Table 8-8 are also excellent tests.

9

Personality Assessment
Projective Techniques

Many different definitions of personality have been proposed. One of the most useful is that of Kleinmuntz (1967, p. 9), who indicated that "the term personality refers to the unique organization of factors which characterize an individual and determines his pattern of interaction with the environment." Factors in Kleinmuntz' definition include a variety of characteristics, including needs, fears, reactions to stress, self-perceptions, and perceptions of others. It is these characteristics that personality tests try to measure. The exact nature of the characteristics assessed by any particular test depends to a large extent on the theoretical convictions of the test's constructor. A person with a psychoanalytic orientation might design a test to assess constructs such as ego strength or castration anxiety, whereas a person with a learning orientation would probably focus on such variables as eliciting and maintaining stimuli, reinforcers, and generalization.

In Chapter 4 we discussed the differences between tests of maximum perform-ance and tests of typical performance. Personality tests belong to the latter category. When we use personality tests we are interested in how a person usually behaves in a situation or class of situations, and there are no right or wrong answers to the items.

In dealing with intelligence tests, we often refer to how much intelligence a person has. High scores on such tests typically indicate more of the construct being assessed. In spite of colloquial references to people having "a lot of personality" or "not much personality," it is not appropriate to think of personality tests as indicating how much personality people have. Rather, they tell us what *kinds* of personalities they have.

Intelligence tests typically yield one or several scores to indicate a person's performance. Some personality tests yield a wide array of scores and indices of various aspects of personality. Other personality tests yield no scores at all, relying instead on the subjective interpretations of responses.

For tests of maximum performance, the selection of appropriate criteria for validation is relatively easy. Intelligence tests usually are validated by comparing test scores with school performance. Tests of musical aptitude can be compared with actual musical performance. It is more difficult to select criterion measures for most personality tests. For example, what is the appropriate criterion for a test of ego strength? Sometimes several acceptable measures are available, and test scores may relate differently to each of them. An anxiety test could be compared to a physiological index such as galvanic skin response, to observable behaviors such as chain smoking or nail biting, to ratings of anxiety by subjects' therapists, or to all three. Test scores could relate to all three measures of anxiety or to some but not to others.

PROJECTIVE VERSUS OBJECTIVE TESTS

Personality tests often are classified as projective or objective. As discussed in Chapter 4, the distinction usually is made according to the nature of the stimulus presented to the subject and to the response format available to the subject (Hirt & Kaplan, 1967).

Stimuli can range from those that are very ambiguous at one extreme to those that are clear and definite at the other extreme. An inkblot, which easily can be interpreted in several different ways, is an example of a very ambiguous stimulus. A statement in a personality questionnaire, which is likely to be interpreted in about the same way by almost everyone who reads it, is an example of a clear and definite stimulus. Semiambiguous pictures, such as those found in the Thematic Apperception Test (TAT), represent an intermediate position on the stimulus continuum. To the extent that a personality test employs ambiguous stimuli, the test is considered to be projective. To the extent that clear and definite stimuli are employed, a test is considered to be objective.

Response formats can range from very unstructured to very structured. A test in which the subject is given minimal direction about how to respond (for example, "What does this remind you of?") and in which many different kinds and numbers of responses are acceptable is very unstructured. In contrast, a test in which the subject is limited to a true-or-false response is a very structured format. Tests with less structured formats are considered to be more projective, whereas those with more structured formats are considered to be more objective.

By a simultaneous consideration of the stimulus and response dimensions, tests can be classified as more projective, more objective, or intermediate. Figure 9–1 illustrates the classification system. A test having very ambiguous stimuli (e.g., inkblots) and an unstructured response format (e.g., "What does this remind you of?") would fall into quadrant A and would be considered most projective. A test having very clear and definite stimuli (for example, inventory statements) and structured response format (for example, true or false) would fall into quadrant D and would be considered most objective. Tests falling into quadrants B (ambiguous stimuli and structured response format) and C (clear and definite stimuli and unstructured response format) have elements of both projective and objective tests and would be classified as intermediate.

The Rorschach test, in which subjects are shown inkblots and instructed to indicate what each one looks like or reminds them of, is a good example of a quadrant A (most projective) test. The Minnesota Multiphasic Personality Inventory (MMPI), which requires the subject to read statements and answer true or false to each, is a good example of a quadrant D (most objective) test. The group Rorschach, in which groups of subjects are shown the standard Rorschach inkblots and asked to choose from among alternatives the one that each inkblot most resembles, falls into quadrant B (intermediate). A sentence-completion test, which re-

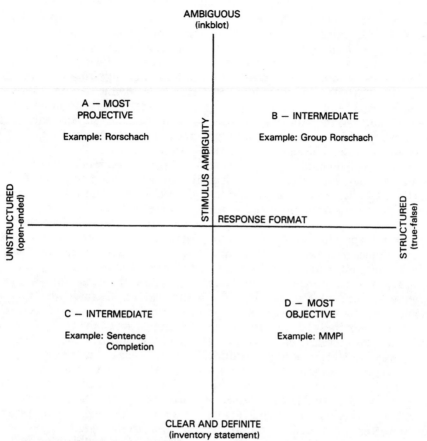

AMBIGUOUS
(inkblot)

A — MOST
PROJECTIVE

Example: Rorschach

B — INTERMEDIATE

Example: Group Rorschach

STIMULUS AMBIGUITY

UNSTRUCTURED
(open-ended)

RESPONSE FORMAT

STRUCTURED
(true-false)

C — INTERMEDIATE

Example: Sentence
Completion

D — MOST
OBJECTIVE

Example: MMPI

CLEAR AND DEFINITE
(inventory statement)

FIGURE 9–1 Schema for classifying personality tests as projective or objective. (Hirt, M. L., and Kaplan, M. L., 1967, Psychological testing. II. Current practice. *Comprehensive Psychiatry, 8,* 310–320. Copyright 1967 by Grune and Stratton, Inc. Adapted by permission of authors.)

quires the subject to complete sentences for which stems are given, falls into the other intermediate quadrant (C). It should be obvious that the classification system does not result in a dichotomous labeling of tests as either projective or objective. Rather, tests are ordered along a continuum, ranging from most projective to most objective.

The importance of the projective versus objective distinction lies in the fact that several important assumptions traditionally have been made concerning the use of one or the other of the approaches. The more important of these assumptions are

1. Because of their ambiguous nature, projective tests elicit more meaningful information about the subject's personality and conflicts.
2. Projective tests are less susceptible to faking than are objective tests.
3. Projective tests reveal more unconscious aspects of personality, whereas objective tests deal with more surface aspects of personality.

That subjects will reveal more about their personalities and problems when responding to more ambiguous and less structured conditions has been referred to as the *projective hypothesis.* Several studies have been conducted as partial tests of this hypothesis. If it is valid, subjects should reveal more about themselves when responding to more ambiguous stimuli. In a study by Laskowitz (1959) undergraduate students were asked to describe TAT cards that differed in ambiguity. Ambiguity was manipulated by showing slides of cards in varying degrees of focus. The resulting descriptions were analyzed to determine the extent to which they went beyond the actual physical aspects. Results indicated that as ambiguity increased, descriptions went more and more beyond the physical aspects of the cards. The author interpreted his data as supporting the projective hypothesis. In a similar study Kenny and Bijou (1953) divided TAT cards into three ambiguity categories (high, medium, and low). Stories told about these cards were analyzed to determine the amount of "revealingness" under the varying conditions. The researchers found that the most revealing stories occurred under medium ambiguity. Kagan (1956) found that boys rated as nonaggressive were differentiated from boys rated as aggressive by stories told about highly structured hostile pictures but were not differentiated by more ambiguous pictures.

From these and similar studies we conclude that data relevant to the validity of the projective hypothesis are equivocal. Murstein (1963, p. 193) reviewed relevant studies and concluded that low and medium structured stimuli are most sensitive to the direct expression of drive. However, high structured materials may also be useful because they can assess differences in the subjects' avoidance of stories that are strongly suggested by the stimuli. It appears that there is some relationship between stimulus ambiguity and amount of information revealed, but the relationship is not as direct and as simple as many projective test users assume.

Many test users assume that objective techniques, such as personality questionnaires, are susceptible to faking because of the obvious nature of the content. For example, a subject who is trying to appear extremely well adjusted will not answer "true" to an item suggesting the presence of delusions or hallucinations. Projective techniques are thought to be less susceptible to faking because subjects are less likely to know what represents adjusted or maladjusted responses.

There is evidence that early personality inventories, based on face validity, were easily faked (for example, Fosberg, 1941). Subjects could create an impression of greater or lesser psychopathology than actually existed. Even inventories that have less obvious content are susceptible to deliberate distortion (Dahlstrom et al., 1975, pp. 133–135). Meehl and Hathaway (1946) acknowledged the susceptibility of inventories to faking, and they developed several scales of the Minnesota Multiphasic Personality Inventory (MMPI) to detect faking and other deviant test-taking attitudes. Gough (1950) and others showed that the validity scales of the MMPI can effectively identify persons who are trying to create unrealistically negative or positive impressions of themselves.

Fosberg (1938) claimed to have demonstrated that the Rorschach is not susceptible to faking. He administered the test to subjects by using standard instructions and also instructing them to create the best impression and the worst impression possible. According to Fosberg, the Rorschach is not sensitive to such faking because it assesses more permanent aspects of personality. Cronbach (1949), in a critical review of Rorschach studies, pointed out that the statistics used by Fosberg were completely inappropriate, and as a result his conclusions were not justified.

Subsequent research demonstrated that the Rorschach is quite susceptible to faking. When subjects are given instructions to create a very favorable or unfavorable picture of themselves, they are able to do so quite effectively (for example, Carp & Shavzin, 1950; Feldman & Graley, 1954). Similar evidence exists for other projective techniques such as the TAT (Kaplan & Eron, 1965; Weisskopf & Dieppa, 1951), the Rosensweig Picture Frustration Test (Schwartz et al., 1964), and sentence-completion procedures (Meltzoff, 1951).

It would appear that when subjects want to fake responses in order to appear either better or worse than they really are, they can do so. Turnbull (1971) demonstrated that the effectiveness of such faking is related to the subjects' familiarity with the condition they are trying to simulate. Also, normal subjects are more capable of distorting their responses on personality tests than are psychiatric patients. Both objective and projective techniques are susceptible to such distortion. However, most objective techniques include quantitative ways of identifying such distortions, whereas projective techniques do not.

It has been suggested by some projective test advocates that because of the tests' ambiguous nature, subjects tend to be less defensive, and as a result, more unconscious aspects of personality are assessed, whereas objective tests assess more surface or conscious aspects. Because it is impossible to define the term *conscious* operationally, this assumption is untestable. However, when the behavioral correlates for objective and projective tests are examined, there is no obvious distinction along the unconscious-conscious dimension as it has been described theoretically.

In summary, it appears that the assumptions associated with the use of projective versus objective tests have little validity. Thus the distinction between the two types of techniques should not be emphasized. The utility of any assesssment technique, objective or projective, depends on the extent to which it permits accurate understanding of and inferences about individuals. This issue will be addressed in later sections that deal with specific projective and objective tests.

INTERPRETATION OF PERSONALITY TESTS

After the assessment data are collected, the clinician is faced with the task of interpreting the data and generating descriptions, inferences, or hypotheses about individuals. In the assessment of ability, interest, aptitude, and achievement, reasonably standardized approaches to interpretation exist. Such is not the case with most personality tests. Rather, interpretations vary from one user to another. There may be as many different approaches to personaltiy test interpretation as there are personality test users.

In trying to understand the variety of approaches, it might be helpful to think of them as falling along a continuum. One end of the continuum can be labeled *impressionistic* and the other end *empirical* (See Figure 9–2). In the impressionistic approach, the user examines responses or scores and bases interpretations on what makes sense. For example, if a subject tells several TAT stories about a person thinking about suicide, it would make sense to infer that the storyteller might also have suicidal ideas. If a person's Rorschach responses contain much aggressive content (for example, squashed cat or animal ripped apart) it might seem reasonable to attribute significant aggression to that individual. If a person obtains an extremely high score on the schizophrenia scale of the MMPI, a diagno-

FIGURE 9–2 Interpretation of Personality Tests

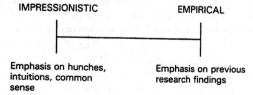

IMPRESSIONISTIC   EMPIRICAL

Emphasis on hunches, intuitions, common sense

Emphasis on previous research findings

sis of schizophrenia could be inferred. It should be noted that in the impressionistic approach, there is little concern about research evidence that might support the validity of the inferences. However, examiners who use this approach may believe that their inferences are justified on the basis of research data. Typically, when asked to present evidence supporting their hypotheses, they make vague references to "past experience."

In the empirical approach to interpretation, the examiner limits inferences, hypotheses, and descriptions to what can be supported by existing research data. A subject's responses or scores have meaning only to the extent that previous research has demonstrated reliable relationships between such responses or scores and the behaviors or characteristics to be predicted or inferred. Recalling our earlier example of the subject who tells TAT stories about a person thinking about attempting suicide, we can illustrate how the empirical approach to interpretation works. Having obtained such stories from a subject, the empirically oriented interpreter would recall (or if necessary consult appropriate books and journals) research that might have been conducted concerning the relationship between TAT stories about suicide attempts and actual attempts by subjects who told such stories. If such research indicates a positive relationship, the interpreter would infer the possibility of suicide attempts for the current subject who tells such stories. If research indicates no relationship or if appropriate research has not been done, the interpreter would refrain from predicting possible suicide attempts for persons who tell such stories, although such a prediction might be quite appealing intuitively. Likewise, prediction about aggression would be inferred on the basis of aggressive content in Rorschach responses only if previous research data support it. Many times no inferences or predictions are made on the basis of some test responses simply because the appropriate data do not exist.

Most clinicians would agree that the empirical approach 'o interpretation is preferable *when adequate research has been done relevant to a particular prediction or inference.* However, persons working in applied settings often find themselves in situations where inferences, predictions, or decisions have to be made and adequate research data do not exist. For example, it is important to be able to predict violent behavior, particularly for persons who previously exhibited such behavior, but little research data exist to guide the practitioner in making such predictions. In such instances practitioners are likely to function on a more subjective or intuitive level. Often their past experience is offered as justification for their inferences.

Theoretically, the approach to test interpretation utilized is independent of the kind of tests employed. Projective tests can be interpreted in either an impressionistic or an empirical manner. Likewise, objective tests also can be interpreted either way. In practice, however, projective tests tend to be interpreted more subjectively or intuitively, whereas objective tests tend to be interpreted more empirically. This difference is due in part to the fact that the scores and profiles of scores yielded by objective tests lend themselves more readily to research studies that underlie the empirical approach. In addition, practitioners of different orientations are attracted to the different tests. Typically, persons with more empirical leanings find the more psychometrically sound objective tests more to their liking, whereas those with less empirical orientations find the less psychometrically developed projective tests more appealing.

PROJECTIVE TECHNIQUES

Dozens, and perhaps even hundreds, of projective techniques have been developed for clinical use. They range from the more traditional and familiar ones, such as the Rorschach inkblot test (Rorschach, 1921) to more recent and unfamiliar ones, such as the Water Association Test (Kataguchi &

Matsuoka, 1979), in which subjects are simply told to draw a picture of water. In this chapter we will discuss in considerable detail several of the more commonly used projective techniques. This should serve as an introduction to readers who will later encounter these tests professionally, and it should also provide a framework for considering and evaluating lesser known techniques that we do not consider in detail.

RORSCHACH INKBLOT TEST

History and Development

The most widely used individually administered personality test is the Rorschach inkblot test. Lubin et al. (1971) found that

FIGURE 9–3 Hermann Rorschach (1884–1922) was a Swiss psychiatrist who first used ink blots to assess personality. (Courtesy National Library of Medicine.)

the Rorschach was used in 90 percent of the clinical settings that they surveyed. The Rorschach also is one of the most thoroughly researched psychological tests. The 360 Rorschach studies published between 1971 and 1978 were second only to the 1,188 MMPI studies published during the same period (Buros, 1978).

Although inkblots previously had been utilized to measure creativity and intelligence, a Swiss psychiatrist, Hermann Rorschach, was the first person to use them systematically to assess personality. Rorschach envisioned his inkblot technique as a clinical tool that would help the clinician understand more completely unconscious factors in personality (Kleinmuntz, 1967).

Rorschach developed a series of ten inkblots that have come to be accepted as standardized stimuli for the technique. The blots are essentially symmetrical, five with various shades of gray, two with gray and red, and three with combinations of pastel colors. An inkblot similar to those used in the Rorschach is presented in Figure 9–4. Rorschach asked patients what each inkblot reminded them of, and apparently he intended to develop a systematic and empirical system for interpreting their responses. Unfortunately, he died in 1922, shortly after publishing his original work on the inkblot technique. Except for the set of ten inkblots, which are the same ones used today, Rorschach left little else to guide those

FIGURE 9–4 Inkblot similar to those used in Rorschach Test.

who would adopt and develop his technique.

As Exner (1969) pointed out, there has been little standardization or consistency among those who developed systems for scoring and interpreting the Rorschach. That is, there is not much agreement about how it should be administered, scored, or interpreted. Major Rorschach systems were developed by Beck (1937), Hertz (1938), Klopfer and Kelly (1942), Piotrowski (1947), and Rappaport et al. (1945, 1956). Although there have been some commonalities in these various systems, there also have been many significant differences.

Exner and Exner (1972) surveyed clinicians who used the Rorschach regularly and found considerable variability in their approaches. About 20 percent did not score the test at all, and about 75 percent of those who did score the test personalized the scoring in some way, usually combining elements of various systems. Exner (1969) compared the various systems and developed a Comprehensive System (Exner, 1974, 1978; Exner and Weiner, 1982) that includes the best elements of each. The reader who is likely to use the Rorschach professionally is encouraged to become familiar with Exner's system, because its attempts at standardization and empirical interpretation represent a major effort toward overcoming some of the shortcomings of the Rorschach technique as it currently is used.

Materials and Administration

The Rorschach technique involves ten standardized inkblots printed on individual cardboard cards. Although there are differences among clinicians concerning how the Rorschach should be administered, it is possible to describe typical procedures utilized by examiners.

Instructions given to subjects purposefully are vague in order not to create an instructional set that might unduly influence them. Typically, subjects are told that they will be shown some inkblots one at a time, and they are to tell the examiner what each one looks like or might be. Any questions or requests by the subject for more structure are handled in a noncommittal way (for example, "It's up to you").

The administration usually involves two parts, free association and inquiry, and sometimes a third part, testing the limits. During the free association, the examiner hands the subject the inkblots one at a time and records the subject's responses verbatim. The examiner also records the time that elapses between presentation of the blot and the first response (reaction time) and the total time that the subject spends responding to the inkblot. The position of the inkblot during each response and any unusual behaviors (such as laughing or nervousness) also are recorded.

After all ten cards have been presented in this manner, the inquiry begins. The subject again is shown each card individually and is asked questions designed to help the examiner determine the way in which the subject arrived at each response. This step usually involves determining to what part of the inkblot the subject was responding and what about the inkblot suggested the particular response. The examiner avoids suggesting explanations to the subject by asking general questions such as "Where on the card did you see the person?" or "What about this inkblot suggested a person to you?" Information obtained in the inquiry is especially essential if the examiner plans to utilize one of the systematic Rorschach scoring systems. Record blanks and location charts containing miniature versions of the ten inkblots are available to facilitate data collection in both the free association and inquiry parts of the administration.

The testing the limits section is optional and typically is used only when the subject failed to give responses commonly obtained to some of the cards. The purpose of this section is to determine if the subject is capable of giving the common response but has chosen instead to give another, perhaps more creative response, or if the subject simply cannot perceive the inkblots in the way most other people do.

The following responses of a subject to an inkblot similar to the one in Figure 9–4 illustrate the procedures for administration:

Reaction time: 1 second
Total time: 14 seconds

Free Association*

Wow—it looks like two birds on a headless, cloaked person—probably—you know—birds of prey on a headless person with his arms thrown up. The birds tore his head off—beheaded him. The way the feathers are fluttered and all, the wings and the head makes two birds attacking. They're huge birds and you can see their legs clamped into or on the person. There's a lot of movement and fluttering.

Inquiry

Examiner: Where on the inkblot did you see the person and the birds?
Subject: It was all of it. The person is in the middle and the birds on each side.
Examiner: What about the inkblot suggested this response to you?
Subject: I don't know for sure—just looks like the shape of a person's body in the middle with their hands up—and these look like wings and feathers fluttering.

Testing the Limits

Examiner: Sometimes people see this inkblot as a bug or winged creature of some kind. Can you see that on this one?
Subject: Sure—looks like a moth or a butterfly—has a small body in the middle and large wings on the sides.

*This free association part of the response is from Maloney, M. P., and Ward, M. P. (1976), *Psychological assessment: A conceptual approach.* Oxford University Press, p. 375. Copyright 1976 by Oxford University Press. Reproduced by permission. The inquiry and testing limits sections have been added by the present authors for illustrative purposes.

Interpretation

After data have been collected, the manner in which they are interpreted varies among clinicians. Some clinicians approach interpretation in subjective, intuitive ways, whereas others tend to rely more heavily on previous research data.

INTUITIVE APPROACHES. Many clinicians do not score Rorschach responses. Rather they examine the subject's responses and make inferences about the subject based on intuition and previous clinical experience. For example, the response of birds attacking and beheading a person would probably lead to inferences that the subject is quite hostile and aggressive or perhaps that the subject feels threatened and vulnerable to attack from the environment. This approach to interpretation usually relies heavily on content and symbolism and also on a belief that subjects reveal important aspects of their own behavior and personality in responding to the unstructured and ambiguous Rorschach task.

Other intuitive approaches seem to assume that the subject's response to the inkblots can be viewed as a miniature of responses in other, more significant areas of life. Thus, the person who gives many responses to small, insignificant areas of the blots to the exclusion of larger, more significant parts is likely to be seen as obsessive-compulsive and preoccupied with trivial details of life to the exclusion of significant life problems. Subjects who give primarily or exclusively common responses are seen as conforming and unwilling to try to be original or creative for fear of failure.

What these various intuitive approaches have in common is that they are not dependent on formal scoring or on research data. Some of the inferences made in this intuitive way could be supported in empirical research literature, but clinicians utilizing the intuitive approach rarely seem concerned about, or knowledgeable of, relevant research data.

SCORING. To some extent it is not correct to refer to Rorschach scoring, since the procedure does not involve determing right or wrong responses and does not result in sophisticated quantification of responses. Rather, it involves designating the part of the inkblot used for a response and determining the subject's reasons for arriving at that particular percept. Although scoring systems typically include frequency counts of categories and ratios and indices based on the counts, scores do not have the psychometric properties associated with those on tests of achievement, aptitude, and so forth.

As discussed earlier, at least five major scoring systems have been developed for the Rorschach. Because Exner's Comprehensive System (Exner, 1974, 1978; Exner & Weiner, 1982) attempts to combine the best features of the other systems, it will be discussed briefly here.

Location is the first and usually the easiest category to be scored for each response. The score represents the area of the inkblot used by the subject in formulating the response. The subject may use the whole blot or may respond only to part of it. The following symbols are used to designate location:

W whole inkblot
D a part of the inkblot commonly used by subjects
Dd a part of the inkblot not commonly used by subjects
S the white space

Most responses can be scored by using these four categories, but occasionally one of three other location categories has to be used. These occur infrequently and generally are thought to reflect serious psychopathology. An example would be a DW response in which the subject attends to a detailed area as justification and then generalizes from this area to the entire blot even though the percept really doesn't fit in with what the entire blot looks like.

Developmental level takes into account the cognitive, integrative quality of the response. Some responses are simple and unorganized whereas others are creative, complex, and integrative. Four categories are available for scoring developmental level for each response:

+ synthesis response integrating separate areas of the blot into a meaningful whole
O ordinary response in which a single area is selected and adequately articulated without gross distortions
V vague response in which no specific form has been articulated and the impression is of a diffuse response
− arbitrary response which is extremely inconsistent with the structural properties of the area of the blot used.

Determinants refer to how the subject used particular features of the blot to construct the response. Exner sees determinants as the most complex and most important category reflecting the perceptual-cognitive processes that the subject uses in organizing stimuli. Exner's system involves the following seven major categories of determinants, and typically subjects combine determinants in a variety of ways:

1. Form. Shape or outline of blot or part of blot is significant reason for response.
2. Movement. Subject attributes movement of any kind (human, animal, inanimate) to percept; can be active ("a man jumping") or passive ("a dog lying down").
3. Color. The red or pastel features of blots are instrumental in a percept.
4. Achromatic color. The black, white, or gray areas are used as colors that are important in arriving at a response.
5. Shading. Subject refers to the light and dark features of the blot as entering into a response.
6. Form dimension. Dimensionality or perspective is based only on form and not on shading.
7. Pairs or reflections. Symmetry of the blot is a deciding factor in producing a response.

Form quality is scored to indicate the goodness of fit between the subject's response and the physical, structural properties of the blot or part of the blot to which the response is given. This rating takes into account the frequency with which responses are given by normal subjects and the examiner's judgment of the quality of the percept and the congruence between the response and the physical characteristics of the blot.

Organizational activity (Z) is scored when the subject integrates two or more areas of the blot into a meaningful relationship.

Content is coded by using twenty-two categories provided by Exner. Examples of content categories are human, animal, blood, X-ray, and so forth.

Popular responses are those frequently given by large numbers of subjects. To be considered popular a response must occur in at least one in three protocols.

Perseveration occurs when the subject persists in the same or very similar responses inappropriately.

Unusual verbalizations include the use of faulty or disorganized language that interferes with clear communication with the examiner (deviant verbalizations), the statement of unrealistic relationships such as "a person with a rabbit's head on" or "a butterfly carrying two rabbits on its wings" (inappropriate combinations), or the use of concrete or circumstantial thinking in justifying an answer ("It must be a man and a woman because they're together and men and women belong together").

Once the subject's responses have all been scored for the categories described, the scoring is summarized on a record form called a Structural Summary Blank. The blank provides space for the scoring of each response and facilitates frequency counts on the various categories and computations of ratios and indices based on these categories. Although these ratios and indices play an important part in Rorschach interpretation, they are too numerous and too complex to discuss in detail here. The interested reader is referred to Exner's work (1974, 1978; Exner & Weiner, 1982) for more detailed discussion.

The reader perhaps can gain a clearer perception of how Exner's system works if we apply it to the sample response reported previously to an inkblot similar to the one in Figure 9–4. Because the response used the entire inkblot, the appropriate scoring category for location is W (whole). Developmental level of the response is categorized as + because the subject integrated separate areas of the blot into a meaningful whole. In the inquiry the subject mentioned shape, so form is scored as a determinant. The clear reference to movement in the response also justifies scoring movement (human, animal, and inanimate) as a determinant. The form quality of the response is reasonably high because the response was well articulated and fits well with the physical properties of the blot. Organizational activity is scored because of the integration of separate parts of the blot (person, birds) into a meaningful whole. Human and animal are both scored as content categories. This is not a popular response because it does not occur in at least one in three protocols. Because only the response to the one card is available, we cannot determine if perseveration would be scored for this subject. Although the content of the response was rather unusual, there is nothing about the manner in which it was given that would justify scoring any unusual verbalizations.

Rorschach scores, ratios, and indices, whether from Exner's system or from some other, can be interpreted intuitively or empirically. Many clinicians rely on the symbolic hypotheses of Klopfer and other early Rorschach systematizers concerning the meanings of location, determinants, and other scoring categories. For example, it often is assumed that above-average use of shading as a determinant is related to exaggerated dependency needs, that absence of color determinants suggests emotional constriction, or that presence of human content is predictive of good interpersonal skills. It should be noted that the interpretive hypotheses were generated intuitively and should not be assumed to be correct.

Other Rorschach interpreters, such as Exner, prefer to base their interpretations on the results of careful research into relationships between Rorschach scores and patterns of scores and actual behavior of individuals outside the testing situation. If previous research demonstrated that subjects with certain kinds of Rorschach scores are more likely than other subjects to have certain characteristics, when a subject produces such scores it is inferred that the subject also will have these nontest characteristics. For example, if research verifies that subjects giving an above-average number of popular responses tend to be rather conventional and unimaginative, the examiner who encounters a Rorschach record having mostly popular responses would infer that the subject producing the responses is likely to be conventional and unimaginative.

PERCEPTUAL OR COGNITIVE STYLES. Maloney and Ward (1976) discussed yet another approach to Rorschach interpretation. Rather than dealing with content, symbolism, or scoring categories, subjects' responses are used as vehicles for observing verbal, perceptual, and cognitive styles. The Rorschach presents the subject with a set of ambiguous stimuli to which responses must be made. The examiner can gain insight into how the subject organizes percepts, the quality of perceptions, the speed of the process, and other aspects of the perceptual process. Likewise, the subjects' responses can provide information about how a subject approaches problems (trial and error versus methodical), motivation (perseverance versus giving up quickly), and the quality of performance (creative, integrated responses versus ordinary and simple ones). If one can assume some consistency of perceptual and cognitive styles from one situation to another, the observations made during the Rorschach administration could permit insight concerning those aspects of the subject's responses in other, more important situations. Although this approach to interpretation is potentially useful, it depends on the examiner having the experience and skill required to make subtle and sometimes complex observations. Additionally, there is little research data concerning the congruence of behavior in the testing situation and in other important aspects of a person's life. Maloney and Ward (1976) illustrated this approach to interpretation of the sample response previously reported. They noted that the subject responded quickly to the stimulus (one second), and yet the resulting percept was well organized and of good form level. The response suggests quick, efficient perceptual functioning with good results, and intelligence can be estimated as average or above. It should be noted that in this approach the examiner resisted the rather strong tendency to infer aggression based on the content of the response.

Evaluation of the Rorschach

As a psychometric instrument the Rorschach leaves much to be desired. Except for using the same ten inkblots there is little standardization of instructions, administration, scoring, or interpretation. Given this lack of standardization it is almost impossible to determine the extent to which Rorschach responses and interpretations of them differ because of differences in personality characteristics of subjects and to what extent such differences can be attributed to other variables. For example, Sachman (cited in Anastasi, 1982) found that Rorschach responses were related to verbal aptitude, age, and educational levels of subjects. There also are data suggesting that subtle behaviors of the examiner, such as a nod of the head, can lead subjects to increase certain kinds of responses (Gross, 1959).

Unlike the tests of general ability that we discussed in earlier chapters, the Rorschach does not have universally accepted normative data. Some normative data have been published for various groups of children, adolescents, and adults (Ames et al., 1971, 1973, 1974; Levitt & Truumaa, 1972). However, it is not clear to what extent these data are applicable in settings other than those in which they were collected. In addition, the impressionistic way in which Rorschach responses typically are interpreted is not based on comparison with established norms.

It is difficult to apply most traditional measures of reliability and validity to the

Rorschach. Although some subjects (and examiners) seem to feel that it is ridiculous to try to assess personality by responses to inkblots, many others attribute face validity to the Rorschach. Psychology and the Rorschach technique have been associated historically, and many subjects expect to be given the inkblot test and may express disappointment if they are not. Split-half reliability cannot be determined for the Rorschach since the equivalence of blots would be difficult, if not impossible, to demonstrate. Test-restest reliability of the Rorschach also is problematic. If the Rorschach assesses personality characteristics, should not responses change to reflect changes in personality? If so, should such change be viewed as unreliability attributable to error variance or as accurate assessment of actual changes in personality? Also, because of the uniqueness of the Rorschach, it is easy for subjects to remember responses given during previous administrations. Should the consistency resulting from this memory factor be viewed as indicative of test reliability? According to McArthur (1972) empirical studies that examined stability of Rorschach performance over time found reliability to be quite variable. Test-retest coefficients ranged from .80 or .90 for some aspects of responses to near zero for others.

The approach that one utilizes in studying Rorschach validity depends on the interpretive strategies involved. For the test to have validity, there should be demonstrable relationships between performance and criterion measures of appropriate behaviors or characteristics. For example, validity of the shading determinant as an indicator of dependency should be demonstrated through significant relationships between the frequency with which shading is used as a determinant and criterion measures of dependency, such as ratings by psychotherapists or others who know the subjects well. Recent reviews of the Rorschach research literature concluded that evidence concerning its validity is overwhelmingly negative (Dana, 1972; Klopfer & Taulbee,

1976; Reznikoff, 1972). Several noteworthy exceptions can be cited. There has been considerable empirical support for Rorschach's hypothesis that human movement responses are related to intelligence and creative ability (Klopfer & Taulbee, 1976). Likewise, the Prognostic Rating Scale (Phillips, 1953), an index based on several Rorschach variables, may permit prediction of change in traditional psychotherapy (Klopfer & Taulbee, 1976).

Reviewers of Rorschach research seem to be in clear agreement that the subjective, intuitive interpretation of responses, often involving symbols, cannot be justified by existing data (Anastasi, 1982; Dana, 1972; Klopfer & Taulbee, 1976). Faced with these overwhelmingly negative results, some Rorschach advocates suggested that the Rorschach is not really a test at all and that applying psychometric standards to it is not fair or appropriate (McArthur, 1972; Rabin, 1972). Various writers suggested that the Rorschach should be viewed as a direct sample of behavior (McArthur, 1972), a clinical technique (Rabin, 1972), or a structured interview (Goldfried et al., 1971). Others suggested that the Rorschach should be viewed as a sample of the subject's cognitive and perceptual processes (Maloney & Ward, 1976). However, as Peterson (1978) pointed out, regardless of how the Rorschach is conceptualized, one must still evaluate the extent to which it results in accurate answers to important questions or predictions about relevant behaviors. Peterson concluded that except for a few isolated areas, existing data do not offer much hope.

In several studies expert Rorschach interpreters have been given responses and asked to describe or make inferences about the personality and behavior of the subjects using whatever interpretive approaches they preferred (Golden, 1964; Kostlan, 1954; Little & Shneidman, 1959; Sines, 1959). Accuracy was determined by comparing the Rorschach interpreters' descriptions with those provided by psychotherapists or those based on extensive case histories. Accuracy of descriptions and inferences was quite low, and in one study in which judges were exposed sequentially to various kinds of data including the Rorschach, descriptive accuracy actually lessened after judges were exposed to Rorschach data (Kostlan, 1954). Also discouraging is the finding that different Rorschach interpreters independently analyzing Rorschach data from the same subject did not agree in their descriptions and inferences (Little & Shneidman, 1959; Kostlan, 1954).

In summary, it can be concluded that the Rorschach is inadequate as a psychometric instrument and that existing research data do not support its continued clinical use. Viewing the Rorschach not as a test but as a behavior sample or a structured interview is an interesting alternative approach, but data concerning the validity of such an approach are lacking. As Peterson (1978) suggested, it is the responsibility of the strong advocates of the Rorschach procedure to provide the validity data on which they base their predictions.

HOLTZMAN INKBLOT TEST

The Holtzman Inkblot Test (HIT) (Holtzman et al., 1961) was developed to overcome some of the psychometric shortcomings of the Rorschach. The HIT consists of two equivalent forms, each containing forty-five inkblots. Some of the blots are symmetrical and some are not; some are achromatic and some are chromatic. As in the Rorschach administration, the subject is asked to respond to the blots one at a time, but only one response is permitted per blot and the inquiry is completed after each card. Responses are scored for twenty-two possible variables. Some of these are similar to Rorschach variables (for example, location, determinants, content), whereas others, such as hostility, anxiety, barrier, and penetration, are unique to the HIT.

Although the HIT is more psychometrically sound than the Rorschach, and early research indicates good reliability (Holtzman et al., 1961) and potential validity and clinical utility (Klopfer & Taulbee, 1976), the technique has not found widespread use among clinicians. This lack of acceptance probably resulted from clinicians' reluctance to try another inkblot test when they are still convinced of the utility of the Rorschach.

THEMATIC APPERCEPTION TEST

The Thematic Apperception Test (TAT) was developed initially by Christiana Morgan and Henry Murray (1935) to assess important constructs in Murray's theory of personality. Subsequently, the TAT has found widespread use in a variety of settings by clinicians with diverse theoretical orientations.

Materials and Administration

The TAT consists of twenty-nine cards containing semiambiguous pictures, most of which include one or more human figures, and one completely blank card. Although the stimuli tend to be less ambiguous physically than the Rorschach inkblots, enough psychological ambiguity exists so that different interpretations of the situations depicted are possible. Figure 9–6 presents a picture similar to those included in the TAT.

In the TAT manual Murray (1943) suggested a complex and time-consuming procedure for administration involving two sets of ten cards each administered on two different days with different instructions. In current practice most clinicians select approximately ten of the thirty cards and administer them on one occasion. Although there are some variations in procedure among clinicians, the examiner typically introduces the TAT as a test of imagination and instructs subjects to make up a story about each picture. Subjects are asked to include what is happening in the picture, what led up to the situation, how the people in

FIGURE 9–5 Henry Murray (1893–) is an American psychologist who collaborated with Christiana Morgan in developing the Thematic Apperception Test. (Courtesy of Harvard University News Office)

FIGURE 9–6 Picture similar to those used in the TAT. (McClelland et al., 1976. Copyright 1976 by Irvington Publishers, Inc. Reproduced with permission.)

years, and is an intelligent boy. He entered the classroom with his fellows and is now listening to the teacher. He is trying to understand the subject which is new to him. The teacher also is trying his best to make the student understand. The student will understand the subject and will go out of the class happy about his success in grasping it. He will be a success in life.*

The primary task for the examiner is to record the stories verbatim as they are told. Sometimes examiners ask subjects to write their own stories. Although there is no formal research concerning the effects of written versus oral responses on the TAT, clinical experience suggests that written stories tend to be more formal and controlled and less spontaneous than oral ones (Stein, 1978). In addition, written administration precludes potentially important observation of the subject by the examiner.

Interpretation of TAT Stories

As is the case with Rorschach, there is no single standardized procedure for interpreting TAT stories. Interpretive strategies

the picture feel, and how things will turn out. If the subject fails to include any of the elements in a story, the examiner reminds the subject after the spontaneous response is completed. When the blank card is administered, the subject is told to imagine a picture and then to tell a story about it. The following story was told by a subject in response to the picture in Figure 9–6:

A student in a classroom is listening to a teacher explain the contents of a book which lies before the student. He is very interested in the subject. He has passed through all preceding school

*McClelland et al., 1976, p. 100. Copyright 1976 by Irvington Publishers, Inc.

range from intuitive and subjective approaches to more quantitative and empirical ones.

NEED-ORIENTED INTERPRETATION. Murray's original approach involved identifying the hero in the story and then specifying the needs, press, outcome, and thema expressed by the hero. The *hero* is the person in the story with whom the subject seems to be identifying, and it is not necessarily the character in the picture most similar to the subject in age, sex, or other personal characteristics. *Needs* are forces emanating from the hero. They are the things that the hero wants, anticipates, or is willing to work for. Among Murray's list of twenty-eight needs are aggression, affiliation, autonomy, and dependency. *Press* are forces emanating from the environment and are the hero's perceptions of the extent to which the environment facilitates or impedes satisfaction of needs. Murray's press include environmental characteristics such as rejection, association, physical injury, loss, and dominance. Needs and each press are assigned values on a scale from one to five to express their importance in the story. *Outcome* is judged as optimistic or pessimistic depending on the consequences for the hero. *Thema* are combinations of the hero's needs, environmental forces, and outcome of the story. In Murray's interpretive approach it is assumed that the hero's needs and perceptions of the environment will reflect those characteristics of the subject. Emphasis is placed on needs, press, and thema that recur in several or more stories told by a subject.

In the story told about the picture in Figure 9-6 the hero obviously is the boy in the plaid shirt. The primary need expressed by the hero is achievement because the boy clearly is interested in learning and excelling as a student. The press is quite positive and is classified as nurturance because the boy sees his teacher as trying to help him attain his goals. The outcome is optimistic because the boy will be happy and will be a success in life. The thema could be summarized as a need for achievement, a supportive environment, and an optimistic outcome.

QUANTITATIVE SCORING. Perhaps the best example of a more quantitative approach to TAT interpretation is the work of McClelland and his colleagues (1976). McClelland found Murray's constructs useful, but he was not satisfied with the subjective way in which Murray suggested they be assessed. Initially, McClelland and his colleagues developed a quantitative system for scoring the achievement need in TAT stories, but subsequently similar systems also were developed for other needs such as affiliation and power (Veroff et al., 1974).

McClelland provided detailed procedures for scoring the achievement need, and there is evidence that the scoring system can be applied reliably (Feld & Smith, 1958). In using the McClelland system each story first is classified into one of three categories. If the story includes no reference to achievement at all, it is classified as unrelated imagery (UI) and a score of −1 is assigned. If a story includes some reference to achievement, but achievement is not central to the story, it is classified as doubtful achievement (TI) and a score of zero is assigned. When achievement is central to the story, the classification is achievement imagery (AI) and a score of +1 is assigned. If the story is classified as either UI or TI, no additional analysis is done. However, if the classification is AI, a set of ten additional criteria is applied to the story and one additional point is assigned for each criterion that is met. For example, additional points are given if the hero states directly a desire to achieve something, if the hero is doing something to attain the achievement goal, and so forth. Thus, each story can receive a score ranging from −1 to +11, higher scores suggesting greater achievement need. A total score for need for achievement is obtained by summing scores from all the stories. In McClelland's original research, four pictures were used, only two of which were originally in the TAT: men working on a machine, a boy at a desk with a book (Figure 9–6), a father and a son, and a boy who seems to be daydreaming.

When McClelland's system is applied to the story told about the picture in Figure 9–6, the story is classified as AI and a score of +1 is assigned because achievement is a central part of the story. When the additional criteria are applied to the story, four more points are assigned. Additional points are given because the hero actually is doing something about attaining an achievement goal, because he is experiencing positive emotional affect associated with attaining an achievement goal, because someone in the story (the teacher) is helping him to attain the achievement goal, and because the entire story revolves around an achievement situation. Thus, this subject's achievement need score for this story is +5.

TAT AS BEHAVIOR SAMPLE. Some clinicians (for example, Maloney & Ward, 1976) suggested that TAT interpretation is the most useful when the stories are treated as verbal productions and are analyzed in terms of stylistic variables such as word usage, flow of speech, quality and appropriateness of syntax, and similar language-related characteristics. The stories also can offer insight into subjects' creativity, defensiveness, conformity, and related attributes. Little emphasis is placed on the actual content of the stories, and it is not necessary to assume that the needs, perceptions, and conflicts of the hero in the story actually are those of the subject. Rather, the TAT is used to produce a behavioral sample that can offer important information about the subject's style of performing and interacting. Unfortunately, this approach to TAT interpretation is dependent on the observational and inferential skills of the examiner, and novice TAT users may not gain much useful information from it.

If we treat the story told about the picture in Figure 9–6 as a behavior sample, several potentially important observations can be made. The story about a boy trying to master schoolwork is one that often is told

about this picture, and all aspects of the story are appropriate given the stimulus properties of the picture. Although the story is not an especially creative one, it is elaborated to an above-average extent. The description of motives and feelings in the story suggests that the subject is not being especially defensive and is trying to fulfill the expectations of the examiner. The vocabulary and grammar are suggestive of a reasonably well-educated person and someone who is probably of above-average intelligence.

Evaluation of the TAT

Since its inception the TAT has been the subject of numerous investigations. Most reviewers of the resulting TAT research seem to agree with Dana (1972), who concluded that the studies do not form a cohesive body of knowledge about the TAT or its application to personality evaluation, and with Swartz (1978), who concluded that TAT results are complicated, not easy to interpret, and equivocal at best. Swartz added that "one has to wonder about the usefulness of an instrument that yields such mixed results after 40 years of investigation" (p. 1,130).

As with other projective techniques, there has been little standardization of TAT administration, scoring, or interpretation. Almost no one adheres to the complex and time-consuming instructions presented in the test manual (Murray, 1943), and routine utilization of any of the numerous TAT scoring systems is noticeably absent in applied settings. It seems that the TAT has remained a popular clinical assessment tool not because of demonstrated reliability or validity but because of its compatability with the emphasis on human needs in contemporary psychology.

RELIABILITY. Because of the lack of standardization and absence of one or more generally accepted scores, traditional measures of reliability are difficult to apply. The differences in stimulus properties among the TAT cards lead to generally low coefficients of internal consistency for scores reflecting Murray's needs (Murstein, 1963). Interrater or interscorer reliability varies considerably depending on the scoring system used and the training of the raters. Tomkins (1947) reported interrater reliability coefficients as high as .95 for objective scoring systems and well-trained raters.

Test-retest reliability was reported for scores reflecting Murray's categories of need and press (Tomkins, 1947). The coefficients ranged from .80 for a two-month retest interval to .50 for a ten-month interval. These coefficients may be spuriously high because subjects often recall and repeat during the second administration stories that were told during the first. Lindzey and Herman (1955) tried to take this memory variable into account by asking subjects not to repeat stories given during the first administration of the TAT when they were tested again two months later. These investigators reported an average test-retest coefficient of .51 under these conditions.

Although the reliability coefficients reported for TAT scores are similar to those found for other projective test measures, it must be remembered that most clinicians do not utilize any formal scoring system when they employ the TAT in practice. Perhaps more relevant to the way the TAT is used in applied settings are studies that compared the inferences or interpretations of different clinicians based on the same sets of TAT responses. As part of a more comprehensive study of personality assessment procedures, Little and Shneidman (1959) asked twelve expert TAT interpreters to examine TAT responses of twelve subjects and to assign a diagnosis to each, to rate the overall degree of maladjustment for each subject, to describe each subject by using a Q-sort procedure, and to complete a large number of true-false descriptive items about each subject. They found that for all judgments based on TAT data, considerable variability existed among judges examining the same data. Further, the reliability of judgments based on TAT responses was considerably lower than for other instruments included in the study (Rorschach, MMPI, Make-a-Picture Story Test).

VALIDITY. Studies that have compared TAT responses or inferences based on those responses with external, nontest measures at best provide only limited evidence that the TAT is a valid assessment procedure. Murstein (1963, 1965) reported that although TAT data may permit gross diagnostic distinctions (schizophrenia versus neurosis versus character disorder), in general the TAT has little utility in specific issues of diagnosis. This conclusion was supported by the results of the Little and Shneidman (1959) study that found limited accuracy of diagnosis from TAT responses.

A large number of studies have reported significant differences in TAT responses for various criterion groups (Adcock, 1965). For example, parents of schizophrenic and normal children gave significantly different TAT responses as did women with good versus poor emotional adjustment following childbirth. These kinds of studies are difficult to evaluate because of uncontrolled differences between criterion groups and because of lack of standardization in the way the responese were scored and interpreted.

Weiner (1976) concluded that there is little doubt that the TAT reflects a wide variety of need states such as achievement, affiliation, power, and sex. However, the relationship between TAT measures of these needs and real life behavioral measures is complex. Relationships between the two kinds of measures generally are positive but of such limited magnitude that prediction of behavior in individual cases is not likely to be accurate.

In the study by Little and Shneidman (1959) that was described earlier, the accuracy of TAT-based judgments and descriptions was determined by comparing them with similar judgments based on extensive anamnestic (social history) data. It was found that accuracy of judgments based on the TAT was not different from accuracy of judgments based on the Rorschach, MMPI, or Make-a-Picture Story Test. However, the accuracy levels for all instruments, including the TAT, were quite low and offered little support for the validity of TAT interpretations.

Although there is evidence to suggest some modest relationship between TAT responses and nontest behaviors, most research suggests that variables other than personality characteristics of subjects significantly influence TAT responses. Especially important are the stimulus properties of the TAT pictures (Murstein, 1963). The stories that subjects tell are determined primarily by the characteristics of the pictures. Any interpretation of TAT stories must take into account the kinds of stories typically told by subjects to the various pictures. For example, one of the TAT cards portrays a young man standing with his head buried in his arms. Behind him is the figure of a woman lying in bed. Holt (1978) examined typical responses to this picture and found that most subjects see the woman as dead for one reason or another (childbirth, illness, murder, suicide, and so on) and the man as feeling guilt. To infer that a subject who tells a story about the woman dying has an abnormal degree of hostility toward women would be quite inappropriate given the typical response to the card. In fact, more interpretive significance should probably be attributed to stories that do not include a description of the woman as dead. In summary, the stimulus properties of the TAT pictures are such that they tend to elicit or "pull" certain kinds of stories from subjects. Any meaningful interpretation must take into account this tendency. Holt (1978) published an excellent summary of normative responses to the various TAT cards.

There is also evidence that variables such as the sex or social status of the subject, perceived status of the examiner, and instructions or time limits all influence responses to the TAT pictures (Weiner, 1976). Additionally, situational variables such as hunger, frustration, and mood influence responses (Stein, 1978). Any approach to interpretation that does not take into account the numerous factors that influence story production is too simplistic and cannot be expected to yield accurate inferences or predictions.

TAT-LIKE TECHNIQUES

Because of the great popularity of the story construction technique among clinicians, numerous tests similar to the TAT have been developed. In the Make-a-Picture Story Test (MAPS) (Shneidman, 1949), the subject selects some from a set of numerous cutout characters, arranges the characters on background cards, and then tells stories about the scenes that have been created.

Based on the assumption that it is easier for children to identify with animals than with humans, Bellak and Bellak (1949) devised the Children's Apperception Test (CAT). The CAT has ten pictures of animals in human situations designed to tap important psychoanalytic circumstances including feeding, toileting, aggression, and attitudes toward parents and siblings. A supplementary CAT (CAT-S) involves an additional ten pictures designed to deal with more transitory problems associated with play, school, physical illness, and so forth. Although the CAT authors claim some advantages for their test over the TAT, subsequent research has indicated that children identify as well, and perhaps even better, with human as with animal figures (Bills, 1950; Budoff, 1963; Furuya, 1957). Thus, another version of the CAT was developed with human characters (CAT-H).

Thompson (1949) hypothesized that TAT cards involving black characters would elicit greater fantasy material from black subjects than would the standard TAT cards. Initial data indicated that his modified cards elicited longer stories from black subjects, but subsequent research failed to demonstrate any advantage of the Thompson modification for black or white subjects (Cook, 1953; Korchin et al., 1950; Light, 1954; Riess et al., 1950).

Other attempts to modify the stimulus pictures to make them more similar to adolescent subjects (Symonds, 1948) or to elderly subjects (Wolk & Wolk, 1971) also did not result in differing levels of identification or fantasy production (Pasewark et al., 1976). Although there does not seem to be any clear evidence that modifications of TAT pictures produce greater identification or more fantasy production than the standard pictures, the modifications may still serve a purpose inasmuch as subjects may attribute greater validity (face validity) to the techniques and might feel more comfortable in responding to them. It should be noted that all these modifications are based on the same assumptions as the standard TAT and that the interpretive strategies used with them are basically the same as those used with the TAT. However, there has been much less research conducted with these modifications than with the standard TAT.

DRAWINGS

Many psychologists believe that analysis of drawings and other expressive productions (paintings, sculpture, and so on) permits accurate inferences about a subject's personality characteristics and adjustment level. There is not a single drawing test; rather, subjects may be asked to draw persons of each sex (Machover, 1949); their families doing something (Kwiatkowska, 1967); a house, a tree, and a person (Buck, 1948); or other things. Drawings are commonly used in conducting personality assessments (Lubin et al., 1971). The drawing technique is popular because it is easy and efficient to administer and because most subjects, particularly children, become readily involved in the task. Further, to many persons, examiners as well as subjects, the technique has considerable face validity. On the surface, it seems reasonable that people might reveal important personal characteristics in their drawings.

Because she presented detailed interpretive information for her technique, Machover's Draw-a-Person Test (DAP) (1949) is the most popular drawing technique among clinicians. In the DAP the subject is given a blank piece of paper and is told to draw a person. After the first drawing is completed the subject is told to draw another person, this time of the sex opposite of the first figure drawn. After both figures are drawn the subject is asked to tell something about the personal characteristics of each figure.

Unlike the Draw-a-Man Test (Goodenough, 1926; Harris, 1963), where a quantitative score is derived from the drawings to serve as an estimate of intellectual functioning, interpretation of the DAP is entirely intuitive and is based on Machover's hypotheses concerning the relationship between structural (size, placement on page, and so on) and content (for example, body detail or clothing) aspects of drawings and personality. It should be noted that Machover's hypotheses were based on her clinical experience rather than on any research findings.

Several examples of Machover's hypotheses will give the reader an idea of how the interpretation is conducted. Machover stated that the head is the center of intellectual power, social balance, and control of body impulses. A disproportionately large or small head indicates difficulties in one of these areas of psychic functioning. Persons who are suspicious and therefore interested in maintaining close contact with the outside world were thought to draw exaggerated eyes. In drawings by males it was hypothesized that massive shoulders emphasized at the expense of other parts of the figure tend to be drawn by adolescents and sexually ambivalent individuals as an overcompensation for feelings of body inadequacy.

Numerous studies have been conducted in an attempt to evaluate hypotheses concerning the relationship between drawing characteristics and attributes of test subjects. Several comprehensive reviews of this research literature (Robak, 1968; Swensen, 1957, 1968) concluded that there is little or no support for most of the hypotheses. Some hypotheses have not been tested adequately, but those that have undergone careful testing have not been supported.

Clearly, significant relationships do not exist between specific drawing characteristics and nontest personality characteristics. However, research has demonstrated a positive relationship between judged overall quality of drawings and gross level of psychological adjustment (Lewinsohn, 1965; Robak, 1968; Swensen, 1957, 1958). There is not sufficient evidence to determine if the relationship is strong enough to permit prediction of adjustment for individual subjects, but it is very doubtful that such prediction would be possible.

In summary, the DAP and other drawing techniques often are used to assess personality characteristics. Their appeal seems to be their ease and efficiency of administration and their face validity. However, existing research does not support their use for making inferences or predictions about personality characteristics or adjustment levels for individual subjects.

INCOMPLETE SENTENCES BLANK

In the sentence-completion technique, subjects are given a list of sentence stems, ususally printed, and are asked to complete

FIGURE 9–7 Julian Rotter (1916–) is an American psychologist who collaborated with Janet Rafferty in constructing the Incomplete Sentences Blank. (Courtesy Julian Rotter)

each sentence, usually in writing, in a way that reflects how they think, feel, or act. Sentence-completion procedures were used in the late 1800s and early 1900s in the study of intellectual ability. Payne (1928), Tendler (1930), and Cameron (1938) were among the first to use the technique for assessing personality. During World War II the sentence-completion method was used widely in a variety of settings, and its popularity in clinical settings continued after the war ended. The ease with which sets of sentence stems can be generated led to the development of many different sentence-completion instruments. Probably the best known and most widely used is the Incomplete Sentences Blank (ISB) (Rotter & Rafferty, 1950).

Materials and Administration

The ISB consists of forty printed sentence stems that are presented to a subject with instructions to complete each sentence in writing to express "your real feelings." The following stems are similar to those included in the ISB:

I believe . . .
Friends . . .
My life . . .
Parents . . .

Although the ISB is available in three forms (high school, college, adult), the test manual, scoring procedures, and normative data are available only for the college form. The three forms are essentially equivalent with some minor modifications to make items more appropriate for each age group.

Rotter and Rafferty (1950) stated in the ISB manual that the instrument was developed to serve as an objective way of screening for emotional disturbance and to provide information to the clinician that could permit more advantageous structuring of early interviews with clients or patients. They acknowledged that the ISB was not developed to describe "whole personality" and that it probably does not provide the clinician with information that cannot be obtained in a lengthy interview. Rather, the brevity and efficiency of the instrument make it a useful way to gain initial information about subjects. Rotter and Rafferty also acknowledged that the ISB responses tend to provide information that the subject is *willing to give* rather than that which the subject cannot help giving.

Interpretation

Two approaches to ISB interpretation were suggested by its authors. The manual presents a quantitative scoring system that can be applied to responses to indicate general adjustment level. In addition, a suggested strategy for qualitative, clinical interpretation is discussed.

SCORING. The ISB scoring system assigns a value ranging from zero to six to each item to yield an overall adjustment score. Responses indicating an unhealthy or maladjusted frame of mind (conflict responses) receive the highest scores. Responses indicating a healthy or hopeful frame of mind (positive responses) receive the lowest scores. Neutral responses, ones that are simply descriptive in nature or avoid the purpose of the test, are given intermediate scores. The following sample responses should help the reader better understand how the scoring systems works:

I believe . . . that life is not worth living. (6)

I believe . . . that most people are smarter than me. (5)

I believe . . . that I am failing my math class. (4)

I believe . . . for every drop of rain that falls a flower grows. (3)

I believe . . . that Joe is a very good friend. (2)

I believe . . . that I get along with almost everyone. (1)

I believe . . . that the future will be great. (0)

Higher scores obviously are suggestive of greater maladjustment. By referring to definitions, examples, and sample protocols in the test manual, users quickly can master the scoring system and reliably score the items. A subject's conflict score is compared with norms presented in the manual, and percentile equivalents can be determined.

The clinical analysis of ISB responses is qualitative and subjective in nature and is intended to help the clinician arrive at an early understanding and structuring of cases. Although Rotter and Rafferty indicated that many different approaches to clinical interpretation are possible, they illustrated an approach that included analysis of familial attitudes, social and sexual attitudes, general attitudes, and character traits.

Evaluation

RELIABILITY. Interscorer reliability coefficients for two trained scorers have ranged from .88 to .96 (Lah & Rotter, 1981; Rotter & Rafferty, 1950). When scores for a trained scorer were compared with scores generated by a clinical psychologist whose only knowledge of the ISB was based on a careful reading of the manual, a coefficient of .90 was obtained (Rotter & Rafferty, 1950). Data such as these suggest that the ISB scoring system leads to reliable scores. When the items were divided into halves and deemed as nearly equivalent as possible, corrected split-half reliability coefficients of .84 and .83 were obtained for records of 124 male and 71 female college students, respectively. No test-retest reliability data were reported for the ISB scores.

NORMATIVE DATA. The ISB manual presents distributions of scores for 85 female and 214 male college students at Ohio State University. From these distributions percentile equivalents for ISB raw scores can be determined. It should be noted that similar normative data have not been presented for high school or adult samples. More recent data suggested that these original norms are outdated and that new norms are needed (Lah & Rotter, 1981).

VALIDITY. In the ISB manual, data are presented for several different groups of adjusted and maladjusted college students.

One comparison involved 82 female and 124 male college students rated by their instructors as adjusted or maladjusted. Although the scores of the adjusted and maladjusted groups had some overlap, a cutting score of 135 correctly identified 78 percent of the adjusted females, 89 percent of the adjusted males, 59 percent of the maladjusted females, and 52 percent of the maladjusted males. A second comparison involved ten college students who were judged by graduate student clinicians as "definitely adjusted or maladjusted." Although the sample size in this comparison was quite small, there was no overlap of ISB scores for the two groups of subjects. Rotter and Rafferty also presented data indicating that relatively high ISB scores were obtained by 46 males who were referred to a psychological clinic for personal therapy. Data such as these suggest that ISB scores can be helpful in screening for overall maladjustment. However, the optimal cutoff score may vary and should be established in each setting where the ISB is to be used.

Goldberg (1965, 1968) presented summaries of research conducted with the ISB and other sentence-completion instruments. He cited studies indicating that ISB scores correlated significantly with criterion measures of overall adjustment, achievement, anxiety, aggression, dependency, and other personality characteristics. Goldberg concluded that there is impressive validity data to support the use of the ISB in clinical practice. However, it should be noted that these validity data were based on formal scoring of the ISB. In clinical practice almost no such scoring occurs.

SOME OTHER PROJECTIVE TECHNIQUES

The approach in this chapter has been to discuss in considerable detail several projective techniques that are widely used and for which adequate research data exist to permit some conclusions about utility. We recognize that many other projective techniques currently are being used in applied settings, and some of these other techniques will now be described briefly.

The Rosenzweig Picture Frustration Test (Rosenzweig, 1945) involves a series of cartoon pictures in which one person is doing something to frustrate another person. The subject fills in a blank space to indicate how the frustrated person probably would respond. Responses can be scored to yield indices of type and direction of aggression expressed by the frustrated person (and therefore by the subject as well). This test is related closely to Rosenzweig's theoretical notions about frustration and aggression and does not seem to be suitable for assessing the wide variety of behaviors in which clinicians typically are interested.

Animal Crackers (Adkins & Ballif, 1975) is a technique designed to assess achievement motivation in children. Subjects are told that they have their own animals that like things and do things that the subject likes and does. The examiner presents pairs of physically identical animals, describes different behaviors for each one, and asks subjects to indicate which one is theirs. Virtually no validity data are available for this technique, and its major use to date has been as a research tool.

The Blacky Pictures (Blum, 1950) were designed to assess stages of psychosexual development. Stimuli are drawings of a dog named Blacky and its family. Subjects are asked to make up a story about each picture, to answer some multiple-choice questions about the pictures, and to indicate which cards are liked and disliked. Although its author has developed complex scoring systems for this instrument (Blum, 1950, 1962), there is little published evidence concerning its utility. Certainly, it has found virtually no acceptance except among clinicians with strong psychoanalytical orientations.

Although the Bender Visual Motor Gestalt Test (Bender, 1946) initially was developed to assess visual-motor coordination, some clinicians use it also as a projective technique for assessing personality. The test requires subjects to reproduce a series of nine geometric designs. Inferences about personality and behavior are based on qualitative features of the drawing such as relative size, placement on the page, and so forth. Lanyon and Goodstein (1971) concluded that research data have not supported the use of the Bender-Gestalt technique in the assessment of personality.

The Hand Test (Wagner, 1962) is a technique in which subjects are presented line drawings of human hands in various ambiguous poses and are asked to tell what each hand is doing. Responses are scored for variables such as affection, tension, and aggression, and indices are calculated from these scores. Wagner (1978) reported that thirty-five of the forty Hand Test validity studies that he examined yielded positive findings. However, he added that he personally was involved in thirty of the forty studies, and he recommended more independent verification of the test's validity.

GENERAL CONCLUSIONS ABOUT PROJECTIVE TECHNIQUES

Although projective techniques continue to find widespread use among clinicians, the existing research indicates that most of them, and especially the more popular ones, are psychometrically unsound. The lack of standardization of administration, scoring, and interpretation makes it difficult to determine to what extent the responses reflect important personality characteristics and to what extent they are influenced by other factors, such as the examiner's characteristics or situational variables. The literature is especially clear in indicating that the subjective, qualitative, and symbolic approaches to interpretation typically used with these techniques cannot be justified.

It has been suggested by some that projective techniques really are not tests at all and that traditional psychometric criteria should not be used in evaluating them. Rather, they should be viewed as clinical tools, structured interviews, or samples of verbal, cognitive, and perceptual functioning. Perhaps projective techniques should be viewed in these alternate ways, but such conceptualizations do not negate the importance of demonstrating through empirical research that they are useful when so used. Currently, there is not sufficient evidence to justify the routine use of projective techniques in either more traditional or more innovative ways. Responsibility for providing such evidence rests with those who advocate their continued clinical use.

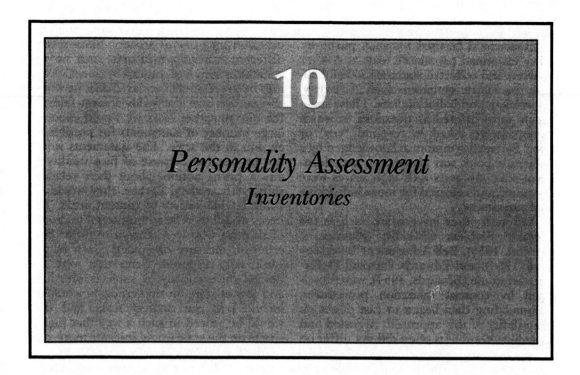

10
Personality Assessment
Inventories

In Chapter 9 we defined objective techniques for assessing personality as those involving clear, unambiguous stimuli and a structured response format. Although techniques such as Q-sort, semantic differential, adjective checklist, and rating scales qualify as objective techniques, the most widely used are personality questionnaires or inventories. These instruments present statements or questions and require specific responses, usually of a true-or-false or yes-or-no variety.

STRATEGIES FOR INVENTORY CONSTRUCTION

Content Validation

Several different strategies have been used in constructing personality inventories. Many early inventories resulted from content validation procedures. In this approach the test constructor decides what is to be measured (for example, anxiety, introversion, ego strength, general maladjustment) and selects items for inclusion in the inventory because they seem on some a priori or logical grounds to measure the relevant constructs or characteristics. For example, suppose that we want to develop a scale to measure anxiety. The content validation approach would involve writing or selecting from existing sources, such as textbooks or clinical reports, items that seem to be related to anxiety. We might choose items such as "I often feel nervous and shaky" or "It is difficult for me to keep my mind on what I am doing." We do not require evidence that persons who respond in the affirmative are more anxious than those who respond negatively. Rather, we are satisfied that the items seem to be related to anxiety.

An example of an inventory constructed by this procedure is the Woodworth Personal Data Sheet (Woodworth, 1920). As large numbers of men were being inducted into military service during World War I, the need for an efficient method of screening for emotional fitness became obvious. Robert Woodworth, an experimental psychologist, and some of his colleagues agreed to try to develop a paper-and-pencil test that could be used for such purposes. They examined psychiatric texts and other sources, and collected statements that dealt with psychiatric symptoms such as anxiety, depression, and hallucinations. These statements were printed as questions to which subjects were asked to respond "yes" or "no." For each symptom acknowledged by a subject, a point was given on a maladjustment scale. Subjects with high scores were identified and referred for more individualized assessment.

Although other inventories, such as the Mooney Problem Checklist (Mooney & Gordon, 1950), Bell Adjustment Inventory (Bell, 1934), and Edwards Personal Preference Schedule (Edwards, 1954), were developed by content validation procedures, accumulating data began to cast doubt on the validity of this approach. Adjusted and maladjusted subjects often did not differ on scales constructed in this manner, and in some instances the adjusted subjects answered items in the maladjusted direction more often than maladjusted subjects did. Another problem that became apparent was that these inventories were easily faked. Because the content of items was obvious, subjects easily could make themselves appear to be more adjusted or more maladjusted than they really were. Although this approach fell into disrepute for many years, it has regained some respectability in recent years through the work of Jackson (1970) and Hase and Goldberg (1967). This more recent use of content validation procedures will be discussed later in this chapter.

Criterion (Empirical) Keying

In the criterion or empirical keying approach the test constructor also decides what is to be measured. However, instead of on an intuitive basis, items are selected on the basis of observed relationships between item endorsements and external criterion measures. If we were to develop an anxiety scale using criterion keying procedures, the first step would be to select some acceptable criterion measure of anxiety. Since several different criterion measures such as galvanic skin response, ratings by peers, or ratings by professionals are available, we would choose the one that seemed most relevant for our purpose. Next we would choose a large number of statements for possible inclusion in the scale. The statements would not be selected because of face validity or any a priori notions about their relationships with anxiety. Rather, they would include a wide variety of content areas. The items would then be administered to groups of subjects who were known to differ on a criterion measure of anxiety, such as galvanic skin response. Items that were endorsed differentially by subjects with high and low anxiety on that criterion would be included in our anxiety scale, and they would be scored in such a way that higher scores on the scale would indicate more anxiety. What is important to note in this procedure is that items are not selected on the basis of face validity; they are selected because subjects who differ on the criterion measure endorse the items differentially.

The first substantial use of the criterion approach was made by Strong (1927) in the development of the Strong Vocational Interest Blank. He developed scales for various occupational groups by comparing item responses of persons in a particular occupational group with responses given by people in general. For example, responses of a group of lawyers were analyzed to determine on which items they differed from a group of men in general. A high score on the resulting scale indicated that a subject had interests similar to lawyers and therefore would be more likely to enjoy law as a career than would people with lower scores.

Although several early personality inventories, such as the Bernreuter Personality Inventory (Bernreuter, 1931) and the Humm-Wadsworth Temperament Scale (Humm & Wadsworth, 1935), utilized the criterion keying approach, the development of the Minnesota Multiphasic Personality

Inventory (MMPI) by Hathaway and McKinley (1940) represented the most notable use of this procedure. Hathaway and McKinley were aware of the problems that had been associated with the content validation approach, and they wanted to develop a paper-and-pencil test to be used in psychiatric diagnosis that would overcome these problems. They used psychiatric diagnosis as a criterion measure, and they identified items for inclusion in the MMPI scales that were endorsed differentially by members of a particular psychiatric group, such as depression or paranoia, and by groups of normal subjects and groups of other psychiatric patients. It was assumed that subjects who obtained high scores on a scale such as depression should receive a psychiatric diagnosis corresponding to that scale (that is, depression). Development of the MMPI scales will be discussed in more detail later in this chapter.

Factor-Analytic Approaches

In the factor-analytic approach to inventory construction the test constructor does not begin with any preconceptions about what particular traits or characteristics are to be measured. A large pool of items from a variety of content areas is assembled. The items are administered to a large number of subjects, and the responses of these subjects are intercorrelated. The resulting intercorrelations are factor analyzed to identify clusters or groups of items that seem to be related to each other but are independent of other groups of items. The content of items included in a cluster is examined, and a label is given to the cluster based on this content. What is being measured by an inventory constructed in this manner is only determined after the inventory has been constructed and it can be decided how many different sets of items are present in the inventory and what each set of items seems to be measuring. It is important to note that in this procedure, as in content validation, external criterion measures typically are not

involved. Although items are grouped together according to factor-analytic procedures, the determination of what each set of items is measuring is made intuitively.

One of the earliest inventories to use this approach was the Guilford-Zimmerman Temperament Survey (Guilford & Zimmerman, 1949). This inventory was developed by intercorrelating responses to items from many existing inventories. The resulting test included 300 items, 30 items representing each of 10 different traits. Among the traits assessed were restraint, sociability, objectivity, and personal relations.

The most widely used inventory constructed according to factor-analytic procedures is the Sixteen Personality Factor Questionnaire (16 PF) developed by R. B. Cattell (1949). Cattell identified more than 4,000 adjectives that he believed described various personality characteristics. He was then able to derive a set of 171 adjectives that he judged to be relatively independent of each other. Close acquaintances of subjects rated them on each of these adjectives, and through a series of factor analyses of these ratings Cattell developed sixteen scales that he concluded measured the relevant dimensions of personality.

Among his scales were Reserved vs. Outgoing, Expedient vs. Conscientious, Trusting vs. Suspicious, and Group-dependent vs. Self-sufficient. The 16 PF will be discussed in greater detail later in this chapter.

Sequential Strategy

Jackson's (1970) sequential strategy for inventory construction uses a combination of content validation, internal consistency, and criterion keying. The first step in sequential strategy is to decide what theoretical constructs are to be measured. Next, clear concise definitions are generated for the constructs. A pool of items to measure each construct is generated intuitively by referring to the definitions. Tentative scales are constructed from these intuitively generated items. The scales are administered to subjects and are refined by internal consistency procedures. Finally, the resulting scales are validated by comparing scores on the scales with appropriate external criterion measures.

Jackson (1974) used the sequential strategy in constructing the Personality Research Form (PRF). Murray's need system (Morgan & Murray, 1935) was selected as the theoretical basis for the inventory. Definitions were written for each of Murray's twenty needs (for example, achievement, affiliation, autonomy), and items were written for each need by examining the definitions. The resulting scales were refined by comparing item responses with total scale scores and with a measure of social desirability. The refined scales were then compared with scales from other inventories and with criterion peer ratings of relevant behaviors. The PRF will be discussed in more detail later in this chapter.

FREQUENTLY USED PERSONALITY INVENTORIES

In deciding which inventories to consider in detail two primary criteria were utilized: frequency of use in applied settings and adequate research data. Table 10–1 summarizes data concerning applied use (Lubin et al., 1971) and research references (Buros, 1978) for some of the more popular personality inventories. Because the Minnesota Multiphasic Personal Inventory (MMPI), Edwards Personal Preference Schedule (EPPS), California Psychological Inventory (CPI), and Sixteen Personality Factor Questionnaire (16 PF) are commonly used and widely researched, they were selected for detailed consideration. In addition, the Personality Research Form (PRF) will be included. Although the PRF was not among the ten most frequently used inventories, it illustrated the sequential strategy of inven-

TABLE 10-1 Frequency of clinical use and number of research references for personality inventories

Inventory	Frequency of Clinical Use (Rank Order)[a]	Number of Research References (1971–1978)[b]
Minnesota Multiphasic Personality Inventory	1	1,118
Edwards Personal Preference Schedule	2	334
California Psychological Inventory	3	452
Mooney Problem Check List	4	48
Sixteen Personality Factor Questionnaire	5	619
IPAT Anxiety Scale Questionnaire	6	85
Guilford-Zimmerman Temperament Survey	7	72
Bell Adjustment Inventory	8	c
Interpersonal Check List	9	c
California Test of Personality	10	67

[a]Source: Lubin et al., (1971); 1 = most frequent.
[b]Source: Buros (1978).
[c]No data concerning number of research references were presented in Buros (1978) because the cumulative total (1936–1978) was less than 100.

tory construction and has been used in considerable research recently.

MINNESOTA MULTIPHASIC PERSONALITY INVENTORY

Rationale and Development

The Minnesota Multiphasic Personality Inventory was developed in the late 1930s and early 1940s and was published in 1943 (Hathaway & McKinley, 1967). Hathaway and McKinley were working at the University of Minnesota Hospitals where assessments of psychiatric patients typically involved individual interviews or mental status examinations and administration of individual projective and intellectual tests. They hoped that the MMPI would be a more efficient, and perhaps more reliable, way of assigning psychiatric diagnostic labels.

Because they were aware of the problems associated with earlier inventories constructed according to content validation procedures, Hathaway and McKinley utilized a criterion keying approach in constructing the MMPI (Hathaway & McKinley, 1940). They assembled a large pool of self-reference statements from textbooks, psychological reports, and other sources. From this pool, 504 statements were judged to be relatively nonambiguous and independent of each other. The following statements are similar to the ones included in the MMPI:

FIGURE 10–A Starke Hathaway (1903–) is an American psychologist who collaborated with a psychiatrist, J. Charnley McKinley, in constructing the Minnesota Multiphasic Personality Inventory. (Courtesy News Service, University of Minnesota)

I have trouble going to sleep at night.
Other people don't seem to like me.
I can't keep my mind on what I'm doing.
I feel unhappy most of the time.

Next, appropriate criterion groups were identified. Normal subjects included visitors to the hospitals, recent high school graduates attending precollege conferences, and other persons without histories of psychiatric problems. Clinical subjects were psychiatric patients who had received diagnoses of hypochondriasis, depression, hysteria, psychopathic deviate, paranoia, psychasthenia, schizophrenia, or hypomania. The 504 statements were administered to all normal and clinical subjects. The items were analyzed to identify statements that discriminated between a particular criterion group and all other diagnostic groups combined. These statements were selected for a scale for that clinical group, and higher scores indicated that more items were endorsed as the subjects in that clinical group had endorsed them. The scale was then cross-validated by comparing scores on the scale for new groups of normal subjects, clinical subjects belonging to the particular clinical group for which the scale was being constructed, and subjects from other clinical groups combined. These procedures were repeated for each of the eight clinical groups represented, and the result was a set of eight clinical scales for the MMPI.

Later, two additional scales were added, and they also have come to be considered standard clinical scales. The Masculinity-femininity (Mf) scale was designed to identify homosexual male subjects. Because few items were found that differentiated between homosexual and heterosexual males, items also were included in the Mf scale if they were answered differently by normal male and female subjects. In addition, forty-six items from a previously published masculinity-femininity interest scale were added to the MMPI item pool and were included in the Mf scale. The Social Introversion (Si) scale was developed by Drake (1946). He contrasted the responses of college women who were more involved in extracurricular activities with those who were less involved.

Because Hathaway and McKinley were aware that earlier inventories were susceptible to faking, they developed four validity indicators to detect faking and other deviant test-taking attitudes (for example, not reading items or answering all or most items either true or false). The first of these, the Cannot Say (?) scale, is simply the number of omitted items in the inventory. Obviously, large numbers of omitted items tend to produce lower scores on the clinical scales and to limit the interpretability of those scores. The L scale was constructed rationally to detect attempts to present oneself in an unrealistically positive way by claiming many virtuous characteristics and denying even minor flaws. Subjects receive points on the L scale by claiming that their manners are as good when at home as when out in company, that they never get mad, that they

read every editorial in the newspapers every day, and that they engage in other similar behaviors.

The F scale is made up of items very infrequently endorsed in the scored direction by normal subjects. High F scale scores suggest deviant responses and may indicate that subjects have not read the items, that they are trying to appear to be very disturbed emotionally, or that they have approached the test with some other deviant attitudes.

The K scale was developed to assess clinical defensiveness in subjects. K scale items are ones that normal and defensive clinical subjects answered differently, and higher scores are reflective of greater defensiveness. The K scale score for a subject also is used as a correction factor for some of the clinical scales. Because defensive subjects tend to obtain artificially lower scores on clinical scales, scores are adjusted upward to reflect the defensiveness. The appropriate correction for each clinical scale was determined empirically by comparing the ability of scores on each clinical scale to discriminate between subjects in the appropriate diagnostic group and other subjects when various proportions of their K scale scores were added to their raw scores on the clinical scales. The K correction, if any, for each clinical scale is indicated at the bottom of the sample MMPI profile sheet in Figure 10–1.

Through these procedures, 14 scales were developed from the MMPI item pool. Four of them assess test-taking attitudes, eight were based on diagnostic categories, and two assess other aspects of personality and behavior. Since the MMPI was published, over 500 additional scales have been developed from the item pool, but the 14 scales described here provide the data base for most MMPI interpretations. Table 10–2 lists these MMPI scales and presents several characteristics associated with high and low scores on each scale.

Materials, Administration, Scoring

The MMPI is easy to administer and score. Subjects are presented with self-

TABLE 10-2 Sample interpretive inferences for standard Minnesota Multiphasic Personality Inventory scales

Scale Name	Scale Abbreviation	Scale No.	Interpretation of High Scores	Interpretation of Low Scores
—	L	—	Trying to create favorable impression by not being honest in responding to items; conventional; rigid; moralistic; lacks insight	Responded frankly to items; confident; perceptive; self-reliant; cynical
—	F	—	May indicate invalid profile; severe pathology; moody; restless; dissatisfied	Socially conforming; free of disabling psychopathology; may be "faking good"
—	K	—	May indicate invalid profile; defensive; inhibited; intolerant; lacks insight	May indicate invalid profile; exaggerates problems; self-critical; dissatisfied; conforming; lacks insight; cynical
Hypochondriasis	Hs	1	Excessive bodily concern; somatic symptoms; narcissistic; pessimistic; demanding; critical; long-standing problems	Free of somatic preoccupation; optimistic; sensitive; insightful
Depression	D	2	Depressed; pessimistic; irritable; dissatisfied; lacks self-confidence; introverted; overcontrolled	Free of psychological turmoil; optimistic; energetic; competitive; impulsive; undercontrolled; exhibitionistic
Hysteria	Hy	3	Physical symptoms of functional origin; lacks insight; self-centered; socially involved; demands attention and affection	Constricted; conventional; narrow interests; limited social participation; untrusting; hard to get to know; realistic
Psychopathic Deviate	Pd	4	Asocial or antisocial; rebellious; impulsive; poor judgment; immature; creates good first impression; superficial relationships; aggressive; free of psychological turmoil	Conventional; conforming; accepts authority; low drive level; concerned about status and security; persistent; moralistic
Masculinity-femininity	Mf	5	Male: aesthetic interests; insecure in masculine role; creative; good judgment; sensitive; passive; dependent; good self-control Female: rejects traditional female role; masculine interests; assertive; competitive; self-confident; logical; unemotional	Male: overemphasizes strength and physical prowess; adventurous; narrow interests; inflexible; contented; lacks insight Female: accepts traditional female role; passive; yielding to males; complaining; critical; constricted
Paranoia	Pa	6	May exhibit frankly psychotic behavior; suspicious; sensitive; resentful; projects; rationalizes; moralistic; rigid	May have frankly psychotic symptoms; evasive; defensive; guarded; secretive; withdrawn
Psychasthenia	Pt	7	Anxious; worried; difficulties in concentrating; ruminative; obsessive; compulsive; insecure; lacks self-confidence; organized; persistent; problems in decision making	Free of disabling fears and anxieties; self-confident; responsible; adaptable; values success and status

TABLE 10-2 (Continued)

Scale Name	Scale Abbreviation	Scale No.	Interpretation of High Scores	Interpretation of Low Scores
Schizophrenia	Sc	8	May have thinking disturbance; withdrawn; self-doubts; feels alienated and unaccepted; vague goals	Friendly, sensitive, trustful; avoids deep emotional involvement; conventional; unimaginative
Hypomania	Ma	9	Excessive activity; impulsive; lacks direction; unrealistic self-appraisal; low frustration tolerance; friendly; manipulative; episodes of depression	Low energy level; apathetic; responsible; conventional; lacks self-confidence; overcontrolled
Social Introversion	Si	0	Socially introverted; shy; sensitive; overcontrolled; conforming; problems in decision making	Socially extroverted; friendly; active; competitive; impulsive; self-indulgent

Graham, J. R. (1978), The Minnesota Multiphasic Personality Inventory (MMPI). In B. B. Wolman (Ed.), *Clinical diagnosis of mental disorders: A handbook.* New York: Plenum Press. Copyright 1978 by Plenum Press. Reproduced by permission.

reference statements and are asked to indicate whether each statement is true or false as applied to them. Although subjects are permitted to omit items that deal with things they do not know about, they are encouraged to try to respond to most of the items. In the test manual (Hathaway & McKinley, 1967) it is suggested that the MMPI is appropriate for subjects sixteen years old or older who have at least a sixth-grade reading level. However, younger subjects and those with lower reading levels can complete the test if they are supervised carefully (Graham, 1977).

Originally the MMPI items were printed on individual cards, and subjects were instructed to sort the cards into three categories—true, false, and cannot say. The examiner then recorded the responses on an answer sheet. Currently the 566 MMPI items* are printed in reusable booklets, and subjects mark their responses on separate answer sheets. The answer sheets can be scored by hand with templates or by computer. There also is a tape-recorded version, and the test has been translated into numerous languages (for example, Spanish, Ger-

man, Chinese, and Japanese). There is no time limit for completing the test, and testing time varies considerably among subjects. Most subjects who are not seriously maladjusted complete the test in fewer than ninety minutes.

Regardless of the form used or the scoring method chosen, each subject's MMPI protocol yields raw scores on the four validity and ten clinical scales.* After the appropriate K correction, if any, has been added to each raw score, scores are plotted on a profile sheet in such a way that they are converted to T-scores. This conversion permits direct comparison among scales. The standardization samples used for the T-score conversions are the same normal subjects used in constructing the scales, and there are separate norms available for males and females. Thus, the theoretically normal or average person would have T-scores of approximately fifty on all of the scales. Scores above fifty suggest responses more similar to the clinical subjects used in developing the scales. Because there are significant differences in scores for nor-

*There are only 550 unique items in the MMPI. In order to facilitate early machine scoring, 16 items appeared twice.

*The MMPI item pool has been used to develop numerous additional scales for special purposes, such as identification of substance abusers. Readers interested in learning more about these additional scales should consult Dahlstrom, et al. (1975) or Graham (1977).

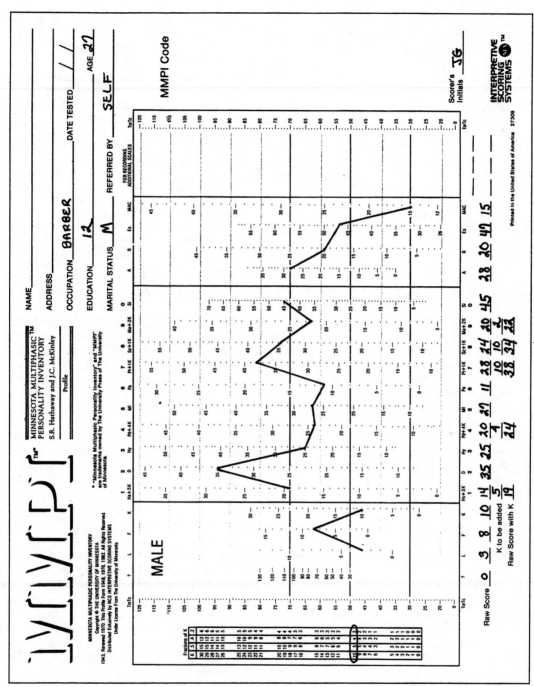

FIGURE 10–1 Sample MMPI profile. (Data from Graham (1977). Copyright 1977 by Oxford University Press, Inc. Reproduced with permission. Profile sheet copyright 1948, 1976, 1982 by University of Minnesota. Reproduced with permission.)

239

mal adult and normal adolescent subjects, special adolescent norms are available for subjects younger than eighteen (Marks et al., 1974). Figure 10–1 presents a sample MMPI profile.

Interpretation

Soon after the original MMPI scales were developed it became apparent that there were no direct, simple relationships between scores and diagnoses of patients. Patients scoring high on a clinical scale often did not fit into the diagnostic category corresponding to that scale. Further, it was noted that nonclinical subjects often obtained high scores on one or more of the clinical scales. However, it was learned that consideration of the pattern of scores on the MMPI scales often permitted accurate inferences about test subjects. Although the MMPI clinical scales were not simply measures of the symptom syndromes on which they were based, subsequent studies revealed numerous significant relationships between MMPI scores and patterns of scores and important nontest behaviors and characteristics. When subjects obtain certain scores on the MMPI scales, the inference is made that they are likely to have characteristics similar to other persons who have scored similarly on the scales. It should be emphasized that inferences about subjects are not based on the labels of the scales but on previous empirical research concerning what the scales measure. To avoid attributing excess meaning because of the names of the clinical scales, many MMPI users refer to the scales by number (see Table 10–2).

To be able to interpret MMPIs accurately, users must familiarize themselves with the many empirical studies that have been conducted. To facilitate this process, several excellent summaries and syntheses of the interpretive data are available (for example, Dahlstrom et al., 1972; Duckworth, 1979; Good & Bratner, 1961; Graham, 1977). These sources present interpretive information for high scores and low scores on the MMPI scales and for configurations of high scores. Table 10–2 gives some

sample interpretive information for the MMPI validity and clinical scales.

Graham (1977) suggested that interpretation of MMPI scores should focus on trying to answer the following questions:

1. What was the test-taking attitude of the examinee and how should this attitude be taken into account in interpreting the scores?
2. What is the general level of adjustment of the person who produced the MMPI scores?
3. What kinds of behaviors (symptoms, attitudes, defenses, and so on) can be inferred about or expected from the person who produced the scores?
4. What circumstances or conditions underlie the person's behaviors?
5. What are the most appropriate diagnostic labels for the person who produced the scores?
6. What are the implications for treatment of the person who produced the scores?

In order to illustrate MMPI interpretation, we will develop some interpretive inferences about the MMPI profile in Figure 10–1.* These inferences represent how a clinical psychologist might use the MMPI in understanding a patient. The subject (JAK) is a twenty-seven-year-old, white, married barber who came to an outpatient clinic complaining of depression, irritability, moodiness, lack of self-confidence, and difficulty in making decisions. He dated the onset of his problems to five years earlier when he was discharged from military service and felt on his own for the first time in his life. His father and mother were both dead. Although they did not show much affection toward him as a child, neither did they make demands on him. JAK expressed some ambivalence about being a barber, and he talked about getting a job as a photographer. He had been married for a little over a year, and his wife was pregnant with their first child. He was pleased with the prospect of being a father, but he also was afraid of the increased responsibility.

*This sample interpretation is based on material previously published by Graham (1977). Copyright 1977 by Oxford University Press. Reproduced with permission.

JAK finished the MMPI in an average amount of time (1½ hours), indicating that he was neither excessively indecisive nor impulsive in responding to the items. He omitted no items, suggesting that he was cooperative and did not use this rather simple way of avoiding unfavorable self-references. His L scale was about average, indicating that he was not particularly defensive, an inference supported by a reasonably low score on the K scale. The F scale T-score of 62 suggests that he was admitting to some deviant attitudes and behaviors, but it was not high enough to suggest an invalid approach to the test. In general, it seems that JAK approached the test in an honest, open manner, and there is no reason to believe that the test is not a representative sample of his behavior.

JAK's scores on the clinical scales are elevated, suggesting moderate to severe psychopathology and somewhat serious problems in functioning in everyday activities. High scores on scales 2 and 7 indicate that he is in considerable emotional turmoil. JAK has T-scores greater than 70 on scales 2, 7, 8, and 0. Reference to appropriate research data concerning high scorers on these scales produces inferences that JAK feels anxious, depressed, and overwhelmed by his problems. Although he continues to meet his daily responsibilities, he does so at a reduced level of efficiency. Most of the time JAK is likely to be rather unemotional and unexcitable, but he also has episodes of unexplainable excitement and restlessness. He is very pessimistic about life, and he may have concluded that life is no longer worthwhile. He may have had periods during which he was unaware of what he was doing, and these episodes, coupled with obsessive thoughts, may cause him to fear that he is losing his mind. JAK has strong needs to achieve and to excel, but feelings of insecurity and inadequacy keep him from involving himself in directly competitive situations. He views the environment as threatening and nonsupportive, and often he feels like he is at the mercy of forces beyond his control. He usually reacts to stress and problems by denying their existence, and when this mechanism fails, he feels overwhelmed and his behavior may become disorganized and maladaptive.

JAK has long-standing feelings of inadequacy, and he is especially likely to feel uncomfortable around women. He harbors doubts about his own masculinity, and he views women as sources of gratification for his strong dependency needs. JAK typically inhibits direct expression of negative feelings, but passive, indirect expressions of aggression are to be expected. He has the capacity for forming deep emotional ties, but fear of rejection and exploitation keeps him from getting too involved with other people.

The most appropriate diagnostic label for JAK is either depressive neurosis or anxiety neurosis. Because he is so emotionally uncomfortable, he is likely to be receptive to psychotherapy, although initially he may rationalize and intellectualize excessively in treatment. However, he is likely to remain in therapy, and slow but steady progress can be expected.

Evaluation

STANDARDIZATION AND NORMS. Unlike the projective techniques discussed in Chapter 9, the MMPI is well standardized in terms of materials, administration, and scoring. The same normative data have been used since its publication. Although some critics suggested that the norms are outdated and not generalizable (for example, Anastasi, 1982), current research indicates that they are remarkably good given the rather unsophisticated way in which they were collected (Colligan et al., 1982). Although there are variations in the ways in which scores are interpreted, most users base interpretations on the sizable research literature that has accumulated since the MMPI's publication.

RELIABILITY. Temporal stability data for MMPI scores have been reported for several different normal and clinical populations and for varying test-retest intervals. In summarizing these reliability data, Graham

(1977) reported that for both normal and psychiatric samples, the typical test-retest coefficients for short intervals (one day to two weeks) range from .70 to .85, and that for considerably longer intervals (one year or more), the typical coefficients range from .35 to .45. Data reviewed by Graham suggest that configurations of MMPI scores are not as reliable as they often are assumed to be. For example, only about 40 to 60 percent of subjects will have the same highest clinical scale on two separate administrations of the test, and only 20 to 40 percent will have the same two highest clinical scales on two administrations. In summary, the temporal stability of MMPI scores over short periods of time compares favorably with other personality scales. The extent to which the instability that is found should be attributed to error variance and the extent to which it reflects actual changes in the behaviors being assessed have not yet been determined.

Data concerning internal consistency of MMPI scales have been summarized by Dahlstrom et al. (1975). Although specific internal consistency values vary considerably (−.05 to .96), typical values for college students range from .60 to .90, and they seem to be only somewhat lower for psychiatric patients. Factor analyses of items within each MMPI scale indicate that most of the scales are complex and not unidimensional (Comrey, 1957a, b, c; Comrey, 1958 a, b, c, d, e; Comrey & Margraff, 1958; Graham et al., 1971).

VALIDITY. Since the MMPI was published in 1943, voluminous additional research concerning its validity has been reported. Dahlstrom et al. (1975) cited over 6,000 studies involving the MMPI. In trying to reach some conclusions about its validity from these studies, it seems helpful to group them into three general categories.

The first category involves studies that compared MMPI profiles of relevant criterion groups. Most of these studies have identified significant differences on one or more of the MMPI scales among groups formed on the basis of diagnosis, severity of disturbance, treatment regimes, and many other criteria. Average or typical profiles for many of these criterion groups were published by Lanyon (1968). Efforts to develop classification rules to discriminate among groups (for example, neurotic versus psychotic) also are included in this first category (Goldberg, 1965; Henrichs, 1964; Meehl & Dahlstrom, 1960; Peterson, 1954; Taulbee & Sisson, 1957).

A second category of validity studies includes attempts to identify reliable nontest correlates of scores on MMPI scales and configurations of MMPI scores. Nontest correlates of high or low scores on individual clinical scales were identified for adolescents (Hathaway & Monachesi, 1963; Marks et al., 1974), normal college students (Black, 1953; Graham & McCord, 1982), student nurses (Hovey, 1953), normal adults (Hathaway & Meehl, 1952), normal Air Force officers (Block & Bailey, 1955; Gough et al., 1955), medical patients (Guthrie, 1949), and college counselees (Mello & Guthrie, 1958). Correlates for configurations of two or more MMPI scales were reported for normal adults (Hathaway & Meehl, 1952), normal college students (Black, 1953), medical patients (Guthrie, 1949), and psychiatric patients (Boerger et al., 1973; Gilberstadt & Duker, 1965; Gynther et al., 1973; Lewandowski & Graham, 1972; Marks et al., 1974; Meehl, 1951). The results of these numerous studies were summarized and synthesized by Graham (1977), Dahlstrom et al. (1972), and others, providing MMPI users with meaningful interpretive data for persons obtaining particular scores and configurations of scores on the MMPI.

A third category of MMPI studies considers the MMPI and the person who interprets it as an integral unit and examines the accuracy of inferences based on the MMPI. The Little and Shneidman (1959) study, discussed in an earlier chapter, illustrates the methodology used. The reader will remember that Little and Shneidman asked expert interpreters to provide diagnoses, ratings, and descriptions of subjects from test data (MMPI, Rorschach, TAT, MAPS). The accuracy of judgments was determined by comparing them with criterion judgments based on extensive case histories. In summarizing the research of which the Little and Shneidman study is a part, Goldberg (1968) concluded that clinical judgments tend to be unreliable and low in absolute validity. In spite of this rather pessimistic conclusion, some positive results also can be cited. Compared with the Rorschach and other projective techniques, personality descriptions based on the MMPI are relatively more accurate (Kostlan, 1954; Little & Shneidman, 1959). Also, descriptions based on the MMPI are more accurate than descriptions based on base rate information (Graham, 1967). When MMPI data are used in conjunction with social history and/or interview data, the resulting descriptions are more valid than when the MMPI data are used alone (Kostlan, 1954; Sines, 1959).

CONCLUSIONS. Although the many differences in subjects, settings, criterion measures, methodologies, and statistical analyses make it difficult, if not impossible, to reach precise conclusions about the MMPI's validity, we believe the existing data indicates considerable clinical utility. Other recent reviews seem to reach similar conclusions. Alker (1978) concluded that the MMPI can provide reliable indications of psychological treatments that will or will not work for specific patients. King (1978) concluded his MMPI review by stating that " . . . the MMPI remains matchless as the objective instrument for the assessment of psychopathology . . . and still holds the place as the *sine qua non* in the psychologist's armamentarium of psychometric aids" (p. 938).

CALIFORNIA PSYCHOLOGICAL INVENTORY

Rationale and Development

Although the California Psychological Inventory (CPI) (Gough, 1975) also was constructed primarily by empirical keying procedures, it differs from the MMPI because it was designed primarily for normal subjects. Whereas the original MMPI scales emphasized psychiatric symptomatology, the CPI emphasizes interpersonal behavior and social interactions. Gough intended the CPI to measure "folk constructs," which he defined as attributes of interpersonal behavior found in all cultures and societies. Because of this emphasis, he believed that the CPI would be useful in predicting an individual's behavior in a wide variety of contexts and situations.

The CPI item pool consists of 480 statements to which true-or-false responses are made. Approximately half the items are from the MMPI; the rest, written specifically for the CPI, are similar in content to the MMPI items. Several different strategies were used in constructing the CPI scales. Most scales resulted from an empirical or criterion keying procedure in which items were selected for inclusion if they were endorsed differentially by groups of subjects known to differ on relevant criterion measures. For example, the Dominance (Do) scale resulted from a comparison of responses by subjects identified as high or low in dominance according to peer nomination. Four of the CPI scales were developed rationally or intuitively to access flexibility, social poise, emotional control, and self-worth. A final scale, Communality (Cm), was developed statistically and consists of items to which 95 percent or more of respondents answered in one direction. Table 10–3 lists each of the eighteen CPI scales, describes what the scale was intended to measure, and summarizes the construction procedures used.

Three CPI scales, Sense of Well-being (Wb), Good Impression (Gi), and Communality (Cm), are primarily validity scales. Subjects with extremely high scores on the Wb scale could be minimizing or denying problems unrealistically, whereas extremely low scorers could be trying to make themselves appear more maladjusted than they really are. Extremely high scores on the Gi scale also suggest that subjects are minimizing problems and denying existing psychopathology, but the meaning of extremely low scores on this scale is unclear. Very low

TABLE 10-3 Summary of California Psychological Inventory Scales

Scale	Purpose*	Construction Procedures
1. Dominance (Do)	To assess factors of leadership ability, dominance, persistence, and social initiative	Empirical; peer nominations of dominance among fraternity and sorority members
2. Capacity for Status (Cs)	To identify individual's capacity for status (not actual or achieved status)	Empirical; scores of high school seniors on objective measure of socioeconomic status
3. Sociability (Sy)	To identify persons of outgoing, sociable, participative temperament	Empirical; number of extracurricular activities of high school seniors
4. Social Presence (Sp)	To assess factors such as poise, spontaneity, and self-confidence in personal and social interaction	Rational
5. Self-acceptance (Sa)	To assess factors such as sense of personal worth, self-acceptance, and capacity for independent thinking and action	Rational
6. Sense of Well-being (Wb)	To identify persons who minimize their worries and complaints and who are relatively free of self-doubts and disillusionment	Empirical; comparison of neurotic patients and normal subjects trying to feign neurosis
7. Responsibility (Re)	To identify persons of conscientious, responsible, and dependable disposition and temperament	Empirical; peer nominations of fraternity members; teachers' and principals' ratings of junior high school and high school students
8. Socialization (So)	To indicate the degree of social maturity, integrity, and rectitude which the individual has attained	Empirical; delinquent vs. nondelinquent adolescents
9. Self-control (Sc)	To assess the degree and adequacy of self-regulation and self-control and freedom from impulsivity and self-centeredness	Rational
10. Tolerance (To)	To identify persons with permissive, accepting, and nonjudgmental social beliefs and attitudes	Empirical; scores on the California Ethnocentrism and Authoritarianism scales
11. Good Impression (Gi)	To identify persons capable of creating a favorable impression and who are concerned about how others react to them	Empirical; comparison of responses under standard and "fake good" instructions
12. Communality (Cm)	To indicate the degree to which an individual's reactions and responses correspond to the modal pattern established for the inventory	Statistical; includes items endorsed 95 percent or more of the time in one direction
13. Achievement via Conformance (Ac)	To identify factors of interest and motivation which facilitate achievement in any setting where conformance is a positive behavior	Empirical; academic achievement of high school students
14. Achievement via Independence (Ai)	To identify those factors of interest and motivation which facilitate achievement in any setting where autonomy and independence are positive behaviors	Empirical; grades of college students enrolled in psychology courses
15. Intellectual Efficiency (Ie)	To indicate the degree of personal and intellectual efficiency which the person has attained	Empirical; correlations of items with scores on intelligence tests
16. Psychological-mindedness (Py)	To measure the degree to which the individual is interested in and responsive to the inner needs, motives, and experiences of others	Empirical; comparisons of responses of psychologists and nonpsychologists

TABLE 10-3 *(Continued)*

Scale	Purpose*	Construction Procedures
17. Flexibility (Fx)	To indicate the degree of flexibility and adaptability of a person's thinking and social behavior	Rational
18. Femininity (Fe)	To assess the masculinity or femininity of interests	Empirical; comparison of male and female responses; comparison of homosexual and heterosexual males

*Reproduced by special permission of the publisher, Consulting Psychologists Press, Inc., from the California Psychological Inventory Manual by Harrison Gough, Copyright 1957, 1975.

scores on the Cm scale indicate that subjects are endorsing many items in the statistically deviant (infrequent) direction, indicating that they may have responded to the items randomly or in some other unacceptable way. Although these three validity scales seem to have great potential for identifying invalid protocols, only limited research has been conducted to determine how well the scales actually work for this purpose.

Materials, Administration, Scoring

The CPI consists of 480 statements printed in a reusable booklet. Subjects are instructed to respond true or false to each statement on separate answer sheets. Gough (1975) suggested that testing time usually is between forty-five minutes to one hour. The CPI can be used successfully with subjects ranging from early teens to late seventies or older. Although the manual does not state the reading level required to complete the CPI, it probably is approximately the same as for the MMPI (sixth grade).

After the CPI has been administered, raw scores are obtained for eighteen scales. Hand-scoring templates are available, and if special answer sheets are used, computer scoring also is possible. Raw scores are transformed to T-scores and are plotted on a profile sheet similar to that used with the MMPI (Figure 10–2). In contrast to the MMPI, higher scores on CPI scales are intended to reflect more positive attributes. The T-scale transformations are based on data from 6,200 normal males and 7,150 normal females. Although Gough claims that these standardization samples include a

wide range of ages, socioeconomic groups, and geographical areas, no specific data concerning these characteristics are provided in the test manual.

On the profile sheet, scales are grouped into four intuitive or logical classes. Class I scales (Do, Cs, Sy, Sp, Sa, Wb) share a common emphasis on feelings of interpersonal adequacy. Class II scales (Re, So, Sc, To, Gi, Cm) emphasize character and are concerned with the acceptance or rejection of social norms and values. Class III scales (Ac, Ai, Ie) are grouped together because of their relations to academic and intellectual variables. Class IV includes other scales (Py, Fx, Fe) that have little relationship with each other.

Interpretation

The T-scores on the eighteen CPI scales provide the data base from which interpretations are made. Average scores are those that fall at about 50 on the profile, with scores above 50 considered as high and those below 50 are considered low. Gough (1975) suggests a systematic approach to CPI interpretation. Interestingly, he does not suggest that a first step in interpretation should be to examine the Wb, Gi, and Cm scales to consider the possibility of random responding or some other deviant test-taking attitude that could invalidate the results. Extremely high or low scores on these scales should raise the possibility of invalidity and suggest caution in further interpretation of results. If the profile is judged to be valid, Gough's step-by-step approach to interpretation can be followed.

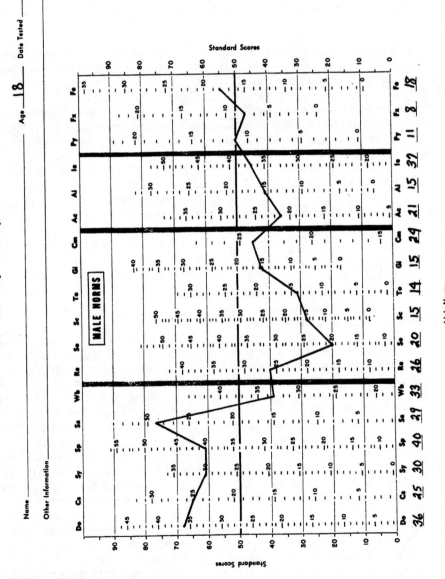

FIGURE 10–2 Sample CPI profile. (Reproduced by special permission of the publisher, Consulting Psychologists Press, Inc., from the California Psychological Inventory Manual by Harrison Gough, Copyright 1957, 1975.)

Step 1 involves noting overall profile elevation. If most scores are above the mean (T = 50), it is likely that the subject is functioning effectively both socially and intellectually. If most scores are below the mean, it is likely that the subject has significant difficulties in interpersonal adjustment. In step 2 differential elevations of the four classes of scales are noted. For example, a subject with high Class I scores and low Class III scores is thought to be a person whose social skills are highly developed but whose intellectual skills and academic drives are weaker. Step 3 involves examining high and low scores on the individual scales and referring to a table in the test manual that presents behavioral descriptors for high and low scores on each scale. Gough does not define precisely how high or how low scores must be in order to be considered "high" or "low." However, he does suggest that the adjectives associated with more extreme high or low scores are more likely to characterize such subjects than is the case for more moderate scores. He claims that the adjectives presented for each scale are based on empirical research, but as we shall see, the research underlying scale descriptors is not very impressive. Although Gough's step 4 involves studying unique features of a profile, he does not give enough information about this aspect of interpretation to be helpful to most CPI users. Step 5 involves consideration of the internal variability of the profile, which includes determining a mean score for each subject that could be different from the standardization sample mean of 50. Gough suggests that considering scale deviations from this "personal mean" can lead to greater accuracy of prediction of behavioral characteristics. In this final stage, any specialized purpose for testing should be considered. He offers the example that T-scores of 60 on Sy and Sp would probably not be high enough to predict success in sales engineering even though such scores are well above the standardization sample mean of 50.

Gough's interpretive strategy was illustrated in the test manual for the profile in Figure 10–2. The interpretation of this profile, which was produced by an eighteen-year-old male, was as follows:

This profile is marked by a general elevation on those scales having to do with poise, ascendancy, and self-assurance, and a general lowering of those indicative of socialization, maturity, and sense of responsibility. These trends are highlighted by the elevation on the self-acceptance scale and the low point on the measure of socialization. In order to arrive at an interpretation beyond what is already suggested by the listing of high and low scales, the descriptive words and phrases for each scale should be consulted.

From a reading of these interpretational guides, a picture of this boy can be evolved. Our expectation is that he would be assertive, socially forward, probably self-centered and overbearing, rebellious, impulsive, undependable, and overconcerned with personal gain and pleasure. Because of his very considerable social skills he might function adequately, in the sense of attaining his own ends and objectives; yet, his deficiencies in the area of responsibility and interpersonal maturity seem almost certainly to destine him for social friction and difficulty.*

In addition, it could be noted that none of the validity scales in this profile is high or low enough to suggest profile invalidity. Gough added that this boy was one of the three in his class of over 400 high school students who was identified by the principal as a serious disciplinary problem.

Evaluation

STANDARDIZATION AND NORMS. As is the case with most objective techniques, the CPI is well standardized in terms of test materials, administration, and scoring. As stated earlier, the standardization samples were quite large, and efforts were made to include persons of varying ages, socioeconomic levels, and geographical areas. Separate norms are provided for males and

*Reproduced by special permission of the publisher, Consulting Psychologists Press, Inc., from the California Psychological Inventory Manual by Harrison Gough, Copyright 1957, 1975.

females. In addition, the test manual presents means and standard deviations for nineteen different samples, including psychiatric patients, prison inmates, juvenile delinquents, and members of several different occupational groups.

RELIABILITY. Megargee (1972) summarized test-retest reliability data for the various CPI scales. Short-term (one to four weeks) stability coefficients ranged from .71 to .89 (average: .76) for college females and from .49 to .84 for male prisoners (average: .77). Over a longer period of time (one year) average coefficients for normal high school students and adults ranged from .38 to .77 (average: .66). These data suggest that the temporal stability of the CPI compares favorably with other personality scales and is only slightly less for longer than for shorter periods of time. It should be noted that the lowest coefficients for all groups tended to be for the Cm and Py scales. Gough (1975) attributed the lower values for the Cm scale to the limited variability in various samples and for the Py scale to its relative brevity (twenty-two items).

Megargee also provided data concerning the internal consistency of the CPI scales. Kuder-Richardson coefficients for samples of high school males and females and college females ranged from .29 for the Fe scale to .94 for the Ac scale in high school females. The average Kuder-Richardson value for these groups was .79. Corrected split-half values for adult males and females ranged from .63 to .86 (average: .78). In general, the CPI scales seem to be relatively more homogeneous than are the MMPI scales. Interestingly, the CPI scales derived from internal consistency analyses do not have notably higher coefficients of internal consistency than those constructed by the empirical strategy.

VALIDITY. As we reported in Table 10–1, the CPI has been the subject of numerous investigations. Unfortunately, many of these studies contributed little to establishing its validity. Rather, the CPI scales have been accepted as adequate measures of

characteristics suggested by their labels and used to evaluate the effects of some other variables. For example, the So scale has been used to assess success of a program designed to make delinquent adolescents more accepting of social standards and values. Studies that have dealt directly with validity of CPI scales primarily have been of four kinds: (1) factor analytic, (2) group comparisons, (3) multiple regression, and (4) behavioral correlates.

Many factor analyses have been conducted on the CPI. Megargee (1972) concluded that most of them suggest the existence of five factors among the eighteen scale scores. Factor 1 generally is labeled *positive adjustment,* and the Sc and Gi scales correlate most highly with it. This factor is very similar to Gough's Class II. Factor 2 includes most of the scales from Gough's Class I and has been labeled *social poise, extraversion,* or *interpersonal effectiveness* by some investigators. The remaining three factors are considerably smaller and less stable than factors 1 and 2. Factor 3 seems to be concerned with independent thought and action as suggested by high correlations with the Ai and Fx scales. Factor 4 is defined primarily by the Cm scale and often is described as reflecting test-taking attitudes. Factor 5 appears only in some factor analyses, but when it is present it is defined by a high correlation with the Fe scale. Thus, it has been given labels such as *masculine-feminine* or *femininity.*

Research studies involving group comparisons of CPI scores seem to have been of two major kinds. Some have involved the study of groups that logically or intuitively might be expected to differ on one or more of the CPI scales. Identification of group differences has been most successful in academic achievement and delinquency. For example, Peterson et al. (1959) compared scores of delinquent and nondelinquent males on the Socialization (So) scale. As expected, delinquents obtained significantly lower So scores than nondelinquents. Benjamin (1970) found that black high school males achieving at higher levels scored higher on six CPI scales, including Achievement via Conformity (Ac) and Intellectual Efficiency (Ie), compared with similar males achieving at lower levels.

Other CPI studies compared CPI scores of groups of interest to investigators without any specific hypotheses or expectations concerning what CPI differences might be found. For example, Query (1966) compared CPI scores of seminary students rated as more or less successful. Significant differences were found on five of eighteen scales, but it was difficult to explain or interpret the obtained results.

From the very beginning of his work with the CPI, Gough recommended that scores be used as variables in multiple regression analyses to predict the specific behavior of interest. This procedure involves obtaining the eighteen CPI scores for subjects for whom some criterion measure (for example, academic grades) is available. Each CPI score is treated as a potential predictor measure, and statistically a prediction equation is developed to determine the optimal weights to be given to each score in the prediction of the criterion behavior. Research was reported indicating that CPI scores can predict with reasonable accuracy a variety of different behaviors, including academic achievement (Gough, 1964), success as an airline stewardess (Gough, 1968) or psychiatric resident (Gough et al., 1972), or delinquent behavior (Gough, 1966). Although the results of these studies have been encouraging, Gough (1975) emphasized the need to replicate the prediction equations in new and different settings.

In the most frequent way of using the CPI, the examiner infers specific personality characteristics based on a subject's high and low scores on individual CPI scales. Thus, evaluation of the validity of such inferences is critical. In the manual Gough (1975) presented a table listing descriptors associated with high or low scores on each CPI scale. This table typically is the major interpretive source for CPI users. Although Gough claimed that the descriptors were derived from research projects in which sub-

jects were studied and rated by psychologists, few meaningful details concerning the research underlying these descriptors were given. A similar set of descriptors for high and low scorers on each scale was published by Gough (1968), and more details about methodology were included. The descriptors were based on ratings given to college men and women by their sorority or fraternity peers.

Several additional studies identified descriptors for high or low scorers on specific CPI scales (Gough, 1953; Gough, 1965; Gough & Peterson, 1952). Attempts by other investigators to replicate Gough's descriptors met with mixed success (Bienen & Magoon, 1965; Gregory & Morris, 1978). Some of the descriptors identified in these more recent studies are similar to those reported earlier by Gough and his colleagues, but some are markedly different. It seems clear to us that research designed to identify correlates or descriptors of high or low scorers on the CPI scales adds considerably to their utility. It is equally clear, however, that more research of this kind is needed. In addition, Gynther and Gynther (1976) and Megargee (1972) indicated that research is lacking concerning charcteristics of persons who obtain particular configurations of scores on two or more CPI scales.

Although the CPI was not designed specifically for clinical subjects, there are some data available concerning its utility with such subjects. Goodstein et al. (1961) found that students who were seeking professional help for personal problems obtained significantly lower scores on most CPI scales than students who were not seeking professional help. Rosenberg (1962) concluded that better-adjusted subjects, as suggested by correspondence of real-self and ideal-self ratings, tended to score higher on many CPI scales. Heilbrun (1961) reported that clients with higher Fe scores tended to terminate therapy prematurely. Several studies reported increases in some or all CPI scores following counseling or psychotherapy (Nichols & Beck, 1960; Rudolph & Bennett, cited by Megargee, 1972; Shaver & Scheibe,

1967). Megargee (1972) concluded that although CPI scores tend to be related to overall measures of emotional adjustment, the CPI is not very effective with emotionally disturbed subjects. He recommended using the MMPI with such subjects and limiting the use of the CPI to groups, such as delinquents or criminals, whose problems stem from conflicts between individual and social values rather than from intrapsychic conflicts.

CONCLUSIONS. Our review of CPI research leads us to conclude that the instrument has the potential for considerable utility if it is used appropriately. We agree with Megargee's conclusion that it is of limited utility with emotionally disturbed subjects and is likely to be most useful in predicting behaviors or characteristics involving the individual's interaction with social standards and values. The extent to which the CPI can be used to infer or predict other kinds of behaviors will not be known until further research has been conducted.

SIXTEEN PERSONALITY FACTOR QUESTIONNAIRE

Rationale and Development

The Sixteen Personality Factor Questionnaire (16 PF) is the result of more than three decades of work by Raymond B. Cattell and numerous colleagues. Many reports of this work exist in the psychological literature, but the most concise source is the *Handbook for the Sixteen Personality Factor Questionnaire (16 PF)* by Cattell et al. (1970).

Cattell developed the 16 PF in order to define and measure the components of human personality. He did not have a priori notions concerning what those components were. Rather, his procedures identified the important components and also produced scales for assessing them.

Cattell reasoned that our language should provide information concerning what characteristics are important in human

FIGURE 10–B Raymond B. Cattell (1905–) is an American psychologist who used factor analytic procedures to develop the Sixteen Personality Factor Questionnaire. (Courtesy News Bureau, University of Illinois)

behavior. Starting with a list of more than 4,500 trait names culled from an unabridged dictionary, Cattell combined synonyms to arrive at 171 terms. College students rated peers on these terms, and intercorrelations and cluster analyses of these ratings identified 36 dimensions that Cattell labeled as surface traits. These 36 dimensions, plus some others that Cattell judged intuitively to be important, were used to obtain more peer ratings from subjects in several different kinds of settings. Factor analyses of these ratings identified 15 factors (plus intelligence) that accounted for intercorrelations among variables, and these were called *primary personality factors*. Items were written to represent these 16 factors, and the resulting scales were refined through subsequent factor analyses.

Table 10-4 lists the sixteen scales developed in this manner. Because each scale is thought to be unidimensional, with high and low scores representing opposite characteristics, scale names include labels for both high and low scores (for example, Reserved vs. Outgoing). Cattell assigned technical labels to most scales to avoid confusion with trait names used in ordinary language (for example, Sizothymia instead of Reserved), but these labels were so unfamiliar and confusing that in current practice they have been replaced by the more familiar terms presented in Table 10-4. Cattell also identified some second-order factors de-

rived from the sixteen primary ones, and the four secondary factors that have been studied sufficiently to justify their practical use also are presented in Table 10-4.

Although the original published version of the 16 PF did not include scales to assess test-taking attitudes, several such scales subsequently were developed (Cattell et al., 1970; Karson & O'Dell, 1976). The Motivational Distortion (MD) scale is made up of items endorsed in the scored direction more often by subjects instructed to provide the most favorable picture of themselves than by subjects taking the test under standard instructions. High scores on the MD scale indicate that the subject may have been "faking good" in taking the test, and caution should be exercised in interpreting the resulting scores. The Faking Bad scale was constructed like the MD scale, except that experimental subjects were instructed to give as bad an impression as possible in responding to the items. High scores on the Faking Bad scale also call into question the interpretability of the test scores. The Random scale of the 16 PF is similar to the F scale of the MMPI and consists of items very infrequently endorsed in the scored direction by subjects. High scores on the Random scale suggest that the subject responded to test items without reading them and considering their content. Obviously, scores resulting from such an approach to the test should not be interpreted.

Materials, Administration, Scoring

Cattell and his colleagues used factor-analytic procedures to develop questionnaires that could be used for subjects aged six years though adulthood. The 16 PF is an adult-level test and is intended for subjects sixteen years of age or older. Five forms of the 16 PF are available. Forms A and B are considered equivalent, each containing 187 items, and the reading level required is about that required for reading newspapers. Forms C an D also are equivalent. Each scale has only 105 items and has a somewhat lower reading level than Forms A

TABLE 10-4 Summary of Sixteen Personality Factor Questionnaire scales

Factor Symbol	
	Primary Factor Scales
A	Reserved vs. Warmhearted
B	Less Intelligent vs. More Intelligent
C	Affected by Feelings vs. Emotionally Stable
E	Humble vs. Assertive
F	Sober vs. Happy-go-lucky
G	Expedient vs. Conscientious
H	Shy vs. Venturesome
I	Tough-minded vs. Tender-minded
L	Trusting vs. Suspicious
M	Practical vs. Imaginative
N	Forthright vs. Shrewd
O	Unperturbed vs. Apprehensive
Q1	Conservative vs. Experimenting
Q2	Group Oriented vs. Self-sufficient
Q3	Undisciplined Self-conflict vs. Controlled
Q4	Relaxed vs. Tense
	Second-Order Factor Scales
QI	Introversion vs. Extraversion
QII	Low Anxiety vs. High Anxiety
QIII	Tender-minded Emotionality vs. Tough Poise
QIV	Subduedness vs. Independence

and B. Form E is designed for subjects with reading levels below sixth grade, and it has 142 items. Items in all forms are statements. For Forms A, B, C, and D, subjects respond by a three-alternative format (for example, yes, perhaps, no; yes, once in a while, no), but for Form E a two-response format is used.

The items for each 16 PF form are printed in booklets that can be reused if separate answer sheets are used. Answer sheets can be scored by hand using templates or by machine if appropriate answer sheets are used. The test can be administered to individual subjects or to groups of subjects. Instructions for completing the test are printed on each test booklet. There is no time limit, but most subjects can complete Form A or Form B in about fifty minutes and Form C or Form D in about thirty minutes. Time needed to complete Form E is quite variable because of reading problems among subjects for whom this form is appropriate. Because any single form of the test includes a rather limited number of items, it is recommended that more than one form (A + B or C + D) be used whenever possible (Karson & O'Dell, 1976). In practice, however, only one form usually is used.

Although the manual for the 16 PF does not stress the importance of assessing test-taking attitudes, an important first step in scoring is to obtain scores for the three validity scales (Motivational Distortion, Faking Bad, Random). A scoring key for the MD scale is provided by the publisher for Forms C and D. If the MD scale is to be scored for other forms or if the Faking Bad or Random scales are to be scored for any form, the test user must construct scoring keys according to directions provided by Karson and O'Dell (1976).

If scores on the validity scales suggest that the test was completed in an acceptable manner, raw scores are then obtained for the sixteen primary and the four second-order factor scales. When done by hand it involves assigning the specified number of points (one or two) for each item that is an-swered in the scored direction. A score of two is given whenever the scored alternative is one of the extreme ones (for example, yes or no). When a middle alternative is chosen for an item in a scale, a score of one is given. However, for the scale dealing with intelligence in Forms A, B, C, or D and for all scales for Form E, only one point is given for an item answered in the scored direction. A raw score for each scale is determined by adding scores for all items included in the scale.

Raw scores are then transformed to specialized standard scores called *sten scores*. Sten scores range from 1 to 10 and have a mean of 5.5 and a standard deviation of 2. These transformations are accomplished by referring to norm tables included in a supplement to the *16 PF Handbook*. Normative data are provided for individual forms and combinations of forms; for males and females separately and combined; and for samples of high school juniors and seniors, college students, and adults. Norm groups are large, ranging from 400 to more than 4,000 subjects in particular groups, and care was taken to make the samples representative of the U.S. population in terms of geographic location, family income, age, and race.

After sten scores are obtained for the various scales, they can be plotted on a profile sheet to facilitate comparisons and interpretation. A sample 16 PF profile is presented in Figure 10–3. Average scores, compared with the normative sample utilized, fall at or about a sten score of 5.5. Scores above 7 typically are considered high scores, and scores below 4 are considered low.

Interpretation

In their *16 PF Handbook* Cattell et al. (1970) suggested two approaches to 16 PF interpretations: profile matching and criterion estimation. The former involves comparing a particular subject's profile of scores with average or typical profiles of appropriate groups (for example, neurotics or

ipat

16 PF TEST PROFILE

FACTOR	Row Score Form A/C/E	Row Score Form B/D	Total	Standard Score	LOW SCORE DESCRIPTION	HIGH SCORE DESCRIPTION
A	10	9	19	5	RESERVED, DETACHED, CRITICAL, ALOOF, STIFF (Sizothymia)	OUTGOING, WARMHEARTED, EASY-GOING, PARTICIPATING (Affectothymia)
B	7	7	14	5	LESS INTELLIGENT, CONCRETE-THINKING (Lower scholastic mental capacity)	MORE INTELLIGENT, ABSTRACT-THINKING, BRIGHT (Higher scholastic mental capacity)
C	4	4	8	1	AFFECTED BY FEELINGS, EMOTIONALLY LESS STABLE, EASILY UPSET, CHANGEABLE (Lower ego strength)	EMOTIONALLY STABLE, MATURE, FACES REALITY, CALM (Higher ego strength)
E	17	17	39	8	HUMBLE, MILD, EASILY LED, DOCILE, ACCOMMODATING (Submissiveness)	ASSERTIVE, AGGRESSIVE, STUBBORN, COMPETITIVE (Dominance)
F	15	15	30	6	SOBER, TACITURN, SERIOUS (Desurgency)	HAPPY-GO-LUCKY, ENTHUSIASTIC (Surgency)
G	10	10	20	3	EXPEDIENT, DISREGARDS RULES (Weaker superego strength)	CONSCIENTIOUS, PERSISTENT, MORALISTIC, STAID (Stronger superego strength)
H	14	13	17	5	SHY, TIMID, THREAT-SENSITIVE (Threctia)	VENTURESOME, UNINHIBITED, SOCIALLY BOLD (Parmia)
I	18	17	35	10	TOUGH-MINDED, SELF-RELIANT, REALISTIC (Harria)	TENDER-MINDED, SENSITIVE, CLINGING, OVERPROTECTED (Premsia)
L	11	10	21	8	TRUSTING, ACCEPTING CONDITIONS (Alaxia)	SUSPICIOUS, HARD TO FOOL (Protension)
M	16	15	31	7	PRACTICAL, "DOWN-TO-EARTH" CONCERNS (Praxernia)	IMAGINATIVE, BOHEMIAN, ABSENT-MINDED (Autia)
N	8	7	15	3	FORTHRIGHT, UNPRETENTIOUS, GENUINE BUT SOCIALLY CLUMSY (Artlessness)	ASTUTE, POLISHED, SOCIALLY AWARE (Shrewdness)
O	22	22	44	10	SELF-ASSURED, PLACID, SECURE, COMPLACENT, SERENE (Untroubled adequacy)	APPREHENSIVE, SELF-REPROACHING, INSECURE, WORRYING, TROUBLED (Guilt proneness)
Q₁	9	8	17	5	CONSERVATIVE, RESPECTING TRADITIONAL IDEAS (Conservatism of temperament)	EXPERIMENTING, LIBERAL, FREE-THINKING (Radicalism)
Q₂	13	12	25	8	GROUP-DEPENDENT, A "JOINER" AND SOUND FOLLOWER (Group adherence)	SELF-SUFFICIENT, RESOURCEFUL, PREFERS OWN DECISIONS (Self-sufficiency)
Q₃	4	3	7	1	UNDISCIPLINED SELF-CONFLICT, LAX, FOLLOWS OWN URGES, CARELESS OF SOCIAL RULES (Low integration)	CONTROLLED, EXACTING WILL POWER, SOCIALLY PRECISE, COMPULSIVE (High strength of self-sentiment)
Q₄	24	23	47	10	RELAXED, TRANQUIL, UNFRUSTRATED, COMPOSED (Low ergic tension)	TENSE, FRUSTRATED, DRIVEN, OVERWROUGHT (High ergic tension)

STANDARD TEN SCORE (STEN)

A sten of	1	2	3	4	5	6	7	8	9	10	Is obtained
by about	2.3%	4.4%	9.2%	15.0%	19.1%	19.1%	15.0%	9.2%	4.4%	2.3%	of adults

Name:

FB _____ Sten Score

FG _____

FIGURE 10–3 Sample 16 PF profile. (Karson & O'Dell (1976). Copyright © 1976 by Institute for Personality and Ability Testing, Inc. Reproduced with permission. Profile sheet copyright 1956, 1973 by Institute for Personality and Ability Testing. Reproduced with permission.)

delinquents) as determined by previous research. The more similar a subject's profile is to the typical profile for a group, the more likely it is that the subject should be diagnosed or classified as belonging to that group.

The latter approach of Cattell et al. involves the application of mathematical equations to a subject's 16 PF scores. These equations give appropriate weights to each scale and permit prediction of group membership or other nontest behaviors. Although scientifically sound, both of these interpretive procedures are complex and require information and skills that the average 16 PF user is not likely to have. Because of the complexity of interpretation, computer programs are available for many interpretive tasks.

Karson and O'Dell (1976) presented a less statistically complicated strategy for interpeting the 16 PF. The first step is to examine the three validity scales (Motivational Distortion, Faking Bad, Random) to determine if any deviant test-taking attitudes are present that would suggest that the resulting scores are invalid and should not be interpreted. It should be noted again that the only scoring key provided by the publisher is for the Motivational Distortion scale for Forms C and D. Other keys must be prepared by test users based on information provided by Karson and O'Dell (1976).

If the scores are judged to be valid and interpretable, the next step is to examine the second-order scores, particularly anxiety and extraversion. This is followed by a scale-by-scale examination of the eighteen primary scores on the test. For both secondary and primary scales, descriptors or inferences are generated for scores that are unusually higher or lower than the mean for the standardization sample. These descriptors and inferences are based in part on research about what people are like who score high or low on specific 16 PF scales, but they also seem to result to a large extent from clinical intuitions about behaviors that

are likely to be associated with the personality dimensions that specific scales are designed to assess.

After each scale is analyzed, hypotheses are formulated concerning the nature of the problem that led to the referral for assessment. Karson and O'Dell state that the "clinician's fund of clinical lore is invaluable . . ." at this stage (1976, p. 96). Inferences are made about combinations of 16 PF scales, about the relationship of scores to general personality theory, and about a subject's scores and observations of patients seen in the past.

The next step involves a succinct summary of the case, including a psychiatric diagnosis if one is appropriate. Hypotheses are then compared with other assessment data, and they are modified if necessary. Finally, an effort is made to obtain follow-up data for each subject. Such feedback permits clinicians to check their accuracy and to improve their predictions.

The strategy of Karson and O'Dell (1976) can be illustrated by presenting their interpretation of the profile in Figure 10–3:

PRESENTING PROBLEM:

Mr. Richard M. was a final quality control inspector for a large corporation. He was referred for psychological evaluation because of increasing difficulty in keeping his temper. He had never attacked anyone, but once, in disgust, he had smashed a tray of dishes in the company cafeteria. This erratic behavior led to a request on the part of the company physician for an evaluation, since he was in a position of considerable responsibility.

IN-DEPTH INTERPRETATION:

This man's profile indicates that he has very low emotional stability (C = 1). Guilt proneness is also remarkably high (O = 10), indicating that he is a chronic worrier. Free-floating anxiety is also at maximum (Q4 = 10). The Q3 of 1 suggests that he has little ability to use obsessive-compulsive mechanisms to bind anxiety. Finally, on the last of the anxiety primaries, L, he earns a score of 8, showing a strong tendency to project and displace heavily. We often prefer to call L+ "anxious insecurity" rather than "suspiciousness," since it is a primary component of the second-order anxiety factor. L+ seems to measure anxiety as much as pure tendencies toward projection, hence the term "anxious insecurity." As you'd expect, since almost all of the anxiety indicators are up, the second-order anxiety factor itself is at the highest possible score. This degree of discomfort makes us wonder about how much his personal problems and the disrupting effects of anxiety are interfering with his ability to perform effectively.

He is very markedly emotionally sensitive (I), especially considering the job he occupies. We can also hypothesize that this maximum score on I, combined with the maximum second-order anxiety score and high scores on the anger factors (E and L), imply a good deal of sensitivity to hostility in this man, coupled with a strong mother-figure identification. High I scores are believed to spring from an overprotected early childhood in which there has not been much interaction with one's peer group, or much participation in the rough and tumble of everyday life. Further, the comparatively low score on cortertia, combined with a Q3 of 1, implies relatively few effective cognitive controls. His response patterns appear to be largely determined by idiosyncratic and personal considerations. High cortertia implies a person capable of making rapid, accurate cognitive decisions when necessary. It is essential in occupations where fast responses to a changing situation are necessary. In such jobs one must be alert, ready to respond, open to new information, and able to adjust quickly under pressure of time. Persons low on cortertia are often not able to do this on a sustained basis.

The combination of 8's on E and L suggests problems in handling anger. A mixture of overwhelming anxiety, low ego strength and high emotional sensitivity as well as difficulty with anger suggests paranoid ideation in this man. A punitive superego is implied by the low group conformity (G = 3), accompanied by the maximum score on guilt proneness (O = 10).

In many ways he looks like a severe anxiety neurotic; however, his major difficulty with angry impulses (E+, L+) makes it apparent that he does not quite fit this picture. These dynamics would be better fit by a paranoid personality, since some of the basic dynamics frequently encountered are psychosexual problems, many angry impulses, low ego strength, and displacement and projection, all found in this case.

FOLLOW-UP:

Beyond the fact that this man was not retained in his job, we know little about what actually happened to him. However, we do have access to psychiatric and psychological reports, done independently of the present evaluation.

The psychiatric evaluation pictures an emotion-starved life as a child; the patient grew up in an orphanage. The psychiatrist notes feelings that people were against him, that they were mocking him, and a certain degree of thought disturbance. The diagnosis made was that of paranoid schizophrenia. The psychological report mentions excessive vigilance, generalized suspiciousness, and mistrust of others. The diagnosis made by the psychologist was that of an ambulatory paranoid schizophrenic. Upon further evaluation a year later, he was diagnosed a paranoid personality.*

Evaluation

The 16 PF is an instrument that has been researched thoroughly. As can be seen in Table 10–1, it is second only to the MMPI in number of research references between 1971 and 1978. Cattell and his colleagues have continued to produce research concerning the 16 PF, and they have been joined in this effort by many other investigators.

SCALE DEVELOPMENT. Cattell utilized sophisticated and sound factor-analytic procedures in developing the 16 PF scales. The current scales resulted from repeated analyses with a variety of populations. No items appear in more than one 16 PF scale, increasing the likelihood that scores on the individual scales will be relatively independent of each other. Data presented by Cattell et al. (1970) suggest that the 16 PF scales are relatively independent. Although a few correlations among 16 PF scales range as high as −.71 and +.66, many of the intercorrelations are in a range from −.20 to +.20.

NORMS. Tables for converting raw scores on 16 PF scales to sten scores are not included in the test manual. Rather they are published as supplements to the *16 PF Handbook* (Cattell et al., 1970). Separate tables are available for the various forms and combinations of forms. Data are presented for three major groups—high school juniors and seniors, college students, and general adult population—and for each of these groups data are presented separately for males and females. The samples on which the norm tables are based are relatively large, ranging from 468 to 2,984 for Forms A and B. The manual claims that the samples were selected to obtain a stratified representation of various educational levels, geographical areas, ages, occupations, and races as they occur in the general U.S. population. However, no data are presented to permit an evaluation of how effectively such stratification was accomplished. Although the norms for the 16 PF seem quite adequate, it is unfortunate that they are not included in the manual. In addition, because so many tables are presented for the various forms and samples, the user of the 16 PF should be very careful in determining that the appropriate table is being utilized for each particular subject.

RELIABILITY. The *Manual for the 16 PF* (1972) reports correlations between 16 PF scores on Forms A and B for a sample of more than 6,000 male and female subjects. The correlations ranged from .21 to .71, with a median of .49. Correlations between 16 PF scores on Forms C and D for a sample of 377 male and female subjects range from .16 to .55, with a median of .38. These data have been interpreted by reviewers as indicating that the 16 PF forms are not equivalent and that significantly different scores could result depending on which form is used (Bloxom, 1978; Walsh, 1978).

Test-retest reliability data also are reported in the test manual. Over a short test-retest interval (four to seven days), reliability coefficients range from .58 to .83 (median: .79) for Form A and from .54 to .89 (median: .78) for Form B. Corresponding data are not reported for Forms C and D. Because each 16 PF form consists of relatively few items, the manual recommends that whenever possible more than one form of the test should be administered. Test-retest reliability data for combinations of forms are somewhat better than for a single form. When Forms A and B are combined, the reliability coefficients over a short period of time range from .65 to .93 (median: .87). Coefficients for a combination of Forms C and D range from .67 to .86.

As is true with most other inventory scale scores, test-retest reliability coefficients decrease as the test-retest interval increases. Coefficients for an interval of about two months range from .35 to .85 (median: .66) for Form A and from .63 to .88 (median: .78) for a combination of Forms A and B. With a four-year test-retest interval, coefficients for Form A range from .28 to .63 (median: .49) for males and from .21 to .64 (median: .51) for females.

In summary, the temporal stability of the 16 PF scales is not as great as for many other personality inventory scales. Careful examination of these reliability data suggest that some of the 16 PF scales produce consistently higher reliability coefficients than others. The rather low correlations between scores from the various forms on the 16 PF are undesirable and suggest that the forms should not be considered equivalent.

VALIDITY. Cattell's primary concern with the validity of the 16 PF centers on what he has labeled *concept validity*, that is, correlations between 16 PF scores and the "pure factors" they were designed to measure. Data resulting from complex factor-analytic procedures suggest that the 16 PF scales are strongly related to the corresponding pure factors (Cattell et al., 1970). However, data concerning concept validity are of little or no value in helping to understand relationships between 16 PF scores and important nontest behaviors of subjects.

In the *16 PF Handbook* (Cattell et al., 1970) two additional kinds of validity data are presented. Mean profiles are given for a large number of occupational-vocational groups (for example, engineers, psychologists, lawyers) and for other groups such as neurotics, delinquents, and physically ill patients. Cattell and his colleagues also present numerous regression equations for determining group membership (for example, neuroticism) and for predicting behaviors such as academic achievement or success as a psychotherapist. However, these data are not presented in a way that is useful to the practitioner, and data concerning accuracy rates for classification and prediction are noticeably absent (Walsh, 1978). The few data of this kind that are reported are not particularly impressive. For example, when 16 PF scores were used in multiple regression analyses to predict academic grades, the correlations ranged from .55 to .63. Equally impressive prediction probably is possible from simpler, more efficient measures such as intelligence tests or previous grade point averages.

Although the test manual and the *16 PF Handbook* both present descriptions of persons who score high or low on 16 PF scales, the source of these descriptions is unclear. Some of the information undoubtedly comes from empirical research, but much of it seems to stem from general psychological theory related to the personality constructs that the 16 PF is thought to measure. Cattell and his colleagues have not undertaken systematic research to determine empirically characteristics associated with high or low 16 PF scores. Several investigators who have compared 16 PF scores with peer ratings failed to find much congruence between them (Becker, 1960; Peterson, 1965; Schaie, 1962).

Conclusions

A great deal of statistical sophistication was involved in the development of the 16 PF. Although existing data suggest that the personality factors identified by Cattell are found in many different groups of people, data concerning whether the 16 PF actually measures the underlying major dimensions of human personality are unclear and not compelling (Bolton, 1978). Other investigators, using other items and other statistical procedures, have identified different sets of dimensions (for example, Comrey, 1970; Edwards, 1967). The rather considerable body of research that has accumulated for the 16 PF is of limited utility to those who use the instrument in applied ways. Perhaps Gynther and Gynther (1976) were not far wrong when they suggested that " . . . almost certainly the main reason that Cattell's work has not received acclaim in proportion to its volume and elegance is that psychologists who do not understand factor analysis—and this is perhaps the majority— tend to be defensive about this approach or to think of factors merely as 'mathematical abstractions' "(p. 235). Cattell and his colleagues did not seem motivated to present their data in a manner that would be more acceptable and more helpful to those who use the 16 PF in practical ways.

EDWARDS PERSONAL PREFERENCE SCHEDULE

Rationale and Development

According to Edwards (1959), "the Edwards Personal Preference Schedule (EPPS) was designed primarily as an instrument for research and counseling purposes, to provide quick and convenient measures of a number of relatively independent *normal* personality variables" (p. 5). The personality variables underlying the EPPS scales are from Henry Murray's list of manifest needs.

Edwards was concerned about the extent to which subjects endorse items because of their perceptions about the social acceptability or desirability of the content rather than because of their actual behaviors, attitudes, and other personal characteristics. This concern about social desirability led Edwards to include procedures for minimizing such influence in response to test items.

As a first step in developing the EPPS scales, Edwards generated lists of statements whose content appeared to assess each of the fifteen needs selected for inclusion in the schedule. Table 10–5 presents the fifteen need scales of the EPPS and a brief description of each. Each statement was then rated by a group of judges in terms of how socially desirable or undesirable it would be for a subject to admit to its content. The EPPS consists of 210 pairs of statements in which items from each of the fifteen need scales are paired with items from the other fourteen need scales. The statements in each pair are approximately equal in terms of judged social desirability. Subjects are asked to choose from each pair the one statement that is more characteristic of them. Because the statements have been equated for social desirability, it is assumed that subjects' choices reflect the relative strength of their needs. Each time a subject chooses a statement from a particular need scale, one raw score point is scored for that scale. For example, one pair of demonstration items reads:*

A. I like to talk about myself to others.
B. I like to work toward some goal that I have set for myself.

A subject who chooses statement A as more characteristic would receive a point on one scale, whereas the choice of statement B would lead to a point on another scale.

Two validity indices are included in the EPPS. A consistency score is based on a comparison of the number of identical choices for fifteen items that are repeated in the test. If a subject is responding in a meaningful way, there should be considerable consistency in these repeated items. Low consistency suggests the possibility of random or other nonmeaningful response to the test items. The manual suggests that a consist-

*Copyright 1954, 1959 by the Psychological Corporation. Reproduced with permission.

TABLE 10-5 Summary of Edwards Personal Preference Schedule Scales

Scale	Definition
Achievement (ach)	To do one's best, to be successful.
Deference (def)	To follow instructions and do what is expected, to accept the leadership of others.
Order (ord)	To have things organized, to keep things neat and orderly.
Exhibition (exh)	To say witty and clever things, to be the center of attention.
Autonomy (aut)	To be independent of others in making decisions, to feel free to do what one wants.
Affiliation (aff)	To be loyal to friends, to do things with friends rather than alone.
Intraception (int)	To analyze one's motives and feelings, to analyze the behavior of others.
Succorance (suc)	To have others provide help when in trouble, to seek encouragement from others.
Dominance (dom)	To argue for one's point of view, to be a leader in groups to which one belongs.
Abasement (aba)	To feel guilty when one does something wrong, to accept blame when things do not go right.
Nurturance (nur)	To help friends when they are in trouble, to show a great deal of affection toward others.
Change (chg)	To do new and different things, to experience novelty and change in daily routine.
Endurance (end)	To keep at a job until it is finished, to avoid being interrupted while at work.
Heterosexuality (het)	To go out with members of the opposite sex, to be in love with someone of the opposite sex.
Aggression (agg)	To attack contrary points of view, to become angry.

ency score of less than nine should call into question scores on the fifteen need scales.

Profile stability scores can be obtained by correlating partial scores for each scale with other partial scores for that scale. However, this calculation involves a correlation formula, and typically examiners do not determine these stability scores for individual subjects. The manual gives no meaningful information for interpreting these stability scores for individual subjects even if the examiner goes to the considerable effort of calculating them.

Materials, Administration, Scoring

The EPPS consists of 225 pairs of statements printed in reusable booklets. Subjects are instructed to read each pair of statements and to choose the one more characteristic of them. Responses are made by circling letters on a separate answer sheet. Special answer sheets are required if the responses are to be machine scored. The manual indicates that the average testing time for college students is about forty minutes. Although no age range for the EPPS is indicated in the manual, it clearly is an adult test. No reading level for the items has been reported, but the reading level may be somewhat higher than the sixth-grade level suggested for the MMPI.

Using a scoring template available from the publisher, one can obtain a consistency score by comparing responses on fifteen pairs of identical items. Raw scores for the fifteen need scales are obtained by counting the number of "A" choices in each row of the answer sheet and the number of "B" choices in each column of answers. Appropriate row and column scores are added together to obtain total raw scores for the fifteen scales. An index of profile stability can be calculated by correlating the fifteen row scores with the fifteen column scores.

After raw scores have been determined for the fifteen need scales and for the consistency scale, they are transferred to a profile sheet that appears on the reverse side of the answer sheet. A sample EPPS profile is presented in Figure 10–4. Percentile equivalents are determined by reference to tables presented in the test manual, and a profile of scores based on these percentiles is constructed. Percentile equivalents are presented separately for 760 college males, 749

college females, 4,031 adult males, and 4,932 adult females. The college sample included students at "various universities and colleges," and no additional demographic data are provided for this sample. The adult sample was made up of members of a consumer purchase panel used for market surveys. The adult sample included subjects from urban and rural areas and covered 1,181 counties in 48 states. The manual suggests that percentiles between 17 and 84 should be considered average; percentiles between 85 and 96, high; and percentiles of 97 and above, very high. Low scores are percentiles between 4 and 16, and very low scores are percentiles of 3 and below.

Interpretation

The manual gives some general suggestions for using the EPPS but no detailed interpretive strategy or sample profiles. The major emphasis of these suggestions is on discussing the results of the EPPS with vocational or educational counselees. Through this process it is hoped that counselees will gain insight about their needs and that the counselor will gain a better understanding of the counselees.

Users of the EPPS who want more guidance in interpreting test scores have little on which to rely. A reasonable approach would be to examine first the consistency score for a subject to determine if the test was answered in a meaningful way. If the consistency score is greater than nine, interpretation of the fifteen need scales would be appropriate. Interpretation of high or very high scores or low or very low scores would involve reference to the definitions of each need that are presented in the test manual (and in Table 10–5 of this chapter). It would be necessary to assume that each scale is assessing the need as defined in these tables, and as we shall see, there is not much support in the research literature for such an assumption.

To illustrate briefly a possible approach to EPPS interpretation, let us now turn to the sample profile presented in Figure 10–4. First, we note that the subject's con-

Edwards Personal Preference Schedule

NAME _____
LAST   FIRST

SEX ____(M)____ NORMS USED _____ ADULT MEN

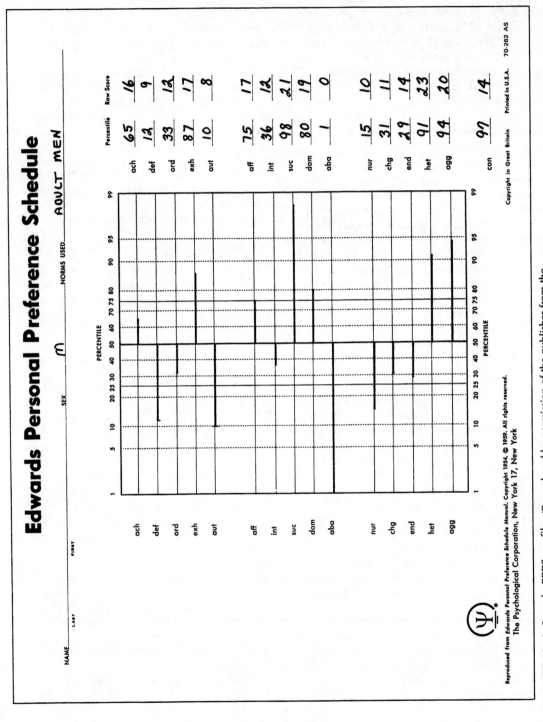

	Percentile	Raw Score
ach	65	16
def	12	9
ord	33	12
exh	87	17
aut	10	8
aff	75	17
int	36	12
suc	98	21
dom	80	19
aba	1	0
nur	15	10
chg	31	11
end	29	14
het	91	23
agg	94	20
con	99	14

FIGURE 10–4 Sample EPPS profile. (Reproduced by permission of the publisher from the Edwards Personal Preference Schedule Manual. Copyright 1954, © 1959 by The Psychological Corporation. All rights reserved.)

sistency score of fourteen is high enough to indicate that he responded to the items in a meaningful way. Thus, we turn to the scores on the need scales. The subject's only very high score was for the Succorance scale. Reference to the definition of succorance in Table 10–5 would lead to the inference that he has a very strong need to receive help, affection, and encouragement from others, especially when he is having personal problems or is feeling sick or depressed. High scores for this subject were on the Aggression, Heterosexuality, and Exhibition scales. Reference to the definitions of these needs would lead to additional inferences that the subject tends to become angry easily, to criticize others, and to express his views openly; that he is attracted by members of the opposite sex and likes to interact with them; and that he likes to be the center of attention and to talk about himself. The subject's only very low score was for Abasement, indicating that he does not feel inferior to others and does not tend to blame himself when things go wrong. Low scores on Autonomy, Deference, and Nurturance suggest that he does not have a strong need to be independent of others; that he does not tend to accept leadership from others; and that he is not likely to be particularly sympathetic, kind, or helpful to others.

Evaluation

SCALE DEVELOPMENT. Except for indicating that statements were generated for each need whose content seemed to assess that need, the manual gives little information about the origin of the statements included in the EPPS. Based on experience with other inventories constructed by these intuitive or face valid methods exclusively, we question how adequately the statements selected for each need adequately assess the strength of that need. The test was constructed to minimize the influence of social desirability on responses, and Edwards equated each pair of items in terms of judged social desirability. Correlations between EPPS scores and scores on a scale de-

signed to measure social desirability that are reported in the manual were quite low, suggesting to Edwards that social desirability is not a major factor in EPPS scores. However, other investigators concluded that the EPPS reduces but does not eliminate the effects of social desirability (Radcliffe, 1965). Other research (for example, Heilbrun & Goodstein, 1961) indicated that the predictive usefulness of personality questionnaires appears to be greater when effects of social desirability are not removed from the questionnaires.

NORMS. As reported earlier, the manual presents normative data separately for college males and females and for adult males and females. Although the adult sample seems to have been reasonably representative of the general population, insufficient information is given about the college samples to judge their representativeness. The rather significant differences in normative data for the adult and college samples emphasize the importance of using appropriate group norms for tests such as the EPPS.

IPSATIVE SCORES. In responding to each item, subjects are asked to indicate which of two statements is more descriptive of them. The resulting raw scores indicate the relative strength of fifteen needs within the personality of each subject. Such scores are referred to as *ipsative* scores. They permit comparison of needs for an individual subject, but they do not communicate any information about the strength of needs compared with other persons. However, the raw scores are converted to percentile equivalents based on normative data. Such conversion is legitimate only if we consider each scale individually and compare an individual's score with the normative sample. It is not appropriate to construct a profile of these converted scores and to make comparisons among needs for individual subjects. The ordering of strength of needs based on raw scores will not be the same as that based on percentile equivalents. The confounding of ipsative scores with normative data is confusing and produces some serious problems in trying to determine the internal consistency of scores, the degree of intercorrelation among scales, and the relationship of scores to external behavioral variables (Hicks, 1970).

RELIABILITY. The manual reports split-half reliability coefficients or coefficients of internal consistency for the fifteen need scales. The reported values range from .60 for Deference to .87 for Heterosexuality (median: .78). These coefficients are reasonably high and compare favorably with values for other personality scales. However, as McKee (1972) noted, the item overlap among the EPPS scales tends to produce artificially inflated coefficients.

The manual also reports data for eighty-nine college students who took the EPPS twice, a one-week interval separating the two administrations. The test-retest reliability coefficients range from .74 to .97 (median: .79). These values compare favorably with other personality scales and suggest that EPPS scores are quite stable over a brief time interval.

SCALE INTERCORRELATIONS. Intercorrelations among the EPPS scores are reported in the manual for large samples of male and female college students. The values are quite low, leading the test's author to conclude that the variables being measured are relatively independent. However, the use of ipsative scores confounds the meaning of the intercorrelations and precludes reaching a definite conclusion about the independence of scores (Stricker, 1965).

VALIDITY. The manual for the EPPS presents some preliminary data concerning validity. Several studies are described in which the EPPS scores were compared with other self-ratings of the needs. For some subjects the agreement between the two sets of data was remarkably high, but for others agreement was disappointingly low. Edwards concluded that the extent of agreement is a function of variables, such as how the needs are defined; the degree of complexity of the needs; the amount of knowledge, insight,

and ability of raters; and the extent to which raters are influenced by standards of social desirability. The manual also presents correlations between the EPPS scales and Guilford-Martin Personnel Inventory scales and the Taylor Manifest Anxiety Scale. The correlations are interpreted as falling in the expected directions.

As indicated by the data in Table 10–1, the EPPS has been the subject of numerous studies since its publication. Data have been compared for groups such as counseled versus .control students, smokers versus nonsmokers, honors versus nonhonors students, and many others (Gynther & Gynther, 1976). The relative strength of needs of groups such as medical students, nursing assistants, and handicapped employees has been reported. Noticeably lacking in the literature are studies in which strength of needs as measured by the EPPS is compared directly with adequate external criterion measures such as peer ratings.

CONCLUSIONS. The development of the EPPS served a useful purpose by focusing attention on the role of social desirability in inventory responses and scores. Unfortunately, the use of ipsative scores created considerable confusion about the meaning of EPPS scores. Reviewers who examined the hundreds of studies that have been conducted on the EPPS are in clear agreement that there is not adequate evidence that the EPPS scales measure the constructs they were designed to measure or that the scales are useful in predicting important nontest variables (Heilbrun, 1972; Radcliffe, 1965; Stricker, 1965). Even Edwards seems to have lost interest in the EPPS, and he has published a new inventory bearing his name (Edwards, 1967).

PERSONALITY RESEARCH FORM

Rationale and Development

Although the Pesonality Research Form (PRF) authored by Jackson (1974) has not gained much popularity in applied settings, we will discuss it in this chapter because it illustrates the sequential strategy for inventory construction and because it represents one of the most psychometrically sound efforts to construct personality scales. The PRF was designed to provide "... personality scales and an item pool which might be useful in personality research, and, secondly, to provide an instrument for measuring broadly relevant personality traits in settings such as schools and colleges, clinics and guidance centers, and in business and industry (Jackson, 1974, p. 4)."

The PRF focuses on areas of normal functioning rather than on psychopathology. Its basic theoretical orientation stems from Murray's list of needs. The sequential strategy discussed earlier in this chapter was used to construct scales to assess these needs. The first step was to develop clear and precise definitions for each of Murray's needs. Then, items were written that intuitively seemed to assess each need as it had been defined. Preliminary sets of items were administered to a group of college students, and the tentative scales were refined. Items were retained if they correlated highly with a total score on the scale in which they were included, if they did not correlate highly with total scores on other scales, and if they were not highly correlated with a measure of social desirability. Thus, the final scales to measure Murray's needs were thought to be internally consistent, to have both convergent and discriminant validity, and to be relatively free of the influence of social desirability.

The current version of the PRF includes twenty scales to assess needs plus two validity scales. Table 10–6 lists all twenty-two scales and presents several representative adjectives describing high scorers on each scale (Jackson, 1967, 1974).

The Desirability (Dy) and Infrequency (In) scales of the PRF are validity scales designed to assess subjects' test-taking attitudes. Items in the Dy scale had been previously rated by judges as indicating either highly desirable or undesirable characteristics if endorsed in the scored direction. High scores on the Dy scale may indicate that subjects consciously or unconsciously

TABLE 10-6 Summary of Personality Research Form Scales

Scale	Descriptive Adjectives For High Scorers
Abasement (Ab)	humble, self-blaming, self-subordinating
Achievement (Ac)	achieving, ambitious, competitive, driving
Affiliation (Af)	affiliative, friendly, sociable, gregarious
Aggression (Ag)	aggressive, hostile, argumentative, belligerent
Autonomy (Au)	autonomous, independent, self-reliant, non-conforming
Change (Ch)	changeable, inconsistent, unpredictable, adaptable
Cognitive Structure (CS)	precise, definite, avoids ambiguity, needs structure
Defendence (De)	defensive, self-protecting, guarded, suspicious
Dominance (Do)	dominant, controlling, persuasive, authoritative
Endurance (En)	enduring, persistent, determined, has stamina
Exhibition (Ex)	exhibitionistic, colorful, immodest, showy
Harmavoidance (Ha)	fearful, self-protective, unadventurous, avoids risk
Impulsivity (Im)	impulsive, hasty, reckless, impatient
Nurturance (Nu)	sympathetic, caring, comforting, consoling
Order (Or)	neat, organized, methodical, disciplined
Play (Pl)	playful, pleasure-seeking, fun-loving, jovial
Sentience (Se)	aesthetic, enjoys physical sensations, sensuous, perceptive
Social Recognition (SR)	approval-seeking, socially proper, obliging
Succorance (Su)	dependent, appealing for help, seeks support, pleading
Understanding (Un)	inquiring, curious, rational, probing
Desirability (Dy)	validity scale—presents favorable picture of self in response to personality statements
Infrequency (In)	validity scale—responds to statements in random or implausible manner

Adapted from Table 1 of *Personality Research Form Manual* (Jackson, 1974, pp. 6-7). Copyright © 1974 by Douglas N. Jackson. Reproduced with permission.

have responded largely in terms of saying socially desirable things about themselves, whereas low scores on this scale may suggest that subjects could be malingering or "faking bad" by saying very undesirable things about themselves. However, Jackson (1974) pointed out that scores on the Dy scale can indicate important personality characteristics. High scores can mean that subjects have atypically high self-regard or a high degree of conventional socialization. Very low scores can indicate atypically low self-regard.

Materials, Administration, Scoring

There are five forms of the PRF. Forms A and B are parallel forms each containing 300 items divided into fifteen 20-item scales. Forms AA and BB also are parallel forms, each containing 440 items that can be scored for the same fifteen scales as in Forms A and B plus seven additional 20-item scales. Form E has 352 items representing the best items from Forms AA and BB, and it yields scores for twenty-two scales.

The PRF can be administered to individual subjects or to groups of subjects. Items are printed in reusable booklets, and responses (true or false) are marked on separate answer sheets. There is no time limit for the test, and the manual estimates average testing time to range from thirty to forty-five minutes for Forms A, B, or E and from forty to seventy minutes for Forms AA or BB. The manual does not indicate the reading level required to complete the PRF meaningfully, but examination of the items suggests that the difficulty level may be somewhat higher than the sixth-grade level of the MMPI.

After the PRF has been administered, it can be scored by machine or by hand. Machine scoring requires the use of special answer sheets that can be processed by optical scanning equipment. Hand scoring involves a single scoring template, counting the number of items endorsed in the score direction for each scale, and recording these raw scores in appropriate blanks at the bottom of the answer sheet.

Raw scores are then transferred to separate profile sheets that have male norms on one side and female norms on the other. A sample PRF profile is presented in Figure 10–5. A profile is constructed by plotting scores on the sheet. Scores in the profile are in the form of normalized T-scores (mean: 50; SD: 10). Tables in the manual also permit transformation of raw scores to percentile equivalents. The T-scores and percentile equivalents are based on data from large samples of male and female college students selected to include a diversity of schools in terms of size, geographical setting, public versus private support, and nature of student body. For Forms A, B, AA, and BB, the samples included 1,029 males and 1,002 females. For Form E the male and female sample sizes were 1,350 and 1,415, respectively.

Interpretation

A careful reading of the manual makes it clear that Jackson was more interested in constructing psychometrically sound scales than he was in offering a technique that would be maximally useful to practitioners. The manual reports reliability, validity, and other psychometric data in great detail, but little direction is given concerning how the PRF scores and profile are to be interpreted for individual subjects. However, given the way in which the scales were constructed and the manner in which the resulting scores are reported, it seems reasonable to use an interpretive approach similar to that previously described for the MMPI and the CPI.

A first step in interpreting the PRF should involve consideration of scores on the two validity scales, Dy and In. Very high or very low scores on the Dy scale should alert the examiner to the possibility that the subject consciously or unconsciously responded so as to create an unrealistically favorable (high score) or unfavorable (low score) impression. A high score on the In scale suggests carelessness, random answers, or other nonpurposeful responses on the part of the subject or scoring errors on the

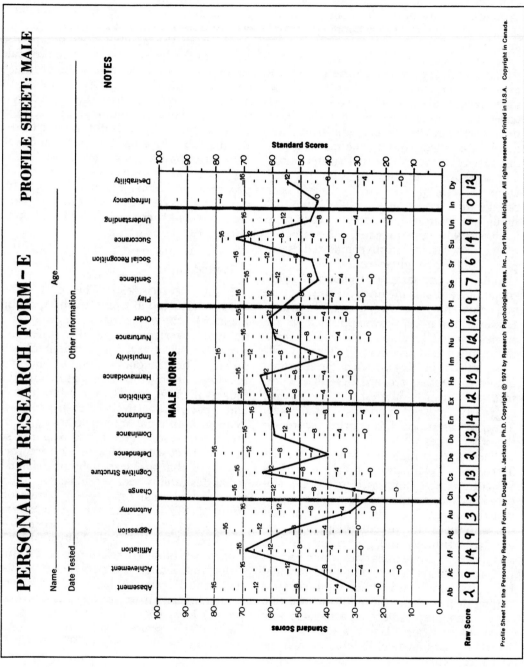

FIGURE 10–5 Sample PRF profile. (Profile sheet copyright © 1974 by Douglas N. Jackson. Reproduced with permission.)

part of the examiner. The manual does not indicate how high or low In scores must be in order to indicate test invalidity, but the expected T-score on the In scale when responses have been totally random is approximately 90 to 95.

If scores on the validity scales indicate that the subject approached the test in the manner intended, scores on the content scales can be interpreted. For each of these scales, the manual presents a description of high scorers and lists several adjectives characteristic of such scorers. The manual does not specify the source of these descriptions and adjectives, but they probably resulted from research that compared self- and peer ratings with scores on each PRF scale. Although the manual indicates that each scale is bipolar, low scores meaning the opposite of high scores, descriptive material is reported only for high scores.

Illustrative or sample profiles and interpretations are not included in the manual and have not been reported elsewhere. However, the interpretive approach we are suggesting can be illustrated by the profile in Figure 10–5. The scores on the two validity scales (Dy and In) do not suggest profile invalidity. Neither score is deviant enough from the mean to suggest that the subject approached the test in an unacceptable way. Thus, we can proceed to interpret scores on the other scales.

The subject's highest scores are for the Succorance, Affiliation, and Cognitive Structure scales. Reference to the descriptive adjectives in the test manual suggests that the subject is a rather dependent person who seeks support and help from others. He is friendly and gregarious, and he searches out interactions with other people, perhaps in order to seek their support and help. In addition, he is a person who prefers a great deal of structure in his life and who avoids ambiguity. Adjectives associated with other scales whose T-scores are approximately 60 (Dominance, Exhibition, Harmavoidance, Nurturance, and Order) suggest that the subject tends to be somewhat ma-

nipulative and controlling in relationships, but that he is capable of displaying sympathy and empathy toward others. He is organized and orderly, and he does not like to take risks.

Although the manual does not present adjectives for low scores, because the scales are bipolar, we can reverse some of the adjectives to provide interpretations of the subject's low scores. Thus, the low scores on the Abasement, Autonomy, and Change scores suggest that he is not humble or self-blaming; that he is not independent or self-reliant; and that he is rather predictable, consistent, and perhaps rigid in his approach to problems. It should be noted that the adjectives derived from the high scores are quite congruent with those based on the low scores.

Evaluation

SCALE DEVELOPMENT. The PRF scales were constructed in a careful and thorough manner by the sequential strategy. There is no item overlap among the scales, and scores are relatively independent of each other. The median absolute intercorrelations among the scales, as reported in the test manual, are .16 and .17 for females and males, respectively. Because half the items in each scale are keyed true and half are keyed false, acquiescence response sets do not affect scores. Jackson's efforts to select items that are reasonably unrelated to social desirability seem to have been effective. The manual reports the results of a study of 135 male and female college students in which the other PRF scores were correlated with the desirability scale. The median absolute correlation was .20, indicating that less than 5 percent of the variance in PRF scales can be explained in terms of tendencies to respond desirably. Reviewers have been in clear agreement that the PRF scales are quite sound psychometrically. Wiggins (1972) concluded that "...the PRF is among the most methodologically sophisticated personality inventories presently available" (p. 303) and Anastasi (1972) stated that "... technically the PRF appears to be exemplary" (p. 298).

NORMS. The norms for the PRF are based on large samples of male and female college students. Although strictly random sampling was not used, Jackson (1974) reported that the stability of normative data was high from one college to another. However, he recommended caution in using the PRF with groups that are quite different from college students without first evaluating the appropriateness of the standard PRF norms for such groups.

RELIABILITY. The intention of developing personality scales that would be quite homogeneous and internally consistent seems to have been met. The median Kuder-Richardson value for the twenty content scales is .91 (Jackson, 1974). Odd-even reliability coefficients also were reported in the test manual. These values for the twenty content scales ranged from .48 to .86 (median: .76) for Form AA and from .51 to .90 (median: .81) for Form BB. For Form E the odd-even reliability coefficients ranged from .50 to .91 (median: .70) for a college student sample. These data clearly indicate that the PRF scales are homogeneous and internally consistent.

The test-retest reliability coefficients for the PRF tend to be higher than for most other personality scales. Jackson (1974) reported an unpublished study by Bentler in which the PRF Form AA was administered twice to 135 male and female college students with a one-week interval between administrations. The reliability coefficients ranged from .46 for the Desirability scale to .90 for the Harmavoidance scale. The median value for all twenty-two scales was .81. Test-retest reliability data have not been published for Form E.

The manual also reported data indicating that Forms AA and BB are equivalent. The means and standard deviations for scores on the parallel forms were remarkably similar.

Data concerning equivalence of Forms A and B have not been reported.

VALIDITY. The primary evidence for the validity of the PRF comes from a series of studies in which scores on the PRF content scales were compared with self- and peer ratings (Jackson, 1974; Kusyszyn, 1968; Merrens, 1975). The data from these studies indicated that scores on the PRF scales were correlated substantially with relevant self- and peer ratings and were relatively independent of ratings of nonrelevant characteristics. Such data offer evidence of both convergent and discriminant validity. For example, Jackson reported results of an unpublished study by Jackson and Guthrie in which PRF scores of 202 college students were correlated with corresponding behavior ratings by peers. The correlations ranged from .16 for the Understanding scale to .64 for the Order scale (median: .29). In another study involving 36 students who shared living quarters and hence would be expected to have a better opportunity to observe one another, the correlations between eight PRF scales and corresponding peer ratings ranged from .35 to .71 (median: .47). Data such as these suggest that the PRF scales are measuring the characteristics they were designed to measure.

Although the manual does not report relationships between PRF scales and other nontest data, more recent research has shown the PRF scales to be related to a wide variety of variables. For example, Antarctic explorers (Butcher & Ryan, 1974) and college student activists (Pierce & Schwartz, 1971) differed from control subjects on PRF scores. Depressed and control subjects differed on a number of PRF scales (Hoffman, 1970), and PRF scores were related to cigarette smoking (Williams, 1973), alcohol use (Nerviano, 1976), and drug use among college students (Holroyd & Kahn, 1974). Although PRF scores of alcoholics changed significantly during a treatment program (Hoffman, 1971), the scores could not predict subjects who dropped out of such treatment (Gross & Nerviano, 1973). Academic achievement and attrition were predicted from PRF scores (Harper, 1975; Maudal et al., 1974; Rothman, 1973), as were therapist type (Berzins et al., 1971) and success as paraprofessional mental health workers (Sandler, 1972). Results such as these demonstrate the potential usefulness of the PRF in personality research and in some applied settings.

Some information concerning construct validity was reported in the form of correlations of PRF scales with scales from the Strong Vocational Interest Blank (SVIB) and the California Psychological Inventory (CPI) (Jackson, 1974). For example, the PRF Dominance scale correlated .78 with the CPI Dominance scale. The PRF Achievement scale correlated .62 with the CPI Achievement via Conformance scale but only .49 with the Achievement via Independence scale. The Cognitive Structure scale of the PRF correlated −.70 with the Flexibility scale of the CPI.

Some of the correlations between PRF scores and the SVIB scales also are interesting. For example, the Clinical Psychologist scale correlated .40 with the PRF Exhibition scale, whereas the Exhibition scale correlated −.51 with the Experimental Psychologist scale. The Understanding scale of the PRF correlated .49 with the Biological Scientist scale and −.51 with the Banker scale. These patterns of correlations between the PRF and scales from other inventories support the notion that the PRF scales are measuring the characteristics they were designed to measure.

CONCLUSIONS. Our review of the development of the PRF and of subsequent research suggests that it is one of the most psychometrically sound instruments available. There is adequate evidence to indicate potential utility in a variety of settings. Yet the PRF is not used commonly in applied settings, partly because of Jackson's emphasis on test construction and his relative disinterest in applications. Even the name of the test, Personality *Research* Form, discourages

its use in applied settings. Also, research with the instrument has been rather unsystematic and scattered, and no one has attempted to summarize and synthesize the results of the research in a manner that would be helpful to those working in applied settings. In his review of the PRF, Hogan (1978) summarized the status of the test by characterizing it as " . . . an interesting and marvelously well-constructed test whose empirical validity (after 10 years) has yet to be demonstrated" (p. 1,008).

OTHER PERSONALITY INVENTORIES

The additional inventories that we now will discuss briefly are ones that are used relatively frequently but for which research data are limited; several have been published so recently that it is too soon to judge how useful they will be in applied settings. The reader who requires more information about these tests should consult *Tests in Print II* (Buros, 1974).

Adjustment Inventory (AI)

The AI (Bell, 1934, 1963) was one of the earliest objectively scored personality tests. The scales were constructed by content validation procedures, they were refined by internal consistency methods, and their validity was checked against external criteria. There are separate forms for students (grades nine to sixteen) and for adults. The most recent revision of the student form yields scores for the following six scales: home, health, submissiveness, emotionality, hostility, and masculinity. Reliability of scores is adequate; some positive results were obtained from studies in which AI scores were correlated with scores from other tests and with independent judgments of the variables represented by the AI scores. Because the content of the AI scales is obvious, test subjects can easily distort responses. Other problems with the AI are the small size and the unrepresentativeness of the normative samples. Although the AI was one of the most promising of the earlier personality inventories, in most settings it has been replaced by more widely researched inventories such as the MMPI or the CPI.

California Test of Personality (CTP)

Although the CTP (Thorpe et al., 1953) is still used fairly often in applied settings, it is an outdated inventory for which acceptable empirical validity has never been demonstrated. Forms of the test are available for subjects ranging from kindergarten age through adulthood. There are three summary scores—self-adjustment, social adjustment, and total adjustment— and thirteen subscales with labels such as Self-reliance, Nervous Symptoms, Social Skills, Family Relations, and so on. The scales were constructed with content validation procedures. The summary scores seem to be adequately reliable, but the subscale scores have poor reliability. In spite of the authors' unsubstantiated claims that the test is of great value in counseling, and some data suggesting that summary scores are somewhat related to other global measures of adjustment, there are not sufficient validity data to recommend the CTP for routine use.

Comrey Personality Scales (CPS)

The CPS (Comrey, 1970) was developed by factor-analytic procedures. Subjects respond to each item on a seven-point scale ("always" to "never" or "definitely" to "definitely not"). Scores are generated for the following substantive scales: Trust vs. Defensiveness, Orderliness vs. Lack of Compulsion, Activity vs. Lack of Energy, Social Conformity vs. Rebelliousness, Emotional Stability vs. Introversion, Masculinity vs. Femininity, and Empathy vs. Egocentrism. In addition, two validity scales are included in the test. Reliability of scales compares favorably with other personality scales, but the normative samples are not very representative. Although initial validity data were very encouraging, the test has not become

popular in applied settings and adequate additional data concerning validity have not emerged.

Edwards Personality Inventory (EPI)

The EPI (Edwards, 1967) was developed to assess personality characteristics that would vary among normal subjects. The format of the EPI is unique in that it requires subjects to respond to items as would someone who knew them well. Although this approach is an interesting variation, available data suggest that scores obtained with these instructions are virtually identical to those obtained when subjects are asked to provide direct self-descriptions. The test is a long one, with 1,500 items distributed among five booklets. Through a combination of face validation and factor-analytic procedures, Edwards developed fifty-three scales, such as Intellectually Oriented, Self-confident, Anxious About His Performance, Feels Misunderstood, and Critical of Others. Normative data are based on several very small and unrepresentative samples of high school and college students. Internal consistency coefficients are satisfactory, but no temporal stability data are presented in the test manual. The most serious problem with the EPI is that no external validity data are presented in the manual. Edwards justified publishing the test before such data were available on the basis that its publication would stimulate other investigators to collect such data. Unfortunately, there still is not adequate evidence of empirical validity to justify use of the EPI.

Eysenck Personality Inventory (EPI)

The EPI (Eysenck & Eysenck, 1969) is the product of considerable factor-analytic research by its authors on the structure of personality. Unlike most other factor-analytically based tests, the EPI yields scores on only two substantive scales—Neuroticism and Extraversion. In addition, a validity scale is scored to assess test-taking attitudes. Temporal stability of the scales is quite high.

Scores on the two scales have been related significantly to scores on other tests, to self-ratings, and to criterion judgments provided by external raters. In spite of these significant validity data, there is not much evidence that the EPI provides information that will be helpful in practical, applied settings. This may explain, to a large extent, why the EPI has been more popular among personality researchers than among practitioners.

Guilford-Zimmerman Temperament Survey (GZTS)

The GZTS (Guilford & Zimmerman, 1949) was one of the earliest self-report inventories constructed with factor-analytic procedures. The GZTS yields scores for three validity scales and for the following ten substantive scales: General Activity, Restraint, Ascendance, Sociability, Emotional Stability, Objectivity, Friendliness, Thoughtfulness, Personal Relations, and Masculinity. Normative samples are adequate, and reliability coefficients compare favorably with other personality scales. Data have been reported indicating that GZTS scores are related to a variety of other personality variables. However, as is the case with 16 PF, very little data exist concerning the relationship between GZTS scores and behaviors of importance in applied settings.

IPAT Anxiety Scale Questionnaire (ASQ)

The ASQ (Cattell & Scheier, 1957, 1963) is a frequently used self-report measure of trait anxiety. Although the details of scale construction are not provided in the manual, it seems clear that anxiety is one of the constructs that emerge when scores from the 16 PF are factor-analyzed. The ASQ has forty items to which subjects respond by using a three-alternative format (for example, yes, no, in between). The scale yields a total anxiety score and seven subscale scores. Normative data based on samples of high school and college students are provided only for the total score. Adequate reliability has been demonstrated for the total score. Validity data are in the form of corre-

lations with other anxiety scales and with clinical ratings of anxiety and comparisons of groups of subjects such as neurotics and normals. Most validity data suggest that the ASQ is a satisfactory measure of trait anxiety.

Interpersonal Check List (ICL)

The ICL (Leary et al., 1956) was developed as a self-rating adjective checklist to measure variables found in Leary's interpersonal system of personality. Using 128 adjectives, subjects can describe themselves or other persons (wife, parent, and so on). Scores are obtained for eight interpersonal traits: Managerial-Autocratic, Competitive-Narcissistic, Aggressive-Sadistic, Rebellious-Distrustful, Self-effacing-Masochistic, Docile-Dependent, Cooperative-Overconventional, and Responsible-Hypernormal. These traits are considered to be present in everyone to some extent; however, extreme amounts of any of the traits are considered to be undesirable. No normative data are available for the ICL, and no reliability or valdity data have been reported. The ICL has some utility as a personality research tool, but its use in applied settings is not advised.

Jackson Personality Inventory (JPI)

The JPI (Jackson, 1976) was constructed with the same sequential strategy used with the PRF. However, instead of assessing needs, as did the PRF, the JPI was designed to measure a variety of interpersonal, cognitive, and value orientations. The following fifteen substantive scales are scored: Anxiety, Breadth of Interest, Complexity, Conformity, Energy Level, Innovation, Interpersonal Affect, Organization, Responsibility, Risk Taking, Self-Esteem, Social Adroitness, Social Participation, Tolerance, and Value Orthodoxy. In addition, an Infrequency scale is available to detect nonmeaningful responses to the items. Normative data are presented for large and carefully selected samples of male and female college students. Surprisingly, no temporal stability data are reported in the manual. Validity data are in the form of correlations of JPI scores with other personality scales and with self-ratings and peer ratings of variables assessed by the JPI. These data suggest that at least some of the JPI scales have promising validity. However, data concerning the utility of the JPI in applied settings are not yet available.

Millon Clinical Multiaxial Inventory (MCMI)

The MCMI (Millon, 1977) was developed to provide separate scales for relatively enduring personality characteristics and for acute clinical states. A sequential strategy—involving the intuitive generation of items, refinement through internal consistency procedures, and external validation—was used in constructing the MCMI scales. In addition to three validity scales for detecting nonmeaningful responses, the MCMI has twenty substantive scales grouped under three general headings: Basic Personality Styles (Asocial, Narcissistic), Pathological Personality Syndromes (Schizoid-Schizophrenic), and Symptom Disorders (Anxiety, Alcoholic Misuse, Psychotic Delusions). The scales have adequate reliability, and initial validity data indicate that diagnostic groups (for example, psychotic depressives) differ from psychiatric control subjects on appropriate scales. However, it is still too soon to know if adequate validity data will emerge to recommend the MCMI for general clinical use.

Mooney Problem Check List (MPCL)

The MPCL (Mooney & Gordon, 1950) was designed to facilitate communication between counselees and counselors. It really is not a measuring device. Rather, it consists of a series of lists of problems commonly experienced by high school and college students. Subjects are asked to check the problems that they have and to indicate the problems that are of most concern to them. By examining the checked problems and discussing them with clients, counselors may facilitate the counseling relationship. No formal scores as such are generated, but it is possible to count the number of problems checked in areas such as school adjustment, social-psychological relations, sex and marriage, and so on. No normative data, reliability coefficients, or validity information are presented in the manual. Although psychometrically the MPCL is inadequate, it continues to be a popular technique because many counselors believe that the information it provides facilitates the counseling relationship.

PERSONALITY INVENTORIES FOR CHILDREN

Although inventories such as the MMPI, CPI, and 16 PF can be used effectively with adolescents as young as fourteen or fifteen years of age, they are not appropriate for younger children. The biggest problem in using self-report techniques with young subjects is that they do not have the reading ability required. In addition, even when items can be read, some of the content of most inventories is not appropriate for young children. For example, an item such as "I am pleased with my sex life" would have little meaning to a ten-year-old boy even if he could read it. Because of these difficulties, projective techniques and observational procedures tend to be more commonly used with children.

Several different approaches have been utilized in developing personality inventories specifically for children. One approach, to substitute pictures for printed items, was used in the development of the Missouri Children's Picture Series (Sines et al., 1971). Another approach, to have a parent or other caregiver respond to statements about the subject's behavior and personality, was used in the development of the Personality Inventory for Children (Wirt et al., 1977).

Missouri Children's Picture Series (MCPS)

The MCPS is an objective, nonverbal, empirically derived test of personality to be used with children from ages five through sixteen. Because of some of the problems involved in using verbal stimuli with children, the MCPS uses as items simple line drawings of children engaged in a variety of activities that children have indicated that they like or do not like to do. There are 238 such drawings printed on small cards. The pictures show a child of indefinite age and supposedly unclear sex engaged in a variety of activities in different settings. A sample drawing from the MCPS is presented in Figure 10–6. The cards are shuffled before each administration, and the child is told to look at each picture, to decide if it looks like fun or does not look like fun, and to sort the cards into two piles. After all cards are sorted, the examiner records the responses on an answer sheet and uses scoring templates to obtain raw scores for the various MCPS scales (see Table 10–7). Normative data are provided separately for boys and girls at each year level from five to sixteen years. The T-score equivalents for each raw score are plotted on a profile sheet similar in format to those of other inventories discussed in this chapter.

The Conformity-Communality scale consists of items for which there was agreement on the direction of sorting by at least 80 percent of subjects in the norm samples. The items in the Masculinity-Feminity scale are ones that were sorted differently by boys and girls of various ages in the normative samples. The Maturity scale is made up of items that were sorted differentially by boys

TABLE 10-7 Summary of Missouri Children's Picture Series Scales

Scale 1	Conformity-Communality
Scale 2	Masculinity-Femininity
Scale 3	Maturity
Scale 4	Aggression
Scale 5	Inhibition
Scale 6	Activity Level
Scale 7	Sleep Disturbance
Scale 8	Somatization

and girls in the seven- and thirteen-year-old groups in the normative samples.

The remaining MCPS scales (Aggression, Inhibition, Activity Level, Sleep Disturbance, Somatization) were constructed empirically on the basis of symptoms reported by parents of children being seen for psychological evaluations in hospitals and clinics. For each scale, a group of children was identified for whom the appropriate symptom was rated by parents as severe. This group was compared with a general sample of children from the same clinical settings to determine which MCPS drawings were sorted differently by the two groups. These drawings comprised a scale for the particular symptom.

Split-half reliability coefficients vary considerably for the MCPS scales, ranging from .33 to .91 for boys and from .44 to .88 for girls. Test-retest reliability coefficients with a ten-day interval between administrations range from .45 to .71 for normal boys and from .48 to .77 for normal girls. Both the internal consistency and test-retest coefficients are considerably lower than for most other personality inventories. Of even more concern are the very low test-retest coefficients (.01 to .70) obtained for some of the scales with clinical samples.

The authors of the MCPS reported some initial validity data that were rather encouraging. Scores on some of the scales were compared with behavioral characteristics of test subjects derived from hospital and clinical records. For the most part the behavioral characteristics associated with the test scores were consistent with the constructs that the scales were designed to

FIGURE 10–6 Sample item from Missouri Children's Picture Series. (Copyright 1964 by J. O. Sines, J. D. Pauker, and L. K. Sines. Reproduced with permission.)

measure. Subsequent validity studies by other researchers have not yielded very encouraging results, particularly when the test is used in settings different from the ones in which it was developed (Miller, 1978).

The authors of the MCPS should be commended for utilizing a very ingenious approach to obtaining self-report from children. However, the MCPS is still in the process of development, and its users should consider the test to be tentative and experimental at this time. Whether future research will demonstrate enough validity to recommend routine clinical use of the MCPS remains to be determined.

Personality Inventory for Children (PIC)

The PIC is an empirically derived instrument whose format is very similar to the MMPI. Instead of children directly reporting their behavior, parents or other caregivers describe their children by responding to various kinds of statements, such as "My child is nervous," "At times my child curses," and "Others think my child is depressed." The PIC is intended for use with children between the ages of three and sixteen.

The PIC includes three validity scales designed to assess the respondent's attitudes in completing the task. The Lie (L), F, and Defensiveness (DEF) scales are similar in construction and intent to the L, F, and K scales of the MMPI. The Adjustment (ADJ) scale is intended as a screening device to identify children who are in need of a psychological evaluation and as a general measure of poor psychological adjustment. Items were selected for the ADJ scale by contrasting responses of parents of normal and maladjusted children.

The clinical scales of the PIC are listed in Table 10–8. Although each scale involved a slightly different methodology in its construction, most were developed by contrasting the responses of children known to differ on relevant characteristics (for example, delinquent versus nondelinquent) or by

asking experienced clinical child psychologists to identify statements in the PIC that they judged to be indicative of relevant characteristics. In addition to the three validity scales, the adjustment scale, and the twelve clinical scales, seventeen supplemental scales can also be scored (See Table 10–8). These supplemental scales are ones whose validities are rather tentative and/or whose intended purposes are not as directly relevant to routine clinical assessment as those of the clinical scales.

After the respondent has completed items in the inventory, raw scores are obtained for the various scales by using templates available from the publisher. The raw scores are converted to T-scores, and these are used to construct a profile similar to that used with the MMPI. Separate norms are available for boys and girls and for the three-to-five-year and six-to-sixteen-year age ranges.

The test manual (Wirt et al., 1977) reports considerable empirically based information about the meaning of scores on the

TABLE 10-8 Summary of Personality Inventory for Children Scales

Profile Scales	Supplemental Scales
Validity and Screening Scales	Adolescent Maladjustment
	Aggression
	Asocial Behavior
Lie	Cerebral Dysfunction
F	Delinquency Prediction
Defensiveness	Ego Strength
Adjustment	Excitement
	Externalization
	Infrequency
Clinical Scales	Internalization
	Introversion-Extraversion
Achievement	K
Intellectual Screening	Learning Disability
Development	Prediction
Somatic Concern	Reality Distortion
Depression	Sex Role
Family Relations	Social Desirability
Delinquency	Somatization
Withdrawal	
Anxiety	
Psychosis	
Hyperactivity	
Social Skills	

various scales. It also suggests a general strategy for profile interpretation, and a number of sample interpretations are included.

The manual reports test-retest reliability coefficients for normal and clinical samples. The average test-retest coefficient for the validity and clinical scales for a clinical sample with an average interval of fifteen days between administrations was .86. Clearly, the reliability of the PIC scales compares favorably with other personality scales.

One of the most positive features of the PIC is that its authors have continued to collect validity data for its scales. Much of this information is reported in the manual, and additional data continue to appear in psychological journals. Most of these studies compared PIC scores of children known to differ on some important variables. For example, in one study described in the manual, the PIC profiles of groups of delinquent boys and girls were studied. As expected, both sexes showed pronounced elevation of the Delinquency scale when compared with the normal standardization samples. In another study, boys and girls between the ages of five and twelve who had received diagnoses of childhood psychosis were compared with the standardization samples. For both sexes the profiles of the psychotic children were dominated by extreme elevations of the Psychosis scale. In addition, the psychotic boys and girls showed significant elevations on the Achievement, Intellectual Screening, Developmental, and Social Skills scales, reflecting the cognitive and social deficits usually manifested by psychotic children.

The PIC is one of the most promising techniques for assessing personality variables in children. It overcomes many of the problems encountered in using direct self-report with young subjects, and it can be used appropriately whenever there is access to an adult informant who knows the child well. If future validity data are as positive as those already reported, the PIC may well become the technique of choice in the assessment of children's personalities.

11

Interviewing
and
Behavioral Assessment

In earlier chapters we considered in detail psychological tests as sources of assessment data. However, there are other sources of information available to the assessor. Among these are self-report interview data, data obtained from significant others who are in positions to know the subject, social history or case history information, and direct observational data. It is to some of these other sources that we turn our attention in this chapter.

INTERVIEWING

The interview is by far the most common technique utilized in psychological assessments. Garfield (1974, p. 77) defined the interview as involving " . . . some form of communication between two or more persons, organized around a specific purpose." It is the specific purpose underlying the interview that differentiates it from the numerous, more casual verbal interactions that most of us have on a daily basis. The purposes for which interviews are conducted are quite varied. An employer can interview applicants for a job in order to determine which, if any, of the applicants will be successful if hired. A teacher can interview a child's parents to try to understand why the child is misbehaving in the classroom. A national pollster can interview members of a community to try to determine their attitudes about a political candidate. A psychologist can interview patients or clients in order to understand better their problems and to try to determine the most appropriate treatments.

Types of Interviews

The interviews that are most often conducted by psychologists can be characterized as selection, therapeutic, or assessment interviews. In *selection interview* the purpose is to determine an interviewee's suitability for some position or program. It can involve applicants for jobs, for academic training programs (for example, graduate school in psychology, medical school, law school), or for other positions or programs. Sometimes the goal of the interview is to decide if a particular applicant is suitable, but more often several or more applicants are interviewed with the goal of identifying the *most suitable* person. The most important factor in the selection interview is that the interviewer has considerable familiarity with the job or position for which selection is taking place. Either explicitly or implicitly the interviewer must conduct an analysis of the abilities, experiences, and other characteristics required for success in the job or program. The interview then is devoted primarily to obtaining information about these relevant characteristics of the applicant.

The major goal of the *therapeutic interview* is to help clients or patients solve problems or bring about desired changes in personality or behavior. The exact nature of the therapeutic interview is determined to a large extent by the theoretical orientation of the interviewer. A person with a strong psychoanalytic orientation might tend to concentrate on childhood experiences and memories. A client-centered therapist might focus on the client's current perceptions and feelings. A learning-oriented interviewer would probably emphasize factors that are reinforcing the interviewee's behavior. Regardless of the theoretical orientation of the psychologist, therapeutic interviews tend to have several common features. They typically are instigated by interviewees who desire to bring about changes in their life. In addition, therapeutic interviews occur over a reasonably extended time period (for example, once a week for six months).

The major goal of the *assessment interview* is to gather information about the interviewee so that the interviewer can make accurate inferences about or descriptions of the interviewee. The nature of the inferences or descriptions will differ as a function of the goal of the assessment process. Sometimes the product of the interview will be an inference about whether the interviewee has significant emotional problems, whether professional intervention is indica-

ted, and what treatment is likely to be most effective. At other times the interviewer will be asked to make specific predictions about important behaviors such as suicide or homicide. Still other situations will require the interviewer to describe the interviewee's personality and behavior in as much detail as possible.

Structured versus Unstructured Interviews

The most important dimension of the assessment interview is the extent to which it is structured. Structure refers to the extent to which an interviewer asks exactly the same questions in the same manner of each interviewee. An extremely structured interview is one in which a specific set of questions is asked or read by the interviewer. Such an approach was recommended by Spitzer et al. (1964), who provide interviewers with a standard set of 82 questions to be used with all interviewees. Based on the responses to these questions, the interviewer completes a 248 item true-or-false questionnaire about the interviewee. A less extreme example of a structured interview is one in which the interviewer is guided by an outline or list of topics. However, the exact manner and order in which the topics are discussed vary from interview to interview. An extremely unstructured interview is one in which the interviewer follows no specific plan. Open-ended questions (for example, "Will you tell me about yourself?") are asked, and few constraints are placed on what the interviewee can discuss and how he or she can discuss it.

The most obvious advantage of the structured interview is that it assures that specific information required for the assessment will be covered. This is especially important because the assessment interview typically takes place on a single occasion. If important material is not covered in an initial interview, there may not be another opportunity to do so. Another advantage of the structured interview is that relatively inexperienced interviewers typically find it easier to conduct an interview when they have a definite outline or agenda to guide them. An important advantage of the more unstructured interview is that it offers an opportunity to determine what the interviewee judges to be significant enough to talk about. Such interviews also permit the interviewer more flexibility in pursuing important topics that were not anticipated before the interview but that became evident as the interview progressed. Finally, the unstructured interview allows the interviewer to observe the interviewee's behavior in a rather unstructured situation. In practice most interviewers use a combination of structured and unstructured techniques. A common approach is to begin the interview with some open-ended questions and to permit the interviewee to respond without imposing constraints. Then, more structure is introduced by the interviewer to assure that important topics are covered.

The Interview Process

GOALS OF THE INTERVIEW. It is important for the interviewer to have specific goals in mind before the interview begins. Why is the person being interviewed? What inferences, decisions, or descriptions will be required of the interviewer upon completion of the interview? Having clearly formulated goals assures that relevant information and topics will be covered during the interview. For example, if the goal of an interview is to determine if someone should be involuntarily hospitalized, the interview would focus on the person's potential danger to oneself and others and ability to care for oneself if not hospitalized. If the purpose of the interview is to determine the most appropriate vocational rehabilitation program, the interview probably would focus on that person's vocational interests, aspirations, and past employment.

PHYSICAL SETTING. Korchin (1976) suggested that all that is needed for a successful interview is a quiet, comfortable room free from distractions. Such surroundings facilitate the concentration and attention of both the interviewer and the interviewee, and they emphasize the confidential, private nature of the interview. It does not matter much whether the interview is conducted with parties on opposite sides of a desk or on side-by-side chairs as long as both parties feel comfortable and attentive. Plush furnishings and decorating are not important, but comfortable surroundings tend to relax interviewees and to increase the likelihood that they will be cooperative and will discuss important topics.

ESTABLISHING RAPPORT. *Rapport* refers to a feeling of mutual trust and respect between the interviewer and the interviewee. Rapport is important in testing and in interviews because it increases the likelihood that interviewees will be cooperative and motivated. In our opinion, in most instances the best way to establish rapport is to discuss with interviewees the purpose of the interview and what will happen as a result. If interviewees understand these things and believe that the interviewer is sincerely interested in them, and if they are convinced that it is in their best interests to be cooperative and honest, the interview is likely to be successful.

VERBAL AND NONVERBAL BEHAVIOR. Obviously, what subjects say in reponse to questions is of great interest. However, many writers (for example Garfield, 1974; Korchin, 1976) emphasized the importance of nonverbal behavior in the interview. How the person says something may be as important as what is said. Nervous laughter, problems with concentration or attention, and other nonverbal behaviors can provide important information. For example, if the interviewee expresses sadness about some event or behavior but does not seem sad behaviorally, we may want to question the self-reported emotion. If an interviewee becomes restless and avoids eye contact when talking about members of the opposite sex, we may wish to hypothesize anxiety in heterosexual relationships.

CONDUCTING THE INTERVIEW. As should be evident from our previous comments, it is the responsibility of the interviewer to initiate the interview, to ensure that appropriate topics are covered, and to bring the interview to its end. After discussing the purpose of the interview, it generally is best to ask several opened-ended questions and then to introduce more structure as required to ensure that relevant topics are covered. Table 11-1 presents a sample outline for an assessment interview. Obviously, the outline can be modified according to the interviewee's characteristics and/or the purpose of the interview. Note that some information from the interview comes directly from the subject's responses (for example identifying data, nature of the problem, school history), but other information is based on observations of the client's behavior during the interview (physical appearance and motor activity). Still other information is based on a combination of the subject's self-report and observations made during the interview (dominant emotions, attention, and orientation).

There are several important things to keep in mind when conducting interviews. First, do not suggest answers to the interviewee by asking questions such as "Was your relationship with your mother a good one?" It would be much preferable to ask "How did you get along with your mother?" Second, allow the interviewee to

TABLE 11-1 Sample outline for assessment interview

I. General observations
  A. Circumstances and setting of interview
  B. Description of client
    1. Identifying data (age, sex, race, etc.)
    2. Physical appearance (dress, grooming, outstanding physical characteristics)
    3. General behavior (cooperativeness, general demeanor)
II. Current problem
  A. Nature of problem
  B. Duration and severity of problem
  C. Previous professional help
  D. Insight and expectations
III. History
  A. Developmental (pregnancy and delivery, developmental rates, illness and injury)
  B. Family constellation (mother, father, siblings, significant others living in home; relationships among family members; family style)
  C. School (achievement, activities, behavioral problems)
  D. Military (rank, experiences, difficulties)
  E. Occupation (level, aspirations, reliability, quality of performance)
  F. Current family (spouse, children; relationships, atmosphere, style)
IV. Mental status and current functioning
  A. Emotions and behavior
    1. Emotions (dominant emotions or mood, stability of emotions, appropriateness of emotions)
    2. Behavior (activity level, abnormalities of behavior, potentiality for destructive or negative behaviors)
  B. Central organizing processes
    1. Intelligence (vocabulary, memory, judgment)
    2. Thought processes (speed, coherence, abstract thinking, flexibility)
    3. Thought content (central themes, abnormalities, insight)
  C. Perceptions (misperceptions, hallucinations, attention, clarity of consciousness, depersonalization, orientation)
  D. Interpersonal relations (perceptions of and reactions to significant others, interpersonal sensitivity, primary role assumed)
  E. Sources of and reactions to stress and conflict
    1. Satisfaction of important needs
    2. Perceptions of environment
    3. Conflicting needs
    4. Task-oriented reactions
    5. Defenses
    6. Life-style

answer the questions; the interviewer should not answer them. For example, an inexperienced interviewer might ask "How did you feel when you lost your job?" and without giving the interviewee time to answer might add "Probably terrible, huh?" Third, learn to be comfortable with periods of silence. Often interviewees are using such periods to formulate answers or to think about topics they would like to discuss. Inexperienced interviewers often become uncomfortable during silences, feeling that they are doing something wrong, and they quickly break the silence by asking another question.

That the interviewer's behavior influences the interviewee's responses has been well documented by Matarazzo and his colleagues (Matarazzo et al., 1965). For example, these investigators determined that as the length of the interviewers' utterances increased, the interviewees showed a corresponding increase in the length of their utterances. Likewise, shorter interviewer utterances tended to produce shorter utterances by the interviewee. Other, perhaps more obvious characteristics of the interviewer that could influence response might include sex, age, race, degree of perceived authority, and extent of perceived interest and understanding.

Evaluating the Interview

Because the interview has been used in different ways for different purposes by persons with varying skills and experience, it is difficult to reach any definite conclusions about its utility. That an interview is included in almost every assessment conducted by psychologists attests to the psychologists' beliefs concerning its value. However, before we can accept the interview as a useful source of assessment data, we must consider the scientific evidence concerning its reliability and validity.

RELIABILITY. The typical process used to determine the reliability of the interview is to have two or more interviewers interview the same persons or view videotapes of interviews and independently to make some ratings, inferences, or predictions about them. If the interviewers agree in their perceptions, the interview is thought to be reliable. This process really determines the reliability of the clinical judgments based on the interview, since it is not possible to separate meaningfully these judgments from the interview itself.

Research data concerning reliability of interview procedures have been quite mixed. For example, Hunt et al. (1953) reported the results of a study in which 794 enlisted naval personnel underwent two independent psychiatric interviews. Based on each interview a judgment was made concerning whether each man was suitable or unsuitable for military service. There was 93.7 percent agreement among the psychiatrists. However, less agreement was reported when the psychiatrists were asked to make more specific inferences about the men (for example, specific psychiatric diagnosis). More negative results were reported in an early study by Hollingsworth (1922). Twelve experienced sales managers each interviewed fifty-seven applicants for a sales position. Each manager rank-ordered all fifty-seven applicants from best (1) to worst (57). Overall, there was little agreement among the managers, and one applicant was rated best (1st) by one manager and worst (57th) by another.

Although the data concerning reliability of interviews are far from conclusive, several tentative conclusions can be reached. Reliability is likely to be greater when interviewers are more experienced, when a more structured interview is used, and when the inferences based on the interview are more general or global in nature.

VALIDITY. The validity of the interview must be established in terms of the accuracy of judgments of the interviewers based on information obtained and observations made during the interview. This process typically involves having psychologists or others interview subjects and make inferences, predictions, or other judgments about them. The accuracy of the judgments is determined by comparing them with some external criterion measure. For example, we could have personnel directors interview job applicants and predict their job performance by using some rather specific measure (say, amount of life insurance sold in six months). The accuracy of these predictions could be checked against actual sales.

Some studies on the validity of judgments based on interview data suggest that the interview is potentially a useful technique. Table 11-2 summarizes the results of a study reported by Wittson & Hunt (1951). Psychiatrists interviewed 944 naval personnel who, during aptitude placement testing, were identified as possibly having psychiatric problems. On the basis of the interviews, each man was placed by the interviewer into one of the following categories: mild symptoms—treatment not indicated; moderate symptoms—shore duty only indicated; severe symptoms—hospitalization indicated. One year after the psychiatric interviews the military status of 932 of the men was studied. As can be seen in Table 11-2, a much higher proportion of the men with severe symptoms (89.7 percent) had been discharged than was the case for the other two groups. Although the data from this study support the utility of the interview, we must be concerned about a possible flaw in the study's methodology. Although the authors

stated that the psychiatrists' categorization did not systematically become a part of the men's records, there is no assurance that in at least some cases those making decisions about discharge were not aware of the psychiatric categorization and based decisions on it rather than on the men's actual military performance.

In Chapters 9 and 10 we discussed a study by Sines (1959) that bears on the issue of validity. Sines asked clinicians to produce Q-sort descriptions of patients based on one or more of the following sources of assessment data: biographical data sheet, MMPI, Rorschach, interview. The accuracy of these descriptions was determined by comparing them with similar descriptions generated by the patients' therapists. The results indicated that the biographical data sheet yielded the most accurate descriptions, but the interview data added more to biographical data than did either the MMPI or the Rorschach. The average correlation between the Q-sort descriptions based on biographical data plus interview data and descriptions generated by therapists was .566, whereas corresponding correlations for the biographical data sheet plus MMPI and biographical data sheet plus Rorschach were .378 and .368, respectively.

Not all validity data have been positive. For example, it has been reported that the interview did not add significantly to test scores and high school achievement in the prediction of college success (Sarbin, 1943) and was of little practical use in predicting the success of graduate students in clinical psychology training programs (Kelly & Fiske, 1951). Reviewers seem to be in agreement that interviews generally do not have sufficient validity to justify their use in personnel selection (Arvey, 1979; Mayfield, 1964; Reilly & Chao, 1982 Ulrich & Trumbo, 1965; Wagner, 1949; Wright, 1969). For example, Reilly and Chao (1982) reviewed twelve studies and reported that the average correlation between interview-based estimates of job performance and supervisors' ratings of actual performance was only .19. These reviewers pointed out that

TABLE 11-2 Psychiatric discharge as a function of interviewers' judgments about severity of psychiatric condition

Severity	Subsequent Psychiatric Discharge	
	N	Percent
Mild (N = 527)	34	6.5
Moderate (N = 367)	74	20.2
Severe (N = 38)	34	89.7

Adapted from Wittson, C. L., and Hunt, W. A. (1951), The predictive value of the brief psychiatric interview. *American Journal of Psychiatry, 107,* 582-585. Copyright 1951, the American Psychiatric Association.

this average validity coefficient is considerably lower than corresponding coefficients based on standardized test data.

In spite of some of these negative findings, the interview is still widely used for a variety of assessment purposes. As was mentioned earlier in relation to reliability, interviews tend to be more valid when interviewers are skilled, when the procedures are more structured, and when the inferences based on the interview are more general or global in nature. Because interviews require considerable amounts of time, their cost effectiveness must be assessed in each setting where they are thought to have some potential utility.

BEHAVIORAL ASSESSMENT

Probably one of the most important changes that has occurred in the field of psychology since World War II has been the increasing emphasis on behavioral approaches to the treatment of maladaptive behaviors. Behavior therapy originally involved the application of classical and operant learning principles to the treatment of maladaptive behavior, but more recently its scope has been changing to include more emphasis on cognitive, as well as behavioral, variables. The successful implementation of behavior therapy techniques requires an adequate assessment of the specific behaviors in need of change and the variables eliciting and maintaining these behaviors. Behavior therapists have not found traditional assessment procedures, such as the Rorschach or MMPI, to be particularly useful in identifying these specific behaviors and variables, and they have developed some alternative approaches to assessment that have come to be labeled *behavioral assessment*.

Comparison of Traditional and Behavioral Approaches

Goldfried and Kent (1972) provided by far the most cogent discussion of the similarities and differences between traditional and behavioral approaches to assessment. They pointed out that although the ultimate goal of both approaches is to predict human behavior, there are important differences in the assumptions underlying the approaches, in the methodologies used to develop assessment procedures, and in the manner in which the assessments are conducted.

A major difference between the approaches is that behavioral assessors contend that the information obtained in the assessment process should be directly relevant to the specific goals of the assessment. For example, behavioral assessors seeking to help a couple with marital problems would focus on how the couple actually interact on a day-to-day basis rather than how they respond to items on a personality inventory (Kendall & Norton-Ford, 1982).

Traditional assessment approaches typically assume that behavior is motivated by certain underlying personality dynamics. By clearly understanding inferred personality constructs (for example, needs, traits, defenses), we should be able to predict overt behavior. Responses to test items are thought to be "signs" of underlying personality constructs. As illustrated in Figure 11-1, the test responses are used to make inferences about underlying personality constructs. Theories of personality then predict target behaviors of persons with particular constellations of characteristics. For example, a set of TAT stories in which the char-

FIGURE 11–1 Inferential processes in traditional and behavioral assessment.

TRADITIONAL ASSESSMENT

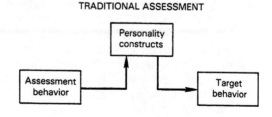

BEHAVORIAL ASSESSMENT

acters, and particularly the hero, are arguing and fighting would probably be seen as evidence of a strong aggression need in the subject's personality. Having inferred this need, we would then expect the subject to be hostile and aggressive in a wide variety of situations.

In behavioral assessment the observed behavior is seen as a "sample" of the actual behavior in which we are interested. For example, if we are interested in determining how hostile or aggressive a child is with the child's peers, we could sample that behavior directly, perhaps through observation of the child interacting with peers on a school playground. As illustrated in Figure 11-1, the behavioral assessment approach does not make inferences about underlying personality constructs. Rather, because the observed behavior is seen as a sample of the target behavior, inferences are made directly from observed behavior to target behavior. If we see the child on the playground behaving aggressively with peers, we probably will infer directly that the child also will be aggressive with peers on other occasions, at least when the situational variables are similar to those in which we made the observations.

Because traditional approaches to assessment assume that consistencies in behavior exist independently of situational variables, the selection of test items is based primarily on the constructor's theory of personality, with little or no attempt to represent different situational variables. For example, a traditional personality scale to measure anxiety might include items such as "I feel nervous much of the time," "It is difficult for me to relax," or "I worry excessively." Note that none of these items mentions particular situations or circumstances. It is assumed that the anxious person will be anxious in most or all situations and circumstances. By contrast a behavioral anxiety scale, such as the S-R Inventory of Anxiousness (Endler et al., 1962), would ask subjects about behaviors in a variety of situations. On the S-R Inventory of Anxiousness subjects are asked to indicate how they would feel and/or behave in

eleven different situations, such as meeting a new date, crawling along a ledge high on a mountainside, or getting up to give a speech before a large group. The inventory also recognizes that anxiety can be felt in several different ways. Subjects are asked to indicate reactions to each of the situations on fourteen different dimensions (for example, "heart beats faster," "becomes immobilized," "experiences nausea"). Thus, whereas a traditional anxiety scale yields a single score indicating how anxious a person is, behavioral inventories typically yield multiple scores, indicating subjects' experiences or behaviors in a variety of situations and in different response modes.

Traditional and behavioral assessment approaches also differ in the relationship between assessment and intervention. Traditional assessment emphasizes gathering information before intervention. When assessment continues during or after the intervention, it typically is brief and informal. In contrast, behavioral assessors emphasize that assessment must continue on a formal basis throughout intervention. Only in this way can the success of an intevention procedure be assessed. For example, if a person is involved in a behavioral intervention program to reduce or eliminate stuttering, it would be essential throughout the intervention to assess the frequency with which stuttering occurs and in what situations.

Steps Involved in Behavioral Assessment

Mischel (1968) believes the following steps to be necessary in every behavioral assessment:

1. Define problem behaviors and desired changes with clear behavioral referents.
2. Describe the exact circumstances provoking the problem behaviors.
3. Identify the conditions maintaining the problem behaviors.
4. Select intervention (treatment) strategies most likely to produce the desired changes.
5. Evaluate the efficacy of the treatment interventions.

Persons seeking professional help usually are quite willing to talk about their problems and about changes they want to make in their lives. However, their reports rarely are in the specific behavioral terms required for an adequate assessment. A client may report being "unhappy" or "depressed," assuming that others will know exactly what is meant by these labels. However, these terms mean quite different things to different people. For one person *depression* might mean psychomotor retardation, withdrawal from everyday activities, and perhaps even suicidal ideation. For another person *depression* might mean being bored and not especially stimulated by one's life. Different intervention strategies would be indicated by these different sets of circumstances.

The behavioral assessor must help the client be more specific in describing problems and desired changes. The client could be asked to describe exactly what behaviors are of concern (for example, crying, sleep disturbance, not going to work), how often they occur (four times per day), and how long they last (a few minutes versus several weeks or months). Clients often do not give accurate accounts of their behaviors unless given adequate structure. We are aware of a client who was asked to report how often he engaged in some self-abusive behavior. His estimate was 10 to 12 times per day. However, when he was given a counter and asked to record each incident, it was learned that the behaviors occurred more than 200 times each day.

Kanfer and Saslow (1969) suggested that problem behaviors can be categorized as either excesses or deficits. An excess is any behavior or class of behaviors described as problematic by the individual because of excess in its frequency, intensity, or duration or because of its inappropriateness. Bedwetting, child abuse, and rape are examples of obvious behavior excesses. Other behaviors are considered excesses only when carried to extremes. For example, it is quite normal for a person to consume food on a daily basis. However, for people who eat so much and so often that they become grossly over-weight, eating would be classified as a behavior excess. Taking a shower on a daily basis also would be normal behavior under most circumstances. However, taking showers eight or ten times every day would be considered a behavior excess.

Behavior deficits are classes of behavior described as problematic because they fail to occur with sufficient frequency, adequate intensity, in appropriate form, or under socially expected conditions. Put more simply, behavior deficits are things that people should or would like to be doing but are not. Examples include not initiating conversations with other people, not being able to say no to unreasonable requests, or not being able to participate appropriately in class discussions. There are individual differences among people in the ease with which these behaviors can be performed. They become problematic and a target for change only when they are impossible or so difficult for the person to do that functioning is impaired significantly.

Once the problem behaviors are specified, behavioral assessment focuses on the exact circumstances provoking or eliciting them. It is important to know when and where the behaviors occur (or do not occur), who is present, and the activities taking place at the time. Does the child abuse occur only when the person has been drinking excessively or when there have been problems at work or under other special circumstances? Is the person unable to initiate conversations only with members of the opposite sex and has no difficulties doing so with same-sex peers? A thorough understanding of the circumstances provoking the problem behaviors is important because it may help to understand the reasons for them. It also is necessary to understand these circumstances if effective treatment programs are to be designed. For example, if a man has great anxiety only when talking to persons judged to be more knowledgeable or in some other way superior to himself, that aspect of the situation would have to be incorporated into a treatment strategy.

Probably the most critical step in

behavioral assessment is identifying the conditions that maintain the problem behaviors. Behavioral approaches emphasize that the problem behaviors are learned in the same way as all other behaviors. Behavior is maintained because it is being reinforced in some way. The behavioral assessor must understand what reinforcement contingencies are operating for each problem behavior. It should not be assumed that the same reinforcers exist for all persons. For example, for some people money and the material possessions it can buy are extremely powerful reinforcers. For others, recognition from significant others for achievements or other behaviors is a much more powerful reinforcer than money. Sometimes the reinforcers are quite obvious, and other times they are subtle and complex. For example, when the school-age child develops stomachaches when it is time to go to school, often the child avoids going to school and thereby avoids anxiety-producing situations such as examinations, gym activities, and so forth.

As an example of a less obvious reinforcer, consider the adolescent female who refuses to eat to such an extent that her health, and perhaps even her life, are at risk. What could be reinforcing such apparently self-destructive behavior? It has been suggested that for many persons, not eating is a way of experiencing some sense of control over their lives (Davidson & Neale, 1982). Often their situations are such that they feel that they have little or no control over events in their lives. By steadfastly refusing to eat, even when encouraged to do so by parents and others, they are able to feel some control, and this feeling is very reinforcing. Of course, there often is the additional positive reinforcer of added attention from parents and others when they do not eat.

Information concerning the specific problem behaviors and desired changes, circumstances provoking or eliciting the problem behaviors, and circumstances reinforcing or maintaining the reinforcement behaviors are all considered in designing intervention strategies to produce the desired changes in behavior. The behavior therapists have developed a wide array of techniques, procedures, and programs to bring about behavioral change. For example, a mother of the child who is having temper tantrums probably would be advised to stop reinforcing the behavior by not giving the child what he or she is trying to get by having the tantrum. The client who has been having difficulties in initiating relationships could undergo a social skills program. The adolescent girl who is not eating could be taught more positive ways of feeling that she has some control over her life.

Once the intervention program has been initiated, it is necessary to evaluate its effectiveness. Typically this involves comparing some aspect of the problem behavior (usually frequency) before and after the intervention. Kaplan and Saccuzzo (1982) reported a case study that illustrates how assessment is important in evaluating the effectiveness of an intervention procedure. A seven-year-old boy was brought to a psychologist because he was reluctant to eat all but a few select foods. His usual menu consisted of cold cereal for breakfast, a peanut butter sandwich for lunch, and plain spaghetti for dinner. He refused to eat meat or vegetables. His physical condition deteriorated to the point that his physician indicated he would have to be hospitalized if his eating did not change. It was learned that at age four the boy had suffered from an illness in which he was unable to eat solid food for twenty-five days because it made him gag. His eating problems continued even after he had recovered from the illness. A behavioral assessment revealed that the boy probably was having the eating problem because of the negative consequences of eating that he experienced during his earlier physical illness and because of the attention and other secondary gains that he received at that time. The problem behaviors probably were being reinforced by the continuing concern of parents and others.

An intervention strategy was developed in which the boy received points for the number of calories that he consumed each day. His mother kept track of the calories that he consumed, and the number of points that he earned were recorded on a bulletin board in the boy's room so that he could see his own progress. The points could be accumulated and exchanged for things that the boy wanted (for example, baseball cards, or a miniature pinball machine). The boy's daily calorie intake was recorded for one week before the intervention program was begun and for one week after it had been in effect. These data are reported in Figure 11-2. It can be seen clearly that the boy's calorie intake increased markedly after one week of the intervention, suggesting that the intervention had been successful. Of course, it would be desirable to continue to monitor calorie intake for a longer period of time to determine if the effects of the intervention were maintained.

Techniques Used in Behavioral Assessment

The two major techniques used by behavioral assessors are observation and self-report. The major purpose of this section is to consider briefly the ways in which these two techniques are utilized in behavioral assessments.

OBSERVATION. Because behavior assessment emphasizes an understanding of specific behaviors of subjects and specific circumstances in their environments, direct observation is almost always the preferred assessment technique. When a subject is observed in real situations (a child in a classroom or a family at home) the observation is referred to as *naturalistic*. An obvious advantage of naturalistic observation is that we are able to observe the subject behaving with people and in situations where the problem behaviors actually occur. A major disadvantage of naturalistic observation is that it often is difficult, if not impossible, to accomplish. It is relatively easy to go into a classroom to observe a child who has been reported as engaging in disruptive behavior. However, it would not be very practical to go to an office to observe an employee's personal problems with a supervisor.

When naturalistic observation is not prac-

FIGURE 11–2 Eating behavior before and after intervention. (Adapted from *Psychological Testing: Principles, Applications, and Issues*, by R. M. Kaplan and D. P. Saccuzzo. Copyright © 1982 by Wadsworth, Inc. Reprinted by permission of the publisher, Brooks/Cole Publishing Company, Monterey, California.)

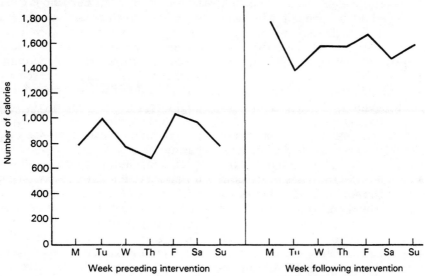

tical, often it is possible to observe subjects in situations designed to resemble or simulate the naturalistic ones. For example, a subject could role-play interactions with a supervisor. Another approach might be to present the subject with a video-taped situation similar to one that has been self-reported as problematic. The actors on the tape talk and respond to the subject (viewer), and the subject's responses are observed. Although these simulations have the obvious advantages of being more practical and of permitting more control of the situations than is possible in naturalistic observation, we must always be concerned about how representative they are of the actual situations they are designed to simulate.

Observation in either naturalistic or simulated situations can be made with varying degrees of formality. An observer can simply watch what is occurring and form some rather general impressions of the subject and the circumstances. Generally, more useful data are obtained from observations when the behaviors to be observed have been defined in advance, when the observers have had some training in making the observations, and when there is some systematic procedure for recording the behaviors of interest. For example, it would be advantageous to define "disruptive classroom behavior" operationally. Such behavior might be judged to be present whenever children get out of their seats without the teacher's permission or whenever they talk aloud except in response to the teacher's questions.

Because any observation represents a sampling of behavior, consideration must be given to obtaining samples that are representative of the population of behaviors of interest. For example, the child's behavior in the classroom typically should be observed at several different times of day and when several different kinds of activities are taking place (recitation, free play, quiet time).

Reactivity is a phenomenon that occurs when people who are being observed alter their actions from their normal patterns because of the presence of observers (Roberts & Renzaglia, 1965). For example, if children are aware that someone is observing their classroom behavior, they may refrain from engaging in typical behaviors in order to make a good impression on the observer. To reduce reactivity, the observer should be as unobtrusive as possible. An observer in a classroom might choose to sit quietly in a back corner of the room from which behavior of interest can be observed without the teacher or the children being constantly reminded of the observer's presence. An even better situation is one in which observations can be made without the observer being visible to those involved in the situation. This is possible through the use of one-way mirrors, closed-circuit television, and similar devices. It also has been noted that if observers are present repeatedly in a situation they have less effect on the participants (for example, Heynes & Lippitt, 1954). Thus, an observer wanting to make classroom observations might be well advised to visit the classroom several times before recording data.

Observer bias occurs whenever observers have information about people they are observing that might lead them to alter their observations because of assumptions about how people should be acting (Kent et al., 1974). Thus, a teacher who is given a child's IQ score, which creates an expectation that the child should be doing well or poorly in certain classroom situations, could perceive behaviors differently depending on the teacher's expectations. Psychiatrists who know a patient was diagnosed as depressed might report different perceptions of the patient than what they would have reported if they knew the patient was diagnosed as paranoid.

Of central importance to all observations is that they be made reliably. Reliability generally is determined by having two or more persons observe the same behavior and report independently on their perceptions. If they agree on what they have observed the observations are considered to be reliable. Generally, more reliable observations result when the observers have been trained, when the observations to be made are specific rather than general, when the behaviors to be observed have been defined specifically, and when an unambiguous system for reporting observations is utilized (Kent & Foster, 1977).

Although there are limitations on the situations in which psychologists or other professionals can make observations, often other persons who are involved significantly with subjects can be used as observers. The reliability of observations made by these nonprofessional observers generally is quite acceptable (Evans & Nelson, 1977). Teachers can observe and report classroom behavior of children. Parents can observe children's behavior in the home. Nurses or nursing assistants can observe ward behavior of psychiatric patients. However, problems of reliability, bias, and expectancy that exist with professional observers are even more important when nonprofessional observers are utilized. It is important to train these observers concerning the specific behaviors that are to be observed and how they are to be reported or recorded.

In efforts to standardize the observation process, checklists and rating scales have been developed for a variety of situations. Teachers can record classroom behavior such as aggression, vocalization, or being out of one's seat (O'Leary et al., 1970). The Behavior Problems Checklist (Achenbach & Edelbrock, 1979) is used by parents to indicate behaviors that their children display at home in categories such as aggression, hyperactivity, and social withdrawal. The ward behavior of psychiatric patients can be rated with instruments such as the Nurse's Observation Scale for Inpatient Evaluation (NOSIE) (Honingfeld et al., 1966). The NOSIE requires nursing staff to observe patients on the ward for three days and to rate specific behaviors such as "refuses to speak" or "keeps himself clean" on a five-point scale.

SELF-REPORT. One of the easiest and most obvious ways to find out about people's behavior is to ask them to tell us about it. Self-report is a potentially rich source of behavioral assessment data because the person providing the information always is present when problem behaviors and other significant events occur. In addition, self-report is the only way in which private or covert behaviors (thoughts or feelings) can be recorded and quantified. In spite of its convenience and potential utility, self-report has some serious problems. The individual is reporting self-perceptions of events. Although such perceptions often are as important as a more objective account, one must not assume that self-report can always be accepted as an objective and accurate account of behavior. In addition, people often are unaware of or insensitive to behaviors and events that can be very important in behavioral assessment.

Both psychoanalytically oriented theorists and classical behaviorists have been reluctant to accept the validity of self-report (Lanyon & Goodstein, 1982). There is concern that the person might not be motivated to give accurate information or be able to remember accurately events that occurred in the past. Parry and Crossley (1950) asked 900 respondents for information that could be externally verified (for example, having a telephone, contributing to a particular charity). They found that for information about which subjects had little or no motivation to distort (having a telephone) there was almost perfect correspondence between self-report and external verification. For information about which the motivation to distort might be greater (contributing to a charity) there was approximately a 40 percent error in self-report. In a review of the research relevant to validity of self-reported interview information, Walsh (1967) concluded that about half the studies indicated high validity and about half indicated only moderate or low validity. Kendall and Norton-Ford (1982, p. 393) concluded that "research investigations have demonstrated that the information that people report about themselves can be accurate and valid, and behavioral assessors add that this is particularly true if the questions that are used to elicit self-report data are focused on specific behaviors that occur in specific situations."

Three primary forms of self-report are used by behavioral assessors. Most frequently self-report information is obtained in an interview. However, self-monitoring and self-report scales and questionnaires also are utilized to collect data.

The characteristics of the general assessment interview that were discussed earlier in this chapter also apply to behavioral interviews. The interviewer should establish rapport with the subject and should know clearly the information that is to be obtained in the interview. Subjects must be given opportunities to express themselves, but the interviewer is responsible for ensuring that appropriate areas are discussed. The major difference between the general assessment interview and the behavioral interview is that the latter places much greater emphasis on specific content areas (Haynes, 1978). In keeping with the general purposes of behavioral assessment, the behavioral interview focuses on the specification, in clearly behavioral terms, of problem behaviors, antecedent events, and maintaining circumstances. Most subjects initially do not report problems and events in specific behavioral terms. Rather, they talk in more general ways, using trait names and other constructs to communicate perceptions. It is the job of the behavioral interviewer to help subjects think and talk about problems and events in more clearly behavioral ways.

Haynes (1978) included the following among the goals for a behavioral interview:

1. *Problem Specification.* The interviewer surveys for multiple problems and then obtains detailed behavioral information relevant to each problem. Because of the difficulties associated with self-report, the interviewer develops hypotheses that can be collaborated later from other data sources.
2. *Assessment of Antecedent and Consequent Factors.* The interviewer attempts to obtain specific information about the situations in which problem behaviors occur, who is present and

what is happening when the problem behaviors occur, and what behaviors or events typically follow the occurrence of the problem behaviors. Subjects often do not readily remember this kind of information, and it often is helpful to ask them to recall and describe recent examples of the problem behavior.

3. *Gathering Historical Data.* Unlike the typical general assessment interview, the behavioral interview focuses on historical information only to the extent that it seems directly relevant to the current problem behavior.
4. *Assessing Mediation Potential.* The interviewer tries to assess the probability of successful intervention with the problem behaviors. Factors relevant to this prediction might include degree of insight, amount of emotional distress, and value of events that would follow successful behavioral change. This aspect of the behavioral interview is far less quantitative than other aspects, and it usually involves inferences on the part of the interviewer.
5. *Reinforcement of Clients.* The interviewer uses the interview to increase the likelihood that the client will return for intervention. This can be accomplished by showing an interest in the client and an understanding of the problem behaviors. In their efforts to extract specific behavioral data from clients, behavioral interviewers sometimes become mechanical in their approach, and this is not likely to increase the client's motivation to return for intervention.,
6. *Education of Client in Behavioral Language and Principles.* Through modeling of speech content and selective reinforcement of the client's comments, the interviewer provides information to the client about important behavioral terms and principles. This education increases the behavioral information that the client is likely to provide in the interview, and it prepares the client for the interview that is to follow.
7. *Making Explicit to the Client the Intervention Program.* The interviewer makes sure that the client clearly understands what will be involved in any intervention program resulting from the assessment and that informed consent for such intervention is obtained. Any special procedures (for example, physiological monitoring or videotaping) are described, and any dangers or risks involved in the intervention are stated clearly.
8. *Motivating the Client.* The interview is used to

increase the client's motivation to accomplish the stated behavioral changes. This can be done by reinforcing any positive changes that might be observed during the interview, no matter how small these changes might be, and by reinforcing the client's statements suggesting that positive change is possible or probable.

In self-monitoring people observe and report on various aspects of their own behavior. It differs from self-report during an interview in that the former involves current or immediate events, whereas the latter typically involves behaviors that have occurred at some time in the past. The problems created by inaccurate memory of past events are overcome by self-monitoring procedures.

Kendall and Norton-Ford (1982) described the steps involved in self-monitoring. First, the subject must decide whether certain behaviors, thoughts, or feelings have occurred. Subjects who are self-monitoring cigarette smoking must determine if they have smoked cigarettes during some specified time period. Second, subjects must record data concerning the behavior that is being self-monitored. Subjects could make a small mark on an index card each time a cigarette is smoked or could push a button on a mechanical or electronic counter. Finally, the recorded data must be displayed in a form that permits their use in assessment and intervention. A very useful way of displaying such data is in a graph or chart. Figure 11–3 illustrates a display of data concerning self-monitored smoking for one week.

Although frequency data are the most commonly collected form of self-monitoring information, subjects also are often asked to observe and record information concerning the circumstances surrounding each occurrence of the target behavior. When and where did the behaviors occur? Who was present? What was happening? What was the subject thinking or feeling immediately before the behavior occurred? What events followed the occurrence of the behavior? Information of this type almost always is re-

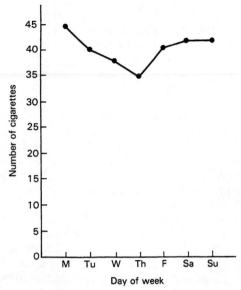

FIGURE 11–3 Sample display of self-monitored cigarette smoking behavior.

corded in written narrative form by the subject. Although such recording is more inconvenient than simply recording frequency data, the additional information it yields to the behavioral assessor often makes it worthwhile. Analyses of information concerning antecedent and consequent events can help the assessor and the client better understand what is eliciting the target behavior and what is reinforcing it. For example, persons who are self-monitoring smoking might observe that they are more likely to smoke when under particular kinds of stress or that smoking usually is accompanied by social interaction with other smokers. These observations would have considerable significance in understanding the problem behavior and in designing intervention strategies.

Although self-monitoring is an efficient and potentially valuable method for collecting data, there are some problems associated with its use. First, there is considerable evidence that the act of self-monitoring tends to produce changes in the behavior that is being monitored (Ciminero et al., 1977). Self-monitoring makes subjects more aware of occurrences of the target behaviors, and this awareness in turn can cause the subject to reduce the frequency of the behaviors. For example, Rutner and Bugle (1969) had a schizophrenic woman record the frequency of her auditory hallucinations. During the first three days of self-monitoring the reported frequency decreased from 181 to 10 per day. Although this reduction in target behaviors during self-monitoring makes it difficult to obtain accurate base line data for target behaviors, it can be viewed as therapeutic in itself and therefore desirable.

Another potential problem has to do with representativeness of the behavior that is sampled for self-monitoring. There is no problem in this regard when event recording is utilized. In event recording the subject records each and every occurrence of the target behavior. Thus, no sampling is involved. However, event recording is difficult to utilize when dealing with covert events (like thoughts or feelings) that might have no clearly delineated starting and stopping points or with behavior that occurs with such great frequency that it would be a burden for the subject to record all its occurrences. Time sampling is an alternative to event recording in situations such as these. In time sampling, time is divided into units (for example, one hour or five minutes) and the subject is asked to record whether or not the target behavior occurred during each unit. Although this simplifies the self-monitoring process considerably, information is lost in this approach. We may know, for example, whether a subject smoked during an hour unit, but we do not know how many times smoking occurred during the unit. Sometimes a combination of event recording and time sampling is utilized. Subjects are asked to record each occurrence of target behavior during certain time periods. For example, the day could be divided into hourly units, and the subject could record the frequency of cigarette smoking during three or four of the twenty-four hours in a day. We would not want the units all to be at meal times or all when the subject is at work.

Paper-and-pencil self-report scales and questionnaires are yet another technique utilized by behavioral assessors. The primary function of such instruments is consistent with that of other behavioral assessment procedures, namely, identifying problems in specific behavioral terms. Self-report instruments tend to be more practical and efficient than direct observation and interview because they are self-administered. They have the additional advantage of offering the potential for greater standardization than can be expected from interviews or most types of observation.

Most behavioral self-report instruments have been developed informally by clinicians for applied use or by researchers to assess treatment effects in experimental studies. Few of these instruments have been developed psychometrically to the extent that more traditional questionnaires, such as the MMPI, have been. Helpful lists and summaries of previously published self-report behavioral questionnaires were provided by Tasto (1977) and Haynes (1978). Cautela (1977) compiled a number of previously unpublished behavioral scales and questionnaires. Instruments have been developed for obtaining self-report concerning specific fears, assertiveness, depression, social interactions, and other problem behaviors. Efforts also have been made to develop questionnaires for assessing sources of reinforcement.

The psychometric sophistication of behavioral scales and questionnaires varies considerably. The Fear Thermometer (Walk, 1956) is an example of a very simple instrument. As illustrated in Figure 11-4, the subject is asked to indicate fear of some object or situation (for example, "a live harmless snake") by drawing a circle around the number that best represents the degree of fear. Although the Fear Thermometer has been used in several behavioral therapy research studies, there is virtually no information available concerning its psychometric properties.

Much more sophisticated procedures were used in developing and refining the

Consider your fear of a live harmless snake, then draw a circle around the number that best represents the degree of that fear. High fear is toward the top. Low fear is toward the bottom. The numbers in between represent gradations in fear from complete calm to extreme fright. Be as accurate as you can.

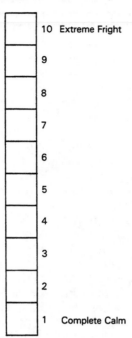

10 Extreme Fright

9

8

7

6

5

4

3

2

1 Complete Calm

FIGURE 11–4 Example of a fear thermometer. (Constructed according to a description provided in Walk, 1956. Copyright © 1956 by American Psychological Association, Inc.)

Fear Survey Scehdule (FSS) (Akutagawa, 1956). Although the original FSS was a 50-item scale, several other versions, varying in length from 51 to 122 items, have been used in research. The various measures consist of items to which subjects respond on a five-point scale (not at all, a little, a fair amount, much, very much) to rate their fear of a variety of objects (for example, snakes, blood), feelings (feeling angry, feeling rejected), activities (masturbation, witnessing surgical operations), and situations (being alone, being in a strange place). Norms have been published so that a subject's fear for any item can be compared with a standardizatin sample (Manosevitz & Lanyon, 1965). A total fear score can also be determined by summing responses to all items. Factor analysis of a 122-item version of the FSS (Tasto et al., 1971) revealed that the items can be divided into five primary groups: (1) fears related to small animals, (2) fears of precipitators and manifestations of hostility, (3) moralistically related fears and sexual fears, (4) fears of isolation and loneliness, and (5) fears of anatomical destruction and physical pain.

Internal consistency coefficients greater than .90 were reported for the FSS (Geer, 1965; Hersen, 1971). Test-retest reliability coefficients for the total score and for factor scores typically ranged from .70 to .85. These data suggest that scores on the FSS tend to be quite reliable.

Several types of validity data exist for the FSS. Numerous studies utilized the FSS before and after some behavioral intervention to assess the effects of the intervention

(Lang & Lazovik, 1963; Lang et al., 1965). These studies demonstrated consistently that scores on the FSS were lower after treatment than before treatment. If we assume that the therapeutic interventions reduced fear, the decreases in FSS scores can be seen as evidence that the instrument was sensitive to the changes in fear that occurred. More direct evidence for the validity of the FSS comes from studies in which subjects have rated their fears on the FSS and then have been subjected to behavioral assessment of the same fears. For example, Robinson and Suinn (1969) had subjects who claimed to be fearful of spiders actually try to approach and touch a harmless spider. Their approach behaviors corresponded to their self-reported fear of spiders on the FSS. When the approach behavior changed after successful treatment, corresponding changes in the self-reported fear on the FSS were noted.

It is important for behavioral assessors to be able to identify reinforcers that are maintaining problem behaviors and ones that can be used in intervention programs to bring about positive behavioral changes. The Reinforcement Survey Schedule (RSS) (Cautela & Kastenbaum, 1967) is a self-report questionnaire designed to identify such reinforcers. In the first two sections of the RSS, subjects are asked to describe how much pleasure they receive from a variety of activities such as eating particular foods, listening to various kinds of music, reading, playing sports, shopping, talking with people, or making love. They respond to each activity on a five-point scale (not at all, a little, a fair amount, much, very much). Another section of the RSS requires subjects to indicate on the same five-point scale how much they enjoy being in each of six situations, such as the following (p. 1,121):

You have just completed a difficult job. Your superior comes by and praises you highly for a "job well done." He also makes it clear that such good work is going to be rewarded very soon.

Information from the RSS is used by the behavioral assessor to understand the kinds of reinforcers that are important to individual subjects.

Keehn et al., (1970) reported internal consistency coefficients for the RSS ranging from .89 to .96. Test-retest reliability coefficients for college students were reported for periods of one week, three weeks, and five weeks (Kleinknecht et al., 1973). Although some of the specific items in the RSS had coefficients as low as .19, its temporal stability was generally quite satisfactory. Median test-retest coefficients for the one-week, three-week, and five-week intervals were .73, .67, and .71, respectively. Kleinknecht et al. concluded that " . . . the RSS is sufficiently stable over time intervals up to 5 weeks to warrant its use as a clinical and research instrument" (pp. 410–411).

The validity of the RSS must be judged according to how well potential reinforcers identified with the instrument actually work in reinforcing behaviors. Cautela and Wisocki (1969) showed that highly rated items actually can serve to reinforce changes in attitudes toward the elderly. Herr (1969) reported the utility of the RSS in identifying effective reinforcers for token economy programs.

TRADITIONAL TESTS FOR BEHAVIORAL ASSESSMENT. In Chapter 9 we discussed Maloney and Ward's suggestion that projective tests, such as the Rorschach or TAT, are most useful clinically when they are viewed as behavioral samples. Emphasis is placed on how the person completes the task rather than on the content of responses. Subjects' perceptual and cognitive styles, verbal ability, creativity, problem-solving strategies, and other important behaviors can be observed through the use of more traditional tests. Although some behavioral assessors recognize their potential utility, most tend to ignore traditional tests, or to minimize their importance because of their strong ties with psychodynamic theory and trait psychology. Readers who want more information about this behavioral use of traditional tests are referred to the work of Maloney and Ward (1976), Friedman (1953), and Greenspoon and Gersten (1967).

Evaluation

Although the same evaluative criteria that are applied to traditional assessment instruments also should be applied to behavioral assessment procedures, the latter have failed to incorporate the usual psychometric properties of validity and reliability into their development (Curran, 1979; Goldfried, 1979; Lanyon & Goodstein, 1982), and there has been little systematic effort to assess the psychometric properties of existing behavioral techniques. Many of the techniques used in applied settings resulted from intuitions and biases of the clinicians who developed them. When behavioral techniques were used in research, the techniques focusing on a given behavior (for example, anxiety or assertiveness) differed from one study to another (Goldfried & Linehan, 1977). This lack of standardization precludes the collection of meaningful normative data and limits the generalization of research findings.

RELIABILITY. Establishing reliability of behavioral assessment most often has involved demonstrating that independent evaluators observe and record behavioral data in similar ways. There are adequate data to conclude that trained individuals can reliably observe and record behavior of interest, particularly if the target behaviors have been clearly and specifically defined (Goldfried & Linehan, 1977). Although the temporal stability of self-report scales and questionnaires can be established in traditional ways, such data have not been reported for most of these instruments. Some of the more adequately researched instruments (FSS and RSS) have test-retest reliability coefficients approximately equivalent to those of more traditional personality questionnaires.

VALIDITY. The validity of any assessment procedure reflects the extent to which it measures what it has been designed to measure. Because behavioral assessment typically involves direct sampling of the behavior of interest, content validity is of primary importance (Lanyon & Goodstein, 1982). The behaviors sampled by observation, interview, self-monitoring, or questionnaire must be representative of the total population of target behaviors that could be measured. Goldfried and D'Zurilla (1969) described an analytic model for identifying appropriate behaviors. The suggested procedure is really quite simple. Populations of interest (such as college students or hospitalized psychiatric patients) are studied extensively to identify relevant behaviors, and these behaviors are then sampled systematically. For example, Goldsmith and McFall (1975) were interested in assessing personal competence among psychiatric patients. They interviewed many patients in order to identify relevant problematic interpersonal situations. By sampling systematically from the situations they identified, they constructed a scale of fifty-five common problem situations (dating, having a job interview, and so on). In a similar effort MacPhillamy and Lewinsohn (1972) identified items for their Pleasant Events Schedule by asking many college students to list events or situations that were pleasurable for them.

Criterion-related (empirical) validity is not particularly relevant to behavioral assessment if the assessment involves direct observation of the target behavior. In this case the assessment behavior and the criterion behavior are one and the same, and no prediction from assessment to criterion is necessary. As long as we are satisfied with the representativeness of the behavior that we observe (content validity), we can be confident that we also are measuring criterion behavior. For example, if the behavior that we are trying to understand is a child's disruptive actions in a classroom, we probably would choose to observe that behavior directly. By doing so we are assessing the criterion behavior directly.

Criterion-related validity is relevant to behavioral assessment when we do not observe the target behavior directly. If we ask a child or a teacher about problem behavior, either in an interview or through appropriate scales or questionnaires, we must be concerned about the extent to which their reports correspond with what actually is happening in the classroom. Typically we demonstrate the validity of these kinds of reports by comparing them with direct observation of appropriate behaviors. We previously discussed efforts that have been made to validate self-report. The study in which subjects expressed the degree of their fear of spiders on a questionnaire and then were actually asked to approach and touch a harmless spider (Robinson & Suinn, 1969) illustrates the approach used to compare self-report and direct observation of behavior. In general, existing data suggest that self-report and report by others who are involved with subjects are reasonably valid if subjects have had some training and if the relevant behaviors have been defined specifically (Kendall & Norton-Ford, 1982).

Construct validity refers to the extent to which we understand the factors underlying performance on an assessment task. For example, when we discussed individual intelligence tests, we stated that scores on most intelligence tests are related to a person's verbal facility. This kind of information is very helpful in understanding the construct of intelligence. Many behavioral assessors would maintain that construct validity is inapplicable to behavioral assessment because of the emphasis on specific behaviors rather than on more general traits or constructs. However, constructs such as fear, assertiveness, or social competence are of central importance in behavioral research and practice. It is just as important to understand the meaning of these constructs as it is to do so for more general constructs such as intelligence (Lanyon & Goodstein, 1982).

Validity of behavioral constructs can be assessed in several different ways. We can identify groups of people known to differ on a particular dimension (such as assertiveness) and determine if they are differentiated by our behavioral measures. We also can assess construct validity by noting changes in a measure as a function of some experience or intervention. For example, if ratings of assertiveness change as a function of an assertiveness program, we have additional information about what our rating scale is measuring. As is the case with more traditional assessment procedures, construct validity of a behavioral measure cannot be established in a single study (Lanyon & Goodstein, 1982). Rather, construct validity is established over time through the accumulation of research and clinical data.

Comparative Validity of Traditional and Behavioral Assessment

Because traditional and behavioral assessment procedures typically appeal to different kinds of assessors and are often applied to different types of assessment tasks, information concerning the relative utility of the two approaches is scanty and unsystematic. Indirect evidence for the superiority of behavioral approaches can be found in reports that using projective test responses as behavioral samples often leads to more accurate predictions than concentrating on the content of such responses (Friedman, 1953; Murstein, 1963).

Paul (1966) administered many different measures of anxiety before desensitization treatment for anxiety in public speaking. Using subjects' self-reported confidence when actually speaking in public as a criterion measure, Paul concluded that the more behavioral scale, the S-R Inventory of Anxiousness, was a better predictor than more traditional instruments such as the IPAT Anxiety Scale. Other investigators (Hase & Goldberg, 1967; Wallace & Sechrest, 1963) demonstrated that simple self-ratings corresponded more closely with criterion ratings of several personality characteristics than did scores on traditional instruments such as the Rorschach.

Critics of behavioral assessment point out that most of the techniques apply only to a limited number of specific problem behaviors and cannot be used meaningfully with the wide variety of problems encountered in applied settings. Lanyon and Goodstein

(1982, p. 36) concluded that " . . . although a few isolated studies have tended to support a more behaviorally oriented approach to assessment, there are insufficient findings at present to draw any conclusions regarding the comparative validity of both orientations." It seems to us that both approaches have utility, depending on the behavior to be assessed, the skill of the assessor, and the importance of situational variables. It is unlikely that assessors will soon adopt one approach to the exclusion of the other. Rather, as traditional and behavioral treatment strategies become more integrated, we expect to see more integration of the two assessment approaches.

12

Measuring Interests, Values, Attitudes, and Personal Orientation

The instruments to be discussed in this chapter are all self-report, typical performance tests. They measure aspects of human behavior similar to those measured by the personality inventories discussed in Chapter 10. In this regard, they have many of the same characteristics associated with personality tests (the possibility of faking, change over even short periods of time, and a variety of construction techniques).

Interest inventories have their origin in educational, vocational, and career counseling. In the United States the pursuit of happiness is one of the inalienable rights stated in the Declaration of Independence. A person is thus expected to be happy or satisfied with one's occupational choice. That is, one is supposed to be *interested* in one's job. Typically, interest inventories present large numbers of items asking whether or not various activities, occupations, and types of people are liked or disliked. The goal is to discover the kinds of activities and occupations in which people are interested. Although interests are not the

sole or even the most important determiner of occupational or educational choice or satisfaction, they are certainly one factor to consider. It is also true that some jobs are judged to be intrinsically uninteresting, boring, and even dangerous. Interest inventories contribute little toward understanding which people will take such jobs. Thus, most interest inventories are useful mainly in helping reasonably intelligent people choose among relatively high-status occupations. Despite their limitations, Tittle and Zytowski (1978) estimated that over 3.5 million interest inventories are scored annually in the United States, which means that they are certainly among the most commonly used tests in this country.

Measures of values and attitudes emerge from social psychology. Values are usually defined as being more basic, unchanging viewpoints on life. Attitudes may be rather specific and of limited duration. Religious and moral concerns, for example, are often considered to be values. On the other hand, we may have an attitude or an opinion about a presidential candidate, social groups, or a particular political issue (abortion, environmental protection, capital punishment, or foreign automobiles). Attitudes reflect how favorable people are toward groups, people, ideas, or issues. Most attitude scales or surveys are used for research and are not commercially published. It appears to us that interests, attitudes, and values are very similar to each other when the actual measurement instruments are examined.

Personal orientation inventories measure how a person relates to the environment. Sex-role preference and health-related behaviors are two examples of personal orientations that have recently been extensively studied. Again, the inventories and scales available have largely been used in research. Such scales are typically not part of personality inventories, although it seems to us that the constructs they measure could be regarded as personality traits.

INTEREST INVENTORIES

Strong-Campbell Interest Inventory (SCII)

The SCII has over a fifty-year history of use. Edward K. Strong, Jr. published the first version of this inventory in 1927. The Strong Vocational Interest Blank (SVIB) has been one of the most widely used and studied inventories in psychology. Buros (1978) lists 1,720 references to the various editions of this inventory. A survey of university counseling centers found that the SCII was the most frequently used test (Sell & Torres-Henry, 1979), and a survey of 335 secondary schools also found the SCII to be used frequently for career guidance (Engen et al., 1982). The SVIB was developed by empirical rather than theoretical techniques of inventory construction. We will focus our discussion almost exclusively on the SCII because it is the dominant interest inventory in current use. We will note briefly, however, several other inventories that are available.

HISTORY. This section draws heavily on Campbell's (1971, Chapter 11) informal history of the SVIB. In 1927, Strong published the first version of the interest inventory that still bears his name. A professor at Stanford University, Strong was intimately involved in revising and improving his inventory until his death in 1963. The voluminous data that he collected and analyzed, largely before the computer age, are impressive. He was a tireless, dedicated researcher. The 1927 inventory contained 420 items and had ten occupational scales. The earliest inventories were to be used only with adult men, but in 1933, a 410-item inventory for women was published.

FIGURE 12–1 Edward K. Strong, Jr. (1884–1963), a psychologist from Stanford University, developed the first interest inventory, a form of which is still in use. (Courtesy News Service, Stanford University)

These earliest editions were based on four assumptions that are still made. First, a person will be more effective and satisfied in a vocation if engaged in work that he or she enjoys. Second, people who continue working at a given occupation and are successful like that occupational environment fairly well. Third, interests remain fairly permanent from early adulthood throughout life. Interests of young people are thus important determiners of their chosen careers. Fourth, people who select the same responses as do those in the occupational group will enjoy that occupation.

Strong used an empirical approach in developing his scoring keys. A criterion group of successful persons in an occupation (for example, architecture) was administered the inventory. The items that differentiated this group from a "men-in-general" sample were then used as a scale for that occupational group. The "men-in-general" were persons in other occupations. Once an occupational scale was developed, persons taking the inventory who scored high on the architect scale, for example, would be told they had interests similar to those of architects. Strong's inventory was thus *criterion-keyed*. Items were placed on occupational scales not for any theoretical reason but because they empirically differentiated between a criterion occupational group, and those in other occupations. Computers now make such analyses relatively easy to accomplish. The basic idea, however, remains the same.

The SVIB for men was revised in 1938 and for women in 1946. The revisions contained thirty-eight and twenty-five occupational scales, respectively. Occupations were also clustered into eleven groups for ease of use and plotted on a profile. In 1943, Strong published a massive volume entitled *Vocational Interests of Men and Women*. This book described twenty years of research on interest measurement and gave many statistical details regarding the construction of the SVIB.

In 1949, Strong retired from Stanford University but continued to work and pub-

lish on his inventory. In 1963, shortly before Strong's death, the Center for Interest Measurement Research was established at the University of Minnesota. The criterion group data and other archival materials were transferred from Stanford to Minnesota. David P. Campbell assumed the major responsibility for maintaining, revising, and researching the SVIB.

In 1966, a revised SVIB for men was published; in 1969, a revised form for women. The two forms contained 399 and 398 items, for men and women, respectively. Campbell (1971, Appendix A) describes the many revisions made at that time. Maintaining separate forms for men and women seemed justified at the time, but having the men's form blue in color and the women's form pink gave at least the appearance of a sexist orientation. Campbell also published a handbook on SVIB that was, in many ways, an updating of Strong's 1943 book.

In 1974, the SVIB was revised again and retitled The Strong-Campbell Interest Inventory (SCII, Form 325), which reflected the contribution of Campbell. A single form containing 325 items for both men and women was produced and is in use at the present time. A theoretical structure was added to the reported profile and several important steps were taken to reduce sex bias in the inventory. Besides the use of a single form, these included eliminating items that appeared to have any sexual bias, eliminating references to gender in the inventory (for example, *policeman* was changed to *police officer*), adding new scales so that both sexes could be scored on all scales, and eliminating the masculinity-femininity scale entirely.

Although the inventory has not been revised since 1974, the manual was extensively revised in 1981. More important, the profile now includes 162 occupational scales, 99 of which were developed after 1977. Thus, many new samples were collected to increase the usefulness of the inventory. In the following discussion of the revised and expanded profile of the SCII, we have made extensive use of the current edition of the manual (Campbell & Hansen, 1981).

CONTENT. The SCII consists of 325 items. Subjects respond to most items by indicating "like," "indifferent," or "dislike" on an answer sheet. There are seven sections in the inventory. The variation in format should help maintain subjects' motivation and "interest." The following descriptions of the types of items are taken from the manual (p. 5):

Section I. Occupation (131 items). These items are all names of occupations, and this is the best section in terms of measurement power; that is, these items elicit more variability in response from one occupation to the next than any other section. People respond to the stereotypic nature of occupational titles, and their responses signal their own occupational orientation.

Section II. School Subjects (36 items). The school subjects cover a wide range of educational situations, including academic and other areas. Most people, even students as young as 13 or 14, have little trouble in deciding how they feel about a given subject, even though they may never have studied it.

Section III. Activities (51 items). This section contains a diverse collection of activities, such as Repairing electrical wiring, Making statistical charts, and Interviewing clients. This is another powerful section; occupations differ widely in the percentage of people answering "Like" or "Dislike" to these items.

Section IV. Amusements (39 items). These items cover spare-time activities, hobbies, games, and a variety of entertainments. Some examples are Poker, Symphony concerts, and Preparing dinner for guests.

Section V. Types of People (24 items). This section asks whether the respondent would enjoy working day-to-day with various types of people, such as Highway construction workers, High school students, and Babies.

Section VI. Preference Between Two Activities (30 items). This section asks the respondent to contrast two activities or circumstances, such as Taking a chance versus Playing safe, or Having a few close friends versus Having many acquaintances, and to decide which is the more appealing, or whether the two should be marked as equally attractive or unattractive.

Section VII. Your Characteristics (14 items). The respondent is asked to read a statement such as Usually start activity of my group, and to respond either "Yes," "?," or "No" to indicate if the statement is an apt self-description.

The items in the SCII were selected largely from earlier editions of the SVIB according to the following guidelines:

1. Each item should elicit a wide range of responses among occupations. Thus, items that were almost univerally liked or disliked would not be useful in differentiating among occupations. A wide range of responses to an item was the principal criterion used in selecting it.
2. Items should cover a wide range of occupational content.
3. Items should be free of sex-role bias. Items were modified whenever possible to eliminate any reference to gender, for example.
4. Items should not be culture-bound. This criterion makes it possible for the inventory to be translated more easily into foreign languages and to be used in subcultures within the United States. A Spanish version of the SCII, for example, already exists.
5. Items should be kept up to date. Occupational titles no longer commonly in use, for example, were eliminated.
6. Items should be unambiguous. That is, everyone should interpret items in the same way.
7. Items should be in good taste. Items that are offensive to a person can produce an emotional response that will limit the inventory's utility.
8. Items should have predictive as well as concurrent validity. That is, items were selected that could differentiate between two groups already in two different occupations (concurrent validity). Because interest inventories are used to make plans for the future, items should also discriminate among people who will enter different occupations in the future (predictive validity). Longitudinal studies are thus very important.
9. Items should be easy to read. The SCII has a reading level at about the junior high level.
10. Responding to the items should be interesting. The face validity of the items, that is,

their relevance to vocational interests, is an important factor in gaining a subject's cooperation.

ADMINISTRATION AND SCORING. The SCII is essentially self-administered. Because of the number of scales scored and the weighting procedures used, subjects must respond on answer sheets that are optically scanned and scored by computer. The SCII can be administered individually or in groups. According to the manual, an average adult can complete the inventory in about thirty minutes.

Responses to each item are weighted +1, 0, or −1 depending on the scale being scored. The resulting raw scores are then converted to T-scores (mean: 50; SD: 10) for each scale. The T-scores are reported on a computer-printed profile, and often a computer-generated interpretation of the profile is obtained. It is important to note that the SCII can only be scored by a commercial scoring service, Interpretative Scoring Systems in Minneapolis. In fact, the items that make up the individual scales are not published in the manual. The SCII has been criticized for this secrecy on the grounds that scientific research and discussion is thereby impeded (Dolliver, 1978; Johnson, 1976).

Scores are provided in four separate areas, and as indicated, are presented in a profile (an example is given in Figure 12–2). On the reverse side of the profiles are descriptive materials useful in interpreting the results. This material is reproduced in Figure 12–3. We will next describe the four types of reported scores.

Section I: Administrative index and special scales. The Administrative Indexes report the percentage of "like," "indifferent," and "dislike" responses for all parts of the inventory and the total. In addition, the total number of item responses is reported. Finally, the number of infrequent responses is given. Infrequent responses were defined empirically as those endorsed infrequently by the General Reference Sample. The Administrative Indexes are used to detect problems in test administration and scoring. The two special scales are Academic Comfort and Introversion-Extroversion. The first indicates the degree of comfort in being in an academic setting, and the second reflects a person's interest in being alone as opposed to working with other people.

Section II: General occupational themes. These six themes represent Holland's theory of an occupational-classification system (Holland, 1959, 1973). It assumes that people and occupations can be categorized into six types—Realistic, Investigative, Artistic, Social, Enterprising, or Conventional. Of course, people and occupations may possess one or more of these types. Descriptions of Holland's six types are given in Figure 12–3. A hexagon indicating the degree of intercorrelations among the six types is given in Figure 12–4. By referring back to Figure 12–2 the reader can determine which occupations score high on Holland's six themes.

Section III: Basic interest scales. Scores for twenty-three Basic Interest Scales are reported. They are organized within Holland's six themes and were constructed by grouping statistically related items. These scales are broader than specific occupations (for example, science rather than chemistry) and have the advantage of interpreting a homogeneous set of items.

Section IV: Occupational scales. The 1981 SCII reports scores on 162 Occupational Scales (for example, air force officer or dental assistant). The profile is plotted and labels are attached to the scores to aid in interpreting the profile. High scores, for example, suggest very similar interests to a particular occupational group; low scores suggest very dissimilar interests. Although every attempt was made to score all occupational scales for both sexes, this proved to be impossible. Thus, four Occupational Scales (dental assistant, dental hygienist, home economics teacher, and secretary) are normed only for females, and four scales (agribusiness manager, investment fund manager, skilled crafts, and vocational agriculture teacher) are normed only for males.

Despite much progress in opening all occupations to persons of either sex, some still remain largely the domain of either females (dental assistant) or males (vocational agriculture teacher). The 1981 SCII has, however, greatly improved the number of scales available for both sexes over that in the 1974 SCII.

In summary, the 1981 SCII yields a total of 189 scores based on weighted combinations of various but unspecified sets of the 325 items in the inventory. With the exceptions noted, all scores are provided for both males and females. However, separate norms are used for the two sexes. No other characteristics of the individual, such as age, are considered in scoring.

RELIABILITY. The SCII manual (Campbell & Hansen, 1981) presents evidence concerning the stability of scores from the General Occupational Themes, Basic Interest Scales, Occupational Scales, and Special Scales. The stability coefficients are based on test-retest correlations over two-week, thirty-day, and three-year intervals. The median test-retest correlations for the four types of scores and the three time intervals are given in Table 12–1. As can be seen, scores are generally quite stable, even over a three-year period. There is some decline in stability over a three-year period, however, suggesting some changes in how subjects respond to the SCII. Although based on relatively small samples and groups not representative of the general population, the results indicate that scores are fairly consistent over time.

For earlier editions of the SVIB, test-retest correlations over time intervals up to twenty-three years are available. Johansson and Campbell (1971) summarized the results of several studies over various retest intervals. They found that for very short intervals, the median test-retest correlations were in the low .90s. Test-retest intervals of one to five years yielded median correlations in the high .70s. For intervals ten years or longer, the age at which the initial testing occurred was important. If subjects were tested during their late teens, correlations of about .65 would be expected; if tested in the early twenties, correlations of about .70 would be expected; if tested after age thirty, correlations of about .80 would be expected. Although longitudinal research on the current SCII is not yet available, the results from the SVIB suggest that long-term stability will probably be found. However, all these results on the SVIB are based on males. The long-term stability of scores for females has generated much less research.

VALIDITY. Because Strong's original work focused mainly on differentiating among the interests of various occupational groups, we will discuss the validity of the Occupational Scales in more detail than the other scoring areas. For example, Holland's six General Occupational Themes represent a theoretical structure, which has been extensively presented by its author (Holland, 1973).

To evaluate the *content validity* of the Occupational Scales, we will first describe the construction techniques that were used. For the 1981 SCII, all scales based on data collected before 1966 were revised. The manual reports that all but 35 of 162 scales were based on samples tested with the SCII (Form T325). The 35 scales were based on samples tested with the preceding inventory used with males or with females. Several examples of criterion groups tested in various occupations are given in Table 12–2 (see pages 308-309).

There is no doubt that obtaining representative samples of persons in a particular occupation is a difficult task. Campbell and Hansen (1981, p. 46) note that the following characteristics are important: (1) The persons tested are *satisfied* with their jobs. (2) Whenever possible, the persons tested are *successful* at their chosen occupation. (3) Whenever possible, samples are restricted to those between the *ages* of twenty-five and fifty-five. (4) Samples are limited to *experienced* workers, those who have been on the job for at least three years. (5) Samples are limited to those performing an occupation

	Category	Rating	Code	Code	Occupation		
R	ADVENTURE	42 LOW					
	MILITARY ACTIVITIES	41 V-LOW	A	A	REPORTER	16	16
	MECHANICAL ACTIVITIES	57 HIGH	A	AS	ENGLISH TEACHER	14	17
I	SCIENCE	52 HIGH	SA	SA	SPEECH PATHOLOGIST	18	31
	MATHEMATICS	51 MOD-H	SA	SA	SOCIAL WORKER	24	18
			SA	SIE	MINISTER	18	20
	MEDICAL SCIENCE	41 MOD-L	SI	(IRS)	REGISTERED NURSE	10	(17)
	MEDICAL SERVICE	45 AVER	(RC)	S	LICENSED PRAC. NURSE	(21)	24
A	MUSIC/DRAMATICS	42 AVER	S	S	SPECIAL ED TEACHER	23	20
			S	S	ELEMENTARY TEACHER	19	29
	ART	52 AVER	SR	SR	PHYSICAL ED TEACHER	20	9
	WRITING	46 AVER	SRE	SRE	RECREATION LEADER	17	15
	TEACHING	47 AVER	SE	SE	YWCA/YMCA DIRECTOR	29	11
			SE	SE	SCHOOL ADMINISTRATOR	26	25
			SEC	SCE	GUIDANCE COUNSELOR	33	1A
S	SOCIAL SERVICE	45 AVER	SEC	SEC	SOCIAL SCIENCE TEACHER	34	13
	ATHLETICS	32 V-LOW	EA	EA	FLIGHT ATTENDANT	14	26
	DOMESTIC ARTS	53 MOD-H	E	EA	BEAUTICIAN	26	26
			E	E	DEPT. STORE MANAGER	27	18
	RELIGIOUS ACTIVITIES	37 MOD-L	E	E	REALTOR	12	14
			E	E	LIFE INSURANCE AGENT	20	6
	PUBLIC SPEAKING	51 AVER	E	E	ELECT. PUBLIC OFFICIAL	26	20
	LAW/POLITICS	54 AVER	E	(CA)	PUBLIC ADMINISTRATOR	35	(27)
			N/A	B	INVESTMENT FUND MGR	N/A	N/A
			EI	B	MARKETING EXECUTIVE	39	19
			E	E	PERSONNEL DIRECTOR	33	26
E	MERCHANDISING	42 MOD-L	EC	E	CHAMBER OF COMM. EXEC.	22	9
			EC	E	RESTAURANT MANAGER	31	19
	SALES	39 LOW	EC	EC	BUYER	15	13
			EC	EC	PURCHASING AGENT	31	30
	BUSINESS MANAGEMENT	49 AVER	N/A	ENC	AGRIBUSINESS MANAGER	N/A	16
			EB	N/A	HOME ECON. TEACHER	19	N/A
			EC	ECS	NURSING HOME ADMIN	17	13
			EC	ECR	DIETITIAN	41	33
C	OFFICE PRACTICES	56 HIGH			EXECUTIVE HOUSEKEEPER		
			CES	CES	BUSINESS ED. TEACHER		
			CE	CE	BANKER		
			CR	CE	CREDIT MANAGER		
			CR	CS	IRS AGENT		
			EB	CA	PUBLIC ADMINISTRATOR		
			C	C	ACCOUNTANT		
					SECRETARY		
			N/A		DENTAL ASSISTANT		

SCII ■ STRONG-CAMPBELL INTEREST INVENTORY — FORM T325

FIGURE 12–2 Sample profile from the Strong-Campbell Interest Inventory, Form T325. (Copyright © 1982 by National Computer Systems. Reproduced by permission.)

FIGURE 12–3 Descriptive materials for subject's use in interpreting scores on the Strong-Cambell Interest Inventory, Form T325. (Copyright ©1982 by National Computer Systems. Reproduced by permission.)

Understanding Your Results on the SCII

First, a caution. There is no magic here. Your answers to the test booklet were used to determine your scores; your results are based on what you said you liked or disliked. The results can give you some useful systematic information about yourself, but you should not expect miracles.

More important, *this test does not measure your abilities*; it can tell you something about the patterns in your interests, and how these compare with those of successful people in many occupations, but the results are based on your *interests*, not your abilities. The results may tell you, for example, that you like the way engineers spend their day; they do *not* tell you whether you have an aptitude for the mathematics involved.

Although most of us know something of our own interests, we're not sure how we compare with people actively engaged in various occupations. We don't know "what it would be like" to be a writer, or receptionist, or scientist, or whatever. People using these results are frequently guided to considering occupations to which they had never given a thought before. In particular, this inventory may suggest occupations that you might find interesting but have not considered simply because you have not been exposed to them. Or the inventory may suggest occupations that you ignored because you thought they were open only to members of the opposite sex. Sexual barriers are now falling, and virtually all occupations are open to qualified people of either sex—so don't let imagined barriers rule out your consideration of any occupation.

Men and women, even those in the same occupation, tend to answer some items on the test differently. Research has shown that these differences should not be ignored—that separate scales for men and women provide more meaningful results. Generally, the scales for your sex—those marked with the "Sex Norm" corresponding to your sex ("m" or "f")—are more likely to be good predictors for you than scales for the other sex would be. Still, you have been scored on *all* the scales, female and male, so that you can make use of the maximum possible information. In a few cases, such as AGRIBUSINESS MANAGER and HOME ECONOMICS TEACHER, Occupational Scales have not been established yet for both sexes.

Studies of employed people who completed this form as students have shown that about one-half are happily employed in occupations compatible with their profile scores. Among those in occupations not compatible with their results, many say they don't like their work, or are doing the job in some unusual manner.

Your answers have been analyzed in three main ways: first, under "General Occupational Themes," for similarity to six important overall patterns; second, under "Basic Interest Scales," for similarity to clusters of specific activities; third, under "Occupational Scales," for similarity to the interests of men and women in 85 occupations. The other two groups of data on the profile—labeled "Administrative Indexes" and "Special Scales"—are of interest mainly to your counselor. The first are checks to make certain that you made your marks on the answer sheet clearly and that your answers were processed correctly. The second are scales that have been developed for use in particular settings and require special interpretation; your counselor will discuss them with you.

The Six General Occupational Themes

Psychological research has shown that vocational interests can be described in a general way by six overall occupational-interest themes. Your scores for these six themes were calculated from the answers you gave to the test booklet. The range of these scores is roughly from 30 to 70, with the average person scoring 50. If your score on one of these themes is considerably above average, say 60, you share many of the characteristics of that theme; if your score is low, say below 40, you share very few; and if your score is close to the average, you share some characteristics but not many.

Men and women score somewhat differently on some of these themes, and this is taken into account by the printed statement for each score; this statement, which might be, for example, "Very high," is based on a comparison between your score and the average score for your sex. Thus, you can compare your score either with the scores of a combined male-female sample, by noting your numerical score, or with the scores of only the members of your own sex, by noting the phrasing of the printed comment.

If you indicated your sex on the answer form, then one of the following will be printed to help you interpret your score: V-HI (very high), HIGH, MOD-H (moderately high), AVER. (average), MOD-L (moderately low), LOW, or V-LOW (very low). If you did not indicate your sex on the answer form, then your counselor will help you with these scores.

The differences between the sexes in these themes are also shown on the profile: the open bars indicate the middle 50 percent of female scores, the shaded bars the middle 50 percent of male scores. The extending, thinner lines cover the middle 80 percent of the scores; and the mark in the middle is the average.

Following are descriptions of the "pure," or extreme, types for the six General Occupational Themes. These descriptions are only generalizations; none will fit any one person exactly. In fact, most people's interests combine all six themes to some degree or other.

R-THEME: People scoring high here are usually rugged, robust, practical, physically strong; they usually have good physical skills, but sometimes have trouble expressing themselves or in communicating their feelings to others. They like to work outdoors and to work with tools, especially large, powerful machines. They prefer to deal with things rather than with ideas or people. They generally have conventional political and economic opinions, and are usually cool to radical new ideas. They enjoy creating things with their hands and prefer occupations such as mechanic, construction work, fish and wildlife management, laboratory technician, some engineering specialties, some military jobs, agriculture, or the skilled trades. Although no single word can capture the broad meaning of the entire theme, the word REALISTIC has been used here, thus the term R-THEME.

I-THEME: This theme centers around science and scientific activities. Extremes of this type are task-oriented; they are not particularly interested in working around other people. They enjoy solving abstract problems, and they have a great need to understand the physical world. They prefer to think through problems rather than act them out. Such people enjoy ambiguous challenges and do not like highly structured situations with many rules. They frequently have unconventional values and attitudes and tend to be original and creative, especially in scientific areas. They prefer occupations such as design engineer, biologist, social scientist, research laboratory worker, physicist, technical writer, or meteorologist. The INVESTIGATIVE characterizes this theme, thus I-THEME.

A-THEME: The extreme type here is artistically oriented, and likes to work in artistic settings that offer many opportunities for self-expression. Such people have little interest in problems that are highly structured or require gross physical strength, preferring those that can be solved through self-expression in artistic media. They resemble I-THEME types in preferring to work alone, but have a greater need for individualistic expression, are usually less assertive about their own opinions and capabilities, and are more sensitive and emotional. They score higher on measures of originality than any of the other types do. They describe themselves as independent, original, unconventional, expressive, and tense. Vocational choices include artist, author, cartoonist, composer, singer, dramatic coach, poet, actor or actress, and symphony conductor. This is the ARTISTIC theme, or A-THEME.

S-THEME: The pure type here is sociable, responsible, humanistic, and concerned with the welfare of others. These people usually express themselves well and get along well with others; they like attention and seek situations that allow them to be near the center of the group. They prefer to solve problems by discussions with others, or by arranging or rearranging relationships between others; they have little interest in situations requiring physical exertion or working with machinery. Such people describe themselves as cheerful, popular, and achieving, and as good leaders. They prefer occupations such as school superintendent, clinical psychologist, high school teacher, marriage counselor, playground director, speech therapist, or vocational counselor. This is the SOCIAL theme, or S-THEME.

E-THEME: The extreme type of this theme has a great facility with words, especially in selling, dominating, and leading; frequently these people are in sales work. They see themselves as energetic, enthusiastic, adventurous, self-confident, and dominant, and they prefer social tasks where they can assume leadership. They enjoy persuading others to their viewpoints. They are impatient with precise work or work involving long periods of intellectual effort. They like power, status, and material wealth, and enjoy working in expensive settings.

Vocational preferences include business executive, buyer, hotel manager, industrial relations consultant, political campaigner, realtor, sales work, sports promoter, and television producer. The word ENTERPRISING summarizes this pattern, thus E-THEME.

C-THEME: Extremes of this type prefer the highly ordered activities, both verbal and numerical, that characterize office work. People scoring high fit well into large organizations but do not seek leadership; they respond to power and are comfortable working in a well-established chain of command. They dislike ambiguous situations, preferring to know precisely what is expected of them. Such people describe themselves as conventional, stable, well-controlled, and dependable. They have little interest in problems requiring physical skills or intense relationships with others, and are most effective at well-defined tasks. Like the E-THEME type, they value material possessions and status. Vocational preferences are mostly within the business world, and include bank examiner, bank teller, bookkeeper, some accounting jobs, financial analyst, computer operator, inventory controller, tax expert, statistician, and traffic manager. The word CONVENTIONAL more or less summarizes the pattern, hence C-THEME.

These six themes can be arranged in a hexagon with the themes most similar to each other falling *next* to each other, and those most dissimilar falling directly *across* the hexagon from each other.

Few people are "pure" types, scoring high on one and only one theme. Most score high on two, three, or even four, which means they share some characteristics with each of these; for their career planning, such people should look for an occupational setting that combines these patterns.

A few people score low on all six themes: this probably means they have no consistent occupational orientation and would probably be equally comfortable in any of several working environments. Some young people score this way because they haven't had the opportunity to become familiar with a variety of occupational activities.

The Basic Interest Scales

These scales are intermediate between the General Occupational Themes and the Occupational Scales. Each is concerned with one specific area of activity. The 23 scales are arranged in groups corresponding to the strength of their relationship to the six General Themes.

For each scale, the level of your score shows how consistent you answered "Like" to the activities in that area. If, for example, you consistently answered "Like" to such items as *Making a speech, Expressing judgments publicly,* and *Be a TV announcer,* you will have a high score on the PUBLIC SPEAKING scale, and you will probably have a higher than average score on the E-THEME.

On these scales, the average adult scores about 50, with most people scoring between 30 and 70. If your score is substantially higher than 50, say about 60, then you have shown more consistent preferences for these activities than the average adult does, and you should look upon that area of activity as an important focus of your interests. The opposite is true for low scores.

As with the other scales, your scores are given both numerically and graphically, and an interpretive comment, based on a comparison between your scores and the average score for your sex, is also provided.

Your scores on some of the Basic Interest Scales might appear to be inconsistent with scores on the corresponding Occupational Scales. You might, for example, score high on the MATHEMATICS scale and low on the MATHEMATICIAN scale. These scores are not errors; they are in fact a useful finding. What they usually mean is that although you have an interest in the subject matter of an occupation (mathematics), you share with people in that occupation (mathematicians) very few of their other likes or dislikes, and you probably would not enjoy the day-to-day life of their working world.

The Occupational Scales

Your score on an Occupational Scale shows how similar your interests are to the interests of people in that occupation. If you reported the same likes and dislikes as they do, your score will be high and you would probably enjoy working in that occupation or a closely related one. If your likes and dislikes are different from those

of the people in the occupation, your score will be low and you would probably not be happy in that kind of work. Remember that the scales for your sex—those in the "Norm" column for the sex corresponding to yours—are more likely to be good predictors for you than scales for the other sex would be.

Your score for each scale is printed in numerals—for those scales normed for your sex—and also plotted graphically. Members of an occupation score about 50 on their own scale—that is, female dentists score about 50 on the DENTIST "f" scale, male artists score about 50 on the ARTIST "m" scale, and so forth. If you score high on a particular scale—say 45 or 50—you have many interests in common with the workers in that occupation. The higher your score, the more common interests you have. *But note that on these scales your scores are being compared with those of people working in those occupations;* in the scoring of the General Themes and the Basic Interest Scales you were being compared with "people-in-general." If your score on any of the Occupational Scales is in the "Mid-Range"—between 28 and 39—you have responded *in the way people-in-general do.*

The Occupational Scales differ from the other scales also in considering your dislikes as well as your likes. If you share the same *dislikes* with the workers in an occupation, you will score moderately high on their scale, even if you don't agree with their *likes.* For example, farmers, artists, and physicists generally dislike working with large groups of people; if you don't like working with large groups, you share this attitude with the people in these occupations, and may score fairly high—40, for example—on these scales even if you don't like agriculture, art, or science. But a higher score—50—reflects an agreement on likes *and* dislikes.

Occupational Groupings

The Occupational Scales have been arranged on the profile in six clusters corresponding to the six General Occupational Themes. Within each cluster, occupations expressing similar interests are listed together.

To the left of each Occupational Scale name are one to three letters indicating the General Themes characteristics of that occupation for each sex. These will help you to understand the interest patterns found among workers in that occupation, and to focus on occupations that might be interesting to you. In some instances "N/A" appears which indicates that a scale for that sex is not available; in other instances, the code letters are in parentheses which indicates the scale for that sex is located elsewhere on the profile and the code letters indicate where. If you score high on two themes, for example, you should scan the list of Occupational Scales and find any that have the same two theme letters, in any order. If your scores there are also high—as they are likely to be—you should find out more about those occupations, and about related occupations not given on the profile. Your counselor can help you.

Using Your Scores

Your scores can be used in two main ways: first, to help you understand how your likes and dislikes fit into the work; and second, to help you identify possible problems by pointing out areas where your interests differ substantially from those of people working in occupations that you might be considering. Suppose, for example, that you have selected some field of science, but the results show that you have only a moderate interest in the daily practice of the mathematical skills necessary to that setting. Although it is discouraging to learn, you are at least prepared for the choice between (1) abandoning that field of science as a career objective, (2) trying to increase your enthusiasm for mathematics, and (3) finding some branch of the field that requires less use of mathematics.

In the world of work there are many hundreds of specialties and professions. Using these results and your scores on other tests as guides, you should search out as much information as you can *about those occupational areas where your interests and aptitudes are focused.* Ask your librarian for information on these jobs and talk to people working in these fields. Talk with your counselor, who is trained to help you, about your results on this test and other tests, and about your future plans. Keep in mind that choosing an occupation is not a single decision, but a series of decisions that will go on for many years; whenever a new decision must be made, you should seek the best possible information about yourself and about the work areas you are considering. Your scores on this inventory should help.

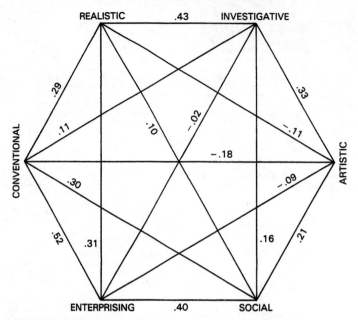

FIGURE 12–4 Intercorrelations among Holland's six General Occupational Themes, arranged in hexagonal order. Correlations are based on a sample of 300 females and 300 males. (From Campbell, D. P. and Hansen, J. C. Manual for the Strong-Campbell Interest Inventory, 3rd ed. Stanford University Press, 1981. Reproduced by permission of Stanford University Press.)

TABLE 12-1 Median and range of test-retest correlations (stability coefficients) for three time intervals for the four scoring areas of the Strong-Campbell Interest Inventory[a]

	Time Interval		
Scoring Area	*Two Weeks*	*Thirty Days*	*Three Years*
General Occupational Themes	.91[b]	.86	.81
	(.85–.93)	(.84–.91)	(.78–.87)
Basic Interest Scales	.91	.88	.82
	(.82–.93)	(.79–.93)	(.74–.92)
Occupational Scales	.91	.89	.87
	(.78–.96)	(.68–.95)	(.71–.93)
Special Scales	(AC)[c] .91	.86	.85
	(IE)[d] .91	.90	.82

[a]Based on tables given in Campbell and Hansen (1981): two-week sample, $n = 180$; thirty-days sample, $n = 102$; three-years sample, $n = 140$.
[b]The top number in each line is the median test-retest correlation; figures in parentheses give the range of test-retest correlations.
[c]Academic Comfort Scale; actual test-retest correlations are given.
[d]Introversion-Extroversion Scale; actual test-retest correlations are given.

in the *typical manner*. That is, a physician who is performing some other occupational role would not be included in the physician's sample. (6) Since most data collection is done by mail, only those persons willing to cooperate are included. *Self-selection* of subjects inevitably occurs and may introduce some bias in the sample, a possibility discussed at length in the manual. However, the validity of the Occupational Scales will determine the adequacy of the construction techniques. The most crucial issue is not the sampling method but the characteristics of the final sample. The fact that, for example, the occupational samples are all reasonably large, varying in size from 100 male licensed practical nurses to 498 male ministers, suggests a fairly successful testing program.

A General Reference Sample (GRS) was used in constructing the Occupational Scales. The GRS consists of 300 men and 300 women, referred to as the Men-in-General (MIG) and Women-in-General (WIG) samples, respectively. These 600 people from diverse occupations were selected to match the previous MIG and WIG samples with respect to responses to items in the SVIB. Thus, an Occupational Scale was constructed by determining which items distinguished that group from the MIG or WIG sample. The manual provides relatively little descriptive information about these samples. The mean ages are 33.4 and 35.2 for MIG and WIG, respectively. Both groups' average educational level is two years beyond high school.

We will now turn to the evidence concerning the validity of the Occupational Scales. The *concurrent validity* refers to the power to differentiate among people presently in different occupations. The manual provides information on the extent of overlap of the occupational groups with the MIG or WIG sample. If the Occupational Scales were perfect, for example, the MIG or WIG distribution of scores on the scale would not overlap the criterion group at all. The Occupational Scales do differ in their concurrent validities. Thus, occupations that are quite distinct, such as artist, physicist, chemist, and interior decorator, exhibit the highest concurrent validities. The poorest scale is the male college professor, for which the criterion sample is fairly heterogeneous. In general, the Occupational Scales do satisfactorily distinguish between the criterion group and the MIG or WIG sample. However, since these groups were used to construct the scales, it is not surprising that such concurrent validity exists.

The *predictive validity* of the SCII is, of course, the most critical to evaluate. Because the SCII may help choose future careers, it should be able to differentiate among people who will eventually enter different occupations and be satisfied with their choices. Thus, the long-range predictive validity of the SCII must be determined through longitudinal studies. Strong (1935) recognized the importance of predictive validity if his inventory was to be useful in vocational counseling. The evidence for high validity includes the following (Campbell & Hansen, 1981, p. 69):

1. People continuing in occupation X should obtain higher interest scores on the scale for X than they do on scales for any other occupations.
2. Interest scores on scale X should be higher for people continuing in occupation X than for people in occupation Y.
3. Interest scores on scale X should be higher for people continuing in occupation X than for people who change from X to occupation Y.
4. People changing from occupation Y to occupation X should score higher on the X scale prior to the change than they scored on the Y scale.

In addition to his earlier work, Strong published an extensive follow-up study of students' vocational interests eighteen years after graduation from college. He found general support for his first three propositions but only marginal support for his fourth (Strong, 1955). Campbell (1971) also summarized several studies that demon-

TABLE 12-2 Example Descriptions of Occupational Criterion Groups for the Strong-Campbell Interest Inventory[a]

Scale/sample[b]	N	Year tested	Mean age	Mean years education	Mean years experience	Composition and comments
Computer Programmer (f)	243	1975	33.0	15.7	6.9	Rosters provided by the Society for Data Processors and write-in responses to articles in *Computerworld;* those selected for criterion sample spent at least 50% of their time programming, 13% had high school diplomas, 54% completed BA degrees, 14% MA. 71% worked in business-related areas, 14% in scientific areas, and 5% in educational areas.
Computer Programmer (m)	203	1979	34.3	15.6	8.6	See women's sample above. Those selected for criterion sample spent at least 50% of their time programming. 25% had high school diplomas, 42% completed BA degrees, 12% MA. 76% worked in business-related areas, 7% in educational areas, and 3% in scientific areas.
Farmer (f)	207	1977	40.8	13.3	17.7	National sample collected through write-in responses to articles in rural or farm-directed publications, and with the assistance of organizations such as the American National Cowbelles, Washington State Dairy Wives, United Farm Wives, Wisconsin State Grange, California Women for Agriculture, and Indiana Women in Agriculture. 58% had high school diplomas, 23% completed BA degrees. Women selected for sample spent about the same amount of time managing their farms (32 hours per week) as they did managing their homes (37 hours per week), and most of their farm management time was in outdoor work, as opposed to accounting and bookkeeping. Major farm products included dairy (41%), grain (36%), and livestock (18%).
Farmer (m)	200	1979	40.8	13.4	24.4	National sample from names provided by participants in the female sample, write-in responses to articles in agricultural magazines, and with the assistance of the Minnesota Agricultural Extension Service. 59% had high school diplomas, 23% completed BA degrees. They averaged 65 hours per week in farm management, and 8 hours per week in home

TABLE 12-2 (Continued)

Scale/sample[b]	N	Year tested	Mean age	Mean years education	Mean years experience	Composition and comments
						management; 75% of work time was spent outdoors. Major farm products included grain (33%), dairy (27%), and livestock (24%).
Librarian (f)	280	1977	37.6	17.7	9.9	Members, American Library Association. 92% completed MA degrees or higher. 43% were employed by community or county, 30% by colleges or universities, and 9% by high schools.
Librarian (m)	315	1977	39.1	18.4	11.6	Members, American Library Association. 98% completed MA degrees or higher, 46% were employed by colleges or universities, 37% by community or county libraries.
Psychologist (f)	275	1966	43.0	Phd+	13.0	National Sample from *American Psychological Association Directory*, 1966.
Psychologist (m)	245	1967	44.0	Phd+	14.3	National sample from *American Psychological Association Directory*, 1966.

[a]This table is based on the complete list of criterion groups presented in Campbell and Hansen (1981, Appendix C).
[b]f = female sample; m = male sample.
Reproduced by permission of Stanford University Press.

strate a substantial relationship between high scores on the Occupational Scales and the eventual occupation entered. The manual of the 1981 SCII thus presents evidence for relatively good predictive validity of the Occupational Scales based on previous inventories. By inference, we assume that the 1981 SCII will exhibit comparable predictive validity. Worthington and Dolliver (1977) also reported results on the predictive validity of the SVIB over eighteen-, twelve-, and six-year time intervals. As might be expected, these investigators found better prediction over shorter intervals of time but did find evidence for the predictive validity of the SVIB.

Perhaps because the SVIB was originally developed for use with men, there have been comparatively few validity studies using women as subjects. Spokane (1979) found only two such studies relating directly to the concurrent or predictive validity of

the SVIB. Spokane studied a sample of 232 women and 386 men who were college seniors and had taken the SVIB before enrolling in college. The occupational preferences of the seniors were related to SCII scores obtained 3½ years earlier. Spokane found that the predictive validity estimates for women were substantially lower than those for men. The reasons for this difference are not immediately apparent. However, the SCII did demonstrate modest predictive validity for both sexes, as judged by the seniors' occupational preferences rather than the actual occupation entered.

The use of the Strong inventories with blacks has not been extensively researched. Nevertheless, the available studies suggest that the SCII can be used effectively with black college men (Borgen & Harper, 1973; Whetstone & Hayles, 1975).

The two special scales, Academic Comfort (AC) and Introversion-Extroversion

(IE), have relatively little validity information about them in the manual. The AC scale was constructed with a criterion group of 421 college professors, whereas for women, criterion samples of psychologists ($n = 275$) and mathematicians ($n = 119$) were used. All persons in the criterion group had Ph.D. degrees. The mean AC score for 198 occupational samples is the principal evidence for the validity of the AC scale. Thus, occupational groups such as biologists, chemists, and physicists have high scores on the AC scale; occupational groups such as farm supply managers, corrections officers, and florists have low scores. In interpreting the AC scale, the manual (Campbell & Hansen, 1981) suggested that persons having higher AC scores will be comfortable in an academic setting. Thus, persons who are well educated or have aspirations for high levels of education will tend to have higher AC scores. There is, however, relatively little research to aid in interpreting the AC scale. Wright (1976), for example, found that the 1974 version of the AC scale was unrelated to attrition among college students. That is, the score was unrelated to whether or not a student would graduate from college.

The IE scale was originally constructed by comparing responses of two groups of students at the University of Minnesota. Students in the two groups were defined as either introverts or extroverts based on their responses to the MMPI (Campbell, 1971). The only validity information on the IE scale in the manual is the mean IE scores for 200 occupational samples. Thus, farmers, sewing machine operators, and physicists have high (introverted) average scores; stockbrokers, auto sale dealers, and elected public officials have low (extroverted) average scores. The manual suggests that persons earning high IE scores (introverts) would rather work with things or ideas, whereas persons earning low scores would enjoy working with others, especially in sales and social services (Campbell & Hansen, 1981, p. 88). Compared to the Occupational Scales, relatively little is known about the validity of the IE scale.

PROFILE INTERPRETATION. Unlike aptitude or personality tests, interest inventories are relatively easy to understand. The scores should help a person identify possible educational or vocational careers, for example. A computer-generated interpretation of the SCII profile, available from Interpretative Scoring Systems in Minneapolis, summarizes the salient features of a profile. This interpretative report also provides references for the occupations of demonstrated interest as well as for general career planning. A portion of the sample report is given in Figure 12–5.

The interpretation of a profile by a counselor begins by considering the Administrative Indexes. If the indexes are not within "normal limits," the profile should not be interpreted. Thus, if a person omits many items, endorses too many infrequent responses, or has a high percentage of "dislike" responses, the profile should probably not be interpreted. In our example in Figure 12–4, these indexes are within normal limits.

The AC and IE scales are examined next for the client's general orientation and how a counseling session might proceed. Thus, a person with a high IE score might be rather quiet in an interview. The AC score would give some indication of the client's interest in further education. In our example in Figure 12–4, the high AC score suggests that the person's interests are similar to those who graduate from college. The high IE score suggests that this person would enjoy working with things more than with groups of people.

The next step in interpreting the profile is to explain and discuss the General Occupational Themes, the Basic Interest Scales, and Occupational Scales with the client. In our example, the person has a code type of CRI (conventional, realistic, investigative) on the General Occupational Themes and appears particularly suited to occupations such as systems analyst and computer programmer, which appear on the Occupational Scales. High scores on the Basic Interest Scales occur in the areas of mechanical activities, science, and mathematics. In summary, a counselor might suggest that the student in our example should consider careers in computer science or engineering, if he had not already been leaning in those directions.

SUMMARY. The SCII profile thus offers a vehicle for helping people make educational and occupational choices. It may also be helpful in focusing discussions between a student and a counselor. Finally, the inventory can be a useful tool for parent-student discussions in planning a student's future. However, reviewers have noted some problems with the SCII. Crites (1978), for example, noted that response style (percentage of likes, indifferents, or dislikes) can affect scores and that low scores are considerably more predictive of eventual occupation than are high scores. This latter point simply means that the low scores (lack of interest) help eliminate certain occupational areas. Crites (1978) and Dolliver (1978) both suggest that asking people which occupation they want to enter or using a base rate is as accurate as the SCII. These two reviewers and Lunneborg (1978) expressed concern about the necessity of maintaining separate norms for men and women. This may imply sex restrictions, for example, on some occupations. As we suggested earlier, interests are only one of many factors that should be considered in exploring career choices. Academic aptitude and achievement are obviously other factors to be considered. Persons may also be content in an occupation even though their interests are not typical of those in the occupation. Test-users should also be cautioned against over-interpreting the test results. "The test says I should be a forest ranger," for example, is an easy interpretation for students to make. On the other hand, the SCII may well suggest alternate careers that a student had not pre-viously considered. Thus, students who had always wanted to be physicians might be enlightened to discover their interests were also similar to those of a biologist or a college professor.

Despite its weaknesses, we agree with Dolliver's (1978) conclusion that the SCII is the best vocational interest inventory currently available.

Other Interest Inventories

We will mention very briefly several other interest inventories that are in wide use. These inventories have acceptable psychometric characteristics (item statistics, reliability, and validity) but are less researched than the SCII.

KUDER OCCUPATIONAL INTEREST SURVEY (KOIS). For many years, the most common alternative to the Strong inventory was one developed by G. Frederic Kuder. First published in 1934, the Kuder Preference Record originally consisted of homogeneous scales. That is, items that correlated with one another were used to form scales. However, the current edition, the KOIS, now has empirically derived scales (Kuder & Diamond, 1979). Thus, the Kuder inventory, which originally stood in sharp contrast to the SVIB's empirically derived scales, now has empirically determined scales. The SCII, on the other hand, has now developed homogeneous scales (the Basic Interest Scales and General Occupational Themes). The original Kuder inventory was taken with a pin, the answer sheet being perforated by the respondent. Hand-scoring was then possible.

The KOIS is now computer-scored, providing scores on 176 scales. It provides scores on 119 occupational scales such as office clerk, auto mechanic, librarian, physician, and travel agent. The complete list of occupations appears in the sample report of scores in Figure 12–6. The scores reported for the various occupations are actually correlations. The scales are also presented in rank order so that the user can readily see

FIGURE 12–5 Sample pages of computer-generated interpretation of occupational scales from Figure 12–3. (Copyright © 1982 by National Computer Systems. Reproduced by permission.)

OCCUPATIONAL SCALES

THE OCCUPATIONAL SCALES INDICATE THE DEGREE OF SIMILARITY BETWEEN YOUR INTERESTS AND THOSE OF EMPLOYED PEOPLE IN VARIOUS OCCUPATIONS. IF YOU REPORTED THE SAME LIKES AND DISLIKES AS THEY DO, YOUR SCORE WILL BE HIGH AND YOU WOULD PROBABLY ENJOY WORKING IN THAT OCCUPATION OR A CLOSELY RELATED ONE—MEMBERS OF AN OCCUPATION SCORE ABOUT 50 ON THEIR OWN SCALE. IF YOUR LIKES AND DISLIKES ARE DIFFERENT FROM THOSE OF PEOPLE IN THE OCCUPATION, YOUR SCORE WILL BE LOW AND YOU WOULD PROBABLY NOT BE HAPPY IN THAT KIND OF WORK. IF YOUR SCORE IS IN THE MID–RANGE, BETWEEN 28 AND 39, YOU HAVE RESPONDED IN THE WAY PEOPLE–IN–GENERAL DO.

RESEARCH HAS INDICATED THAT PEOPLE WHO ENTER AN OCCUPATION WHERE THEY HAVE SIMILAR SCORES TEND TO REMAIN IN THAT OCCUPATION AND ARE MORE SATISFIED THAN IF THEY ENTER AN OCCUPATION WHERE THEY HAVE DISSIMILAR SCORES. FURTHERMORE, THESE SCORES MAY INDICATE INTEREST IN AN OCCUPATION THAT YOU MAY NOT HAVE CONSIDERED BEFORE AND THEY CAN HELP YOU THINK ABOUT VARIOUS CAREERS. THE FOLLOWING SCORES INDICATE HOW YOUR INTERESTS MATCH THOSE OF MALES IN VARIOUS OCCUPATIONS.

VERY SIMILAR 55+	SIMILAR 54–46	MODERATELY SIMILAR 45–40	MID–RANGE 39–28
60 SYSTEMS ANALYST	50 ENGINEER	44 PHYSICIST	39 ACCOUNTANT
55 COMPUTER PROGR.	48 COLLEGE PROF.	43 BIOLOGIST	39 FORESTER
	48 CHEMIST	43 MATH–SCI. TCHR.	38 GEOLOGIST
	47 SOCIOLOGIST	42 IRS AGENT	37 MUSICIAN
	47 GEOGRAPHER	41 LIBRARIAN	37 ARCHITECT
	46 MATHEMATICIAN		37 PSYCHOLOGIST
			35 FOR. LANG. TCHR.
			35 SKILLED CRAFTS
			34 MEDICAL TECH.
			33 DIETITIAN
			33 FARMER
			33 X–RAY TECHNICIAN
			32 OPTOMETRIST
			32 BANKER
			32 INVEST. FUND MGR
			31 EXEC HOUSEKEEPER
			31 AIR FORCE OFF.
			31 SPEECH PATHOL.
			31 PHOTOGRAPHER

30 CREDIT MANAGER
30 CHIROPRACTOR
30 PURCHASING AGENT
29 NAVY OFFICER
29 BUSINESS ED. TCH
29 ELEM. TEACHER
29 PHYSICIAN
28 LIC. PRAC. NURSE

VERY DISSIMILAR
12-
11 YMCA DIRECTOR
10 ART TEACHER
10 POLICE OFFICER
9 PHYS. ED. TCHR.
9 CHAM. OF COMM.
7 ADVERTISING EXEC
6 LIFE INS. AGENT
6 PUBLIC REL. DIR.

DISSIMILAR
21-13
21 PHARMACIST
20 VOC AGRIC. TCHR.
20 MINISTER
20 SPECIAL ED. TCHR
20 ELECT. PUBL. OFF
19 RESTAURANT MGR.
19 MARKETING EXEC.
18 GUIDANCE COUNS.
18 INT. DECORATOR
18 SOCIAL WORKER
18 DEPT. STORE MGR.
17 REGISTERED NURSE
17 VETERINARIAN
17 ENGLISH TEACHER
16 REPORTER
16 AGRIBUS. MANAGER
15 FINE ARTIST
15 PHYS. THERAPIST
15 RECREAT. LEADER
14 REALTOR
13 BUYER
13 NURS. HOME ADM.
14 SOCIAL SCI. TCHR
13 COMMERCIAL ART.

MODERATELY DISSIMILAR
27-22
27 PUBLIC ADMINIST.
27 DENTIST
26 PERSONNEL DIR.
26 BEAUTICIAN
26 FLIGHT ATTENDANT
25 OCCUP. THERAPIST
25 LAWYER
25 SCHOOL ADMINIST.
25 ARMY OFFICER

* * * * * * * *

FIGURE 12-5 (Continued)

YOUR HIGHEST SCORES APPEARED ON THE FOLLOWING SCALES AND INDICATE THE GREATEST DEGREE OF SIMILARITY BETWEEN YOUR ANSWERS AND THOSE OF MALES IN THESE OCCUPATIONS. AS BEFORE, REFERENCES ARE GIVEN FOR THE OCCUPATIONAL OUTLOOK HANDBOOK (OOH) WHICH GIVES ADDITIONAL INFORMATION ON EMPLOYMENT OPPORTUNITIES AND RELEVANT WORK SITUATIONS. ALSO, REFERENCES ARE LISTED FOR THE DICTIONARY OF OCCUPATIONAL TITLES (DOT), FOURTH EDITION. THE DOT GIVES DETAILED JOB DESCRIPTIONS OF THE DUTIES AND FUNCTIONS OF EACH OCCUPATION AND SHOULD BE AVAILABLE IN YOUR LOCAL LIBRARY OR LOCAL COUNSELING OFFICE. THE FIRST DOT REFERENCE IS FOR PAGE NUMBER AND THE SECOND DOT REFERENCE IS FOR THE DOT CODE FOR THAT OCCUPATION.

YOUR HIGHEST SCORES APPEARED ON THE FOLLOWING SCALES AND INDICATE THE GREATEST DEGREE OF SIMILARITY BETWEEN YOUR ANSWERS AND THOSE OF MALES IN THESE OCCUPATIONS-

60 SYSTEMS ANALYST----------
   OOH 100-101
   DOT 29
   DOT 012.167

SYSTEMS ANALYSTS SOLVE DATA PROCESSING PROBLEMS BY ANALYZING THE TYPE OF DATA THAT IS REQUIRED AND FINDING THE MOST EFFICIENT WAY OF PROVIDING IT. A FOUR-YEAR COLLEGE DEGREE, ESPECIALLY IN A COMPUTER-RELATED FIELD, IS DESIRABLE FOR MOST POSITIONS. SYSTEMS ANALYSTS MUST BE GOOD AT WORKING WITH DETAILS, BE ABLE TO THINK LOGICALLY, AND LIKE WORKING WITH IDEAS. RELATED OCCUPATIONS INCLUDE COMPUTER PROGRAMMER AND MATHEMATICIAN. EMPLOYMENT FOR THIS OCCUPATION IS EXPECTED TO GROW FASTER THAN THE AVERAGE FOR ALL OCCUPATIONS THROUGH THE 1980S.

55 COMPUTER PROGRAMMER----------
   OOH 98-100
   DOT 38-39
   DOT 020.162-.187

COMPUTER PROGRAMMERS ANALYZE PROBLEMS AND CONVERT
THEM TO A FORM SUITABLE FOR SOLUTION BY A COMPUTER.
TRAINING FOR THIS FIELD RANGES FROM SOME DATA
PROCESSING TRAINING TO A FOUR-YEAR COLLEGE DEGREE,
DEPENDING UPON THE TYPE OF PROGRAMMING IN WHICH A
PERSON IS INTERESTED. LOGICAL THINKING, PATIENCE,
PERSISTENCE, ACCURACY, AND INGENUITY ARE NECESSARY
TRAITS FOR THIS FIELD. RELATED FIELDS ARE SYSTEMS
ANALYST AND COMPUTER OPERATOR. EMPLOYMENT OF
COMPUTER PROGRAMMERS IS EXPECTED TO GROW FASTER THAN
THE AVERAGE FOR ALL OCCUPATIONS THROUGH THE 1980S.

50 ENGINEER----------
   OOH 282-292
   DOT 15-31
   DOT 002.061-015.061

ENGINEERS WORK IN RESEARCH AND DEVELOPMENT, DESIGN
PRODUCTION, CONSULTING, TECHNICAL WRITING, AND
TECHNICAL SALES. AT LEAST FOUR YEARS OF COLLEGE
TRAINING ARE REQUIRED. ENGINEERS MUST BE CREATIVE
AND ANALYTICAL, ABLE TO WORK AS PART OF A TEAM, AND
WILLING TO CONTINUE THEIR EDUCATION THROUGHOUT THEIR
CAREER. ENGINEERING SPECIALTIES INCLUDE
AERONAUTICAL, CHEMICAL, CIVIL, ELECTRICAL,
MECHANICAL, AND METALLURGICAL. EMPLOYMENT
OPPORTUNITIES ARE EXPECTED TO BE GOOD THROUGH THE
1980S.

FIGURE 12-6 Example score report for Kuder Occupational Interest Inventory, Form DD. (From *Kuder Occupational Interest Survey, Form DD; General Manual,* by G. Frederic Kuder. © 1979, G. Frederic Kuder. Reprinted by permission of the publisher, Science Research Associates, Inc.)

Report of Scores   Kuder Occupational Interest Survey   Form DD

NAME POLONSKI WANDA S   FEMALE   003 00001   DATE 06/18/79

OCCUPATIONAL SCALES	NORMS M	NORMS F
PRIMARY SCH TCHR		.50*
STENOGRAPHER		.49*
BEAUTICIAN		.48*
OFFICE CLERK		.48*
DEPT STORE SALES		.47*
NURSE		.47*
BANK CLERK		.45*
>FLORIST		.45*
SECRETARY		.45*
>BOOKKEEPER		.43
DENTAL ASSISTANT		.43
HOME DEMONST AGT		.40
>LIBRARIAN		.40
X-RAY TECHNICIAN		.40
SOC WORKR-SCHOOL		.39
>AUDIOL>SP PATHOL		.38
>BOOKSTOR MANAGER		.38
SOC WORKER-MEDIC		.38
>COUNSELOR-HI SCH		.37
>MATH TCHR-HI SCH		.37
RELIGIOUS ED DIR		.37
>SOCIAL CASEWORKER		.37
>SOC WORKER-PSYCH		.37
>DENTIST		.35
OCCUPA THERAPIST		.35
DIETITIAN-ADMIN		.34
DIETITIAN-SCHOOL		.34

OCCUPATIONAL SCALES	NORMS M	NORMS F
PEDIATRICIAN	.17	
UNIV PASTOR	.17	
YMCA SECRETARY	.17	
ARCHITECT	.16	
CARPENTER	.16	
OSTEOPATH	.16	
BUYER	.15	
CLOTHIER-RETAIL	.15	
>DENTIST	.15	
ELECTRICIAN	.15	
POLICE OFFICER	.15	
WELDER	.15	
AUTO MECHANIC	.14	
AUTO SALESPERSON	.14	
>FLORIST	.14	
MACHINIST	.14	
MATHEMATICIAN	.14	
>MATH TCHR-HI SCH	.14	
PHARMACIST	.14	
>PHYSICIAN	.14	
>PSYCH-CLINICAL	.13	
PSYCH-COUNSELING	.13	
SCHOOL SUPT	.13	
SUPERVISR-INDUSTR	.13	
COUNTY AGRI AGT	.12	
>LAWYER	.12	
PLUMBER	.12	

COLLEGE MAJOR SCALES	NORMS M	NORMS F
>ELEMENTARY EDUC	.44*	.44*
HOME ECON EDUC		.44*
NURSING		.43*
>PHYSICAL EDUC		.43*
>FOREIGN LANGUAGE		.40*
TCHG CATH SISTER		.40*
BUS ED & COMMERC		.39*
HEALTH PROFES		.39*
>ENGLISH		.38*
SOCIAL SCI-GENL		.38*
>MUSIC & MUSIC ED		.37
MATHEMATICS		.36
>SOCIOLOGY		.35
>ART AND ART EDUC		.34
DRAMA		.34
>HISTORY		.34
>BIOLOGICAL SCI		.33
>PSYCHOLOGY		.33
>POLITICAL SCI		.27
>ART AND ART EDUC	.25*	
>FOREIGN LANGUAGE	.25*	
>ELEMENTARY EDUC	.21*	
>ENGLISH	.21*	
>MUSIC & MUSIC ED	.20*	

316

>PHYS THERAPIST .34	>SCIENCE TCHR, HS .12	>PHYSICAL EDUC .18
DEAN OF WOMEN .33	STATISTICIAN .12	>SOCIOLOGY .17
>PHYSICIAN .33	TRAVEL AGENT .12	>HISTORY .13
>SOCIAL WORKER-GROUP .33	TV REPAIRER .12	PREMED/PHAR/DENT .12
NUTRITIONIST .32	INSURANCE AGENT .11	
>INTERIOR DECORAT .31	PHARMACEUT SALES .11	>PSYCHOLOGY .12
>PSYCH, CLINICAL .30	PSYCHOLOGY PROF .11	>BIOLOGICAL SCI .11
ELEM SCHL TCHR .30*	REAL ESTATE AGT .11	ANIMAL HUSBANDRY .10
>ACCOUNTANT .29	FORESTER .10	AGRICULTURE .09
HOME EC TCHR COL .29	PLANT NURSRY WKR .10	ARCHITECTURE .09
>SCIENCE TCHR, HS .29	RADIO STATON MGR .10	>MATHEMATICS .09
>LAWYER .27	BANKER .09	>POLITICAL SCI .09
PSYCHOLOGIST .27	PERSONNEL MANAGR .08	FORESTRY .08
>COMPUTR PROGRAMR .25	>COMPUTR PROGRAMR .08	
>INTERIOR DECORAT .25*	FARMER .08	LAW-GRAD SCHOOL .08
MINISTER .24*	PLUMBING CONTRAC .08	BUS MANAGEMENT .07
POSTAL CLERK .24*	PSYCH,INDUSTRIAL .08	PHYSICAL SCIENCE .07
>LIBRARIAN .23	VETERINARIAN .08	AIR FORCE CADET .07
PRINTER .23	CHEMIST .07	BUS ACCT AND FIN .06
>AUDIOL/SP PATHOL .22	ENGINEER, ELEC .07	BUS & MARKETING .06
>BOOKSTOR MANAGER .22	METEOROLOGIST .07	ECONOMICS .05
TRUCK DRIVER .21	ENG,HEAT/AIR CON .06	MILITARY CADET .05
>SOCIAL CASEWORKR .20	ENG,MINING/METAL .06	
>SOC WORKER-PSYCH .20	>ACCT-CERT PUBLIC .05	ENGINEERING-CHEM .04
>X-RAY TECHNICIAN .19	BLDG CONTRACTOR .05	ENGINEERING-ELEC .04
>BOOKKEEPER .19	ENGINEER, CIVIL .05	ENGINEERING-MECH .04
JOURNALIST .19	ENGINEER, MECH .04	ENGINEERING,CIVIL .03
PAINTER, HOUSE .19	SALES ENG-HT/AIR .04	
>PHYS THERAPIST .19	ENGINEER, INDUS .03	
>COUNSELOR-HI SCH .18		
PHOTOGRAPHER .18		
PODIATRIST .18		
PSYCHIATRIST .18		
>SOC WORKER-GROUP .18		
BRICKLAYER .17		
OPTOMETRIST .17		

V 48

M	.14	S	.18
MBI	.05	F	.14
W	.47	D	.54
WBI	.08	MO	.50

> INDICATES TWIN SCALES, WITH SCORES IN M AND F COLUMNS.

Your scores are reported to you in rank order, on all scales. They show to what extent the choices you marked were like those typical of satisfied people in the occupations and college majors listed. Your top scores are followed by an asterisk (*). (For additional information and for an alphabetical list of scales, see the other side of this report.)

317

which occupation group was most similar to the person's responses. The KOIS thus provides correlations between the person's responses and those of a large number of occupational groups.

In addition, the KOIS provides scores on 48 college-major scales, including such ones as agriculture, history, psychology, and nursing. The "scores" reported are again correlation coefficients, indicating how similar the subject's responses were to those in various college majors. The SCII, it will be recalled, had no scales dealing with the interests of college majors.

The KOIS differs from the SCII by not using a general reference group in developing occupational scales. Responses were correlated with membership in occupational groups. It also presents items in a forced-choice mode. Subjects are presented 100 triads of activities and are required to choose the one liked most and the one liked least. Separate norms for men and women are used. Suggestions for the interpretation of the KOIS are available (Zytowski, 1973) as is evidence on its predictive validity over long periods of time (Zytowski, 1974, 1976).

ACT ASSESSMENT. As we noted briefly in Chapter 8, the ACT Assessment program includes a 90-item interest inventory (*Your ACT Assessment Results*, 1980c), to which students respond "dislike," "indifferent," or "like." Students then receive scores in six Basic Interest Areas—science, creative arts, social service, business contact, business detail, and technical. These scores can be used to locate a student's possible college major on a two-dimensional map. One coordinate represents people-related versus things-related activities. The second coordinate represents data-related versus ideas-related activities. A similar mapping procedure is used in locating a student's interests in the "world of work." An example appears in Figure 12–7.

The ACT mapping is based on Holland's (1973) theory of occupational types. Prediger (1976) described the rationale for developing the world-of-work mapping and

its utility for vocational guidance and research (Prediger, 1981). The ACT approach provides students with information that largely interprets itself and could be particularly helpful to those who have no desire or need to seek professional help or guidance for college or career planning.

MINNESOTA VOCATIONAL INTEREST INVENTORY (MVII). The interest inventories noted so far are mainly used with high school and college students who typically wish to enter professions. Kenneth E. Clark of the University of Minnesota pioneered in measuring the interests of nonprofessional men (Clark, 1961). The MVII was developed specifically for men in nonprofessional occupations, mainly in skilled trades (Clark & Campbell, 1965). Like the Kuder, the MVII has 138 triads of statements from which the person chooses the activities most and least liked. It is a forced-choice format, in other words. The MVII reports scores in twenty-one occupational areas such as printer, electrician, and plumber. The empirical method of the SVIB was used to construct these scales. Scores are also reported for nine area (homogeneous) scales such as mechanical, health service, and outdoors. Barnette (1973) described the use of the MVII and gave information on its reliability and validity. A major shortcoming, of course, is that it cannot be used with women.

MEASURING VALUES

As we suggested at the beginning of this chapter, values are basic dimensions of personality that indicate an individual's philosophy of life. Oskamp (1977, p. 13), for example, defines a value as an important life-goal or standard of behavior. Values are the most important and basic elements in a person's system of attitudes and beliefs. Viewing values as goals, we can see that they thus help to determine many of a person's other attitudes, beliefs, and interests.

In this section, we will discuss three measures of values. However, we should also

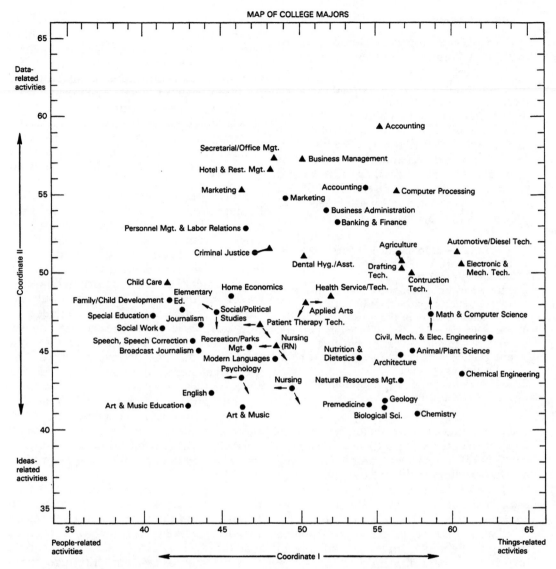

FIGURE 12–7 ACT assessment mapping of student interests into possible college majors. Students use their scores on the two coordinates to locate college majors having interests similar to theirs. For example, a student with a Coordinate I score of 55 and a Coordinate II score of 42 has interests similar to students majoring in premedicine, geology, biological sciences, and chemistry. (From American College Testing Program, 1980, p. 17. Reproduced by permission.)

note that values and attitudes are very similar. In fact, empirically they can be measured in similar ways. Thus, whether a particular measuring instrument is called an attitude scale or a value scale appears to be largely a semantic question. The preference of the person constructing the scale largely determines its label.

Study of Values Scale

Originally developed by Gordon Allport and Philip Vernon to measure six types of values arising from Spranger's (1928) theorizing, the most widely researched measure of values is published under the title the *Study of Values* (Allport & Vernon, 1931). Buros (1978) listed 1,027 references to this test, which first appeared in 1931. The most recent version of this scale was constructed by the original two authors and Gardner Lindzey (Allport et al., 1960).

The Allport-Vernon-Lindzey Study of Values (AVL) provides scores for six values:

1. Theoretical—a dominant interest in the discovery of truth along with a rational approach to problems.
2. Economic—an emphasis on useful, practical values, reflecting a businesslike attitude.
3. Aesthetic—a value in the artistic side of life.
4. Social—a value of unselfishly helping others.
5. Political—an interest in dominating others and gaining influence but not limited to political activities or office.
6. Religious—a value in understanding the meaning of existence.

Some of these values are obviously similar to some of the occupational themes from Holland (1973), which were described in the previous section of this chapter.

The AVL has two parts, both of which use a forced-choice format. The scale is thus an *ipsative* one. That is, a person cannot receive a high score in all areas. Ipsative scoring by definition forces a high score in one area to be complemented by lower scores in other areas. In Part I, there are thirty items. Each of the six values is paired twice with each of the other values. Different statements, however, are used. In Part I, three points are divided between the two statements—either three points to one statement and zero to the other, or two points to one statement and one to the other. Part II consists of fifteen items. A statement is presented, and respondents must rank order four alternatives that reflect four of the six different values. In Part II, then, all possible

combinations of four values chosen from among the six available are presented once (yielding fifteen items). Different statements are used, however, in each of the fifteen items. Several sample items from the AVL are given in Figure 12-8.

The AVL is easy to administer and score. It is a self-report instrument that is rather transparent in its purpose. Thus, cooperative, honest subjects are assumed to be taking the test, which would be relatively easy to fake.

Scores are typically reported on a profile. Because the AVL is an ipsative test, the total raw score for all subjects is always the same. Thus, profiles are interpretable intra-individually. The scores are scaled so that the "average" person has a score of forty on the six scales. The ipsative scoring, however, makes the use of the AVL across subjects much more difficult. The manual does provide normative data (means for the six values for various normative samples) but recognizes that the ipsative nature of the test makes percentiles and other standard scores virtually useless.

The manual reports test-retest (one- and two-month intervals) reliabilities that average about .90 for the six scales. Split-half reliabilities range from .84 to .95. Thus, the six values seem to be reliably measured by the AVL.

The validity of the AVL has been examined in literally hundreds of studies. Its popularity indicates that many investigators want to measure values and have concluded that the AVL is among the best available tests for such assessment. Although it has been used with high school students, it was originally intended for college students and college graduates. The bulk of studies in which the AVL has been used reflect the original purpose of the test.

In evaluating the validity of the AVL, many studies contrast the average scores of different groups. Thus, Hogan (1972) concludes that the scores predict a variety of criteria in the expected manner. Compared with the standardization group, for example, "gifted" students have higher average

FIGURE 12-8 Example Items from the Allport-Vernon-Lindzey Study of Values. (Copyright ©, 1960, by Gordon W. Allport, Philip E. Vernon, and Gardner Lindzey. Reproduced by permission of the Publisher, The Riverside Publishing Company.)

Part I: Subjects indicate preference for the two alternatives by dividing 3 points between them (e.g., 3, 0; 2, 1; 1, 2; or 0, 3).

1. The main object of scientific research should be the discovery of truth rather than its practical application.
   (a) Yes   (b) No
2. Assuming that you have sufficient ability, would you prefer to be:
   (a) a banker?
   (b) a politician?

Part II: Alternatives are rank ordered in preference—highest preference, 4; next highest, 3; next, 2; least preferred, 1.

1. If you could influence the educational policies of the public schools of some city, would you undertake
   _____a. to promote the study and participation in music and fine arts?
   _____b. to stimulate the study of social problems?
   _____c. to provide additional laboratory facilities?
   _____d. to increase the practical value of courses?
2. Should one guide one's conduct according to, or develop one's chief loyalties toward
   _____a. one's religious faith?
   _____b. ideals of beauty?
   _____c. one's occupational organization and associates?
   _____d. ideals of charity?

---

scores on the theoretical and aesthetic scales than do "nongifted" peers (Gowan, 1956; Warren & Heist, 1960). The AVL has also been related to measures of creativity. For example, creative research mathematicians were found to have lower scores on the religious scale than did average Ph.D. mathematicians (Helson & Crutchfield, 1970). Among architects, it also was found that the economic, social, and religious scales were predictive of creativity in architecture as rated by peers (Hall & MacKinnon, 1969). It was also reported that scores on the religious scale correlate highly ($r = .79$) with church attendance (Bender, 1958). Boys and girls from a strongly independent religious group (Mennonites) were found to have higher average scores on the religious scale, as would be predicted (Wiebe & Vraa, 1976).

As another example of findings in an expected direction, Whittaker (1971) reported data on intellectual, nonconformist, collegiate dropouts. The subjects were 151 former students at the Univesity of California, Berkley, who were still living in the university community. These former students were found, on the average, to have extremely high scores on the aesthetic scale and very low scores on the economic scale.

There continues to be interest in measuring the impact college has on students' attitudes, values, abilities, and other such variables. That is, do students change in any significant way as a result of four years of college? Do different colleges have different kinds of effects? These are questions of great interest to college administrators and faculty as well as to the parents of college students. Feldman and Newcomb (1969) reviewed the results of a large number of studies that examined the changes that occur in students over the four years of college. With respect to AVL values, they found two strong and consistent changes. First, aesthetic values were of more importance to seniors than to first-year students. Second, religious values were of less importance to seniors than to first-year students. These changes are, again, in the direction we would expect.

Although some values apparently do change over the four years of college, some studies suggest that values remain fairly constant over long periods of time after college. For example, after four or five years, there were no changes in values for persons who had been enrolled in teacher preparation courses (Kirchner & Hogan, 1972). Similarly, after twelve years, the average scores for a group of business administrators did not change (Singer & Abramson, 1973). This study also found no relationship between success in business and scores on any of the value scales.

However, other studies have found some changes occurring after college. Hoge and Bender (1974), for example, found that little change occurred in the economic, social, and political scales. Theoretical values, however, tended to strengthen after graduation. Aesthetic and religious values changed rather dramatically but in opposite directions, depending on the time at which the initial testing occurred. Thus, students tested in 1940, 1955, and 1969 showed an increase in religious value and then a decrease. The aesthetic value was just the opposite. Longitudinal studies such as the one by Hoge and Bender at least begin to illuminate how people develop and adapt during adulthood.

Despite AVL's widespread use, its ipsative scoring presents a very serious limitation. Hicks (1970) cogently reviewed the properties of ipsative measures and concluded that they should, in general, not be used. For example, the fact that a high score on one scale can only be obtained if scores on other scales are low forces negative intercorrelations among the scales. Because the scores are not independent, it is also not justified to use ipsative scores for prediction or to examine group differences. As Hicks (p. 182) concluded,

... It is necessary to reevaluate thoroughly the extensive body of research that has utilized purely ipsative forced-choice tests and that has employed statistical techniques predicated upon assumptions which such instruments necessarily violate.

Unless an investigator is strictly interested in intraindividual comparisons, we suggest that the AVL should not be used in research. An equivalent normative test should be substituted.

In an attempt to improve the AVL, Shorr (1953) developed a test measuring the intensity of four kinds of values—theoretical, social, aesthetic, and economic-political. Shorr's test is a normative one. Unfortunately, virtually no additional work has been done on this scale.

Other Measures of Value

ROKEACH VALUE SURVEY. Another ipsative measure of values is that developed by Rokeach (1968). This survey provides a ranking of two types of values—instrumental and terminal. Instrumental values are preferred modes of behavior, whereas terminal values are preferable end states of development in a person's life. There are eighteen values of each type. Examples of instrumental values include ambition, courage, honesty, and responsibility. Examples of terminal values include a comfortable life, a world of beauty, national security, and true friendship. Subjects rank order the eighteen instrumental and eighteen terminal values to establish a hierarchy.

PERSONAL VALUE SCALES. Scott (1965) developed a scale to measure college students' ideas of ideal relationships between people. Twelve values were assessed, including intellectualism, social skills, physical development, and religiousness. Subjects respond to items reflecting each of these values by choosing one of three alternatives—"always admire," "depends on situation," or "always dislike." The following items are examples of several of the values measured:

intellectualism—having a strong intellectual curiosity

social skills—dressing and acting in a way that is appropriate to the occasion

physical development—being good in some form of sport

religiousness—always attending religious services regularly and faithfully

Originally only sixty items were used, each value being measured by only four to six items. However, Scott provided additional items so that twenty for each value are now available. For researchers interested in studying the values of college students, Scott's scale merits further use. It is a normative rather than an ipsative test.

For additional tests measuring values and a concise summary of the historical and theoretical framework of the empirical study of values, the interested reader might consult Robinson and Shaver's (1969, Ch. 7) monograph on attitude measurement.

MEASURING ATTITUDES

There have undoubtedly been thousands of studies in which measuring people's attitudes toward some particular concept, person, or group have been of central importance. Scales have been developed to measure attitudes toward such diverse topics as evolution, the existence of God, mental hospitals, old people, and people in general. In this section, we will focus on several ways in which attitudes have been measured rather than on particular scales. Researchers interested in finding scales focused on particular attitudes could begin with the book by Shaw and Wright (1967), in which 176 scales are published, or the series of monographs on measuring attitudes published at the Institute for Social Research at the University of Michigan

(Robinson & Shaver, 1969; Robinson et al., 1968, 1969). Our discussion in this section generally parallels, although it is much briefer, that found in Oskamp's (1977) first two chapters.

Oskamp (p. 10) notes that attitudes are often conceptualized as having three components. (1) A *cognitive* component is the set of ideas one has about an object. (2) An *affective (emotional)* component refers to the feelings and emotions one has toward the object. (3) A *behavioral* component refers to a person's action tendencies toward the object. In fact, however, it is probably difficult to differentiate among the three components because they are highly interrelated. The *evaluative* aspect of attitudes is probably most often stressed currently (p. 9). Thus, the tendency to respond favorably or unfavorably toward particular ideas, objects, people, or groups seems to be the most important characteristic of an attitude.

Attitudes, of course, are never observed directly. We infer their existence by the responses an individual makes. Campbell (1963) suggests that a social attitude is inferred when a person exhibits consistency in responding to social objects. Oskamp (1977) suggests that "attitudes are the result of past experiences (both vicarious and actual), and that they combine with the present stimulus situation to determine [a person's] responses" (p. 14). This view of attitudes is illustrated in Figure 12-9.

Although the definition and conceptualization of attitudes is somewhat abstract, several viable techniques for measuring attitudes are available. As is true in developing any test, extensive pretesting of items will usually be required before a reliable and useful scale becomes available. A fairly large technical literature exists on measuring attitudes (Edwards, 1957; Scott, 1968; Thurstone & Chave, 1929).

Likert Scale

By far the most common approach to measuring attitudes is the Likert scale

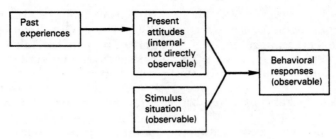

FIGURE 12–9 Attitudes are unobservable intervening variables which influence the relationship between stimulus events and behavioral responses. (From S. Oskamp, *Attitudes and Opinions*, 1977, p. 15. Copyright © 1977 by Prentice-Hall. Reproduced by permission.)

(Likert, 1932). A Likert scale typically consists of a number of statements to which subjects respond on a five-point scale of agreement to disagreement, approval to disapproval, or favorable to unfavorable, depending on how the statement is worded.

For example, if we were developing a scale to measure students' attitudes toward psychology we might use the following statement:

Psychology has contributed to a better understanding of human behavior.

    __Strongly agree
    __Agree
    __Neither agree nor disagree
    __Disagree
    __Strongly disagree

In this example, a person responding "strongly agree" would receive a 5, "agree" would receive a 4, and so on, with "strongly disagree" receiving a 1. Many such statements about psychology (both favorable and unfavorable) would be constructed, and the "score" on each item added to give a total. Each item or statement is presumed to be measuring a small part of what psychology means to the subjects. We expect people who regard psychology favorably to have high scores and those who have low scores to be less favorable.

In constructing attitude scales, it is assumed that the items will be intercorrelated and that they will each correlate positively with the total score. It is relatively easy, of course, to verify these assumptions with well-established statistical procedures. It follows from these assumptions that the attitude scale should be unidimensional. That is, it should measure only one attitude and not two or more. This too can be verified statistically. Finally, as is true of any test, the reliability and validity of the attitude scale should be demonstrated. As an example, a Likert scale measuring attitude toward socialized medicine is given in Figure 12-10.

Thurstone Scaling

Louis L. Thurstone was a psychologist who developed many quantitative techniques. He published early papers in mathematical learning theory, psychometrics, and factor analysis. He also developed scaling techniques that could be applied to the measurement of attitudes. Edwards (1957) and Torgerson (1958), among others, presented good summaries and discussion of Thurstone's scaling methods.

Scaling methods are techniques for assigning numerical values to attributes of interest. The numerical values have some of the usual properties we ordinarily assume numbers will have. Thus, for example, the distance between the numbers 10 and 20 should be the same as the distance between 40 and 50. Such scales are commonly called *interval scales*. They may be changed by any linear transformation of the numerical

FIGURE 12–10 A Likert Scale to Measure Attitudes Toward Socialized Medicine† (I. Mahler. Attitudes toward socialized medicine. *Journal of Social Psychology*, 1953, 38, 273–282.) Copyright © 1953 by *The Journal Press*, Provincetown, Mass. Reproduced by permission.

Please indicate your reaction to the following statements, using these alternatives:

Strongly Agree = SA
Agree = A
Undecided = U
Disagree = D
Strongly Disagree = SD

*1. The quality of medical care under the system of private practice is superior to that under a system of compulsory health insurance.

2. A compulsory health program will produce a heathlier and more productive population.

*3. Under a compulsory health program there would be less incentive for young persons to become doctors.

4. A compulsory health program is necessary because it brings the greatest good to the greatest number of people.

*5. Treatment under a compulsory health program would be mechanical and superficial.

6. A compulsory health program would be a realization of one of the true aims of a democracy.

*7. Compulsory medical care would upset the traditional relationship between the family doctor and the patient.

*8. I feel that I would get better care from a doctor whom I am paying than from a doctor who is being paid by the government.

9. Despite many practical objections, I feel that compulsory health insurance is a real need of the American people.

10. A compulsory health program could be administered quite efficiently if the doctors would cooperate.

*These items would be reversed in scoring; the same alternatives are used for each item.
†These are ten items from among twenty developed by Mahler (1953) to measure attitude toward socialized medicine.

---

values. That is, they are like the relationship between degrees centrigrade and Fahrenheit in measuring temperatures. Thurstone scaling techniques are designed mathematically to yield interval scales. Although Likert-type scales are usually treated as though they are interval scales, they are in fact probably ordinal scales. That is, the summed total for a Likert scale conveys the rank order of individuals but probably does not tell us numerically how much stronger one person's attitude is than another's.

Through one of the scaling methods developed by Thurstone, scale values are determined for each statement. Three of the most common scaling methods used are the method of equal-appearing intervals, paired comparisons, and successive intervals. All methods require a large sample of subjects to rate the statements. These raters or judges provide the raw data from which the scale values are derived.

METHOD OF EQUAL-APPEARING INTERVALS. In this method, a large number of raters are asked to sort the statements into eleven categories such that the distance between them (and the statements in them) appears to be equal. The median category assigned a statement by all judges determines the scale value. A measure of variability is also computed for each statement. Statements are then selected for inclusion in the final attitude scale so that a wide range (from high to low) of scale values are included. These are spread evenly across the attitude continuum. Statements having great variability would be eliminated because there would be no consensus regarding their location on the scale.

METHOD OF PAIRED COMPARISONS. In this technique, each statement is paired with every other statement. Again, a large number of judges is required. Their task is simply to indicate which statement is preferred or which statement is more favorable. Statements high on the attitude continuum, for example, would be judged more favorable than those on the low end. Mathematical techniques then transform these ratings into scale values. A serious limitation of this method is the large number of judgments required for relatively small numbers of statements. For example, 20 statements generate 190 different comparisons. For this reason, the technique has been infrequently used in constructing attitude scales.

SUCCESSIVE INTERVALS. In successive interval scaling, a number of statements are rated in a number of categories (seven to nine being commonly used). The ratings are, however, not assumed to give direct numerical information. With mathematical techniques, the data from a large number of judges is used to derive scale values from the ratings. In choosing the final set of attitude statements, the same criteria are used as for the method of equal-appearing intervals.

Thurstone attitude scales thus have a theoretical and mathematical basis that Likert-type scales lack. However, Thurstone scales require somewhat more time and technical knowledge to construct. They ask the subject only to agree with each statement. In theory, one will agree only with those items close to one's position on the attitude contin-

uum. A person's score is typically the mean of the scale values associated with all the statements with which a person agreed. In constructing the scale, however, the judges do not have to have a favorable (or unfavorable) attitude toward the object. They should still be able to rate where a statement would lie on the continuum, whether they personally agree with it or not.

Figure 12-11 is an example of a Thurstone-type scale for measuring attitudes toward capital punishment. Shaw and Wright (1967) present many other examples. For technical details on Thurstone scaling methods, several excellent sources are available (Baird & Noma, 1979; Edwards, 1957; Thurstone, 1959; Thurstone & Shave, 1929; Torgerson, 1958).

Semantic Differential

A third method of measuring attitudes comes from the work of Osgood and his colleagues (1957). Osgood was interested in connotative meaning. That is, he was not interested in dictionary definitions but in the emotional reactions people had as part of a word's meaning. He had subjects rate concepts (like police officer) on bipolar adjective scales (like good-bad). The results of many such analyses suggest that there are three primary dimensions of connotative meaning. The *evaluative* dimension is defined by adjective scales such as good-bad, favorable-unfavorable, and pleasant-unpleasant. In most studies, this dimension is the most important. The second is called the *potency* dimension and is defined by adjective scales such as strong-weak, heavy-light, and hard-soft. The third is the *activity* dimension, defined by adjective scales such as active-passive, fast-slow, and hot-cold.

The semantic differential technique is a general one that can be applied to any object of interest. There is fairly convincing evidence that the evaluative dimension is the most important one in "semantic space," which makes it especially useful for measuring attitudes. In addition, there is ev-

FIGURE 12-11 Twelve items from among twenty-four developed by Peterson and Thurstone (1933) to measure attitudes toward capital punishment. The items are ordered in terms of scale values, which would not be the case in actual use; the scale values would, of course, not be listed.

This is a study of attitude toward capital punishment. Below you will find a number of statements expressing different attitudes toward capital punishment.

√ Put a check mark if you agree with the statement.
X Put a cross if you disagree with the statement.

Try to indicate either agreement or disagreement for each statement. If you simply cannot decide about a statement you may mark it with a question mark.

This is not an examination. There are no right or wrong answers to these statements. This is simply a study of people's attitudes toward capital punishment. Please indicate your own convictions by a check mark when you agree and by a cross when you disagree.

Scale Value	Item Number	
(0.1)	12	I do not believe in capital punishment under any circumstances.
(0.9)	16	Execution of criminals is a disgrace to civilized society.
(2.0)	21	The state cannot teach the sacredness of human life by destroying it.
(2.7)	8	Capital punishment has never been effective in preventing crime.
(3.4)	9	I don't believe in capital punishment but I'm not sure it isn't necessary.
(3.9)	11	I think the return of the whipping post would be more effective than capital punishment.
(5.8)	18	I do not believe in capital punishment but it is not practically advisable to abolish it.
(6.2)	6	Capital punishment is wrong but is necessary in our imperfect civilization.
(7.9)	23	Capital punishment is justified only for premeditated murder.
(9.4)	20	Capital punishment gives the criminal what he deserves.
(9.6)	17	Capital punishment is just and necessary.
(11.0)	7	Every criminal should be executed.

idence that the evaluation, potency, and activity dimensions have cross-cultural generality (Osgood, 1962; Osgood et al., 1975).

In using the semantic differential to measure attitudes, subjects rate the objects of interest on three or four bipolar adjective scales from each of the three dimensions. Subjects appear to accept such ratings as quite reasonable and are able to do them reliably. Scores are then obtained for three dimensions by adding the ratings for the ad-

jective scales used for each dimension. Figure 12-12 gives an example of a semantic differential form for measuring attitudes toward capital punishment.

PERSONAL ORIENTATION

In this section, we will discuss several tests that measure various individual traits or characteristics. These scales could be re-

FIGURE 12-12 Semantic Differential to Measure Attitudes Toward Capital Punishment. Typically more scales would be used and several concepts would be rated. The semantic dimensions would, of course, not be printed on the page. (Adapted from Osgood, Suci, & Tannenbaum, 1957, p. 82-84.)

Typical Instructions

The purpose of this study is to measure the meanings of certain things to various people by having them judge them against a series of descriptive scales. In taking this test, please make your judgments on the basis of what these things mean to you. On each page of this booklet you will find a different concept to be judged and beneath it a set of scales. You are to rate the concept on each of these scales in order.

Here is how you are to use these scales:

If you feel that the concept at the top of the page is very closely related to one end of the scale, you might place your check mark as follows:

fair   X   : _____ : _____ : _____ : _____ : _____ : _____   unfair

If you feel that the concept is quite closely related to one or the other end of the scale (but not extremely), you might place your check mark as follows:

strong_____ :   X   : _____ : _____ : _____ : _____ : _____   weak

If the concept seems only slightly related to one side as opposed to the other side (but is not really neutral), then you might check as follows:

active_____ : _____ :   X   : _____ : _____ : _____ : _____   passive

The direction toward which you check, of course, depends on which of the two ends of the scale seem most characteristic of the thing you are judging.

If you consider the concept to be neutral on the scale, if both sides of the scale are equally associated with the concept, or if the scale is completely irrelevant, unrelated to the concept, then you should place your check mark in the middle space:

safe   _____ : _____ : _____ :   X   : _____ : _____ : _____   dangerous

Make each item a separate and independent judgment. Work at fairly high speed through this test. Do not worry or puzzle over individual items. It is your first impressions, the immediate "feelings" about the items, that we want.

Capital Punishment

Dimension				
(Evaluative)	1. good	___ : ___ : ___ : ___ : ___ : ___ : ___	bad
(Potency)	2. weak	___ : ___ : ___ : ___ : ___ : ___ : ___	strong
(Activity)	3. passive	___ : ___ : ___ : ___ : ___ : ___ : ___	active
(Evaluative)	4. favorable	___ : ___ : ___ : ___ : ___ : ___ : ___	unfavorable
(Potency)	5. hard	___ : ___ : ___ : ___ : ___ : ___ : ___	soft
(Activity)	6. fast	___ : ___ : ___ : ___ : ___ : ___ : ___	slow

garded as measures of aspects of personality, but they are not included in personality inventories. Literally, hundreds of such scales have been developed, each one to measure a particular aspect of human behavior. We will discuss several which currently appear to be quite popular with substantial numbers of researchers. These scales, as is true for attitude scales, are used primarily in research. They are usually not used for individual counseling, although they might contribute to a clinical psychologist's understanding of a particular patient.

Type A Behavior

There is little doubt that cardiovascular disease is a major health problem in the United States. Heart disease causes more deaths (about 640,000 annually) than any other single disease. The prevention of heart disease is, therefore, a major public health issue in the United States (Hamberg et al., 1982). Although physiological factors such as atherosclerosis (hardening of the arteries) occurring as a function of age are important in producing coronaries, it has been long recognized that behavior and emotions are related to heart disease. In the popular press, this is now referred to as Type A behavior, a coronary-prone behavior pattern, defined by "extreme competitiveness, striving for achievement, aggressiveness, impatience, haste, restlessness, and feelings of being challenged by responsibility and under the pressure of time" (Jenkins et al., 1979, p. 3).

As Burish (1980) suggested, Type A behavior is a function of the individual and of the environment. Type A individuals are thus more likely to exhibit Type A behaviors in competitive environments and competitive environments are presumably more likely to produce Type A persons. Modern industrial societies appear to have the kind of environments that both encourage Type A behaviors and produce Type A individuals. Being able to predict which persons are coronary-prone would clearly be of great importance in reducing deaths and disabling conditions.

The concept of Type A or coronary-prone behavior originated with two cardiologists, Meyer Friedman and Ray Rosenman. These two physicians initially relied on their own and other physicians' clinical judgments to determine which patients exhibited such behavior, but then they and their colleagues developed a structured interview that could be used more objectively (Rosenman et al., 1964). The structured interview remains a viable method of assessing Type A behavior. It does, of course, require extensive training and is very time-consuming. It would be inefficient and impractical, for example, to use in large-scale studies or to screen large numbers of patients.

In order to provide a psychometrically valid test as an alternative to the interview, C. David Jenkins developed a self-report inventory to assess Type A behavior. The most recent edition of this test is the Jenkins Activity Survey, Form C (JAS) (Jenkins et al., 1979). This, the fifth edition of the JAS, is a refined version of the earlier editions. Changes were based on research on the previous editions.

The JAS (Form C) consists of fifty-two multiple-choice items with two to eight alternatives per item. The following are two examples*:

How often do you actually "put words in the person's mouth" in order to speed things up?
  A. Frequently
  B. Occasionally
  C. Almost never

How often do you go to your place of work when you are not expected to be there (such as nights or weekends)?
  A. It is not possible on my job
  B. Rarely or never
  C. Occasionally (less than once a week)
  D. Once a week or more

The JAS (Form C) may be administered to a group. Subjects respond on the test form, which is machine scorable. According to the manual, most subjects can complete the test in fifteen to twenty minutes. Each response is weighted according to statistically derived formulas based on research, and raw scores are determined by totaling these weighted responses.

*Reproduced by permission of the publisher from the Jenkins Activity Survey Manual. Copyright © 1979 by The Psychological Corporation. All rights reserved.

In addition to a score for Type A behavior, three component scores are also reported: Speed and Impatience, Job Involvement, and Hard-Driving and Competitive. Standard scores and associated percentile scores are provided for all four scales. In contrast to most tests, the standard scores have a mean of zero and a standard deviation of ten. Thus, positive scores (above the mean of zero) are in the direction of Type A behavior; negative scores denote Type B behavior. The normative sample for the JAS consisted of 2,588 males in relatively high-level jobs in the San Francisco Bay and Burbank areas of California. These males were tested in 1969 and were part of the Western Collaborative Group Study, a large-scale study of heart disease (Jenkins et al., 1979, p. 10). In addition to the normative group, the manual presents means and standard deviations for thirty-five other groups, ranging from male supermarket workers in Georgia ($n=178$) to a random sample of the male European population of Auckland, New Zealand ($n=300$).

The internal consistency of the JAS is good. A value of .85 is reported in the manual for the Type A behavior scale, for example. The internal consistency reliabilities for the three component scales range from .83 to .73. The manual also reports test-retest reliabilities for four samples in time intervals from four to six months up to four years. For Type A behavior scores, these reliabilities range from a low of .64 (four years) to a high of .76 (four to six months). Thus, the JAS scores appear to be reasonably stable over time as well as internally consistent.

Jenkins et al. provide several lines of evidence on the validity of the JAS. (1) Scores were positively correlated with those from the structured interview. (2) At least eight studies demonstrated a relationship between Type A behavior and the prevalence of coronary disease. Thus, patients suffering from coronary disease tended to have higher average Type A scores than did patients with other medical problems. (3) Those patients in the upper third on the

Type A scale had 1.7 times the incidence of coronary disease than those in the lower third (Type B). This predictive (or prospective) study is an important validation of the JAS. (4) Among patients who had already had one coronary, those with Type A scores were more likely to have a second attack. (These results are illustrated in Figure 12-13.) (5) There is also some evidence that Type A behavior is related to the amount of coronary atherosclerosis present. This evidence all supports the validity of the JAS as a measure of Type A behavior.

Despite the encouraging results obtained to date, Burish (1980) made three critical points. (1) Although Type A behavior is correlated with the incidence of coronary heart disease (CHD), the evidence available does not yet demonstrate that Type A behavior *causes* CHD. (2) Although the correlation between Type A behavior and CHD is statis-

FIGURE 12–13 Rate of recurrent myocardial infarction per hundred male survivors (ages 39 to 59) of first episode of coronary heart disease, arrayed by type A score. (Reproduced by permission of the publisher from the Jenkins Activity Survey Manual. Copyright © 1979 by The Psychological Corporation. All rights reserved.)

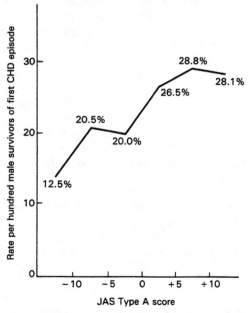

tically significant, it is not high enough to permit great confidence in predicting CHD for individuals. (3) The relationship of stress to CHD and Type A behavior remains to be untangled. Burish also noted that most research on Type A behavior involved white, middle-class, middle-aged males. Whether other populations will produce similar or different results remains to be demonstrated.

Matthews (1982) has reviewed the psychological nature of the Type A behavior pattern. She concluded that different measures of Type A have minimal overlap, largely because each measures different aspects of the Type A behavior pattern. She also concluded that individuals receiving high scores on the JAS Type A are competitive, aggressive, and achievement-oriented. Matthews also noted that the studies using the JAS usually did not focus on the emotional correlates of Type A behavior, particularly anger and hostility.

In summary, the JAS provides an additional method of detecting coronary-prone individuals. The interest in Type A behavior as it is related to coronary disease will undoubtedly continue unabated for the forseeable future, unless or until this major health problem is eliminated or perhaps at least better understood.

Sex-Role Orientation
(Masculinity-Femininity)

Spence and Helmreich (1978) suggested that differences between men and women can be clarified by distinguishing among four categories: biological gender, sexual orientation, sex role, and masculinity and femininity as characteristics of a person's self-concept. In this classification, *gender* refers to the biological categories of male or female. *Sexual orientation* refers to a person's preference for a same- or opposite-sexed partner. As used by psychologists, *sex role* "refers to the distinguishing characteristics of women and men themselves—to differences in behavior, personality, abilities, preferences, and the like" (p. 13). The mas-

culine versus feminine distinction has traditionally been bipolar and refers to a psychological dimension that distinguishes between males and females. Thus, women are presumed to be emotional, sensitive, and dependent, whereas men are considered aggressive, independent, and insensitive (Spence & Helmreich, 1978, p. 17).

Several authors have discussed the problems in defining sex-role orientation and other problems associated with assessing differences between males and females. The interested reader should consult these sources for further information on the issues. (Bem, 1979; Constantinople, 1973; Kelly & Worell, 1977; Locksley & Colten, 1979; Maccoby & Jacklin, 1974; Orlofsky, 1980; Pedhazur & Tetenbaum 1979; Spence & Helmreich, 1978, 1979; Unger, 1979; Wittig & Peterson, 1979; Worell, 1978).

We will now turn to two scales that are used to measure masculinity and femininity in a manner that no longer considers these psychological characteristics to be bipolar opposites. The first scale to be discussed is the Personal Attributes Questionnaire. The second, the Bem Sex Role Inventory, popularized the notion of psychological androgyny. An androgynous person is one having both masculine and feminine personality attributes. Both scales permit the classification of persons into one of four categories based on scores on a masculine (M) and feminine (F) scale. Thus, persons scoring high on both M and F would be called androgynous; a person high on M but low on F would be called masculine; one high on F and low on M would be called feminine; one low on both M and F would be classified as undifferentiated. Practically speaking, median or mean scores can be used as division points. Figure 12-14 indicates this division into four categories.

PERSONAL ATTRIBUTES QUESTIONNAIRE (PAQ). The PAQ was developed by Janet Taylor Spence and her colleagues (1974, 1975). The long version contains fifty-five items that empirically differentiate between

	Masculinity	
	Above median	Below median
Femininity — Above median	Androgynous	Feminine
Femininity — Below median	Masculine	Undifferentiated

FIGURE 12–14 Method of classifying individuals on separate masculinity and femininity scales based on their scores above or below the median.

the two sexes. That is, the PAQ consists of items that raters commonly agreed differentiated between the sexes and on which men and women reported themselves as differing as well. The items reflect socially desirable characteristics.

The items are divided into three scales: Masculine, Feminine, and Masculine-Feminine. Masculine (M) items are defined as those being socially desirable for both sexes but occurring to a greater degree among males. There are twenty-three such items on this scale. Feminine (F) items are similarly defined except they occurred to a greater degree among females. There are eighteen such items on the F scale. Thirteen items are assigned to the M-F scale because they represent attributes that are socially desirable for one sex but undesirable for the other. The M-F scale thus reflects the more traditional manner of measuring masculinity and femininity. One of the fifty-five items could not be classified.

Subjects respond by rating themselves on each bipolar item on a five-point scale. Three separate scores, M, F, and M-F are determined for each subject. An example from each of the scales is given in Figure 12-15.

Spence and Helmreich (1978) constructed a short form of the PAQ consisting of twenty-four items, eight items for each scale. Items were selected from among the fifty-four available on the basis of their correlation with the appropriate total scale score. (Items from the short form appear in Figure 12-15.) The authors reported that internal consistency reliabilities for the short

FIGURE 12-15 Instructions and Sample Items from Personal Attributes Questionnaire. (From Spence, J. T. & Helmreich, R. L. Masculinity and femininity: Their psychological dimensions, correlate and antecedents. Austin: University of Texas, 1978, p. 231. Reproduced by permission.)

The items below inquire about what kind of a person you think you are. Each item consists of a pair of characteristics, with the letters A-E in between. For example:

Not at all Artistic   A. . . .B. . . .C. . . .D. . . .E   Very Artistic

Each pair describes contradictory characteristics—that is, you cannot be both at the same time, such as very artistic and not at all artistic.

The letters form a scale between the two extremes. You are to choose a letter which describes where you fall on the scale. For example, if you think you have no artistic ability, you would choose A. If you think you are pretty good, you might choose D. If you are only medium, you might choose C, and so forth.

Scale*

M-F	1. Not at all aggressive	A. . . .B. . . .C. . . .D. . . .E *Very aggressive***
M	2. Not at all independent	A. . . .B. . . .C. . . .D. . . .E *Very independent*
F	3. Not at all emotional	A. . . .B. . . .C. . . .D. . . .E *Very emotional*

*The scale to which each item is assigned is indicated by M (Masculinity), F (Femininity), and M-F (Masculinity-Femininity).
**Italics indicate the extreme masculine response for the M and M-F scales and the extreme feminine response for the F scale. Each extreme masculine response on the M and M-F scales and extreme feminine response on the F scale are scored 4, the next most extreme scored 3, etc.

form are .85, .82, and .78 for M, F, and M-F scales, respectively. Thus, it appears the PAQ possesses satisfactory reliability for a research scale, although additional information on reliability would be useful.

Spence and Helmreich presented a large amount of data bearing on the validity of the PAQ, primarily the short form. For example, they consistently found that male college and high school students scored significantly higher on M and M-F scales than did females. In addition, college students (and high school students) tended to be categorized in the correct cell of the four-fold table, but rarely in the opposite sex cell. However, a sizeable percentage were androgynous or undifferentiated. In one study (p. 55), college males were classified as follows: (1) androgynous: 32 percent, (2) feminine: 8 percent, (3) masculine: 34 percent, and (4) undifferentiated: 25 percent. College females were classified as follows: (1) androgynous: 27 percent, (2) feminine: 32 percent, (3) masculine: 14 percent, and (4) undifferentiated: 28 percent.

The intercorrelations of the scales support a dualistic conception of masculinity and femininity. That is, low positive correlations between M and F were found for both males and females, as was an expected relationship between a measure of self-esteem and the sex categories. The highest self-esteem scores were obtained from the androgynous group, followed by the masculine, feminine, and undifferentiated groups. Data from several criterion groups (homosexuals, female varsity athletes, female Ph.D. scientists, and male Ph.D. scientists) also demonstrated interesting and interpretable relations to PAQ scores. The PAQ merits further use in research as a measure of sex-role orientation.

BEM SEX-ROLE INVENTORY (BSRI). The first systematic attempt to avoid a bipolar masculinity-femininity dimension was made by Sandra Bem, who in 1974 published the Bem Sex-Role Inventory (BSRI). The items were selected for inclusion on the masculinity (M) or the femininity (F) scale if they were rated more desirable in American society for one sex than for the other. The raters were two separate samples of undergraduate students at Stanford University. In both samples, half were males and half were females. Words and phrases that could be used to describe people comprise the items.

An item was placed on the M scale if males and females in both samples rated it significantly more desirable for a man than for a woman. The converse was true for items on the F scale. Neutral (social desirability) items were those judged approximately equally desirable for both men and women. As a result of the statistical criteria used, twenty items were selected for each scale. The BSRI thus consists of sixty items.

A subject's task is to indicate how well each of the sixty items describes the subject. Ratings are made on a seven-point scale, in which a "1" means "never or almost never true," and "7" means "always or almost always true." Examples from the masculine, feminine, and neutral items are given in Figure 12-16.

Originally, three scores were obtained: masculinity, femininity, and androgyny. The masculinity score is the mean self-rating for all masculine items that have been endorsed. The femininity score is analogously obtained. These scores reflect the degree to which a subject endorses masculine or feminine personality characteristics as being self-descriptive. The androgyny score reflects the relative amount of masculinity and femininity. This score is somewhat more complicated to obtain but essentially reflects the difference (F-M) between femininity and masculinity. For example, a male having a high M and low F would receive a high negative score on androgyny. He would thus be "appropriately" sex typed. A person becomes more androgynous when he or she tends to endorse M and F items to about the same degree; that is, the difference will be close to zero. Note that Bem's original definition of *androgyny* would include subjects with high M and high F scores as well as those with low scores on both M and F. This original definition is different from that used by Spence and Helmreich in their PAQ test, which in-

FIGURE 12-16 Sample Items from the Bem Sex Role Inventory. (Reproduced by special permission of the Publisher, Consulting Psychologists Press, Inc., Palo Alto, CA 94306, from *Bem Sex Role Inventory*, by Sandra Bem, Ph.D. Copyright 1978.)

Instructions: Subjects indicate how well each of 60 personality characteristics describes them. The scale ranges from 1 ("Never or almost never true") to 7 ("Always or almost always true").

Masculine Items	*Feminine Items*	*Neutral Items*
Acts as a leader	Affectionate	Adaptable
Aggressive	Cheerful	Conceited
Ambitious	Childlike	Conscientious

---

cluded an undifferentiated category (low M, low F). These are individuals who do not describe themselves with gender-specific terms.

Bem (1974) administered the BSRI to two additional groups of college students to determine its psychometric characteristics. For the two samples, internal consistency reliabilities were .86 and .86 for the M scale and .80 and .82 for the F scale. The androgyny scale had corresponding reliabilities of .85 and .86 for the two samples. In addition, test-retest reliabilities during a four-week period were about .90 for all scales, suggesting reasonable stability over short periods of time. It thus appears to us that the BSRI has acceptable reliability when used with college students.

Bem also found that the M and F scores were essentially unrelated in her two samples for both males and females. Thus, she has evidence that M and F are not opposite ends of a single dimension. In addition, she noted that the BSRI scores did not correlate in any simple way with traditional M-F scales on the CPI or Guilford-Zimmerman personality inventories. Bem also found that males scored higher on M than did females. The converse was true for females.

Bem (1977) later reported that the four-fold categorization illustrated in Figure 12-14 did appear worthwhile. She found that the undifferentiated group did differ from the androgynous group on two varia-

bles (self-esteem and a behavioral measure of responsiveness). Bem (p. 204) also noted that androygynous and undifferentiated persons are alike in that they are not being sex typed.

Factor analyses of the BSRI found several factors in the scale and suggested that additional refinement of the items would be useful. These studies, in general, do support the concept of developing separate scales for measuring femininity and masculinity (Bohannon & Mills, 1979; Gaudreau, 1977; Moreland et al., 1978; Waters, et al., 1977).

The BSRI will undoubtedly continue to be used as a measure of sex-role orientation. It merits further use by researchers interested in exploring the relationship between sex-role orientation and other personality and ability variables.

One study (Kelly et al., 1978) that compared the BSRI and PAQ, as well as two other sex-role inventories, raises an interesting problem, however. Kelly et al. found that the BSRI and PAQ correlations were .85 and .73 for the M and F scales, respectively. Although these correlations are obviously high, they are far from perfect. More importantly, the inventories do not place subjects into the same categories (for example, androgynous). Gaa and Liberman (1981) reported similar results. This finding means that results of research based on different sex-role orientation inventories will not necessarily be comparable.

The two sex-role orientation inventories we have discussed have been mostly developed with college students. Nonstudent populations largely remain to be examined. Thus, these two inventories do not have extensive normative samples to help in interpreting their scores. Although it is easy to suggest but difficult to do, it would be of major interest to perform longitudinal studies on changes in sex-role orientation and development. Assessing aspects of sex-role orientation in children remains a challenging and important task.

State-Trait Anxiety Inventory

We have already referred to test anxiety as a factor that can reduce scores on maximum performance tests. However, the twentieth century is often called the age of anxiety. There is, in fact, a good deal to be afraid of in the modern world. Psychologists have been actively studying and attempting to measure anxiety for many years. As an example of one test that has been widely used (Buros, 1978, lists 333 references), we will briefly discuss the State-Trait Anxiety Inventory (STAI) developed by Spielberger and his colleagues (1970). One reviewer (Katkin, 1978) suggests that research with the STAI has proliferated to such a point that it is the dominant anxiety measure in current use.

The STAI is based on a theoretical distinction between state and trait anxiety. *State anxiety* refers to relatively short-term tension, perhaps because of a specific situation. *Trait anxiety* refers to a relatively long-term tendency to be generally anxious in many situations. The STAI consists of twenty items to assess how a person feels right now (state anxiety) and twenty items to assess how a person generally feels (trait anxiety). These two measures are not necessarily correlated, since even persons who have low A-Trait scores may have high A-State scores under the right set of conditions (for example, just before surgery).

The STAI is a self-report test in which subjects indicate the intensity or frequency of their feelings (anxiety) on a four-point scale. Two scores are provided by adding the responses to the A-State and A-Trait items. Examples for the A-State are "I feel calm" and "I feel secure"; for the A-Trait scale examples are "I wish I could be as happy as others seem to be" and "I am calm, cool, and collected."

The psychometric properties of the STAI are quite good. The manual reports internal consistency reliabilities of .83 to .92 for A-State scores and .86 to .92 for A-Trait scores. The test-retest reliabilities reported in the manual demonstrate that A-Trait scores are more reliable (stable) over time than are the A-State scores, as would be expected from the definitions of state and trait anxiety. For example, over a 104-day test-retest interval, A-State scores correlated in the low .30s whereas A-Trait scores correlated in the .70s. Other investigators (Joesting, 1977; Metzger, 1976; Nixon & Steffeck, 1977) found the STAI to exhibit a similar pattern of test-retest reliability.

The validity of the STAI has been examined, at least indirectly, in many studies. Reviewers (Dreger, 1978; Katkin, 1978) concluded that the distinction between state and trait anxiety is justified by good evidence. Researchers often administer the STAI under stress and no-stress conditions. The stress may be a real situation (before surgery) or an imagined one ("imagine you are scheduled for surgery"). These studies in general support the construct validity of the STAI, since A-State scores increase under stress whereas A-Trait scores remain largely unchanged. For example, in several studies the STAI was administered to patients just before surgery and then again after recovery from surgery. The A-State scores were high just before surgery but decreased significantly after. The A-Trait scores, however, remained largely unchanged (Auerbach, 1973; Martinez-Urrutia, 1975; Spielberger et al., 1973).

Factor analysis has also been used to study the state-trait distinction (Endler & Magnusson, 1976; Kendall et al., 1976; Loo, 1979). Kendall et al., for example, found a single trait anxiety factor, which they labeled *Cognitive Anxiety*. They also found two state anxiety factors that they labeled *Negative Descriptors* ("I am jittery") and *Positive Descriptors* ("I feel content"). Thus, the A-State scale may have two components, whereas the A-Trait scale appears to be largely unidimensional. Endler and Magnusson (1976), however, found no support for the state-trait distinction, and Loo (1979) suggested that the A-Trait scale was multidimensional. These correlational analyses remain complex and difficult to interpret. The experimental evidence as well as A-Trait correlations with other measures of anxiety still convince us that the STAI is probably the most valid self-report inventory currently available for measuring anxiety.

As an indication of its popularity the STAI has been translated into Spanish, Hindi, Portuguese, French, Turkish, Greek, Italian, and Swedish. The cross-cultural study of anxiety represents an interesting line of inquiry (Spielberger & Diaz-Guerrero, 1976). In addition, Smith and Lay (1974) published an extensive annotated bibliography on state and trait anxiety that includes over 100 references to the STAI.

As a cautionary note to its use, the STAI can be faked. That is, the content of the STAI items makes it fairly obvious what the test is designed to measure. Smith (1974), for example, found that subjects can "simulate" responses that would be expected under stressful conditions. For his subjects both A-State and A-Trait scores were elevated under instructions to simulate stress. Although Smith suggested a possible strategy for detecting the exaggeration of stress, we have found no other studies specifically examining this issue. Researchers should thus be certain that subjects have little or no reason to fake their responses on the STAI.

Another measure of trait anxiety that has been widely used was developed by Janet Taylor (now Janet Taylor Spence). She selected fifty items from the MMPI on the basis of their ability to detect clinical anxiety. The resulting scale was called the Manifest Anxiety Scale (MAS) (Taylor, 1953). This scale was often used as a measure of drive in the context of Hull-Spence learning theory. Because the MAS did not distinguish between state and trait anxiety, it has, it seems, been largely replaced in research by the STAI. The MAS is still a popular measure in clinical work, however. Those interested in other measures of anxiety, including physiological indices, should consult Marinelli's excellent chapter on the clinical assessment of anxiety (Marinelli, 1980).

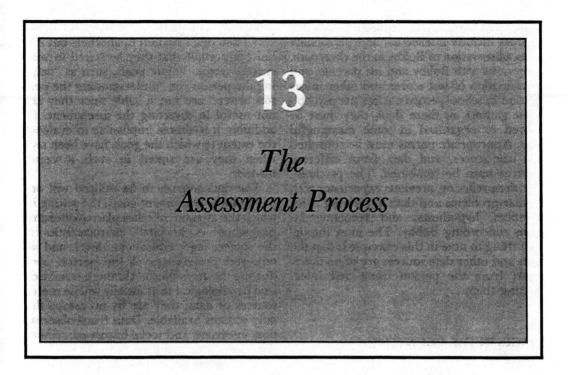

13

The Assessment Process

In Chapter 1 a distinction was made between the terms *test* and *assessment*. A *test* was defined as a standardized sample of behavior from which other, more important behaviors can be inferred or predicted. *Assessment,* a broader term, refers to the entire process involved in collecting information about persons and using it to make important predictions or inferences. Tests represent only one of many sources of information. The purpose of this chapter is to describe in some detail the assessment process.

IMPORTANCE OF THE INTERPRETER

In Chapters 3 and 4 we considered the important psychometric characteristics of psychological tests. A test that is not reliable and valid, that has not been well standardized, and that does not have adequate norms cannot be very useful. However, even a test that possesses all these desirable technical qualities might not be useful. A

test is useful only to the extent that the person using it has the training and experience necessary to give meaning to the results. The test user is involved in virtually all aspects of the assessment process. The user formulates goals for the assessment, makes decisions about data to be collected, gathers the data, scores it if appropriate, and calls on previous experience and training to make inferences or predictions about the subject based on the data collected.

An example should help to illustrate the importance of the test user. Bobby has been referred to the school psychologist by his teacher who is concerned that "he isn't keeping up with his classmates in any of his school subjects." The psychologist's first step in the assessment probably is to talk with Bobby's teacher to obtain more information about the problem. The goals of the assessment depend in part on what else the psychologist learns from the teacher but probably are to understand the reasons for Bobby's poor performance and to suggest remediation. The next step is to decide on sources of data to be collected. Possible sources include intellectual and personality tests, observation of Bobby in the classroom, interviews with Bobby and his parents, and examination of test scores and other information in school records. After the psychologist gathers all these data, they must be scored or organized in some meaningful way. Appropriate norms must be consulted for test scores, and data from different sources must be combined. The psychologist then relies on previous experience with similar problems and data in arriving at inferences, hypotheses, and recommendations concerning Bobby. The most important thing to note in this example is that the tests and other data sources are of no utility apart from the person using and interpreting them.

STAGES IN THE ASSESSMENT PROCESS

Kleinmuntz (1967, pp. 339–355) likened the assessment process to any other data processing system. He suggested that it involves three primary stages—input, processing, and output (see Figure 13–1).

Input

In the input stage the goals of the assessment are formulated, data sources are selected, data are collected, and data are arranged or organized in a manner suitable for "reading in" to the human data processor. The goals of the assessment will vary from one situation to another, but it is most important that they be stated in very specific terms. Vague goals, such as "helping the person" or "understanding the person better," are not suitable since they are not useful in directing the assessment. In addition, it is almost impossible to evaluate the extent to which the goals have been met when they are stated in such a vague manner.

The data sources to be utilized will depend on the assessment goals, the setting in which the assessment takes place (for example, school vs. hospital), characteristics of the subject (age, educational level, and so on), and preferences of the person conducting the assessment. Although standardized psychological tests usually will be useful sources of data, they are by no means the only sources available. Data from observation, interview, and social history contribute significantly to many assessments.

The collection of data is an important function that should be carried out by a well-trained and qualified person. Many standardized tests must be administered by a doctoral level psychologist or someone with equivalent training. Obtaining useful information from an interview requires a thorough understanding of that process and considerable experience. Observational techniques also require adequate training and experience if they are to yield useful information.

Scoring tests in some cases involves a simple clerical process such as placing a scoring

FIGURE 13–1 Stages in the assessment process.

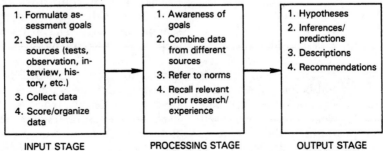

template over an answer sheet and counting the number of marks appearing in the holes. In other cases, scoring can be complicated and may require considerable training and experience. Organizing data sources in a meaningful way usually involves summarizing information in some manner (for example, MMPI profile sheet, Rorschach psychogram, IQ and subtest scores from the WISC-R, list of needs and press from the TAT).

Processing

In the processing stage the test user is aware of the goals formulated in the input stage and typically has a wide array of test scores and other data available. A first step in this stage usually is to refer to appropriate norms for available test scores. For example, the user may consult the appropriate manual and learn that a test subject's Full Scale IQ score of 87 on the WISC-R places that person at the twentieth percentile compared with other subjects in the standardization sample. Achievement test scores may indicate that the subject is several grade levels below his or her age peers in one or several school subjects.

The next step usually is to compare and combine data from different sources. The assessor looks for consistencies and inconsistencies and places more confidence in data that are consistent across sources.

At this point in the processing stage the assessor compares the subject's data to data from previous assessments and to research findings. The assumption is made that subjects with similar assessment data will also be similar in other important ways.

Output

In this final stage of assessment the assessor makes inferences about the subject. The forms that these inferences take depend on the assessment goals. For employment the inferences could be concerned with the likelihood that the subject will be successful on the job if hired. In an academic setting the final product could be a recommendation concerning admission to college, graduate school, or some other program. In a clinical setting the assessor could make statements about the level of psychopathology or preferred treatment. Sometimes the output of the assessment is a rather global and complete personality description of the subject. It should be emphasized that regardless of the exact nature of the assessment output, it must be in a form that can be understood and utilized by the person to whom it is directed.

BASE RATES

In Chapter 3 *base rate* was defined as the proportion of people possessing a particular characteristic in the population of interest. For example, if we know from past experience that fewer than 1 percent of patients in a particular psychiatric hospital have committed suicide, the base rate for suicide in that hospital would be less than 1 percent. Or if we know that 60 percent of persons hired for a particular type of job in the past were considered to be successful workers, the base rate for success on that particular job would be 60 percent.

As part of the processing stage of the assessment process, the assessor must take base rates into account when making inferences or predictions. If the assessor knows that fewer than 1 percent of patients in a particular hospital will commit suicide, the likelihood of the assessment process leading to greater than 99 percent accuracy (the level that would be achieved if the prediction of no suicide is made for every patient in that setting) is very small. On the other hand, if the base rate for success on a particular job is 60 percent, an increment in accuracy above 60 percent should not be too difficult to achieve through the assessment process.

Rosen (1954) pointed out that sometimes the consequences of not accurately predicting an event (for example, suicide) are so dire that some way of predicting that event must be found. Typically the procedure used is to adjust cutting scores so that all or most of the potential suicides are identified even if in the process many persons who are not suicidal (false positives) are incorrectly classified. Lanyon and Goodstein (1971, pp. 136–137) indicated that in such low probability but serious predictions, it may be possible to identify certain subgroups, such as adolescents or the elderly, for whom the base rate for the event might be higher than for the entire population.

In generating global personality descriptions the assessor must also take base rates into account. For example, if the assessor is describing a patient in a setting where more than 90 percent of the patients are anxious, to include the adjective *anxious* in the description does little to differentiate that particular patient from other patients. However, the inclusion of such a descriptor might have value if the description is to be used by someone who is not familiar with the base rates for this particular setting. Tallent (1958) suggested that many clinicians capitalize on base rates by emphasizing in their personality descriptions attributes that apply to virtually all persons in a given setting. He labeled this tendency the Aunt Fanny error because the descriptors are ones that would be true of anybody's "Aunt Fanny."

CLINICAL VERSUS STATISTICAL PREDICTION

There is not much agreement among experts concerning how data should be combined and interpreted in assessment. Meehl (1954, pp. 3–4) suggested that there are two quite different ways to process assessment data. In the clinical approach the assessor examines all available data and combines and processes them in a subjective or intuitive way in order to arrive at a prediction. By contrast, in the statistical or actuarial approach, data would be combined and processed automatically with empirically derived formulas, equations, or actuarial tables.

An example of how the same prediction in the two approaches would be handled should help to clarify the differences between them. Suppose that a group of patients has completed the MMPI and a judgment is to be made concerning whether each patient is neurotic or psychotic (assuming that all patients fall into one of these two categories). In the clinical approach, a psychologist or other qualified person would examine each MMPI protocol, rely on past experience and subjective impressions of MMPI differences between neurotics and psychotics, and intuitively arrive at a prediction. In the statistical approach, scores on the MMPI scales would be entered into actuarial formulas that had been empirically derived on the basis of MMPI data from other neurotics and psychotics. The formulas, which could be applied by a nonprofessional worker or a computer, would yield a prediction of neurotic or psychotic for each patient.

Although the advantages and disadvantages of the clinical and statistical approaches to prediction have been argued for quite some time (for example, Burgess, 1928; Viteles, 1925), it was Meehl's 1954 book, *Clinical Versus Statistical Prediction*, that first pitted the two approaches against each other. Meehl evaluated existing prediction studies and concluded that in virtually all instances the actuarial approach was either equal or superior to clinical prediction.

Meehl's conclusions generated a great deal of controversy, and for a while clinicians seemed to be lining up on one side or the other of the issue. Fortunately, some investigators used a more reasoned approach to the problem. For example, Holt (1958) pointed out that Meehl had emphasized the data combination or integration stage of the assessment process to the exclusion of other stages. Assessment, according to Holt, involves the following stages: a study of the criterion, choice of intervening variables, choice of measures of these variables, data collection, and data combination. The role of the clinician should be studied in all these steps, not just at the data combination step as Meehl had done.

Sawyer (1966) emphasized the importance of the clinician in the data collection stage of assessment. The clinician's contribution may be providing assessment of characteristics from interview, history, and observation that otherwise would not enter into the prediction process.

Goldman (1961, pp. 210–212) listed situations in which the clinical approach is to be favored over the actuarial approach:

1. When experience tables or base rates are not available for the predictions to be made.
2. In the prediction of low probability events such as suicide or homicide.
3. When personality descriptions are required rather than simple behavioral predictions.

Although this controversy has not been resolved, some conclusions seem possible. It is clear from research that in some predictions the use of actuarial formulas leads to greater accuracy. In these situations the clinician would be wise to rely on the formulas, although the clinician can still have an important role in formulating the goals of the assessment, selecting data sources, and collecting data. When the clinician must make predictions or generate descriptions but adequate base rates and formulas do not exist, the clinical approach must be used.

Although Meehl performed an important function by highlighting the differences between clinical and statistical prediction, he also tended to promote division among assessors. Both clinical and actuarial approaches are important and useful in the assessment process. The assessors who adhere to one approach to the exclusion of the other are greatly limiting their assessment versatility.

AMOUNT OF INFORMATION

Most persons involved in assessment seem to assume that more accurate inferences, predictions, or descriptions will occur as more information is available about the subject. Existing research indicates that having more assessment data does not necessarily mean that the resulting inferences or predictions will be more accurate (Kostlan, 1954; Oskamp, 1965; Sines, 1959; Winch & More, 1956).

An investigation by Sines (1959) illustrates the methodology that can be used to study the relationship between amount of assessment data and accuracy of inferences. Sines gave five clinical psychology trainees a Biographical Data Sheet (BDS) which reported some demographic data (for example, age, sex, marital status) about each of the six psychiatric patients. The trainees were asked to use a ninety-seven-item Q-sort* to provide a description of each patient based on the BDS. Each trainee then interviewed each patient, administered a Rorschach, or was given the patient's MMPI profile. A second Q-sort description was generated for each patient based on the BDS plus the second data source. A third data source was added, and a third Q-sort was generated for the three data sources. Finally, a fourth data source was added, and a fourth Q-sort was generated from all four data sources. The BDS was always the first data source, but the order of presentation of the interview, Rorschach, and MMPI was varied systematically. It was made clear to each trainee that each Q-sort was to be based on the accumulated information available for each subject. After the patients had been seen in psychotherapy for approximately ten sessions, a Q-sort description of each patient was provided by the therapist. The accuracy of the descriptions based on varying amounts of assessment data was determined by correlating the descriptions of the same patients by their therapists.

Table 13–1 reports the average validity coefficients (correlations between assessment-based and therapist-generated Q-sort

*In the Q-sort procedure (Stephenson, 1953) the individual receives a set of cards containing descriptive statements that are to be sorted into piles indicating how characteristic or uncharacteristic each statement is of the person being described. Since Q-sort data typically are analyzed by correlating them with other Q-sort data, a normal distribution of ratings is assured by instructing the sorter to place a specified number of statements (cards) in each pile.

TABLE 13-1 Average validity coefficients of descriptions based on varying amounts of information

Amount of Information	Average Validity Coefficient
One Data Source (BDS)	.396
Two Data Sources	.446
Three Data Sources	.477
Four Data Sources	.480

Adapted from Sines, L. K. (1959), The relative contribution of four kinds of data to accuracy in personal assessment. *Journal of Consulting Psychology, 23,* 483–492. Copyright 1959 by the American Psychological Association. Adapted by permission of the author.

descriptions) as a function of the amount of information available. It can be seen that there was a consistent positive relationship between the amount of data utilized and the accuracy of descriptions. That is, as more data sources were utilized, the resulting descriptions were more accurate. However, the absolute improvement in accuracy as additional data were added to the BDS was quite small. Sines' research indicates that adding some kinds of data leads to increases in accuracy whereas adding other kinds does not. For example, when the interview was added to the BDS, the mean validity coefficient increased from .396 to .566, but when the Rorschach data were added to the BDS, the validity coefficient decreased from .396 to .368. Another interesting conclusion of the Sines study was that the perceptions of the patients crystallized early in the process and were resistant to change as new data were added.

In summary, it appears that having more assessment data available about a subject does not necessarily mean that more accurate inferences will occur. The nature of the material to be added and the sequential position of each data source also must be considered.

EXPERIENCE OF ASSESSOR

It often is assumed that persons with more training and experience with assessment techniques will be able to generate more accurate inferences than those with less training and experience. We expect a psychologist with a Ph.D. and ten years of clinical experience to be more adept at interpreting MMPIs and Rorschachs than a beginning graduate student in clinical psychology. Unfortunately, research does not confirm a direct relationship between experience and accuracy of inferences.

Graham (1971) found that experienced clinical psychologists, clinical psychology trainees, and naive undergraduate students did not differ in the accuracy with which they could differentiate between neurotic and psychotic patients on the basis of their MMPI profiles. In another study (Graham, 1967) judges of varying experience examined MMPI profiles of psychiatric patients and generated Q-sort descriptions of them. Judges with low experience were graduate students in psychology who had studied the MMPI but who had little or no actual experience in interpretation. Judges with medium experience were Ph.D. clinical psychologists who used the MMPI routinely in their work. Judges with high experience were Ph.D. clinical psychologists who had a great deal of experience with the MMPI and also were actively engaged in MMPI research. Accuracy of Q-sort descriptions was determined by comparing them with descriptions based on interviews with patients, relatives, and hospital staff and on examination of patients' clinical records. Table 13–2 reports the average correlations between MMPI-based descriptions and criterion Q-sort descriptions for the three experience levels. Although there was a tendency for

TABLE 13-2 Average correlations between MMPI-based descriptions and criterion descriptions for three experience levels

Experience Level	r
High	.31
Medium	.37
Low	.29

From Graham, J. R. (1967), A Q-sort study of the accuracy of clinical descriptions based on the MMPI. *Journal of Psychiatric Research, 5,* 297-305. Copyright 1967, Pergamon Press, Ltd. Reproduced by permission.

the more experienced judges to generate more accurate descriptions, differences in accuracy did not differ signficantly for the three levels.

There also are data indicating that experience and accuracy of inferences are not highly related when data sources are sentence-completion tests (Walker & Linden, 1967), drawings (Hiler & Nesvig, 1965; Schaeffer, 1964; Stricker, 1967; Watson, 1967), Bender-Gestalt test (Goldberg, 1959), Rorschach and Thematic Apperception Test (Soskin, 1954), or interviews (Grigg, 1958). Even in studies that found more experienced judges to be more accurate, the magnitude of the differences in accuracy among experience levels was small (Jones, 1969; Karson & Freud, 1956; Silverman, 1959).

Although accuracy of inferences based on assessment data does not seem to be related directly to the experience of test users, judges with different experience differ in the amount of confidence they have in the accuracy of their inferences. More experienced judges tend to have less confidence that their inferences are accurate, and their confidence in their inferences changes appropriately as the accuracy of the inferences changes. By contrast, less experienced judges tend to be overly confident about the accuracy of their inferences, and they become even more confident as they are involved more with a particular inferential task, such as predicting diagnosis from the MMPI (Goldberg, 1959; Oskamp, 1962, 1965).

In summary, it seems that the experience of test users is not highly related to accuracy of inferences from test data. However, more experienced judges tend to be more appropriate in the amount of confidence they have in the accuracy of their inferences.

SOURCES OF ASSESSMENT DATA

There is not much agreement among test users concerning which kinds of data contribute most to accurate inferences or predictions. Almost every popular assessment technique has loyal supporters who maintain that their technique is superior to all others. Unfortunately, such individuals often argue for their techniques on the basis of faith or subjective clinical experience rather than objective evidence.

There have been several studies on the comparative utility of various sources of assessment data. A study by Little and Shneidman (1959) illustrates the methodology that typically has been used in these studies, so we will discuss their research in some detail. They compared the accuracy of personality descriptions, diagnoses, and global ratings of adjustment based on data from the Rorschach, TAT, MMPI, and MAPS (Make-a-Picture Story). Data were obtained from normals, neurotics, and psychotics. Clinicians who were acknowledged experts with one of the data sources served as judges for that source. Criterion ratings of the patients were generated by twenty-three psychiatrists and one psychologist based on examination of lengthy clinical case histories. Results indicated that there was little agreement between the test judges and criterion judges concerning diagnosis or level of adjustment. Test judges tended to overrate pathology for all patients, but those using the MMPI were less extreme in this regard than those using other data sources. When Q-sort personality descriptions based on each data source were correlated with criterion descriptions, the overall accuracy was low for all techniques. The average correlations between criterion descriptions and those based on the Rorschach, MAPS, TAT, and MMPI were .16., .11, .17, and .28, respectively. Although, relatively speaking, MMPI descriptions were more accurate than those based on the other data sources, on an absolute level their accuracy was only modest.

Golden (1964) asked experienced clinicians to provide personality descriptions of patients from four data sources (identifying data, MMPI, Rorschach, and TAT). The accuracy of the descriptions was determined by comparing them with descriptions based on case histories. The mean accuracy of all descriptions exceeded a chance level, and those based on any source of test data were more accurate than those based on identifying data alone. However, descriptions based on the MMPI, Rorschach, or TAT did not differ in accuracy from each other.

Kostlan (1954) obtained Rorschach, MMPI, Stein Sentence Completion, and social case history data from five psychiatric outpatients. Various combinations of data sources were presented to twenty clinical psychologists with at least two years of diagnostic experience, and they were asked to complete a 282-item true-false checklist based on the assessment data. The accuracy of the ratings was determined by comparing them with ratings provided by the patients' psychotherapists. Kostlan concluded that all assessment-based descriptions were more accurate than would be expected by chance. When a social case history was not included in the data, the accuracy of inferences based on the other data did not exceed that of inferences based on minimal identifying information (age, marital status, occupation, education, and referral source). The accuracy was greatest for data combinations that included the social case history and the MMPI. Again, as in other studies discussed, the absolute level for assessment-based descriptions was only modest.

The Sines (1959) study, which had as its primary focus the relationship between accuracy of descriptions and amount of data, also compared the accuracy of four individual assessment data sources—biographical data sheet, MMPI, Rorschach, and interview. The mean correlation between Q-sorts based on biographical data and those provided by the patients' therapists exceeded a chance level of accuracy. The mean correlation for the biographical data sheet plus the interview, the biographical data sheet plus the MMPI, and the biographical data sheet plus the Rorschach were .566, .378, and .368, respectively. Clearly the interview added more to the biographical data than did the MMPI or the Rorschach.

What conclusions can be reached from these and similar studies? First, it would appear that assessment data permit more accurate descriptions or inferences than are possible without such data. Second, unless they are used along with social history or biographical data, data from tests add little to the accuracy of description or inference. Third, the interview seems to contribute more to the accuracy of the description or inference than does any other source of assessment data. Fourth, the absolute level of the accuracy of the description or inference based on assessment data is only modest and probably far less than many test users believe.

CLINICAL JUDGMENT RESEARCH

The limited accuracy of descriptions and inferences from assessment data has led some individuals to suggest that we should abandon assessment entirely. Others have been stimulated to try to understand the interpretive process of the test user and to identify procedures for increasing accuracy. Investigations of this kind are called *clinical judgment research.*

Clinical judgment research has proceeded along two major avenues. The first has involved trying to simulate the judgment process. The second has concentrated on manipulating contingencies in the judgment process and observing the effects on judgmental accuracy.

The simulation approach includes the development of mathematical or computer models that accurately reproduce the decisions of human judges in a variety of judgmental tasks. In this approach the emphasis is not on accuracy. Rather, the goal is to duplicate the inferential process of the human judge regardless of how accurate the judgments resulting from that process are.

Several important clinical judgments have been modeled accurately. For example, Dawes (1971) demonstrated that a model based on applicants' undergraduate grade point average, Graduate Record Examination scores, and rating of quality of the undergraduate institutions could accurately predict the decisions of a department of psychology admissions committee. Goldberg (1970) was able to develop a model that accurately duplicated clinicians' diagnoses of neurotic versus psychotic from MMPI profiles. Kleinmuntz (1963) developed a computer program that simulated clinicians' judgments of the maladjustment of college students from MMPIs.

Several other interesting findings came from these simulation studies. In most instances a simple linear or additive model accurately replicated human judgments, although persons involved in such judgments typically claim that they combine data in highly complex and configural ways. For example, in Goldberg's study, a simple unweighted combination of six MMPI scales predicted the diagnoses of clinicians better than some very complex and configural formulas. Dawes (1971) pointed out that often the models are more accurate over the long run than are the human judgments on which the models are based. This can occur because the models are not influenced by extraneous factors, such as boredom or fatigue, which enter into human decisions.

Several different contingencies in the clinical judgment process have been manipulated and the effects on judgmental accuracy observed. Goldberg and Rorer (1965) reasoned that a possible explanation for the relatively low accuracy of clinical judgments is the lack of opportunity for clinicians to improve their accuracy because of the absence of systematic feedback about the correctness of their predictions. Several investigators (Goldberg & Rorer, 1965; Graham, 1971; Sechrest et al., 1967) demonstrated that judges make more accurate inferences if they receive immediate and specific feedback. However, the increment in accuracy associated with such feedback is only modest. In addition, it is not clear whether or not feedback generalizes from one task or sample to another. There also is some question of whether judges actually extract useful information from the feedback or if they simply are more motivated to do well in that situation because the task seems more possible. Obviously, there are important varia-bles in addition to feedback that influence judgmental accuracy.

Graham (1967), using descriptions of psychiatric patients based on the MMPI, concluded that some kinds of inferences (more factual ones) were more accurately made than others. Some judges make more accurate inferences than others, and some patients are more accurately described than others. Graham (1971) found that inferences tend to be more accurate when the behaviors to be inferred are more reliably measured. Rotter (1967) suggested that judges can only utilize feedback effectively if they explicitly state the hypotheses on which their inferences are based. In initial attempts to evaluate Rotter's suggestion, Graham (1970) and Cohen (1972) did not find that explicit hypothesis formulation led to greater accuracy (with or without feedback) when judgments of psychosis versus neurosis were made from MMPI profiles.

What conclusions can be reached from clinical judgment research? First, clinical judgments can be accurately simulated. Second, it appears that judges combine data in a much simpler manner than they maintain. Third, factors such as the nature of the inferential task, availability of feedback concerning accuracy, and as yet unspecified characteristics of the judge and the subject are related to inferential accuracy. Obviously, the clinical judgment process is very complex, and additional research is needed to understand that process better and to intervene in it in order to increase accuracy of judgments.

CONCLUDING COMMENTS

Much of the data reviewed in this chapter seems to point to the human judge or test user as an inadequate, and maybe even hopeless, creature. Judges are of great importance in the assessment process, but their judgments are of limited accuracy. Experience or training are unrelated to accuracy of inferences, as is the amount of assessment data available. Judges tend to crystalize their impressions early in the process and are reluctant to change as more data become available. Judges tend to be overconfident of the accuracy of their inferences, and there is some doubt that they combine data in the highly complex and configural manner that they claim.

Is there anything positive to say about the assessment process? Yes. First, you should recall that inferences and descriptions based on assessment data tend to be more accurate than those made without such data. As long as the assessment process is not too costly (in terms of both time and money) the use of assessment procedures can help us make accurate inferences about people and understand them better.

A study by Cohen (1975) suggests that perhaps human judges are not as inadequate as they have been pictured. Cohen presented psychologists with figure drawings that were said to have been drawn by normal or emotionally disturbed children. Psychologists were asked to indicate whether each drawing was produced by a normal or an emotionally disturbed child. Some judges were given feedback about the accuracy of their judgments and others were not. Cohen artificially constructed his materials in such a way that he could control the reliability of his criterion measure (normal versus emotionally disturbed) and systematically control the relationship between drawing characteristics and the criterion measure. He found that when judges were asked to predict a reliable criterion and were given test materials in which there were valid relationships between drawing characteristics and the criterion, they were able to learn to make the judgment of normal or emotionally disturbed from drawings with great accuracy. Unlike other clinical judgment studies that reported low to moderate accuracy levels, Cohen's judges correctly identified 96 percent of the drawings. Cohen concluded that the clinicians' mediocre accuracy levels may be due to methodological difficulties rather than to inherent limitations in their judgmental ability. He also suggested that we should refocus research toward developing better assessment sources, that is, ones in which there are valid relationships between assessment data and criterion variables.

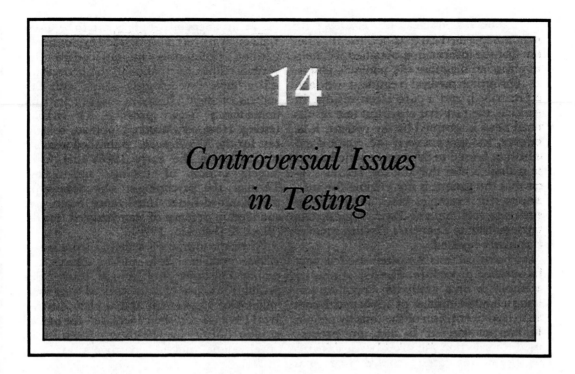

14

Controversial Issues
in Testing

In this chapter, we will discuss several controversial issues regarding the use and interpretation of psychological tests. In the first thirteen chapters we have presented the principles of psychological testing along with examples of many of the more commonly used ability and personality tests. Our hope is that the reader is now prepared to examine the criticisms of psychological testing with an understanding of both the strengths and weaknesses of various tests.

In our opinion, the central problem concerns the misinterpretation and misuse of tests and test scores. That is, tests are not intrinsically good or bad. Tests that are poorly constructed and have poor reliability and validity are easily dismissed. Everyone agrees that such tests should not be used for any legitimate purpose. A more difficult problem concerns the use of psychometrically sound tests. Even tests that have been carefully constructed and demonstrate acceptable reliability can still be misused either because of ignorance or because no better procedure exists to answer the question of interest. The misuse of psychometrically sound tests thus arises because the user does not recognize the validity limits of a particular test.

Two principles should be constantly kept in mind when considering both the criticisms and use of tests. First, a test score represents current performance on a standardized task. As such, the score is a function of both environmental and genetic influences. Second, test scores should not be the only data used in making decisions about people and are rarely the most important factor in such decisions. Both of these principles implicitly recognize that any test score is an imperfect indicator of a variable of interest.

Finally, it seems important to recognize that in many instances tests are not particularly pleasant experiences. No one likes to be evaluated when the results can be negative and unpleasant. When we are ill, physicians subject us to many unpleasant medical tests. Anyone who has had a barium enema or a spinal tap, for example, knows that many medical tests are painful, degrading, and generally unpleasant. However the public accepts medical tests because they believe that the information obtained will help the physician diagnose the patient's illness. An appropriate medical treatment will then be prescribed, and a cure often results. In medicine, the fact that a painful test results in bad news is accepted by the patient. It is, however, less acceptable if the medical examination is used to determine benefits and the patient is told that the test results suggest that the patient is not eligible for such benefits (for example, black lung disease benefits to coal miners). Psychological tests that demonstrate a person's weaknesses may be similarly rejected.

Psychological tests are often used as part of a selection procedure. The use of tests by an employer or a graduate school for selecting a limited number of applicants is certain to lead to criticism of the tests by people who are not selected. In fact, any process used for selection will probably be criticized by those who are excluded from participating in some desirable activity. Psychological testing is generally well accepted when the test results are used for diagnostic purposes. Thus, in psychotherapy, the scores on personality tests can be used in planning the course of a patient's psychotherapy. In education, diagnostic tests of reading and mathematical skills can be used to determine which students need special instruction in these areas. In general, it appears that achievement tests are less criticized than aptitude tests, possibly because achievement tests are more clearly understood not to measure innate characteristics but to reflect the outcome of the educational experiences of the student.

HISTORICAL PERSPECTIVE

Cronbach (1975) and Haney (1981) cogently summarized the history of social controversy surrounding standardized testing. Public controversy first appeared only after standardized tests were developed for recruits for the army during World War I and

large numbers of people began to be tested. Data on army recruits provided evidence regarding differences in intelligence for various ethnic, occupational, and geographical groups. Psychologists, elated with the success of their efforts in military testing, immediately began pressing for civilian testing. However, Walter Lippman, columnist for the *New Republic,* published a series of articles in the early 1920s that were largely critical of testing, and Lewis Terman, the psychologist who developed the Stanford-Binet Intelligence Scale, responded in defense of standardized testing (Block & Dworkin, 1976).

After the flurry of activity in the early 1920s, relatively little public interest in testing appeared until around 1960. Surprisingly, the use of standardized tests with millions of servicemen and women during World War II and their increased use in education during the 1930s produced relatively little public controversy (Haney, 1981).

In 1957, the Soviet Union launched Sputnik and the United States was shocked to find itself behind in the space race. In order to promote academic excellence, standardized tests were used by the National Merit Scholarship Corporation to identify academically gifted students. Also, more and more high school students were enrolling in colleges and were taking standardized tests such as the Scholastic Aptitude Test (SAT). The SAT and other such tests were used as part of the admission procedure for many colleges. Multiple-choice tests and optical scanners permitted tests to be given to large numbers of students, because they could be scored quickly and accurately. A well-known critic of multiple-choice tests was Banesh Hoffman, whose book, *The Tyranny of Testing,* was published in 1962. Hoffman suggested that multiple-choice tests, requiring examinees to pick the "best" answer, contain too many ambiguous questions and penalize creative thinkers. He also suggested that test publishers, such as the Educational Testing Service, were insensitive and unresponsive to legitimate questions from students who took the SAT and other similar tests.

In the early and mid-1960s, additional public comment flared briefly over personality tests. Their use for selection purposes by the federal government was the subject of congressional hearings, to which an entire issue of the *American Psychologist* (Amrine, 1965) was devoted. The hearings raised legitimate questions about invasion of privacy and the usefulness of personality tests for selection. Other popular books critical of personality tests also appeared at this time: *They Shall Not Pass* (Black, 1962), *The Brain Watchers* (Gross, 1962), and *The Naked Society* (Packard, 1962). As the titles suggest, these authors viewed psychological tests as intrusive instruments that threatened an individual's rights.

In 1969, Arthur Jensen published an article in the *Harvard Educational Review* entitled "How Much Can We Boost IQ and Scholastic Achievement?" This long, scholarly article contained the working hypothesis that perhaps the mean difference in IQ between whites and blacks is partially caused by genetic factors. In the late 1960s and early 1970s the suggestion that blacks were inferior to whites in their performance on IQ tests generated a great deal of public commentary. The book of readings edited by Block and Dworkin (1976) gives a good sample of the articles written on this subject. Richard Herrnstein, a Harvard psychology professor, published an article in *The Atlantic Monthly* in 1971 which continued the IQ controversy. The main issue was to what extent intelligence is an inherited trait (genetically determined) versus one determined largely by environmental factors. This debate continues to be of widespread professional and public interest. Minority groups and others suggest that social factors such as discrimination, poor schooling, and poverty are the important determinants of the lower average IQ scores obtained by blacks and Hispanics. They also argue that a genetic explanation of IQ differences legitimizes continued discrimination by the majority in the United States. They also suggest that

most tests are biased against minorities, because the tests were largely developed by and for white, middle-class Americans.

The Civil Rights Act of 1964 produced another set of challenges to psychological tests. Title VII of this act was intended to promote equal treatment of all people and improve the economic position of blacks in particular (Wigdor & Garner, 1982). Tests have been a very visible part of many admission and selection procedures. As such, they have increasingly been the subject of legal rulings and government regulation for the past decade. As part of Title VII, the Equal Employment Opportunity Commission (EEOC) was created to promote compliance with the Civil Rights Act and has issued several statements on employee selection procedures. The EEOC guidelines, which first appeared in 1966 and the latest in 1978, largely say that discrimination exists if a test or any other selection device results in a lower proportion of minority group members being selected than white males. If minorities are underrepresented, the EEOC only permits tests to be used if they meet stringent validity guidelines. The Psychological Corporation (1978) has published an annotated bibliography on 66 court decisions on employment testing for the years 1968 through 1977. This compilation of court decisions was designed to assist those using or considering the use of tests for selecting personnel.

Litigation involving tests continues to be a source of controversy in education as well as employment. In 1972, for example, the case of Larry P. was initiated because black children were being placed in classes for the Educable Mentally Retarded (EMR) in higher proportions than white children. Intelligence tests were used as part of the information in making such assignments. The judge enjoined the San Francisco public schools from using intelligence tests in placing students in EMR classes because of the adverse impact on black children. The tests were judged to be biased against black children.

The debate over standardized testing

shows no signs of diminishing. The National Research Council established a Committee on Ability Testing to conduct a broad examination of the role and function of testing in the United States. The committee conducted a public hearing in November 1978 and published two volumes in 1982 entitled *Ability Testing: Uses, Consequences, and Controversies*. The *American Psychologist* of October 1981 was a special issue entitled *Testing: Concepts, Policy, Practice, and Research*. Both of these publications provide excellent presentations and detailed discussion of controversial issues in testing. In addition, Ralph Nader's consumer organization has examined the Educational Testing Service (ETS) and the Scholastic Aptitude Test with predictable results—tests do more harm than good (Nairn, 1980). The Nader report, of course, produced various rejoinders defending the use of tests (Kaplan, 1982; Lerner, 1980a). Several books critical of testing have also appeared, including *The Testing Trap* (Strenio, 1981), *The Mismeasure of Man* (Gould, 1981), *The Myth of Measurability* (Houts, 1977), and *The Science and Politics of I.Q.* (Kamin, 1974).

TEST BIAS

There now exists a large literature on test bias. In addition to many articles, several integrated summaries have been published, including two technical books (Berk, 1982; Jensen, 1980) and two chapters on bias in assessment (Reschly, 1979; Reynolds, 1982). Unfortunately, despite the literature, no universally accepted definition of *test bias* yet exists. The issues, however, do appear to be coming into sharper focus.

Bias has a precise meaning in statistics. A statistic is biased if, on the average, it does not equal the parameter it is supposed to estimate. Thus, a statistic is biased if it contains systematic rather than random error. In testing, bias is mainly claimed to exist in intelligence and aptitude tests, less often in achievement tests, and rarely in personality tests. It is argued that test bias exists if a minority group receives lower scores on a test than do members of the majority. The assumption, of course, is that minority and majority groups would not differ in test performance if the test were not biased. Although tests could be biased against any minority group, most controversy exists over the fact that blacks, *as a group*, tend to obtain significantly lower scores on tests of cognitive ability than do whites. Given the fact that blacks are a large minority and that they have experienced virulent racial discrimination in the past, it is not surprising that any device or instrument that shows blacks to be lower in ability than whites would be vigorously questioned by members of the affected group and their advocates. If all men and women are in fact created equal, we might expect that an unbiased test would show no significant differences between groups. It is much easier and politically wiser to attack the tests than to address the other factors that could lead to poorer performance.

The Context for Test Bias

We will first discuss the area of cognitive ability tests in which minority groups typically receive lower scores than do the majority. Flaugher (1978) identified several aspects of the controversy over test bias. The first concerns the existence or nonexistence of test bias in achievement tests. The problem here is the failure to recognize the distinction between aptitude and achievement. Thus if students score poorly on an achievement test and it is interpreted as reflecting innate ability, the problem is seen to rest with the students. If, however, the score on the test is interpreted as an indication of a poor education, more resources are advocated for education in order to improve achievement. The fact that mean differences in test performance between blacks and whites exist is the definition of test bias most used by the courts and popular press. This observation has been made by several authors (Cole, 1981; Green, 1978; Reschly, 1981; Reynolds, 1982).

Tests reflect group differences that are produced by many associated variables (socioeconomic status, educational system, family and home environment, and so on). In fact, tests might be criticized if they did *not* show group differences. As Novick (1981), among others, noted, there is a growing concern with equality of outcome or results rather than with equality of opportunity. Tests are judged to be biased because they demonstrate unequal results. The issue of test bias can be legitimately raised when test scores are overinterpreted. Achievement tests can measure a fairly narrow range of individual differences quite well—those related to academic matters. But much else of importance in human affairs we measure much less well. We may choose to exaggerate the importance of what we do measure well.

Test bias has also been identified with sexism. The English language itself, at least as it is commonly used, does have a masculine bias. Thus, tests are scrutinized closely for sexual bias in their language content apart from how the scores are used. Test bias has been identified very often with differential validity. That is, tests make valid predictions for the majority but not for the minority group. Test bias has also been closely identified with content. That is, individual items in a test are somehow identified as being "unfair" to members of a minority group. Methods of detecting item bias include judgmental (Tittle, 1982) as well as statistical ones (Angoff, 1982; Ironson, 1982).

Test bias also is involved in the selection model used. Thus, if a test is used for selection purposes and proportionately more minorities have lower scores on the test, fewer minorities will be selected. Peterson and Novick (1976) discussed the technical characteristics of various selection models, as did Jensen (1980).

Test bias is also related to validating tests against the wrong criterion. Thus the criterion chosen is often the first-semester GPA in college or a supervisor's ratings. When we find there are larger group differences on the predictor (a "biased" test) than on the criterion measure, we may be demonstrating that the criterion is simply less reliable than the predictor.

Test bias is often identified with the atmosphere or situation in which the testing occurs. Minority children who are tested by persons of the majority, for example, are presumed to exhibit less than optimal test performance. Flaugher's (1978) main point is that test bias has no simple definition but rather refers to a context of concerns about tests themselves and their use.

Definitions of Test Bias

Because the validity of any test should determine how it will be used, defining *test bias* in terms of a test's validity seems to us to be a reasonable approach. Reynolds (1982) defines test bias in content, construct, and predictive or criterion-related validity. These definitions are given in Figure 14-1.

Evidence on Bias in Ability Tests

On the basis of the available evidence, ability tests have generally not been shown to be biased when definitions involving content and construct validity are used (Jensen, 1980, Ch. 11; Reynolds, 1982). Regarding bias in construct validity, the following conclusion from Reynolds (p. 200) seems reasonable:

Construct validity of a large number of popular psychometric assessment instruments has been investigated across race and sex with a variety of populations of minority and white children and with a divergent set of methodologies. All roads have led to Rome. No consistent evidence of bias in construct validity has been found with any of the many tests investigated. This leads to the conclusion that psychological tests, especially aptitude tests, function in essentially the same manner across race and sex; test materials are perceived and reacted to in a similar manner; and tests measure the same construct with equivalent accuracy for blacks, whites, Mexican-Americans, and other American minorities for both sexes. Single-group and differential validity have not been found and likely are not an ex-

FIGURE 14–1 Validity definitions of test bias. (Adapted from Reynolds, C. R. The problem of bias in psychology assessment. In C. R. Reynolds and T. B. Gutkin eds. *The handbook of school psychology.* 1982, pp. 188, 194, 201. John Wiley & Sons, Inc. Reproduced by permission.)

Validity Type	Definition of Bias
Content	An item or subscale of a test is considered to be biased in content when it is demonstrated to be relatively more difficult for members of one group than another when the general ability level of the groups being compared is held constant and no reasonable theoretical rationale exists to explain group differences on the item (or subscale) in question.
Construct	Bias exists in regard to construct validity when a test is shown to measure different hypothetical traits (psychological constructs) for one group than another or to measure the same trait but with differing degrees of accuracy.
Predictive	A test is considered biased with respect to predictive validity when the inference drawn from the test score is not made with the smallest feasible random error in an inference or prediction as a function of membership in a particular group.

isting phenomenon with regard to well constructed standardized psychological and educational tests. This means that test score differences across race are real and not an artifact of test bias.

A similar conclusion is warranted for the existence of bias in content validity in ability tests.

The most important use of tests is as predictors of future behaviors. As we suggested, the internal characteristics of most well-standardized ability tests in widespread use suggest that they are not biased against minority groups. Can we, however, still have bias in the predictions we make in the criterion performance of minorities?

Jensen (1980, Ch. 10) and Reynolds (1982) both provide excellent summaries on the research dealing with bias in predictive validity. In general, the research to date strongly suggests that ability tests are equally valid for both minority and majority groups. That is, a single equation can often be used to predict the criterion of interest for both groups. In one of the earlier studies, Cleary (1968) correlated SAT scores with college GPA for samples of black and white students at three universities. The

SAT-Verbal score correlated with GPA at the three schools for blacks and a random sample of whites as follows:

	School 1	School 2	School 3
Blacks	.47	.26	.47
Whites	.45	.38	.47

These results demonstrate that the SAT correlations with GPA are generally similar for both the black and white students.

In evaluating prediction studies, note that the majority and minority groups could differ with respect to (1) the correlation with the criterion, (2) the slope of the regression line relating test to criterion, (3) the standard error of estimate made in predicting the criterion from the test, or (4) the intercept of the regression line. A test could be called biased if one or more of these differences were statistically significant. Methodologically, there are three different situations that are possible when two groups exist (Cleary et al., 1975). These possibilities, along with the case of a single group (or a combined group) are given in Figure 14-2.

Case 1 illustrates the usual bivariate pre-

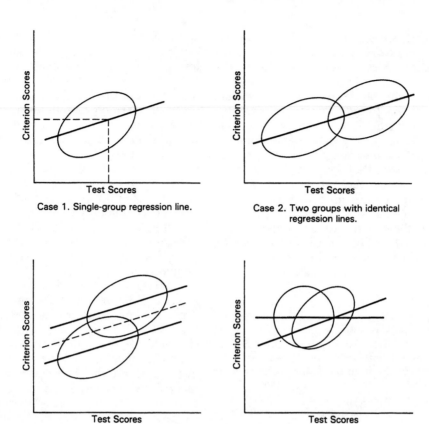

FIGURE 14-2 Relationships between test scores and criterion scores. (From Cleary, T. A., Humphreys, L. G., Kendrick, S. A., and Wesman, A. Educational uses of tests with disadvantaged students. *American Psychologist*, 1975, 30, 15–41. Copyright 1975 by the American Psychological Association, Inc. Reproduced by permission.)

diction situation in which a criterion is predicted from a test. Statistically speaking, the usual prediction equation guarantees with all persons that (1) the average error of prediction is zero and (2) the variance of the errors is a minimum. Case 2 illustrates the situation for two groups having the same regression line. Note that if the majority has a higher average test score than the minority group, the majority group's average criterion score is also higher. However, the same regression line is used for both groups. Case 3 illustrates two groups having the same slopes but differing in intercepts. Thus, the two solid lines represent the re-

gression lines for the two groups. The dotted line represents the regression line based on the two groups combined. Note that if the combined regression line is used for both groups, the result is *overprediction* for the minority group and *underprediction* for the majority group. In a statistical sense, then, use of the combined regression line results in bias against the majority group and in favor of the minority group. Finally, Case 4 illustrates the situation where both the slopes and intercepts differ for the two groups.

Cleary (1968) examined the regression equations as well as the correlations for blacks and whites. She found that the regression lines did not differ in two of the three universities studied. She also found that by using the white or combined regression lines, the black criterion scores were overpredicted. Linn (1973) summarized the results from studies at twenty-two universities in which the regression equations for blacks and whites were compared. In only eight cases were they found to be the same. However, when those derived from the white samples were used to make predictions for blacks, in eighteen of twenty-two instances the equations slightly *overpredicted* the actual GPA of blacks. Cleary et al. (1975, p. 31), in their report on the use of tests with disadvantaged students, concluded the following:

In summary, when the criterion to be predicted is GPA in a regular college program, almost all of the research demonstrates that standardized tests are useful, both within and between groups. The predictions within black and white colleges are comparable, and within integrated colleges the usual regression equations lead to comparable predictions for black and white students.

Jensen (1980, Ch. 10) concluded that test bias is also not evident in employment studies. Boehm (1972) reviewed thirteen studies in which 160 validity coefficients for blacks and whites were compared. Only seven of them revealed a significant black-white difference. Schmidt et al. (1973) added seven more studies to those used by Boehm and also concluded that differential validity is a rare phenomenon and can often be explained as a statistical artifact. Further analyses of differential validity for blacks and whites in employment testing was published by Hunter et al. (1979), who examined thirty-seven studies of 866 validity pairs (correlations) based on 185,487 data points (120,294 for whites and 65,193 for blacks). They concluded that tests that successfully predict criterion performance for whites do so equally successfully for blacks. There is, in other words, no evidence for differential validity.

In Chapters 5, 6, and 7 we discussed the use of several individually administered tests of intelligence (for example, Stanford-Binet, WISC–R, McCarthy). Such tests are often used to place children in special classes when learning disabilities or mental retardation are identified. With respect to differences in average performance, blacks score about one standard deviation lower than whites. Reynolds (1982) and Jensen (1980) again concluded that most available evidence does not indicate that intelligence tests most commonly used with children are biased against minorities. That is, the tests generally predict as well for minority groups as they do for the majority group. Reynolds and Hartlage (1979) found that the WISC–R predicted achievement test scores equally well for black and white children. A similar result was obtained when the WISC-R was used with Hispanics (Reynolds & Gutkin, 1980a). Reschly and Sabers (1979) also used the WISC-R to predict scores on the Metropolitan Achievement Tests in reading and mathematics for four ethnic groups (Anglo-American, black, Chicano, American Indian) in five different grades (one, three, five, seven, and nine). With the use of regression equations, differences among the groups were found to exist, as is illustrated in Table 14-1. Three of the slopes and six of the intercepts differed significantly. The major differences in the regression lines were caused by differences in intercept, non-Anglo-American groups having lower predicted scores. When combined prediction equations (based on all four ethnic groups) were used, the tendency was to overpredict the achievement of non-Anglo-American groups. The Stanford-Binet Intelligence Scale, another commonly used IQ test, has also been found to predict achievement test scores equally well for black and white children (Bossard et al. 1980).

Reynolds (1982) suggested that the results using tests with preschool children are less convincing regarding a lack of predictive bias. For example, Oakland (1978) provided predictive validity coeffi-

TABLE 14-1 Prediction of MAT Reading and Mathematics Scores From WISC-R[a] Scores for Four Ethnic-Racial Groups

Grade and Group	N	S.E. Est. Read.	S.E. Est. Math.	Slope Read.	Slope Math.	Intercept Read.	Intercept Math.	r Read.	r Math.
1st									
Anglo	49	9.28	8.39	.110	.222	45.2	34.2	.16	.34
Black	40	6.09	7.25	.448	.411	8.5	10.7	.70	.61
Chicano	44	8.80	8.35	.406	.424	16.2	14.1	.49	.53
Papago	48	6.63	6.73	.347	.439	15.9	9.8	.48	.57
Total	181	8.32	7.97	.390	.416	15.4	13.0	.55	.59
3rd									
Anglo	51	8.22	8.00	.492	.384	7.4	17.8	.62	.53
Black	40	6.53	7.52	.484	.274	10.2	25.7	.64	.38
Chicano	45	7.21	9.35	.415	.311	14.0	24.1	.53	.34
Papago	51	4.68	6.87	.290	.221	18.5	25.3	.54	.32
Total	187	7.27	8.25	.509	.406	5.0	13.9	.68	.55
5th									
Anglo	52	6.79	7.75	.628	.521	−5.4	4.3	.77	.65
Black	45	6.90	7.09	.373	.460	16.6	10.4	.57	.64
Chicano	48	6.44	6.97	.424	.307	12.2	24.6	.64	.49
Papago	44	6.29	5.59	.137	.274	34.5	21.9	.21	.44
Total	189	6.88	7.09	.473	.457	8.9	10.3	.73	.71
7th									
Anglo	54	7.55	8.77	.376	.401	19.1	15.0	.56	.53
Black	51	6.42	7.72	.582	.427	−2.1	12.8	.77	.59
Chicano	46	7.38	7.50	.388	.496	14.5	6.1	.46	.55
Papago	43	6.43	4.95	.289	.179	20.9	28.3	.47	.39
Total	194	7.10	7.62	.479	.434	7.1	11.1	.71	.65
9th									
Anglo	44	6.25	8.32	.519	.612	4.4	−5.2	.70	.66
Black	46	7.76	6.14	.294	.155	22.1	33.4	.46	.33
Chicano	32	6.77	6.88	.449	.509	10.0	4.5	.63	.67
Papago	37	6.04	5.02	.327	.174	16.8	30.1	.47	.32
Total	159	7.03	7.38	.484	.462	6.2	8.2	.72	.69

[a]WISC-R Full Scale IQ

From Reschly, D., & Sabers, D. L. (1979), Analysis of test bias in four groups with the regression definition. *Journal of Educational Measurement, 16,* 1-9. Copyright 1979, National Council on Measurement in Education, Washington, D.C.

cients for six groups of children—three ethnic groups (Anglo-American, Mexican-American, black) at each of two SES levels (middle, lower). Readiness tests were administered before students entered first grade or in the first three months of grade one. Achievement tests were administered in the spring of second grade and in the spring of fourth grade. Although Oakland did not use regression equations, his results demonstrated generally that the predictive validity was highest for Anglo-American children, followed by Mexican-American and black children. Anglo- and Mexican-American children did not differ markedly in statistically significant correlations (24 percent versus 20 percent), but for black children there were fewer statistically significant correlations (9 percent). The SES differences were even more striking, the readiness tests having much higher predictive validity for middle SES than for lower SES students.

Based on the empirical results in predicting criteria in colleges, elementary and high schools, and employment, there is little evidence that ability tests are biased in a statistical sense against minority groups. If anything, when combined prediction equations are used, there is a rather general finding that test scores *overpredict* the criterion scores of minority groups.

Bias in Personality Measures

Although most of the public controversy concerning racial differences on psychological tests has centered on aptitude or ability tests, there is evidence that blacks and other minority group members score differently from the white majority on most personality measures. Gynther (1979) reviewed the existing research and concluded that blacks, Hispanics, American Indians, and Asian-Americans tend to obtain scores on the MMPI, CPI, and other personality tests that are significantly different from those of majority group subjects. These data have inappropriately been interpreted by some as indicating that minority group members are more deviant or pathological than the white majority.

There is no clear agreement among investigators concerning why the minority groups score differently or the significance of these differences in decisions made about minority group members. Pritchard and Rosenblatt (1980) concluded that minority group differences on the MMPI have been exaggerated and that the MMPI has as much predictive validity with blacks as with whites. Gynther and Green (1980) maintained that the differences between blacks and whites are meaningful and lead to inappropriate treatment of blacks. For example, they reported data suggesting that blacks have been unfairly rejected as police applicants because of MMPI scores and that diagnoses of psychiatric patients based on the MMPI are less accurate for blacks than for whites. However, Genthner and Graham (1976) demonstrated that MMPI differences between black and white psychiatric patients did not lead to different decisions concerning discharge from the hospital. Lachar et al. (1976) found no differences in the accuracy of computer-generated MMPI narratives for black and white patients.

In summary, there is convincing evidence that blacks and other minority group members tend to score differently from the white majority on many personality scales. If used inappropriately, these scales could contribute to discrimination against minorities. However, it appears that the differences on personality scales are indicative of important behavioral and personal differences. If used appropriately, these scales can lead to accurate predictions for both minority and majority group members.

Selection Models

In evaluating tests and their use, there appears to be no clear distinction between the terms *bias* and *fairness*. We have defined *bias* in statistical terms. Of course, an unbiased test could still be used unfairly. The fairness of tests or what is "fair" in selection procedures seems to be a question of values, which are determined more by social, political, regulatory, and legal factors than by scientific methods. Several models have been proposed and compared by several authors (Cole, 1973; Hunter & Schmidt, 1976; Jensen, 1980, Ch. 9; Petersen & Novick, 1976).

It is important to realize, first, that no selection model is universally fair. Thus, a selection model that is designed to favor a minority group is by definition unfair to those in the majority. The best that can be hoped for is that the consequences of each selection model are fully understood and subject to public discussion. Second, we must remember that selection is important only when the selection ratio is low. If almost everyone who applies is selected, regardless of the test scores, then unfair selection is almost impossible to occur. We are thus mainly concerned with situations in which relatively few persons are selected to participate in some desirable activity. The models we will discuss do not exhaust all possibilities, but we will comment on the ones most commonly proposed. Jensen (1980, Ch. 9) provides a very thorough and technical discussion of an even larger number of possible models. Our discussion largely follows that of Cole (1973).

RANDOM MODEL. One possibility is to select persons by lottery. Every person who applies has an equal chance of being selected. Test scores and other predictors are not used in making the selection. This procedure is fair to both minority and majority groups if both are appropriately represented among the applicants. However, this method is decidedly unfair to the institution making the selection. Persons are not selected who would have the maximum chance of success. Average scores on the criterion variable will be lower than if valid predictors were available. Largely for this reason, the lottery system has not been adopted.

QUOTA MODEL. In the quota model, selection is based on proportional representation. Thus, a method that requires half those who are selected be women is a quota model. The proportion of women selected matches the proportion of women in the population. Fairness in selection is thus defined as proportional representation of particular groups. Most affirmative action programs accept quotas as the goal for the recruiting and promotional activities of organizations. This model would not maximize the level of performance on the criterion variable and could be judged unfair to the organization selecting applicants. It might also be judged unfair to the majority group if minority group members with lower predictor scores were selected in order to reach the necessary quota. The rationale for using quotas is to overcome the effects of past discrimination, when members of minority groups were excluded entirely.

REGRESSION MODEL. Cleary (1968) first proposed the regression model, and it appears to be the one most commonly investigated and used. In this model, separate prediction equations are developed for both minority and majority groups. If the prediction equations for the two groups do not differ significantly, a single equation is used for both groups. If they do differ, separate equations are used. Regression equations ensure that the best possible predictions are made and that the average error of prediction in all persons is zero. This method is fair to the selecting institution, because only those persons having the highest predicted scores on the criterion are selected. However, if the minority group mean is considerably lower than the majority group mean, proportionately fewer minority group members will be selected. Thus, from the minority group's perspective, this model is unfair.

SUBJECTIVE REGRESSION MODEL. This model, proposed by Darlington (1971), combines a regression approach with a quota selection explicitly defined. Darlington suggested that we predict the criterion variable $(Y - kC)$ rather than simply Y, where Y equals the criterion variable of interest, C equals the applicant's group membership, and k equals a value determined by the decision-maker. The variable $(Y - kC)$ is a "culture-modified" variable that reflects how desirable the selection of members is in a particular subpopulation. If $k = 0$, we have the regression model. Suppose, however, that we have $C = 1$ if an applicant is a member of the minority group and $C = 0$ for the majority group. If $k = 5$, we are lowering the criterion score (Y) by five points for members of the minority group. The criterion being predicted thus represents a combination of subjectively defined goals (minority group representation) with the usual regression approach to optimize criterion performance. The Darlington approach is interesting in that the criterion variable rather than the predictor variable is modified. That is, points are not added to test scores to equalize the group means. This model would probably be judged fair to minorities but unfair to the majority group. The organization might judge it to be fair if it assisted with affirmative action goals without decreasing productivity by a large amount.

EQUAL RISK MODEL. Einhorn and Bass (1971) proposed this model, which is based on Guion's (1966) definition of discrimination. This model emphasizes the applicant's risk of failure if selected. Applicants are selected who have the same risk of failure regardless of their group membership. Note that this model does not distinguish among various levels of performance on the criterion variable. The only thing essential is to be above a minimally acceptable threshold. This model also permits different cutoff scores to be used for the two groups if such differences are necessary to provide equal probabilities of success. Different regression equations could be used for the two groups.

CONSTANT RATIO MODEL. Thorndike (1971) proposed this model in which the proportion of members of majority and minority groups is considered. For example, suppose that 60 percent of group X is successful and 30 percent of group Y is successful. Fair selection requires that the proportion of group X selected relative to group Y should match the 60:30 success ratio. In this example, two members from group X are selected for every one member from group Y. Note that different cutoff scores could be specified for the two groups and the best applicants available from the two groups selected. This model stresses fairness to the applicants rather than to the selecting organization.

CONDITIONAL PROBABILITY MODEL. Cole (1973) extended the constant ratio model to be even more fair to the applicant. She referred to this extension as the *conditional probability model*. She emphasized being fair to those who would not be selected but who would succeed if given the chance. Cole (p. 240) states that "the basic principle of the conditional probability model is that for both minority and majority groups whose members can achieve a satisfactory criterion score there should be the same probability of selection regardless of group membership."

EXPECTED UTILITY MODEL. Gross and Su (1975) noted that several of the selection models can be viewed in terms of the utilities associated with various outcomes. Figure 14-3 illustrates the situation with two groups, each having applicants that are accepted or rejected and fail or succeed. In this approach, eight possible outcomes are identified. The institution decides explicitly on the desirability or importance of each outcome and assigns a utility to each of them. Then, the institution establishes cutoff scores that maximize the expected utility. Such a selection procedure will be judged fair to the extent that a person agrees with the utilities assigned to the various outcomes. Figure 14-3 reflects the utility that selecting minority group members who are successes is more important than selecting majority group members who are successes. Similarly, rejecting minority group members who would have been successes is a more serious loss than for the majority group. It is important to note that this model does not specify the utilities, but it does make them explicit and open to scrutiny and discussion.

Petersen and Novick (1976) concluded that the regression model, the equal risk model, and the expected utility model are internally consistent and could be used for selection. They also concluded that the subjective regression model is a possible candidate for use. They generally prefer the expected utility model, because the desirability of particular outcomes is explicitly addressed and, therefore, open to public discussion.

SEX BIAS

As Flaugher (1978) noted, *sex bias* is an important issue in the use of tests. Because test bias usually refers to the impact that tests have on ethnic minorities, especially blacks, we did not examine performance differences between men and women in the previous section. In this section we will discuss the evidence regarding sex bias in three different types of tests—ability, personality, and interests.

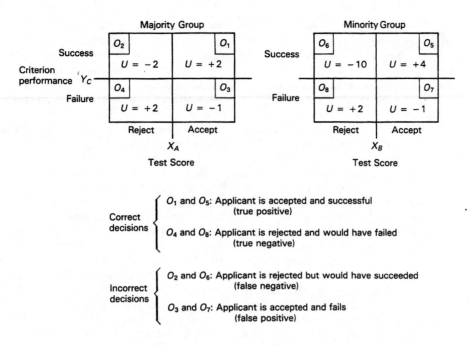

	Majority Group			Minority Group	

Correct decisions
{ O_1 and O_5: Applicant is accepted and successful (true positive)
  O_4 and O_8: Applicant is rejected and would have failed (true negative) }

Incorrect decisions
{ O_2 and O_6: Applicant is rejected but would have succeeded (false negative)
  O_3 and O_7: Applicant is accepted and fails (false positive) }

U = utility associated with each possible outcome

FIGURE 14–3 Expected utility model for selection.

Ability Testing

Do males and females differ significantly on intelligence tests or on other tests designed to measure more specific abilities? If differences do exist, are they *real* differences between males and females or are they artifactual differences because of sex bias in the tests? There are thus two separate questions to be addressed.

Jensen (1980, Ch. 13) has summarized the available research evidence on sex bias in mental testing. Maccoby and Jacklin (1974, Ch. 3) have provided a more extensive review of sex differences in intellectual abilities and cognitive styles. With respect to sex differences, it appears that the following generalizations are justified:

1. The majority of studies do not find significant differences between males and females, and when significant differences are found, they do not always favor one sex over the other (Jensen, 1980, p. 622).

2. Most general intelligence tests, such as the Wechsler scales and the Stanford-Binet, have been successfully constructed to eliminate sex differences. Thus, in measures of general intelligence males and females obtain the same average score.

3. By about age 11, females exceed males on tests of verbal ability. This trend continues at least through high school and probably beyond (Maccoby & Jacklin, 1974, p. 351).

4. Males excel in mathematical ability, beginning at about age 12 (Jensen, 1980, pp. 625–626; Maccoby & Jacklin, 1974, p. 352).

5. The largest and most consistently obtained sex differences occur on tests of visual-spatial ability. This difference, favoring males, appears at puberty and increases through the high school years (Jensen, 1980, p. 626; Maccoby and Jacklin, 1974, p. 351).

Although the differences we have noted are real in a statistical sense, they are not as large as mean differences between racial groups or social classes. Thus, as Jensen (1980, p. 632) suggests, "Sex difference in measured mental abilities is a small-magnitude phenomenon."

Ability tests can, of course, be biased in content or in the way they are used. Although the sex of the examiner is also a potential source of bias, there is no substantial evidence that the sex of the examiner has any large effect on obtained IQ scores (Jensen, 1980, p. 603; Rumenik et al., 1977).

One study that examined the item content of six intelligence tests found that males were referred to in the items much more often than females (Zoref and Williams, 1980). The same study also found that five of the six tests represented both sexes in a stereotypical fashion 40 percent of the time. Test publishers are now much more aware of such "content bias" and appear to be taking steps to eliminate the appearance of such bias (Berk, 1982, Ch. 9).

Does sex bias exist in the predictions that are made from ability tests? The empirical results have demonstrated that the correlation between measures of scholastic aptitude and college GPA is somewhat higher for women than for men (Jensen, 1980, p. 628; Linn, 1982). Linn (1973) has also reported that, when the same regression line is used to predict college GPA from SAT scores for men and women, women's grades are significantly underestimated. Thus, on the surface, it might be argued that the SAT is biased against women because it systematically errs in predicting their college GPAs. However, when sex differences in the choice of college majors are considered, the apparent bias in prediction disappears (Jensen, 1980, p. 630).

In summary, sex bias does not seem to be a major problem with most tests of mental ability. The content of test items, however, should be carefully monitored to eliminate sexist language, representation, and stereotypes.

Personality Testing

Sex bias exists in personality testing whenever the use of personality tests leads to more inappropriate inferences about or descriptions of subjects of one sex than of the other. Tests can be biased in the content of the stimulus materials, in the manner in which they are administered, and in the ways that results are interpreted.

Many personality inventories use sexist language in their items. For example, the MMPI includes items referring to a crook getting away with a crime if *he* can and to any *man* who is willing to work having a good chance of succeeding. More modern inventories have carefully avoided sexist language in items, and some more established inventories, such as the MMPI, are being revised to eliminate sexist language.* One could argue that the pictures in the TAT are sex biased because male figures are shown in employment and competitive situations, whereas female figures tend to be depicted in more stereotypically feminine activities and situations.

In personality testing, especially if projective techniques are utilized, there is the possibility that sex of test examiners can interact with sex of test subjects in influencing responses. Several studies (for example, Harris and Masling, 1970) have demonstrated that female subjects produce more Rorschach responses for male than for female examiners. It has been suggested that female subjects are more anxious to please the male examiner and to comply with his expectations. However, other studies (for example, Milner and Moses, 1972) have found no effects of examiner sex on productivity of subjects on the Rorschach. Garfield et al. (1952) and Eisler (1968) concluded that examiner sex was unrelated to productivity of subjects on the TAT and related thematic tests.

Several investigators have examined the interaction of examiner and subject sex on sexual content of projective test responses. Milner and Moses (1972) found that opposite-sex examiner-subject combinations produced fewer sexual responses on the Rorschach than did same-sex combinations. However, in a similar study Alden and

*Personal communication from Beverly Kaemmer, University of Minnesota Press, 1983.

Benton (1951) found no relationship between examiner and subject sex and sexual content of Rorschach responses. Similarly, Eisler (1968) failed to find any relationship between sex of examiner and sexual content of male subjects' stories in a thematic test. Data such as these suggest that the effect of examiner and subject sex on personality test performance is complex and not yet fully understood.

Perhaps the most important way in which sex bias can enter into personality testing is in the interpretation of test results. It is quite possible that different interpretations will be made of the same data depending on the sex of the test subject and of the person making the interpretations (Broverman et al., 1970). To explore this possibility, Lewittes et al., (1973) presented Rorschach protocols to clinicians and asked them to rate degree of psychopathology, level of intellectual functioning, and diagnosis for each protocol. For random halves of the clinicians, the protocols were designated as male or female. There were no differences in ratings or diagnosis as a function of specified sex of subject. However, clinicians had a tendency to diagnose subjects of their own sex as somewhat less seriously disturbed than subjects of the opposite sex.

There are data suggesting that different interpretations should be made of the same test data depending on the subject's sex. Numerous MMPI investigations have suggested that different behavioral correlates are appropriate for the same profile types for males and females (Gynther, Altman, & Sletten, 1973; Ritzema, 1974; Marks, Seeman, & Haller, 1974). For example, Gynther et al. (1973) found that alcoholism was present for both males and females who had elevated scores on scales 2 (Depression) and 4 (Psychopathic Deviate) of the MMPI. However, women with this pattern also showed symptoms of severe depression, whereas men with the pattern did not.

The possibility of sex bias in personality testing must be considered when new instruments are being constructed and when existing instruments are being administered and interpreted. Existing data suggest that the relationship between examiner and subject sex and test responses and interpretations is complex and not fully understood at this time. There are times when the same test data are inappropriately interpreted differently for male and female subjects and other times when different interpretations for males and females are indicated but may not be made.

Interest Testing

The extent to which sex bias exists in interest testing has been examined in considerable detail by several national panels (Association for Measurement and Evaluation in Guidance Commission on Sex Bias in Measurement; National Institute of Education Career Education Program). In relation to interests tests the NIE panel defined sex bias as "any factor that might influence a person to limit—or might cause others to limit—his or her consideration of a career solely on the basis of gender" (Diamond, 1978, pp. 5–6).

The reports of the national panels have indicated several ways in which interest inventories can be sex biased and have suggested some tentative solutions (AMEG Commission on Sex Bias in Measurement, 1973; Tittle & Zytowski, 1978). Inventories have been criticized for using sex-stereotypic language; for example, use of the generic he or she. Inventory items often have reflected experiences and activities not equally familiar to both sexes. Perhaps the most serious bias has been the practice of not reporting scores on all occupational scales for both sexes. Thus, a woman who does not have a score reported on a farmer scale is less likely to consider farming as an occupation, and a man who does not have a score reported on a nurse scale is less likely to consider nursing as a career.

Recommendations for reducing sex bias in interest tests have included elimination of sexist language, inclusion of items in inventory scales that are equally familiar to males and females whenever possible, having test interpreters give more consideration to environmental and cultural factors that influence vocational interests and choices. Test publishers have responded quite positively to these recommendations, and many changes have occurred in interest inventories (Diamond, 1978). For example, the latest edition of the *Manual for the SVIB-SCII* (Campbell & Hansen, 1981) specifies exactly how each of the NIE guidelines has been incorporated into the latest revision of the Strong-Campbell Interest Inventory. Perhaps the most impressive change is that scores are reported for both males and females for all but eight of the 162 occupational scales. The scales for which scores are not reported for both sexes are for occupations where adequate samples could not be identified for one sex (male dental assistants, female vocational agriculture teachers).

Relevant issues concerning sex bias in interest testing have been discussed, specific remedial guidelines have been published, and significant changes have been made by test publishers. However, as Diamond (1978) has pointed out, sex bias in occupational choices and preferences will continue until societal changes occur that will permit males and females to explore and experience without gender-imposed limitations.

THE IQ CONTROVERSY

There is no way to deny that blacks as a group obtain average scores about one standard deviation below whites on almost all tests of cognitive ability. The interpretation and proposed explanations of this empirical fact generate the IQ controversy. If blacks and whites had the same mean IQ, the controversy would largely disappear. The scientific question of whether IQ is an inherited trait or one determined primarily by environmental factors would be of interest to relatively few people and discussed largely at professional meetings. However, because the difference between black and

white mean IQs does exist, the possible explanations have become highly politicized. To claim that blacks are genetically inferior to whites is unacceptable to most people. On the other hand, to claim that the trait of intelligence is not influenced by genetic factors seems equally absurd. We have already discussed the question of test bias. We will now examine the available evidence on inheritance of intelligence.

As we indicated in the first section of this chapter, the most recent IQ controversy largely originated in 1969 with the publication of Arthur Jensen's article, "How Much Can We Boost IQ and Scholastic Achievement?" in the *Harvard Educational Review*. Jensen (1969) specifically examined the genetic aspects of racial differences in average intelligence while explicitly recognizing the role of environmental factors. He argued that since some human characteristics such as height are partially determined by heredity, there is equally good reason to expect other human characteristics such as intelligence to be biologically determined. To quote from Jensen (p. 80):

There seems to be little question that racial differences in genetically conditioned behavioral characteristics, such as mental abilities, should exist, just as physical differences. The real questions, geneticists tell me, are not whether there are or are not genetic racial differences that affect behavior, because there undoubtedly are. The proper questions to ask, from a scientific standpoint are: What is the direction of the difference? What is the magnitude of the difference? And what is the significance of the difference—medically, socially, educationally, or from whatever standpoint that may be relevant to the characteristic in question? A difference is important only within a specific context. For example, one's blood type in the ABO system is unimportant until one needs a transfusion. And some genetic differences are apparently of no importance with respect to any context as far as anyone has been able to discover—for example, differences in the size and shape of ear lobes. The idea that all genetic differences have arisen or persisted only as a result of natural selection, by conferring sole survival or adaptive benefit on their possessors, is no longer generally held.

And later in his 1969 article (p. 82), he states the following:

There is an increasing realization among students of the psychology of the disadvantaged that the discrepancy in their average performance cannot be completely or directly attributed to discrimination or inequalities in education. It seems not unreasonable, in view of the fact that intelligence variation has a large genetic component, to hypothesize that genetic factors may play a part in this picture.

Cronbach (1975) noted that this particular quotation produced much personal attack on Jensen as well as extensive commentary in the popular press. Jensen (1972) described in detail the personal costs he suffered because he stated an unpopular view. As the following quotation from Jensen (1969, p. 78) certainly suggests, he does not hold racist views:

Furthermore, since, as far as we know, the full range of human talents is represented in all the major races of man and in all socioeconomic levels, it is unjust to allow the mere fact of an individual's racial or social background to affect the treatment accorded to him. All persons rightfully must be regarded on the basis of their individual qualities and merits, and all social, educational, and economic institutions must have built into them the mechanisms for insuring and maximizing the treatment of persons according to their individual behavior.

The literature on the IQ controversy is now extensive and the interested reader can examine a number of books on the topic (Block & Dworkin, 1976; Eckberg, 1979; Eysenck vs. Kamin, 1981; Kamin, 1974; Loehlin et al., 1975).

What is the current evidence on the inheritability of intelligence in human populations? Bouchard and McGue (1981) reviewed 111 studies in the world literature that bear on this question. One of their figures on the familial correlations for IQ is given in Figure 14–4. They reported that this pattern of correlation supports the conclusion that the higher the proportion of genes two family members have in common,

the higher the average correlation between their IQs. This is referred to as a *polygenic inheritance model* in which no dominance, no assortive mating, and no environmental effects occur. These results show that monozygotic twins reared together have the largest average correlation between their IQs (.86). Only three studies (sixty-five sets of twins) are available on monozygotic twins reared apart and these show an average correlation of .72. The magnitude of this correlation makes a strictly environmental interpretation difficult. Monozygotic twins, it will be recalled, are individuals who are genetically identical. Bouchard and McGue (1981, p. 1,058) concluded the following:

That the data support the inference of partial genetic determination for IQ is indisputable; that they are informative about the precise strength of this effect is dubious. Certainly the large amount of unexplained variability within degrees of relationship, while not precluding attempts to model the data, suggests that such models should be interpreted cautiously.

After a careful review of the available evidence, Loehlin et al. (1975) concluded that there is a substantial genetic contribution to IQ within both the black and white populations. They also suggested that the following three general but limited conclusions are justified (pp. 238–239).

1. Observed average differences in the scores of members of different U.S. racial-ethnic groups on intellectual-ability tests probably reflect in part inadequacies and biases in the tests themselves, in part differences in environmental conditions among the groups, and in part genetic differences among the groups. It should be emphasized that these three factors are not necessarily independent, and may interact.

2. A rather wide range of positions concerning the relative weight to be given these three factors can reasonably be taken on the basis of current evidence, and a sensible person's position might well differ for different abilities, for different groups, and for different tests.

3. Regardless of the position taken on the relative importance of these three factors, it seems

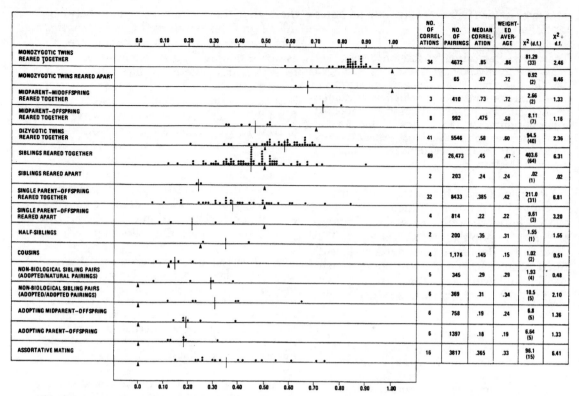

FIGURE 14–4 Familial correlations for IQ. The vertical bar in each distribution indicates the median correlation; the arrow, the correlation predicted by a simple polygenic model. (From Bouchard, T. J., Jr., and McGue, M. "Familial studies of intelligence: A review." *Science*, 1981, *212*, 1055–1059. Copyright 1981 by the American Association for the Advancement of Science. Reproduced by permission of the authors.)

clear that the differences among individuals within racial-ethnic (and socioeconomic) groups greatly exceed in magnitude the average differences between such groups.

The available evidence to date, then, suggest that part of the black-white differences in average IQ could be due to genetic influences. However, *even if* the heritability of IQ is .80 (80 percent of the variance in IQ scores for a given population is produced by genetic factors), most of the variance between groups is not due to genetic factors. That is, within-group variance is considerably larger than between-group variance. In our opinion, it seems impossible to design and execute an acceptable scientific study that will disentangle these highly sensitive is-

sues. We should, rather, focus our efforts on maximizing human potential. A multiply handicapped and profoundly retarded child needs one kind of environment. A child who writes symphonies at age five or six needs another.

ETHICAL ISSUES IN TESTING

Invasion of Privacy

Whenever people respond to psychological test items, answer questions in an interview, or have their personal behavior observed, an invasion of privacy occurs. Ordinarily, persons involved in these situations have decided that whatever invasion of their privacy occurs is not as significant as the benefits they are likely to derive from the assessments. However, psychological tests have been criticized on the basis that they invade privacy and thus deprive individuals of their constitutional rights.

Although concerns about invasions of privacy have existed for many years and still exist today, they seem to have reached a peak when in the summer of 1965 subcommittees of the U.S. Senate and House of Representatives held public hearings concerning alleged invasion of privacy of federal employees who were required to take psychological tests as a condition of employment. Although neither subcommittee found deliberate or widespread misuse of tests, testimony offered during the hearings served to clarify some of the issues involved (Brayfield, 1965).

When psychological tests are criticized on the basis of invasion of privacy, there seem to be two major (and not necessarily related) issues. First, there are some people who maintain that privacy is invaded whenever questions are asked about aspects of personal lives that ordinarily are not openly discussed in our culture. Thus, MMPI items dealing with eliminative functions, religious beliefs, or sexual practices are thought to be inappropriate and invasive. Even when less sensitive issues are involved, some individuals believe that no one has a right to know about another person's intellectual functioning, attitudes, values, or interests. This belief that individuals have a basic right to privacy is referred to as *inviolacy*.

The second issue has to do with potential misuse of information. Many individuals seem to fear that information about them will become known to others who have no need or right to have it. There also seems to be concern that information may be used inappropriately to make decisions about employment, admission to academic programs, legal issues, or other matters.

Concerning the inviolacy issue, there is little doubt that individuals have the right to keep information about themselves private.

However, people may decide that they are willing to permit their privacy to be invaded because of some benefit that they might derive as a result of doing so. For example, persons having significant emotional problems must decide if they are willing to allow professional persons to become aware of some private information in order to facilitate treatment. When people want to gain certain kinds of employment or admission to educational or training programs, they must decide if the benefit of getting the job or being admitted to the program is important enough to warrant some invasion of privacy. The person always has the option of not applying for the job or for admission to the program if the judgment is made that the advantages are not significant enough to incur the invasion. Usually, people do not raise the invasion of privacy issue when they voluntarily agree to take tests or to be assessed in other ways. There is much greater concern when they are obligated to be tested as part of an employment or educational situation. It was the requirement that government employees and potential employees complete psychological tests that resulted, at least in part, in the congressional hearings described earlier.

The issue of misuse of information should not be directed at tests but rather at potential misuse by the professionals who are responsible for the information that is gathered. *Ethical Principles of Psychologists* (American Psychological Association, 1981) and similar guidelines developed by professional groups regulate the use of assessment information and protect clients against misuses. Psychologists have ethical obligations to use such information in their clients' best interests and to assure that such information is not misused by others to whom it is communicated. In general, information about clients is shared with others on a "need to know" basis. For example, within an educational institution or business organization, only persons who need information in order to make important decisions have access to it. In addition, only the information needed to make such decisions is made available. Personal information obtained in the process of assessment that is not relevant to the decisions to be made is kept confidential by the psychologist.

Several rather simple procedures can reduce clients' concerns about invasion of privacy. If clients are informed about why certain information is needed, they are much less likely to resent revealing it. For example, Fink and Butcher (1972) found that telling subjects how MMPI items were selected greatly reduced their concerns about the personal nature of some of the items. Similarly, if subjects are told at the time of testing why the testing is being done, who will have access to the responses, and what interpretations and/or decisions will be made on the basis of the information, very little concern about invasion of privacy is likely to be expressed.

Confidentiality

A basic principle underlying the relationship between psychologists and their clients is that information revealed to the psychologist by the client is to remain confidential. This principle is stated clearly in the *Ethical Principles of Psychologists* (American Psychological Association, 1981). Such information cannot be revealed to a third party without the client's consent. Confidentiality includes, but is not limited to, test information. Information obtained through interview, observation, examination of records, and other methods also is considered to be confidential.

The purpose of the confidentiality principle is to protect the client. It is the client's right to determine what, if any, personal information can be made known to other people. Often clients will judge that it is in their best interests for psychologists to communicate information to other professionals (for example, physicians or lawyers). In such cases the clients are asked to sign forms giving their informed consent for the release of information. *Informed consent* means that the client knows not only *to whom* information is to be released but also exactly *what* information is to be released. Without such informed consent the psychologist generally cannot release information about the client even if it seems to be in the best interests of the client to do so.

In addition to the psychologist's ethical responsibility to maintain confidentiality, further protection of the client's rights is provided through privileged communication legislation that has been enacted in many states. Privileged communication originally applied only to the relationship between attornies and their clients. It has been maintained that attornies cannot represent clients adequately if there is a possibility that in court they could be required to reveal information given to them by clients in preparing their defense. Thus, *privileged communication* means that attornies cannot be required, even in court, to reveal information about clients that was obtained in their professional relationships with the clients. For many years this same privilege has been extended to relationships between individuals and their physicians or clergy. More recently, privileged communication has been extended to the individual's relationship with a psychologist. Such legislation is now in effect in most of the United States. It should be noted that the privilege is extended to the client and not to the psychologist. Thus, it is the client who decides when to waive the privilege and to allow the psychologist to reveal information.

As psychologists have become more involved in the legal arena, it is important for them and their clients to realize that privileged communication is an "all or none" situation. For example, if clients instruct psychologists to reveal some information about them in legal proceedings, the psychologist is obligated to reveal, if asked, any and all information available about the client.

There are some exceptions to these general principles. In *Ethical Principles of Psychologists* (American Psychological Association, 1981), it is stated that information about clients can be released to others without the clients' consent when failure to release such information would result in clear danger to the client or others. For example, if a client tells a psychologist of a contemplated suicide and if the psychologist judges that such an attempt is likely to occur, the psychologist is free to notify relatives, law enforcement officers, or others in order to protect the client's life. Likewise, if a client tells a psychologist of an intent to harm someone else, the psychologist can communicate this information to the intended victim or others in order to protect the well-being of the intended victim.

The courts have made it clear that the psychologist not only may breach confidentiality when there is clear danger to the client or someone else but also is obligated to do so. In the case of *Tarasoff v. Regents of University of California*, the university, psychotherapists employed by the university, and campus police were sued by the parents of a female student who was murdered by a client of one of the psychotherapists. The client told his psychotherapist of his intention to kill the young woman. The psychotherapist notified his superior, and the campus police were asked to confine the client. After talking with the client, the campus police released him when he promised to stay away from the young woman. The client then terminated his relationship with the psychotherapist and killed the young woman. Her parents maintained that the psychotherapist and the others involved had not fulfilled an obligation to warn the girl or her parents of the danger to her life. The California Supreme Court ruled in favor of the parents, concluding that the confidentiality of the therapy relationship is not as important as society's interest in protecting itself from dangerous persons (Leonard, 1977).

Special considerations regarding confidentiality arise when the psychologist's client is a minor. What rights of confidentiality do children have? Do parents have rights to obtain information about their children from psychologists who have examined them? Most states have laws stating that parents have the right to receive information, including test information, obtained from

their children. In many situations it clearly is in the child's best interests for the parents to have such information. However, it is important to consider in what form it should be given to them. For example, it might not be advantageous to report a child's IQ score to parents who do not understand its meaning or who might be likely to misuse the information. It would be preferable to communicate information about performance range and expectations.

The confidentiality issue becomes more complex when the psychologists' clients are institutions or organizations (schools, businesses, and so on) rather than the individuals who are tested. If a child is tested by a school psychologist employed by the school system, must informed consent be obtained from the child's parent or guardian in order to release information to the school system? If a psychologist is employed by a business organization to test job applicants, must the psychologist have the applicants' consent to release information to the business organization?

Ethical Principles of Psychologists (American Psychological Association, 1981) recognizes that psychologists will sometimes find themselves involved in conflicts of interests between their employing institutions or organizations and the individual clients that they test. The suggested resolution is a rather general statement that the psychologists must inform all involved parties of their loyalties and ethical responsibilities and behave appropriately. Anastasi (1982) made a more specific suggestion. She recommended that when tests are administered in institutions (schools, courts, places of employment), the individual being tested (or a parent or guardian in the case of minors) should be informed at the time of the testing of its purpose, how the results will be used, and the availability of results to institutional personnel who have a legitimate need for them. Under these circumstances no further consent is required when results are made available within the institution.

Although we agree with Anastasi's recommendation, we would add an additional caution about what information is released. It is our opinion that only information relevant to the purpose of the testing should be made available. For example, in the course of a psychological evaluation of a job applicant, a psychologist might learn that a subject is a homosexual. Unless the homosexuality is directly relevant to performance in the job for which the person is being considered, it would not be appropriate for that information to be released to the prospective employer.

Client's Right To Information

In *Ethical Principles of Psychologists* (American Psychological Association, 1981) it is stated that clients have the right to know the results of tests, the interpretations made of the results, and bases for conclusions and recommendations made about them. In many counseling settings, such feedback about testing is an integral part of the therapeutic process. In addition, the Family Educational Rights and Privacy Act of 1974 granted the parents of minor students and students 18 years of age or older access to most records maintained by educational institutions (Bersoff, 1981). The right to information about test performance does not mean that clients must be shown their actual scores. Rather, information about performance should be communicated to clients at a level and in language they can understand clearly. For example, it would not be appropriate or meaningful to tell the average client that he or she received an IQ score of 115 on the WAIS–R. Rather, it would be more appropriate to indicate something about the client's standing in relation to other persons in the general population or in some specific normative group. In addition, information should be provided concerning the relationship between IQ test scores and the reason for which the test was given (for example, likelihood of success in a particular educational program or at a specific job). It is the psychologist's obligation to discuss limitations of the assessment procedures utilized and to indicate any reservations about reliability or validity because of the circumstances of the assessment or the inappropriateness of the norms for the person tested.

In summary, clients have a right to receive information about tests they have taken. It is the psychologist's responsibility to communicate the information so that it will not be misunderstood or misused and will be maximally beneficial to the clients.

LEGAL ISSUES

The courts have been progressively more active in examining the legal issues involved in using tests. Bersoff (1981) and Wigdor and Garner (1982, Ch. 3), among others, provide an historical perspective on legal issues. Our discussion is organized around the three themes that Bersoff finds currently most pervasive, (1) test bias, (2) employment testing, and (3) truth-in-testing. We have already discussed the first two topics in this chapter, but we now wish to note several specific court cases and other regulatory activity that relate to these areas. Legal scholars have also commented on these areas (Bersoff, 1979; Booth & Mackay, 1980; Johnson, 1976, Robertson, 1980).

Test Bias In Education

In a previous section of this chapter, we discussed the scientific evidence regarding test bias. Standardized tests are alleged to be biased against minorities because blacks and other groups obtain, on the average, lower scores. The lower scores result in higher proportions of blacks, for example, being placed in EMR classes and, conversely, may also mean fewer being placed in classes for the gifted. Such data often are used as evidence of discrimination. The 1964 Civil Rights Act, of course, prohibits discrimination in any form.

An early case in the area of test bias was that of *Hobson v. Hansen*. This case, reported in 1967, questioned the constitutionality of using group tests to place students in ability tracks in the Washington, D.C., public schools. Essentially, the court found that a group test was constitutional but that *use* of the test was unconstitutional. The basis of the decision was the acceptance of the evidence that blacks were proportionately overrepresented in lower-ability tracks and underrepresented in higher tracks. The court reasoned that since the *outcome* of using test scores for placement was discriminatory, the test was in fact biased against black students (Reschly, 1979).

Two other cases dealt specifically with the placement of students in special education classes and were settled by consent decrees prior to trial. *Diana v. State of California* was a class action suit in 1970 on behalf of Mexican-American children in Monterey, California. A similar suit, *Gudalupe v. Tempe Elementary District*, was filed in 1972 in Arizona. Both questioned the over-representation of bilingual students in classes for the mentally retarded. The intelligence tests used were alleged to be inappropriate because they emphasized verbal facility and middle-class values and symbols. The consent decrees consisted of changes in assessment procedures, such as students would be tested in their primary language (often Spanish) and unfair portions of the test would be eliminated. *Gudalupe's* consent decree required that IQ scores be at least two standard deviations below the mean before the child could be classified as mentally retarded, that intelligence tests not be the sole determiners of mental retardation, that classification decisions be based on performance measures if the child's primary language was not English, and that parents should be interviewed regarding the child's adaptive behavior. According to Reschly (1979), the second point (that IQ tests not be the sole determiners of mental retardation) noted in the Guadalupe consent decree has appeared frequently in both legislation and regulation.

The present legal situation, however, seems ambiguous. Two court decisions from the school year 1979–1980 have yielded completely opposite rulings on test bias. In the case of *Larry P. v. Riles,* a California court ruled that individually administered IQ tests were biased against blacks and enjoined the California State Department of Education from using standardized tests for diagnosis or placement of black children. In the case of *PASE v. Hannon,* an Illinois court ruled specifically that the WISC, WISC–R, and Stanford-Binet could be used for diagnostic and placement purposes by the Chicago public schools. Thus, these tests did not discriminate against blacks.

The *Larry P.* case was discussed by Lambert (1981), who noted specifically that after the moritorium on IQ testing, the percentage of minorities in EMR classes remained essentially the same, although fewer children in total were assigned to these classes. She also listed numerous other problems with the court's finding in this case. Sattler (1981) prepared a mock interview with the judges in the *Larry P.* and *PASE v. Hannon* cases. Sattler's presentation, using quotations from the two judges' rulings, highlights areas where the two judges agreed and disagreed. The reader can contrast their differing opinions to several mock questions in Figure 14-5. The permissible use of tests for placement in schools will undoubtedly be determined by further court rulings.

Employment Testing

The legal issues and regulations in employment testing appear to be as unclear as those in education. *Griggs v. Duke Power Co.* was the first major challenge to the use of ability tests in hiring and promoting employees. The U.S. Supreme Court ruled on this case in 1971. Black employees charged that the use of general ability tests unfairly discriminated against them. The court ruled that employment practices having an adverse impact on blacks must be related to the job. It based its decision on Title VII of the 1964 Civil Rights Act and also referred to EEOC Guidelines on Employment Testing. The important aspect of the *Griggs* ruling was that general ability tests could not

FIGURE 14-5 Some differences between the rulings of Judge Peckham (*Larry P.*) and Judge Grady (*PASE v. Hannon*). (Adapted from "An Interview with Judges Robert F. Peckham and John F. Grady," *Journal of School Psychology*, 1981, *19*, 359-369. New York: Human Sciences Press, Inc.)

1. How are children selected for EMR classes?
   Judge Peckham: Primarily on the basis of IQ test.
   Judge Grady: Classroom difficulty noted, then IQ test administered, and finally case study evaluation by staff.
2. How important is the IQ test in placement?
   Judge Peckham: Of primary importance.
   Judge Grady: Only one component in placement decision.
3. Was test validity important in the decision?
   Judge Peckham: Yes; IQ tests had not been validated for placing black children in EMR classes.
   Judge Grady: No; this is a broader question not involved in this case.
4. Do socioeconomic factors account for the fact that black children have lower average scores than white children?
   Judge Peckham: Not entirely; the tests were not designed to eliminate cultural biases against blacks.
   Judge Grady: Largely yes; it is poverty rather than racism leading to the difference.
5. Generally speaking, are intelligence tests racially biased?
   Judge Peckham: Yes.
   Judge Grady: No.

be used and only tests that were job related could be used in employment testing. No test could be administered that was designed, intended, or used to discriminate. However, the guidelines for determining whether or not tests were job related were left unstated by the court (Bersoff, 1981; Ledvenka & Schoenfeldt, 1978).

A second ruling by the U.S. Supreme Court in 1975 extended the law on employment testing. In *Albemarle Paper Co. v. Moody*, four black employees challenged the use of tests because they were discriminatory against blacks, too few of whom were being promoted to higher-level jobs. The Supreme Court's ruling found that EEOC guidelines for the use of discriminatory tests were not being met. Ledvinka and Schoenfeldt (1978) noted that Albemarle's testing program was found insufficient because it was (1) using a test for jobs on which it had not been validated, (2) using subjective supervisory ratings as criteria, (3) using

a test for entry-level jobs that had been validated only on upper-level jobs, and (4) validating tests on a group not representative of job applicants. The *Griggs* and *Albemarle* decisions have largely made EEOC guidelines the law of the land for employment testing and litigation based on Title VII of the 1964 Civil Rights Act. As Wigdor and Garner (1982, p. 106) stated:

In the early litigation, employment testing cases usually involved very weak testing programs, often introduced just as Title VII went into effect and with little or no attempt to evaluate the usefulness of the instrument for the jobs in question. That is no longer true. Carefully constructed and researched tests are now the subject of litigation, and they, too, seldom withstand legal challenge. Judges are requiring, in the face of evidence of differential impact, a degree of technical adequacy that tests and test users apparently cannot provide.

These same authors later concluded (p. 107):

Employment testing is being subjected to a degree of governmental scrutiny that few human contrivances could bear. Many interests may be served by testing: efficiency or productivity; the sense of fairness that results from cloaking the allocation of scarce positions with the mantle of objective selection; better matching of people and jobs; the identification of talent that might otherwise go undetected and unrealized. But these interests are not at present strong enough to compete with the commitment of the government to finally break the pattern of economic disadvantage and estrangement that has characterized the position of blacks, women, and members of other specific groups in the society. Hundreds of cases and a decade and a half later, the dilemma remains unchanged. Until a constitutional principle evolves that incorporates into the idea of equality an acceptable rationale for compensatory treatment of the disadvantaged, national perceptions of fairness and national interest in productivity will continue to suffer.

Another U.S. Supreme Court decision, however, contributes to the confusion. In *Washington v. Davis* (1976) the use of a verbal ability test was challenged because it disproportionately discriminated against black police applicants in Washington, D.C. This suit was brought under the Fifth Amendment to the U.S. Constitution (the equal protection clause) rather than Title VII. In this case, the court found that even though the tests had an adverse impact on blacks, the plaintiffs had not demonstrated that the tests were intentionally used to discriminate against them.

Bersoff (1981) cited several cases, which the U.S. Supreme Court refused to review, that have begun to threaten the use of content valid tests. At issue was the use of job-related tests that were not empirically correlated with job performance. It appears that current rulings require that highly abstract attributes be validated in predictive, criterion-related studies but that more job-related tests could be judged on a content-construct validity continuum.

As Tenopyr (1981) noted, employers are well aware of the legal difficulties that can arise from using tests to help make personnel decisions. She suggested that the pros-pect of legal battles has contributed to a decline in the use of tests even though they are useful selection tools. We illustrate the complexities by reproducing in Figure 14-6 a portion of the 1978 EEOC Uniform Guidelines on Employee Selection Procedures. Although the EEOC calls for a search for alternatives, there appears to be no viable alternatives that are as valid as tests. Tenopyr (1981), for example, noted that interviews and experience and educational variables are not as valid as tests. Reilly and Chao (1982) reviewed the literature on alternatives and suggested that only biodata and peer evaluation have validities similar to those of tests. These reviewers also noted that none of the alternatives, when valid, had less adverse impact on minority groups than did tests.

Schmidt and Hunter (1981) emphasized three conclusions based on a large amount of empirical research. First, standardized ability tests are valid predictors of job performance and of training for jobs. Second, ability tests are equally valid for minority and majority groups. Third, the use of ability tests for selection can save organizations large amounts of money. That is, using selection tests will increase productivity and decrease costs. Balancing the needs of organizations to have productive employees against the legitimate needs of minority groups to have equal opportunities for economic advancement remains a most perplexing and emotional problem. We see no immediate resolution. Employment decisions will continue to be made. If tests are not used, other less valid mechanisms will be.

Consumerism

Test materials are usually unavailable to the general public. Obviously if questions were generally available, a person scheduled to take a particular test could study the questions beforehand. That person's score would be invalid because the test assumes no previous experience with its content. In other words, the test would be assessing how

FIGURE 14-6 Sample section of EEOC Uniform Guidelines on Employee Selection Procedures (From Equal Employment Opportunity Commission, *Federal Register*, 43 No. 166, 1978, p. 38,298.)

Sec. 5. *General standards for validity studies*—A. *Acceptable types of validity studies*. For the purposes of satisfying these guidelines, users may rely upon criterion-related validity studies, content validity studies or construct validity studies, in accordance with the standards set forth in the technical standards of these guidelines, section 14 below. New strategies for showing the validity of selection procedures will be evaluated as they become accepted by the psychological profession.

B. *Criterion-related, content, and construct validity*. Evidence of the validity of a test or other selection procedure by a criterion-related validity study should consist of empirical data demonstrating that the selection procedure is predictive of or significantly correlated with important elements of job performance. See section 14B below. Evidence of the validity of a test or other selection procedure by a content validity study should consist of data showing that the content of the selection procedure is representative of important aspects of performance on the job for which the candidates are to be evaluated. See section 14C below. Evidence of the validity of a test or other selection procedure through a construct validity study should consist of data showing that the procedure measures the degree to which candidates have identifiable characteristics which have been determined to be important in successful performance in the job for which the candidates are to be evaluated. See section 14D below.

C. *Guidelines are consistent with professional standards*. The provisions of these guidelines relating to validation of selection procedures are intended to be consistent with generally accepted professional standards for evaluating standardized tests and other selection procedures, such as those described in the Standards for Educational and Psychological Tests prepared by a joint committee of the American Psychological Association, the American Educational Research Association, and the National Council on Measurement in Education (American Psychological Association, Washington, D.C. 1974) (hereinafter "A.P.A. Standards") and standard textbooks and journals in the field of personnel selection.

D. *Need for documentation of validity*. For any selection procedure which is part of a selection process which has an adverse impact and which selection procedure has an adverse impact, each user should maintain and have available such documentation as is described in section 15 below.

E. *Accuracy and standardization*. Validity studies should be carried out under conditions which assure insofar as possible the adequacy and accuracy of the research and the report. Selection procedures should be administered and scored under standardized conditions.

F. *Caution against selection on basis of knowledges, skills, or ability learned in brief orientation period*. In general, users should avoid making employment decisions on the basis of measures of knowledges, skills, or abilities which are normally learned in a brief orientation period, and which have an adverse impact.

G. *Method of use of selection procedures*. The evidence of both the validity and utility of a selection procedure should support the method the user chooses for operational use of the procedure, if that method of use has a greater adverse impact than another method of use. Evidence which may be sufficient to support the use of a selection procedure on a pass/fail (screening) basis may be insufficient to support the use of the same procedure on a ranking basis under these guidelines. Thus, if a user decides to use a selection procedure on a ranking basis, and that method of use has a greater adverse impact than use on an appropriate pass/fail basis (see section 5H below), the user should have sufficient evidence of validity and utility to support the use on a ranking basis. See sections 3B, 14B (5) and (6), and 14C (8) and (9).

H. *Cutoff scores*. Where cutoff scores are used, they should normally be set so as to be reasonable and consistent with normal expectations of acceptable proficiency within the work force. Where applicants are ranked on the basis of properly validated selection procedures and those applicants scoring below a higher cutoff score than appropriate in light of such expectations have little or no chance of being selected for employment, the higher cutoff score may be appropriate, but the degree of adverse impact should be considered.

I. *Use of selection procedures for higher level jobs*. If job progression structures are so established that employees will probably, within a reasonable period of time and in a majority of cases, progress to a higher level, it may be considered that the applicants are being evaluated for a job or jobs at the higher level. However, where job progression is not so nearly automatic, or the time span is such that higher level jobs or employees' potential may be expected to change in significant ways, it should be considered that applicants are being evaluated for a job at or near the entry level. A "reasonable period of time" will vary for different jobs and employment situations but will seldom be more than 5 years. Use of selection procedures to evaluate applicants for a higher level job would not be appropriate:

(1) If the majority of those remaining employed do not progress to the higher level job;

(2) If there is a reason to doubt that the higher level job will continue to require essentially similar skills during the progression period; or

(3) If the selection procedures measure knowledges, skills, or abilities required for advancement which would be expected to develop principally from the training or experience on the job.

J. *Interim use of selection procedures.* Users may continue the use of a selection procedure which is not at the moment fully supported by the required evidence of validity, provided: (1) The user has available substantial evidence of validity, and (2) the user has in progress, when technically feasible, a study which is designed to produce the additional evidence required by these guidelines within a reasonable time. If such a study is not technically feasible, see section 6B. If the study does not demonstrate validity, this provision of these guidelines for interim use shall not constitute a defense in any action, nor shall it relieve the user of any obligations arising under Federal law.

K. *Review of validity studies for currency.* Whenever validity has been shown in accord with these guidelines for the use of a particular selection procedure for a job or group of jobs, additional studies need not be performed until such time as the validity study is subject to review as provided in ection 3B above. There are no absolutes in the area of determining the currency of a validity study. All circumstances concerning the study, including the validation strategy used, and changes in the relevant labor market and the job should be considered in the determination of when a validity study is outdated.

---

well the person remembered the correct answers rather than the ability it was designed to measure. The public disclosure of test materials has, therefore, never been routine, although sample items have been published.

The late 1960s and 1970s found consumers demanding more information about products and more protection from harmful ones. Ralph Nader has often epitomized an advocate for the rights of consumers. The federal government has several agencies that are supposed to perform a watch-dog function: Federal Trade Commission, Environmental Protection Agency, and Federal Drug Administration.

Bersoff (1981) notes that the Family Education Rights and Privacy Act passed in 1974 was the first legislation that affected the disclosure of test results. In addition to protecting the records of students, this act also gives parents access to their children's school records and the right to challenge those records in a hearing. Bersoff also notes that Public Law 94-142 gives the parents of handicapped children access to all records bearing on the placement of their children in special classes. Bersoff concludes that the availability of test protocols under these laws is still not clear. It is probable, although far from certain, that students and their parents could get access to test protocols.

Can employees gain access to test materials used in hiring and promotion decisions? The answer to this question appears to be largely no. The U.S. Supreme Court ruled against test disclosure in 1979 in the case of *Detroit Edison v. NLRB.* In this case, a union charged that workers had been wrongly denied promotion after taking the necessary aptitude tests. In essence, the NLRB held that the employees' grievances could not be adequately addressed unless full disclosure of test scores was obtained. The court held that the rights of individual employees to privacy was paramount.

Roskind (1980) suggests that the ruling means that the failure to disclose test scores without employee consent is not an act of bad faith or an unfair labor practice. Lerner (1980b) further notes three other facts about the *Detroit Edison* case. (1) The test had been validated. (2) The criterion validity method had been used. (3) The criterion was clearly job-related. The fact that employees failed the test and thus were ineligible for promotion produced the law suit. Thus the union could not question the criterion-related validity of the test and understandably (from the worker's perspective) chose to attack its content validity. This could not be done successfully without full access to test materials.

However, "truth-in-testing" laws have been passed in two states, California and New York. The New York law, passed in 1980, is the more stringent and requires testing companies to give results and correct answers to any person requesting information about his or her score. The tests included under the law are aptitude tests, like the SAT, used for college admission and other tests used for admission to professional schools. As Bersoff (1981) notes, however, the enforcement of the law with respect to the Medical School Admission Test was enjoined to prevent disclosure of its items.

Although testing companies such as the Educational Testing Service had originally objected to truth-in-testing laws, such objections are now less strident. Lefkowitz (1980) listed the major provisions of the New York law. They include limiting disclosure to aptitude portions of aptitude tests for postsecondary and graduate schools for which applicants pay a fee, requiring that background information on test development and validation be filed with the New York State Commissioner of Education, requiring that background information on the test be given to the student upon application to take the test, filing a copy of all items used to obtain a raw score along with the correct answers (these are provided to the student upon request and payment of a fee to cover the cost of dissemination), releasing test scores only to those institutions designated to receive them by the student, and allowing scores (not identified by the individual) to be released for research.

The fact that tests like the SAT are "open" in New York means they are also no longer secure in other states as well. Copies of the test administered in New York could be made available to students in other states. There is no way to guarantee that content would not be compromised. Certainly the truth-in-testing law in New York places an extra burden on testing companies. Tests must perhaps be revised more often than they formerly were. If the law were applied to achievement tests, where a limited number of valid items were available, its effect would be to eliminate standardized testing in this area. Quaintance (1980) persuasively argues that test security is also basic to public merit systems (civil service) and the New York law does not apply to this system.

Further legislation, even a federal truth-in-testing law, may occur in the future. The delicate balance is between an individual's and the public's right to know and the need for valid tests to predict important aspects of human behavior.

AUTOMATED PSYCHOLOGICAL TESTING

Advancements in computer technology over the past several decades have been almost unbelievable. A silicone chip as thin as the nail on one's little finger and less than half its area can perform operations which not long ago required computer hardware that would almost completely fill a large room. In an era of rapidly expanding computer technology it is not surprising that there have been increasing efforts to automate the testing process.

Automation in psychological testing occurs whenever a computer performs functions previously carried out by the human examiner. Computers can administer, score, and interpret some psychological tests. A subject can be seated at a computer terminal; test items can be displayed on a screen; the subject can respond to items by pressing buttons on the terminal or typing responses on the terminal's keyboard; responses can be fed automatically into the computer's central processing unit, yielding one, several, or even hundreds of scores in a matter of seconds; and the scores can be entered into a computer program that will print appropriate interpretive statements about the subject.

Although personality questionnaires, such as the MMPI, lend themselves most readily to automation, automated procedures also have been applied to other instruments, including the Rorschach, Wechsler intelligence scales, Thematic Apperception Test, and Incomplete Sentences Blank (Lanyon & Goodstein, 1982). The major advantages of automated procedures are efficiency and accuracy. Operations that would take a psychologist or clerk several minutes or even hours to complete can be performed by the computer in a few seconds. Assuming that accurate information has been programmed into the computer, there is almost complete reliability in the functions that it performs.

Programming a computer to administer many psychological tests is not complex. Almost any experienced programmer can accomplish this task with ease. Similarly, there is not much sophistication involved in programming a computer to score objective tests like the MMPI. The computer's memory stores information concerning which items and which responses are scored for the various scales. The computer quickly processes a subject's responses, computing scores for as many scales as have been previously programmed. Raw scores can be converted to percentiles, standard scores, or other convenient scores by referring to normative data that also are stored in the computer's memory. The computer can even construct a profile of a subject's scores. More creativity and sophistication are involved in developing programs that can examine Rorschach responses or TAT stories electronically and code them so that scores and indices can be computed (for example, see Piotrowski, 1980).

Automated interpretations of psychological tests are not as simple and straightforward as are administration and scoring. Interpretive statements are written for various patterns of responses and scores that subjects might produce on a particular test and these statements are stored in the computer's memory. When the test is administered, the computer scans the results and searches its memory for interpretive statements previously determined to be appropriate for the subject's scores. These statements are then printed on the computer terminal.

It is important to distinguish between automated and actuarial interpretations. *Automation* refers to the use of computers to store descriptive statements and to assign appropriate statements to particular test responses or scores. The decisions about which statements are to be assigned to which responses or scores may be based on research, actuarial tables, or experience. Regardless of the basis for the decisions, they are made automatically by the computer. *Actuarial interpretations* are ones in which the assignment of particular interpretive statements to subjects' responses and scores is based entirely on previously established empirical relationships between the responses and scores and the behaviors or characteristics included in the statements. Experience and intuition are not part of actuarial interpretations, which can be carried out by people or by computers. Thus, all computerized interpretations of psychological tests are automated, but they may or may not be actuarial.

The interpretive statements included in most automated interpretation programs have been written by psychologists experienced in the use of the test being interpreted. The psychologists have decided which statements are to be printed for particular responses and scores. These decisions typically are based on both the psychologists' understanding of previous research and on experience and intuition. The computer simply carries out the process in a rapid and efficient manner.

As stated earlier, automated interpretations are used most often with objective tests. The structured responses and the objectively determined scores make these tests ideally suited for automated scoring and interpretation. As an example of automated interpretation, we will now present a computer-generated report based on the MMPI results discussed in detail in Chapter 10. The subject's MMPI responses were recorded on a special answer sheet provided by the scoring and interpretation service. The completed sheet was mailed to the service, and the report was received by return mail about one week later.*

In addition to the narrative interpretation of the MMPI, reproduced in Figure 14-7, the automated report includes a profile of the validity and clinical scales,† a profile of scores on sixteen supplementary scales, raw scores and T-scores for fifty more supplementary scales, and several summary indices. Finally, the report lists critical items endorsed in the scored direction by the subject. Critical items are ones whose contents are especially indicative of serious emotional problems (for example, depression, suicidal ideation, mental confusion).

A comparison of this automated report with the clinician-generated interpretation for this same MMPI profile (presented in Chapter 10) indicates considerable agreement between the interpretations. Both conclude that the MMPI is valid, that the subject has considerable emotional discomfort, and that he is seeking help with his problems. Both interpretations state that the subject is likely to be depressed and pessimistic about the future, but the automated report states more directly that suicide is a significant concern. Both interpretations also note that under stress the subject could become quite disorganized and maladaptive. There is agreement that interpersonal relationships are likely to be unsatisfactory because of distrust and fear of rejection. The general diagnostic picture presented by the two interpretations is congruent, although the automated report uses diagnostic labels from a more current classification system.

There are, however, several areas where the two interpretations vary significantly. The automated report states that the subject does not appear to have sex-role conflict, whereas the clinician-generated interpretation suggests that he harbors doubts about his masculinity. Concerning treatment, both reports agree that the subject needs professional help and that he is likely to be receptive to such help because he is so emotionally uncomfortable. However, the automated report suggests a rather negative prognosis, emphasizing psychotropic medication and supportive psychotherapy. The clinician-generated interpretation offers a somewhat more positive prognosis, suggesting that the subject is likely to remain in therapy and to make slow but steady progress.

Overall, the agreement between the automated and clinician-generated interpretations of this MMPI is remarkable. Although there are several specific differences, the general pictures that emerge from the two reports are quite similar. The agreement is not unexpected when one recognizes that the clinician that generated the report and the clinician who developed the program for the automated interpretation were largely basing their interpretations on the same research data. Although the automated service does not reveal the approach to interpretation used in its program, analysis of the resulting report indicates that the approach is similar to the one described in Chapter 10 and used by the clinician who interpreted this MMPI.

This automated report would be useful to a clinician. Its inferences could be obtained by the clinician efficiently and with little expenditure of professional time. However, it would be important for the clinician to integrate the data from this report with other information available about the

*We gratefully acknowledge the cooperation of Interpretive Scoring Systems in providing this report and in granting permission to reproduce it in part here.

†This profile contains the same information as that in Figure 10-1. The reader is encouraged to refer back to that profile.

client. For example, the automated report makes inferences about a history of poor work and achievement, inadequacy and insecurity in the marriage, and potential for suicide. These inferences could be compared with data available from interviews with the client and his wife, observations of the client, and his performance on other psychological tests.

There are some important potential benefits to associate with automated scoring and interpretation services. Savings in professional time can reduce the cost of psychological testing and can free the professional for other activities that cannot be easily automated. The reliability of scoring and interpretation by computer is almost perfect. Since experts usually develop the interpretive programs that determine which descriptive statements will be assigned to particular sets of test results, a level of interpretive sophistication greater than that of which the typical psychologist is capable can be expected.

In spite of these important potential benefits, there are some significant problems and concerns. The most important is that the validity of the resulting interpretations has not been established adequately. As we stated earlier, the automated interpretations typically are based on the knowledge and experience of those who write the interpretive programs. When these professional persons understand the instruments and their limitations, are knowledgeable about previous research concerning the tests, and have adequate previous experience in assessment, high-quality reports are likely to be produced. Unfortunately, there seems to be great variability among persons writing interpretive programs, and some of the resulting products are incomplete, inaccurate, and misleading (Adair, 1978; Butcher, 1978).

Regardless of the qualifications of the professionals who develop the interpretive programs, consumers should require evidence that the resulting interpretations are valid. To date, efforts to establish accuracy or validity of automated interpretations have involved ratings by users of reports prepared on their clients (Butcher, 1978). This procedure is of limited scientific utility because raters typically have seen the test data and the reports before they made their ratings. A much better procedure would be for persons who are well acquainted with test subjects to rate personality characteristics and behaviors without knowledge of MMPI results or interpretations and to compare these ratings with the automated interpretations.

Another important concern about automated interpretations focuses on the qualifications of the users of these services. Although all services purport to assess the qualifications of potential users to make sure they are adequately trained and experienced enough to use the interpretive reports appropriately, many users of the services are not qualified to use the particular tests that are being interpreted. Some psychologists who are trained and licensed to practice psychology are not adequately informed about a specific test, such as the MMPI, to evaluate the appropriateness of automated interpretations of it. Of even greater concern are nonpsychological users, such as psychiatrists, nonpsychiatric physicians, and chiropractors, who have little or no experience or training in psychological assessment in general or specifically in the tests being interpreted. Although one might argue that it is the professional and ethical responsibility of users of automated services to obtain sufficient training, we maintain that it is the responsibility of the automated services to ensure the qualifications of potential users. This belief is consistent with test publishers' responsibility for limiting the sale of psychological tests to qualified professionals.

There is little doubt that when automated interpretations are based on programs developed by qualified professionals and are used by qualified professionals, the potential benefits are considerable. However, such interpretations should be considered as only part of the assessment process. Unfortunately, the automated interpretation

THE MINNESOTA REPORT ^{TM*}   Page 1

for the Minnesota Multiphasic Personality Inventory ^{TM} : Adult System

By James N. Butcher, Ph.D.

Client No. :   985   Gender : Male
Setting : Mental Health Outpatient   Age : 27
Report Date : 13-SEP-83
ISS Code Number : 00000985 581 0005

PROFILE VALIDITY

The client has responded to the items in a frank and open manner,
producing a valid MMPI profile. He appears to be a relatively cooperative
person who took the test seriously.

He has admitted to a number of psychological problems that warrant
attention. He may be experiencing some difficulties managing his life
situation and is seeking assistance at this time.

SYMPTOMATIC PATTERN

A pattern of chronic psychological maladjustment characterizes
individuals with this MMPI profile. The client is overwhelmed by anxiety,
tension, and depression. He feels helpless and alone, inadequate and
insecure, and believes that life is hopeless and that nothing is working
out right. He attempts to control his worries through intellectualization
and unproductive self-analyses, but he has difficulty concentrating and
making decisions.

He is functioning at a very low level of efficiency. He tends to
overreact to even minor stress, and may show rapid behavioral
deterioration. He also tends to blame himself for his problems. His
life-style is chaotic and disorganized, and he has a history of poor work
and achievement.

He may be preoccupied with occult or obscure religious ideas.
Obsessive-compulsive and phobic behavior are likely to make up part of the
symptom pattern. He has a wide range of interests, and appears to enjoy
aesthetic and cultural activities. Interpersonally, he appears to be
sensitive, concerned, and able to easily express his feelings toward
others. He appears to have no sex-role conflict.

His response content indicates that he is preoccupied with feeling
guilty and unworthy, and feels that he deserves to be punished for wrongs
he has committed. He feels regretful and unhappy about life, complains
about having no zest for life, and seems plagued by anxiety and worry about
the future. He has difficulty managing routine affairs, and the item
content he endorsed suggests a poor memory, concentration problems, and an
inability to make decisions. He appears to be immobilized and withdrawn
and has no energy for life. According to his response content, there is a
strong possibility that he has seriously contemplated suicide. A careful
evaluation of this possibility is suggested.

INTERPERSONAL RELATIONS

NOTE: This MMPI interpretation can serve as a useful source of hypotheses
about clients. This report is based on objectively derived scale indexes
and scale interpretations that have been developed in diverse groups of
patients. The personality descriptions, inferences and recommendations
contained herein need to be verified by other sources of clinical
information since individual clients may not fully match the prototype.
The information in this report should most appropriately be used by a
trained, qualified test interpreter. The information contained in this
report should be considered confidential.

FIGURE 14–7 Sample of computer-generated test interpretation. (From Minnesota Multiphasic
Personality Inventory. Copyright © The University of Minnesota, 1943, renewed 1970. This report
1982. All rights reserved. Scored and distributed exclusively by NCS Interpretive Scoring Systems under
license from The University of Minnesota. Reproduced by permission.)

Problematic personal relationships are also characteristic of his life. He seems to lack basic social skills and is behaviorally withdrawn. He may relate to others ambivalently, never fully trusting or loving anyone. Many individuals with this profile never establish lasting, intimate relationships. His marital situation is likely to be unrewarding and impoverished. He seems to feel inadequate and insecure in his marriage.

He is a rather introverted person who has some difficulties meeting other people. He is probably shy and may be uneasy and somewhat rigid and overcontrolled in social situations.

BEHAVIORAL STABILITY

This is a rather chronic behavioral pattern. Individuals with this profile live a disorganized and pervasively unhappy existence. They may have episodes of more intense and disturbed behavior resulting from an elevated stress level.

DIAGNOSTIC CONSIDERATIONS

Individuals with this profile show a severe psychological disorder and would probably be diagnosed as severely neurotic with an Anxiety Disorder or Dysthymic Disorder in a Schizoid Personality. The possibility of a more severe psychotic disorder, such as Schizophrenic Disorder, should be considered, however.

TREATMENT CONSIDERATIONS

Individuals with this profile typically receive psychotropic medication for their acute distress. Since they have many psychological concerns, they may have difficulty focusing upon a problem. They tend not to do well in insight oriented or "uncovering" psychotherapy, and may actually deteriorate if they are asked to be introspective. They might, however, respond to supportive treatment of a directive, goal-oriented type. They might present some suicide risk, and precautions and further evaluation should be undertaken.

often is used instead of a more complete assessment. Without the services of an experienced and skilled psychologist to integrate the interpretations from a particular test with interviews, social history, observation, and other test data, the automated interpretations are at best insufficient and at worst potentially dangerous (Graham, 1977).

Although computers are becoming more and more familiar to the average person, there is still a great tendency to attribute considerable scientific authenticity to any of

FIGURE 14-8 Automated Test Interpretation Practices: An Interim Standard for Members of the APA and for Organizations By Whom Members are Employed. Adopted by the Council of Representatives of the American Psychological Association, September 1966. (From Fowler, R. D. Automated interpretation of personality test data. In J. N. Butcher Ed., *MMPI: Research developments and clinical applications.* New York: McGraw-Hill, 1969. Copyright 1969 by McGraw Hill Book Company. Reproduced by permission.)

The advent of sophisticated computer technology and recent psychological research has made it feasible and desirable for consulting and service organizations to offer computer-based interpretation services for diverse clinical psychological measurement instruments. Since these services will be rendered to clients with varying degrees of training in psychological measurement and since improper use of such interpretations could be detrimental to the well-being of individuals, it is considered proper for the American Psychological Association to establish various conditions which must be met before such services should be offered to clients.

1. Any organization offering the services described above must have on its staff or as an active consultant a member of the American Psychological Association who is a Diplomate of the American Board of Examiners in Professional Psychology or who has essentially equivalent qualifications.
2. Such services will be offered only to individuals or organizations for use under the active supervision of qualified professional personnel with appropriate training. The qualified person must be either a staff member or a responsible, active consultant to the individual or organization receiving such services.
3. Organizations offering scoring services must maintain an active quality control program to assure the accuracy and correctness of all reported scores.
4. Organizations offering interpretation services must be able to demonstrate that the computer programs or algorithms on which the interpretations rest are based on appropriate research to establish the validity of the programs and procedures used in arriving at interpretations.
5. The public offering of an automated test interpretation service will be considered as a professional-to-professional consultation. In this the formal responsibility of the consultant is to the consultee but his ultimate and overriding responsibility is to the client.
6. The organization offering service is responsible that their reports adequately interpret the test materials. They should not misinterpret nor over-interpret the data nor omit important interpretations that the consultee would reasonably expect to be included.
7. The organization offering services is responsible that their report be interpretable by the consultee. The technical level of the report should be understandable and not misleading to the consultee. The professional consultee is responsible for integrating the report into his client relationship. Where technical interpretations could be misleading, the organization offering service would be responsible either not to accept the referral, to modify the form of their report, or to avoid otherwise its misinterpretation.

their output. There is a danger that uninformed users of the automated interpretations will assume accuracy and validity of interpretations not justified by existing data (Graham, 1977). In fact, Ziskin (1981) suggested that psychologists serving as expert witnesses in court bring into the courtroom automated interpretations of MMPI data because judges and juries are likely to be impressed with the apparent scientific authenticity of these interpretations.

A final concern about automated interpretations is that the interpretive systems often become crystalized and fixated at a rather naive level (Butcher, 1978). Although the potential exists for modifying interpretive systems as new data become available, there is a tendency for services not to change a program that is operating smoothly and is producing a profit for the company. Butcher discussed several instances where, in response to critics, only cosmetic changes or no changes at all were made in existing interpretive programs.

In an effort to address some of the potential problems associated with automated test interpretation, in 1966 the American Psychological Association developed some interim standards for such services (Fowler, 1969), which are reproduced in Figure 14–8. The standards address most of the problems discussed, making it clear that the organizations offering the services have primary responsibility for demonstrating validity and accuracy of their interpretations and for assuring appropriate use. Unfortunately, the standards are general and do not provide specific guidelines or procedures for accomplishing their intended purposes. Although the standards were labeled "interim" in 1966, no updated version has yet been published. More current and more detailed standards regulating automated interpretations of psychological tests are needed.

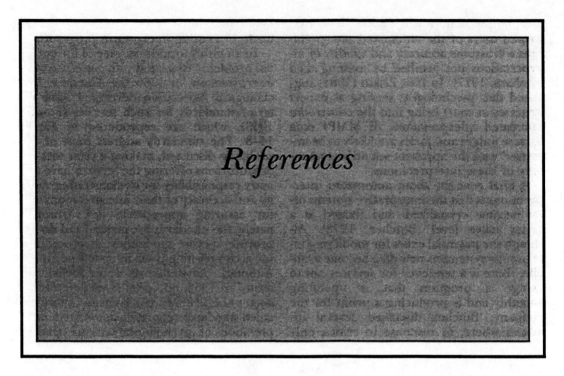

References

ACHENBACH, T. M., & EDELBROCK, C. S. (1979). The child behavior profile: II. Boys aged 12–16 and girls aged 6–11 and 12–16. *Journal of Consulting and Clinical Psychology, 47,* 223–233.

ADAIR, F. L. (1978). Review of MMPI computerized scoring and interpreting services. In O. K. Buros (Ed.). *Eighth mental measurements yearbook.* Highland Park, N.J.: Gryphon.

ADCOCK, C. J. (1965). Thematic Apperception Test. In O. K. Buros (Ed.). *Sixth mental measurements yearbook.* Highland Park, N.J.: Gryphon.

ADKINS, D. C., & BALLIF, B. L. (1975). *Animal Crackers: A test of motivation to achieve. Examiner's manual.* Monterey, Calif.: CTB/McGraw-Hill.

AKUTAGAWA, D. A. (1956). *A study in construct validity of the psychoanalytic concept of latent anxiety and a test of projection distance hypothesis.* Unpublished doctoral dissertation, University of Pittsburgh.

ALDEN, P., & BENTON, A. L. (1951). Relationship of sex of examiner to incidence of Rorschach responses with sexual content. *Journal of Projective Techniques, 15,* 231–234.

ALEAMONI, L. M., & OBOLER, L. (1978). ACT versus SAT in predicting first semester GPA. *Educational and Psychological Measurement, 38,* 393–399.

ALKER, H. A. (1978). Minnesota Multiphasic Personality Inventory. In O. K. Buros (Ed.). *Eighth mental measurements yearbook.* Highland Park, N.J.: Gryphon.

ALLEN, M. J., & YEN, W. M. (1979). *Introduction to measurement theory.* Monterey, Calif.: Brooks/Cole.

ALLPORT, G. W., & VERNON, P. E. (1931). A test for personal values. *Journal of Abnormal Psychology, 26,* 231–248.

ALLPORT, G. W., VERNON, P. E., & LINDZEY, G. (1960). *Study of values* (3rd ed.). Boston: Houghton Mifflin.

AMEG COMMISSION ON SEX BIAS IN MEASUREMENT (1973). Report on sex bias in interest measurement. *Measurement and Evaluation in Guidance, 6,* 171–177.

AMERICAN COLLEGE TESTING PROGRAM (1973a). *Assessing students on the way to college: Technical report for the ACT Assessment Program.* Iowa City, Iowa: Author.

AMERICAN COLLEGE TESTING PROGRAM (1973b). *Highlights of the ACT Technical Report.* Iowa City, Iowa: Author.

AMERICAN COLLEGE TESTING PROGRAM (1980a). *College student profiles: Norms for the ACT Assessment (1980–81 ed.).* Iowa City, Iowa: Author.

AMERICAN COLLEGE TESTING PROGRAM (1980b).

Content of the tests in the ACT Assessment. Iowa City, Iowa: Author.

AMERICAN COLLEGE TESTING PROGRAM (1980c). *Your ACT Assessment results.* Iowa City, Iowa: Author.

American heritage dictionary of the English language (1976). Boston: Houghton Mifflin.

AMERICAN PSYCHOLOGICAL ASSOCIATION (1953, 1966, 1977). *Ethical standards of psychologists.* Washington, D.C.: Author.

AMERICAN PSYCHOLOGICAL ASSOCIATION (1966). *Standards for educational and psychological test manuals.* Washington, D.C.: Author.

AMERICAN PSYCHOLOGICAL ASSOCIATION (1974). *Standards for educational and psychological tests.* Washington, D.C.: Author.

AMERICAN PSYCHOLOGICAL ASSOCIATION (1981). Ethical principles of psychologists. *American Psychologist, 36,* 633–638.

AMES, L. B., METRAUX, R. W., RODELL, J. L., & WALKER, R. N. (1973). *Rorschach responses in old age.* New York: Brunner/Mazel.

AMES, L. B., METRAUX, R. W., RODELL, J. L., & WALKER, R. N. (1974). *Child Rorschach responses: Developmental trends from two to ten years.* New York: Brunner/Mazel.

AMES, L. B., METRAUX, R. W., & WALKER, R. N. (1971). *Adolescent Rorschach responses: Developmental trends from ten to sixteen years.* New York: Brunner/Mazel.

AMRINE, M. (1965). The 1965 Congressional inquiry into testing: A commentary. *American Psychologist, 20,* 859–870.

ANASTASI, A. (1978). Personality Research Form. In O. K. Buros (Ed.). *Eighth mental measurements yearbook.* Highland Park, N.J.: Gryphon.

ANASTASI, A. (1980). Abilities and the measurement of achievement. In W. B. Schrader (Ed.). *Measuring achievement: Progress over a decade.* San Francisco: Jossey-Bass.

ANASTASI, A. (1982). *Psychological testing* (5th ed.) New York: Macmillan.

ANDERSON, B. (1982). Test use today in elementary and secondary schools. In A. K. Wigdor and W. R. Garner (Eds.). *Ability testing: Uses, consequences, and controversies (Part II).* Washington, D.C.: National Academy Press.

ANDERSON, R. J., & SISCO, F. H. (1977). Standardization of the WISC-R Performance Scale for deaf children (Series T. No. 1). Washington, D.C.: Gallaudet College Office of Demographic Studies.

ANGOFF, W. A. (1982). Use of difficulty and discrimination indices for detecting item bias. In R. A. Berk (Ed.). *Handbook of methods for detecting test bias.* Baltimore: The Johns Hopkins University Press.

ANGOFF, W. A. (Ed.). (1971). *The College Board Admissions Testing Program: A technical report on research and development activities relating to the Scholastic Aptitude Test and Achievement Tests.* Princeton, N.J.: College Entrance Examination Board.

ANTHONY, J. J. (1973). A comparison of Wechsler Preschool and Primary Scale of Intelligence and Stanford-Binet Intelligence Scale scores for disadvantaged preschool children. *Psychology in the Schools, 10,* 297–299.

APPELBAUM, A. S., & TUMA, J. M. (1977). Social class and test performance: Comparative validity of the Peabody with the WISC and WISC-R for two socioeconomic groups. *Psychological Reports, 40,* 139–145.

ARVEY, R. D. (1979). Unfair discrimination in the employment interview: Legal and psychological aspects. *Psychological Bulletin, 86,* 736–765.

ASHEM, B., & JANES, M. D. (1978). Deleterious effects of chronic undernutrition on cognitive abilities. *Journal of Child Psychology and Psychiatry and Allied Disciplines, 19,* 23–31.

ASSOCIATION OF AMERICAN MEDICAL COLLEGES (1977). *New Medical College Admission Test: Interpretative manual.* Washington, D.C.: Author.

ASTIN, A. W., KING, M. R., & RICHARDSON, G. T. (1978). *The American freshman: National norms for fall 1978.* Los Angeles: University of California, Los Angeles, and the American Council on Education.

AUERBACH, S. M. (1973). Emotional reactions to surgery. *Journal of Consulting and Clinical Psychology, 40,* 264–271.

BAIRD, J. C., & NOMA, E. (1979). *Fundamentals of scaling and psychophysics.* New York: Wiley.

BALINSKY, B., & SHAW, H. W. (1956). The contribution of the WAIS to a management appraisal program. *Personnel Psychology, 9,* 207–209.

BALOH, R., STURM, R., GREEN, B., & GLESER, G. (1975). Neuropsychological effects of chronic asymptomatic increased lead absorption: A controlled study. *Archives of Neurology, 32,* 326–330.

BARAHENI, M. N. (1974). Raven's Progressive Matrices as applied to Iranian children. *Educational and Psychological Measurement, 34,* 983–988.

BARNES, T. R. (1978). Dumber by the dozen or by the decade? *Psychological Reports, 42,* 970.

BARNETTE, W. L., JR. (1973). The Minnesota Vocational Interest Inventory. In D. G. Zytowski (Ed.). *Contemporary approaches to interest measurement.* Minneapolis: University of Minnesota Press.

BATEMAN, B. (1968). "Clinically" obtained IQs versus "production line" IQs in a mentally retarded sample. *Journal of School Psychology, 7,* 29–33.

BAUM, D. D., & KELLY, T. J. (1979). The validity of Slosson Intelligence Test with learning disabled kindergarteners. *Journal of Learning Disabilities, 12,* 268–270.

BAYLEY, N. (1933). Mental growth during the first three years. *Genetic Psychology Monographs, 14,* 1–92.

BAYLEY, N. (1969). *Manual for the Bayley Scales of Infant Development.* New York: Psychological Corporation.

BEATON, A. E., HILTON, T. L., & SCHRADER, W. B. (1977). *Changes in verbal abilities of high school seniors, college entrants, and SAT candidates between 1960 and 1972.* New York: College Entrance Examination Board.

BECK, S. J. (1937). Introduction to the Rorschach method: A manual of personality study. *American Orthopsychiatric Association Monograph,* No. 1.

BECKER, W. C. (1960). The matching of behavior rating and questionnaire personality factors. *Psychological Bulletin, 57,* 201–212.

BECKER, W. C. (1974). Some necessary conditions for the controlled study of achievement and aptitude. In D. R. Green (Ed.). *The aptitude-achievement distinction.* Monterey, Calif.: CTB/McGraw-Hill.

BELL, H. M. (1963). *The Adjustment Inventory manual.* Palo Alto, Calif.: Consulting Psychologists Press.

BELLAK, L., & BELLAK, S. S. (1949). *Manual of instructions for the Children's Apperception Test.* New York: C.P.S. Co.

BEM, S. L. (1974). The measurement of psychological androgyny. *Journal of Consulting and Clinical Psychology, 42,* 155–162.

BEM, S. L. (1977). On the utility of alternate procedures for assessing psychological androgyny. *Journal of Consulting and Clinical Psychology, 45,* 196–205.

BEM, S. L. (1979). Theory and measurement of androgyny: A reply to Pedhazur-Tetenbaum and Locksley-Colten critiques. *Journal of Personality and Social Psychology, 37,* 1047–1054.

BENDER, I. E. (1958). Changes in religious interest: A retest after fifteen years. *Journal of Abnormal and Social Psychology, 57,* 41–46.

BENDER, L. (1946). *Instructions for the use of the Visual Motor Gestalt Test.* New York: American Orthopsychiatric Association.

BENJAMIN, A. D. (1981). *The helping interview* (3rd ed.). Boston: Houghton Mifflin.

BENJAMIN, J. A. (1970). A study of the social psychological factors related to the academic success of Negro high school students. *Dissertation Abstracts International, 30* (8-A), 3543.

BENNETT, G. K., SEASHORE, H. G., & WESMAN, A. G. (1974). *Manual for the Differential Aptitude Tests (Forms S and T).* New York: Psychological Corporation.

BENNETT, G. K., SEASHORE, H. G., & WESMAN, A. G. (1982a). *Differential Aptitude Tests (Forms V and W): Administrator's handbook.* New York: Psychological Corporation.

BENNETT, G. K., SEASHORE, H. G., & WESMAN, A. G. (1982b). *Differential Aptitude Tests (Forms V and W): Directions for administering and scoring.* New York: Psychological Corporation.

BERK, R. (1979). The discrimination efficiency of the Bayley Scales of Infant Development. *Journal of Abnormal Child Psychology, 7,* 113–119.

BERK, R. A. (1980). A consumer's guide to criterion-referenced test reliability. *Journal of Educational Measurement, 17,* 324–349.

BERK, R. A. (Ed.). (1982). *Handbook of methods for detecting test bias.* Baltimore: The Johns Hopkins University Press.

BERNREUTER, R. G. (1931). *The Personality Inventory.* Palo Alto, Calif.: Consulting Psychologists Press.

BERRY, K., & SHERRETS, S. (1975). A comparison of the WISC and WISC-R for special education. *Pediatric Psychology, 3,* 14.

BERSOFF, D. N. (1979). Regarding psychologists testily: Legal regulation of psychological assessment in the public schools. *Maryland Law Review, 39,* 27–120.

BERSOFF, D. N. (1981). Testing and the law. *American Psychologist, 36,* 1047–1056.

BERZINS, J. I., BARNES, D. F., COHEN, D. I., & Ross, E. F. (1971). Reappraisal of the A-B therapist "type" distinction in terms of the Personality Research Form. *Journal of Consulting and Clinical Psychology, 36,* 360–369.

BIEMILLER, L. (1981, October 7). 18-year decline in aptitude-test scores halted this year, College Board reports. *Chronicle of Higher Education,* pp. 1, 8.

BIENEN, S., & MAGOON, T. (1965). Adjective check list adjectives associated with differential status on CPI scales. *Personnel and Guidance Journal, 44,* 286–291.

BILLS, R. E. (1950). Animal pictures for obtaining children's projections. *Journal of Clinical Psychology, 6,* 291–293.

BISHOP, D., & BUTTERWORTH, G. E. (1979). A longitudinal study using the WPPSI and WISC-R with an English sample. *British Journal of Educational Psychology, 49,* 156–168.

BLACK, H. (1962). *They shall not pass.* New York: Random House.

BLACK, J. D. (1953). *The interpretation of MMPI profiles of college women.* Unpublished doctoral dissertation, University of Minnesota.

BLACK, R., & DANA, R. H. (1977). Examiner sex bias and Wechsler Intelligence Scale for Children scores. *Journal of Consulting and Clinical Psychology, 45,* 500.

BLOCK, J., & BAILEY, D. (1955). *Q-sort item analyses of a number of MMPI scales.* Officer Education Research Laboratory, Technical Memorandum, OERL-TM-55-7.

BLOCK, N. J., & DWORKIN, G. (EDS.). (1976). *The IQ controversy.* New York: Pantheon.

BLOOM, A. S., & RASKIN, L. M. (1980). WISC-R Verbal-Performance IQ discrepancies: A comparison of learning disabled children to the normative sample. *Journal of Clinical Psychology, 36,* 322–323.

BLOOM, B. S. (1964). *Stability and change in human characteristics.* New York: Wiley.

BLOXOM, B. M. (1978). The Sixteen Personality Factor Questionnaire. In O. K. Buros (Ed.). *Eighth mental measurements yearbook.* Highland Park, N.J.: Gryphon.

BLUM, G. S. (1950). *The Blacky Pictures.* New York: Psychological Corporation.

BLUM, G. S. (1962). A guide for research use of the Blacky Pictures. *Journal of Projective Techniques, 26,* 3–29.

BOEHM, V. R. (1972). Negro-white differences in validity of employment and training selection procedures: Summary of research evidence. *Journal of Applied Psychology, 56,* 33–39.

BOERGER, A. R., GRAHAM, J. R., & LILLY, R. S. (1974). Behavioral correlates of single-scale MMPI code types. *Journal of Consulting and Clinical Psychology, 42,* 398–402.

BOHANNON, W. E., & MILLS, C. J. (1979). Psychometric properties and underlying assumptions of two measures of masculinity/femininity. *Psychological Reports, 44,* 431–450.

BOLTON, B. F. (1978). The Sixteen Personality Factor Questionnaire. In O. K. Buros (Ed.). *Eighth mental measurements yearbook.* Highland Park, N.J.: Gryphon.

BOOTH, D., & MACKAY, J. (1980). Legal constraints on employment testing and evolving trends in the law. *Emory Law Journal, 29,* 121–194.

BORGEN, F. H., & HARPER, G. T. (1973). Predictive validity of measured vocational interests with black and white college men. *Measurement and Evaluation in Guidance, 6,* 19–27.

BORING, E. G. (1923). Intelligence as the tests test it. *The New Republic, 34,* 35–36.

BOSSARD, M. D., REYNOLDS, C. R., & GUTKIN, T. B. (1980). A regression analysis of test bias on the Stanford-Binet Intelligence Scale for black and white children referred for psychological services. *Journal of Clinical Child Psychology, 9,* 52–54.

BOUCHARD, T. J., JR. (1978). Review of the Differential Aptitude Tests. In O. K. Buros (Ed.). *Eighth mental measurements yearbook.* Highland Park, N.J.: Gryphon.

BOUCHARD, T. J., JR., & MCGUE, M. (1981). Familial studies of intelligence: A review. *Science, 212,* 1055–1059.

BRACKEN, B. A. (1981). McCarthy scales as a learning disability diagnostic aid: A closer look. *Journal of Learning Disabilities, 14,* 128–130.

BRADLEY, F. O., HANNA, G. S., & LUCAS, B. A. (1980). The reliability of scoring the WISC-R. *Journal of Consulting and Clinical Psychology, 48,* 530–531.

BRAYFIELD, A. H. (Ed.). (1965). Testing and public policy. *American Psychologist, 20,* 857–1005.

BRITTAIN, M. (1968). A comparative study of the use of the Wechsler Scale for children and the Stanford-Binet Intelligence Scale (Form L-M) with eight-year-old children. *British Journal of Educational Psychology, 38,* 103–104.

BROOKS, C. R. (1977). WISC, WISC-R, S-B L & M, WRAT: Relationships and trends among children ages six to ten referred for psychological evaluation. *Psychology in the Schools, 14,* 30–33.

BROVERMAN, I. K., BROVERMAN, D. M., CLARKSON, F. E., ROSENKRANTZ, P. S., & VOGEL, S. R. (1970). Sex-role stereotypes and clinical judgments of mental health. *Journal of Consulting and Clinical Psychology, 34,* 1–7.

BROWN, H. S., & MAY, A. E. (1979). A test-retest reliability study of the Wechsler

Adult Intelligence Scale. *Journal of Consulting and Clinical Psychology, 47,* 601–602.

BROWN, W. B., & McGUIRE, J. M. (1976). Current psychological assessment practices. *Professional Psychology, 7,* 475–484.

BRYANT, C. K., & ROFFE, M. W. (1978). A reliability study of the McCarthy Scales of Children's Abilities. *Journal of Clinical Psychology, 34,* 401–406.

BUCK, J. N. (1948). The H-T-P test. *Journal of Clinical Psychology, 4,* 151–159.

BUDOFF, M. (1963). Animal vs. human figures in a picture story test for young mentally backward children. *American Journal of Mental Deficiency, 68,* 245–250.

BURGESS, E. W. (1928). Factors determining success or failure on parole. In A. A. Bruce (Ed.). *The workings of the indeterminate sentence law and the parole system in Illinois.* Springfield, Illinois: Board of Parole.

BURISH, T. G. (1980). Type A/B behavior patterns. In R. H. Wood (Ed.). *Encyclopedia of clinical assessment.* San Francisco: Jossey-Bass.

BURKE, H. R. (1958). Raven's Progressive Matrices: A review and critical evaluation. *Journal of Genetic Psychology, 93,* 199–228.

BURKE, H. R. (1972). Raven's Progressive Matrices: Validity, reliability, and norms. *Journal of Psychology, 82,* 253–257.

BURKE, H. R., & BINGHAM, W. C. (1969). Raven's Progressive Matrices: More on construct validity. *Journal of Psychology, 72,* 247–251.

BUROS, O. K. (Ed.). (1941–1978, irregular). *Mental measurements yearbooks.* Highland Park, N.J.: Gryphon.

BUROS, O. K. (Ed.). (1974). *Tests in print II.* Highland Park, N.J.: Gryphon.

BUROS, O. K. (Ed.). (1978). *Eighth mental measurements yearbook.* Highland Park, N.J.: Gryphon.

BUSCH, R. F. (1980). Predicting first-grade reading achievement. *Learning Disability Quarterly, 3,* 38–48.

BUTCHER, J. N. (1978). Review of computerized scoring and interpreting services. In O. K. Buros (Ed.). *Eighth mental measurements yearbook.* Highland Park, N.J.: Gryphon.

BUTCHER, J. N., & RYAN, M. (1974). Personality stability and adjustment to an extreme environment. *Journal of Applied Psychology, 59,* 107–109.

CAMERON, N. (1938). A study of thinking in senile deterioration and schizophrenic disorganization. *American Journal of Psychology, 51,* 650–664.

CAMPBELL, D. P. (1971). *Handbook for the Strong*

Vocational Interest Blank. Stanford, Calif.: Stanford University Press.

CAMPBELL, D. P., & HANSEN, J. C. (1981). *Manual for the Strong-Campbell Interest Inventory* (3rd ed.). Stanford, Calif.: Stanford University Press.

CAMPBELL, D. T. (1963). Social attitudes and other acquired behavioral dispositions. In S. Koch (Ed.). *Psychology: A study of a science* (Vol. 6). New York: McGraw-Hill.

CAMPBELL, D. T., & FISKE, D. W. (1959). Convergent and discriminant validation by the multitrait-multimethod matrix. *Psychological Bulletin, 56,* 81–105.

CARP, A. L., & SHAVZIN, A. R. (1950). The susceptibility to falsification of the Rorschach psychodiagnostic technique. *Journal of Consulting Psychology, 14,* 230–233.

CARROLL, J. B. (1974). The aptitude-achievement distinction: The case of foreign language aptitude and proficiency. In D. R. Green (Ed.). *The aptitude-achievement distinction.* Monterey, Calif.: CTB/McGraw-Hill.

CARROLL, J. R. (1972). Review of the ITPA. In O. K. Buros (Ed.). *Seventh mental measurements yearbook.* Highland Park, N.J.: Gryphon.

CARVER, R. P. (1974). Two dimensions of tests: Psychometric and edumetric. *American Psychologist, 29,* 512–518.

CATRON, D. W., & THOMPSON, C. C. (1979). Test-retest gains in WAIS scores after four retest intervals. *Journal of Clinical Psychology, 35,* 352–357.

CATTELL, P. (1960). *The measurement of intelligence of infants and young children* (reprinted). New York: Psychological Corporation.

CATTELL, R. B. (1949). *Manual for forms A and B: Sixteen Personality Factor Questionnaire.* Champaign, Ill.: Institute for Personality and Ability Testing.

CATTELL, R. B. (1963). Theory of fluid and crystallized intelligence: A critical experiment. *Journal of Educational Psychology, 54,* 1–22.

CATTELL, R. B. (1971). *Abilities: Their structure, growth, and action.* Boston: Houghton Mifflin.

CATTELL, R. B., EBER, H. W., & TATSUOKA, M. M. (1970). *Handbook for the Sixteen Personality Factor Questionnaire (16PF).* Champaign, Ill.: Institute for Personality and Ability Testing.

CATTELL, R. B., & SCHEIER, I. H. (1963). *The IPAT Anxiety Scale Questionnaire manual.* Champaign, Ill.: Institute for Personality and Ability Testing.

CAUTELA, J. R. (1977) *Behavior analysis forms for*

clinical intervention. Champaign, Ill.: Research Press.

CAUTELA, J. R., & KASTENBAUM, R. (1967). A Reinforcement Survey Schedule for use in therapy, training, and research. *Psychological Reports, 20,* 1115–1130.

CAUTELA, J. R., & WISOCKI, P. A. (1963). The use of imagery in the modification of attitudes toward the elderly: A preliminary report. *The Journal of Psychology, 73,* 193–199.

CHARLESWORTH, W. R. (1976). Human intelligence as adaptation: An ethological approach. In L. B. Resnick (Ed.). *The nature of intelligence.* Hillsdale, N.J.: Erlbaum.

CHASE, C. I. (1972). Review of the ITPA. In O. K. Buros (Ed.). *Seventh mental measurements yearbook.* Highland Park, N.J.: Gryphon.

CHISSOM, B. S., & HOENES, R. L. (1976). A comparison of the D-48 Test and the IPAT Culture Fair Intelligence Test to predict SRA Achievement test scores for 8th and 9th grade students. *Educational and Psychological Measurement, 36,* 561–564.

CIEUTAT, V. J., & FLICK, G. L. (1967). Examiner differences among Stanford-Binet items. *Psychological Reports, 21,* 613–622.

CIMINERO, A. R., NELSON, R. O., & LIPINSKI, D. P. (1977). Self-monitoring procedures. In A. R. Ciminero, K. S. Calhoun, and H. E. Adams (Eds.). *Handbook of behavioral assessment.* New York: Wiley.

CLARK, K. E. (1961). *Vocational interests of nonprofessional men.* Minneapolis: University of Minnesota Press.

CLARK, K. E., & CAMPBELL, D. P. (1965). *Manual for the Minnesota Vocational Interest Inventory.* New York: Psychological Corporation.

CLEARY, T. A. (1968). Test bias: Prediction of grades of negro and white students in integrated colleges. *Journal of Educational Measurement, 5,* 115–124.

CLEARY, T. A., HUMPHREYS, L. G., KENDRICK, S. A., & WESMAN, A. (1975). Educational uses of tests with disadvantaged students. *American Psychologist, 30,* 15–41.

CLEMANS, W. V. (1971). Test administration. In R. L. Thorndike (Ed.). *Educational measurement* (2nd ed.). Washington, D.C.: American Council on Education.

COATES, S., & BROMBERG, P. M. (1973). Factorial structure of the Wechsler Preschool and Primary Scale of Intelligence between the ages of 4 and 6½. *Journal of Consulting and Clinical Psychology, 40,* 365–370.

COCHRAN, M. L., & PEDRINI, D. T. (1969). The concurrent validity of the 1965 WRAT with adult retardates. *American Journal of Mental Deficiency, 73,* 654–656.

COHEN, R. A. (1972). *Accuracy of inference as a function of cues and hypothesis formulation.* Unpublished master's thesis, Kent State University.

COHEN, R. A. (1975). *Accuracy and confidence level in clinical inference as a function of cue validity, feedback and specific practice.* Unpublished doctoral dissertation, Kent State University.

COLE, N. S. (1973). Bias in selection. *Journal of Educational Measurement, 10,* 237–255.

COLE, N. S. (1981). Bias in testing. *American Psychologist, 36,* 1067–1077.

COLEMAN, W., & CURETON, E. E. (1954). Intelligence and achievement: The "jangle fallacy" again. *Educational and Psychological Measurement, 14,* 347–351.

COLEMAN, W., & WARD, A. W. (1956). Further evidence of the jangle fallacy. *Educational and Psychological Measurement, 16,* 524–526.

COLLEGE ENTRANCE EXAMINATION BOARD (1965). *Effect of coaching on Scholastic Aptitude Test scores.* New York: Author.

COLLEGE ENTRANCE EXAMINATION BOARD (1977). *On further examination: Report of the advisory panel on the scholastic aptitude test decline.* New York: Author.

COLLEGE ENTRANCE EXAMINATION BOARD (1981). *An SAT: Test and technical data for the Scholastic Aptitude Test administered in March 1980.* New York: Author.

COLLIGAN, R. C., OSBORNE, D., & SWENSON, W. M. (1982). *The MMPI: A contemporary normative study.* Paper presented at the 17th Annual Symposium on Recent Developments in the Use of the MMPI, Tampa, Florida.

COLVIN, S. S. (1921). Intelligence and its measurement: A symposium. *Journal of Educational Psychology, 12,* 136–139.

COMREY, A. L. (1957a). A factor analysis of items on the MMPI depression scale. *Educational and Psychological Measurement, 17,* 578–585.

COMREY, A. L. (1957b). A factor analysis of items on the MMPI hypochondriasis scale. *Educational and Psychological Measurement, 17,* 566–577.

COMREY, A. L. (1957c). A factor analysis of items on the MMPI hysteria scale. *Educational and Psychological Measurement, 17,* 586–592.

COMREY, A. L. (1958a). A factor analysis of items on the F scale of the MMPI. *Educational and Psychological Measurement, 18,* 621–632.

COMREY, A. L. (1958b). A factor analysis of items on the MMPI hypomania scale. *Educational and Psychological Measurement, 18,* 313–323.

COMREY, A. L. (1958c). A factor analysis of items on the MMPI paranoia scale. *Educational and Psychological Measurement, 18,* 99–107.

COMREY, A. L. (1958d). A factor analysis of items on the MMPI psychasthenia scale. *Educational and Psychological Measurement, 18,* 293–300.

COMREY, A. L. (1958e). A factor analysis of items on the MMPI psychopathic deviate scale. *Educational and Psychological Measurement, 18,* 91–98.

COMREY, A. L. (1970). *Comrey Personality Scales manual.* San Diego, Calif.: Educational and Industrial Testing Service.

COMREY, A. L., & MARGRAFF, W. (1958). A factor analysis of items on the MMPI schizophrenia scale. *Educational and Psychological Measurement, 18,* 301–311.

CONRY, R., & PLANT, W. T. (1965). WAIS and group test predictions of an academic success criterion: High school and college. *Educational and Psychological Measurement, 25,* 493–500.

CONSTANTINOPLE, A. (1973). Masculinity-femininity: An exception to the famous dictim? *Psychological Bulletin, 80,* 389–407.

COOK, R. A. (1953). Identification of ego defensiveness in thematic apperception. *Journal of Projective Techniques, 17,* 312–319.

COOLEY, N. R. (1977). The Wechsler Preschool and Primary Scale of Intelligence: Difficulty order of subtest questions. *Psychology in the Schools, 14,* 24–29.

COVENY, T. E. (1976). Standardized tests for visually handicapped children: A review of research. *New Outlook for the Blind, 70,* 232–236.

COVIN, T. M. (1976). Comparison of Otis-Lennon Mental Ability Test, Elementary I Level, and WISC-R IQs among suspected mental retardates. *Psychological Reports, 38,* 403–406.

COVIN, T. M. (1977a). Comparison of SIT and WISC-R IQs among special education candidates. *Psychology in the Schools, 14,* 19–23.

COVIN, T. M. (1977b). Stability of the WISC-R for 9-year-olds with learning disabilities. *Psychological Reports, 40,* 1297–1298.

COVIN, T. M., & COVIN, J. N. (1976). Comparability of Peabody and WAIS scores among adolescents suspected of being mentally retarded. *Psychological Reports, 39,* 33–34.

COWDEN, J. E., PETERSON, W. M., & PACHT, A. R. (1971). The validation of a brief screening test for verbal intelligence at several correctional institutions in Wisconsin. *Journal of Clinical Psychology, 27,* 216–218.

CRAMER, B. (1978, July 12). Egypt's students do battle . . . against a national exam. *Akron (Ohio) Beacon Journal,* sect. D, p. 5.

CRITES, J. O. (1978). Review of the Strong-Campbell Interest Inventory. In O. K. Buros (Ed.). *Eighth mental measurements yearbook.* Highland Park, N.J.: Gryphon.

CROCKETT, B. K., RARDIN, M. W., & PASEWARK, R. A. (1975). Relationship between WPPSI and Stanford-Binet IQs and subsequent WISC IQs in headstart children. *Journal of Consulting and Clinical Psychology, 43,* 922.

CROCKETT, B. K., RARDIN, M. W., & PASEWARK, R. A. (1976). Relationship of WPPSI and subsequent Metropolitan Achievement Test scores in Head Start children. *Psychology in the Schools, 13,* 19–20.

CROFOOT, M. J., & BENNET, T. S. (1980). A comparison of three screening tests and the WISC-R in special education evaluations. *Psychology in the Schools, 17,* 474–478.

CRONBACH, L. J. (1949). Statistical methods applied to Rorschach scores: A review. *Psychological Bulletin, 46,* 393–432.

CRONBACH, L. J. (1951). Coefficient alpha and the internal structure of tests. *Psychometrika, 16,* 297–334.

CRONBACH, L. J. (1970). *Essentials of psychological testing* (3rd ed.). New York: Harper & Row.

CRONBACH, L. J. (1975). Five decades of public controversy over mental testing. *American Psychologist, 30,* 1–14.

CRONBACH, L. J. (1978). Review of USES Basic Occupational Literacy Test. In O. K. Buros (Ed.). *Eighth mental measurements yearbook.* Highland Park, N.J.: Gryphon.

CRONBACH, L. J. (1980). Validity on parole: How can we go straight? In W. Schrader (Ed.). *New directions for testing and measurement: Measuring achievement progress over a decade* (Vol. 5). San Francisco: Jossey-Bass.

CRONBACH, L. J., & GLESER, G. C. (1965). *Psychological tests and personnel decisions.* Urbana: University of Illinois Press.

CRONBACH, L. J., GLESER, G. C., NANDA, N., & RAJARATNAM, N. (1972). *The dependability of behavioral measurements: Theory of generalizability for scores and profiles.* New York: Wiley.

CRONBACH, L. J., & MEEHL, P. E. (1955). Construct validity in psychological tests. *Psychological Bulletin, 52,* 281–302.

CUMMINS, J. P., & DAS, J. P. (1980). Cognitive processing, academic achievement, and WISC-R performance in EMR children. *Journal of Consulting and Clinical Psychology, 48,* 777–779.

CURRAN, J. P. (1979). Pandora's box reopened? The assessment of social skills. *Journal of Behavioral Assessment, 1,* 55–72.

DAHLSTROM, W. G., WELSH, G. S., & DAHLSTROM, L. E. (1972). *An MMPI handbook. Volume I: Clinical interpretation.* Minneapolis: University of Minnesota Press.

DAHLSTROM, W. G., WELSH, G. S., & DAHLSTROM, L. E. (1975). *An MMPI handbook, Volume II: Research applications.* Minneapolis: University of Minnesota Press.

DALTON, S. (1976). A decline in the predictive validity of the SAT and high school achievement. *Educational and Psychological Measurement, 36,* 445–448.

DANA, R. H. (1972). Thematic Apperception Test. In O. K. Buros (Ed.). *Seventh mental measurements yearbook.* Highland Park, N.J.: Gryphon.

DANA, R. H. (1978). Rorschach. In O. K. Buros (Ed.). *Eighth mental measurements yearbook.* Highland Park, N.J.: Gryphon.

DARLINGTON, R. B. (1971). Another look at "culture fairness." *Journal of Educational Measurement, 8,* 71–82.

DAVIDSON, G. C., & NEALE, J. M. (1982). *Abnormal psychology: An experimental approach.* New York: Wiley.

DAVIS, E. E. (1975). Concurrent validity of the McCarthy Scales of Children's Abilities. *Measurement and Evaluation in Guidance, 8,* 101–104.

DAVIS, E. E., & ROWLAND, T. (1974). A replacement for the venerable Stanford-Binet? *Journal of Clinical Psychology, 30,* 517–521.

DAVIS, E. E., & SLETTEDAHL, R. W. (1976). Stability of the McCarthy Scales over a 1-year period. *Journal of Clinical Psychology, 32,* 798–800.

DAVIS, E. E., & WALKER, C. (1976). Validity of the McCarthy Scales for southwestern rural children. *Perceptual and Motor Skills, 42,* 563–567.

DAVIS, E. E., & WALKER C. (1977). McCarthy Scales and WISC-R. *Perceptual and Motor Skills, 44,* 966.

DAWES, R. M. (1971). A case study of graduate admissions: Application of three principles of human decision making. *American Psychologist, 26,* 180–188.

DEAN, R. S. (1978). Distinguishing learning-disabled and emotionally disturbed children on the WISC-R. *Journal of Consulting and Clinical Psychology, 46,* 381–382.

DEAN, R. S. (1979). Predictive validity of the WISC-R with Mexican-American children. *Journal of School Psychology, 17,* 55–58.

DIAMOND, E. E. (1978). Issues of sex bias and sex-fairness in career interest measurement: Background and current status. In C. K. Tittle & D. C. Zytowski (Eds.). *Sex-fair interest measurement: Research and implications.* Washington, D.C.: National Institute of Education.

DIAMOND, J., & EVANS, W. (1973). The correction for guessing. *Review of Educational Research, 43,* 181–191.

DINNING, W. D., ANDERT, J. N., & HUSTAK, T. L., (1977). Reliability and stability of WAIS IQs for institutionalized adult retardates. *Psychological Reports, 40,* 929–930.

DLUGOKINSKI, E., WEISS, S., & JOHNSTON, S. (1976). Preschoolers at risk: Social, emotional, and cognitive consideration. *Psychology in the Schools, 13,* 134–139.

DOLLIVER, R. H. (1978). Review of the Strong-Campbell Interest Inventory. In O. K. Buros (Ed.). *Eighth mental measurements yearbook.* Highland Park, N.J.: Gryphon.

DONLON, T. F., & ANGOFF, W. H. (1971). The Scholastic Aptitude Test. In W. H. Angoff (Ed.). *The college board admissions testing program: A technical report on research and development activities relating to the Scholastic Aptitude Test and Achievement Tests.* Princeton, N.J.: College Entrance Examination Board.

DRAKE, L. E. (1946). A social I.E. scale for the MMPI. *Journal of Applied Psychology, 30,* 51–54.

DREGER, R. M. (1978). Review of the State-Trait Anxiety Inventory. In O. K. Buros (Ed.). *Eighth mental measurements yearbook.* Highland Park, N.J.: Gryphon.

DROEGE, R. (1966). Effects of practice on aptitude test scores. *Journal of Applied Psychology, 50,* 306–310.

DUBOIS, P. H. (1970). *A history of psychological testing.* Boston: Allyn & Bacon.

DUBOIS, P. H. (1972). Review of the Scholastic Aptitude Test. In O. K. Buros (Ed.). *Seventh mental measurements yearbook.* Highland Park, N.J.: Gryphon.

DUCKWORTH, J. (1979). *The MMPI interpretation manual for counselors and clinicians.* Muncie, Ind.: Accelerated Development.

DUNN, L. M. (1965). *Peabody Picture Vocabulary Test expanded manual.* Circle Pines, Minn.: American Guidance Service.

DUNN, L. M., & DUNN, L. M. (1981). *Peabody Pic-*

ture Vocabulary Test–Revised. Manual for Forms L and M. Circle Pines, Minn.: American Guidance Service.

DUVALL, S., & MALONEY, M. P. (1978). Comparison of the WAIS and Leiter International Performance Scale in a large urban community mental health setting. Psychological Reports, 43, 235–238.

EAKINS, D. J., GREEN, D. S., & BUSHNELL, D. (1976-77). The effects of an instructional test-taking unit on achievement test scores. The Journal of Educational Research, 70, 67–71.

EBEL, R. L. (1978). Review of the Stanford Achievement Test. In O. K. Buros (Ed.). Eighth mental measurements yearbook. Highland Park, N.J.: Gryphon.

ECKBERG, D. L. (1979). Intelligence and race: The origins and dimensions of the IQ controversy. New York: Praeger.

EDUCATIONAL TESTING SERVICE (1980). Test use and validity: A response to charges in the Nader/Nairn report on ETS. Princeton, N.J.: Author.

EDUCATIONAL TESTING SERVICE (1981). Guide to the use of the Graduate Record Examinations. Princeton, N.J.: Author.

EDUCATIONAL TESTING SERVICE (1982). GRE 1982-83 information bulletin. Princeton, N.J.: Author.

EDUCATIONAL TESTING SERVICE (1983). ETS 1982 annual report. Princeton, N.J.: Author.

EDWARDS, A. E. (1957). Techniques of attitude scale construction. New York: Appleton-Century-Crofts.

EDWARDS, A. J. (1971). Individual mental testing: Part I history and theories. San Francisco: Intext Educational Publishers.

EDWARDS, A. L. (1959). Edwards Personal Preference Schedule manual. New York: Psychological Corporation.

EDWARDS, A. L. (1967). Edwards Pesonality Inventory manual. Chicago: Science Research Associates.

EINHORN, H. J., & BASS, A. R. (1971). Methodology consideration relevant to discrimination in employment testing. Psychological Bulletin, 75, 261–269.

EISERT, D. C. (1980). Mothers' reports of their low birth weight infants' subsequent development on the Minnesota Child Development Inventory. Journal of Pediatric Psychology, 5, 353–364.

EISLER, R. M. (1968). Thematic expression of sexual conflict under varying stimulus conditions. Journal of Consulting and Clinical Psychology, 32, 216–220.

ELASHOFF, J. D., & SNOW, R. E. (1971). "Pygmalion" reconsidered. Worthington, Ohio: Charles A. Jones Publishing Co.

ELKIND, D. (1969) Piagetian and psychometric conceptions of intelligence. Harvard Educational Review, 39, 319–337.

ENDLER, N. S., HUNT, J. McV., & ROSENSTEIN, A. J. (1962). An S-R inventory of anxiousness. Psychological Monographs, 76 (Whole No. 536).

ENDLER, N. S., & MAGNUSSON, D. (1976). Multidimensional aspects of state and trait anxiety: A cross-cultural study of Canadian and Swedish college students. In C. D. Spielberger & R. Diaz-Guerro (Eds.). Cross-cultural anxiety. Washington, D.C.: Hemisphere Publishing.

ENGEN, H. B., LAMB, R. R., & PREDIGER, D. J. (1982). Are secondary schools still using standardized tests? Personnel and Guidance Journal, 60, 287–290.

EQUAL EMPLOYMENT OPPORTUNITY COMMISSION (1978). Uniform guidelines on employee selection procedures. Federal Register, 43 (No. 166), 38290–38315.

ERNHART, C. B., LANDA, B., & CALLAHAN, R. (1980). The McCarthy Scales: Predictive validity and stability of scores for urban black children. Educational and Psychological Measurement, 40, 1183–1188.

EVANS, I. M., & NELSON, R. O. (1977). Assessment of child behavior problems. In A. R. Ciminero, K. S. Calhoun, and H. E. Adams (Eds.). Handbook of behavioral assessment. New York: Wiley.

EXNER, J. E. (1969). The Rorschach systems. New York: Grune & Stratton.

EXNER, J. E. (1974). The Rorschach: A comprehensive system. New York: Wiley.

EXNER, J. E. (1978). The Rorschach: A comprehensive system. Volume II. Current research and advanced interpretation. New York: Wiley.

EXNER, J. E., & EXNER, D. E. (1972). How clinicians use the Rorschach. Journal of Personality Assessment, 36, 402–408.

EXNER, J. E., & WEINER, I. B. (1982). The Rorschach: A comprehensive system. New York: Wiley.

EYSENCK, H. J. (1973). The inequality of man. London: Temple Smith.

EYSENCK, H. J., & EYSENCK, S. G. G. (1969). Eysenck Personality Inventory manual. San Diego, Calif.: Educational and Industrial Testing Service.

EYSENCK, H. J., versus KAMIN, L. (1981). The intelligence controversy. New York: Wiley.

FEDERAL TRADE COMMISSION, BOSTON REGIONAL OFFICE (1978, September). *Staff memorandum of the Boston Regional Office of the Federal Trade Commission: The effects of coaching on standardized admission examinations*. Boston: Author.

FEDERAL TRADE COMMISSION, BUREAU OF CONSUMER PROTECTION (1979, March). *Effects of coaching on standardized admission examinations: Revised statistical analyses of data gathered by Boston Regional Office of the Federal Trade Commission*. Washington, D.C.: Author.

FELD, S., & SMITH, C. P. (1958). An evaluation of the method of content analysis. In J. W. Atkinson (Ed.). *Motives in fantasy, action, and society*. Princeton, N.J.: Van Nostrand.

FELDMAN, K. A., & NEWCOMB, T. M. (1969). *The impact of colleges on students (Vol. 1): An analysis of four decades of research*. San Francisco: Jossey-Bass.

FELDMAN, M. J., & GRALEY, J. (1954). The effects of an experimental set to simulate abnormality on group Rorschach performance. *Journal of Projective Techniques, 18*, 326–334.

FERGUSON, R. L. (1976). The decline in ACT scores: What does it mean? *Educational Technology, 16*, 21–27.

FIELD, J. G. (1960). Two types of tables for use with Wechsler's intelligence scales. *Journal of Clinical Psychology, 16*, 3–7.

FINCHER, C. (1974). Is the SAT worth its salt? An evaluation of the Scholastic Aptitude Test in the university system of Georgia over a thirteen-year period. *Review of Educational Research, 44*, 293–305.

FINK, A. M. & BUTCHER, J. N. (1972). Reducing objections to personality inventories with special instructions. *Educational and Psychological Measurement, 32*, 631–639.

FISHER, G. M. (1960). A corrected table for determining the significance of the difference between verbal and performance IQs on the WAIS and the Wechsler-Bellevue. *Journal of Clinical Psychology, 16*, 7–8.

FISHER, G. M., KILMAN, B. A., & SHOTWELL, A. M. (1961). Comparability of intelligence quotients of mental defectives on the WAIS and the 1960 revision of the SB. *Journal of Consulting Psychology, 25*, 192–195.

FITZ-GIBBON, C. T. (1974). The identification of mentally gifted "disadvantaged" students at the eighth grade level. *Journal of Negro Education, 43*, 53–66.

FITZPATRICK, A. R. (1983). The meaning of content validity. *Applied Psychological Measurement, 7*, 3–13.

FLAUGHER, R. L. (1978). The many definitions of test bias. *American Psychologist, 33*, 671–679.

FLAVELL, J. H. (1963). *The developmental psychology of Jean Piaget*. Princeton, N.J.: Van Nostrand.

FLAVELL, J. H. (1977). *Cognitive development*. Englewood Cliffs, N.J.: Prentice-Hall.

FLETCHER, J. M., TODD, J., & SATZ, P. (1975). Culture-fairness of three intelligence tests and a short-form procedure. *Psychological Reports, 37*, 1255–1262.

FLODEN, R. E., PORTER, A. C., SCHMIDT, W. H., & FREEMAN, D. J. (1980). Don't they all measure the same thing? Consequences of standardized test selection. In E. L. Baker and E. S. Quellmalz (Eds.). *Educational testing and evaluation: Design, analysis, and policy*. Beverly Hills, Calif.: Sage.

FLORES, M. B., & EVANS, G. T. (1972). Some differences in cognitive abilities between selected Canadian and Filipino students. *Multivariate Behavioral Research, 7*, 175–192.

FOSBERG, I. A. (1938). Rorschach reactions under varied instructions. *Rorschach Research Exchange, 3*, 12–30.

FOSBERG, I. A. (1941). An experimental study of the reliability of the Rorschach psychodiagnostic technique. *Rorschach Research Exchange, 5*, 72–84.

FOWLER, R. D. (1969). Automated interpretation of personality test data. In J. N. Butcher (Ed.). *MMPI: Research developments and clinical applications*. New York: McGraw-Hill.

FREEMAN, F. S. (1962). *Theory and practice of psychological testing* (3rd ed.). New York: Holt, Rinehart & Winston.

FREIDES, D. (1978). Review of WISC-R. In O. K. Buros (Ed.). *Eighth mental measurements yearbook*. Highland Park, N.J.: Gryphon.

FRIEDMAN, H. (1953). Perceptual regression in schizophrenia: An hypothesis suggested by the use of the Rorschach test. *Journal of Projective Techniques, 17*, 171–185.

FRIEDMAN, T., & WILLIAMS, E. B. (1982). Current use of tests for employment. In A. K. Wigdor and W. R. Garner (Eds.). *Ability testing: Uses, consequences, and controversies (Part II)*. Washington, D.C.: National Academy Press.

FUEYO, V. (1977). Training test-taking skills: A critical analysis. *Psychology in the Schools, 14*, 180–184.

FURUYA, K. (1957). Responses of school children to human and animal pictures. *Journal of Projective Techniques, 21*, 248–252.

GAA, J. P., & LIBERMAN, D. (1981). Categorization agreement of the Personality Attributes Questionnaire and the Bem Sex-Role Inventory. *Journal of Clinical Psychology, 37,* 593–601.

GARDNER, E. F., MADDEN, R., RUDMAN, H. C., KARLSEN, B., MERWIN, J. C., CALLIS, R., & COLLINS, C. S. (1983). *Stanford Achievement Test Series: Multilevel norms booklet (national).* New York: Psychological Corporation.

GARDNER, E. F., RUDMAN, H. C., KARLSEN, B., & MERWIN, J. C. (1982). *Directions for administering the complete battery of the Stanford Achievement Test (Primary 2, Form E).* New York: Psychological Corporation.

GARFIELD, S. L. (1974). *Clinical psychology: The study of personality and behavior,* Chicago: Aldine.

GARFIELD, S. L., BLEK, L., & MELKER, F. (1952). The influence of administration and sex differences on selected aspects of TAT stories. *Journal of Consulting Psychology, 16,* 140–144.

GARFINKEL, R., & THORNDIKE, R. L. (1976). Binet item difficulty then and now. *Child Development, 47,* 959–965.

GAUDREAU, P. (1977). Factor analysis of the Bem Sex-Role Inventory. *Journal of Consulting and Clinical Psychology, 45,* 299–302.

GEER, J. H. (1965). The development of a scale to measure fear. *Behavior Research and Therapy, 3,* 45–53.

GENTHNER, R. W., & GRAHAM, J. R. (1976). Effects of short-term public psychiatric hospitalization for both black and white patients. *Journal of Consulting and Clinical Psychology, 44,* 118–124.

GERKEN, K. C. (1978). Performance of Mexican American children on intelligence tests. *Exceptional Children, 44,* 438–443.

GERKEN, K. C., HANCOCK, K. A., & WADE, T. H. (1978). A comparison of the Stanford-Binet Intelligence Scale and the McCarthy Scales of Children's Abilities with preschool children. *Psychology in the Schools, 15,* 468–472.

GESELL, A. (1925). *The mental growth of the preschool child.* New York: Macmillan.

GHISELLI, E. E., CAMPBELL, J. P., & ZEDECK, S. (1981). *Measurement theory for the behavioral sciences.* San Francisco: W. H. Freeman.

GIANGRECO, C. J. (1966). The Hiskey-Nebraska Test of Learning Aptitude compared with several achievement tests. *American Annals of the Deaf, 111,* 566–577.

GIBSON, J., & LIGHT, P. (1967). Intelligence among university scientists. *Nature, 213,* 441–443.

GILBERSTADT, H., & DUKER, J. (1965). *A handbook for clinical and actuarial MMPI interpretation.* Philadelphia: Saunders.

GIRONDA, R. J. (1977). A comparison of WISC and WISC-R results of urban educable mentally retarded students. *Psychology in the Schools, 14,* 271–275.

GLASER, R. (1963). Instructional technology and the measurement of learning outcomes. *American Psychologist, 18,* 519–521.

GLASER, R., & NITKO, A. J. (1971). Measurement in learning and instruction. In R. L. Thorndike (Ed.). *Educational measurement* (2nd ed.). Washington, D.C.: American Council on Education.

GLASS, G. V. (1978). Standards and criteria. *Journal of Educational Measurement, 15,* 237–261.

GOH, D. S., & YOUNGQUIST, J. (1979). A comparison of the McCarthy Scales of Children's Abilities and the WISC-R. *Journal of Learning Disabilities, 12,* 344–348.

GOLDBERG, L. R. (1959). The effectiveness of clinicians' judgment: The diagnosis of organic brain damage from the Bender-Gestalt test. *Journal of Consulting Psychology, 23,* 25–33.

GOLDBERG, L. R. (1965). Diagnosticians vs. diagnostic signs: The diagnosis of psychosis vs. neurosis from the MMPI. *Psychological Monographs, 79,* 9 (Whole No. 602).

GOLDBERG, L. R. (1968). Simple models or simple processes. *American Psychologist, 23,* 483–496.

GOLDBERG, L. R. (1970). Man versus model of man: A rationale, plus some evidence, for a method of improving on clinical inference. *Psychological Bulletin, 73,* 422–432.

GOLDBERG, L. R., & RORER, L. G. (1965). Learning clinical inferences: The results of intensive training on clinicians' ability to diagnose psychosis vs. neurosis from the MMPI. *American Psychologist, 20,* 736.

GOLDBERG, P. A. (1965). A review of sentence completion methods in personality assessment. *Journal of Projective Techniques and Personality Assessment, 29,* 12–45.

GOLDBERG, P. A. (1968). The current status of sentence completion methods. *Journal of Projective Techniques and Personality Assessment, 32,* 215–221.

GOLDEN, M. (1964). Some effects of combining psychological tests on clinical inferences. *Journal of Consulting Psychology, 28,* 440–446.

GOLDFRIED, M. R. (1979). Behavioral assessment: Where do we go from here? *Behavioral Assessment, 1,* 19–22.

GOLDFRIED, M. R., & D'ZURILLA, T. J., (1969). A behavior-analytic model for assessing competence. In C. D. Spielberger (Ed.). *Current topics in clinical and community psychology* (Vol. 1). New York: Academic Press.

GOLDFRIED, M. R., & KENT, R. N. (1972). Traditional versus behavioral personality assessment: A comparison of methodological and theoretical assumptions. *Psychological Bulletin, 77,* 409–420.

GOLDFRIED, M. R., & LINEHAN, M. M. (1977). Basic issues in behavioral assessment. In A. R. Ciminero, K. S. Calhoun, and H. E. Adams (Eds.), *Handbook of behavioral assessment.* New York: Wiley.

GOLDFRIED, M. R., STRICKER, G., & WEINER, I. B. (1971). *Rorschach handbook of clinical and research applications.* Englewood Cliffs, N.J.: Prentice-Hall.

GOLDMAN, L. (1961). *Using tests in counseling.* New York: Appleton-Century-Crofts.

GOLDMAN, R. D., & SLAUGHTER, R. E. (1976). Why college grade point average is difficult to predict. *Journal of Educational Psychology, 68,* 9–14.

GOLDSMITH, J. B., & McFALL, R. M. (1975). Development and evaluation of an interpersonal skill-training program for psychiatric inpatients. *Journal of Abnormal Psychology, 84,* 51–58.

GOOD, P. K., & BRANTNER, J. P. (1961). *The physician's guide to the MMPI.* Minneapolis: University of Minnesota Press.

GOOD, T. L., & BECKERMAN, T. M. (1978). An examination of teachers' effects on high, middle, and low aptitude students' performance on standardized achievement tests. *American Educational Research Journal, 15,* 477–482.

GOODARD, H. H. (1908). The Binet and Simon tests of intellectual capacity. *The Training School, 5,* 3–9.

GOODARD, H. H. (1911). Two thousand normal children measured by the Binet Measuring Scale of Intelligence. *Pedagogical Seminary, 18,* 232–259.

GOODENOUGH, F. L. (1926). *Measurement of intelligence by drawings.* Yonkers-on-Hudson, N.Y.: World Book Co.

GOODSTEIN, L. R., CRITES, J. O., HEILBRUN, A. B., & REMPEL, P. P. (1961). The use of the California Psychological Inventory in a university counseling service. *Journal of Counseling Psychology, 8,* 147–153.

GORDON, M. A. (1974). Correlation and regression for ACT and SAT test scores. *College and University, 50,* 82–84.

GORSUCH, R. L. (1974). *Factor analysis.* Philadelphia: Saunders.

GOUGH, H. (1950). The F minus K dissimulation index for the MMPI. *Journal of Consulting Psychology, 14,* 408–413.

GOUGH, H. (1952). Identifying psychological femininity. *Educational and Psychological Measurement, 12,* 427–439.

GOUGH, H. (1953). The construction of a personality scale to predict scholastic achievement. *Journal of Applied Psychology, 37,* 361–366.

GOUGH, H., (1957). *Manual for the California Psychological Inventory* (reprinted 1975). Palo Alto, Calif.: Consulting Psychologists Press.

GOUGH, H. (1964). Academic achievement in high school as predicted from the California Psychological Inventory. *Journal of Educational Psychology, 65,* 174–180.

GOUGH, H. (1965). Cross-cultural validation of a measure of asocial behavior. *Psychological Reports, 17,* 379–387.

GOUGH, H. (1966). Appraisal of social maturity by means of the CPI. *Journal of Abnormal Psychology, 17,* 189–195.

GOUGH, H. (1968). An interpreter's syllabus for the California Psychological Inventory. In P. McReynolds (Ed.). *Advances in psychological assessment* (Vol. 1). Palo Alto, Calif.: Science and Behavior Books.

GOUGH, H., FOX, R. E., & HALL, W. B. (1972). Personality inventory assessment of psychiatric residents. *Journal of Counseling Psychology, 19,* 269–274.

GOUGH, H. G., McKEE, M. G., & YANDELL, R. J. (1955). *Adjective check list analyses of a number of selected psychometric and assessment variables.* Officer Education Research Laboratory, Technical Memorandum, OERL-TM-55-10.

GOUGH, H., & PETERSON, D. (1952). The identification and measurement of predispositional factors in crime and delinquency. *Journal of Consulting Psychology, 16,* 207–212.

GOULD, S. J. (1981). *The mismeasure of man.* New York: W. W. Norton.

GOWAN, J. C. (1956). Achievement and personality test scores of gifted college students. *California Journal of Education, 7,* 105–109.

GRAHAM, J. R. (1967). A Q-sort study of the accuracy of clinical descriptions based on the MMPI. *Journal of Psychiatric Research, 5,* 297–305.

GRAHAM, J. R. (1970). *Explicit hypothesis formulation and the learning of clinical inference from the MMPI.* Unpublished manuscript, Kent State University.

GRAHAM, J. R. (1971). Feedback and accuracy of clinical judgments from the MMPI. *Journal of Consulting and Clinical Psychology, 36,* 286–291.

GRAHAM, J. R. (1977). *The MMPI: A practical guide.* New York: Oxford.

GRAHAM, J. R. (1978). The Minnesota Multiphasic Personality Inventory (MMPI). In B. B. Wolman (Ed.). *Clinical diagnosis of mental disorders.* New York: Plenum.

GRAHAM, J. R., & McCORD, G. (1982). *Correlates of "normal range" MMPI scores for nonclinical subjects.* Paper presented at 17th Annual Symposium on Recent Developments in the Use of the MMPI. Tampa, Fla.

GRAHAM, J. R., SCHROEDER, H. E., & LILLY, R. S. (1971). Factor analyses of items on the social introversion and masculinity-femininity scales of the MMPI. *Journal of Clinical Psychology, 27,* 367–370.

GRAZIANO, W. G., VARCA, P. E., & LEVY, J. C. (1982). Race of examiner effects and the validity of intelligence tests. *Review of Educational Research, 52,* 469–498.

GREEN, B. F., JR. (1978). In defense of measurement. *American Psychologist, 33,* 664–670.

GREENSPOON, J., & GERSTEN, C. D. (1967). A new look at psychological testing from the standpoint of a behaviorist. *American Psychologist, 22,* 843–853.

GREGORY, R., & MORRIS, L. (1978). Adjective correlates for women on the CPI scales: A replication. *Journal of Personality Assessment, 42,* 258–264.

GRIGG, A. E. (1958). Experience of clinicians and speech characteristics and statements of clients as variables in clinical judgment. *Journal of Consulting Psychology, 22,* 315–319.

GROSS, A. L., & SU, W. (1975). Defining a "fair" or "unbiased" selection model: A question of utilities. *Journal of Applied Psychology, 60,* 345–351.

GROSS, L. R. (1959). Effects of verbal and nonverbal reinforcement in the Rorschach. *Journal of Consulting Psychology, 23,* 66–68.

GROSS, M. (1962). *The brain watchers.* New York: Random House.

GROSS, W. F., & NERVIANO, V. J. (1973). The prediction of dropouts from an inpatient alcoholism program by objective personality inventories. *Quarterly Journal of Studies on Alcohol, 34,* 514–515.

GUERTIN, W. H., LADD, C. E., FRANK, G. H., RABIN, A. I., & HIESTER, D. S. (1966). Research with the Wechsler intelligence scales for adults: 1960–1965. *Psychological Bulletin, 66,* 385–409.

GUERTIN, W. H., LADD, C. E., FRANK, G. H., RABIN, A. I., & HIESTER, D. S. (1971). Research with the Wechsler intelligence scales for adults: 1965–1970. *The Psychological Record, 21,* 289–339.

GUERTIN, W. H., RABIN, A. I., FRANK, G. H., & LADD, C. E. (1962). Research with the Wechsler intelligence scales for adults: 1955–1960. *Psychological Bulletin, 59,* 1–26.

GUILFORD, J. P. (1954). *Psychometric methods* (2nd ed.). New York: McGraw-Hill.

GUILFORD, J. P. (1967). *The nature of human intelligence.* New York: McGraw-Hill.

GUILFORD, J. P., & HOEPFNER, R. (1971). *The analysis of intelligence.* New York: McGraw-Hill.

GUILFORD, J. P., & ZIMMERMAN, W. S. (1949). *The Guilford Temperament Survey: Manual of instructions.* Beverly Hills, Calif.: Sheridan Supply.

GUION, R. (1966). Employment tests and discriminatory hiring. *Industrial Relations, 5,* 20–37.

GUION, R. (1978). "Content validity" in moderation. *Personnel Psychology, 31,* 205–214.

GULLIKSEN, H. (1950). *Theory of mental tests.* New York: Wiley.

GUSSETT, J. C. (1974). College Entrance Examination Board Scholastic Aptitude Test scores as a predictor for college mathematics grades. *Educational and Psychological Measurement, 34,* 953–954.

GUTHRIE, G. M. (1949). *A study of the personality characteristics associated with the disorders encountered by an internist.* Unpublished doctoral dissertation, University of Minnesota.

GUTKIN, T. B. (1979). Brief reports on the WISC-R: III. WISC-R scatter indices: Useful information for differential diagnosis? *Journal of School Psychology, 17,* 368–371.

GUTKIN, T., & REYNOLDS, C. R. (1980). Factorial similarity of the WISC-R for Anglos and Chicanos referred for psychological services. *Journal of School Psychology, 18,* 34–39.

GYNTHER, M. D. (1979). Ethnicity and personality: An update. In J. N. Butcher (Ed.). *New developments in the use of the MMPI.* Minneapolis: University of Minnesota Press.

GYNTHER, M. D., ALTMAN, H., & SLETTEN, I.

W. (1973). Replicated correlates of MMPI two-point code types: The Missouri Actuarial system. *Journal of Clinical Psychology, 29,* 263–289.

GYNTHER, M. D. & GREEN, S. B. (1980). Accuracy may make a difference, but does a difference make for accuracy? *Journal of Consulting and Clinical Psychology, 48,* 268–272.

GYNTHER, M. D., & GYNTHER, R. A. (1976). Personality inventories. In I. B. Weiner (Ed.). *Clinical methods in psychology.* New York: Wiley.

HALE, R. L. (1978). The WISC-R as a predictor of WRAT performance. *Psychology in the Schools, 15,* 172–175.

HALE, R. L. (1979). The utility of WISC-R subtest scores in discriminating among adequate and underachieving children. *Multivariate Behavioral Research, 14,* 245–253.

HALE, R. L., & LANDINO, S. A. (1981). Utility of WISC-R subtest analysis in discriminating among groups of conduct problem, withdrawn, mixed, and nonproblem boys. *Journal of Consulting and Clinical Psychology, 49,* 91–95.

HALL, V. C., & KAYE, D. B. (1977). Patterns of early cognitive development among boys in four subcultural groups. *Journal of Educational Psychology, 69,* 66–87.

HALL, W. B., & MacKINNON, D. W. (1969). Personality inventory correlates of creativity among architects. *Journal of Applied Psychology, 53,* 322–326.

HALPIN, G., HALPIN, G., & HAUF, B. (1976). Incremental validity of the ACT test battery for predicting success in a school of nursing over a 10-year period. *Educational and Psychological Measurement, 36,* 433–437.

HALPIN, G., HALPIN, G., & SCHAER, B. B. (1981). Relative effectiveness of the California Achievement Tests in comparison with the ACT Assessment, College Board Scholastic Aptitude Test, and high school grade point average in predicting college grade point average. *Educational and Psychological Measurement, 41,* 821–827.

HAMBLETON, R. K., SWAMINATHAN, H., ALGINA, J., & COULSON, D. B. (1978). Criterion-referenced testing and measurement: A review of technical issues and developments. *Review of Educational Research, 48,* 1–47.

HAMBURG, D. A., ELLIOTT, G. R., & PARRON, D. L., (EDS.) (1982). *Health and behavior: Frontiers of research in the biobehavioral sciences.* Washington, D.C.: National Academy Press.

HAMM, H. A., & EVANS, J. G. (1978). WISC-R subtest patterns of severely emotionally

disturbed students. *Psychology in the Schools, 15,* 188–190.

HANEY, W. (1981). Validity, vaudeville, and values: A short history of social concerns over standardized testing. *American Psychologist, 36,* 1021–1034.

HANNA, G. S. (1974). Review of the Differential Aptitude Tests. *Journal of Educational Measurement, 11,* 145–149.

HARGADON, F. (1981). Tests and college admissions. *American Psychologist, 36,* 1112–1119.

HARMAN, H. (1976). *Modern factor analysis* (3rd ed.). Chicago: University of Chicago Press.

HARPER, F. B. (1975). The validity of some alternative measures of achievement motivation. *Educational and Psychological Measurement, 35,* 905–909.

HARRIS, D. B. (1963). *Children's drawings as measures of intellectual maturity: A revision and extension of the Goodenough Draw-a-Man Test.* New York: Harcourt Brace Jovanovich, Inc.

HARRIS, S., & MASLING, J. (1970). Examiner sex, subject sex, and Rorschach productivity. *Journal of Consulting and Clinical Psychology, 34,* 60–63.

HARRISON, K. A., & WIEBE, M. J. (1977). Correlational study of McCarthy, WISC, and Stanford-Binet Scales. *Perceptual and Motor Skills, 44,* 63–68.

HARRISON, P. L. (1981). Mercer's Adaptive Behavior Inventory, the McCarthy Scales, and dental development as predictors of first-grade achievement. *Journal of Educational Psychology, 73,* 78–82.

HARRISON, P. L., KAUFMAN, A. S., & NAGLIERI, J. A. (1980). Subtest patterns and recategorized groupings of the McCarthy Scales for EMR children. *American Journal of Mental Deficiency, 85,* 129–134.

HARRISON, P. L., & NAGLIERI, J. A. (1978). Extrapolated general cognitive indexes on the McCarthy Scales for gifted and mentally retarded children. *Psychological Reports, 43,* 1291–1296.

HARTLAGE, L. C., LUCAS, T. L., & GODWIN, A. (1976). Culturally biased and culture-fair tests correlated with school performance in culturally disadvantaged children. *Journal of Clinical Psychology, 32,* 658–660.

HARTLAGE, L. C., & STEELE, C. T. (1977). WISC and WISC-R correlates of academic achievement. *Psychology in the Schools, 14,* 15–18.

HARTNETT, R., & FELDMESSER, D. (1980, March).

College admissions testing and the myth of selectivity: Unresolved questions and needed research. *AAHE Bulletin, 32* (7). Washington, D.C.: American Association for Higher Education.

HASE, H. D., & GOLDBERG, L. R. (1967). The comparative validity of different strategies of devising personality inventory scales. *Psychological Bulletin, 67,* 231–248.

HATHAWAY, S. R., & McKINLEY, J. C. (1940). A multiphasic personality schedule (Minnesota): I. Construction of the schedule. *Journal of Psychology, 10,* 249–254.

HATHAWAY, S. R., & McKINLEY, J. C. (1967). *Manual for the Minnesota Multiphasic Personality Inventory.* New York: Psychological Corporation.

HATHAWAY, S. R., & MEEHL, P. E. (1952). *Adjective check list correlates of MMPI scores.* Unpublished materials, University of Minnesota.

HATHAWAY, S. R., & MONACHESI, E. D. (1963). *Adolescent personality and behavior: MMPI patterns of normal, delinquent, dropout, and other outcomes.* Minneapolis: University of Minnesota Press.

HAYNES, S. M. (1978). *Principles of behavioral assessment.* New York: Gardner Press.

HEATH, D. H. (1977). Academic predictors of adult maturity and competence. *Journal of Higher Education, 48,* 613–632.

HEBB, D. O. (1949). *The organization of behavior.* New York: Wiley.

HEIL, J., BARCLAY, A., & ENDRES, J. M. (1978). A factor analytic study of WPPSI scores of educationally deprived and normal children. *Psychological Reports, 42,* 727–730.

HEILBRUN, A. B. (1961). Male and female personality correlates of early termination in counseling. *Journal of Counseling Psychology, 8,* 31–36.

HEILBRUN, A. B. (1972). The Edwards Personal Preference Schedule. In O. K. Buros (Ed.). *Seventh mental measurements yearbook.* Highland Park, N.J.: Gryphon.

HEILBRUN, A. B., & GOODSTEIN, L. D. (1961). Social desirability response set: Error or predictor variable? *Journal of Psychology, 51,* 321–329.

HELSON, R., & CRUTCHFIELD, R. S. (1970). Mathematicians: The creative researchers and the average Ph.D. *Journal of Consulting and Clinical Psychology, 34,* 250–257.

HENDERSON, R. W., & RANKIN, R. J. (1973). WPPSI reliability and predictive validity with disadvantaged Mexican-American children. *Journal of School Psychology, 11,* 16–20.

HENNING, J. J., & LEVY, R. H. (1967). Verbal-Performance IQ differences of white and Negro delinquents on the WISC and WAIS. *Journal of Clinical Psychology, 23,* 164–168.

HENRICHS, T. F. (1964). Objective configural rules for discriminating MMPI profiles in a psychiatric population. *Journal of Clinical Psychology, 20,* 157–159.

HERR, W. S. (1969). The natural history of a behavior modification program. *Newsletter of the Association for Advancement of Behavior Therapy, 4,* 11–12.

HERRNSTEIN, R. J. (1971). I.Q. *Atlantic Monthly, 228,* 43–64.

HERSEN, M. (1971). Fear scale norms for an inpatient population. *Journal of Clinical Psychology, 27,* 375–378.

HERTZ, M. R. (1938). Scoring the Rorschach inkblot test. *Journal of Genetic Psychology, 52,* 16–64.

HESS, A. K., & NEVILLE, D. (1977). Testwiseness: Some evidence for the effect of personality testing on subsequent test results. *Journal of Personality Assessment, 41,* 170–177.

HEYNES, R., & LIPPITT, R. (1954). Systematic observational techniques. In G. Lindzey (Ed.). *Handbook of social psychology.* Vol. 1. Cambridge, Mass.: Addison-Wesley.

HICKS, L. E. (1970). Some properties of ipsative, normative, and forced-choice normative measures. *Psychological Bulletin, 74,* 167–184.

HILER, E. W., & NESVIG, D. (1965). An evaluation of criteria used by clinicians to infer pathology from figure drawings. *Journal of Consulting Psychology, 29,* 520–529.

HILLS, J. R. (1978). ACT assessment. In O. K. Buros (Ed.). *Eighth mental measurements yearbook.* Highland Park, N.J.: Gryphon.

HIMELSTEIN, P. (1966). Research with the Stanford-Binet, Form L-M: The first five years. *Psychological Bulletin, 65,* 156–164.

HIRSHOREN, A., & KAVALE, K. (1976). Profile analysis of the WISC-R: A continuing malpractice. *The Exceptional Child, 23,* 83–87.

HIRT, M. L., & KAPLAN, M. L. (1967). Psychological testing: II. Current practice. *Comprehensive Psychiatry, 8,* 310–320.

HISKEY, M. S. (1966). *Hiskey-Nebraska Test of Learning Aptitudes: Manual.* Lincoln, Neb.: Union College Press.

HODAPP, A. F., & HODAPP, J. B. (1980). Correlation of the PPVT and WISC-R: A function of diagnostic category. *Psychology in the Schools, 17,* 33–36.

HOFFMAN, B. (1962). *The tyranny of testing.* New York: Collier.

HOFFMAN, H. (1970). Personality patterns of depression and its relation to acquiesence. *Psychological Reports, 26,* 459–464.

HOFFMAN, H. (1971). Personality changes of hospitalized alcoholics after treatment. *Psychological Reports, 29,* 948–950.

HOGAN, R. (1972). Review of Study of Values. In O. K. Buros (Ed.). *Seventh mental measurements yearbook.* Highland Park, N.J.: Gryphon.

HOGAN, R. (1978). Personality Research Form. In O. K. Buros (Ed.). *Eighth mental measurements yearbook.* Highland Park, N.J.: Gryphon.

HOGE, D. R., & BENDER, I. E. (1974). Factors influencing value change among college graduates in adult life. *Journal of Personality and Social Psychology, 29,* 572–585.

HOLLAND, J. L. (1959). A theory of vocational choice. *Journal of Counseling Psychology, 6,* 35–45.

HOLLAND, J. L. (1973). *Making vocational choices: A theory of careers.* Englewood Cliffs, N.J.: Prentice-Hall.

HOLLENBECK, G. P., & KAUFMAN, A. S. (1973). Factor analysis of the Wechsler Preschool and Primary Scale of Intelligence (WPPSI). *Journal of Clinical Psychology, 29,* 41–45.

HOLLINGSWORTH, H. L. (1922). *Judging human character.* New York: Appleton.

HOLYROD, K., & KAHN, M. (1974). Personality factors in student drug use. *Journal of Consulting and Clinical Psychology, 42,* 236–243.

HOLT, R. R. (1958). Clinical and statistical prediction: A reformulation and some new data. *Journal of Abnormal and Social Psychology, 56,* 1–12.

HOLT, R. R. (1978). *Methods in clinical psychology: Vol. 1. Projective assessments.* New York: Plenum.

HOLTZMAN, W. H., THORPE, J. S., SWARTZ, J. D., & HERRON, E. W. (1961). *Inkblot perception and personality: Holtzman inkblot technique.* Austin: University of Texas Press.

HONINGFELD, G., GILLIS, R. D., & KLETT, C. J. (1966). NOSIE-30: A treatment sensitive ward behavior scale. *Psychological Reports, 19,* 180–182.

HONZIK, M. P., MacFARLANE, J. W., & ALLEN, L. (1948). The stability of mental test performance between two and eighteen years. *Journal of Experimental Education, 17,* 309–324.

HOPKINS, K. D., & STANELY, J. C. (1981). *Educational and psychological measurement* (6th ed.). Englewood Cliffs, N.J.: Prentice-Hall.

HORN, J. L., & KNAPP, J. R., (1973). On the subjective character of the empirical base of Guilford's structure-of-intellect model. *Psychological Bulletin, 80,* 33–43.

HORNER, T. M. (1980). Test-retest and home-clinic characteristics of the Bayley Scales of Infant Development in nine- and fifteen-month-old infants. *Child Development, 51,* 751–758.

HOUTS, P. L. (1975). Standardized testing in America, II. *The National Elementary Principal, 54,* 2–3.

HOUTS, P. L. (ED.). (1977). *The myth of measurability.* New York: Hart.

HOVEY, H. B. (1953). MMPI profiles and personality characteristics. *Journal of Consulting Psychology, 17,* 142–146.

HOYT, D. P. (1966). College grades and adult accomplishments: A review of research. *Educational Record, 47,* 70–75.

HUBBLE, L. M. (1978). Comparability and equivalence of estimates of IQs from Revised Beta Examination and Wechsler Adult Intelligence Scale among older male delinquents. *Psychological Reports, 42,* 1030.

HUMM, D. G., & WADSWORTH, G. W. (1935). The Humm-Wadsworth Temperament Scale. *American Journal of Psychiatry, 92,* 163–200.

HUMPHREYS, L. G. (1974). The misleading distinction between aptitude and achievement tests. In D. R. Green (Ed.). *The aptitude-achievement distinction.* Monterey, Calif.: CTB/McGraw Hill.

HUNT, E. (1976). Varieties of cognitive power. In L. B. Resnick (Ed.). *The nature of intelligence.* Hillsdale, N.J.: Erlbaum.

HUNT, W. A., WITTSON, C. L., & HUNT, E. B. (1953). A theoretical and practical analysis of the diagnostic process. In P. H. Koch & J. Zubin (Eds.). *Current problems in psychiatric diagnosis.* New York: Grune & Stratton.

HUNTER, J. E. & SCHMIDT, F. L. (1976). A critical analysis of the statistical and ethical implications of various definitions of test "bias." *Psychological Bulletin, 83,* 1053–1071.

HUNTER, J. E., SCHMIDT, F. L. & HUNTER, R. (1979). Differential validity of employment tests by race: A comprehensive review and analysis. *Psychological Bulletin, 86,* 721–735.

HUTTON, J. (1969). Practice effects on intelligence and school readiness tests for preschool children. *Training School Bulletin, 65,* 130–134.

INGLE, R. B., & DE AMICO, G. (1969). The effect of physical conditions of the test room on standardized achievement test scores. *Journal of Educational Measurement, 6,* 237–240.

INSTITUTE FOR PERSONALITY AND ABILITY TESTING (1972). *Manual for the 16PF.* Champaign, Ill.: Author.

INSTITUTE FOR PERSONALITY AND ABILITY TESTING (1973a). *Measuring Intelligence with the Culture Fair Tests: Manual for Scales 2 and 3.* Champaign, Ill.: Author.

INSTITUTE FOR PERSONALITY AND ABILITY TESTING (1973b). *Technical supplement for the Culture Fair Intelligence Tests: Scales 2 and 3.* Champaign, Ill.: Author.

IRONSON, G. H. (1982). Use of chi-square and latent trait approaches for detecting item bias. In R. A. Berk (Ed.). *Handbook of methods for detecting test bias.* Baltimore: The Johns Hopkins University Press.

IRVINE, S. H. (1969). Figural tests of reasoning in Africa: Studies in the use of Raven's Progressive Matrices across cultures. *International Journal of Psychology, 4,* 217–228.

IVIMY, J. K., & TAYLOR, R. L. (1980). Differential performance of learning disabled and non-learning disabled children on the McCarthy Scales, WISC-R, and WRAT. *Journal of Clinical Psychology, 36,* 960–963.

IWANICKI, E. F. (1980). A new generation of standardized achievement test batteries: A profile of their major features. *Journal of Educational Measurement, 17,* 155–162.

JACKSON, D. N. (1967). *Personality Research Form manual* (reprinted 1974). Goshen, N.Y.: Research Psychologists Press.

JACKSON, D. N. (1970). A sequential system for personality scale development. In C. D. Speilberger (Ed.). *Current topics in clinical and community psychology* (Vol. 2). New York: Academic Press.

JACKSON, D. N. (1976). *Jackson Personality Inventory manual.* Goshen, N.Y.: Research Psychologists Press.

JASTAK, J., BIJOU, S., & JASTAK, S. (1976). *The Wide Range Achievement Test.* Wilmington: Guidance Associates of Delaware.

JENKINS, C. D., ZYZANSKI, S. J., & ROSENMAN, R. H. (1979). *Jenkins Activity Survey manual.* New York: Psychological Corporation.

JENSEN, A. R. (1969). How much can we boost IQ and scholastic achievement? *Harvard Educational Review, 39,* 1–123.

JENSEN, A. R. (1972). *Genetics and education.* New York: Harper & Row.

JENSEN, A. R. (1980). *Bias in mental testing.* New York: The Free Press.

JOESTING, J. (1977). Test-retest correlations for the State-Trait Anxiety Inventory. *Psychological Reports, 40,* 671–672.

JOHANSSON, C. B., & CAMPBELL, D. P. (1971). Stability of the Strong Vocational Interest Blank for Men. *Journal of Applied Psychology, 55,* 34–36.

JOHNSON, J. (1976). *Albemarle Paper Company vs. Moody:* The aftermath of *Griggs* and the death of employee testing. *Hastings Law Journal, 28,* 1239–1262.

JOHNSON, R. W. (1976). Review of the Strong-Campbell Interest Inventory. *Measurement and Evaluation in Guidance, 9,* 40–45.

JONES, L. V. (1949). A factor analysis of the Stanford-Binet at four age levels. *Psychometrika, 14,* 299–331.

JONES, L. V. (1954). Primary abilities in the Stanford-Binet, age 13. *Journal of Genetic Psychology, 84,* 125–147.

JONES, L. V. (1981). Achievement test scores in mathematics and science. *Science, 213,* 412–416.

JONES, N. F. (1969). The validity of clinical judgments of schizophrenic pathology based on verbal responses to intelligence test items. *Journal of Clinical Psychology, 15,* 396–400.

JORDAN, J. E., & FELTY, J. (1968). Factors associated with intellectual variation among visually impaired children. *American Foundation for the Blind Research Bulletin, 15,* 61–70.

KAGAN, J. (1956). The measurement of overt aggression from fantasy. *Journal of Abnormal and Social Psychology, 52,* 390–393.

KAMIN, L. J. (1974). *The science and politics of I.Q.* Hillsdale, N.J.: Erlbaum.

KANFER, F. H., & SASLOW, G. (1969). Behavioral analysis: An alternative to diagnostic classification. *Archives of General Psychiatry, 12,* 529–538.

KANGAS, J., & BRADWAY, K. (1971). Intelligence at middle-age: A thirty-eight year follow up. *Developmental Psychology, 5,* 333–337.

KAPLAN, M. F., & ERON, L. K. (1965). Test sophistication and faking in the TAT situation. *Journal of Projective Techniques, 29,* 498–503.

KAPLAN, R. M. (1982). Nader's raid on the testing industry: Is it in the best interest of the consumer? *American Psychologist, 37,* 15–23.

KAPLAN, R. M., & SACCUZZO, D. P. (1982). *Psychological testing: Principles, applications, and issues.* Monterey, Calif.: Brooks/Cole.

KARNES, F. A., & BROWN, K. E. (1980). Factor analysis of the WISC-R for the gifted. *Journal of Educational Psychology, 72,* 197–199.

KARSON, S., & FREUD, S. L. (1956). Predicting diagnoses with the MMPI. *Journal of Clinical Psychology, 12,* 376–379.

KARSON, S., & O'DELL, J. W. (1976). *A guide to the clinical use of the 16 PF.* Champaign, Ill.: Institute for Personality and Ability Testing.

KATAGUCHI, Y., & MATSUOKA, M. (1979). Basic research on the Water Association Test (WAT). *Proceedings of the Japanese Psychological Association 43rd Annual Convention,* Tokyo, p. 629.

KATKIN, E. S. (1978). Review of the State-Trait Anxiety Inventory. In O. K. Buros (Ed.). *Eighth mental measurements yearbook.* Highland Park, N.J.: Gryphon.

KATOFF, L. (1978, August). The development and evaluation of the KID scale. *Dissertation Abstracts International,* Vol. 39, Section B, Issue No. 2, 98.

KATOFF, L., & REUTER, J. (1979). A listing of infant tests. *Catalog of Selected Documents in Psychology, 9,* 56.

KATOFF, L., & REUTER, J. (1980). Review of developmental screening tests for infants. *Journal of Clinical Child Psychology, 9,* 30–34.

KATOFF, L., REUTER, J., & DUNN, V. (1979). *The Kent Infant Development Scale manual.* Kent, Ohio: Kent State University.

KAUFMAN, A. S. (1973a). Comparison of the WPPSI, Stanford-Binet, and McCarthy Scales as predictors of first-grade achievement. *Perceptual and Motor Skills, 36,* 67–73.

KAUFMAN, A. S. (1973b). The relationship of WPPSI IQs to SES and other background variables. *Journal of Clinical Psychology, 29,* 354–357.

KAUFMAN, A. S. (1975a). Factor analysis of the WISC-R at eleven age levels between 6½ and 16½ years. *Journal of Consulting and Clinical Psychology, 43,* 135–147.

KAUFMAN, A. S. (1975b). Factor structure of the McCarthy at five age levels between 2½ and 8½. *Educational and Psychological Measurement, 35,* 641–656.

KAUFMAN, A. S. (1975c). Note on interpreting profiles of McCarthy Scale indexes. *Perceptual and Motor Skills, 4,* 262.

KAUFMAN, A. S. (1976a). Do normal children have "flat" ability profiles? *Psychology in the Schools, 13,* 284–285.

KAUFMAN, A. S. (1976b). Verbal-Performance IQ discrepancies on the WISC-R. *Journal of Consulting and Clinical Psychology, 44,* 739–744.

KAUFMAN, A. S. (1978). The importance of basic concepts in the individual assessment of preschool children. *Journal of School Psychology, 16,* 207–211.

KAUFMAN, A. S. (1979a). *Intelligent testing with the WISC-R.* New York: Wiley.

KAUFMAN, A. S. (1979b). WISC-R research: Implications for interpretation. *School Psychology Digest, 8,* 5–27.

KAUFMAN, A. S., & HOLLENBECK, G. P. (1973). Factor analysis of the standardization edition of the McCarthy Scales. *Journal of Clinical Psychology, 29,* 358–362.

KAUFMAN, A. S., & KAUFMAN, N. L. (1975). Social-class on the McCarthy Scales for black and white children. *Perceptual and Motor Skills, 41,* 205–206.

KAUFMAN, A. S., & KAUFMAN, N. L. (1977a). *Clinical evaluation of young children with the McCarthy Scales.* New York: Grune & Stratton.

KAUFMAN, A. S., & KAUFMAN, N. L. (1977b). Research on the McCarthy Scales and its implications for assessment. *Journal of Learning Disabilities, 10,* 284–291.

KAUFMAN, A. S., & VAN HAGEN, J. (1977). Investigation of the WISC-R for use with retarded children: Correlation with the 1972 Stanford-Binet and comparison of WISC and WISC-R profiles. *Psychology in the Schools, 14,* 10–14.

KAUFMAN, A. S., ZALMA, R., & KAUFMAN, N. L. (1978). The relationship of hand dominance to the motor coordination, mental ability, and right-left awareness of young normal children. *Child Development, 49,* 885–888.

KAUFMAN, N. L., & KAUFMAN, A. S. (1974). Comparison of normal and minimally brain dysfunctioned children on the McCarthy Scales of Children's Abilities. *Journal of Clinical Psychology, 30,* 69–72.

KAVALE, K. (1981). Functions of the Illinois Test of Psycholinguistic Abilities (ITPA): Are they trainable? *Exceptional Children, 47,* 496–510.

KEEHN, J. D., BLOOMFIELD, F. F., & HUG, M. A. (1970). Uses of the Reinforcement Survey Schedule with alcoholics. *Quarterly Journal of Studies on Alcohol, 31,* 602–615.

KELLEY, E. L. (1967). *Assessment of human characteristics.* Belmont, Calif.: Brooks/Cole.

KELLY, E. L., & FISKE, D. W. (1951). *The predic-*

tion of performance in clinical psychology. Ann Arbor: University of Michigan Press.

KELLY, J. A., FURMAN, W., & YOUNG, V. (1978). Problems associated with the typological measurement of sex roles and androgyny. *Journal of Consulting and Clinical Psychology, 46,* 1574–1576.

KELLY, J. A., & WORELL, J. (1977). New formulations of sex roles and androgyny. *Journal of Consulting and Clinical Psychology, 45,* 1101–1115.

KELLEY, T. L. (1927). *Interpretation of educational measurements.* Chicago, Ill.: World Book Company.

KENDALL, P. C., FINCH, A. J., JR., AUERBACH, S. M., HOOKE, J. F., & MIKULA, P. J. (1976). The State-Trait Anxiety Inventory: A systematic evaluation. *Journal of Consulting and Clinical Psychology, 44,* 406–412.

KENDALL, P. C., & LITTLE, V. L. (1977). Correspondence of brief intelligence measures to the Wechsler scales with delinquents. *Journal of Consulting and Clinical Psychology, 45,* 660–666.

KENDALL, P. C., & NORTON-FORD, J. D. (1982). *Clinical psychology: Scientific and professional dimensions.* New York: Wiley.

KENDRICK, D. C., & POST, F. (1967). Differences in cognitive status between healthy, psychiatrically ill, and diffusely brain-damaged elderly subjects. *British Journal of Psychiatry, 113,* 75–81.

KENNEDY, W. A., VAN DE REIT, V., & WHITE, J. C. (1963). A normative sample of intelligence and achievement of Negro elementary school children in the southeastern United States. *Monographs of the Society for Research in Child Development, 28,* No. 6.

KENNY, D. T., & BIJOU, S. W. (1953). Ambiguity of pictures and extent of personality factors in fantasy responses. *Journal of Consulting Psychology, 17,* 283–288.

KENT, R. N., & FOSTER, S. L. (1977). Direct observational procedures: Methodological issues in naturalistic settings. In A. R. Ciminero, K. S. Calhoun, and H. E. Adams (Eds.). *Handbook of behavioral assessment.* New York: Wiley.

KENT, R. N., O'LEARY, K. D., DIAMENT, C., & DIETZ, A. (1974). Expectation biases in observational evaluation of therapeutic change. *Journal of Consulting and Clinical Psychology, 42,* 774–780.

KING, A. D. (1978). Minnesota Multiphasic Personality Inventory. In O. K. Buros (Ed.). *Eighth mental measurements yearbook.* Highland Park, N.J.: Gryphon.

KIRCHNER, J. H., & HOGAN, R. A. (1972). Values of college seniors enrolled in teacher preparation four to five years later. *Psychology in the Schools, 9,* 79–83.

KIRK, S. A., & KIRK, W. D. (1971). *Psycholinguistic learning disabilities: Diagnosis and remediation.* Urbana: University of Illinois Press.

KIRK, S. A., & KIRK, W. D. (1978). Uses and abuses of the ITPA. *Journal of Speech and Hearing Disorders, 43,* 58–75.

KLEIN, A. E. (1979). Further evidence on the redundancy of the Stanford Achievement Test. *Educational and Psychological Measurement, 39,* 1061–1065.

KLEINBAUM, D. G., & KUPPER, L. L. (1978). *Applied regression analysis and other multivariable methods.* North Scituate, Mass.: Duxbury Press.

KLEINKNECHT, R. A., McCORMICK, C. E., & THORNDIKE, R. M. (1973). Stability of stated reinforcers as measured by the Reinforcement Survey Schedule. *Behavior Therapy, 4,* 407–413.

KLEINMUNTZ, B. (1963). MMPI decision rules for the identification of college maladjustment: A digital computer approach. *Psychological Monographs, 77,* 14 (Whole No. 577).

KLEINMUNTZ, B. (1967). *Personality measurement: An introduction.* Homewood, Ill.: Dorsey.

KLINEGELHOFER, E. L. (1967). Performance of Tanzanian secondary pupils on the Raven Standard Progressive Matrices Test. *Journal of Social Psychology, 72,* 205–215.

KLOPFER, B., & KELLY, D. (1942). *The Rorschach technique.* Yonkers-on-Hudson, N.Y.: World Book.

KLOPFER, W. G., & TAULBEE, E. S. (1976). Projective tests. In M. R. Rosensweig & L. W. Porter (Eds.). *Annual review of psychology.* Palo Alto, Calif.: Annual Reviews.

KNOBLOCH, H., & PASAMANICK, B. (1974). *Gesell and Amatruda's developmental diagnosis: The evaluation and management of normal and abnormal neuropsychologic development in infancy and early childhood* (3rd ed.). New York: Harper & Row.

KORCHIN, S. J. (1976). *Modern clinical psychology: Principles of intervention in the clinic and community.* New York: Basic Books.

KORCHIN, S. J., MITCHELL, H. E., & MELTZOFF, J. (1950). A critical evaluation of the Thompson Thematic Apperception Test. *Journal of Projective Techniques, 14,* 445–452.

KOSTLAN, A. A. (1954). A method for the empirical study of psychodiagnosis. *Journal of Consulting Psychology, 18,* 83–88.

KRAMER, M. S., ROOKS, Y., & PEARSON,

H. A. (1978). Growth and development in children with sickle-cell trait: A prospective study of matched pairs. *New England Journal of Medicine, 299*, 686–689.

KUBEY, R. W. (1979). Radiation and decline of scholastic aptitude scores. *Psychological Reports, 45*, 862.

KUDER, F., & DIAMOND, E. F. (1979). *Kuder DD Occupational Interest Survey: General manual* (2nd ed.). Chicago: Science Research Associates.

KUDER, G. F., & RICHARDSON, M. W. (1937). The theory of the estimation of test reliability. *Psychometrika, 2*, 151–160.

KUSYSZYN, I. (1968). A comparison of judgmental methods with endorsements in the assessment of personality traits. *Journal of Applied Psychology, 52*, 227–233.

KWIATKOWSKA, H. (1967). Family art therapy. *Family Process, 6*, 37–55.

KYLE, J. G. (1977). Raven's Progressive Matrices: 30 years later. *Bulletin of the British Psychological Society, 30*, 406–407.

LACHAR, D., KLINGE, V., & GRISELL, J. L. (1976). Relative accuracy of automatic MMPI narratives generated from adult norm, and adolescent norm profiles. *Journal of Consulting and Clinical Psychology, 44*, 20–24.

LAH, M. I., & ROTTER, J. B. (1981). Changing college student norms on the Rotter Incomplete Sentences Blank. *Journal of Consulting and Clinical Psychology, 49*, 985.

LAMBERT, N. M. (1981). Psychological evidence in *Larry P. v. Wilson Riles:* An evaluation by a witness for the defense. *American Psychologist, 36*, 937–952.

LANG, P. J., & LAZOVIK, A. D. (1963). Experimental desensitization of a phobia. *Journal of Abnormal and Social Psychology, 66*, 519–525.

LANG, P. J., LAZOVIK, A. D., & REYNOLDS, D. J. (1965). Desensitization, suggestibility, and pseudotherapy. *Journal of Abnormal Psychology, 70*, 395–402.

LANGLEY, M. B. (1978-79). Psychoeducational assessment of the multiply handicapped blind child: Issues and methods. *Education of the Visually Handicapped, 10*, 97–114.

LANYON, R. I. (1968). *A handbook of MMPI group profiles.* Minneapolis: University of Minnesota Press.

LANYON, R. I., & GOODSTEIN, L. D. (1971). *Personality assessment* (rev. ed. 1982). New York: Wiley.

LARSON, J. R., & SCONTRINO, M. P. (1976). The consistency of high school grade point average

and of the verbal and mathematical portions of the Scholastic Aptitude Test of the College Entrance Examination Board, as predictors of college performance. *Educational and Psychological Measurement, 36*, 439–443.

LASKOWITZ, D. (1959). *The effect of varied degrees of pictorial ambiguity on fantasy evocation.* Unpublished doctoral dissertation, New York University.

LAWLIS, G. F., STEDMAN, J. M., & CORTNER, R. H. (1980). Factor analysis of the WISC-R for a sample of bilingual Mexican-Americans. *Journal of Clinical Child Psychology, 9*, 57–58.

LEARY, T., LaFORGE, R., & SUCZEK, R. (1956). *Interpersonal Check List manual.* Cambridge, Mass.: Psychological Consultation Service.

LEDVINKA, J., & SCHOENFELDT, L. F. (1978). Legal developments in employment testing: *Albermarle* and beyond. *Personnel Psychology, 31*, 1–13.

LEFKOWITZ, J. (1980). Pros and cons of "truth in testing" legislation. *Personnel Psychology, 33*, 17–24.

LEHMAN, I. J. (1975). The Stanford Achievement Test Series—1973. *Journal of Educational Measurement, 12*, 297–306.

LENNING, O. T., & MAXEY, E. J. (1973). ACT versus SAT prediction for present-day colleges and students. *Educational and Psychological Measurement, 33*, 397–406.

LEONARD, J. B. (1977). A therapist's duty to potential victims. *Law and Human Behavior, 1*, 309–317.

LERNER, B. (1980a). The war on testing: David, Goliath, and Gallup. *Public Interest, 60*, 119–147.

LERNER, B. (1980b). The war on testing: Detroit Edison in perspective. *Personnel Psychology, 33*, 11–16.

LEVENSON, R. L., & ZINO, T. C. (1979a). Assessment of cognitive deficiency with the McCarthy Scales and Stanford-Binet: A correlational analysis. *Perceptual and Motor Skills, 48*, 291–295.

LEVENSON, R. L., & ZINO, T. C. (1979b). Using McCarthy Scales extrapolated general cognitive indexes below 50: Some words of caution. *Psychological Reports, 45*, 350.

LEVINE, E. S. (1974). Psychological tests and practices with the deaf: A survey of the state of the art. *Volta Review, 76*, 298–319.

LEVITT, E. E., & TRUUMAA, A. (1972). *The Rorschach technique with children and adolescents: Application and norms.* New York: Grune & Stratton.

LEWANDOWSKI, D., & GRAHAM, J. R. (1972). Empirical correlates of frequently occurring two-point MMPI code types: A replicated study. *Journal of Consulting and Clinical Psychology, 39,* 467–472.

LEWINSOHN, P. M. (1965). Psychological correlates of overall quality of figure drawings. *Journal of Consulting Psychology, 29,* 504–512.

LEWIS, J., & TODD, R. (1978). The relationship of cognitive abilities scores with social studies achievement. *Educational and Psychological Measurement, 38,* 463–464.

LEWITTES, D. J., MOSELLE, J. A., & SIMMONS, W. L. (1973). Sex role bias in clinical judgments based on Rorschach interpretations. *Proceedings of the 81st Annual Convention of the American Psychological Association* (Summary), *8,* 495–496.

LIEBERT, R. M., & MORRIS, L. W. (1967). Cognitive and emotional components of test anxiety: A distinction and some initial data. *Psychological Reports, 20,* 975–978.

LIGHT, B. H. (1954). Comparative study of a series of TAT & CAT cards. *Journal of Clinical Psychology, 10,* 179–181.

LIKERT, R. (1932). A technique for the measurement of attitudes. *Archives of Psychology,* No. 140.

LINDVALL, C. M., & NITKO, A. J. (1975). *Measuring pupil achievement and aptitude* (2nd ed.). New York: Harcourt Brace Jovanovich, Inc.

LINDZEY, G., & HERMAN, P. S. (1955). TAT: A note on reliability and situational validity. *Journal of Projective Techniques, 19,* 36–42.

LINN, R. L. (1973). Fair test use in selection. *Review of Educational Research, 43,* 139–161.

LINN, R. L. (1978). Review of the Differential Aptitude Tests. In O. K. Buros (Ed.). *Eighth mental measurements yearbook.* Highland Park, N.J.: Gryphon.

LINN, R. L. (1982). Ability testing: Individual differences, prediction and differential prediction. In A. K. Wigdor and W. R. Garner (Eds.). *Ability testing: Uses, consequences, and controversies. Part II: Documentation section.* Washington, D.C.: National Academy Press.

LITTELL, W. M. (1960). The Wechsler Intelligence Scale for Children: Review of a decade of research. *Psychological Bulletin, 57,* 132–156.

LITTLE, K. B., & SCHNEIDMAN, E. S. (1959). Congruencies among interpretations of psychological test and anamnestic data. *Psychological Monographs, 73,* 6 (Whole No. 476).

LOCKSLEY, A., & COLTEN, M. E. (1979). Psychological androgyny: A case of mistaken identity? *Journal of Personality and Social Psychology, 37,* 1017–1031.

LOEHLIN, J. C., LINDZEY, G., & SPUHLER, J. N. (1975). *Race differences in intelligence.* San Francisco: W. H. Freeman.

LONGSTAFF, H. (1954). Practice effects on the Minnesota Vocational Test for Clerical Workers. *Journal of Applied Psychology, 38,* 18–20.

LOO, R. (1979). The State-Trait Anxiety Inventory A-Trait Scale: Dimensions and their generalization. *Journal of Personality Assessment, 43,* 50–53.

LORD, F. M. (1953). The relation of test score to the trait underlying the test. *Educational and Psychological Measurement, 13,* 517–549.

LORD, F. M. (1975). Formula scoring and number-right scoring. *Journal of Educational Measurement, 12,* 7–11.

LORD, F. M., & NOVICK, M. (1968). *Statistical theories of mental test scores.* Reading, Mass.: Addison-Wesley.

LORGE, I., THORNDIKE, R. L., & HAGEN, E. P. (1964). *Lorge-Thorndike Intelligence Tests: Multilevel Education (Forms 1 and 2).* Lombard, Ill.: Riverside Publishing Company.

LORO, B., & WOODWARD, J. A. (1976). Verbal and Performance IQ for discrimination among psychiatric diagnostic groups. *Journal of Clinical Psychology, 32,* 107–114.

LOWE, C. M. (1967). Prediction of post-hospital work adjustment by use of psychological tests. *Journal of Counseling Psychology, 14,* 248–252.

LOWRANCE, D., & ANDERSON, H. N. (1979). A comparison of the Slosson Intelligence Test and the WISC-R with elementary school children. *Psychology in the Schools, 16,* 361–364.

LUBIN, B., WALLIS, R. R., & PAINE, C. (1971). Patterns of psychological test usage in the United States: 1935–1969. *Professional Psychology, 2,* 70–74.

LUMSDEN, J. (1976). Test theory. *Annual Review of Psychology, 27,* 251–280.

LUMSDEN, J. (1978). Review of the Illinois Test of Psycholinguistic Abilities, Revised Edition. In O. K. Buros (Ed.). *Eighth mental measurements yearbook.* Highland Park, N.J.: Gryphon.

LUNNEBORG, P. W. (1978). Review of the Strong-Campbell Interest Inventory. In O. K. Buros (Ed.). *Eighth mental measurements yearbook.* Highland Park, N.J.: Gryphon.

LYMAN, H. B. (1978). *Test scores and what they mean* (3rd ed.). Englewood Cliffs, N.J.: Prentice-Hall.

MACCOBY, E. E., & JACKLIN, C. N. (1974). *The psychology of sex differences*. Stanford, Calif.: Stanford University Press.

MACDONALD, H. A., & NETHERTON, A. H. (1969). Contribution of a nonverbal general ability test to the educational assessment of pupils in the cross-cultural setting of the Canadian North. *Journal of Educational Research, 62,* 315–319.

MACHOVER, K. (1949). *Personality projection in the drawing of the human figure*. Springfield, Ill.: Thomas.

MACPHILLAMY, D. J., & LEWINSOHN, P. M. (1972). Measuring reinforcing events. *Proceedings of the 80th Annual Convention of the American Psychological Association* (Summary) 7, 399–400.

MAHLER, I. (1953). Attitudes toward socialized medicine. *Journal of Social Psychology, 38,* 273–282.

MALONEY, M. P., NELSON, D., DUVALL, S., & KIRKENDALL, A. (1978). Performance of psychiatric inpatients on three standard tests of intelligence. *Psychological Reports, 43,* 1289–1290.

MALONEY, M. P. & WARD, M. P. (1976). *Psychological assessment: A conceptual approach*. New York: Oxford.

MANDLER, G., & SARASON, S. B. (1952). A study of anxiety and learning. *Journal of Abnormal and Social Psychology, 47,* 166–173.

MANDLER, G., & SARASON, S. B. (1953). The effects of prior experience and subjective failure on the evocation of test anxiety. *Journal of Personality, 21,* 338–341.

MANOSEVITZ, M., & LANYON, R. I. (1965). Fear survey schedule: A normative study. *Psychological Reports, 17,* 699–703.

MARINELLI, R. P. (1980). Anxiety. In R. H. Wood (Ed.). *Encyclopedia of clinical assessment*. San Francisco: Jossey-Bass.

MARKS, P. A., SEEMAN, W., & HALLER, D. L. (1974). *The actuarial use of the MMPI with adolescents and adults*. Baltimore: Williams & Wilkins.

MARTIN, J.D., & RUDOLPH, L. (1972). Correlates of the Wechsler Adult Intelligence Scale, the Slosson Intelligence Scale, ACT scores, and grade point averages. *Educational and Psychological Measurement, 32,* 459–462.

MARTINEZ-URRUTIA, A. (1975). Anxiety and pain in surgical patients. *Journal of Consulting and Clinical Psychology, 43,* 437–442.

MARUYAMA, G., RUBIN, R. A., & KINGSBURG, G. G. (1981). Self-esteem and educational achievement: Independent constructs with a common cause. *Journal of Personality and Social Psychology, 40,* 962–975.

MASLING, J. (1960). The influence of situational and interpersonal variables in projective testing. *Psychological Bulletin, 57,* 65–85.

MATARAZZO, J. D. (1972). *Wechsler's measurement and appraisal of adult intelligence*. Baltimore: Williams and Wilkins.

MATARAZZO, J. D., WIENS, A. N., & SASLOW, G. (1965). Studies of interview speech behavior. In L. Krasner & L. P. Ulmann (Eds.). *Research in behavior modification: New developments and their clinical implications*. New York: Holt.

MATARAZZO, R. G., WIENS, A. N., MATARAZZO, J. D., & MANAUGH, T. S. (1973). Test-retest reliability of the WAIS in a normal population. *Journal of Clinical Psychology, 29,* 194–197.

MATEFY, R. E. (1978). Evaluation of remediation program using senior citizens as psychoeducational agents. *Community Mental Health Journal, 14,* 327–336.

MATTHEWS, K. A. (1982). Psychological perspectives on the Type A behavior pattern. *Psychological Bulletin, 91,* 293–323.

MAUDAL, G. R., BUTCHER, J. N., & MAUGER, P. A. (1974). A multivariate study of personality and academic factors in college attrition. *Journal of Counseling Psychology, 21,* 560–567.

MAUGER, P. A., & KOLMODIN, C. A. (1975). Long-term predictive validity of the Scholastic Aptitude Test. *Journal of Educational Psychology, 67,* 847–851.

MAYFIELD, E. C. (1964). The selection interview: A re-evaluation of published research. *Personnel Psychology, 17,* 239–260.

MCARTHUR, C. C. (1972). Rorschach. In O. K. Buros (Ed.). *Seventh mental measurements yearbook*. Highland Park, N.J.: Gryphon.

MCCALL, R. B. (1980). The development of intellectual functioning in infancy and the prediction of later IQ. In J. D. Osofsky (Ed.). *Handbook of infant development*. New York: Wiley.

MCCARTHY, D. (1972). *Manual for the McCarthy Scales of Children's Abilities*. New York: Psychological Corporation.

MCCLELLAND, D. C., ATKINSON, J. W., CLARK, R. A., & LOWELL, E. L. (1976). *The achievement motive*. New York: Irvington Publishers.

MCKEE, M. G. (1972). The Edwards Personal Preference Schedule. In O. K. Buros (Ed.).

Seventh mental measurements yearbook. Highland Park, N.J.: Gryphon.

McLAURIN, W. A., & FARRAR, W. E. (1973). Validities of the Progressive Matrices Tests against IQ and grade point average. *Psychological Reports, 32,* 803–806.

McLAURIN, W. A., JENKINS, J. F., FARRAR, W. E., & RUMORE, M. C. (1973). Correlations of IQs on verbal and nonverbal tests of intelligence. *Psychological Reports, 33,* 821–822.

McMANMAN, K. M., & COHN, M. J. (1978). The performance of English speaking and Spanish speaking children on a measure of nonverbal intelligence. *Journal of Instructional Psychology, 5,* 2–5.

McNEMAR, Q. (1942). *The revision of the Stanford-Binet Scale: An analysis of the standardization data.* Boston: Houghton Mifflin.

McNEMAR, Q. (1957). On WAIS difference scores. *Journal of Consulting Psychology, 21,* 239–240.

McNEMAR, Q. (1964). Lost: Our intelligence? Why? *American Psychologist, 19,* 871–882.

McNEMAR, Q. (1969). *Psychological statistics* (4th ed.). New York: Wiley.

MEEHL, P. E. (1951). *Research results for counselees.* St. Paul, Minn.: State Department of Education.

MEEHL, P. E. (1954). *Clinical versus statistical prediction.* Minneapolis: University of Minnesota Press.

MEEHL, P. E., & DAHLSTROM, W. G. (1960). Objective configural rules for discriminating psychotic from neurotic MMPI profiles. *Journal of Consulting Psychology, 24,* 375–387.

MEEHL, P. E., & HATHAWAY, S. R. (1946). The K factor as a suppressor variable in the MMPI. *Journal of Applied Psychology, 30,* 526–564.

MEEHL, P. E., & ROSEN, A. (1955). Antecedent probability and the efficiency of psychometric signs, patterns, or cutting scores. *Psychological Bulletin, 52,* 194–216.

MEER, B., & BAKER, J. A. (1965). Reliability of measurements of intellectual functioning of geriatric patients. *Journal of Gerontology, 20,* 410–414.

MEGARGEE, E. I. (1972). *The California Psychological Inventory handbook.* San Francisco: Jossey-Bass.

MELLO, N. K., & GUTHRIE, G. M. (1958). MMPI profiles and behavior in counseling. *Journal of Counseling Psychology, 5,* 125–129.

MELTZOFF, J. (1951). The effect of mental set and item structure upon response to a projective test. *Journal of Abnormal and Social Psychology, 46,* 177–189.

MERRENS, M. R. (1975). The relationship between personality inventory scores and self-ratings. *Journal of Social Psychology, 97,* 139–140.

MERRIFIELD, P., & HUMMEL-ROSSI, B. (1976). Redundancy in the Stanford Achievement Test. *Educational and Psychological Measurement, 36,* 997–1001.

MESSICK, S. (1980a). Test validity and the ethics of assessment. *American Psychologist, 35,* 1012–1027.

MESSICK, S. (1980b). *The effectiveness of coaching for the SAT: Review and reanalysis of research from the fifties to the FTC.* Princeton, N.J.: Educational Testing Service.

MESSICK, S., & JUNGEBLUT, A. (1981). Time and method in coaching for the SAT. *Psychological Bulletin, 89,* 191–216.

METZGER, R. L. (1976). A reliability and validity study of the State-Trait Anxiety Inventory. *Journal of Clinical Psychology, 32,* 276–278.

MILLER, L. C. (1978). Missouri Children's Picture Series. In O. K. Buros (Ed.). *Eighth mental measurements yearbook.* Highland Park, N.J.: Gryphon.

MILLIREN, A. P., & NEWLAND, T. E. (1968–69). Statistically significant differences between subtest scaled scores for the WPPSI. *Journal of School Psychology, 7,* 16–19.

MILLMAN, J., BISHOP, C., & EBEL, R. (1965). An analysis of testwiseness. *Educational and Psychological Measurement, 25,* 707–726.

MILLON, T. (1977). *Millon Clinical Multiaxial Inventory: Manual.* Minneapolis, Minn.: NCS Interpretive Scoring Systems.

MILNER, J. S., & MOSES, T. H. (1972). Effects of administrator's gender on sexual content and productivity in the Rorschach. *Journal of Clinical Psychology, 30,* 159–161.

MISCHEL, W. (1968). *Personality and assessment.* New York: Wiley.

MISHRA, S. P. (1981). Factor analysis of the McCarthy Scales for groups of white and Mexican-American children. *Journal of School Psychology, 19,* 178–182.

MITCHELL, K. R., & NG, K. T. (1972). Effects of group counseling and behavior therapy in the academic achievement of test anxious subjects. *Journal of Counseling Psychology, 19,* 491–497.

MIZE, J. M., CALLAWAY, B., & SMITH, J. W. (1979). Comparison of reading disabled children's scores on the WISC-R, Peabody Picture Vocabulary Test, and Slosson Intelligence Test. *Psychology in the Schools, 16,* 356–358.

MOONEY, R. L., & GORDON, L. V. (1950). *Mooney Problem Check List manual.* New York: Psychological Corporation.

MORELAND, J. R., GULANICK, N., MONTAGUE, E. R., & HARREN, V. A. (1978). The psychometric properties of the Bem Sex-Role Inventory. *Applied Psychological Measurement, 2,* 247–256.

MORGAN, C., & MURRAY, H. A. (1935). A method for investigating fantasies: The Thematic Apperception Test. *Archives of Neurology and Psychiatry, 34,* 289–306.

MORROW, B. H. (1979). Elementary school performance of offspring of young adolescent mothers. *American Educational Research Journal, 16,* 423–429.

MORSBACH, G., McGOLDRICK, G., & YOUNGER, J. (1978). Inter-scorer reliability of the Geometric Design subtest of the WPPSI. *Journal of Behavioral Science, 2,* 279–284.

MULAIK, S. A. (1972). *The foundations of factor analysis.* New York: McGraw-Hill.

MUNDAY, L. A. (1967). Predicting college grades using ACT data. *Educational and Psychological Measurement, 27,* 401–406.

MUNDAY, L. A. (1976). Declining admissions test scores. *ACT Research Reports, 71,* 1–34.

MURRAY, H. A. (1943). *Thematic Apperception Test manual.* Cambridge, Mass.: Harvard University Press.

MURSTEIN, B. I. (1963). *Theory and research in projective techniques (emphasizing the TAT).* New York: Wiley.

MURSTEIN, B. I. (1965). The stimulus. In B. I. Murstein (Ed.). *Handbook of projective techniques.* New York: Basic Books.

MYERS, J. L. (1979). *Fundamentals of experimental design* (3rd ed.). Boston: Allyn and Bacon.

NAGLE, R. J. (1979). The McCarthy Scales of Children's Abilities: Research implications for the assessment of young children. *School Psychology Review, 8,* 319–326.

NAGLIERI, J. A., & HARRISON, P. L. (1979). Comparison of McCarthy Cognitive Indexes and Stanford-Binet IQs for educable mentally retarded children. *Perceptual and Motor Skills, 48,* 1251–1254.

NAGLIERI, J. A., KAUFMAN, A. S., & HARRISON, P. L. (1981). Factor structure of the McCarthy Scales for school-age children with low GCIs. *Journal of School Psychology, 19,* 226–232.

NAIRN, A. (1980). *The reign of ETS: The corporation that makes up minds.* Washington D.C.: Ralph Nader.

NATIONAL ASSOCIATION OF SECONDARY SCHOOL PRINCIPALS (1976). *Competency tests and graduation requirements.* Reston, Va.: Author.

NERVIANO, V. J. (1976). Common personality patterns among alcoholic males: A multivariate study. *Journal of Consulting and Clinical Psychology, 44,* 104–110.

NEVO, B. (1976). The effects of general practice, specific practice, and item familiarization on change in aptitude test scores. *Measurement and Evaluation in Guidance, 91,* 16–20.

NEWCOMER, P. L. (1974–75). The ITPA and academic achievement. *Academic Therapy, 10,* 401–406.

NEWLAND, T. E. (1972). Review of the Hiskey-Nebraska Test of Learning Aptitude. In O. K. Buros (Ed.). *Seventh mental measurements yearbook.* Highland Park, N.J.: Gryphon.

NICHOLS, R. C., & BECK, K. W. (1960). Factors in psychotherapy change. *Journal of Consulting Psychology, 24,* 388–399.

NICHOLSON, C. L. (1977). Correlations between the Quick Test and the Wechsler Intelligence Scale for Children–Revised. *Psychological Reports, 40,* 523–526.

NIXON, G. F., & STEFFECK, J. C. (1977). Reliability of the State-Trait Anxiety Inventory. *Psychological Reports, 40,* 357–358.

NOVICK, M. R. (1981). Burden of proof/Burden of remedy. *Public Personnel Management Journal, 10,* 333–342.

NUNNALLY, J. C. (1978). *Psychometric theory* (2nd ed.). New York: McGraw-Hill.

OAKLAND, T. (1978). Predictive validity of readiness tests for middle and lower socioeconomic status Anglo, Black, and Mexican-American children. *Journal of Educational Psychology, 70,* 574–582.

OGDON, D. P. (1975). Extrapolated WISC-R IQs for gifted and mentally retarded children. *Journal of Consulting and Clinical Psychology, 43,* 216.

OGUNLADE, J. O. (1978). The predictive validity of the Raven Progressive Matrices with some Nigerian children. *Educational and Psychological Measurement, 38,* 465–467.

O'LEARY, K. D., KAUFMAN, K. F., KASS, R. E., & DRABMAN, R. S. (1970). The effects of loud and soft reprimands on the behavior of disruptive students. *Exceptional Children, 37,* 145–155.

OLLENDICK, T. H. (1979). Discrepancies between Verbal and Performance IQs and subtest scatter on the WISC-R for juvenile delinquents. *Psychological Reports, 45,* 563–568.

ORLOFSKY, J. L. (1980). Sex-role orientation. In R. H. Wood (Ed.). *Encyclopedia of clinical assessment*. San Francisco: Jossey-Bass.

OSBORNE, R. T. (1975). Fertility, IQ, and school achievement. *Psychological Reports, 37,* 1067–1073.

OSGOOD, C. E. (1957a). A behavioristic analysis of perception and language as cognitive phenomena. In *Contemporary approaches to cognition.* Cambridge, Mass.: Harvard University Press.

OSGOOD, C. E. (1957b). Motivational dynamics of language behavior. In M. R. Jones (Ed.). *Nebraska symposium on motivation.* Lincoln: University of Nebraska Press.

OSGOOD, C. E. (1962). Studies on the generality of affective meaning systems. *American Psychologist, 17,* 10–28.

OSGOOD, C. E., MAY, W. H., & MURRAY, M. S. (1975). *Cross-cultural universals of affective meaning.* Urbana: University of Illinois Press.

OSGOOD, C. E., SUCI, G. J., & TANNENBAUM, P. H. (1957). *The measurement of meaning.* Urbana: University of Illinois Press.

OSKAMP, S. (1962). The relationship of clinical experience and training methods to several criteria of clinical prediction. *Psychological Monographs, 76,* 28 (Whole No. 547).

OSKAMP, S. (1965). Overconfidence in case-study judgments. *Journal of Consulting Psychology, 29,* 261–265.

OSKAMP, S. (1977). *Attitudes and opinions.* Englewood Cliffs, N.J.: Prentice-Hall.

OSOFSKY, J. D. (ED.). (1980). *Handbook of infant development.* New York: Wiley.

PACKARD, V. (1964). *The naked society.* New York: McKay.

PARASKEVOPOULOS, J. N., & KIRK, S. A. (1969). *The development and psychometric characteristics of the revised Illinois Test of Psycholinguistic Abilities.* Urbana: University of Illinois Press.

PARRY, H., & CROSSLEY, H. (1950). Validity of response to survey questions. *Public Opinion Quarterly, 14,* 61–80.

PASEWARK, R. A., FRITZGERALD, B. J., DEXTER, V., & CANGEMI, A. (1976). Responses of adolescent, middleaged, and aged females on the Gerontological and Thematic Apperception Tests. *Journal of Personality Assessment, 40,* 588–591.

PASEWARK, R. A., SCHERR, S. S., & SAWYER, R. N. (1974). Correlations of scores on the Vane Kindergarten, Wechsler Preschool and Primary Scale of Intelligence and Metropolitan Reading Readiness Tests. *Perceptual and Motor Skills, 38,* 518.

PAUL, G. L. (1966). *Insight vs. desensitization in psychotherapy: An experiment in anxiety reduction.* Stanford, Calif.: Stanford University Press.

PAYNE, A. F. (1928). *Sentence completions.* New York: Guidance Clinic.

PEDHAZUR, E. J. (1982). *Multiple regression in behavioral research* (2nd ed). New York: Holt Rinehart & Winston.

PEDHAZUR, E. J., & TETENBAUM, T. J. (1979). Bem Sex Role Inventory: A theoretical and methodological critique. *Journal of Personality and Social Psychology, 37,* 996–1016.

PETERSEN, N. S., & NOVICK, M. R. (1976). An evaluation of some models for culture-fair selection. *Journal of Educational Measurement, 13,* 3–29.

PETERSON, D. R. (1954). Predicting hospitalization of psychiatric outpatients. *Journal of Abnormal and Social Psychology. 49,* 260–265.

PETERSON, D. R. (1965). Scope and generality of verbally defined personality factors. *Psychological Reports, 72,* 48–59.

PETERSON, D., QUAY, H., & ANDERSON, A. (1959). Extending the construct validity of a socialized scale. *Journal of Consulting and Clinical Psychology, 23,* 182.

PETERSON, R. A. (1978). Rorschach. In O. K. Buros (Ed.). *Eighth mental measurements yearbook.* Highland Park, N.J.: Gryphon.

PETERSON, R. C., & THURSTONE, L. L. (1933). *Motion pictures and the social attitudes of children.* New York: Macmillan.

PETRIE, I. (1975). Characteristics and progress of a group of language disordered children with severe receptive difficulties. *British Journal of Disorders of Communication, 10,* 123–133.

PHILLIPS, B. L., PASEWARK, R. A., & TINDALL, R. C. (1978). Relationship among McCarthy Scales of Children's Abilities, WPPSI, and Columbia Mental Maturity Scale. *Psychology in the Schools, 15,* 352–356.

PHILLIPS, C. J., & BANNON, W. J. (1968). Stanford-Binet Form L-M Third Revision: A local English study of norms, concurrent validity and social differences. *British Journal of Educational Psychology, 38,* 148–161.

PHILLIPS, D. (1976). An investigation of the relationship between musicality and intelligence. *Psychology of Music, 4,* 16–31.

PHILLIPS, L. (1953). Case history data and prognosis in schizophrenia. *Journal of Nervous and Mental Disease, 117,* 515–525.

PIAGET, J. (1950). *The psychology of intelligence.* New York: Harcourt Brace Jovanovich, Inc..

PIAGET, J. (1954). *Construction of reality in the child.* New York: Basic Books.

PIAGET, J., & INHELDER, B. (1969). *The psychology of the child.* New York: Basic Books.

PIAGET, J., & INHELDER, B. (1973). *Memory and intelligence.* New York: Basic Books.

PIERCE, R. A., & SCHWARTZ, A. J. (1971). Personality styles of student activists. *Journal of Psychology, 79,* 227–231.

PIKE, L. W. (1978). Short-term instruction, testwiseness, and the Scholastic Aptitude Test: A literature review with research recommendations. (CBRDR 77-78, No. 2 and ETS RB 78-2.) Princeton, N.J.: Educational Testing Service.

PINTER, R. (1921). Intelligence and its measurement: A symposium. *Journal of Educational Psychology, 12,* 139–143.

PIOTROWSKI, R. J. (1978). Abnormality of subtest score differences on the WISC-R. *Journal of Consulting and Clinical Psychology, 46,* 569–570.

PIOTROWSKI, R. J. (1981). Abnormality of the difference and the WISC-R: Comment on Silverstein. *Journal of Consulting and Clinical Psychology, 49,* 467.

PIOTROWSKI, Z. A. (1947). A Rorschach compendium. *Psychiatric Quarterly, 21,* 70–101.

PIOTROWSKI, Z. A. (1980). The psychological X-ray in mental disorders. In J. B. Sidowski, J. H. Johnson, & T. W. Williams (Eds.). *Technology in mental health care delivery systems.* Norwood, N.J.: Ablex.

PLANT, W. T., & LYND, C. (1959). A validity study and a college freshman norm group for the WAIS. *Personnel and Guidance Journal, 38,* 560–578.

POOL, D. A., & BROWN, R. (1970). The PPVT as a measure of general adult intelligence. *Journal of Consulting and Clinical Psychology, 34,* 8–11.

POPHAM, W. J. (1975). *Educational evaluation.* Englewood Cliffs, N.J.: Prentice-Hall.

POPHAM, W. J., & HUSEK, T. R. (1969). Implications of criterion-referenced measurement. *Journal of Educational Measurement, 6,* 1–9.

PREDIGER, D. J. (1976). A world-of-work map for career exploration. *Vocational Guidance Quarterly, 24,* 198–208.

PREDIGER, D. J. (1981). Mapping occupations: A graphic aid for vocational guidance and research. *Vocational Guidance Quarterly, 30,* 20–36.

PRICE, F. W., & KIM, S. H. (1976). The association of college performance with high school grades and college entrance test scores. *Educational and Psychological Measurement, 36,* 965–970.

PRITCHARD, D. A., & ROSENBLATT, A. (1980). Racial bias in the MMPI: A methodological review. *Journal of Consulting and Clinical Psychology, 48,* 263–267.

PSYCHOLOGICAL CORPORATION (1978). *Summaries of court decisions on employment testing: 1968–1977.* New York: Author.

PSYCHOLOGICAL CORPORATION (1981). *Miller Analogies Test manual (1981 revision).* New York: Author.

QUAINTANCE, M. K. (1980). Test security: Foundation of public merit systems. *Personnel Psychology, 33,* 25–31.

QUERY, W. (1966). CPI factors and success of seminary students. *Psychological Reports, 18,* 665–666.

RABIN, A. I. (1972). Rorschach. In O. K. Buros (Ed.). *Seventh mental measurements yearbook.* Highland Park, N.J.: Gryphon.

RADCLIFFE, J. A. (1965). The Edwards Personal Preference Schedule. In O. K. Buros (Ed.). *Sixth mental measurements yearbook.* Highland Park, N.J.: Gryphon.

RAMANAIAH, N. V., & ADAMS, M. L. (1979). Confirmatory factor analysis of the WAIS and the WPPSI. *Psychological Reports, 45,* 351–355.

RAMEY, C. T., & CAMPBELL, F. A. (1979). Early childhood education for psychosocially disadvantaged children: Effects on psychological processes. *American Journal of Mental Deficiency, 83,* 645–648.

RAMEY, C. T., CAMPBELL, F. A., & NICHOLSON, J. E. (1973). The predictive power of the Bayley Scales of Infant Development and the Stanford-Binet intelligence test in a relatively constant environment. *Child Development, 44,* 790–795.

RAMSEY, P. H., & VANE, J. R. (1970). A factor analytic study of the Stanford-Binet with young children. *Journal of School Psychology, 8,* 278–284.

RAPPAPORT, D., GILL, M., & SCHAFER, R. (1945, 1946). *Diagnostic psychological testing* (2 vols.). Chicago: Yearbook Publishers.

RASBURY, W., McCOY, J. G., & PERRY, N. W., JR. (1977). Relation of scores on WPPSI and WISC-R at a one-year interval. *Perceptual and Motor Skills, 44,* 695–698.

RASKIN, L. M., BLOOM, A. S., KLEE, S. H., & REESE, A. (1978). The assessment of developmentally disabled children with the WISC-R, Binet, and other tests. *Journal of Clinical Psychology, 34,* 111–114.

RAVEN, J. C. (1938). *Progressive Matrices: A per-*

ceptual test of intelligence, 1938, Individual Form. London: H. K. Lewis.

RAVEN, J. C. (1960). Guide to the Standard Progressive Matrices, Sets A, B, C, D, and E. London: H. K. Lewis.

RAVEN. J. C. (1965a). Advanced Progressive Matrices, Sets I and II. London: H. K. Lewis.

RAVEN. J. C. (1965b). Coloured Progressive Matrices. London: H. K. Lewis.

REEVE, R. E., HALL, R. J., & ZAKRESKI, R. S. (1979). The Woodcock-Johnson Tests of Cognitive Ability: Concurrent validity with the WISC-R. Learning Disability Quarterly, 2, 63–69.

REILLY, R. R., & CHAO, G. T. (1982). Validity and fairness of some alternative employee selection procedures. Personnel Psychology, 35, 1–62.

RESCHLY, D. J. (1978). WISC-R factor structures among Anglos, Blacks, Chicanos, and Native-American Papagos. Journal of Consulting and Clinical Psychology, 46, 417–422.

RESCHLY, D. J. (1979). Nonbiased assessment. In G. D. Phye and D. J. Reschly (Eds.). School psychology: Perspectives and issues. New York: Academic Press.

RESCHLY, D. J. (1981). Psychological testing in educational classification and placement. American Psychologist, 36, 1094–1102.

RESCHLY, D. J., & RESCHLY, J. E. (1979). Brief reports on the WISC-R:I. Validity of WISC-R factor scores in predicting achievement and attention for four sociocultural groups. Journal of School Psychology, 17, 355–361.

RESCHLY, D., & SABERS, D. L. (1979). Analysis of test bias in four groups with the regression definition. Journal of Educational Measurement, 16, 1–9.

RESNICK, L. B. (ED.). (1976). The nature of intelligence. Hillsdale, N.J.: Erlbaum.

RESNICK, L. B., & GLASER, R. (1976). Problem solving and intelligence. In L. B. Resnick (Ed.). The nature of intelligence. Hillsdale, N.J.: Erlbaum.

REYNOLDS, C. R. (1979a). Methodological and statistical problems in discerning profile reliability: Comment on Roffe and Bryant. Psychology in the Schools, 16, 505–507.

REYNOLDS, C. R. (1979b). Objectivity of scoring for the McCarthy drawing tests. Psychology in the Schools, 16, 367–368.

REYNOLDS, C. R. (1982). The problem of bias in psychological assessment. In C. R. Reynolds and T. B. Gutkin (Eds.). The handbook of school psychology. New York: Wiley.

REYNOLDS, C. R., & GUTKIN, T. B. (1980a). A regression analysis of test bias on the WISC-R for Anglos and Chicanos referred for psychological services. Journal of Abnormal Child Psychology, 8, 237–243.

REYNOLDS, C. R., & GUTKIN, T. B. (1980b). Stability of the WISC-R factor structure across sex at two age levels. Journal of Clinical Psychology, 36, 775–777.

REYNOLDS, C. R., GUTKIN, T. B., DAPPAN, L., & WRIGHT, D. (1979). Differential validity of the WISC-R for boys and girls referred for psychological services. Perceptual and Motor Skills, 48, 868–870.

REYNOLDS, C. R., & HARTLAGE, L. (1979). Comparison of WISC and WISC-R regression lines for academic prediction with black and white referred children. Journal of Consulting and Clinical Psychology, 47, 589–591.

REZNIKOFF, M. (1972). Rorschach. In O. K. Buros (Ed.). Seventh mental measurements yearbook. Highland Park, N.J.: Gryphon.

RICHARDS, J. M., HOLLAND, J. L., & LUTZ, S. W. (1967). Prediction of student accomplishment in college. Journal of Educational Psychology, 58, 343–355.

RICHARDS, J. T. (1970). Internal consistency of the WPPSI with the mentally retarded. American Journal of Mental Deficiency, 74, 581–582.

RIESS, B. F., SCHWARTZ, E. K., & COTTINGHAM, A. (1950). An experimental critique of assumptions underlying the Negro version of the TAT. Journal of Abnormal and Social Psychology, 45, 700–709.

RITZEMA, R. J. (1974). The effect of demographic variables on the behavioral correlates of MMPI two point code types. Unpublished master's thesis, Kent State University.

RIVERSIDE PUBLISHING COMPANY (1982). Technical manual for Form 3, Levels 1 & 2 and Levels A-H Cognitive Abilities Test. Chicago: Author.

ROBAK, H. B. (1968). Human figure drawings: Their utility in the clinical psychologist's armamentarium for personality assessment. Psychological Bulletin, 70, 1–19.

ROBERTS, R. R., & RENZAGLIA, G. A. (1965). The influence of tape recording on counseling. Journal of Counseling Psychology, 12, 10–16.

ROBERTSON, D. (1980). Examining the examiners: The trend toward truth in testing. Journal of Law and Education, 9, 167–199.

ROBINSON, C., & SUINN, R. M. (1969). Group desensitization of a phobia in massed sessions. Behaviour Research and Therapy, 7, 319–321.

ROBINSON, J. P., ATHANASIOU, R., & HEAD, K. B, (1969). Measures of occupational attitudes and occupational characteristics. Ann Arbor, Mich.: Institute for Social Research.

ROBINSON, J. P., RUSK, J. G., & HEAD, K. B. (1968). *Measures of political attitudes.* Ann Arbor, Mich.: Institute for Social Research.

ROBINSON, J. P., & SHAVER, P. R. (1969). *Measures of social psychological attitudes.* Ann Arbor, Mich.: Institute for Social Research.

ROFFE, M. W., & BRYANT, C. K. (1979). How reliable are MSCA profile interpretations? *Psychology in the Schools, 16,* 14–18.

ROKEACH, M. (1968). *Beliefs, attitudes, and values.* San Francisco: Jossey-Bass.

RORSCHACH, H. (1921). *Psychodiagnostik.* (Trans. Haus Huber Verlag, 1942.) Bern: Haus Huber.

ROSEN, A. (1954). Detection of suicidal patients: An example of some limitations in the prediction of infrequent events. *Journal of Consulting Psychology, 18,* 397–403.

ROSEN, M., SALLINGS, L., FLOOR, L., & NAWAKIWSKA, M. (1968). Reliability and stability of Wechsler IQ scores for institutionalized mental subnormals. *American Journal of Mental Deficiency, 73,* 218–225.

ROSENBERG, L. A. (1962). Idealization of self and social adjustment. *Journal of Consulting Psychology, 26,* 487.

ROSENMAN, R. H., FRIEDMAN, M., STRAUS, R., WURM, M., KOSITCHEK, R., HAHN, W., & WERTHESSEN, N. T. (1964). A predictive study of coronary heart disease: The Western Collaborative Group Study. *Journal of the American Medical Association, 189,* 15–22.

ROSENTHAL, R. (1966). *Experimenter effects in behavioral research.* New York: Appleton-Century-Crofts.

ROSENTHAL, R., & JACOBSON, L. (1968). *Pygmalion in the classroom.* New York: Holt, Rinehart & Winston.

ROSENZWEIG, S. (1945). The picture-association method and its application in a study of reactions to frustration. *Journal of Personality, 21,* 3–23.

ROSKIND, W. L. (1980). DECO v. NLRB, and the consequences of open testing in industry. *Personnel Psychology, 33,* 3–9.

ROTHMAN, A. I. (1973). A comparison of persistent high and low achievers through four years of undergraduate medical training. *Journal of Medical Education, 48,* 180–182.

ROTTER, J. B. (1967). Can the clinician learn from experience? *Journal of Consulting Psychology, 31,* 12–15.

ROTTER, J. B., & RAFFERTY, J. E. (1950). *Manual: The Rotter Incomplete Sentences Blank.* New York: Psychological Corporation.

ROWLEY, G. L., & TRAUB, R. E. (1977). Formula scoring, number-right scoring, and test-taking strategy. *Journal of Educational Measurement, 14,* 15–22.

RUBIN, R. A. (1978). Stability of self-esteem ratings and their relation to academic achievement. *Psychology in the Schools, 15,* 430–433.

RUMENIK, D. K., CAPASSO, D. R., & HENDRICK, C. (1977). Experimenter sex effects in behavioral research. *Psychological Bulletin, 84,* 852–877.

RUNYON, R. P., & HABER, A. (1980). *Fundamentals of behavioral statistics* (4th ed.). Reading, Mass.: Addison-Wesley.

RUSCHIVAL, M. A., & WAY, J. G. (1971). The WPPSI and the Stanford-Binet: A validity and reliability study using gifted preschool children. *Journal of Consulting and Clinical Psychology, 37,* 163.

RUTNER, R. I., & BUGLE, C. (1969). An experimental procedure for the modification of psychotic behavior. *Journal of Consulting and Clinical Psychology, 33,* 651–653.

SAMUELS, W. (1977). Observed IQ as a function of test atmosphere, tester expectation, and race of tester: A replication for female subjects. *Journal of Educational Psychology, 69,* 593–604.

SANDLER, I. N. (1972). Characteristics of women working as child aides in a school-based preventive mental health program. *Journal of Consulting and Clinical Psychology, 39,* 56–61.

SARASON, I. G. (1957). Test anxiety, general anxiety, and intellectual performance. *Journal of Consulting Psychology, 21,* 485–490.

SARASON, I. G. (1972). Experimental approaches to test anxiety: Attention and the uses of information. In C. D. Spielberger (Ed.). *Anxiety: Current trends in theory and research* (Vol. 2). New York: Academic Press.

SARASON, I. G. (1975). Test anxiety, attention and the general problem of anxiety. In C. D. Spielberger and I. G. Sarason (Eds.). *Stress and anxiety* (Vol. 1). Washington, D.C.: Hemisphere/Wiley.

SARASON, S. B., & MANDLER, G. (1952). Some correlates of test anxiety. *Journal of Abnormal and Social Psychology, 47,* 810–817.

SARBIN, T. R. (1943). A contribution to the study of actuarial and individual methods of prediction. *American Journal of Sociology, 48,* 593–602.

SATTLER, J. M. (1970). Racial "experimenter effects" in experimentation, testing, interviewing, and psychotherapy. *Psychological Bulletin, 73,* 137–160.

SATTLER, J. M. (1974). *Assessment of children's in-*

telligence (rev. reprint). Philadelphia: W. B. Saunders.

SATTLER, J. M. (1976). Scoring difficulty of the WPPSI Geometric Design subtest. *Journal of School Psychology, 14,* 230–234.

SATTLER, J. M. (1981). Intelligence tests on trial: An "interview" with Judges Robert F. Peckham and John F. Grady. *Journal of School Psychology, 19,* 359–369.

SATTLER, J. M. (1982). *Assessment of children's intelligence and special abilities.* Boston: Allyn and Bacon.

SATTLER, J. M., ANDRES, J. R., SQUIRE, L. S., WISELY, R., & MALOY, C. F. (1978). Examiner scoring of ambiguous WISC-R responses. *Psychology in the Schools, 15,* 486–489.

SATTLER, J. M., & GWYNNE, J. (1982). White examiners generally do not impede test performance of black children: To debunk a myth. *Journal of Consulting and Clinical Psychology, 50,* 196–208.

SAWYER, J. (1966). Measurement and prediction, clinical and statistical. *Psychological Bulletin, 66,* 178–200.

SCHAEFFER, R. W. (1964). Clinical psychologists' ability to use the Draw-A-Person Test as an indicator of personality adjustment. *Journal of Consulting Psychology, 28,* 383.

SCHAIE, K. W. (1962). On the equivalence of questionnaire and rating data. *Psychological Reports, 10,* 521–522.

SCHERR, S. S., PASEWARK, R. A., & SAWYER, R. N. (1973). Relationship of the Vane Kindergarten Test and Wechsler Preschool and Primary Scale of Intelligence. *Journal of Clinical Psychology, 29,* 466–468.

SCHMIDT, F. L., BERNER, J. G., & HUNTER, J. E. (1973). Racial differences in validity of employment tests: Reality or illusion? *Journal of Applied Psychology, 58,* 5–9.

SCHMIDT, F. L., & HUNTER, J. E. (1980). The future of criterion-related validity. *Personnel Psychology, 33,* 41–60.

SCHMIDT, F. L., & HUNTER, J. E. (1981). Employment testing: Old theories and new research findings. *American Psychologist, 36,* 1128–1137.

SHNEIDMAN, E. S. (1949). *The Make-a-Picture Story Test.* New York: Psychological Corporation.

SCHOLL, G., & SCHNUR, R. (1976). *Measures of psychological, vocational, and educational functioning in the blind and visually handicapped.* New York: American Foundation for the Blind.

SCHRADER, W. B. (1971). The predictive valid-ity of college board admissions tests. In W. G. Angoff (Ed.). *The College Board Admissions Testing Program: A technical report on research and development activities relating to the Scholastic Aptitude Test and Achievement Tests.* New York: College Entrance Examination Board.

SCHWARTING, F. G. (1976). A comparison of the WISC and WISC-R. *Psychology in the Schools, 13,* 139–141.

SCHWARTZ, M. M., COHEN, B. D., & PAVLIK, W. D. (1964). The effects of subject- and experimenter-induced defensiveness response sets of picture-frustration test reactions. *Journal of Projective Techniques, 28,* 341–345.

SCOTT, W. A. (1965). *Values and organizations: A study of fraternities and sororities.* Chicago: Rand McNally.

SCOTT, W. A. (1968). Attitude measurement. In G. Lindzey and E. Aronson (Eds.). *The handbook of social psychology* (Vol. 2) (2nd ed.). Reading, Mass.: Addison-Wesley.

SECHREST, L., GALLIMORE, R., & HERSCH, P. D. (1967). Feedback and accuracy of clinical prediction. *Journal of Consulting Psychology, 31,* 1–11.

SELL, J. M., & TORRES-HENRY, R. (1979). Testing practices in university and college counseling centers in the United States. *Professional Psychology, 10,* 774–779.

SERWER, B. J., SHAPIRO, B. J., & SHAPIRO, P. P. (1972). Achievement prediction of "high risk" children. *Perceptual and Motor Skills, 35,* 347–354.

SEWELL, T. E. (1977). A comparison of WPPSI and Stanford-Binet Intelligence Scale (1972) among lower SES black children. *Psychology in the Schools, 14,* 158–161.

SEWELL, T. E., & SEVERSON, R. A. (1974). Learning ability and intelligence as cognitive predictors of achievement in first-grade black children. *Journal of Educational Psychology, 66,* 948–955.

SHARE, J. B., KOCH, R., WEBB, A., & GRALIKER, B. (1964). The longitudinal development of infants and young children with Down's Syndrome (Mongolism). *American Journal of Mental Deficiency, 68,* 685–692.

SHAVER, P. R., & SCHEIBE, K. E. (1967). Transformation of social identity: A study of chronic mental patients and college volunteers in a summer camp setting. *Journal of Psychology, 66,* 19–37.

SHAW, M. E., & WRIGHT, J. M. (1967). *Scales for the measurement of attitudes.* New York: McGraw-Hill.

SHAYCOFT, M. F. (1979). *Handbook of criterion-referenced testing: Development, evaluation, and use.* New York: Garland STPM Press.

SHIEK, D. A., & MILLER, J. E. (1978). Validity generalization of the WISC-R factor structure with 10½-year-old children. *Journal of Consulting and Clinical Psychology, 46,* 583.

SHORR, J. (1953). The development of a test to measure the intensity of values. *Journal of Educational Psychology, 44,* 266–274.

SHUEY, A. M. (1966). *The testing of negro intelligence* (2nd ed.). New York: Social Science Press.

SHURRAGER, H. C., & SHURRAGER, P. S. (1964). *Haptic Intelligence Scale for the Blind.* Chicago: Psychology Research.

SHUTT, D. L., & HANNON, T. A. (1974). The validity of the HNTLA for evaluation of the abilities of bilingual children. *Educational and Psychological Measurement, 34,* 429–432.

SILVERMAN, L. H. (1959). A Q-sort study of the evaluations made from projective techniques. *Psychological Monographs, 73,* 7 (Whole No. 477).

SILVERSTEIN, A. B. (1978). Note on the construct validity of the ITPA. *Psychology in the Schools, 15,* 371–372.

SILVERSTEIN, A. B. (1981a). Reliability and abnormality of test score differences. *Journal of Clinical Psychology, 37,* 392–394.

SILVERSTEIN, A. B. (1981b). Verbal-Performance IQ discrepancies on the WISC-R: One more time. *Journal of Consulting and Clinical Psychology, 49,* 465–466.

SILVERSTEIN, A. B. (1982). Factor structure of the Wechsler Adult Intelligence Scale—Revised. *Journal of Consulting and Clinical Psychology, 50,* 661–664.

SIMON, H. (1976). Identifying basic abilities underlying intelligent performance of complex tasks. In L. B. Resnick (Ed.). *The nature of intelligence.* Hillsdale, N.J.: Erlbaum.

SINES, J. O., PAUKER, J. D., & SINES, L. K. (1971). *Missouri Children's Picture Series manual.* Iowa City, Iowa: Psychological Assessment Services.

SINES, L. K. (1959). The relative contribution of four kinds of data to accuracy in personality assessment. *Journal of Consulting Psychology, 23,* 483–492.

SINGER, H. A., & ABRAMSON, P. R. (1973). Values of business administrators: A longitudinal study. *Psychological Reports, 33,* 43–46.

SISCO, F. H., & ANDERSON, R. J. (1978). Current findings regarding the performance of deaf children on the WISC-R. *American Annals of the Deaf, 123,* 115–121.

SKAGER, R. (1982). On the use and importance of tests of ability in admission to postsecondary education. In A. K. Wigdor and W. R. Garner (Eds.). *Ability testing: Uses, consequences, and controversies (Part II).* Washington, D.C.: National Academy Press.

SMITH, A. L., HAYS, J., & SOLWAY, K. S. (1977). Comparison of the WISC-R and Culture Fair Intelligence test in a juvenile delinquent population. *Journal of Psychology, 97,* 179–182.

SMITH, R. C. (1974). Response bias in the State-Trait Anxiety Inventory: Detecting the exaggeration of stress. *Journal of Psychology, 86,* 241–246.

SMITH, R. C., & LAY, C. D. (1974). State and trait anxiety: An annotated bibliography. *Psychological Reports, 34,* 519–594.

SNART, F. (1979). Strategy training for children with learning difficulties. *Mental Retardation Bulletin, 7,* 61–73.

SNOW, R. (1969), Unfinished Pygmalion. *Contemporary Psychology, 14,* 197–199.

SNOWMAN, J., LEITNER, D. W., SNYDER, V., & LOCKHART, L. (1980). A comparison of the predictive validities of selected academic tests of the American College Test (ACT) Assessment Program and the descriptive tests of language skills for college freshmen in a basic skills program. *Educational and Psychological Measurement, 40,* 1159–1166.

SOSKIN, W. F. (1954). Bias in postdiction from projective tests. *Journal of Abnormal and Social Psychology, 49,* 69–74.

SPEARMAN, C. (1904). The proof and measurement of association between two things. *American Journal of Psychology, 15,* 72–101.

SPEARMAN, C. (1907). Demonstration of formula for true measurement of correlation. *American Journal of Psychology, 18,* 161–169.

SPEARMAN, C. (1910). Correlation calculated with faulty data. *British Journal of Psychology, 3,* 271–295.

SPEARMAN, C. (1927). *The abilities of man.* New York: Macmillan.

SPENCE, J. T., COTTON, J. W., UNDERWOOD, B. J., & DUNCAN, C. P. (1983). *Elementary statistics* (4th ed.). Englewood Cliffs, N.J.: Prentice-Hall.

SPENCE, J.T., & HELMREICH, R. L. (1978). *Masculinity and femininity: Their psychological dimensions, correlates, and antecedents.* Austin: University of Texas Press.

SPENCE, J. T., & HELMREICH, R. L. (1979). The

many faces of androgyny: A reply to Locksley and Colten. *Journal of Personality and Social Psychology, 37,* 1032–1046.

SPENCE, J. T., HELMREICH, R., & STAPP, J. (1974). The Personal Attributes Questionnaire: A measure of sex-role stereotypes and masculinity-femininity. *JSAS Catalog of Selected Documents in Psychology, 4,* 43.

SPENCE, J. T., HELMREICH, R., & STAPP, J. (1975). Ratings of self and peers on sex-role attributes and their relation to self-esteem and conceptions of masculinity and femininity. *Journal of Personality and Social Psychology, 32,* 29–39.

SPIELBERGER, C. D., ANTON, W. D., & BEDELL (1976). The nature and treatment of test anxiety. In M. Zuckerman and C. D. Spielberger (Eds.). *Emotions and anxiety: New concepts, methods and applications.* Hillsdale, N.J.: Erlbaum.

SPIELBERGER, C. D., AUERBACH, S. M., WADSWORTH, A. P., DUNN, T. M., & TAULBEE, E. S. (1973). Emotional reactions to surgery. *Journal of Consulting and Clinical Psychology, 40,* 33–38.

SPIELBERGER, C. D., & DIAZ-GUERRERO, R. (EDS.) (1976). *Cross-cultural anxiety.* Washington, D.C.: Hemisphere Publishing Corporation.

SPIELBERGER, C. D., GORSUCH, R. C., & LUSHENE, R. E. (1970). *Manual for the State-Trait Anxiety Inventory.* Palo Alto, Calif.: Consulting Psychologists Press.

SPITZER, R. L., FLEISS, J. L., BURDOCK, E. I., & HARDESTY, A. S. (1964). The mental status schedule: Rationale, reliability and validity. *Comprehensive Psychiatry, 5,* 384–395.

SPOKANE, A. R. (1979). Occupational preference and the validity of the Strong-Campbell Interest Inventory for college men and women. *Journal of Counseling Psychology, 26,* 312–318.

SPRANGER, G. (1928). *Types of men.* New York: Hafner.

STANLEY, J. C. (1976). Test better finder of great math talent than teachers are. *American Psychologist, 31,* 313.

STEIN, M. I. (1978). Thematic Apperception Test and related materials. In B. B. Wolman (Ed.). *Clinical Diagnosis of Mental Disorders.* New York: Plenum.

STEPHENSON, W. (1953). *The study of behavior.* Chicago: University of Chicago Press.

STOKES, E. H., BRENT, D., HUDDLESTON, N. J., ROZIER, J. S., & MARRERO, B. (1978). A comparison of WISC and WISC-R scores for sixth grade students: Implications for validity. *Educational and Psychological Measurement, 38,* 469–473.

STREITFELD, J. W., & AVERY, C. D. (1968). The WAIS and HIS tests as predictors of academic achievement in a residential school for the blind. *The International Journal for the Education of the Blind, 18,* 73–76.

STRENIO, A. J., JR. (1981). *The testing trap.* New York: Rawson, Wade Publisher.

STRICKER, G. (1967). Actuarial, naive clinical, and sophisticated clinical prediction of pathology from figure drawings. *Journal of Consulting Psychology, 31,* 492–494.

STRICKER, L. J. (1965). The Edwards Personal Preference Schedule. In O. K. Buros (Ed.). *Sixth mental measurements yearbook.* Highland Park, N.J.: Gryphon.

STRICKER, L. J. (1969). "Test-wiseness" on personality scales. *Journal of Applied Psychology Monograph, 53* (3, Part 2).

STRONG, E. K., JR. (1927). A vocational interest test. *Educational Record, 8,* 107–121.

STRONG, E. K., JR. (1935). Predictive value of the Vocational Interest Test. *Journal of Educational Psychology, 26,* 331–349.

STRONG, E. K., JR. (1943). *Vocational interests of men and women.* Stanford, Calif.: Stanford University Press.

STRONG, E K., JR. (1955). *Vocational interests 18 years after college.* Minneapolis: University of Minnesota Press.

SUDDICK, D. E., & BOWEN, C. L. (1981). Longitudinal study of mathematics scores of the Stanford Achievement Test. *Psychological Reports, 49,* 284–286.

SUPER, D. E. (1982). *DAT Career Planning Program: Counselor's manual* (2nd ed.). New York: Psychological Corporation.

SUPER, D. E., BRAASCH, W. F., & SHAY, J. B. (1947). The effect of distractions on test results. *Journal of Educational Psychology, 38,* 373–377.

SWALLOW, R. (1981). Fifty assessment instruments commonly used with blind and partially seeing individuals. *Journal of Visual Impairment and Blindness, 75,* 65–72.

SWARTZ, J. D. (1978). Thematic Apperception Test. In O. K. Buros (Ed.). *Eighth mental measurements yearbook.* Highland Park, N.J.: Gryphon.

SWENSEN, C. H. (1957). Empirical evaluation of human figure drawings. *Psychological Bulletin, 54,* 431–66.

SWENSEN, C. H. (1968). Empirical evaluation of

human figure drawings. 1957–1966. *Psychological Bulletin, 70,* 20–44.

SWERDLIK, M. E. (1977). The question of the comparability of the WISC and WISC-R: Review of the research and implications for school psychologists. *Psychology in the Schools, 14,* 260–270.

SWERDLIK, M. E., & SCHWEITZER, J. (1978). A comparison of factor structures of the WISC and WISC-R. *Psychology in the Schools, 15,* 166–172.

SYMONDS, P. M. (1948). *Symonds Picture-Story Test.* New York: Bureau of Publications, Teachers College, Columbia University.

TALLENT, N. (1958). On individualizing the psychologist's clinical evaluation. *Journal of Clinical Psychology, 14,* 243–244.

TASTO, D. L. (1977). Self-report schedules and inventories. In A. R. Ciminero, K. S. Calhoun, and H. E. Adams (Eds.). *Handbook of behavioral assessment.* New York: Wiley.

TASTO, D. L., HICKSON, R., & RUBIN, S. E. (1971). Scaled profile analysis of fear survey schedule factors. *Behavior Therapy, 2,* 543–549.

TAULBEE, E. S., & SISSON, B. D. (1957). Configural analysis of MMPI profiles of psychiatric groups. *Journal of Consulting Psychology, 21,* 413–417.

TAYLOR, H. C., & RUSSELL, J. T. (1939). The relationship of validity coefficients to the practical effectiveness of tests in selection. *Journal of Applied Psychology, 23,* 565–578.

TAYLOR, J. A. (1953). A personality scale of manifest anxiety. *Journal of Abnormal and Social Psychology, 48,* 285–290.

TAYLOR, R. L. (1979). Comparison of the McCarthy Scales of Children's Abilities and the Peabody Picture Vocabulary Test. *Psychological Reports, 45,* 196–198.

TEICH, H. E. (1976). Practice effects on the Peabody Picture Vocabulary Test: An investigation of uncontrolled coaching and other factors. *Dissertation Abstracts International, 36,* 5820B–5821B.

TENDLER, A. D. (1930). A preliminary report on a test for emotional insight. *Journal of Applied Psychology, 14,* 123–126.

TENOPYR, M. L. (1977). Content-construct confusion. *Personnel Psychology, 30,* 47–54.

TENOPYR, M. L. (1981). The realities of employment testing. *American Psychologist, 36,* 1120–1127.

TERMAN, L. M. (1906). Genius and stupidity: A study of some of the intellectual processes of seven "bright" and seven "stupid" boys. *Pedagogical Seminary, 13,* 307–373.

TERMAN, L. M. (1916). *The measurement of intelligence.* Boston: Houghton Mifflin.

TERMAN, L. M. (1921). Intelligence and its measurement: A symposium. *Journal of Educational Psychology, 12,* 127–133.

TERMAN, L. M., & CHILDS, H. G. (1912). Tentative revision and extension of the Binet-Simon Measuring Scale of Intelligence. *Journal of Educational Psychology, 3,* 61–74.

TERMAN, L. M., & MERRILL, M. A. (1937). *Measuring intelligence.* Boston: Houghton Mifflin.

TERMAN, L. M., & MERRILL, M. A. (1960). *Stanford-Binet Intelligence Scale.* Boston: Houghton Mifflin.

TERMAN, L. M., & MERRILL, M. A. (1973). *Stanford-Binet Intelligence Scale (1973 Norms Edition).* Boston: Houghton Mifflin.

THIEL, G. W., & REYNOLDS, C. R. (1980). Predictive validity of the Revised Stanford-Binet Intelligence Scale with trainable mentally retarded students. *Educational and Psychological Measurement, 40,* 509–512.

THOMAS, C. L. (1979). Relative effectiveness of high school grades for predicting college grades: Sex and ability level effects. *Journal of Negro Education, 48,* 6–13.

THOMAS, P. J. (1980). A longitudinal comparison of the WISC and WISC-R with special education students. *Psychology in the Schools, 17,* 437–441.

THOMPSON, C. E. (1949). The Thompson modification of the Thematic Apperception Test. *Rorschach Research Exchange, 13,* 469–478.

THOMPSON, G. H. (1939). *The factorial analysis of human ability.* London: University of London Press.

THOMPSON, R. J. (1980). The diagnostic utility of WISC-R measures with children referred to a developmental evaluation center. *Journal of Consulting and Clinical Psychology, 48,* 440–447.

THORNDIKE, E. L. (1921). Intelligence and its measurement: A symposium. *Journal of Educational Psychology, 12,* 124–127.

THORNDIKE, R. L. (1968). Review of *Pygmalion in the classroom,* by R. Rosenthal and L. Jacobson. *American Educational Research Journal, 5,* 708–711.

THORNDIKE, R. L. (1971). Concepts of culture fairness. *Journal of Educational Measurements, 8,* 63–70.

THORNDIKE, R. L., & HAGEN, E. (1978a). *Cogni-*

tive Abilities Test, Form 3; Examiner's manual. Boston: Houghton Mifflin.

THORNDIKE, R. L., & HAGEN, E. (1978b). *Examiner's manual: Cognitive Abilities Test, Primary Battery standardization edition, Level 1, Form 3.* Boston: Houghton Mifflin.

THORNDIKE, R. L., & HAGEN, E. (1978c). *Examiner's manual: Cognitive Abilities Test, Primary Battery, standardization edition, Level 2, Form 3.* Boston: Houghton Mifflin.

THORPE, L. P., CLARK, W. W., & TIEGS, E. W. (1953). *California Test of Personality manual.* Monterey, Calif.: CTB/McGraw-Hill.

THURSTONE, L. L. (1938). Primary mental abilities. *Psychometric Monographs* (Whole No. 1).

THURSTONE, L. L. (1959). *The measurement of values.* Chicago: University of Chicago Press.

THURSTONE, L. L., & CHAVE, E. J. (1929). *The measurement of attitude.* Chicago: University of Chicago Press.

TITTLE, C. K. (1982). Use of judgmental methods in item bias studies. In R. A. Berk (Ed.). *Handbook of methods for detecting test bias.* Baltimore: The Johns Hopkins University Press.

TITTLE, C. K., & ZYTOWSKI, D. G. (EDS.). (1978). *Sex-fair interest measurement: Research and implications.* Washington, D.C.: National Institute of Education.

TOMKINS, S. S. (1947). *The Thematic Apperception Test.* New York: Grune & Stratton.

TORGERSON, W. S. (1958). *Theory and methods of scaling.* New York: Wiley.

TOWN, C. H. (1914). *A method of measuring the development of the intelligence of young children.* Chicago: Chicago Medical Book Co.

TOWNES, B. D., TRUPIN, E. W., MARTIN, D. C., & GOLDSTEIN, D. (1980). Neuropsychological correlates of academic success among elementary school children. *Journal of Consulting and Clinical Psychology, 48,* 675–684.

TRENTHAM, L. L. (1975). The effect of distractions on sixth-grade students in a testing situation. *Journal of Educational Measurement, 12,* 13–18.

TROUTMAN, J. G. (1978). Cognitive predictors of final grades in finite mathematics. *Educational and Psychological Measurement, 38,* 401–404.

TUCKMAN, B. W. (1978). Review of USES Basic Occupational Literary Test. In O. K. Buros (Ed.). *Eighth mental measurements yearbook.* Highland Park, N.J.: Gryphon.

TULKIN, S. R., & NEWBROUGH, J. R. (1968). Social class, race, and sex differences on the Ra-ven (1956) Standard Progressive Matrices. *Journal of Consulting and Clinical Psychology, 32,* 400–406.

TUMA, J. M., & APPELBAUM, A. S. (1980). Reliability and practice effects of WISC-R IQ estimates in a normal population. *Educational and Psychological Measurement, 40,* 671–678.

TUMA, J. M., APPELBAUM, A. S., & BEE, D. E. (1978). Comparability of the WISC and the WISC-R in normal children of divergent socioeconomic backgrounds. *Psychology in the Schools, 15,* 339–346.

TURNBULL, W. (1971). *A role theory of faking: The case of the MMPI.* Unpublished master's thesis, University of North Carolina.

ULRICH, L., & TRUMBO, D. (1965). The selection interview since 1949. *Psychological Bulletin, 63,* 100–116.

UNGER, R. K. (1979). Toward a redefinition of sex and gender. *American Psychologist, 34,* 1085–1094.

U.S. DEPARTMENT OF LABOR, EMPLOYMENT AND TRAINING ADMINISTRATION (1979). *Guide for occupational exploration.* Washington, D.C.: U.S. Government Printing Office.

UZGIRIS, I. C., & HUNT, J. McV. (1975). *Assessment in infancy: Ordinal Scales of Psychological Development.* Urbana: University of Illinois Press.

VALENCIA, R. R. (1979). Comparing of intellectual performance of Chicano and Anglo third-grade boys on the Raven Coloured Progressive Matrices. *Psychology in the Schools, 16,* 448–453.

VANCE, H. B. (1975–76). Instructional strategies with the ITPA. *Academic Therapy, 11,* 223–231.

VANCE H. B., BLIXT, S., ELLIS, R., & DEBELL, S. (1981). Stability of the WISC-R for a sample of exceptional children. *Journal of Clinical Psychology, 37,* 397–399.

VANCE, H. B., HANKINS, N., WALLBROWN, F., ENGIN, A., & McGEE, H. (1978). Analysis of cognitive abilities for mentally retarded children on the WISC-R. *Psychological Record, 28,* 391–397.

VANCE, H. B., SINGER, M. G., & ENGIN, A. W. (1980). WISC-R subtest differences for male and female LD children and youth. *Journal of Clinical Psychology, 36,* 953–957.

VANDER KOLK, C. J. (1977). Intelligence testing for visually impaired persons. *Journal of Visual Impairment and Blindness, 71,* 158–163.

VAN HAGAN, J., & KAUFMAN, A. S. (1975). Factor analysis of the WISC-R for a group of mentally retarded children and adolescents. *Journal of Consulting and Clinical Psychology, 43,* 661–667.

VERNON, P. E. (1954). Symposium on the effects of coaching and practice in intelligence tests: Conclusions. *British Journal of Educational Psychology, 24,* 57–63.

VERNON, P. E. (1969). *Intelligence and cultural environment.* London: Methuen.

VERNON, P. E. (1979). *Intelligence: Heredity and environment.* San Francisco: W. H. Freeman.

VEROFF, J., ATKINS, J. W., FELF, S. C., & JURIN, G. (1974). The use of thematic apperception to assess motivation in a nationwide interview study. In J. W. Atkinson and J. O. Raynor (Eds.). *Motivation and achievement.* Washington, D.C.: Winston.

VINCENT, K. R., & COX, J. A. (1974). A reevaluation of Raven's Standard Progressive Matrices. *Journal of Psychology, 88,* 299–303.

VITELES, M. S. (1925). The clinical viewpoint in vocational selection. *Journal of Applied Psychology, 9,* 131–138.

VOSS, J. F. (1976). The nature of "the nature of intelligence." In L. B. Resnick (Ed.). *The nature of intelligence.* Hillsdale, N.J.: Erlbaum.

WADDELL, D. D. (1980). The Stanford-Binet: An evaluation of the technical data available since the 1972 restandardization. *Journal of School Psychology, 13,* 203–209.

WAGNER, E. E. (1962). *Hand Test: Manual for administration, scoring and interpretation.* Los Angeles: Western Psychological Services.

WAGNER, E. E. (1978). Diagnostic applications of the Hand Test. In B. B. Wolman (Ed.) *Clinical diagnosis of mental disorders.* New York: Plenum.

WALD, A. (1950). *Statistical decision function.* New York: Wiley.

WALK, R. D. (1956). Self-ratings of fear in a fear-invoking situation. *Journal of Abnormal and Social Psychology, 52,* 171–178.

WALKER, C. D., & LINDEN, J. D. (1967). Varying degrees of psychological sophistication in the interpretaton of sentence completion data. *Journal of Clinical Psychology, 23,* 229–231.

WALKER, H. M., & LEV, J. (1953). *Elementary statistical methods.* New York: Holt Rinehart & Winston.

WALLACE, J. (1966). An abilities conception of personality: Some implications for personality measurement. *American Psychologist, 21,* 132–138.

WALLACE, J., & SECHREST, L. (1963). Frequency hypothesis and content analysis of projective techniques. *Journal of Consulting Psychology, 27,* 387–393.

WALLACE, W. L. (1972a). American College Testing Program. In O. K. Buros (Ed.). *Seventh mental measurements yearbook.* Highland Park, N.J.: Gryphon.

WALLACE, W. L. (1972b). Review of the Scholastic Aptitude Test. In O. K. Buros (Ed.). *Seventh mental measurements yearbook.* Highland Park, N.J.: Gryphon.

WALLACH, M. A. (1976). Tests tell us little about talent. *American Scientist, 64,* 57–63.

WALLBROWN, F. H., BLAHA, J., & WHERRY, R. J. (1973). The hierarchical factor structure of the Wechsler Preschool and Primary Scale of Intelligence. *Journal of Consulting and Clinical Psychology, 41,* 356–362.

WALSH, J. A. (1978). The Sixteen Personality Factor Questionnaire. In O. K. Buros (Ed.). *Eighth mental measurements yearbook.* Highland Park, N.J.: Gryphon.

WALSH, W. B. (1967). Validity of self-report. *Journal of Counseling Psychology, 14,* 18–23.

WARREN, J. R., & HEIST, P. A. (1960). Personality attributes of gifted college students. *Science, 132,* 330–337.

WATERS, C. W., WATERS, L. K., & PINCUS, S. (1977). Factor analysis of masculine and feminine sex-typed items from the Bem Sex-Role Inventory. *Psychological Reports, 40,* 567–570.

WATKINS, E. O., & WIEBE, M. J. (1980). Construct validity of the McCarthy Scales of Children's Abilities: Regression analysis with preschool children. *Educational and Psychological Measurement, 40,* 1173–1182.

WATSON, C. G. (1967). Relationship of distortion to DAP diagnostic accuracy among psychologists at three levels of sophistication. *Journal of Consulting Psychology, 31,* 142–146.

WATSON, C. G., & KLETT, W. G. (1973). Prediction of WAIS scores from group ability tests. *Journal of Clinical Psychology, 29,* 46–49.

WECHSLER, D. (1939). *The measurement of adult intelligence.* Baltimore: Williams & Wilkins.

WECHSLER, D. (1944). *The measurement of adult intelligence* (3rd ed.). Baltimore: Williams & Wilkins.

WECHSLER, D. (1949). *Manual for the Wechsler Intelligence Scale for Children.* New York: Psychological Corporation.

WECHSLER, D. (1955). *Manual for the Wechsler Adult Intelligence Scale.* New York: Psychological Corporation.

WECHSLER, D. (1958). *Measurement and appraisal*

of adult intelligence (4th ed.). Baltimore: Williams and Wilkins.

WECHSLER, D. (1967). Manual for the Wechsler Preschool and Primary Scale of Intelligence. New York: Psychological Corporation.

WECHSLER, D. (1974). Manual for the Wechsler Intelligence Scale for Children–Revised. New York: Psychological Corporation.

WECHSLER, D. (1981). WAIS-R Manual. New York: Psychological Corporation.

WEINER, I. B. (1976). Clinical methods in psychology. New York: Wiley.

WEISS, S. C. (1980). Culture Fair Intelligence Test and Draw-a-Person scores from a rural Peruvian sample. Journal of Social Psychology, 111, 147–148.

WEISSKOPF, E. A., & DIEPPA, J. J. (1951). Experimentally induced faking of TAT responses. Journal of Consulting Psychology, 15, 469–474.

WHARTON, Y. L. (1977). List of hypotheses advanced to explain the SAT score decline. New York: College Entrance Examination Board.

WHETSTONE, R. D., & HAYLES, V. R. (1975). The SVIB and black college men. Measurement and Evaluation in Guidance, 8, 96–100.

WHIPPLE, G. M. (1910). Manual of mental and physical tests. Baltimore: Warwick and York.

WHITE, D. R., & JACOBS, E. (1979). The prediction of first-grade reading achievement from WPPSI scores of preschool children. Psychology in the Schools, 16, 189–192.

WHITTAKER, D. (1971). The psychological adjustment of intellectual, nonconformist, collegiate dropouts. Adolescence, 6, 415–424.

WIEBE, B., & VRAA, C. W. (1976). Religious values of students in religious and in public high schools. Psychological Reports, 38, 709–710.

WIEBE, M. J., & HARRISON, K. A. (1978). Relationships of the McCarthy Scales of Children's Abilities and the Detroit Tests of Learning Aptitude. Perceptual and Motor Skills, 46, 355–359.

WIGDOR, A. K., & GARNER, W. R. (EDS.). (1982). Ability testing: Uses, consequences, and controversies. Part I: Report of the committee. Washington, D.C.: National Academy Press.

WIGGINS J. (1972). Personality Research Form. In O. K. Buros (Ed.). Seventh mental measurements yearbook. Highland Park, N.J.: Gryphon.

WIKOFF, R. L. (1979). The WISC-R as a predictor of achievement. Psychology in the Schools, 16, 364–366.

WILLIAMS, A. F. (1973). Personality and other characteristics associated with cigarette smoking among young teenagers. Journal of Health and Social Behavior, 14, 374–380.

WILLINGHAM, W. W. (1974). Predicting success in graduate education. Science, 183, 273–278.

WILSON, K. M. (1979, June). The validation of GRE scores as predictors of first year performance in graduate study: Report of the GRE Cooperative Validity Studies Project (GRE Board Report 75–8R). Princeton, N.J.: Educational Testing Service.

WILSON, R. S. (1975). Twins: Patterns of cognitive development as measured on the Wechsler Preschool and Primary Scale of Intelligence. Developmental Psychology, 11, 126–134.

WILSON, R. S. (1978). Synchronies in mental development: An epigenetic perspective. Science, 202, 939–948.

WILTSHIRE, E. B., & GRAY, J. E. (1969). Draw-A-Man and Raven's Progressive Matrices (1938) intelligence test performance of reserve Indian children. Canadian Journal of Behavioral Science, 1, 119–122.

WINCH, R. F., & MORE, D. M. (1956). Does the TAT add information to interviews? Statistical analysis of the increment. Journal of Clinical Psychology, 12, 316–321.

WINE, J. (1971). Test anxiety and direction of attention. Psychological Bulletin, 76, 92–104.

WING, H. (1980). Practice effects with traditional mental test items. Applied Psychological Measurement, 4, 141–155.

WIRT, R. D., LACHAR, D., KLINEDINST, J. K., & SEAT, P. D. (1977). Multidimensional description of child personality: A manual for the Personality Inventory for Children. Los Angeles: Western Psychological Services.

WITTIG, M. A., & PETERSON, A. C. (EDS.). (1979). Sex-related differences in cognitive functioning: Developmental issues. New York: Academic Press.

WITTSON, C. L., & HUNT, W. A. (1951). The predictive value of the brief psychiatric interview. American Journal of Psychiatry, 107, 582–585.

WOLF, T. H. (1973). Alfred Binet. Chicago: University of Chicago Press.

WOLK, R. L., & WOLK, R. B. (1971). The Gerontological Appperception Test. New York: Behavioral Publications.

WOODWORTH, R. S. (1920). Personal Data Sheet. Chicago: Stoelting.

WORELL, J. (1978). Sex roles and psychological well-being: Perspectives on methodology. Journal of Consulting and Clinical Psychology, 46, 777–791.

WORTHINGTON, E. L., JR., & DOLLIVER, R. H. (1977). Validity studies of the Strong Vocational Interest Inventories. *Journal of Counseling Psychology, 24,* 208–216.

WRIGHT, C. R. (1969). Summary of research on the selection interview since 1964. *Personnel Psychology, 22,* 391–413.

WRIGHT, J. C. (1976). The SVIB academic achievement score and college attrition. *Measurement and Evaluation in Guidance, 8,* 258–259.

YANG, R. K. (1980). Early infant assessment: An overview. In J. D. Osofsky (Ed.). *Handbook of infant development.* New York: Wiley.

ZAJONC, R. B. (1976). Family configuration and intelligence. *Science, 192,* 227–236.

ZAJONC, R. B., & BARGH, J. (1980). Birth order, family size, and decline of SAT scores. *American Psychologist, 35,* 662–668.

ZIMMERMAN, I. L., & WOO-SAM, J. M. (1972). Research with the Wechsler Intelligence Scale for Children. *Psychology in the Schools, 9,* 232–271.

ZIMMERMAN, I. L., & WOO-SAM, J. M. (1973). *Clinical interpretation of the Wechlser Adult Intelligence Scale.* New York: Grune & Stratton.

ZINGALE, S. A., & SMITH, M. D. (1978). WISC-R patterns for learning disabled children at three SES levels. *Psychology in the Schools, 15,* 199–204.

ZISKIN, J. (1981). *Use of the MMPI in forensic settings (Clinical Notes on the MMPI,* No. 9). Nutley, N.J.: Roche Psychiatric Service Institute.

ZOREF, L., & WILLIAMS, P. (1980). A look at content bias in IQ tests. *Journal of Educational Measurement, 17,* 313–322.

ZYTOWSKI, D. G. (1973). The Kuder Occupational Interest Inventory. In D. G. Zytowski (Ed.). *Contemporary approaches to interest measurement.* Minneapolis: University of Minnesota Press.

ZYTOWSKI, D. G. (1974). Predictive validity of the Kuder Preference Record, Form B, over a 25-year span. *Measurement and Evaluation in Guidance, 7,* 122–129.

ZYTOWSKI, D. G. (1976). Long-term profile stability of the Kuder Occupational Interest Survey. *Educational and Psychological Measurement, 36,* 689–692.

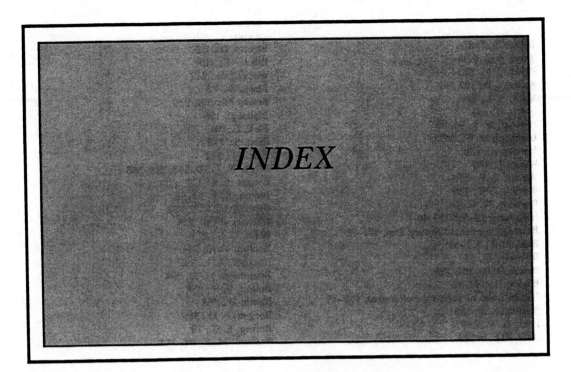

INDEX

B

Bailey, D., 242
Baird, J. C., 326
Baker, J. A., 103
Balinsky, B., 107
Ballif, B. L., 229
Baloh, R., 141
Bannon, W. J., 94, 95
Baraheni, M. N., 157
Barclay, A., 126
Bargh, J., 180
Barnes, D. F., 268
Barnes, T. R., 180
Barnette, W. L., Jr., 318
Base rates, 49–51, 339–40
Basic Occupational Literary Test, 171–72
Bass, A. R., 357–58
Bateman, B., 57
Baum, D. D., 124, 126
Bayley, N., 141–43
Bayley Scales of Infant Development, 142–45
Beaton, A. E., 180
Beck, K. W., 249
Beck, S. J., 6, 214
Becker, W. C., 161, 257
Beckerman, T. M., 166
Bedell, 73
Bee, D. E., 116, 118
Behavioral assessment, 281–95
Bell, H. M., 232
Bell Adjustment Inventory, 234
Bellak, L., 225
Bellak, S. S., 225
Bem, S. L., 331, 333, 334
Bem Sex-role Inventory, 333–35
Bender, I. E., 321, 322
Bender, L., 229
Bender Visual Motor Gestalt Test, 229–30
Benjamin, J. A., 248–49
Bennett, G. K., 169, 170–71
Bennett, T. S., 117
Benton, A. L., 360–61
Berk, R. A., 68, 144, 350, 360
Berner, J. G., 354
Berneuter, R. G., 232
Berry, K., 115
Bersoff, D. N., 368, 370, 371, 373, 374
Berzins, J. I., 268
Bias, 285, 349–62, 368–69
Biemiller, L., 180
Bienen, S., 249
Bijou, S., 116
Bills, R. E., 225
Binet, A., 4–5, 77, 78, 82–83

Bingham, W. C., 156
Bishop, C., 71
Bishop, D., 125
Black, H., 349
Black, J. D., 242
Black, R., 75
Blacky Pictures, 229
Blaha, J., 126
Blek, L., 360
Blixt, S., 113
Block, J., 242
Block, N. J., 79, 348, 349, 363
Bloom, A. S., 117, 119
Bloom, B. S., 91–92
Bloomfield, F. F., 292
Bloxom, B. M., 256
Blum, G. S., 229
Boehm, V. R., 354
Boerger, A. R., 242
Bohannon, W. E., 334
Bolton, B. F., 257
Booth, D., 368
Borgen, F. H., 309
Boring, E. G., 79
Bossard, M. D., 94, 354
Bouchard, T. J., Jr., 169, 171, 363, 364
Bowen, C. L., 205
Braasch, W. F., 57
Bracken, B. A., 140
Bradley, F. O., 13–14
Bradway, K., 103
Bratner, J. P., 240
Brayfield, A. H., 365
Brent, D., 116
Brittain, M., 91
Bromberg, P. M., 126
Brooks, C. R., 115–17
Broverman, D. M., 361
Broverman, I. K., 361
Brown, H. S., 103
Brown, K. E., 118
Brown, R., 106
Brown, W. B., 6
Bryant, C. K., 135, 137
Buck, J. N., 226
Budoff, M., 225
Bugle, C., 290
Burdock, E. I., 276
Burgess, E. W., 340
Burish, T. G., 329
Burke, H. R., 156
Buros, O. K., 4, 105, 151, 156, 170, 172, 181, 197, 213, 234, 268, 294, 320
Busch, R. F., 166
Bushnell, D., 71

H

Haber, A., 8
Hagen, E., 161, 162
Hahn, W., 329
Hale, R. L., 117, 119
Hall, R. J., 117
Hall, V. C., 157, 158
Hall, W. B., 249, 321
Haller, D. L., 240, 242, 361
Halpin, G., 187, 188
Hambleton, R. K., 68
Hamburg, D. A., 329
Hamm, H. A., 119
Hancock, K. A., 138
Handicapped and disabled, 146–50
Hand Test, 230
Haney, W., 348
Hanna, G. S., 113–14, 171
Hannon, T. A., 151
Hansen, J. C., 299, 301, 306–7, 310, 362
Haptic Intelligence Scale for Adult Blind, 150–51
Hardesty, A. S., 276
Hargadon, F., 189
Harman, H., 81
Harper, F. B., 268
Harper, G. T., 309
Harren, V. A., 334
Harris, D. B., 226
Harris, S., 360
Harrison, K. A., 93, 138, 139
Harrison, P. L., 135, 138–40
Hartlage, L. C., 117, 157, 354
Hartnett, B., 189
Hase, H. D., 232, 294
Hathaway, S. R., 6, 210, 233, 235–38, 242
Hauf, B., 188
Hayles, V. R., 309
Haynes, S. M., 288, 290
Hays, J., 154
Heath, D. H., 179
Hebb, D. O., 79–80
Heil, J., 126
Heilbrun, A. B., 249, 262
Heilbrun, A. R., 261
Heist, P. A., 321
Helmreich, R. L., 331–33
Helson, R., 321
Henderson, R. W., 122, 125, 126
Hendrick, C., 75, 360
Henning, J. J., 107, 108
Henrichs, T. F., 242
Heredity-environment issue, 79–80, 362–64
Herman, P. S., 224

Herr, W. S., 292
Herron, E. W., 220
Hersch, P. D., 345
Hersen, M., 291
Hertz, M. R., 214
Hess, A. K., 72
Heynes, R., 286
Hicks, L. E., 262, 322
Hickson, R., 291
Hiester, D. S., 105–7
Hiler, E. W., 343
Hills, J. R., 186, 187, 189
Hilton, T. L., 180
Himelstein, P., 93
Hirt, M. L., 208, 209
Hiskey, M. S., 151
Hiskey-Nebraska Test of Learning Aptitude, 151
Hodapp, A. F., 117
Hodapp, J. B., 117
Hoenes, R. L., 153, 154
Hoepfner, R., 82
Hoffman, B., 348
Hoffman, H., 267
Hogan, R., 268, 320, 322
Hoge, D. R., 322
Holland, J. L., 188, 300, 301, 318, 320
Hollenbeck, G. P., 126, 140
Hollingsworth, M. L., 279
Holroyd, D., 267
Holt, R. R., 225, 340
Holtzman, W. H., 220
Holtzman Inkblot Test, 220
Homogeneous groups, 22, 37–38, 45–46
Honingfeld, G., 287
Honzik, M. P., 91
Hooke, J. F., 335–36
Hopkins, K. D., 197
Horn, J. L., 82
Horner, T. M., 144
Houts, D. L., 196
Hovey, H. B., 242
Hoyt, D. P., 189
Hubble, L. M., 107
Huddleston, N. J., 116
Hug, M. A., 292
Humm, D. G., 232–33
Hummel-Rossi, B., 206
Humphreys, L. G., 160, 352–54
Hunt, E., 78, 279
Hunt, J. McV., 80, 282
Hunt, W. A., 279, 280, 380
Hunter, J. E., 46, 354, 356
Hunter, J. F., 371
Hunter, R., 354

McCarthy Scales of Children's Abilities, 128–41
McClelland, D. C., 221n, 222
Maccoby, E. E., 331, 359
McCord, G., 242
McCormick, C. E., 292
McCoy, J. G., 125
MacDonald, H. A., 156
McFall, 293
MacFarlane, J. W., 91
McGoldrick, G., 123
McGue, M., 363, 364
McGuire, J. M., 6
Machover, K., 226
Mackey, J., 368
McKee, M. G., 242, 262
McKinley, J. C., 6, 233, 235, 236, 238
MacKinnon, D. W., 321
McLaurin, W. A., 156
McManman, K. M., 157
McNemar, Q., 8, 82, 91, 94, 104–5, 171
MacPhillamy, D. J., 293
Magnusson, D., 335, 336
Magoon, T., 249
Mahler, I., 325
Make-a-Picture Story Test, 225
Maloney, M. P., 82, 107, 215, 218–19, 223
Maloy, C. F., 114
Manaugh, T. S., 103
Mandler, G., 73
Manifest Anxiety Scale, 336
Manosevitz, M., 291
Margraff, W., 242
Marinelli, R. P., 366
Marks, P. A., 240, 242, 361
Marrero, B., 116
Martin, D. C., 206
Martin, J. D., 107
Martinez-Urrutia, A., 335
Maruyama, G., 206
Masling, J., 76, 360
Mastery states, 68–69
Matarazzo, J. D., 96, 103, 105–8, 279
Matarazzo, R. G., 103
Matefy, R. E., 206
Matsuoka, M., 212–13
Matthews, K. A., 331
Maudal, G. R., 268
Mauger, P. A., 179, 268
Maxey, E. J., 188
May, A. E., 103
Mayfield, E. C., 280
Mean X̄, 14, 16, 61n
Median, 14–15
Medical College Admission Test, 70, 194
Meehl, P. E., 42, 53, 210, 242, 340, 341

Meer, B., 103
Megargee, E. I., 248, 250
Melker, F., 360
Mello, N. K., 242
Meltzoff, J., 211, 225
Merrens, M. R., 267
Merrifield, P., 206
Merrill, M. M., 5, 85–87, 89–93, 95
Merwin, J. C., 199, 201, 205
Messick, S., 43, 72, 179
Metraux, R. W., 218
Metropolitan Achievement Tests, 199
Metzger, R. L., 335
Midpoints, 10
Mikula, P. J., 335–36
Miller, J. E., 118
Miller, L. C., 273
Miller Analogies Test, 195–96
Milliren, A. P., 123
Millman, J., 71
Millon, T., 271
Millon Clinical Multiaxial Inventory, 271
Mills, C. J., 334
Milner, J. S., 75, 360
Miner, J. B., 7
Minnesota Multiphasic Personality Inventory, 6, 208, 232–43
Minnesota Vocational Interest Inventory, 318
Minority groups, 349–56
Mischel, W., 282
Mishra, S. D., 140
Missouri Children's Picture Series, 271–73
Mitchell, H. E., 225
Mitchell, K. R., 73
Mize, J. M., 117
Mode, 15
Monachesi, E. D., 242
Montague, E. R., 334
Mooney, R. L., 232, 271
Mooney Problem Check List, 234, 271
More, D. M., 341
Moreland, J. R., 334
Morgan, C., 220, 234
Morris, L. W., 73, 249
Morrow, B. H., 206
Morsbach, G., 123
Moselle, J. A., 361
Moses, T. H., 75, 360
Mulaik, S. A., 81
Multiple regression analyses, 26
Multitrait-multimethod matrix, 43–45
Munday, L. A., 187, 188
Murray, H. A., 6, 220–34
Murstein, B. I., 210, 224, 225, 294
Myers, J. L., 35

Profiles, 66–68
Prognostic Rating Scale, 219
Projective hypothesis, 209–10
Projective techniques, 6, 55, 76
Proportions, 12

Q

Q-sort procedure, 341n
Quaintance, M. K., 374
Quay, H., 248
Query, W., 249

R

Rabin, A. I., 105–7, 219
Radcliffe, J. A., 261, 262
Rafferty, J. E., 227–28
Rajaratnam, N., 29, 35, 36
Ramanaiah, N. V., 126
Ramey, C. T., 139
Ramsey, P. H., 95
Range, 16
Rankin, R. J., 122, 125, 126
Rappaport, D., 214
Rapport, 57–58, 277
Rardin, M. W., 124–26
Rasbury, W., 125
Raskin, L. M., 117, 119
Ratings, 36–37
Raven, J. C., 154–56
Raven's Progressive Matrices, 154–58
Reactivity, 286
Reese, A., 117
Reeve, R. E., 117
Regression equations, 23–26
Reilly, R. R., 280, 371
Reinforcement Survey Schedule, 292
Reinforcers, 284
Reliability (r$_{xx}$), 28–39, 46
Rempel, P. P., 249
Renzaglia, G. A., 286
Reschly, D. J., 117–18, 350, 354–55, 369
Reschly, J. E., 117
Research, clinical judgment, 344–45
Resnick, L. B., 78
Response formats, 208
Responses, faked, 210–11
Restriction of range, 37–38
Reuter, J., 141, 145, 146
Reynolds, C. R., 93, 94, 117, 118, 136–37, 350–52, 352n, 354
Reynolds, D. J., 292

Reznikoff, M., 219
Rice, J. M., 6
Richards, J. M., 188
Richards, J. T., 122
Richardson, G. T., 189
Richardson, M. W., 35
Riess, B. F., 225
Ritzema, R. J., 361
Robak, H. B., 226, 227
Roberts, R. R., 286
Robertson, D., 368
Robinson, C., 292, 294
Robinson, J. P., 323
Rodell, J. L., 218
Roffe, M. W., 135, 137
Rokeach, M., 322
Rokeach Value Survey, 322
Rooks, Y., 141
Rorer, L. G., 345
Rorschach, H., 6, 212, 213
Rorschach inkblot test, 208, 213–20
Rosen, A., 50, 53, 339
Rosen, M., 103
Rosenberg, L. A., 249
Rosenblatt, A., 356
Rosenkrantz, P. S., 361
Rosenman, R., 329, 330
Rosenstein, A. J., 282
Rosenthal, R., 75–76
Rosenzweig, S., 229
Rosenzweig Picture Frustration Test, 229
Roskind, W. L., 373–74
Ross, E. F., 268
Rothman, A. I., 268
Rotter, J., 227–28, 345
Rowland, T., 138
Rowley, G. L., 74
Rozier, J. S., 116
Rubin, R. A., 206
Rubin, S. E., 291
Rudman, H. C., 199, 201, 205
Rudolph, L., 107, 249–50
Rumenik, D. K., 75, 360
Rumore, M. C., 156
Runyon, R. P., 8
Ruschival, M. A., 122
Russell, J. T., 50, 51
Rutner, R. I., 290
Ryan, M., 267

S

Sabers, D. L., 354, 355
Saccuzzo, D. P., 284

Wisocki, P. A., 292
Wittig, M. A., 331
Wittson, C. L., 279, 280
Wolf, T. H., 82, 83, 83n
Wolk, R. B., 226
Wolk, R. L., 226
Wolman, B. B., 238n
Woodward, J. A., 108
Woodworth, R. S., 6, 231
Woodworth Personal Data Sheet, 231–32
Woo-Sam, J. M., 105–7, 113–17
Worell, J., 331
Worthington, E. L., Jr., 309
Wright, C. R., 280
Wright, D., 117
Wright, J. C., 310
Wright, J. M., 323, 326
Wurm, M., 329

Y

Yandell, R., 242
Yang, R. K., 141, 146

Yen, W. M., 30, 32
Yerkes, R. M., 5
Yoakum, C. S., 7
Young, V., 334
Younger, J., 123
Youngquist, J., 138, 139

Z

Zajonc, R. B., 180
Zakreski, R., 117
Zalma, R., 140
Zedeck, S., 31
Zimmerman, I. L., 105–7, 113, 115–17
Zimmerman, W. S., 233, 270
Zingale, S. A., 118, 119
Zino, T. C., 135, 138, 139
Ziskin, J., 381
Zoref, L., 154, 360
Zytowski, D. G., 296, 318, 361
Zyzanski, S. J., 329, 330